D0887448

# Masterminds of Programming

Edited by Federico Biancuzzi and Shane Warden

WITHDRAWN
NORTHEASTERN ILLINOIS
UNIVERSITY LIBRARY

O'REILLY®

Beijing • Cambridge • Farnham • Köln • Sebastopol • Taipei • Tokyo

**Masterminds of Programming**
Edited by Federico Biancuzzi and Shane Warden

Copyright © 2009 Federico Biancuzzi and Shane Warden. All rights reserved. Printed in the United States of America.

Published by O'Reilly Media, Inc. 1005 Gravenstein Highway North, Sebastopol, CA 95472

O'Reilly books may be purchased for educational, business, or sales promotional use. Online editions are also available for most titles (*safari.oreilly.com*). For more information, contact our corporate/institutional sales department: (800) 998-9938 or *corporate@oreilly.com*.

| | |
|---|---|
| **Editor:** Andy Oram | **Proofreader:** Nancy Kotary |
| **Production Editor:** Rachel Monaghan | **Cover Designer:** Monica Kamsvaag |
| **Indexer:** Angela Howard | **Interior Designer:** Marcia Friedman |

**Printing History:**

March 2009: First Edition.

The O'Reilly logo is a registered trademark of O'Reilly Media, Inc. *Masterminds of Programming* and related trade dress are trademarks of O'Reilly Media, Inc. Many of the designations used by manufacturers and sellers to distinguish their products are claimed as trademarks. Where those designations appear in this book, and O'Reilly Media, Inc. was aware of a trademark claim, the designations have been printed in caps or initial caps.

While every precaution has been taken in the preparation of this book, the publisher and authors assume no responsibility for errors or omissions, or for damages resulting from the use of the information contained herein.

Ronald Williams Library
Northeastern Illinois University

05-19-09

ISBN: 978-0-596-51517-1
[V]

# CONTENTS

# Foreword

**PROGRAMMING LANGUAGE DESIGN IS A FASCINATING TOPIC.** There are so many programmers who think they can design a programming language better than one they are currently using; and there are so many researchers who believe they can design a programming language better than any that are in current use. Their beliefs are often justified, but few of their designs ever leave the designer's bottom drawer. You will not find them represented in this book.

Programming language design is a serious business. Small errors in a language design can be conducive to large errors in an actual program written in the language, and even small errors in programs can have large and extremely costly consequences. The vulnerabilities of widely used software have repeatedly allowed attack by malware to cause billions of dollars of damage to the world economy. The safety and security of programming languages is a recurrent theme of this book.

Programming language design is an unpredictable adventure. Languages designed for universal application, even when supported and sponsored by vast organisations, end up sometimes in just a niche market. In contrast, languages designed for limited or local use can win a broad clientele, sometimes in environments and for applications that their designers never dreamed of. This book concentrates on languages of the latter kind.

These successful languages share a significant characteristic: each of them is the brainchild of a single person or a small team of like-minded enthusiasts. Their designers are masterminds of programming; they have the experience, the vision, the energy, the persistence, and the sheer genius to drive the language through its initial implementation, through its evolution in the light of experience, and through its standardisation by usage (de facto) and by committee (de jure).

In this book the reader will meet this collection of masterminds in person. Each of them has granted an extended interview, telling the story of his language and the factors that lie behind its success. The combined role of good decisions and good luck is frankly acknowledged. And finally, the publication of the actual words spoken in the interview gives an insight into the personality and motivations of the designer, which is as fascinating as the language design itself.

—*Sir Tony Hoare*

*Sir Tony Hoare, winner of an ACM Turing Award and a Kyoto Award, has been a leader in research into computing algorithms and programming languages for 50 years. His first academic paper, written in 1969, explored the idea of proving the correctness of programs, and suggested that a goal of programming language design was to make it easier to write correct programs. He is delighted to see the idea spread gradually among programming language designers.*

# Preface

**WRITING SOFTWARE IS HARD—AT LEAST, WRITING SOFTWARE THAT STANDS UP UNDER TESTS, TIME,** and different environments is hard. Not only has the software engineering field struggled to make writing software easier over the past five decades, but languages have been designed to make it easier. But what makes it hard in the first place?

Most of the books and the papers that claim to address this problem talk about architecture, requirements, and similar topics that focus on the *software*. What if the hard part was in the *writing*? To put it another way, what if we saw our jobs as programmers more in terms of communication—*language*—and less in terms of engineering?

Children learn to talk in their first years of life, and we start teaching them how to read and write when they are five or six years old. I don't know any great writer who learned to read and write as an adult. Do you know any great programmer who learned to program late in life?

And if children can learn foreign languages much more easily than adults, what does this tell us about learning to program—an activity involving a new language?

Imagine that you are studying a foreign language and you don't know the name of an object. You can describe it with the words that you know, hoping someone will understand what you mean. Isn't this what we do every day with software? We describe the object we have in our mind with a programming language, hoping the description will be clear enough to the compiler or interpreter. If something doesn't work, we bring up the picture again in our mind and try to understand what we missed or misdescribed.

With these questions in mind, I chose to launch a series of investigations into why a programming language is created, how it's technically developed, how it's taught and learned, and how it evolves over time.

Shane and I had the great privilege to let 27 great designers guide us through our journey, so that we have been able to collect their wisdom and experience for you.

In *Masterminds of Programming*, you will discover some of the thinking and steps needed to build a successful language, what makes it popular, and how to approach the current problems that its programmers are facing. So if you want to learn more about successful programming language design, this book surely can help you.

If you are looking for inspiring thoughts regarding software and programming languages, you will need a highlighter, or maybe two, because I promise that you will find plenty of them throughout these pages.

*—Federico Biancuzzi*

## Organization of the Material

The chapters in this book are ordered to provide a varied and provocative perspective as you travel through it. Savor the interviews and return often.

Chapter 1, *C++*, interviews Bjarne Stroustrup.

Chapter 2, *Python*, interviews Guido van Rossum.

Chapter 3, *APL*, interviews Adin D. Falkoff.

Chapter 4, *Forth*, interviews Charles H. Moore.

Chapter 5, *BASIC*, interviews Thomas E. Kurtz.

Chapter 6, *AWK*, interviews Alfred Aho, Peter Weinberger, and Brian Kernighan.

Chapter 7, *Lua*, interviews Luiz Henrique de Figueiredo and Roberto Ierusalimschy.

Chapter 8, *Haskell*, interviews Simon Peyton Jones, Paul Hudak, Philip Wadler, and John Hughes.

Chapter 9, *ML*, interviews Robin Milner.

Chapter 10, *SQL*, interviews Don Chamberlin.

Chapter 11, *Objective-C*, interviews Tom Love and Brad Cox.

Chapter 12, *Java*, interviews James Gosling.

Chapter 13, *C#*, interviews Anders Hejlsberg.

Chapter 14, *UML*, interviews Ivar Jacobson, James Rumbaugh, and Grady Booch.

Chapter 15, *Perl*, interviews Larry Wall.

Chapter 16, *PostScript*, interviews Charles Geschke and John Warnock.

Chapter 17, *Eiffel*, interviews Bertrand Meyer.

*Contributors* lists the biographies of all the contributors.

## Conventions Used in This Book

The following typographical conventions are used in this book:

*Italic*
> Indicates new terms, URLs, filenames, and utilities.

`Constant width`
> Indicates the contents of computer files and generally anything found in programs.

## How to Contact Us

Please address comments and questions concerning this book to the publisher:

> O'Reilly Media, Inc.
> 1005 Gravenstein Highway North
> Sebastopol, CA 95472
> 800-998-9938 (in the United States or Canada)
> 707-829-0515 (international or local)
> 707-829-0104 (fax)

We have a web page for this book, where we list errata, examples, and any additional information. You can access this page at:

> *http://www.oreilly.com/catalog/9780596515171*

To comment or ask technical questions about this book, send email to:

> *bookquestions@oreilly.com*

For more information about our books, conferences, Resource Centers, and the O'Reilly Network, see our website at:

> *http://www.oreilly.com*

## Safari® Books Online

 When you see a Safari® Books Online icon on the cover of your favorite technology book, that means the book is available online through the O'Reilly Network Safari Bookshelf.

Safari offers a solution that's better than e-books. It's a virtual library that lets you easily search thousands of top tech books, cut and paste code samples, download chapters, and find quick answers when you need the most accurate, current information. Try it for free at *http://my.safaribooksonline.com*.

# CHAPTER ONE

# C++

C++ occupies an interesting space among languages: it is built on the foundation of C, incorporating object-orientation ideas from Simula; standardized by ISO; and designed with the mantras "you don't pay for what you don't use" and "support user-defined and built-in types equally well." Although popularized in the 80s and 90s for OO and GUI programming, one of its greatest contributions to software is its pervasive generic programming techniques, exemplified in its Standard Template Library. Newer languages such as Java and C# have attempted to replace C++, but an upcoming revision of the C++ standard adds new and long-awaited features. Bjarne Stroustrup is the creator of the language and still one of its strongest advocates.

# Design Decisions

*Why did you choose to extend an existing language instead of creating a new one?*

**Bjarne Stroustrup:** When I started—in 1979—my purpose was to help programmers build systems. It still is. To provide genuine help in solving a problem, rather than being just an academic exercise, a language must be complete for the application domain. That is, a non-research language exists to solve a problem. The problems I was addressing related to operating system design, networking, and simulation. I—and my colleagues—needed a language that could express program organization as could be done in Simula (that's what people tend to call object-oriented programming), but also write efficient low-level code, as could be done in C. No language that could do both existed in 1979, or I would have used it. I didn't particularly want to design a new programming language; I just wanted to help solve a few problems.

Given that, building on an existing language makes a lot of sense. From the base language, you get a basic syntactic and semantic structure, you get useful libraries, and you become part of a culture. Had I not built on C, I would have based C++ on some other language. Why C? I had Dennis Ritchie, Brian Kernighan, and other Unix greats just down (or across) the hall from me in Bell Labs' Computer Science Research Center, so the question may seem redundant. But it was a question I took seriously.

In particular, C's type system was informal and weakly enforced (as Dennis Ritchie said, "C is a strongly typed, weakly checked language"). The "weakly checked" part worried me and causes problems for C++ programmers to this day. Also, C wasn't the widely used language it is today. Basing C++ on C was an expression of faith in the model of computation that underlies C (the "strongly typed" part) and an expression of trust in my colleagues. The choice was made based on knowledge of most higher-level programming languages used for systems programming at the time (both as a user and as an implementer). It is worth remembering that this was a time when most work "close to the hardware" and requiring serious performance was still done in assembler. Unix was a major breakthrough in many ways, including its use of C for even the most demanding systems programming tasks.

So, I chose C's basic model of the machine over better-checked type systems. What I really wanted as the framework for programs was Simula's classes, so I mapped those into the C model of memory and computation. The result was something that was extremely expressive and flexible, yet ran at a speed that challenged assembler without a massive runtime support system.

*Why did you choose to support multiple paradigms?*

**Bjarne:** Because a combination of programming styles often leads to the best code, where "best" means code that most directly expresses the design, runs faster, is most maintainable, etc. When people challenge that statement, they usually do so by either defining their favorite programming style to include every useful construct (e.g., "generic programming is simply a form of OO") or excluding application areas (e.g., "everybody has a 1GHz, 1GB machine").

*Java focuses solely on object-oriented programming. Does this make Java code more complex in some cases where C++ can instead take advantage of generic programming?*

**Bjarne:** Well, the Java designers—and probably the Java marketers even more so—emphasized OO to the point where it became absurd. When Java first appeared, claiming purity and simplicity, I predicted that if it succeeded Java would grow significantly in size and complexity. It did.

For example, using casts to convert from `Object` when getting a value out of a container (e.g., `(Apple)c.get(i)`) is an absurd consequence of not being able to state what type the objects in the container is supposed have. It's verbose and inefficient. Now Java has generics, so it's just a bit slow. Other examples of increased language complexity (helping the programmer) are enumerations, reflection, and inner classes.

The simple fact is that complexity will emerge somewhere, if not in the language definition, then in thousands of applications and libraries. Similarly, Java's obsession with putting every algorithm (operation) into a class leads to absurdities like classes with no data consisting exclusively of static functions. There are reasons why math uses $f(x)$ and $f(x,y)$ rather than `x.f( )`, `x.f(y)`, and `(x,y).f( )`—the latter is an attempt to express the idea of a "truly object-oriented method" of two arguments and to avoid the inherent asymmetry of `x.f(y)`.

C++ addresses many of the logical as well as the notational problems with object orientation through a combination of data abstraction and generic programming techniques. A classical example is `vector<T>` where `T` can be any type that can be copied including built-in types, pointers to OO hierarchies, and user-defined types, such as strings and complex numbers. This is all done without adding runtime overheads, placing restrictions on data layouts, or having special rules for standard library components. Another example that does not fit the classical single-dispatch hierarchy model of OO is an operation that requires access to two classes, such as `operator*(Matrix,Vector)`, which is not naturally a "method" of either class.

*One fundamental difference between C++ and Java is the way pointers are implemented. In some ways, you could say that Java doesn't have real pointers. What differences are there between the two approaches?*

**Bjarne:** Well, of course Java has pointers. In fact, just about everything in Java is implicitly a pointer. They just call them *references*. There are advantages to having pointers implicit as well as disadvantages. Separately, there are advantages to having true local objects (as in C++) as well as disadvantages.

C++'s choice to support stack-allocated local variables and true member variables of every type gives nice uniform semantics, supports the notion of value semantics well, gives compact layout and minimal access costs, and is the basis for C++'s support for general resource management. That's major, and Java's pervasive and implicit use of pointers (aka references) closes the door to all that.

Consider the layout tradeoff: in C++ a vector<complex>(10) is represented as a handle to an array of 10 complex numbers on the free store. In all, that's 25 words: 3 words for the vector, plus 20 words for the complex numbers, plus a 2-word header for the array on the free store (heap). The equivalent in Java (for a user-defined container of objects of user-defined types) would be 56 words: 1 for the reference to the container, plus 3 for the container, plus 10 for the references to the objects, plus 20 for the objects, plus 24 for the free store headers for the 12 independently allocated objects. Obviously, these numbers are approximate because the free store (heap) overhead is implementation defined in both languages. However, the conclusion is clear: by making references ubiquitous and implicit, Java may have simplified the programming model and the garbage collector implementation, but it has increased the memory overhead dramatically—and increased the memory access cost (requiring more indirect accesses) and allocation overheads proportionally.

What Java doesn't have—and good for Java for that—is C and C++'s ability to misuse pointers through pointer arithmetic. Well-written C++ doesn't suffer from that problem either: people use higher-level abstractions, such as iostreams, containers, and algorithms, rather than fiddling with pointers. Essentially all arrays and most pointers belong deep in implementations that most programmers don't have to see. Unfortunately, there is also lots of poorly written and unnecessarily low-level C++ around.

There is, however, an important place where pointers—and pointer manipulation—is a boon: the direct and efficient expression of data structures. Java's references are lacking here; for example, you can't express a swap operation in Java. Another example is simply the use of pointers for low-level direct access to (real) memory; for every system, some language has to do that, and often that language is C++.

The "dark side" of having pointers (and C-style arrays) is of course the potential for misuse: buffer overruns, pointers into deleted memory, uninitialized pointers, etc. However, in well-written C++ that is not a major problem. You simply don't get those problems with pointers and arrays used within abstractions (such as vector, string, map, etc.). Scoped resource management takes care of most needs; smart pointers and specialized handles can be used to deal with most of the rest. People whose experience is primarily C or old-style C++ find this hard to believe, but scope-based resource management is an immensely powerful tool and user-defined with suitable operations can address classical problems with less code than the old insecure hacks. For example, this is the simplest form of the classical buffer overrun and security problem:

```
char buf[MAX_BUF];
gets(buf); // Yuck!
```

Use a standard library string and the problem goes away:

```
string s;
cin >> s;     // read whitespace separated characters
```

These are obviously trivial examples, but suitable "strings" and "containers" can be crafted to meet essentially all needs, and the standard library provides a good set to start with.

*What do you mean by "value semantics" and "general resource management"?*

**Bjarne:** "Value semantics" is commonly used to refer to classes where the objects have the property that when you copy one, you get two independent copies (with the same value). For example:

```
X x1 = a;
X x2 = x1; // now x1==x2
x1 = b;    // changes x1 but not x2
           // now x1!=x2 ( provided X(a)!=X(b) )
```

This is of course what we have for usual numeric types, such as ints, doubles, complex numbers, and mathematical abstractions, such as vectors. This is a most useful notion, which C++ supports for built-in types and for any user-defined type for which we want it. This contrast to Java where built-in types such and char and int follow it, but user-defined types do not, and indeed cannot. As in Simula, all user-defined types in Java have reference semantics. In C++, a programmer can support either, as the desired semantics of a type requires. C# (incompletely) follows C++ in supporting user-defined types with value semantics.

"General resource management" refers to the popular technique of having a resource (e.g., a file handle or a lock) owned by an object. If that object is a scoped variable, the lifetime of the variable puts a maximum limit on the time the resource is held. Typically, a constructor acquires the resource and the destructor releases it. This is often called RAII (Resource Acquisition Is Initialization) and integrates beautifully with error handling using exceptions. Obviously, not every resource can be handled in this way, but many can, and for those, resource management becomes implicit and efficient.

*"Close to the hardware" seems to be a guiding principle in designing C++. Is it fair to say that C++ was designed more bottom-up than many languages, which are designed top-down, in the sense that they try to provide abstractly rational constructs and force the compiler to fit these constructs to the available computing environment?*

**Bjarne:** I think top-down and bottom-up are the wrong way to characterize those design decisions. In the context of C++ and other languages, "close to the hardware" means that the model of computation is that of the computer—sequences of objects in memory and operations as defined on objects of fixed size—rather than some mathematical abstraction. This is true for both C++ and Java, but not for functional languages. C++ differs from Java in that its underlying machine is the real machine rather than a single abstract machine.

The real problem is how to get from the human conception of problems and solutions to the machine's limited world. You can "ignore" the human concerns and end up with machine code (or the glorified machine code that is bad C code). You can ignore the machine and come up with a beautiful abstraction that can do anything at extraordinary cost and/or lack of intellectual rigor. C++ is an attempt to give a very direct access to hardware when you need it (e.g., pointers and arrays) while providing extensive abstraction mechanisms to allow high-level ideas to be expressed (e.g., class hierarchies and templates).

That said, there has been a consistent concern for runtime and space performance throughout the development of C++ and its libraries. This pervades both the basic language facilities and the abstraction facilities in ways that are not shared by all languages.

## Using the Language

*How do you debug? Do you have any suggestion for C++ developers?*

**Bjarne:** By introspection. I study the program for so long and poke at it more or less systematically for so long that I have sufficient understanding to provide an educated guess where the bug is.

Testing is something else, and so is design to minimize errors. I intensely dislike debugging and will go a long way to avoid it. If I am the designer of a piece of software, I build it around interfaces and invariants so that it is hard to get seriously bad code to compile and run incorrectly. Then, I try hard to make it testable. Testing is the systematic search for errors. It is hard to systematically test badly structured systems, so I again recommend a clean structure of the code. Testing can be automated and is repeatable in a way that debugging is not. Having flocks of pigeons randomly peck at the screen to see if they can break a GUI-based application is no way to ensure quality systems.

Advice? It is hard to give general advice because the best techniques often depend on what is feasible for a given system in a given development environment. However: identify key interfaces that can be systematically tested and write test scripts that exercise those. Automate as much as you can and run those automated tests often. And do keep regression tests and run them frequently. Make sure that every entry point into the system and every output can be systematically tested. Compose your system out of quality components: monolithic programs are unnecessarily hard to understand and test.

*At what level is it necessary to improve the security of software?*

**Bjarne:** First of all: security is a systems issue. No localized or partial remedy will by itself succeed. Remember, even if all of your code was perfect, I could probably still gain access to your stored secrets if I could steal your computer or the storage device holding your backup. Secondly, security is a cost/benefit game: perfect security is probably beyond the reach for most of us, but I can probably protect my system sufficiently that "bad guys" will consider their time better spent trying to break into someone else's system. Actually, I prefer not to keep important secrets online and leave serious security to the experts.

But what about programming languages and programming techniques? There is a dangerous tendency to assume that every line of code has to be "secure" (whatever that means), even assuming that someone with bad intentions messes with some other part of the system. This is a most dangerous notion that leaves the code littered with unsystematic tests guarding against ill-formulated imagined threats. It also makes code ugly, large, and slow. "Ugly" leaves places for bugs to hide, "large" ensures incomplete testing, and "slow" encourages the use of shortcuts and dirty tricks that are among the most fertile sources of security holes.

I think the only permanent solution to security problems is in a simple security model applied systematically by quality hardware and/or software to selected interfaces. There has to be a place behind a barrier where code can be written simply, elegantly, and efficiently without worrying about random pieces of code abusing random pieces of other code. Only then can we focus on correctness, quality, and serious performance. The idea that anyone can provide an untrusted callback, plug-in, overrider, whatever, is plain silly. We have to distinguish between code that defends against fraud, and code that simply is protected against accidents.

I do not think that you can design a programming language that is completely secure and also useful for real-world systems. Obviously, that depends on the meaning of "secure" and "system." You could possibly achieve security in a domain-specific language, but my main domain of interest is systems programming (in a very broad meaning of that term), including embedded systems programming. I do think that type safety can and will be improved over what is offered by C++, but that is only part of the problem: type safety does not equal security. People who write C++ using lots of unencapsulated arrays, casts, and unstructured new and delete operations are asking for trouble. They are stuck in an 80s style of programming. To use C++ well, you have to adopt a style that minimizes type safety violations and manage resources (including memory) in a simple and systematic way.

### Would you recommend C++ for some systems where practitioners are reluctant to use it, such as system software and embedded applications?

**Bjarne:** Certainly, I do recommend it and not everybody is reluctant. In fact, I don't see much reluctance in those areas beyond the natural reluctance to try something new in established organizations. Rather, I see steady and significant growth in C++ use. For example, I helped write the coding guidelines for the mission-critical software for Lockheed Martin's Joint Strike Fighter. That's an "all C++ plane." You may not be particularly keen on military planes, but there is nothing particularly military about the way C++ is used and well over 100,000 copies of the JSF++ coding rules have been downloaded from my home pages in less than a year, mostly by nonmilitary embedded systems developers, as far as I can tell.

C++ has been used for embedded systems since 1984, many useful gadgets have been programmed in C++, and its use appears to be rapidly increasing. Examples are mobile phones using Symbian or Motorola, the iPods, and GPS systems. I particularly like the use of C++ on the Mars rovers: the scene analysis and autonomous driving subsystems, much of the earth-based communication systems, and the image processing.

People who are convinced that C is necessarily more efficient than C++ might like to have a look at my paper entitled "Learning Standard C++ as a New Language" [*C/C++ Users Journal*, May 1999], which describes a bit of design philosophy and shows the result of a few simple experiments. Also, the ISO C++ standards committee issued a technical report on performance that addresses a lot of issues and myths relating to the use of C++ where performance matters (you can find it online searching for "Technical Report on C++ Performance").* In particular, that report addresses embedded systems issues.

* *http://www.open-std.org/JTC1/sc22/wg21/docs/TR18015.pdf*

*Kernels like Linux's or BSD's are still written in C. Why haven't they moved to C++? Is it something in the OO paradigm?*

**Bjarne:** It's mostly conservatism and inertia. In addition, GCC was slow to mature. Some people in the C community seem to maintain an almost willful ignorance based on decade-old experiences. Other operating systems and much systems programming and even hard real-time and safety-critical code has been written in C++ for decades. Consider some examples: Symbian, IBM's OS/400 and K42, BeOS, and parts of Windows. In general, there is a lot of open source C++ (e.g., KDE).

You seem to equate C++ use with OO. C++ is not and was never meant to be just an object-oriented programming language. I wrote a paper entitled "Why C++ is not just an Object-Oriented Programming Language" in 1995; it is available online.[*] The idea was and is to support multiple programming styles ("paradigms," if you feel like using long words) and their combinations. The most relevant other paradigm in the context of high-performance and close-to-the-hardware use is generic programming (sometimes abbreviated to GP). The ISO C++ standard library is itself more heavily GP than OO through its framework for algorithms and containers (the STL). Generic programming in the typical C++ style relying heavily on templates is widely used where you need both abstraction and performance.

I have never seen a program that could be written better in C than in C++. I don't think such a program could exist. If nothing else, you can write C++ in a style close to that of C. There is nothing that requires you to go hog-wild with exceptions, class hierarchies, or templates. A good programmer uses the more advanced features where they help more directly to express ideas and do so without avoidable overheads.

*Why should a programmer move his code from C to C++? What advantages would he have using C++ as a generic programming language?*

**Bjarne:** You seem to assume that code first was written in C and that the programmer started out as a C programmer. For many—probably most—C++ programs and C++ programmers, that has not been the case for quite a while. Unfortunately, the "C first" approach lingers in many curricula, but it is no longer something to take for granted.

Someone might switch from C to C++ because they found C++'s support for the styles of programming usually done with C is better than C's. The C++ type checking is stricter (you can't forget to declare a function or its argument types) and there is type-safe notational support for many common operations, such as object creation (including initialization) and constants. I have seen people do that and be very happy with the problems they left behind. Usually, that's done in combination with the adoption of some C++ libraries that may or may not be considered object-oriented, such as the standard vector, a GUI library, or some application-specific library.

---

[*] *http://www.research.att.com/~bs/oopsla.pdf*

Just using a simple user-defined type, such as vector, string, or complex, does not require a paradigm shift. People can—if they so choose—use those just like the built-in types. Is someone using std::vector "using OO"? I would say no. Is someone using a C++ GUI without actually adding new functionality "using OO"? I'm inclined to say yes, because their use typically requires the users to understand and use inheritance.

Using C++ as "a generic-programming programming language" gives you the standard containers and algorithms right out of box (as part of the standard library). That is major leverage in many applications and a major step up in abstraction from C. Beyond that, people can start to benefit from libraries, such as Boost, and start to appreciate some of the functional programming techniques inherent in generic programming.

However, I think the question is slightly misleading. I don't want to represent C++ as "an OO language" or "a GP language"; rather, it is a language supporting:

- C-style programming
- Data abstraction
- Object-oriented programming
- Generic programming

Crucially, it supports programming styles that combines those ("multiparadigm programming" if you must) and does so with a bias toward systems programming.

## OOP and Concurrency

*The average complexity and size (in number of lines of code) of software seems to grow year after year. Does OOP scale well to this situation or just make things more complicated? I have the feeling that the desire to make reusable objects makes things more complicated and, in the end, it doubles the workload. First, you have to design a reusable tool. Later, when you need to make a change, you have to write something that exactly fits the gap left by the old part, and this means restrictions on the solution.*

**Bjarne:** That's a good description of a serious problem. OO is a powerful set of techniques that can help, but to be a help, it must be used well and for problems where the techniques have something to offer. A rather serious problem for all code relying on inheritance with statically checked interfaces is that to design a good base class (an interface to many, yet unknown, classes) we require a lot of foresight and experience. How does the designer of the base class (abstract class, interface, whatever you choose to call it) know that it specifies all that is needed for all classes that will be derived from it in the future? How does the designer know that what is specified can be implemented reasonably by all classes that will be derived from it in the future? How does the designer of the base class know that what is specified will not seriously interfere with something that is needed by some classes that will be derived from it in the future?

In general, we can't know that. In an environment where we can enforce our design, people will adapt—often by writing ugly workarounds. Where no one organization is in charge, many incompatible interfaces emerge for essentially the same functionality.

Nothing can solve these problems in general, but generic programming seems to be an answer in many important cases where the OO approach fails. A noteworthy example is simply containers: we cannot express the notion of being an element well through an inheritance hierarchy, and we can't express the notion of being a container well through an inheritance hierarchy. We can, however, provide effective solutions using generic programming. The STL (as found in the C++ standard library) is an example.

*Is this problem specific to C++, or does it afflict other programming languages as well?*

**Bjarne:** The problem is common to all languages that rely on statically checked interfaces to class hierarchies. Examples are C++, Java, and C#, but not dynamically typed languages, such as Smalltalk and Python. C++ addresses that problem through generic programming, where the C++ containers and algorithms in standard library provide a good example. The key language feature here is templates, providing a late type-checking model that gives a compile time equivalent to what the dynamically typed languages do at runtime. Java's and C#'s recent addition of "generics" are attempts to follow C++'s lead here, and are often—incorrectly, I think—claimed to improve upon templates.

"Refactoring" is especially popular as an attempt to address that problem by the brute force technique of simply reorganizing the code when it has outlived its initial interface design.

*If this is a problem of OO in general, how can we be sure that the advantages of OO are more valuable than the disadvantages? Maybe the problem that a good OO design is difficult to achieve is the root of all other problems.*

**Bjarne:** The fact that there is a problem in some or even many cases doesn't change the fact that many beautiful, efficient, and maintainable systems have been written in such languages. Object-oriented design is one of the fundamental ways of designing systems and statically checked interfaces provide advantages as well as this problem.

There is no one "root of all evil" in software development. Design is hard in many ways. People tend to underestimate the intellectual and practical difficulties involved in building a significant system involving software. It is not and will not be reduced to a simple mechanical "assembly line" process. Creativity, engineering principles, and evolutionary change are needed to create a satisfactory large system.

*Are there links between the OO paradigm and concurrency? Does the current pervasive need for improved concurrency change the implementation of designs or the nature of OO designs?*

**Bjarne:** There is a very old link between object-oriented programming and concurrency. Simula 67, the programming language that first directly supported object-oriented programming, also provided a mechanism for expressing concurrent activities.

The first C++ library was a library supporting what today we would call *threads*. At Bell Labs, we ran C++ on a six-processor machine in 1988 and we were not alone in such uses. In the 90s there were at least a couple of dozen experimental C++ dialects and libraries attacking problems related to distributed and parallel programming. The current excitement about multicores isn't my first encounter with concurrency. In fact, distributed computing was my Ph.D. topic and I have followed that field ever since.

However, people who first consider concurrency, multicores, etc., often confuse themselves by simply underestimating the cost of running an activity on a different processor. The cost of starting an activity on another processor (core) and for that activity to access data in the "calling processor's" memory (either copying or accessing "remotely") can be 1,000 times (or more) higher than we are used to for a function call. Also, the error possibilities are significantly different as soon as you introduce concurrency. To effectively exploit the concurrency offered by the hardware, we need to rethink the organization of our software.

Fortunately, but confusingly, we have decades' worth of research to help us. Basically, there is so much research that it's just about impossible to determine what's real, let alone what's best. A good place to start looking would be the HOPL-III paper about Emerald. That language was the first to explore the interaction between language issues and systems issues, taking cost into account. It is also important to distinguish between data parallel programming as has been done for decades—mostly in FORTRAN—for scientific calculations, and the use of communicating units of "ordinary sequential code" (e.g., processes and threads) on many processors. I think that for broad acceptance in this brave new world of many "cores" and clusters, a programming system must support both kinds of concurrency, and probably several varieties of each. This is not at all easy, and the issues go well beyond traditional programming language issues—we will end up looking at language, systems, and applications issues in combination.

*Is C++ ready for concurrency? Obviously we can create libraries to handle everything, but does the language and standard library need a serious review with concurrency in mind?*

**Bjarne:** Almost. C++0x will be. To be ready for concurrency, a language first has to have a precisely specified memory model to allow compiler writers to take advantage of modern hardware (with deep pipelines, large caches, branch-prediction buffers, static and dynamic instruction reordering, etc.). Then, we need a few small language extensions: thread-local storage and atomic data types. Then, we can add support for concurrency as libraries. Naturally, the first new standard library will be a threads library allowing portable programming across systems such as Linux and Windows. We have of course had such libraries for many years, but not standard ones.

Threads plus some form of locking to avoid data races is just about the worst way to directly exploit concurrency, but C++ needs that to support existing applications and to maintain its role as a systems programming language on traditional operating systems. Prototypes of this library exist—based on many years of active use.

One key issue for concurrency is how you "package up" a task to be executed concurrently with other tasks. In C++, I suspect the answer will be "as a function object." The object can contain whatever data is needed and be passed around as needed. C++98 handles that well for named operations (named classes from which we instantiate function objects), and the technique is ubiquitous for parameterization in generic libraries (e.g., the STL). C++0x makes it easier to write simple "one-off" function objects by providing "lambda functions" that can be written in expression contexts (e.g., as function arguments) and generates function objects ("closures") appropriately.

The next steps are more interesting. Immediately post-C++0x, the committee plans for a technical report on libraries. This will almost certainly provide for thread pools and some form of work stealing. That is, there will be a standard mechanism for a user to request relatively small units of work ("tasks") to be done concurrently without fiddling with thread creation, cancellation, locking, etc., probably built with function objects as tasks. Also, there will be facilities for communicating between geographically remote processes through sockets, iostreams, and so on, rather like boost::networking.

In my opinion, much of what is interesting about concurrency will appear as multiple libraries supporting logically distinct concurrency models.

*Many modern systems are componentized and spread out over a network; the age of web applications and mashups may accentuate that trend. Should a language reflect those aspects of the network?*

**Bjarne:** There are many forms of concurrency. Some are aimed at improving the throughput or response time of a program on a single computer or cluster, some are aimed at dealing with geographical distribution, and some are below the level usually considered by programmers (pipelining, caching, etc.).

C++0x will provide a set of facilities and guarantees that saves programmers from the lowest-level details by providing a "contract" between machine architects and compiler writers—a "machine model." It will also provide a threads library providing a basic mapping of code to processors. On this basis, other models can be provided by libraries. I would have liked to see some simpler-to-use, higher-level concurrency models supported in the C++0x standard library, but that now appears unlikely. Later—hopefully, soon after C++0x—we will get more libraries specified in a technical report: thread pools and futures, and a library for I/O streams over wide area networks (e.g., TCP/IP). These libraries exist, but not everyone considers them well enough specified for the standard.

Years ago, I hoped that C++0x would address some of C++'s long-standing problems with distribution by specifying a standard form of marshalling (or serialization), but that didn't happen. So, the C++ community will have to keep addressing the higher levels of distributed computing and distributed application building through nonstandard libraries and/or frameworks (e.g., CORBA or .NET).

The very first C++ library (really the very first C with classes) library, provided a lightweight form of concurrency and over the years, hundreds of libraries and frameworks for concurrent, parallel, and distributed computing have been built in C++, but the community has not been able to agree on standards. I suspect that part of the problem is that it takes a lot of money to do something major in this field, and that the big players preferred to spend their money on their own proprietary libraries, frameworks, and languages. That has not been good for the C++ community as a whole.

# Future

## *Will we ever see C++ 2.0?*

**Bjarne:** That depends on what you mean by "C++ 2.0." If you mean a new language built more or less from scratch providing all of the best of C++ but none of what's bad (for some definitions of "good" and "bad"), the answer is "I don't know." I would like to see a major new language in the C++ tradition, but I don't see one on the horizon, so let me concentrate on the next ISO C++ standard, nicknamed C++0x.

It will be a "C++ 2.0" to many, because it will supply new language features and new standard libraries, but it will be almost 100% compatible with C++98. We call it C++0x, hoping that it'll become C++09. If we are slow—so that that *x* has to become hexadecimal—I (and others) will be quite sad and embarrassed.

C++0x will be almost 100% compatible with C++98. We have no particular desire to break your code. The most significant incompatibilities come from the use of a few new keywords, such as static_assert, constexpr, and concept. We have tried to minimize impact by choosing new keywords that are not heavily used. The major improvements are:

- Support for modern machine architectures and concurrency: a machine model, a thread library, thread local storage and atomic operations, and an asynchronous value return mechanism ("futures").

- Better support for generic programming: concepts (a type system for types, combinations of types, and combinations of types and integers) to give better checking of template definitions and uses, and better overloading of templates. Type deduction based on initializers (auto), generalized initializer lists, generalized constant expressions (constexpr), lambda expressions, and more.

- Many "minor" language extensions, such as static assertions, move semantics, improved enumerations, a name for the null pointer (nullptr), etc.

- New standard libraries for regular expression matching, hash tables (e.g., unordered_map), "smart" pointers, etc.

For complete details, see the website of the "C++ Standards Committee."* For an overview, see my online C++0x FAQ.†

---

* *http://www.open-std.org/jtc1/sc22/wg21/*

† *http://www.research.att.com/~bs/C++0xFAQ.html*

Please note that when I talk about "not breaking code," I am referring to the core language and the standard library. Old code will of course be broken if it uses nonstandard extensions from some compiler provider or antique nonstandard libraries. In my experience, when people complain about "broken code" or "instability" they are referring to proprietary features and libraries. For example, if you change operating systems and didn't use one of the portable GUI libraries, you probably have some work to do on the user interface code.

### What stops you from creating a major new language?

**Bjarne:** Some key questions soon emerge:

- What problem would the new language solve?
- Who would it solve problems for?
- What dramatically new could be provided (compared to every existing language)?
- Could the new language be effectively deployed (in a world with many well-supported languages)?
- Would designing a new language simply be a pleasant distraction from the hard work of helping people build better real-world tools and systems?

So far, I have not been able to answer those questions to my satisfaction.

That doesn't mean that I think that C++ is the perfect language of its kind. It is not; I'm convinced that you could design a language about a tenth of the size of C++ (whichever way you measure size) providing roughly what C++ does. However, there has to be more to a new language that just doing what an existing language can, but slightly better and slightly more elegantly.

### What do the lessons about the invention, further development, and adoption of your language say to people developing computer systems today and in the foreseeable future?

**Bjarne:** That's a big question: can we learn from history? If so, how? What kind of lessons can we learn? During the early development of C++, I articulated a set of "rules of thumb," which you can find in *The Design and Evolution of C++* [Addison-Wesley], and also discussed in my two HOPL papers. Clearly, any serious language design project needs a set of principles, and as soon as possible, these principles need to be articulated. That's actually a conclusion from the C++ experience: I didn't articulate C++'s design principles early enough and didn't get those principles understood widely enough. As a result, many people invented their own rationales for C++'s design; some of those were pretty amazing and led to much confusion. To this day, some see C++ as little more than a failed attempt to design something like Smalltalk (no, C++ was not supposed to be "like Smalltalk"; it follows the Simula model of OO), or as nothing but an attempt to remedy some flaws in C for writing C-style code (no, C++ was not supposed to be just C with a few tweaks).

The purpose of a (nonexperimental) programming language is to help build good systems. It follows that notions of system design and language design are closely related.

My definition of "good" in this context is basically "correct, maintainable, and providing acceptable resource usage." The obvious missing component is "easy to write," but for the kind of systems I think most about, that's secondary. "RAD development" is not my ideal. It can be as important to say what is not a primary aim as to state what is. For example, I have nothing against rapid development—nobody in their right mind wants to spend more time than necessary on a project—but I'd rather have lack of restrictions on application areas and performance. My aim for C++ was and is direct expression of ideas, resulting in code that can be efficient in time and space.

C and C++ have provided stability over decades. That has been immensely important to their industrial users. I have small programs that have been essentially unchanged since the early 80s. There is a price to pay for such stability, but languages that don't provide it are simply unsuitable for large, long-lived projects. Corporate languages and languages that try to follow trends closely tend to fail miserably here, causing a lot of misery along the way.

This leads to thinking about how to manage evolution. How much can be changed? What is the granularity of change? Changing a language every year or so as new releases of a product are released is too ad hoc and leads to a series of de facto subsets, discarded libraries and language features, and/or massive upgrade efforts. Also, a year is simply not sufficient gestation period for significant features, so the approach leads to half-baked solutions and dead ends. On the other hand, the 10-year cycle of ISO standardized languages, such as C and C++, is too long and leads to parts of the community (including parts of the committee) fossilizing.

A successful language develops a community: the community shares techniques, tools, and libraries. Corporate languages have an inherent advantage here: they can buy market share with marketing, conferences, and "free" libraries. This investment can pay off in terms of others adding significantly, making the community larger and more vibrant. Sun's efforts with Java showed how amateurish and underfinanced every previous effort to establish a (more or less) general-purpose language had been. The U.S. Department of Defense's efforts to establish Ada as a dominant language was a sharp contrast, as were the unfinanced efforts by me and my friends to establish C++.

I can't say that I approve of some of the Java tactics, such as selling top-down to nonprogramming executives, but it shows what can be done. Noncorporate successes include the Python and Perl communities. The successes at community building around C++ have been too few and too limited, given the size of the community. The ACCU conferences are great, but why haven't there been a continuous series of huge international C++ conferences since 1986 or so? The Boost libraries are great, but why hasn't there been a central repository for C++ libraries since 1986 or so? There are thousands of open source C++ libraries in use. I don't even know of a comprehensive list of commercial C++ libraries. I won't start answering those questions, but will just point out that any new language must somehow manage the centrifugal forces in a large community, or suffer pretty severe consequences.

A general-purpose language needs the input from and approval of several communities, such as, industrial programmers, educators, academic researchers, industrial researchers, and the open source community. These communities are not disjoint, but individual sub-communities often see themselves as self-sufficient, in possession of knowledge of what is right and in conflict with other communities that for some reason "don't get it." This can be a significant practical problem. For example, parts of the open source community have opposed the use of C++ because "it's a Microsoft language" (it isn't) or "AT&T owns it" (it doesn't), whereas some major industrial players have considered it a problem with C++ that *they* don't own it.

This really crucial problem here is that many subcommunities push a limited and paro-chial view of "what programming really is" and "what is really needed": "if everybody just did things the right way, there'd be no problem." The real problem is to balance the vari-ous needs to create a larger and more varied community. As people grow and face new challenges, the generality and flexibility of a language start to matter more than providing optimal solutions to a limited range of problems.

To get to technical points, I still think that a flexible, extensible, and general static type system is great. My reading of the C++ experience reinforces that view. I am also very keen on genuine local variables of user-defined types: the C++ techniques for handling general resources based on scoped variables have been very effective compared to just about anything. Constructors and destructors, often used together with RAII, can yield very elegant and efficient code.

## Teaching

*You left industry to become an academic. Why?*

**Bjarne:** Actually, I haven't completely left industry, because I maintain a link to AT&T Labs as an AT&T fellow, and spend much time each year with industry people. I consider my connection with industry essential because that's what keeps my work anchored in reality.

I went to Texas A&M University as a professor five years ago because (after almost 25 years in "The Labs") I felt a need for a change and because I thought I had something to contribute in the area of education. I also entertained some rather idealistic ideas about doing more fundamental research after my years of very practical research and design.

Much computer science research is either too remote from everyday problems (even from conjectured future everyday problems), or so submerged in such everyday problems that it becomes little more than technology transfer. Obviously, I have nothing against tech-nology transfer (we badly need it), but there ought to be strong feedback loops from industrial practice to advanced research. The short planning horizon of many in industry and the demands of the academic publication/tenure race conspire to divert attention and effort from some of the most critical problems.

*During these years in academia, what did you learn about teaching programming to beginners?*

**Bjarne:** The most concrete result of my years in academia (in addition to the obligatory academic papers) is a new textbook for teaching programming to people who have never programmed before, *Programming: Principles and Practice Using C++* [Addison-Wesley].

This is my first book for beginners. Before I went to academia, I simply didn't know enough beginners to write such a book. I did, however, feel that too many software developers were very poorly prepared for their tasks in industry and elsewhere. Now I have taught (and helped to teach) programming to more than 1,200 beginners and I feel a bit more certain that my ideas in this area can scale.

A beginner's book must serve several purposes. Most fundamentally, it must provide a good foundation for further learning (if successful, it will be the start of a lifelong effort) and also provide some practical skills. Also, programming—and in general software development—is not a purely theoretical skill, nor is it something you can do well without learning some fundamental concepts. Unfortunately, far too often, teaching fails to maintain a balance between theory/principles and practicalities/techniques. Consequently, we see people who basically despise programming ("mere coding") and think that software can be developed from first principles without any practical skills. Conversely, we see people who are convinced that "good code" is everything and can be achieved with little more than a quick look at an online manual and a lot of cutting and pasting; I have met programmers who considered K&R "too complicated and theoretical." My opinion is that both attitudes are far too extreme and lead to poorly structured, inefficient, and unmaintainable messes even when they do manage to produce minimally functioning code.

*What is your opinion on code examples in textbooks? Should they include error/ exception checking? Should they be complete programs so that they can actually be compiled and run?*

**Bjarne:** I strongly prefer examples that in as few lines as possible illustrate an idea. Such program fragments are often incomplete, though I insist that mine will compile and run if embedded in suitable scaffolding code. Basically, my code presentation style is derived from K&R. For my new book, all code examples will be available in a compilable form. In the text, I vary between small fragments embedded in explanatory text and longer, more complete, sections of code. In key places, I use both techniques for a single example to allow the reader two looks at critical statements.

Some examples should be complete with error checking and all should reflect designs that can be checked. In addition to the discussion of errors and error handling scattered throughout the book, there are separate chapters on error handling and testing. I strongly prefer examples derived from real-world programs. I really dislike artificial cute examples, such as inheritance trees of animals and obtuse mathematical puzzles. Maybe I should add a label to my book: "no cute cuddly animals were abused in this book's examples."

# CHAPTER TWO

# Python

---

Python is a modern, general-purpose, high-level language developed by Guido van Rossum as a result of his work with the ABC programming language. Python's philosophy is pragmatic; its users often speak of the Zen of Python, strongly preferring a single obvious way to accomplish any task. Ports exist for VMs such as Microsoft's CLR and the JVM, but the primary implementation is CPython, still developed by van Rossum and other volunteers, who just released Python 3.0, a backward-incompatible rethinking of parts of the language and its core libraries.

---

# The Pythonic Way

*What differences are there between developing a programming language and developing a "common" software project?*

**Guido van Rossum:** More than with most software projects, your most important users are programmers themselves. This gives a language project a high level of "meta" content. In the dependency tree of software projects, programming languages are pretty much at the bottom—everything else depends on one or more languages. This also makes it hard to change a language—an incompatible change affects so many dependents that it's usually just not feasible. In other words, all mistakes, once released, are cast in stone. The ultimate example of this is probably C++, which is burdened with compatibility requirements that effectively require code written maybe 20 years ago to be still valid.

*How do you debug a language?*

**Guido:** You don't. Language design is one area where agile development methodologies just don't make sense—until the language is stable, few people want to use it, and you won't find the bugs in the language definition until you have so many users that it's too late to change things.

Of course there's plenty in the *implementation* that can be debugged like any old program, but the language design itself pretty much requires careful design up front, because the cost of bugs is so exorbitant.

*How do you decide when a feature should go in a library as an extension or when it needs to have support from the core language?*

**Guido:** Historically, I've had a pretty good answer for that. One thing I noticed very early on was that everybody wants their favorite feature added to the language, and most people are relatively inexperienced about language design. Everybody is always proposing "let's add this to the language," "let's have a statement that does X." In many cases, the answer is, "Well, you can already do X or something almost like X by writing these two or three lines of code, and it's not all that difficult." You can use a dictionary, or you can combine a list and a tuple and a regular expression, or write a little metaclass—all of those things. I may even have had the original version of this answer from Linus, who seems to have a similar philosophy.

Telling people you can already do that and here is how is a first line of defense. The second thing is, "Well, that's a useful thing and we can probably write or you can probably write your own module or class, and encapsulate that particular bit of abstraction." Then the next line of defense is, "OK, this looks so interesting and useful that we'll actually accept it as a new addition to the standard library, and it's going to be pure Python." And then, finally, there are things that just aren't easy to do in pure Python and we'll suggest or recommend how to turn them into a C extension. The C extensions are the last line of defense before we have to admit, "Well, yeah, this is so useful and you really cannot do this, so we'll have to change the language."

There are other criteria that determine whether it makes more sense to add something to the language or it makes more sense to add something to the library, because if it has to do with the semantics of namespaces or that kind of stuff, there's really nothing you can do besides changing the language. On the other hand, the extension mechanism was made powerful enough that there is an amazing amount of stuff you can do from C code that extends the library and possibly even adds new built-in functionality without actually changing the language. The parser doesn't change. The parse tree doesn't change. The documentation for the language doesn't change. All your tools still work, and yet you have added new functionality to your system.

*I suppose there are probably features that you've looked at that you couldn't implement in Python other than by changing the language, but you probably rejected them. What criteria do you use to say this is something that's Pythonic, this is something that's not Pythonic?*

**Guido:** That's much harder. That is probably, in many cases, more a matter of a gut feeling than anything else. People use the word Pythonic and "that is Pythonic" a lot, but nobody can give you a watertight definition of what it means for something to be Pythonic or un-Pythonic.

*You have the "Zen of Python," but beyond that?*

**Guido:** That requires a lot of interpretation, like every good holy book. When I see a good or a bad proposal, I can tell if it is a good or bad proposal, but it's really hard to write a set of rules that will help someone else to distinguish good language change proposals from bad change proposals.

*Sounds almost like it's a matter of taste as much as anything.*

**Guido:** Well, the first thing is always try to say "no," and see if they go away or find a way to get their itch scratched without changing the language. It's remarkable how often that works. That's more of a operational definition of "it's not necessary to change the language."

If you keep the language constant, people will still find a way to do what they need to do. Beyond that it's often a matter of use cases coming from different areas where there is nothing application-specific. If something was really cool for the Web, that would not make it a good feature to add to the language. If something was really good for writing shorter functions or writing classes that are more maintainable, that might be a good thing to add to the language. It really needs to transcend application domains in general, and make things simpler or more elegant.

When you change the language, you affect everyone. There's no feature that you can hide so well that most people don't need to know about. Sooner or later, people will encounter code written by someone else that uses it, or they'll encounter some obscure corner case where they have to learn about it because things don't work the way they expected.

Often elegance is also in the eye of the beholder. We had a recent discussion on one of the Python lists where people were arguing forcefully that using dollar instead of self-dot was much more elegant. I think their definition of elegance was number of keystrokes.

*There's an argument to make for parsimony there, but very much in the context of personal taste.*

**Guido:** Elegance and simplicity and generality all are things that, to a large extent, depend on personal taste, because what seems to cover a larger area for me may not cover enough for someone else, and vice versa.

*How did the Python Enhancement Proposal (PEP) process come about?*

**Guido:** That's a very interesting historical tidbit. I think it was mostly started and championed by Barry Warsaw, one of the core developers. He and I started working together in '95, and I think around 2000, he came up with the suggestion that we needed more of a formal process around language changes.

I tend to be slow in these things. I mean I wasn't the person who discovered that we really needed a mailing list. I wasn't the person who discovered that the mailing list got unwieldy and we needed a newsgroup. I wasn't the person to propose that we needed a website. I was also not the person to propose that we needed a process for discussing and inventing language changes, and making sure to avoid the occasional mistake where things had been proposed and quickly accepted without thinking through all of the consequences.

At the time between 1995 and 2000, Barry, myself, and a few other core developers, Fred Drake, Ken Manheimer for a while, were all at CNRI, and one of the things that CNRI did was organize the IETF meetings. CNRI had this little branch that eventually split off that was a conference organizing bureau, and their only customer was the IETF. They later also did the Python conferences for a while, actually. Because of that it was a pretty easy boondoggle to attend IETF meetings even if they weren't local. I certainly got a taste of the IETF process with its RFCs and its meeting groups and stages, and Barry also got a taste of that. When he proposed to do something similar for Python, that was an easy argument to make. We consciously decided that we wouldn't make it quite as heavy-handed as the IETF RFCs had become by then, because Internet standards, at least some of them, affect way more industries and people and software than a Python change, but we definitely modeled it after that. Barry is a genius at coming up with good names, so I am pretty sure that PEP was his idea.

We were one of the first open source projects at the time to have something like this, and it's been relatively widely copied. The Tcl/Tk community basically changed the title and used exactly the same defining document and process, and other projects have done similar things.

*Do you find that adding a little bit of formalism really helps crystallize the design decisions around Python enhancements?*

**Guido:** I think it became necessary as the community grew and I wasn't necessarily able to judge every proposal on its value by itself. It has really been helpful for me to let other people argue over various details, and then come with relatively clear-cut conclusions.

*Do they lead to a consensus where someone can ask you to weigh in on a single particular crystallized set of expectations and proposals?*

**Guido:** Yes. It often works in a way where I initially give a PEP a thumb's up in the sense that I say, "It looks like we have a problem here. Let's see if someone figures out what the right solution is." Often they come out with a bunch of clear conclusions on how the problem should be solved and also a bunch of open issues. Sometimes my gut feelings can help close the open issues. I'm very active in the PEP process when it's an area that I'm excited about—if we had to add a new loop control statement, I wouldn't want that to be designed by other people. Sometimes I stay relatively far away from it like database APIs.

*What creates the need for a new major version?*

**Guido:** It depends on your definition of major. In Python, we generally consider releases like 2.4, 2.5, and 2.6 "major" events, which only happen every 18–24 months. These are the only occasions where we can introduce new features. Long ago, releases were done at the whim of the developers (me, in particular). Early this decade, however, the users requested some predictability—they objected against features being added or changed in "minor" revisions (e.g., 1.5.2 added major features compared to 1.5.1), and they wished the major releases to be supported for a certain minimum amount of time (18 months). So now we have more or less time-based major releases: we plan the series of dates leading up to a major release (e.g., when alpha and beta versions and release candidates are issued) long in advance, based on things like release manager availability, and we urge the developers to get their changes in well in advance of the final release date.

Features selected for addition to releases are generally agreed upon by the core developers, after (sometimes long) discussions on the merits of the feature and its precise specification. This is the PEP process: Python Enhancement Proposal, a document-base process not unlike the IETF's RFC process or the Java world's JSR process, except that we aren't quite as formal, as we have a much smaller community of developers. In case of prolonged disagreement (either on the merits of a feature or on specific details), I may end up breaking a tie; my tie-breaking algorithm is mostly intuitive, since by the time it is invoked, rational argument has long gone out of the window.

The most contentious discussions are typically about user-visible language features; library additions are usually easy (as they don't harm users who don't care), and internal improvements are not really considered features, although they are constrained by pretty stringent backward compatibility at the C API level.

Since the developers are typically the most vocal users, I can't really tell whether features are proposed by users or by developers—in general, developers propose features based on needs they perceived among the users they know. If a user proposes a new feature, it is rarely a success, since without a thorough understanding of the implementation (and of language design and implementation in general) it is nearly impossible to properly propose a new feature. We like to ask users to explain their problems without having a specific solution in mind, and then the developers will propose solutions and discuss the merits of different alternatives with the users.

There's also the concept of a radically major or breakthrough version, like 3.0. Historically, 1.0 was evolutionarily close to 0.9, and 2.0 was also a relatively small step from 1.6. From now on, with the much larger user base, such versions are rare indeed, and provide the only occasion for being truly incompatible with previous versions. Major versions are made backward compatible with previous major versions with a specific mechanism available for deprecating features slated for removal.

*How did you choose to handle numbers as arbitrary precision integers (with all the cool advantages you get) instead of the old (and super common) approach to pass it to the hardware?*

**Guido:** I originally inherited this idea from Python's predecessor, ABC. ABC used arbitrary precision rationals, but I didn't like the rationals that much, so I switched to integers; for reals, Python uses the standard floating-point representation supported by the hardware (and so did ABC, with some prodding).

Originally Python had two types of integers: the customary 32-bit variety ("int") and a separate arbitrary precision variety ("long"). Many languages do this, but the arbitrary precision variety is relegated to a library, like Bignum in Java and Perl, or GNU MP for C. In Python, the two have (nearly) always lived side-by-side in the core language, and users had to choose which one to use by appending an "L" to a number to select the long variety. Gradually this was considered an annoyance; in Python 2.2, we introduced automatic conversion to long when the mathematically correct result of an operation on ints could not be represented as an int (for example, 2**100).

Previously, this would raise an OverflowError exception. There was once a time where the result would silently be truncated, but I changed it to raising an exception before ever letting others use the language. In early 1990, I wasted an afternoon debugging a short demo program I'd written implementing an algorithm that made non-obvious use of very large integers. Such debugging sessions are seminal experiences.

However, there were still certain cases where the two number types behaved slightly different; for example, printing an int in hexadecimal or octal format would produce an unsigned outcome (e.g., –1 would be printed as FFFFFFFF), while doing the same on the mathematically equal long would produce a signed outcome (–1, in this case). In Python 3.0, we're taking the radical step of supporting only a single integer type; we're calling it int, but the implementation is largely that of the old long type.

*Why do you call it a radical step?*

**Guido:** Mostly because it's a big deviation from current practice in Python. There was a lot of discussion about this, and people proposed various alternatives where two (or more) representations would be used internally, but completely or mostly hidden from end users (but not from C extension writers). That might perform a bit better, but in the end it was already a massive amount of work, and having two representations internally would just increase the effort of getting it right, and make interfacing to it from C code even hairier. We are now hoping that the performance hit is minor and that we can improve performance with other techniques like caching.

*How did you adopt the "there should be one—and preferably only one—obvious way to do it" philosophy?*

**Guido:** This was probably subconscious at first. When Tim Peters wrote the "Zen of Python" (from which you quote), he made explicit a lot of rules that I had been applying without being aware of them. That said, this particular rule (while often violated, with my consent) comes straight from the general desire for elegance in mathematics and computer science. ABC's authors also applied it, in their desire for a small number of orthogonal types or concepts. The idea of orthogonality is lifted straight from mathematics, where it refers to the very *definition* of having one way (or one true way) to express something. For example, the XYZ coordinates of any point in 3D space are uniquely determined, once you've picked an origin and three basis vectors.

I also like to think that I'm doing most users a favor by not requiring them to choose between similar alternatives. You can contrast this with Java, where if you need a listlike data structure, the standard library offers many versions (a linked list, or an array list, and others), or C, where you have to decide how to implement your own list data type.

*What is your take on static versus dynamic typing?*

**Guido:** I wish I could say something simple like "static typing bad, dynamic typing good," but it isn't always that simple. There are different approaches to dynamic typing, from Lisp to Python, and different approaches to static typing, from C++ to Haskell. Languages like C++ and Java probably give static typing a bad name because they require you to tell the compiler the same thing several times over. Languages like Haskell and ML, however, use type inferencing, which is quite different, and has some of the same benefits as dynamic typing, such as more concise expression of ideas in code. However the functional paradigm seems to be hard to use on its own—things like I/O or GUI interaction don't fit well into that mold, and typically are solved with the help of a bridge to a more traditional language, like C, for example.

In some situations the verbosity of Java is considered a plus; it has enabled the creation of powerful code-browsing tools that can answer questions like "where is this variable changed?" or "who calls this method?" Dynamic languages make answering such questions harder, because it's often hard to find out the type of a method argument without analyzing every path through the entire codebase. I'm not sure how functional languages like Haskell support such tools; it could well be that you'd have to use essentially the same technique as for dynamic languages, since that's what type inferencing does anyway—in my limited understanding!

### Are we moving toward hybrid typing?

**Guido:** I expect there's a lot to say for some kind of hybrid. I've noticed that most large systems written in a statically typed language actually contain a significant subset that is essentially dynamically typed. For example, GUI widget sets and database APIs for Java often feel like they are fighting the static typing every step of the way, moving most correctness checks to runtime.

A hybrid language with functional and dynamic aspects might be quite interesting. I should add that despite Python's support for some functional tools like map( ) and lambda, Python does *not* have a functional-language subset: there is no type inferencing, and no opportunity for parallellization.

### Why did you choose to support multiple paradigms?

**Guido:** I didn't really; Python supports procedural programming, to some extent, and OO. These two aren't so different, and Python's procedural style is still strongly influenced by objects (since the fundamental data types are all objects). Python supports a tiny bit of functional programming—but it doesn't resemble any real functional language, and it never will. Functional languages are all about doing as much as possible at compile time—the "functional" aspect means that the compiler can optimize things under a very strong guarantee that there are no side effects, unless explicitly declared. Python is about having the simplest, dumbest compiler imaginable, and the official runtime semantics actively discourage cleverness in the compiler like parallelizing loops or turning recursion into loops.

Python probably has the reputation of supporting functional programming based on the inclusion of lambda, map, filter, and reduce in the language, but in my eyes these are just syntactic sugar, and not the fundamental building blocks that they are in functional languages. The more fundamental property that Python shares with Lisp (not a functional language either!) is that functions are first-class objects, and can be passed around like any other object. This, combined with nested scopes and a generally Lisp-like approach to function state, makes it possible to easily implement concepts that superficially resemble concepts from functional languages, like currying, map, and reduce. The primitive operations that are necessary to *implement* those concepts are built in Python, where in functional languages, those concepts *are* the primitive operations. You can write reduce( ) in a few lines of Python. Not so in a functional language.

### When you created the language, did you consider the type of programmers it might have attracted?

**Guido:** Yes, but I probably didn't have enough imagination. I was thinking of professional programmers in a Unix or Unix-like environment. Early versions of the Python tutorial used a slogan something like "Python bridges the gap between C and shell programming," because that was where I was myself, and the people immediately around me. It never occurred to me that Python would be a good language to embed in applications until people started asking about that.

The fact that it was useful for teaching first principles of programming in a middle school or college setting or for self-teaching was merely a lucky coincidence, enabled by the many ABC features that I kept—ABC was aimed specifically at teaching programming to nonprogrammers.

*How do you balance the different needs of a language that should be easy to learn for novices versus a language that should be powerful enough for experienced programmers to do useful things? Is that a false dichotomy?*

**Guido:** Balance is the word. There are some well-known traps to avoid, like stuff that is thought to help novices but annoys experts, and stuff that experts need but confuses novices. There's plenty enough space in between to keep both sides happy. Another strategy is to have ways for experts to do advanced things that novices will never encounter—for example, the language supports metaclasses, but there's no reason for novices to know about them.

## The Good Programmer

*How do you recognize a good programmer?*

**Guido:** It takes time to recognize a good programmer. For example, it's really hard to tell good from bad in a one-hour interview. When you work together with someone though, on a variety of problems, it usually becomes pretty clear which are the good ones. I hesitate to give specific criteria—I guess in general the good ones show creativity, learn quickly, and soon start producing code that works and doesn't need a lot of changes before it's ready to be checked in. Note that some folks are good at different aspects of programming than others—some folks are good at algorithms and data structures, others are good at large-scale integration, or protocol design, or testing, or API design, or user interfaces, or whatever other aspects of programming exist.

*What method would you use to hire programmers?*

**Guido:** Based on my interviewing experience in the past, I don't think I'd be any good at hiring in the traditional way—my interview skills are nearly nonexistent on both sides of the table! I guess what I'd do would be to use some kind of apprentice system where I'd be working closely with people for quite some time and would eventually get a feeling for their strengths and weaknesses. Sort of the way an open source project works.

*Is there any characteristic that becomes fundamental to evaluate if we are looking for great Python programmers?*

**Guido:** I'm afraid you are asking this from the perspective of the typical manager who simply wants to hire a bunch of Python programmers. I really don't think there's a simple answer, and in fact I think it's probably the wrong question. You don't want to hire Python programmers. You want to hire smart, creative, self-motivated people.

*If you check job ads for programmers, nearly all of them include a line about being able to work in a team. What is your opinion on the role of the team in programming? Do you still see space for the brilliant programmer who can't work with others?*

**Guido:** I am with the job ads in that one aspect. Brilliant programmers who can't do teamwork shouldn't get themselves in the position of being hired into a traditional programming position—it will be a disaster for all involved, and their code will be a nightmare for whoever inherits it. I actually think it's a distinct lack of brilliance if you can't do teamwork. Nowadays there are ways to learn how to work with other people, and if you're really so brilliant you should be able to learn teamwork skills easily—it's really not as hard as learning how to implement an efficient Fast Fourier Transform, if you set your mind about it.

*Being the designer of Python, what advantages do you see when coding with your language compared to another skilled developer using Python?*

**Guido:** I don't know—at this point the language and VM have been touched by so many people that I'm sometimes surprised at how certain things work in detail myself! If I have an advantage over other developers, it probably has more to do with having used the language longer than anyone than with having written it myself. Over that long period of time, I have had the opportunity to ponder which operations are faster and which are slower—for example, I may be aware more than most users that locals are faster than globals (though *others* have gone overboard using this, not me!), or that functions and method calls are expensive (more so than in C or Java), or that the fastest data type is a tuple.

When it comes to using the standard library and beyond, I often feel that others have an advantage. For example, I write about one web application every few years, and the technology available changes each time, so I end up writing a "first" web app using a new framework or approach each time. And I still haven't had the opportunity to do serious XML mangling in Python.

*It seems that one of the features of Python is its conciseness. How does this affect the maintainability of the code?*

**Guido:** I've heard of research as well as anecdotal evidence indicating that the error rate per number of lines of code is pretty consistent, regardless of the programming language used. So a language like Python where a typical application is just much smaller than, say, the same amount of functionality written in C++ or Java, would make that application much more maintainable. Of course, this is likely going to mean that a single programmer is responsible for more functionality. That's a separate issue, but it still comes out in favor of Python: more productivity per programmer probably means fewer programmers on a team, which means less communication overhead, which according to *The Mythical Man-Month* [Frederick P. Brooks; Addison-Wesley Professional] goes up by the square of the team size, if I remember correctly.

*What link do you see between the easiness of prototyping offered by Python and the effort needed to build a complete application?*

**Guido:** I never meant Python to be a prototyping language. I don't believe there should be a clear distinction between prototyping and "production" languages. There are situations where the best way to write a prototype would be to write a little throwaway C hack. There are other situations where a prototype can be created using no "programming" at all—for example, using a spreadsheet or a set of find and grep commands.

The earliest intentions I had for Python were simply for it to be a language to be used in cases where C was overkill and shell scripts became too cumbersome. That covers a lot of prototyping, but it also covers a lot of "business logic" (as it's come to be called these days) that isn't particularly greedy in computing resources but requires a lot of code to be written. I would say that most Python code is not written as a prototype but simply to get a job done. In most cases Python is fully up to the job, and there is no need to change much in order to arrive at the final application.

A common process is that a simple application gradually acquires more functionality, and ends up growing tenfold in complexity, and there is never a precise cutover point from prototype to final application. For example, the code review application Mondrian that I started at Google has probably grown tenfold in code size since I first released it, and it is still all written in Python. Of course, there are also examples where Python did eventually get replaced by a faster language—for example, the earliest Google crawler/indexer was (largely) written in Python—but those are the exceptions, not the rule.

## How does the immediacy of Python affect the design process?

**Guido:**  This is often how I work, and, at least for me, in general it works out well! Sure, I write a lot of code that I throw away, but it's much less code than I would have written in any other language, and writing code (without even running it) often helps me tremendously in understanding the details of the problem. Thinking about how to rearrange the code so that it solves the problem in an optimal fashion often helps me think about the problem. Of course, this is not to be used as an excuse to avoid using a whiteboard to sketch out a design or architecture or interaction, or other early design techniques. The trick is to use the right tool for the job. Sometimes that's a pencil and a napkin—other times it's an Emacs window and a shell prompt.

## Do you think that bottom-up program development is more suited to Python?

**Guido:** I don't see bottom-up versus top-down as religious opposites like vi versus Emacs. In any software development process, there are times when you work bottom-up, and other times when you work top-down. Top-down probably means you're dealing with something that needs to be carefully reviewed and designed before you can start coding, while bottom-up probably means that you are building new abstractions on top of existing ones, for example, creating new APIs. I'm not implying that you should start coding APIs without having some kind of design in mind, but often new APIs follow logically from the available lower-level APIs, and the design work happens while you are actually writing code.

*When do you think Python programmers appreciate more its dynamic nature?*

**Guido:** The language's dynamic features are often most useful when you are exploring a large problem or solution space and you don't know your way around yet—you can do a bunch of experiments, each using what you learned from the previous ones, without having too much code that locks you into a particular approach. Here it really helps that you can write very compact code in Python—writing 100 lines of Python to run an experiment once and then starting over is much more efficient than writing a 1,000-line framework for experimentation in Java and then finding out it solves the wrong problem!

*From a security point of view, what does Python offer to the programmer?*

**Guido:** That depends on the attacks you're worried about. Python has automatic memory allocation, so Python programs aren't prone to certain types of bugs that are common in C and C++ code like buffer overflows or using deallocated memory, which have been the bread and butter of many attacks on Microsoft software. Of course the Python runtime itself is written in C, and indeed vulnerabilities have been found here over the years, and there are intentional escapes from the confines of the Python runtime, like the ctypes module that lets one call arbitrary C code.

*Does its dynamic nature help or rather the opposite?*

**Guido:** I don't think the dynamic nature helps or hurts. One could easily design a dynamic language that has lots of vulnerabilities, or a static language that has none. However having a runtime, or *virtual machine* as is now the "hip" term, helps by constraining access to the raw underlying machine. This is coincidentally one of the reasons that Python is the first language supported by Google App Engine, the project in which I am currently participating.

*How can a Python programmer check and improve his code security?*

**Guido:** I think Python programmers shouldn't worry much about security, certainly not without having a specific attack model in mind. The most important thing to look for is the same as in all languages: be suspicious of data provided by someone you don't trust (for a web server, this is every byte of the incoming web request, even the headers). One specific thing to watch out for is regular expressions—it is easy to write a regular expression that runs in exponential time, so web applications that implement searches where the end user types in a regular expression should have some mechanism to limit the running time.

*Is there any fundamental concept (general rule, point of view, mindset, principle) that you would suggest to be proficient in developing with Python?*

**Guido:** I would say pragmatism. If you get too hung up about theoretical concepts like data hiding, access control, abstractions, or specifications, you aren't a real Python programmer, and you end up wasting time fighting the language, instead of using (and enjoying) it; you're also likely to use it inefficiently. Python is good if you're an instant gratification junkie like myself. It works well if you enjoy approaches like extreme programming or other agile development methods, although even there I would recommend taking everything in moderation.

### What do you mean by "fighting the language"?

**Guido:** That usually means that they're trying to continue their habits that worked well with a different language.

A lot of the proposals to somehow get rid of explicit self come from people who have recently switched to Python and still haven't gotten used to it. It becomes an obsession for them. Sometimes they come out with a proposal to change the language; other times they come up with some super-complicated metaclass that somehow makes self implicit. Usually things like that are super-inefficient or don't actually work in a multithreaded environment or whatever other edge case, or they're so obsessed about having to type those four characters that they changed the convention from self to s or capital S. People will turn everything into a class, and turn every access into an accessor method, where that is really not a wise thing to do in Python; you'll just have more verbose code that is harder to debug and runs a lot slower. You know the expression "You can write FORTRAN in any language?" You can write Java in any language, too.

### You spent so much time trying to create (preferably) one obvious way to do things. It seems like you're of the opinion that doing things that way, the Python way, really lets you take advantage of Python.

**Guido:** I'm not sure that I really spend a lot of time making sure that there's only one way. The "Zen of Python" is much younger than the language Python, and most defining characteristics of the language were there long before Tim Peters wrote it down as a form of poetry. I don't think he expected it to be quite as widespread and successful when he wrote it up.

### It's a catchy phrase.

**Guido:** Tim has a way with words. "There's only one way to do it" is actually in most cases a white lie. There are many ways to do data structures. You can use tuples and lists. In many cases, it really doesn't matter that much whether you use a tuple or a list or sometimes a dictionary. It turns out usually if you look really carefully, one solution is objectively better because it works just as well in a number of situations, and there's one or two cases where lists just works so much better than tuples when you keep growing them.

That comes more actually from the original ABC philosophy that was trying to be very sparse in the components. ABC actually shared a philosophy with ALGOL-68, which is now one of the deadest languages around, but was very influentia. Certainly where I was at the time during the 80s, it was very influential because Adriaan van Wijngaarden was the big guy from ALGOL 68. He was still teaching classes when I went to college. I did one or two semesters where he was just telling anecdotes from the history of ALGOL 68 if he felt like it. He had been the director of CWI. Someone else was it by the time I joined.

There were many people who had been very close with ALGOL 68. I think Lambert Meertens, the primary author of ABC, was also one of the primary editors of the ALGOL 68 report, which probably means he did a lot of the typesetting, but he may occasionally also have done quite a lot of the thinking and checking. He was clearly influenced by ALGOL 68's philosophy of providing constructs that can be combined in many different ways to produce all sorts of different data structures or ways of structuring a program.

It was definitely his influence that said, "We have lists or arrays, and they can contain any kind of other thing. They can contain numbers or strings, but they can also contain other arrays and tuples of other things. You can combine all of these things together." Suddenly you don't need a separate concept of a multidimensional array because an array of arrays solves that for any dimensionality. That philosophy of taking a few key things that cover different directions of flexibility and allow them to be combined was very much a part of ABC. I borrowed all of that almost without thinking about it very hard.

While Python tries to give the appearance that you can combine things in very flexible ways as long as you don't try to nest statements inside expressions, there is actually a remarkable number of special cases in the syntax where in some cases a comma means a separation between parameters, and in other cases the comma means the items of a list, and in yet another case it means an implicit tuple.

There are a whole bunch of variations in the syntax where certain operators are not allowed because they would conflict with some surrounding syntax. That is never really a problem because you can always put an extra pair of parentheses around something when it doesn't work. Because of that the syntax, at least from the parser author's perspective, has grown quite a bit. Things like list comprehensions and generator expressions are syntactically still not completely unified. In Python 3000, I believe they are. There's still some subtle semantic differences, but the syntax at least is the same.

## Multiple Pythons

*Does the parser get simpler in Python 3000?*

**Guido:** Hardly. It didn't become more complex, but it also didn't really become simpler.

*No more complex I think is a win.*

**Guido:** Yeah.

*Why the simplest, dumbest compiler imaginable?*

**Guido:** That was originally a very practical goal, because I didn't have a degree in code generation. There was just me, and I had to have the byte code generator behind me before I could do any other interesting work on the language.

I still believe that having a very simple parser is a good thing; after all, it is just the thing that turns the text into a tree that represents the structure of the program. If the syntax is so ambiguous that it takes really advanced parts of technology to figure it out, then human readers are probably confused half the time as well. It also makes it really hard to write another parser.

Python is incredibly simple to parse, at least at the syntactic level. At the lexical level, the analysis is relatively subtle because you have to read the indentation with a little stack that is embedded in the lexical analyzer, which is a counterexample for the theory of separation between lexical and grammatical analysis. Nevertheless, that is the right solution. The funny thing is that I love automatically generated parsers, but I do not believe very strongly in automatically generated lexical analysis. Python has always had a manually generated scanner and an automated parser.

People have written many different parsers for Python. Even port of Python to a different virtual machine, whether Jython or IronPython or PyPy, has its own parser, and it's no big deal because the parser is never a very complex piece of the project, because the structure of the language is such that you can very easily parse it with the most basic one-token lookahead recursive descent parser.

What makes parsers slow is actually ambiguities that can only be resolved by looking ahead until the end of the program. In natural languages there are many examples where it's impossible to parse a sentence until you've read the last word and the arbitrary nesting in the sentence. Or there are sentences that can only be parsed if you actually know the person that they are talking about, but that's a completely different situation. For parsing programming languages, I like my one-token lookahead.

*That suggests to me that there may never be macros in Python because you have to perform another parsing phase then!*

**Guido:** There are ways of embedding the macros in the parser that could probably work. I'm not at all convinced that macros solve any problem that is particularly pressing for Python, though. On the other hand, since the language is easy to parse, if you come up with some kind of hygienic set of macros that fit within the language syntax, it might be very simple to implement micro-evaluation as parse tree manipulations. That's just not an area that I'm particularly interested in.

*Why did you choose to use strict formatting in source code?*

**Guido:** The choice of indentation for grouping was not a novel concept in Python; I inherited this from ABC, but it also occurred in occam, an older language. I don't know if the ABC authors got the idea from occam, or invented it independently, or if there was a common ancestor. The idea may be attributed to Don Knuth, who proposed this as early as 1974.

Of course, I could have chosen not to follow ABC's lead, as I did in other areas (e.g., ABC used uppercase for language keywords and procedure names, an idea I did not copy), but I had come to like the feature quite a bit while using ABC, as it seemed to do away with a certain type of pointless debate common amongst C users at the time, about where to place the curly braces. I also was well aware that readable code uses indentation voluntarily anyway to indicate grouping, and I had come across subtle bugs in code where the indentation disagreed with the syntactic grouping using curly braces—the programmer and any reviewers had assumed that the indentation matched the grouping and therefore not noticed the bug. Again, a long debugging session taught a valuable lesson.

*Strict formatting should produce a cleaner code and probably reduce the differences in the "layout" of the code of different programmers, but doesn't this sound like forcing a human being to adapt to the machine, instead of the opposite path?*

**Guido:** Quite the contrary—it helps the human reader more than it helps the machine; see the previous example. Probably the advantages of this approach are more visible when maintaining code written by another programmer.

New users are often put off by this initially, although I don't hear about this so much any more; perhaps the people teaching Python have learned to anticipate this effect and counter it effectively.

*I would like to ask you about multiple implementations of Python. There are four or five big implementations, including Stackless and PyPy.*

**Guido:** Stackless, technically, is not a separate implementation. Stackless is often listed as a separate Python implementation because it is a fork of Python that replaces a pretty small part of the virtual machine with a different approach.

*Basically the byte code dispatch, right?*

**Guido:** Most of the byte code dispatch is very similar. I think the byte codes are the same and certainly all of the objects are the same. What they do different is when you have a call from one Python procedure to another procedure: they do that with manipulation of objects, where they just push a stack of stack frames and the same bit of C code remains in charge. The way it's done in C Python is that, at that point, a C function is invoked which will then eventually invoke a new instance of the virtual machine. It's not really the whole virtual machine, but the loop that interprets the byte code. There's only one of those loops on the C stack in stackless. In traditional C Python, you can have that same loop on your C stack many times. That's the only difference.

PyPy, IronPython, Jython are separate implementations. I don't know about something that translates to JavaScript, but I wouldn't be surprised if someone had gotten quite far with that at some point. I have heard of experimental things that translate to OCaml and Lisp and who knows what. There once was something that translated to C code as well.

Mark Hammond and Greg Stein worked on it in the late 90s, but they found out that the speedup that they could obtain was very, very modest. In the best circumstances, it would run twice as fast; also, the generated code was so large that you had these enormous binaries, and that became a problem.

*Start-up time hurt you there.*

**Guido:** I think the PyPy people are on the right track.

*It sounds like you're generally supportive of these implementations.*

**Guido:** I have always been supportive of alternate implementations. From the day that Jim Hugunin walked in the door with a more or less completed JPython implementation, I was excited about it. In a sense, it counts as a validation of the language design. It also means that people can use their favorite language on the platform where otherwise they wouldn't have access to it. We still have a way to go there, but it certainly helped me isolate which features were really features of the language that I cared about, and which features were features of a particular implementation where I was OK with other implementations doing things differently. That's where we ended up on the unfortunately slippery slope of garbage collection.

*That's always a slippery slope.*

**Guido:** But it's also necessary. I cannot believe how long we managed to live with pure reference counting and no way to break cycles. I have always seen reference counting as a way of doing garbage collection, and not a particularly bad one. There used to be this holy war between reference counting versus garbage collection, and that always seemed rather silly to me.

*Regarding these implementations again, I think Python is an interesting space because it has a pretty good specification. Certainly compared to other languages like Tcl, Ruby, and Perl 5. Was that something that came about because you wanted to standardize the language and its behavior, or because you were looking at multiple implementations, or something else?*

**Guido:** It was probably more a side effect of the community process around PEPs and the multiple implementations. When I originally wrote the first set of documentation, I very enthusiastically started a language reference manual, which was supposed to be a sufficiently precise specification that someone from Mars or Jupiter could implement the language and get the semantics right. I never got anywhere near fulfilling that goal.

ALGOL 68 probably got the closest of any language ever with their highly mathematical specification. Other languages like C++ and JavaScript have managed with sheer willpower of the standardization committee, especially in the case of C++. That's obviously an incredibly impressive effort. At the same time, it takes so much manpower to write a specification that is that precise, that my hope of getting something like that for Python never really got implemented.

What we do have is enough understanding of how the language is supposed to work, and enough unit tests, and enough people on hand that can answer to implementers of other versions in finite time. I know that, for example, the IronPython folks have been very conscientious in trying to run the entire Python test suite, and for every failure deciding if the test suite was really testing the specific behavior of the C Python implementation or if they actually had more work to do in their implementation.

The PyPy folks did the same thing, and they went one step further. They have a couple of people who are much smarter than I, and who have come up with an edge case probably prompted by their own thinking about how to generate code and how to analyze code in a JIT environment. They have actually contributed quite a few tests and disambiguations and questions when they found out that there was a particular combination of things that nobody had ever really thought about. That was very helpful. The process of having multiple implementations of the language has been tremendously helpful for getting the specification of the language disambiguated.

### Do you foresee a time when C Python may not be the primary implementation?

**Guido:** That's hard to see. I mean some people foresee a time where .NET rules the world; other people foresee a time where JVMs rule the world. To me, that all seems like wishful thinking. At the same time, I don't know what will happen. There could be a quantum jump where, even though the computers that we know don't actually change, a different kind of platform suddenly becomes much more prevalent and the rules are different.

### Perhaps a shift away from the von Neumann architecture?

**Guido:** I wasn't even thinking of that, but that's certainly also a possibility. I was more thinking of what if mobile phones become the ubiquitous computing device. Mobile phones are only a few years behind the curve of the power of regular laptops, which suggests that in a few years, mobile phones, apart from the puny keyboard and screen, will have enough computing power so that you don't need a laptop anymore. It may well be that mobile phones for whatever platform politics end up all having a JVM or some other standard environment where C Python is not the best approach and some other Python implementation would work much better.

There's certainly also the question of what do we do when we have 64 cores on a chip, even in a laptop or in a cell phone. I don't actually know if that should change the programming paradigm all that much for most of the things we do. There may be a use for some languages that let you specify incredibly subtle concurrent processes, but in most cases the average programmer cannot write correct thread-safe code anyway. Assuming that somehow the ascent of multiple cores forces them to do that is kind of unrealistic. I expect that multiple cores will certainly be useful, but they will be used for coarse-grained parallelism, which is better anyway, because with the enormous cost difference between cache hits and cache misses, main memory no longer really serves the function of shared memory. You want to have your processes as isolated as possible.

*How should we deal with concurrency? At what level should this problem be dealt with or, even better, solved?*

**Guido:** My feeling is that writing single-threaded code is hard enough, and writing multi-threaded code is way harder—so hard that most people don't have a hope of getting it right, and that includes myself. Therefore, I don't believe that fine-grained synchronization primitives and shared memory are the solution—instead, I'd much rather see message-passing solutions get back in style. I'm pretty sure that changing all programming languages to add synchronization constructs is a bad idea.

I also still don't believe that trying to remove the GIL from CPython will work. I do believe that some support for managing multiple processes (as opposed to threads) is a piece of the puzzle, and for that reason Python 2.6 and 3.0 will have a new standard library module, multiprocessing, that offers an API similar to that of the threading module for doing exactly that. As a bonus, it even supports processes running on different hosts!

## Expedients and Experience

*Is there any tool or feature that you feel is missing when writing software?*

**Guido:** If I could sketch on a computer as easily as I can with pencil and paper, I might be making more sketches while doing the hard thinking about a design. I fear that I'll have to wait until the mouse is universally replaced by a pen (or your finger) that lets you draw on the screen. Personally, I feel terribly handicapped when using any kind of computerized drawing tool, even if I'm pretty good with pencil and paper perhaps I inherited it from my father, who was an architect and was always making rough sketches, so I was always sketching as a teenager.

At the other end of the scale, I suppose I may not even know what I'm missing for spelunking large codebases. Java programmers have IDEs now that provide quick answers to questions like "where are the callers of this method?" or "where is this variable assigned to?" For large Python programs, this would also be useful, but the necessary static analysis is harder because of Python's dynamic nature.

*How do you test and debug your code?*

**Guido:** Whatever is expedient. I do a lot of testing when I write code, but the testing method varies per project. When writing your basic pure algorithmic code, unit tests are usually great, but when writing code that is highly interactive or interfaces to legacy APIs, I often end up doing a lot of manual testing, assisted by command-line history in the shell or page-reload in the browser. As an (extreme) example, you can't very well write a unit test for a script whose sole purpose is to shut down the current machine; sure, you can mock out the part that actually does the shut down, but you still have to test that part, too, or else how do you know that your script actually works?

Testing something in different environments is also often hard to automate. Buildbot is great for large systems, but the overhead to set it up is significant, so for smaller systems often you just end up doing a lot of manual QA. I've gotten a pretty good intuition for doing QA, but unfortunately it's hard to explain.

### When should debugging be taught? And how?

**Guido:** Continuously. You are debugging your entire life. I just "debugged" a problem with my six-year-old son's wooden train set where his trains kept getting derailed at a certain point on the track. Debugging is usually a matter of moving down an abstraction level or two, and helped by stopping to look carefully, thinking, and (sometimes) using the right tools.

I don't think there is a single "right" way of debugging that can be taught at a specific point, even for a very specific target such as debugging program bugs. There is an incredibly large spectrum of possible causes for program bugs, including simple typos, "thinkos," hidden limitations of underlying abstractions, and outright bugs in abstractions or their implementation. The right approach varies from case to case. Tools come into play mostly when the required analysis ("looking carefully") is tedious and repetitive. I note that Python programmers often need few tools because the search space (the program being debugged) is so much smaller.

### How do you resume programming?

**Guido:** This is actually an interesting question. I don't recall ever looking consciously at how I do this, while I indeed deal with this all the time. Probably the tool I used most for this is version control: when I come back to a project I do a diff between my workspace and the repository, and that will tell me the state I'm in.

If I have a chance, I leave XXX markers in the unfinished code when I know I am about to be interrupted, telling me about specific subtasks. I sometimes also use something I picked up from Lambert Meertens some 25 years ago: leave a specific mark in the current source file at the place of the cursor. The mark I use is "HIRO," in his honor. It is colloquial Dutch for "here" and selected for its unlikeliness to ever occur in finished code. :-)

At Google we also have tools integrated with Perforce that help me in an even earlier stage: when I come in to work, I might execute a command that lists each of the unfinished projects in my workspace, so as to remind me which projects I was working on the previous day. I also keep a diary in which I occasionally record specific hard-to-remember strings (like shell commands or URLs) that help me perform specific tasks for the project at hand—for example, the full URL to a server stats page, or the shell command that rebuilds the components I'm working on.

### What are your suggestions to design an interface or an API?

**Guido:** Another area where I haven't spent a lot of conscious thought about the best process, even though I've designed tons of interfaces (or APIs). I wish I could just include a talk by Josh Bloch on the subject here; he talked about designing Java APIs, but most of what he said would apply to any language. There's lots of basic advice like picking clear names (nouns for classes, verbs for methods), avoiding abbreviations, consistency in naming, providing a small set of simple methods that provide maximal flexibility when combined, and so on. He is big on keeping the argument lists short: two to three arguments is usually the maximum you can have without creating confusion about the order. The worst thing is having several consecutive arguments that all have the same type; an accidental swap can go unnoticed for a long time then.

I have a few personal pet peeves: first of all, and this is specific to dynamic languages, don't make the return type of a method depend on the *value* of one of the arguments; otherwise it may be hard to understand what's returned if you don't know the relationship—maybe the type-determining argument is passed in from a variable whose content you can't easily guess while reading the code.

Second, I dislike "flag" arguments that are intended to change the behavior of a method in some big way. With such APIs the flag is always a constant in actually observed parameter lists, and the call would be more readable if the API had separate methods: one for each flag value.

Another pet peeve is to avoid APIs that could create confusion about whether they return a new object or modify an object in place. This is the reason why in Python the list method sort( ) doesn't return a value: this emphasizes that it modifies the list in place. As an alternative, there is the built-in sorted( ) function, which returns a new, sorted list.

*Should application programmers adopt the "less is more" philosophy? How should they simplify the user interface to provide a shorter learning path?*

**Guido:** When it comes to graphical user interfaces, it seems there's finally growing support for my "less is more" position. The Mozilla foundation has hired Aza Raskin, son of the late Jef Raskin (codesigner of the original Macintosh UI) as a UI designer. Firefox 3 has at least one example of a UI that offers a lot of power without requiring buttons, configuration, preferences or anything: the smart location bar watches what I type, compares it to things I've browsed to before, and makes useful suggestions. If I ignore the suggestions it will try to interpret what I type as a URL or, if that fails, as a Google query. Now that's smart! And it replaces three or four pieces of functionality that would otherwise require separate buttons or menu items.

This reflects what Jef and Aza have been saying for so many years: the keyboard is such a powerful input device, let's use it in novel ways instead of forcing users to do everything with the mouse, the slowest of all input devices. The beauty is that it doesn't require new hardware, unlike Sci-Fi solutions proposed by others like virtual reality helmets or eye movement sensors, not to mention brainwave detectors.

There's a lot to do of course—for example, Firefox's Preferences dialog has the dreadful look and feel of anything coming out of Microsoft, with at least two levels of tabs and many modal dialogs hidden in obscure places. How am I supposed to remember that in order to turn off JavaScript I have to go to the Content tab? Are Cookies under the Privacy tab or under Security? Maybe Firefox 4 can replace the Preferences dialog with a "smart" feature that lets you type keywords so that if I start typing "pass," it will take me to the section to configure passwords.

*What do the lessons about the invention, further development, and adoption of your language say to people developing computer systems today and in the forseeable future?*

**Guido:** I have one or two small thoughts about this. I'm not the philosophical kind, so this is not the kind of question I like or to which I have a prepared response, but here's one thing I realized early on that I did right with Python (and which Python's predecessor, ABC, didn't do, to its detriment). A system should be extensible by its users. Moreover, a large system should be extensible at two (or more) levels.

Since the first time I released Python to the general public, I got requests to modify the language to support certain kinds of use cases. My first response to such requests is always to suggest writing some Python code to cover their needs and put it in a module for their own use. This is the first level of extensibility—if the functionality is useful enough, it may end up in the standard library.

The second level of extensibility is to write an extension module in C (or in C++, or other languages). Extension modules can do certain things that are not feasible in pure Python (though the capabilities of pure Python have increased over the years). I would much rather add a C-level API so that extension modules can muck around in Python's internal data structures, than change the language itself, since language changes are held to the highest possible standard of compatibility, quality, semantic clarity, etc. Also, "forks" in the language might happen when people "help themselves" by changing the language implementation in their own copy of the interpreter, which they may distribute to others as well. Such forks cause all sorts of problems, such as maintenance of the private changes as the core language also evolves, or merging multiple independently forked versions that other users might need to combine. Extension modules don't have these problems; in practice most functionality needed by extensions is already available in the C API, so changes to the C API are rarely necessary in order to enable a particular extension.

Another thought is to accept that you don't get everything right the first time. Early on during development, when you have a small number of early adopters as users, is the time to fix things drastically as soon as you notice a problem, never mind backward compatibility. A great anecdote I often like to quote, and which has been confirmed as truthful by someone who was there at the time, is that Stuart Feldman, the original author of "Make" in Unix v7, was asked to change the dependence of the Makefile syntax on hard tab characters. His response was something along the lines that he agreed tab was a problem, but that it was too late to fix since there were already a dozen or so users.

As the user base grows, you need to be more conservative, and at some point absolute backward compatibility is a necessity. There comes a point where you have accumulated so many misfeatures that this is no longer feasible. A good strategy to deal with this is what I'm doing with Python 3.0: announce a break with backward compatibility for one particular version, use the opportunity to fix as many such issues as possible, and give the user community a lot of time to deal with the transition.

In Python's case, we're planning to support Python 2.6 and 3.0 alongside each other for a long time—much longer than the usual support lifetime of older releases. We're also offering several transitional strategies: an automated source-to-source conversion tool that is far from perfect, combined with optional warnings in version 2.6 about the use of functionality that will change in 3.0 (especially if the conversion tool cannot properly recognize the situation), as well as selective back-porting of certain 3.0 features to 2.6. At the same time, we're not making 3.0 a total rewrite or a total redesign (unlike Perl 6 or, in the Python world, Zope 3), thereby minimizing the risk of accidentally dropping essential functionality.

*One trend I've noticed in the past four or five years is much greater corporate adoption of dynamic languages. First PHP, Ruby in some context, definitely Python in other contexts, especially Google. That's interesting to me. I wonder where these people were 20 years ago when languages like Tcl and Perl, and Python a little bit later, were doing all of these useful things. Have you seen desire to make these languages more enterprise-friendly, whatever that means?*

**Guido:** Enterprise-friendly is usually when the really smart people lose interest and the people of more mediocre skills have to somehow fend for themselves. I don't know if Python is harder to use for mediocre people. In a sense you would think that there is quite a bit of damage you cannot do in Python because it's all interpreted. On the other hand, if you write something really huge and you don't use enough unit testing, you may have no idea what it actually does.

*You've made the argument that a line of Python, a line of Ruby, a line of Perl, a line of PHP, may be 10 lines of Java code.*

**Guido:** Often it is. I think that the adoption level in the enterprise world, even though there are certain packages of functionality that are helpful, is probably just a fear of very conservative managers. Imagine the people in charge of IT resources for 100,000 people in a company where IT is not a main product—maybe they are building cars, or doing insurance, or something else, but everything they do is touched by computers. The people in charge of that infrastructure necessarily have to be very conservative. They will go with stuff that looks like it has a big name attached, like maybe Sun or Microsoft, because they know that Sun and Microsoft screw up all the time, but these companies are obliged to recover from those screwups and fix them, even if it takes five years.

Open source projects traditionally have just not offered that same peace of mind to the average CIO. I don't know exactly if and how and when that will change. It's possible that if Microsoft or Sun suddenly supported Python on their respective VMs, programmers in enterprises would actually discover that they can get higher productivity without any downsides by using more advanced languages.

# CHAPTER THREE

# APL

In the late 1950s, while on the faculty of Harvard University, Kenneth Iverson devised an extension of mathematical notation for the precise description of algorithms. Then, along with Adin Falkoff and other researchers at IBM, the team gradually turned the notation into a full-fledged programming language called APL. The language uses an extended character set requiring a specialized keyboard and appears on the page as strings of sometimes unfamiliar symbols—but the underlying consistency of the language makes it easy to learn, and its unmatched array-processing capabilities make it extraordinarily powerful. Its spiritual descendents, J and K, continue APL's legacy of concise and powerful algebraic manipulations.

# Paper and Pencil

*I read a paper written by you and Ken Iverson, "The Design of APL," which said that the first seven or eight years of development happened without any computer involved! This let you change design aspects without having to worry about legacy issues. How did the first software implementation influence the evolution of the language?*

**Adin Falkoff:** Yes, the first years of the evolution of APL, when it had no name other than "Iverson's notation," were mainly concerned with paper-and-pencil mathematical applications, analysis of digital systems, and teaching. To a great extent, we thought of programming as a branch of mathematics concerned with the discovery and design of algorithms, and this concept was supported by the symbolic form of the notation. The attractiveness of the notation as a general programming language became evident after a while, and was advanced by the efforts of various people (in particular, Herb Hellerman at IBM) who experimented with machine implementations of significant elements of the notation, including primitive functions and array operations. Nevertheless, it is true that throughout this period we had complete freedom to design the language without concern for "legacy" issues.

The most significant early evolution of the language took place in two steps. First was the writing and publication of "The Formal Description of System 360" [*IBM Systems Journal*, 1964]. In order to formally describe some of the behavior of this newly designed computing system, some additions and modifications to the notation described in Iverson's book (*A Programming Language* [Wiley]) were necessary. Second was the design of a type element for Selectric-based terminals, which we undertook in anticipation of using the language on a machine. This imposed significant restraints arising from the linear nature of typewriting, and mechanical requirements of the Selectric mechanism. I believe there is considerable detail on the influence of these two factors on the evolution of the language in the paper you refer to, "The Design of APL" [*IBM Journal of Research and Development*, 1974].

The first comprehensive implementation of the language was, of course, APL\360. It necessarily introduced facilities to write defined functions (i.e., programs)—something taken for granted when using pencil and paper—and for controlling the environment in which programs would be executed. The ideas introduced then, including the workspace and library system, rules for scope of names, and the use of shared variables for communication with other systems, have persisted without significant change. Programs written for APL\360 run without modification on the modern APL systems that I am familiar with.

It is fair to say that the presence of an implementation influenced further evolution of the language by the strict application of the principle that new ideas must always subsume the earlier ones, and, of course, by the constant critical examination of how the language was working for new and different applications.

*When you defined the syntax, how did you picture the typical APL programmer?*

**Adin:** We did not direct our thinking about syntax to programmers as such, but rather conceived the language as being a communication medium for people, which incidentally should also work for people communicating with machines. We did realize that users would have to be comfortable with a symbolic language like algebra, but also felt that they would come to appreciate the power of symbolic representation, as it facilitates formal manipulation of expressions leading to more effective analysis and synthesis of algorithms. Specifically, we did not believe a lot of experience or knowledge of mathematics was necessary, and in fact used the APL system for teaching at the elementary and high school level with some notable success.

As time went on, we found that some of the most skilled and experienced programmers were attracted to APL, used it, and contributed to its development.

*Did the complex syntax limit the diffusion of APL?*

**Adin:** The syntax of APL and its effect on the acceptance of the language is well worth discussing, although I do not agree with the statement that it is "complex." APL was based on mathematical notation and algebraic expressions, regularized by removing anomalous forms and generalizing accepted notation. For example, it was decided that dyadic functions like addition or multiplication would stand between their two arguments, and monadic functions would consistently have the function symbols written before the argument, without exceptions such as are found in traditional math notation, so that absolute value in APL has one vertical bar before the argument and not bars on both sides, and the symbol for factorial in APL comes before the argument rather than following it. In this respect, the syntax of APL was simpler than the syntax of its historical source.

The syntax of APL was also simpler than that of algebraic notation and other programming languages in another very important way: the precedence rule for the evaluation of expressions in APL is simply that all functions have the same precedence, and the user does not have to remember whether exponentiation is carried out before multiplication, or where defined functions fit into the hierarchy. The rule is simply that the rightmost subexpression is evaluated first.

Hence, I don't believe that the syntax of APL limited the diffusion of the language, although the character set, using many nonalphabetic symbols not easily available on standard keyboards, probably did have such an effect.

*How did you decide to use a special character set? How did that character set evolve over time?*

**Adin:** The character set was defined by the use of conventional mathematical notation, augmented by a few Greek letters and some visually suggestive symbols like the quad.

There was also the practical influence of the linear typewriter limitation, leading to the invention of some characters that could be produced by overstriking. Later on, as terminals and input devices became more versatile, these composite characters became primitive symbols in their own right, and a few new characters were introduced to accommodate new facilities, such as the diamond for a statement separator.

*Was there a conscious decision to use the limited resources of the time more productively?*

**Adin:** The character set definitely was influenced by the desire to optimize the use of the limited resources available at the time; but the concise, symbolic form was developed and maintained because of the conviction that it facilitated analysis and formal manipulation of expressions. Also, the brevity of programs compared to equivalent ones written in other languages makes it easier to comprehend the logical flow of a program once the effort is made to read it in the concise APL representation.

*I would think people needed a lot of training to learn the language, especially the character set. Was there a process of natural selection, which meant that APL programmers were experts at the language? Were they more productive? Did they write higher-quality code with fewer bugs?*

**Adin:** Learning APL to the point of being able to write programs at the level of FORTRAN, for example, was actually not difficult or lengthy. Programming in APL was more productive because of the simplicity of the rules, and the availability of primitive functions for data manipulation like sorting, or mathematical functions like matrix inversion. These factors contributed to the conciseness of APL programs, which made them easier to analyze and debug. Credit for productivity must also be given to the APL implementations, using workspaces with all their useful properties, and the interactive terminal-based interpretive systems.

*A super-concise form of expression might be incredibly useful on devices with a small screen like PDAs or smartphones! Considering that APL was first coded on big iron such as IBM System/360, would it be extensible to handle modern projects that need to manage network connections and multimedia data?*

**Adin:** An implementation of APL on a handheld device would at the very least provide a very powerful hand calculator; and I see no problem with networks and multimedia, as such applications have been managed in APL systems for a very long time. Tools for managing GUIs are generally available on modern APL systems.

Early on in the development of APL systems, facilities for managing host operating systems and hardware from within APL functions were introduced, and were utilized by APL system programmers to manage the performance of APL itself. And commercial APL timesharing systems dependent upon networks for their economic viability used APL for managing their networks.

It is true that the first commercially viable APL systems were coded on large machines, but the earliest implementations, which demonstrated the feasibility of APL systems, were done on relative small machines, such as the IBM 1620 and the IBM 1130 family, including the IBM 1500, which had significant usage in educational applications. There was even an implementation on an early experimental desktop machine, dubbed "LC" for "low cost," that had but a few bytes of memory and a low-capacity disk. The evolution of IBM APL implementation is described in some detail in the paper "The IBM Family of APL Systems" [*IBM Systems Journal*, 1991].

## Elementary Principles

*When you pursued standardization, was it a deliberate decision?*

**Adin:** We surely started standardization fairly early; in fact I think I wrote a paper about it, and we got to be part of ISO. We always wanted to standardize things and we managed to a large extent to do that. We discouraged people from fiddling around with the basic structures of the language, adding arbitrary kind of things that would complicate the syntax, or violate some of the elementary principles we were trying to maintain.

*What was your main desire for standardization, compatibility or conceptual purity?*

**Adin:** The desire of standardization is an economic issue. We surely wanted APL to be viable economically, and since a lot of different people were implementing and using it, it seemed a good idea to have a standard.

*Several different vendors had different APL compilers. Without strong standardization, what happens when you have an extension that works on one system but not on another?*

**Adin:** That is something worked on rather carefully by the APL standardization committees, and efforts were made to compromise between extensibility and purity.

*You want people to be able to solve problems you haven't anticipated, but you don't want them to remove the essential nature of your system. Forty years later, how do you think the language holds up? Are the design principles you chose still applicable?*

**Adin:** I think so; I really don't see anything really wrong.

*Is that because you spent a lot of time designing it carefully or because you had a very strong theoretical background with algebra?*

**Adin:** I think we were a couple of reasonably smart people with a belief in the concepts of simplicity and practicality, and an unwillingness to compromise that vision.

I found it too much trouble to try to learn and remember all the rules in other languages so I tried to keep it simple from that standpoint, so that I could use it.

Some of our way of thinking shows up in papers, especially the ones jointly authored by Iverson and me. I myself later wrote a paper that was called "A Note on Pattern Matching: Where do you find the match to an empty array?"[APL Quote Quad, 1979], which used some nice reasoning involving small programs and algebraic principles, to obtain the reported results, which turned out to be consistent and useful. The paper looked at various possibilities, and found that the one simplest to express works out better than any other.

*I found it really fascinating to build a language from a small set of principles and discovering new ideas built on those principles. That seems like a good description of mathematics. What is the role of math in computer science and programming?*

**Adin:** I believe that computer science is a branch of mathematics.

Programming of mathematical computations is obviously part of mathematics, especially the numerical analysis required to constantly maintain compatibility between discrete digital operations and the continuity of theoretical analysis.

Some other thoughts that come to mind are: the impetus from math problems that can be solved only by extensive computations that inspire need for speed; the discipline of logical thought required for math and carried over to programming of all kinds; the notion of algorithms, which are a classical mathematical tool; and the various specialized branches of mathematics, such as topology, that lend themselves to analysis of computational problems.

*I have read some other discussions where you and other people suggested that one of the interesting applications was using APL to teach programming and mathematics at the elementary and high school levels.*

**Adin:** We did some of that, particularly at the beginning, and we had a little fun with it.

At that time we only had typewriter terminals and we made some available to some local private schools. There was one in particular where problem students were supposed to be taught, and we gave them exercises to do on the typewriter and turned them loose.

The fun part was that we found that some of these students who were supposed to be resistant to learning broke into the school after hours so they could do more work on it. They were using typewriter terminals hooked to our time-sharing system.

*So they enjoyed that so much they suddenly had to do it even afterward?*

**Adin:** Yes.

*You used APL to teach "programming thinking" to nonprogrammers. What made APL attractive for nonprogrammers?*

**Adin:** In the early days one of the things was you didn't have all this overhead, you didn't have to make declarations before you added two numbers, so if you wanted to add 7 and 5 you just wrote down 7 + 5, instead of saying there is a number called 7 and there is a number called 5, these are numbers, floating point or not floating point, and the result is a number and I want to store the result here, so there was a lower barrier in APL to doing what you wanted.

*When someone is learning to program, the initial step toward doing that first thing is very small. You basically write down what you want to do, and you don't have to spend time pleasing a compiler to get it to work.*

**Adin:** That's right.

*Easy to start and easy to play with. Does this technique let people become programmers or increase their programming knowledge?*

**Adin:** The easy accessibility makes it easy to experiment, and if you can experiment and try out different things, you learn, and so I think that is favorable toward the development of programming skills.

*The notation that you chose for APL is different from traditional algebraic notation.*

**Adin:** Well, it's not that different…the precedence rules are different. They are very simple: you go from right to left.

*Did you find that much easier to teach?*

**Adin:** Yes, because there is only one rule and you don't have to say that if it's a defined function, you go this way, and if it's exponentiation, it has precedence over multiplication, or stuff like that. You just say, "look at the line of the instructions and take it from right to left."

*Was this a deliberate design decision to break with familiar notation and precedence in favor of greater simplicity?*

**Adin:** That's right. Greater simplicity and greater generality.

I think Iverson was mainly responsible for that. He was quite good at algebra and he was very interested in teaching. One example he liked to use was the representation of polynomials, which is extremely simple in APL.

*When I first saw that notation, even though it was unfamiliar, it did seem conceptually much simpler overall. How do you recognize simplicity in a design or an implementation? Is that a matter of good taste or experience, or is there a rigorous process you apply to try to find optimal simplicity?*

**Adin:** I think to some extent it must be subjective, because it depends somewhat on your experience and where you come from. I would say the fewer there rules are, the simpler it is in general.

*You started from a small set of axioms and you can build from there, but if you understand that small set of axioms, you can derive more complexity?*

**Adin:** Well, let's take this matter of precedence. I think it's simpler to have the precedence based on a simple form from right to left, than on a basis of a table that says this function goes first and that function goes second. I think it is one rule versus an almost limitless number of rules.

You see, in any particular application you set up your own set of variables and functions, and for a particular application you might find it simpler to write some new rules, but if you are looking at a general language like APL, you want to start with the fewest possible number of rules.

*To give people designing systems built with the language more opportunity to evolve?*

**Adin:** People who are building applications are in fact building languages; fundamentally, programming has to do with developing languages suitable for particular applications.

*You express the problem in a language specific to its domain.*

**Adin:** But then those objects, notably the nouns and the verbs, the objects and the functions, they have to be defined in something, for example in a general-purpose language like APL.

So you use APL to define these things, but then you set up your operations to facilitate the kind of things you want to do in that application.

*Is your concern constructing the building blocks people can use to express themselves?*

**Adin:** My concern is giving them the basic building blocks if you like, the fundamental tools for constructing the building blocks that are suitable and appropriate for what they are trying to accomplish in the field in which they are working.

*It seems to be a concern shared by other language designers; I think of Chuck Moore with Forth, or John McCarthy with Lisp, and Smalltalk in the early 70s.*

**Adin:** I'm sure that's the case.

McCarthy, I know, is a theoretical kind of person and he was concerned with developing a system to express the lambda calculus effectively, but I don't think the lambda calculus is as convenient for most purposes as plain old algebra, from which APL derives.

*Suppose I want to design a new programming language. What's the best piece of advice you can give me?*

**Adin:** I guess the best thing I can say is do something that you enjoy, something that pleases you to work with, something that helps you accomplish something that you would like to do.

We were always very personal in our approach, and I think most designers are, as I read what people have to say. They started doing things that they wanted to do, which then turned out to be useful generally.

*When you were designing APL, were you able to see at some point "we are going in the wrong direction here; we need to scale back this complexity" or "we have several different solutions; we can unify them into something much simpler"?*

**Adin:** That is approximately right, but there was usually a question of "is this a generalization which subsumes what we already have, and what is the likelihood that it is going to enable us to do a lot more with very little further complication?"

We paid a lot of attention to end conditions—what happens in a limit when you go from 6 to 5 to 4 down to 0, for example. Thus, in reduction you are applying a function like summation to a vector, and if you are summing up a vector that has $n$ elements and then $n$ minus one elements, and so on, what happens when you eventually have no elements? What's the sum? It has to be 0 because that's the identity element.

In the case of multiplication, the multiplication over an empty vector goes to 1, because that's the identity element for that function.

*You mentioned looking at several different solutions and trying to generalize and asking yourself the question of what happens when approaching 0, for example. If you hadn't already known that when you do a reduction, you need to end up at the identity element for when n is 0, you could look at both those cases and say "Here is the argument we make: it is 0 when this case and it's 1 in this case, because it is the identity element."*

**Adin:** That's right. That's one of the processes we used.

What happens in the special cases is very important. and when you use APL effectively, you keep applying that criterion to the more elaborate functions that you might be developing for a particular application. This often leads to unexpected but gratifying simplification.

*Do the design techniques you use when creating a language inform the design techniques people might use when programming in the language?*

**Adin:** Yes, because as I said before, programming is a process of designing languages. I think that's a very fundamental thing, which is not often mentioned in the literature as far as I know.

*Lisp programmers do, but in a lot of the languages that came afterward, especially Algol and its C derivatives, people don't seem to think this way. Is there a divide between what is built in the language and what's not, where everything else is second class?*

**Adin:** Well, what do we mean by second class? In APL the so-called second class follows the same rules as the first class, and we don't have any problem there.

*You can make the same argument for almost all of Lisp or Scheme or Smalltalk, but C has a distinct division between operators and functions, and user-created functions. Is making that distinction sharp between these entities a design mistake?*

**Adin:** I don't know if I would call it a mistake, but I think it's simpler to have the same rules apply to both what's primitive and not primitive.

*What's the biggest mistake you've made with regard to design or programming? What did you learn from it?*

**Adin:** When work on APL first began, we consciously avoided making design decisions that catered to the computer environment. For example, we eschewed the use of declarations, seeing their use as an unnecessary burden on the user when the machine could easily determine the size and type of a data object from the object itself at the time of its input or generation. In the course of time, however, as APL became more widely used with more and more vested interests, hardware factors were increasingly difficult to avoid.

Perhaps the biggest mistake that I personally made was to underestimate advances in hardware and become too conservative in system design. In contemplating early implementation of APL on the PC, for instance, I advocated leaving out recent language extensions to general arrays and complex numbers because these would strain the capacity of the extant hardware to provide satisfactory performance. Fortunately, I was overruled, and it was not long before major increases in PC memory and processor speeds made such powerful extensions completely feasible.

It is hard to think of big mistakes made in programming because one expects to make errors in the course of writing a program of reasonable complexity. It then depends on the programming tools how the error grows, when it is discovered, and how much has to be redone to recover from it. Modularization and ready reuse of idiomatic code fragments, as follows from the functional programming style fostered by APL, tends to limit the generation and propagation of errors so they don't become big mistakes.

As for mistakes in the design of APL itself, our method of development, using consensus among the designers and implementers as the ultimate deciding factor, and feedback from users gaining practical experience in a diversity of applications as well as our own use of the language before design was frozen, helped us avoid serious errors.

However, one person's exercise of principle may be another's idea of a mistake, and even over long periods of time, differences may not be empirically resolvable. Two things come to mind.

One is the character set. There was from the earliest times considerable pressure to use reserved words instead of the abstract symbols chosen to represent primitive functions. Our position was that we were really dealing with extensions to mathematics, and the evolution of mathematical notation was clearly in the direction of using symbols, which facilitated formal manipulation of expressions. Later on, Ken Iverson, who had an abiding interest in the teaching of mathematics, chose to limit the character set to ASCII in his further work, on the language J, so that J systems could be easily accessible to students and others without specialized hardware. My own inclination was and is to stick with the symbolic approach; it's more in keeping with history and ultimately easier to read. Time will tell if either direction is mistaken, or if it doesn't really matter.

The second thing that comes to mind as possibly leading to a significant mistake in direction that may never be decided is the treatment of general arrays, i.e., arrays whose scalar elements may themselves have an accessible structure within the language. After APL\360 was established as an IBM product (one of the very first such when IBM unbundled its software and hardware in 1966 or 1967), we began to look at extensions to more general arrays and had extensive studies and discussions regarding the theoretical underpinnings. Ultimately APL systems have been built with rival ways of treating scalar elements and syntactic consequences. It will be interesting to see how this evolves as the general interest in parallel programming becomes more commercially important.

## Parallelism

*What are the implications (for the design of applications) of thinking about data in collections rather than as individual units?*

**Adin:** This is a rather large subject, as indicated by the spread of "array languages" and the introduction of array primitives in languages like FORTRAN, but I think there are two significant aspects to thinking in terms of collections.

One, of course, is the simplification of the thought process when not bogged down in the housekeeping details of dealing with individual items. It is closer to our natural way of thinking to say, for example, how many of the numbers in this collection are equal to zero, and write a simple expression that produces the desired result, than to start thinking in terms of a loop in any of its derivative forms.

The second is that possibilities for parallelism are made more evident in programs acting directly on collections, leading to more efficient utilization of modern hardware.

*There's been some talk in modern programming languages about adding higher-order features to languages such as C++ or Java—languages where you spend a lot of time writing the same* for( ) *loop over and over again. For example, I have a collection of things and I want to do something to each one of them. Yet APL solved this problem 40–45 years ago!*

**Adin:** Well, I don't know how many years ago, but there are sort of two stages there. One is the use of arrays as primitive, and second stage was the introduction of the operator called each, which basically applies any arbitrary function to any collection of items. But there were always some questions like "Do we want to put in primitives for looping specifically?" We decided we didn't want to do that because it complicated the syntax too much, and it was easy enough to write the few needed loops in the standard way.

*Complicate the syntax for the implementation or for users?*

**Adin:** For both: people have to read it, machines have to read it; the syntax is either simple or not.

You would put in new kinds of statements, and that's clearly a complication. Now the question is "Is the payoff worth it?", and that's where the design judgment comes in. And we always came down on the side that we didn't want to have new kinds of syntax for handling loops since we could do it quite conveniently with what we had.

*You said that APL really has an advantage for parallel programming. I can understand the use of arrays as the primitive data structure for the language. You also mentioned the use of shared variables. How do they work?*

**Adin:** A shared variable in APL is a variable that is accessible to more than one processor at a time. The sharing processors can both be APL processors or one can be of a different sort. For example, you can have a variable, let's call it X, and, as far as APL is concerned, reading and writing X is not different from an ordinary variable. However there might be another processor, let's say a file processor, which also has access to X, it being a shared variable, and whatever value APL might give to X, the file processor uses that value according to its own interpretation. And similarly, when it gives a value to X, which is then read by APL, the APL processor similarly applies its own knowledge to it, however it chooses to interpret that value. And this X is a shared variable.

What we have in APL systems like APL2 of IBM is some protocol for managing access to this variable so that you don't run into trouble with different kinds of race conditions.

*Is this parallelization you were talking about something the compiler can determine automatically? Suppose that I want to multiply two arrays and add the value to each element of an array. This is easy to express in APL, but can the compiler perform implicit parallelization on that?*

**Adin:** The definition in APL is that it doesn't matter in what order you do the operations on the elements of an array; therefore, the compiler or the interpreter or whatever implementation you have is free to do them simultaneously or in any arbitrary sequence.

*Besides enabling simplicity at the language level, it can give implementers tremendous flexibility to change the way the implementation works, taking advantage of new hardware, or give you a mechanism to exploit things like automatic parallelization.*

**Adin:** That's right, because according to the definition of the language, which is of course the definition of what happens when the processor is applied, it doesn't matter what order you do them. That was a very deliberate decision.

*Was that a unique decision in the history of languages of the time?*

**Adin:** I am not that familiar with the history of languages, but since we were basically the only serious array-oriented language, it probably was unique.

*It's interesting to talk about collections and large data sets, which are clearly preoccupations of modern programmers. APL preceded the invention of the relational database. Now we have a lot of data in structures containing different data types, in relational databases, and in large unstructured collections such as web pages. Can APL handle these well? Does it offer models that people using more popular languages such as SQL, PHP, Ruby, and Java can learn from?*

**Adin:** APL arrays can have as elements both scalars, which have no internal structure, and nonscalars, which may be of any complexity. Nonscalar elements are recursively structured of other arrays. "Unstructured" collections such as web pages can therefore be conveniently represented by APL arrays and manipulated by primitive APL functions.

Regarding very large arrays, APL has the facility to treat external files as APL objects. Once an association has been made between a name in the workspace and an external file, operations can be applied to the file using APL expressions. It appears to the user as if the file is within the workspace, even though in actuality it may be many times larger than the workspace size.

It is very hard to give specific details of what designers of other languages can learn from APL, and it would be presumptuous of me to go into particulars of the languages you mention, as I am not an expert in any of them. However, as I read about them in the literature I see that by and large the principles that guided the design of APL—which we described, for example, in our 1973 paper "The Design of APL"—have continued to inform later work in language design.

Of the two overriding principles, simplicity and practicality, the latter seems to have fared better; simplicity is a more difficult objective to achieve since there are no practical constraints on complexity. We strove for simplicity in APL by carefully defining the scope of the primitive operations it would allow, maintaining the abstract nature of APL objects, and resisting the temptation to include special cases represented by the operations of other systems.

An illustration of this is the fact that the concept of a "file" does not appear in APL. We have arrays that may be treated as files as called for by an application, but there are no primitive functions specifically designed for file manipulation as such. The practical need for efficiency in file management, however, early on fostered the development of the shared-variable paradigm, which itself is a general concept useful in a multitude of applications where the APL program needs to invoke facilities of another (APL or non-APL) auxiliary processor.

Later on, an additional facility, using the general concept of namespaces, was designed to allow APL programs to directly manipulate objects outside of the workspace, including access to Java fields and methods, extremely large data collections, compiled programs in other languages, and others. The user interface to both the shared-variable and namespace facilities rigorously maintains APL syntax and semantics and thereby keeps it simple.

Without going into detail, therefore, it is reasonable to say that the newer languages could benefit by maintaining a strict adherence to their own primitive concepts, defining each to be as general as possible within the context of the applications they are addressing.

As for specific characteristics of APL as a model, APL has demonstrated that declarations are unnecessary, although they may contribute to efficiency of execution in some situations, and that the number of different data types can be quite small. Newer languages may benefit by aiming in these directions rather than taking it for granted that the user has to help out the computer by providing such implementation-related information.

Also, the concept of a pointer is not a primitive in APL, and has never been missed. Of course, where possible the primitive operations in the language should be defined on collections of data having an abstract internal structure, such as regular arrays, trees, and others.

You are correct in noting that APL preceded the invention of the relational database. Both Dr. E. F. (Ted) Codd and the APL group were at the IBM T. J. Watson Research Center in the 1960s, when he was developing the relational database concepts, and I believe that we had a very strong influence on that work. I recall in particular a heated discussion between us one afternoon where we demonstrated that simple matrices, rather than complex scalar pointer systems, could be used for representing the relationships among data entities.

## Legacy

*I know that lots of design influences in Perl came from APL. Some people say some of the crypticness of Perl comes from APL. I don't know if this is a compliment or not.*

**Adin:** Let me give you an example of that kind of compliment. There is a lot of politics involved in the design and use of programming languages, particularly in a place like IBM where it is a business. At various times, people tried to set up competitive experiments to see if APL would do better than, say, PL1 or FORTRAN. The results were always loaded, because the judges were people on the other side, but there is one comment that I always remember from some functionary: he said APL can't be very good because two of the smartest guys he knew, Iverson and Falkoff, can't make people believe in it.

*What do the lessons about the invention, further development, and adoption of your language say to people developing computer systems today and in the foreseeable future?*

**Adin:** Decisions about system design are not purely technical or scientific. Economic and political considerations have a strong influence, and especially so in situations where there is potential flexibility in the underlying technicalities, as in the design of languages and systems.

In the period when APL was taking hold as an important tool being used within IBM in the mid-1960s, and consideration was being given to making it into a product, we had to contend with an IBM "language czar," who decreed that only PL/1 would be supported by the company in the future—except, of course, for FORTRAN and COBOL, which were already entrenched in the industry and could not be totally abandoned.

As history has shown, this was an unrealistic position for the company to take and was bound to fail, but this was not so obvious at the time, considering the dominance of IBM in the computing industry and the dominance of certain factions within the power structure of the company.

We had to fight the policy to get the necessary support for APL to survive. The battle took place on several fronts: as members of the IBM Research Division, we exploited as much as possible opportunities to give professional talks, seminars, and formal classes so as to imbed awareness of APL's unique characteristics in the technical consciousness of the time; we enlisted—wherever we could find them—people of influence within the company to countervail against the administrative power structure; we spread and supported the internal use of our APL\360 system to development and manufacturing locations; we leveraged important customers' interest in APL systems to force the availability of APL outside the company, at least on an experimental basis; and made allies within the ranks of the marketing division. And we were successful, to the point where APL\360 was among the very first IBM program products to be marketed after the unbundling of hardware and software in the late 1960s.

A very significant milestone was accomplished on account of the interest that technical talks and demonstrations had engendered at the NASA Goddard Space Center. In 1966 that facility requested access to our internal APL system in order to experiment with its use. They were a very important customer, and we were urged by the IBM marketing people to comply with their request. However, we demurred, insisting that we would only agree to do this if we were first enabled to give a weeklong instructional course on site at the Goddard Space Center.

We obtained this agreement, but then ran into difficulty implementing it: time-sharing systems like APL\360 at the time required terminals connecting to the central system through acoustic modems working with specialized telephone "data sets." These telephone sets were also used on the other end, attached to the central computer, and they were in short supply. After all the administrative agreements to go ahead with the project had been reached, we found that neither the New York- nor Washington D.C.-area phone companies could provide the units needed for the projected classes at the Space Center.

While it was their normal practice to work only with their own equipment, the D.C. phone company agreed to install any data sets we could somehow provide. But as much as our IBM communication managers tried to persuade the New York phone company to find data sets somewhere, they were not able to produce any, although they somehow conveyed the idea that they would look the other way if we happened to use their equipment already in our possession in ways they could not officially condone.

So we proceeded to disable half of the lines coming into our central computer, and had the data sets thus freed taken down to the Space Center in an IBM station wagon. They were then installed off the record by the local phone company and we were able to go ahead with our course, thus establishing the first off-premises use of the APL\360 system by a non-IBM entity, getting it out the door despite the support-only-PL/1 policy.

### What do you regret most about the language?

**Adin:** We gave the design of APL our best efforts and worked hard in the political arena to have it accepted and widely used. Under the circumstances, I don't find anything to regret about the language. One possible regret in hindsight is that we did not start sooner and put greater effort behind the development of an effective compiler, but we can't know what this might have cost in tradeoffs, given the extant limitations of resources. Furthermore, there is reason to believe that current interest in parallel programming and the adoption of APL-like array operations in traditional compiled languages like FORTRAN will result in the equivalent in due course.

*How do you define success in terms of your work?*

**Adin:** APL proved to be a very useful tool in the development of many aspects of IBM's business. It provided a much simplified approach to using computers that allowed researchers and product developers to apply themselves more efficiently to the substantive problems they were working on, from theoretical physics to development of flat-screen displays. It was also used to prototype major business systems such as assembly lines and warehouses, allowing them to get started quickly and tested before being frozen in implementations using other programming systems.

We were successful in making APL into a whole line of IBM products, and providing leadership for other computer companies to provide their own APL systems conforming to an international standard.

APL also found substantial use in academic institutions as a tool and a discipline, thus fulfilling one of the principal purposes of its development—its use in education.

APL of course was the forerunner of programming languages and systems treating arrays as primitive data objects and using shared variables for managing simultaneity, and as such will no doubt have a strong influence on further developments involving parallel programming. It is very gratifying to see that in the last few months, three separate computer industry consortiums have been established to work in this field.

# CHAPTER FOUR

# Forth

Forth is a stack-based, concatenative language designed by Chuck Moore in the 1960s. Its main features are the use of a stack to hold data, and words that operate on the stack, popping arguments and pushing results. The language itself is small enough that it runs on anything from embedded machines to supercomputers, and expressive enough to build useful programs out of a few hundred words. Successors include Chuck Moore's own colorForth, as well as the Factor programming language.

# The Forth Language and Language Design

*How do you define Forth?*

**Chuck:** Forth is a computer language with minimal syntax. It features an explicit parameter stack that permits efficient subroutine calls. This leads to postfix expressions (operators follow their arguments) and encourages a highly factored style of programming with many short routines sharing parameters on the stack.

*I read that the name Forth stands for fourth-generation software. Would you like to tell us more about it?*

**Chuck:** Forth is derived from "fourth," which alludes to "fourth-generation computer language." As I recall, I skipped a generation. FORTRAN/COBOL were first-generation languages; Algol/Lisp, second. These languages all emphasized syntax. The more elaborate the syntax, the more error checking is possible. Yet most errors occur in the syntax. I determined to minimize syntax in favor of semantics. And indeed, Forth words are loaded with meaning.

*You consider Forth a language toolkit. I can understand that view, given its relatively simple syntax compared to other languages and the ability to build a vocabulary from smaller words. Am I missing anything else?*

**Chuck Moore:** No, it's basically the fact that it's extremely factored. A Forth program consists of lots of small words, whereas a C program consists of a smaller number of larger words.

By small word, I mean one with a definition typically one line long. The language can be built up by defining a new word in terms of previous words and you just build up that hierarchy until you have maybe a thousand words. The challenge there is 1) deciding which words are useful, and 2) remembering them all. The current application I'm working on has a thousand words in it. And I've got tools for searching for words, but you can only search for a word if you remember that it exists and pretty much how it's spelled.

Now, this leads to a different style of programming, and it takes some time for a programmer to get used to doing it that way. I've seen a lot of Forth programs that look very much like C programs transliterated into Forth, and that isn't the intent. The intent is to have a fresh start. The other interesting thing about this toolkit, words that you define this way are every bit as efficient or significant as words that are predefined in the kernel. There's no penalty for doing this.

*Does the externally visible structure consisting of many small words derive from Forth's implementation?*

**Chuck:** It's a result of our very efficient subroutine call sequences. There's no parameter passing because the language is stack-based. It's merely a subroutine call and return. The stack is exposed. The machine language is compiled. A switch to and from a subroutine is literally one call instruction and one return instruction. Plus you can always reach down into the equivalent of an assembly language. You can define a word that will execute actual machine instructions instead of subroutine calls, so you can be as efficient as any other language, maybe more efficient than some.

*You don't have the C calling overhead.*

**Chuck:** Right. This gives the programmer a huge amount of flexibility. If you come up with a clever factoring of a problem, you can not only do it efficiently, you can make it extraordinarily readable.

On the other hand, if you do it badly, you can end up with code that no one else can read— code your manager can't understand, if managers can understand anything. And you can create a real mess. So it's a two-edged sword. You can do very well; you can do very badly.

*What would you say (or what code would you show) to a developer who uses another programming language to make him interested in Forth?*

**Chuck:** It is very hard to interest an experienced programmer in Forth. That's because he has invested in learning the tools for his language/operating system and has built a library appropriate for his applications. Telling him that Forth would be smaller, faster, and easier is not persuasive compared to having to recode everything. A novice programmer, or an engineer needing to write code, doesn't face that obstacle and is much more receptive—as might be the experienced programmer starting a new project with new constraints, as would be the case with my multicore chips.

*You mentioned that a lot of Forth programs you've seen look like C programs. How do you design a better Forth program?*

**Chuck:** Bottom-up.

First, you presumably have some I/O signals that you have to generate, so you generate them. Then you write some code that controls the generation of those signals. Then you work your way up until finally you have the highest-level word, and you call it go and you type go and everything happens.

I have very little faith in systems analysts who work top-down. They decide what the problem is and then they factor it in such a way that it can be very difficult to implement.

*Domain-driven design suggests describing business logic in terms of the customer's vocabulary. Is there a connection between building up a vocabulary of words and using the terms of art from your problem domain?*

**Chuck:** Hopefully the programmer knows the domain before he starts writing. I would talk to the customer. I would listen to the words he uses and I would try to use those words so that he can understand what the program's doing. Forth lends itself to this kind of readability because it has postfix notation.

If I was doing a financial application, I'd probably have a word called "percent." And you could say something like "2.03 percent". And the argument's percent is 2.03 and everything works and reads very naturally.

*How can a project started on punch cards still be useful on modern computers in the Internet era? Forth was designed on/for the IBM 1130 in 1968. That it is the language of choice for parallel processing in 2007 is surely amazing.*

**Chuck:** It has evolved in the meantime. But Forth is the simplest possible computer language. It places no restrictions upon the programmer. He/she can define words that succinctly capture aspects of a problem in a lean, hierarchical manner.

*Do you consider English readability as a goal when you design programs?*

**Chuck:** At the very highest level, yes, but English is not a good language for description or functionality. It wasn't designed for that, but English does have the same characteristic as Forth in the sense that you can define new words.

You define new words by explaining what they are in previously defined words mostly. In a natural language, this can be problematic. If you go to a dictionary and check that out, you find that often the definitions are circular and you don't get any content.

*Does the ability to focus on words instead of the braces and brackets syntax you might have in C make it easier to apply good taste to a Forth program?*

**Chuck:** I would hope so. It takes a Forth programmer who cares about the appearance of things as opposed merely to the functionality. If you can achieve a sequence of words that flow together, it's a good feeling. That's really why I developed colorForth. I became annoyed at the syntax that was still present in Forth. For instance, you could limit a comment by having a left parenthesis and a right parenthesis.

I looked at all of those punctuation marks and said, "Hey, maybe there's a better way." The better way was fairly expensive in that every word in the source code had to have a tag attached to it, but once I swallowed that overhead, it became very pleasant that all of those funny little symbols went away and were replaced by the color of the word which was, to me, a much gentler way of indicating functionality.

I get interminable criticism from people who are color blind. They were really annoyed that I was trying to rule them out of being programmers, but somebody finally came up with a character set distinction instead of a color distinction, which is a pleasant way of doing it also.

The key is the four-bit tag in each word, which gives you 16 things that we're to do, and the compiler can determine immediately what's intended instead of having to infer it from context.

*Second- and third-generation languages embraced minimalism, for example with meta-circular bootstrapping implementations. Forth is a great example of minimalism in terms of language concepts and the amount of hardware support required. Was this a feature of the times, or was it something you developed over time?*

**Chuck:** No, that was a deliberate design goal to have as small a kernel as possible. Predefine as few words as necessary and then let the programmer add words as he sees fit.

The prime reason for that was portability. At the time, there were dozens of minicomputers and then there became dozens of microcomputers. And I personally had to put Forth on lots of them.

I wanted to make it as easy as possible. What happens really is there might be a kernel with 100 words or so that is just enough to generate a—I'll call it an operating system, but it's not quite—that has another couple hundred words. Then you're ready to do an application.

I would provide the first two stages and then let the application programmers do the third, and I was usually the application programmer, too. I defined the words I knew were going to be necessary. The first hundred words would be in machine language probably or assembler or at least be dealing directly with the particular platform. The second two or three hundred words would be high-level words, to minimize machine dependence in the lower, previously defined level. Then the application would be almost completely machine independent, and it was easy to port things from one minicomputer to another.

*Were you able to port things easily above that second stage?*

**Chuck:** Absolutely. I would have a text editor, for instance, that I used to edit the source code. It would usually just transfer over without any changes.

*Is this the source of the rumor that every time you ran across a new machine, you immediately started to port Forth to it?*

**Chuck:** Yes. In fact, it was the easiest path to understanding how the machine worked, what its special features were based on how easy it was to implement the standard package of Forth words.

*How did you invent indirect-threaded code?*

**Chuck:** Indirect-threaded code is a somewhat subtle concept. Each Forth word has an entry in a dictionary. In direct-threaded code, each entry points to code to be executed when that word is encountered. Indirect-threaded code points to a location that contains the address of that code. This allows information besides the address to be accessed—for instance, the value of a variable.

This was perhaps the most compact representation of words. It has been shown to be equivalent to both direct-threaded and subroutine-threaded code. Of course these concepts and terminology were unknown in 1970. But it seemed to me the most natural way to implement a wide variety of kinds of words.

*How will Forth influence future computer systems?*

**Chuck:** That has already happened. I've been working on microprocessors optimized for Forth for 25 years, most recently a multicore chip whose cores are Forth computers.

What does Forth provide? As a simple language, it allows a simple computer: 256 words of local memory; 2 push-down stacks; 32 instructions; asynchronous operation; easy communication with neighbors. Small and low-power.

Forth encourages highly factored programs. Such are well-suited to parallel processing, as required by a multicore chip. Many simple programs encourage thoughtful design of each. And requiring perhaps only 1% the code that would otherwise be written.

Whenever I hear people boasting of millions of lines of code, I know they have greviously misunderstood their problem. There are no contemporary problems requiring millions of lines of code. Instead there are careless programmers, bad managers, or impossible requirements for compatibility.

Using Forth to program many small computers is an excellent strategy. Other languages just don't have the modularity or flexibility. And as computers get smaller and networks of them are cooperating (smart dust?), this will be the environment of the future.

*This sounds like one major idea of Unix: multiple programs, each doing just one thing, that interact. Is that still the best design today? Instead of multiple programs on one computer, might we have multiple programs across a network?*

**Chuck:** The notion of multithreaded code, as implemented by Unix and other OSes, was a precursor to parallel processing. But there are important differences.

A large computer can afford the considerable overhead ordinarily required for multi-threading. After all, a huge operating system already exists. But for parallel processing, almost always the more computers, the better.

With fixed resources, more computers mean smaller computers. And small computers cannot afford the overhead common to large ones.

Small computers will be networked, on chip, between chips and across RF links. A small computer has small memory. Nowhere is there room for an operating system. The computers must be autonomous, with a self-contained ability to communicate. So communication must be simple—no elaborate protocol. Software must be compact and efficient. An ideal application for Forth.

Those systems requiring millions of lines of code will become irrelevant. They are a consequence of large, central computers. Distributed computation needs a different approach.

A language designed to support bulky, syntactical code encourages programmers to write big programs. They tend to take satisfaction, and be rewarded, for such. There is no pressure to seek compactness.

Although the code generated by a syntactic language might be small, it usually isn't. To implement the generalities implied by the syntax leads to awkward, inefficient object code. This is unsuitable for a small computer. A well-designed language has a one-one correlation between source code and object code. It's obvious to the programmer what code will be generated from his source. This provides its own satisfaction, is efficient, and reduces the need for documentation.

*Forth was designed partly to be compact in both source and binary output, and is popular among embedded developers for that reason, but programmers in many other domains have reasons to choose other languages. Are there aspects of the language design that add only overhead to the source or the output?*

**Chuck:** Forth is indeed compact. One reason is that it has little syntax.

Other languages seem to have deliberately added syntax, which provides redundancy and offers opportunity for syntax checking and thus error detection.

Forth provides little opportunity for error detection due to its lack of redundancy. This contributes to more compact source code.

My experience with other languages has been that most errors are in the syntax. Designers seem to create opportunity for programmer error that can be detected by the compiler. This does not seem productive. It just adds to the hassle of writing correct code.

An example of this is type checking. Assigning types to various numbers allows errors to be detected. An unintended consequence is that programmers must work to convert types, and sometimes work to evade type checking in order to do what they want.

Another consequence of syntax is that it must accommodate all intended applications. This makes it more elaborate. Forth is an extensible language. The programmer can create structures that are just as efficient as those provided by the compiler. So all capabilities do not have to be anticipated and provided for.

A characteristic of Forth is its use of postfix operators. This simplifies the compiler and offers a one-one translation of source code to object code. The programmer's understanding of his code is enhanced and the resulting compiled code is more compact.

*Proponents of many recent programming languages (notably Python and Ruby) cite readability as a key benefit. Is Forth easy to study and maintain in relation to those? What can Forth teach other programming languages in terms of readability?*

**Chuck:** Computer languages all claim to be readable. They aren't. Perhaps it seems so to one who knows the language, but a novice is always bewildered.

The problem is the arcane, arbitrary, and cryptic syntax. All the parentheses, ampersands, etc. You try to learn why it's there and eventually conclude there's no good reason. But you still have to follow the rules.

And you can't speak the language. You'd have to pronounce the punctuation like Victor Borgia.

Forth alleviates this problem by minimizing the syntax. Its cryptic symbols @ and ! are pronounced "fetch" and "store." They are symbols because they occur so frequently.

The programmer is encouraged to use natural-language words. These are strung together without punctuation. With good choice of words, you can construct reasonable sentences. In fact, poems have been written in Forth.

Another advantage is postfix notation. A phrase like "6 inches" can apply the operator "inches" to the parameter 6, in a very natural manner. Quite readable.

On the other hand, the programmer's job is to develop a vocabulary that describes the problem. This vocabulary can get to be quite large. A reader has to know it to find the program readable. And the programmer must work to define helpful words.

All in all, it takes effort to read a program. In any language.

### How do you define success in terms of your work?

**Chuck:** An elegant solution.

One doesn't write programs in Forth. Forth is the program. One adds words to construct a vocabulary that addresses the problem. It is obvious when the right words have been defined, for then you can interactively solve whatever aspect of the problem is relevant.

For example, I might define words that describe a circuit. I'll want to add that circuit to a chip, display the layout, verify the design rules, run a simulation. The words that do these things form the application. If they are well chosen and provide a compact, efficient toolset, then I've been successful.

### Where did you learn to write compilers? Was this something everybody at the time had to do?

**Chuck:** Well, I went to Stanford around '60, and there was a group of grad students writing an ALGOL compiler—a version for the Burroughs 5500. It was only three or four of them, I think, but I was impressed out of my mind that three or four guys could sit down and write a compiler.

I sort of said, "Well, if they can do it, I can do it," and I just did. It isn't that hard. There was a mystique about compilers at the time.

### There still is.

**Chuck:** Yeah, but less so. You get these new languages that pop up from time to time, and I don't know if they're interpreted or compiled, but well, hacker-type people are willing to do it anyway.

The operating system is another concept that is curious. Operating systems are dauntingly complex and totally unnecessary. It's a brilliant thing that Bill Gates has done in selling the world on the notion of operating systems. It's probably the greatest con game the world has ever seen.

An operating system does absolutely nothing for you. As long as you had something—a subroutine called disk driver, a subroutine called some kind of communication support, in the modern world, it doesn't do anything else. In fact, Windows spends a lot of time with overlays and disk management all stuff like that which are irrelevant. You've got gigabyte disks; you've got megabyte RAMs. The world has changed in a way that renders the operating system unnecessary.

*What about device support?*

**Chuck:** You have a subroutine for each device. That's a library, not an operating system. Call the ones you need or load the ones you need.

*How do you resume programming after a short hiatus?*

**Chuck:** I don't find a short coding hiatus at all troublesome. I'm intensely focused on the problem and dream about it all night. I think that's a characteristic of Forth: full effort over a short period of time (days) to solve a problem. It helps that Forth applications are naturally factored into subprojects. Most Forth code is simple and easy to reread. When I do really tricky things, I comment them well. Good comments help re-enter a problem, but it's always necessary to read and understand the code.

*What's the biggest mistake you've made with regard to design or programming? What did you learn from it?*

**Chuck:** Some 20 years ago I wanted to develop a tool to design VLSI chips. I didn't have a Forth for my new PC, so I thought I'd try a different approach: machine language. Not assembler language, but actually typing the hex instructions.

I built up the code as I would in Forth, with many simple words that interacted hierarchically. It worked. I used it for 10 years. But it was difficult to maintain and document. Eventually I recoded it in Forth and it became smaller and simpler.

My conclusion was that Forth is more efficient than machine language. Partly because of its interactivity and partly because of its syntax. One nice aspect of Forth code is that numbers can be documented by the expression used to calculate them.

## Hardware

*How should people see the hardware they develop on: as a resource or as a limit? If you think of hardware as a resource, you might want to optimize the code and exploit every hardware feature; if you see it as a limit, you are probably going to write code with the idea that your code will run better on a new and more powerful version of the hardware, and that's not a problem because hardware evolves rapidly.*

**Chuck:** A very perceptive observation that software necessarily targets its hardware. Software for the PC certainly anticipates faster computers and can afford to be sloppy.

But for embedded systems, the software expects the system to be stable for the life of the project. And not a lot of software is migrated from one project to another. So here the hardware is a constraint, though not a limit. Whereas, for PCs, hardware is resource that will grow.

The move to parallel processing promises to change this. Applications that cannot exploit multiple computers will become limited as single computers stop getting faster. Rewriting legacy software to optimize parallel processing is impractical. And hoping that smart compilers will save the day is just wishful thinking.

*What is the root of the concurrency problem?*

**Chuck:** The root of the concurrency problem is speed. A computer must do many things in an application. These can be done on a single processor with multitasking. Or they can be done simultaneously with multiple processors.

The latter is much faster and contemporary software needs that speed.

*Is the solution in hardware, software, or some combination?*

**Chuck:** It's not hard to glue multiple processors together. So the hardware exists. If software is programmed to take advantage of this the problem is solved. However, if the software can be reprogrammed, it can be made so efficient that multiprocessors are not needed. The problem is to use multiprocessors without changing legacy software. This is the intelligent compiler approach that has never been achieved.

I'm amazed that software written in the 1970s hasn't/can't be rewritten. One reason might be that in those days software was exciting; things being done for the first time; programmers working 18-hour days for the joy of it. Now programming is a 9–5 job as part of a team working to a schedule; not much fun.

So they add another layer of software to avoid rewriting the old software. At least that's more fun than recoding a stupid word processor.

*We have access to a big computational power in common computers, but how much actual computing (that is, calculating) are these systems doing? And how much are they just moving and formatting data?*

**Chuck:** You are right. Most computer activity is moving data, not calculating. Not just moving data, but compressing, encrypting, scrambling. At high data rates, this must be done with circuitry so one wonders why a computer is needed at all.

*Can we learn something from this? Should we build hardware in a different way?*

*Don Knuth launched a challenge: check what happens inside a computer during one second of time. He said that what we would discover could change a lot of things.*

**Chuck:** My computer chips recognize this by having a simple, slow multiply. It isn't used very often. Passing data between cores and accessing memory are the important features.

*On one hand you have a language that really enables people to develop their own vocabularies and not necessarily think about the hardware presentation. On the other hand, you have a very small kernel that's very much tied to that hardware. It's interesting how Forth can bridge the gap between the two. On some of these machines, is it true that you have no operating system besides your Forth kernel?*

**Chuck:** No, Forth is really standalone. Everything that needs to exist is in the kernel.

*But it abstracts away that hardware for people who write programs in Forth.*

**Chuck:** Right.

*The Lisp Machine did something similar, but never really was popular. Forth quietly has done that job.*

**Chuck:** Well, Lisp did not address I/O. In fact, C did not address I/O and because it didn't, it needed an operating system. Forth addressed I/O from the very beginning. I don't believe in the most common denominator. I think that if you go to a new machine, the only reason it's a new machine is because it's different in some way and you want to take advantage of those differences. So, you want to be there at the input-output level so you can do that.

*Kernighan and Ritchie might argue for C that they wanted a least common factor to make porting easier. Yet you found it easier to port if you didn't take that approach.*

**Chuck:** I would have standard ways of doing that. I would have a word—I think it was fetchp maybe—that would fetch 8 bits from a port. That would be defined differently on different computers, but it would be the same function at the stack.

*In one sense then, Forth is equivalent to C plus the standard I/O library.*

**Chuck:** Yeah, but I worked with the Standard FORTRAN Library in the early days, and it was awful. It just had the wrong words. It was extremely expensive and bulky. It was so easy to define half a dozen instructions to perform in I/O operation that you didn't need the overhead of a predefined protocol.

*Did you find yourself working around that a lot?*

**Chuck:** In FORTRAN, yeah. When you're dealing with, say, Windows, there's nothing you can do. They won't let you have access to the I/O. I have stayed away from Windows most deliberately, but even without Windows, the Pentium was the most difficult machine to put Forth on.

It had too many instructions. And it had too many hardware features like the lookaside buffers and the different kinds of caching you really couldn't ignore. You had to wade your way through, and the initialization code necessary to get Forth running was the most difficult and the most bulky.

Even if it only had to be executed once, I spent most of my time trying to figure out how to do it correctly. We had Forth running standalone on a Pentium, so it was worth the trouble.

The process extended over 10 years probably, partly chasing the changes in the hardware Intel was making.

*You mentioned that Forth really supports asynchronous operation. In what sense do you mean asynchronous operation?*

**Chuck:** Well, there's several senses. Forth has always had a multiprogramming ability, a multithreading ability called Cooperative.

We had a word called pause. If you had a task and it came to a place where it didn't have anything to do immediately, it would say pause. A round-robin scheduler would assign the computer to the next task in the loop.

If you didn't say pause, you could monopolize the computer completely, but that would never be the case, because this was a dedicated computer. It was running a single application and all the tasks were friendly.

I guess that was in the old days when all of the tasks were friendly. That's one kind of asynchronism that these tasks could run, do their own thing without ever having to synchronize. One of the features, again, of Forth is that that word pause could be buried in lower-level words. Every time you tried to read or write disk, the word pause would be executed for you, because the disk team knew that it was going to have to wait for the operation to complete.

In the new chips, the new multicore chips that I'm developing, we're taking that same philosophy. Each computer is running independently and if you have a task on your computer, and another task on the neighbor, they're both running simultaneously but they're communicating with each other. That's the equivalent of what the tasks would've been doing in a threaded computer.

Forth just factors very nicely into those independent tasks. In fact, in the case of the multi-core computer, I can use not exactly the same programs, but I can factor the programs in the same way to make them run in parallel.

*When you had the cooperative multithreading, did each thread of execution have its own stack, and you switched between them?*

**Chuck:** When you did a task switch, sometimes all you needed to do, depending on the computer, was save the word on top of the stack and then switch the stack pointer. Sometimes you actually had to copy out the stack and load the new one, but in that case, I would make it a point to have a very shallow stack.

*Did you deliberately limit the stack depth?*

**Chuck:** Yes. Initially, the stacks were arbitrarily long. The first chip I designed had a stack that was 256 deep because I thought that was small. One of the chips I designed had a stack 4 deep. I've settled now on about 8 or 10 as a good stack depth, so my minimalism has gotten stricter over time.

*I would've expected it to go the other way.*

**Chuck**: Well, in my VLSI design application, I do have a case where I'm recursively following traces across the chip, in which case, I have to set the stack depths to about 4,000. To do that might require a different kind of stack, a software-implemented stack. But, in fact, on the Pentium it can be a hardware stack.

## Application Design

*You brought up the idea that Forth is an ideal language for many small computers networked together—smart dust, for example. For which kinds of applications do you think these small computers are the most appropriate?*

**Chuck:** Communication certainly, sensing certainly. But I'm just beginning to learn how independent computers can cooperate to achieve a greater task.

The multicore computers we have are brutally small. They have 64 words of memory. Well, to put it differently, they have 128 words of memory: 64 RAM, 64 ROM. Each word can hold up to four instructions. You might end up with 512 instructions in a given computer, period, so the task has to be rather simple. Now how do you take a task like the TCP/IP stack and factor it amongst several of these computers in such a way that you can perform the operation without any computer needing more than 512 instructions? That's a beautiful design problem, and one that I'm just approaching now.

I think that's true of almost all applications. It's much easier to do an application if it's broken up into independent pieces as it is trying to do it in serial on a single processor. I think that's true of video generation. Certainly I think it's true of compressing and uncompressing images. But I'm just learning how to do that. We've got other people here in the company that are also learning and having a good time at it.

*Is there any field of endeavor where this is not appropriate?*

**Chuck:** Legacy software, certainly. I'm really worried about legacy software, but as soon as you're willing to rethink a problem, I think it is more natural to think of it this way. I think it corresponds more closely to the way we think the brain works with Minsky's independent agents. An agent to me is a small core. It may be that consciousness arises in the communication between these, not in the operation of any one of them.

Legacy software is an unappreciated but serious problem. It will only get worse—not only in banking but in aerospace and other technical industries. The problem is the millions of lines of code. Those could be recoded, say in thousands of lines of Forth. There's no point in machine translation, which would only make the code bigger. But there's no way that code could be validated. The cost and risk would be horrendous. Legacy code may be the downfall of our civilization.

*It sounds like you're betting that in the next 10 to 20 years we'll see more and more software arise from the loose joining of many small parts.*

**Chuck:** Oh, yes. I'm certain that's the case. RF communication is so nice. They talk about micro agents inside your body that are fixing things and sensing things, and these agents can only communicate via RF or maybe acoustic.

They can't do much. They're only a few molecules. So this has got to be how the world goes. It's the way our human society is organized. We have six and half billion independent agents out there cooperating.

*Choosing words poorly can lead to poorly designed, poorly maintainable applications. Does building a larger application out of dozens or hundreds of small words lead to jargon? How do you avoid that?*

**Chuck:** Well, you really can't. I find myself picking words badly. If you do that, you can confuse yourself. I know in one application, I had this word—I forget what it was now—but I had defined and then I had modified it, and it ended up meaning the opposite of what it said.

It was like you had a word called right that makes things go to the left. That was hideously confusing. I fought it for a while and finally renamed the word because it was just impossible to understand the program with that word throwing so much noise into your cognition. I like to use English words, not abbreviations. I like to spell them out. On the other hand, I like them to be short. You run out of short meaningful English words after a while and you've got to do something else. I hate prefixes—a crude way to try to create namespaces so you can use the same old words over and over. They just look to me like a cop out. It's an easy way to distinguish words, but you should've been smarter.

Very often Forth applications will have distinct vocabularies where you can reuse words. In this context, the word does this; in that context, it does something else. In the case of my VLSI design, all of this idealism failed. I needed at least a thousand words, and they're not English words; they're signal names or something, and I quickly had to revert to definitions and weirdly spelled words and prefixes and all of that stuff. It isn't all that readable. But on the other hand, it's full of words like nand and nor and xor for the various gates that are involved. Where possible, I use the words.

Now, I see other people writing Forth; I don't want to pretend to be the only Forth programmer. Some of them do a very good job of coming up with names for things; others do a very bad job. Some come up with a very readable syntax, and others don't think that that's important. Some come up with very short definitions of words, and some have words that are a page long. There are no rules; there's only stylistic conventions.

Also, the key difference between Forth and C and Prolog and ALGOL and FORTRAN, the conventional languages tried to anticipate all possible structures and syntax and build it into the language in the first place. That has led to some very clumsy languages. I think C is a clumsy language with its brackets and braces and colons and semicolons and all of that. Forth eliminated all of that.

I didn't have to solve the general problem. I just had to provide a tool that someone else could use to solve whatever problem they encountered. The ability to do anything and not the ability to do everything.

### Should microprocessors include source code so that they can be fixed even decades later?

**Chuck:** You're right, including the source with microcomputers will document them nicely. Forth is compact, which facilitates that. But the next step is to include the compiler and editor so that the microcomputer code can be examined and changed without involving another computer/operating system that may have been lost. colorForth is my attempt to do that. A few K of source and/or object code is all that's required. That can easily be stored on flash memory and be usable in the far future.

### What is the link between the design of a language and the design of a software written with that language?

**Chuck:** A language determines its use. This is true of human-human languages. Witness the difference between Romance (French, Italian), Western (English, German, Russian) and Eastern (Arabic, Chinese) languages. They affect their cultures and their worldview. They affect what is said and how it's said. Of these, English is particularly terse and increasingly popular.

So too with human-computer languages. The first languages (COBOL, FORTRAN) were too verbose. Later languages (Algol, C) had excessive syntax. These languages necessarily led to large, clumsy descriptions of algorithms. They could express anything, but do it badly.

Forth addresses these issues. It is relatively syntax-free. It encourages compact, efficient descriptions. It minimizes the need for comments, which tend to be inaccurate and distract attention from the code itself.

Forth also has a simple, efficient subroutine call. In C, a subroutine call requires expensive setup and recovery. This discourages its use. And encourages elaborate parameter sets that amortize the cost of the call, but lead to large, complex subroutines.

Efficiency allows Forth applications to be very highly factored, into many, small subroutines. And they typically are. My personal style is one-line definitions—hundreds of small subroutines. In such a case, the names assigned this code become important, both as a mnemonic device and as a way to achieve readability. Readable code requires less documentation.

The lack of syntax allows Forth a corresponding lack of discipline. This, to me, allows individual creativity and some very pleasant code. Others view it as a disadvantage, fearing management loss of control and lack of standardization. I think that's more of a management failure than the fault of the language.

*You said "Most errors are in syntax." How do you avoid the other types of errors in Forth programs, such as logic errors, maintainability errors, and bad style decisions?*

**Chuck:** Well, the major error in Forth has to do with stack management. Typically, you leave something on the stack inadvertently and it'll trip you up later. We have a stack comment associated with words, which is very important. It tells you what is on the stack upon entry and what is on the stack upon exit. But that's only a comment. You can't trust it.

Some people did actually execute those and use them to do verification and stack behavior.

Basically, the solution is in the factoring. If you have a word whose definition is one line long, you can read through it thinking how the stack acts and conclude at the end that it's correct. You can test it and see if it works the way you thought it did, but even so, you're going to get caught up in stack errors. The words dup and drop are ubiquitous and have to be used correctly. The ability to execute words out of context just by putting their input parameters and looking at their output parameters is hugely important. Again, when you're working bottom-up, you know that all of the words you've already defined work correctly because you tested them.

Also, there are only a few conditionals in Forth. There's an if-else-then construction, a begin-while construct. My philosophy, which I regularly try to teach, is that you minimize the number of conditionals in your program. Rather than having a word that tests something and either does this or that, you have two words: one that does this and one that does that, and you use the right one.

Now it doesn't work in C because the calling sequences are so expensive that they tend to have parameters that let the same routine do different things based upon the way it's called. That's what leads to all of the bugs and complications in legacy software.

*In trying to work around deficiencies of the implementation?*

**Chuck:** Yeah. Loops are unavoidable. Loops can be very, very nice. But a Forth loop, at least a colorForth loop, is a very simple one with a single entry and a single exit.

*What advice would you give a novice to make programming more pleasant and effective?*

**Chuck:** Well, surely not to your surprise, I would say you should learn to write Forth code. Even if you aren't going to be writing Forth code professionally, exposure to it will teach you some of these lessons and give you a better perspective on whatever language you use. If I were writing a C program, I have written almost none, but I would write it in the style of Forth with a lot of simple subroutines. Even if there were a cost involved there, I think it would be worth it in maintainability.

The other thing is keep it simple. The inevitable trend in designing an aircraft or in writing an application, even a word processor, is to add features and add features and add features until the cost becomes unsupportable. It would be better to have half a dozen word processors that would focus on different markets. Using Word to compose an email is silly;

99% of all of the facilities available are unnecessary. You ought to have an email editor. There used to be such, but the trend seems to be away from that. It's not clear to me why.

Keep it simple. If you're encountering an application, if you're on part of a design team, try to persuade other people to keep it simple. Don't anticipate. Don't solve a problem that you think might occur in the future. Solve the problem you've got. Anticipating is very inefficient. You can anticipate 10 things happening, of which only one will, so you've wasted a lot of effort.

*How do you recognize simplicity?*

**Chuck:** There's I think a budding science of complexity, and one of their tenets is how to measure complexity. The description that I like, and I don't know if there's any other one, is that the shortest description or if you have two concepts, the one with the shorter description is the simpler. If you can come up with a shorter definition of something, you come up with a simpler definition.

But that fails in a subtle way that any kind of description depends on the context. If you can write a very short subroutine in C, you might say this is very simple, but you're relying upon the existence of the C compiler and the operating system and the computer that's going to execute it all. So really, you don't have a simple thing; you have a pretty complex thing when you consider the wider context.

I think it's like beauty. You can't define it, but you can recognize it when you see it—simple is small.

*How does teamwork affect programming?*

**Chuck:** Teamwork—much overrated. The first job of a team is to partition the problem into relatively independent parts. Assign each part to an individual. The team leader is responsible for seeing that the parts come together.

Sometimes two people can work together. Talking about a problem can clarify it. But too much communication becomes an end in itself. Group thinking does not facilitate creativity. And when several people work together, inevitably one does the work.

*Is this valid for every type of project? If you have to write something as feature-rich as OpenOffice.org...it sounds pretty complex, no?*

**Chuck:** Something like OpenOffice.org would be factored into subprojects, each programmed by an individual with enough communication to assure compatibility.

*How do you recognize a good programmer?*

**Chuck:** A good programmer writes good code quickly. Good code is correct, compact, and readable. "Quickly" means hours to days.

A bad programmer will want to talk about the problem, will waste time planning instead of writing, and will make a career out of writing and debugging the code.

*What is your opinion of compilers? Do you think they mask the real skills of programmers?*

**Chuck:** Compilers are probably the worst code ever written. They are written by someone who has never written a compiler before and will never do so again.

The more elaborate the language, the more complex, bug-ridden, and unusable is the compiler. But a simple compiler for a simple language is an essential tool—if only for documentation.

More important than the compiler is the editor. The wide variety of editors allows each programmer to select his own, to the great detriment of collaborative efforts. This fosters the cottage industry of translating from one to another.

Another failing of compiler writers is the compulsion to use every special character on the keyboard. Thus keyboards can never become smaller and simpler. And source code becomes impenetrable.

But the skills of a programmer are independent of these tools. He can quickly master their foibles and produce good code.

*How should software be documented?*

**Chuck:** I value comments much less than others do. Several reasons:

- If comments are terse, they are often cryptic. Then you have to guess what they mean.

- If comments are verbose, they overwhelm the code they're embedded in and trying to explain. It's hard to find and relate code to comment.

- Comments are often badly written. Programmers aren't known for their literary skills, especially if English is not their native language. Jargon and grammatical errors often make them unreadable.

- Most importantly, comments are often inaccurate. Code may change without comments being updated. Although code may be critically reviewed, comments rarely are. An inaccurate comment causes more trouble than no comment. The reader must judge whether the comment or the code is correct.

Comments are often misguided. They should explain the purpose of the code, not the code itself. To paraphrase the code is unhelpful. And if it is inaccurate, downright misleading. Comments should explain why the code is present, what it is intended to accomplish, and any tricks employed in accomplishing it.

colorForth factors comments into a shadow block. This removes them from the code itself, making that code more readable. Yet they are instantly available for reading or updating. It also limits the size of comments to the size of the code.

Comments do not substitute for proper documentation. A document must be written that explains in prose the code module of interest. It should expand greatly the comments and concentrate on literate and complete explanation.

Of course, this is rarely done, is often unaffordable, and is easily lost since it is separate from the code.

*Quoting from* http://www.colorforth.com/HOPL.html:

*"The issue of patenting Forth was discussed at length. But since software patents were controversial and might involve the Supreme Court, NRAO declined to pursue the matter. Whereupon, rights reverted to me. I don't think ideas should be patentable. Hindsight agrees that Forth's only chance lay in the public domain. Where it has flourished."*

*Software patents are still controversial today. Is your opinion about patents still the same?*

**Chuck:** I've never been in favor of software patents. It's too much like patenting an idea. And patenting a language/protocol is especially disturbing. A language will only be successful if it's used. Anything that discourages use is foolish.

*Do you think that patenting a technology prevents or limits its diffusion?*

**Chuck:** It is difficult to market software, which is easy to copy. Companies go to great lengths to protect their product, sometimes making it unusable in the process. My answer to that problem is to sell hardware and give away the software. Hardware is difficult to copy and becomes more valuable as software is developed for it.

Patents are one way of addressing these issues. They have proven a wonderful boon to innovation. But there's a delicate balance required to discourage frivolous patents and maintain consistency with prior art/patents. And there are huge costs associated with granting and enforcing them. Recent proposals to reform patent law threaten to freeze out the individual inventor in favor of large companies. Which would be tragic.

# CHAPTER FIVE

# BASIC

In 1963, Thomas Kurtz and John Kemeny invented BASIC, a general-purpose language intended to teach beginners to program as well as to allow experienced users to write useful programs. Their original goals included abstracting away details of the hardware. The language spread widely after the introduction of microcomputers in the 70s; many personal computers included custom variants. Though the language has moved beyond line numbers and GOTO statements through Microsoft's Visual Basic and Kurtz's BASIC, multiple generations of programmers learned the joy of programming from a language that encouraged experimentation and rewarded curiosity.

# The Goals Behind BASIC

*What is the best way to learn to program?*

**Tom Kurtz:** Beginning programmers should not have to wade through manuals. Most manuals are far too wordy to retain the attention of new students. Simple coding assignments and easy access to easy-to-use implementations are required, and many examples.

*Some educators prefer to teach a language in which programmers need to develop a lot of experience before applying it. You have chosen instead to create a language that any level of programmer can use quickly, where they can improve their knowledge by experience.*

**Tom:** Yes. Once you have learned to program, new computer languages are easy to learn. The first is the hardest. Unless a language is particularly obtuse, the new language will be but a short step from the languages already known. An analogy with spoken languages (which are much more difficult to learn): once you learn your first Romance language, the second is much simpler. First of all, the grammar is similar, there are many words the same, and the syntax is fairly simple (i.e., whether the verb is in the middle, as in English, or at the end).

The simpler the first language, the more easily the average student will learn it.

*Did this evolutionary approach guide your decision to create BASIC?*

**Tom:** When we were deciding to develop BASIC (John Kemeny and I back in 1962 or so), I considered attempting to develop simplified subsets of either FORTRAN or Algol. It didn't work. Most programming languages contain obscure grammatical rules that act as a barrier for the beginning student. We tried to remove all such from BASIC.

Several of the considerations that went into the design of BASIC were:

- One line, one statement.

  We couldn't use a period to end a statement, as JOSS did (I believe.) And the Algol convention of a semicolon made no sense to us, as did the FORTRAN Continuation (C).

- Line numbers are GOTO targets.

  We had to have line numbers since this was long before the days of WYSIWYG. Inventing a new concept of "statement label" didn't seem like a good idea to us. (Later, when creating and editing programs became easier, we allowed the user to *not* use line numbers, as long as he didn't use GOTO statements; by that time, BASIC was fully structured.)

- All arithmetic is floating point.

  One of the most difficult concepts for a beginner to learn is why the distinction between type integer and type floating. Almost all the programming languages at the time bowed to the architecture of the most computer hardware, which included floating point for engineering calculations and integer for efficiency.

In handling all arithmetic in floating point, we protected the user from numeric typing. We did have to do some complicated stuff internally when an integer value was required (as in an array subscript) and the user provided a noninteger (as in 3.1). We simply rounded in such cases.

We had similar problems with the difference between binary and decimal fractions. As in the statement:

```
FOR I = 1 TO 2 STEP 0.1
```

The decimal fraction 0.1 is an infinite repeating binary fraction. We had to use a fuzz factor to determine the completion of the loop.

(Some of these binary-decimal considerations were not included in the original BASIC, but were handled in the much more recent True BASIC.)

- A number is a number (is a number).

  No form requirements when entering a number in the code or in data statements. And the PRINT statement produced answers in a default format. The FORMAT statement, or its equivalent in other languages, is quite difficult to learn. And the beginning user might wonder why would he have to learn it—he just wanted to get a simple answer!

- Reasonable defaults.

If there are any complications for the "more advanced" user, they should not be visible to the beginner. Admittedly, there were not many "advanced" features in the original BASIC, but that idea was, and is, important.

The correctness of our approach was borne out by that fact that it took about an hour to teach freshmen how to write simple programs in BASIC. Our training started out with four one-hour lectures, then was reduced to three, then two, and finally to a couple of videotapes.

I once determined that an introductory computer science course could be taught using a version of BASIC (not the original one, but one that included structured programming constructs). The only thing you could not do was to introduce the student to the ideas of pointers and allocated storage!

Another point: in the early days running a program required several steps: Compiling. Linking and loading. Execution. We decided in BASIC that *all* runs would combine these steps so that the user wouldn't even be aware of them.

At that time in the history of computing, most languages required a multiple-pass compiler, which might consume too much valuable computer time. Thus, we compiled once, and executed many times. But small student programs were compiled and executed once only. It did require us to develop a single-pass compiler, and go directly to execution if the compilation stage was without errors.

Also, in reporting errors to the student, we stopped after five errors. I can recall FORTRAN error printouts many pages in length detailing *all* the syntax errors in a program, usually from omitting but one key punctuation at the beginning.

*I've seen a BASIC manual from 1964. The subtitle is "the elementary algebraic language designed for the Dartmouth Time Sharing system." What's an algebraic language?*

**Tom:** Well, we were both mathematicians, so naturally there are certain things in the language that look mathematical, for example raising numbers to power and things of this sort, and then the functions that we added were mathematical, like sine and cosine, because we were thinking of students doing calculus using BASIC programs. So there was obviously a bias for numerical calculations in contrast to other languages that were developed at the time such as COBOL, which had a different focus.

What we did was look at FORTRAN at the time. Access to FORTRAN on any of the big IBM computers was through the medium of 80-column punch cards. We were introducing a computer in our campus through the use of teletype machines, which were used as input to computers because they were compatible with phone lines, and we wanted the phone lines to connect the terminals in various places on the campus to the central computer. So all that was done using machinery designed originally for communication purposes such as teletype communication, store and forward messages, and so on. So we did away with punch cards.

Second thing we wanted to do was to get away from the requirements that punch cards imposed on users, which was that things had to be in certain columns on the card, and so we wanted to be something more or less free form that somebody could type on a teletype keyboard, which is just a standard "qwerty" keyboard, by the way, but only with upper-case letters.

That's how the form of the language appeared, something that was easy to type, in fact originally it was space-independent. If you put spaces or you didn't put spaces in what you were typing it didn't make any difference, because the language was designed originally so that whatever you typed was always interpreted by the computer correctly, even if there were spaces or no spaces. The reason for that was that some people, especially faculty members, couldn't type very well.

Space insensitivity made its way into some of the early personal computer versions of BASIC, and that led to some quite funny anomalies about the interpretation of what the person typed.

At Dartmouth there was no ambiguity at all. Only in much later years were spaces required as the language evolved; the ending of a variable name had to be either a space or symbol.

*One critic of BASIC said that it is a language designed to teach; as soon as you start writing big programs, they become chaotic. What do you think?*

**Tom:** This is a statement by somebody who hasn't followed the development of BASIC over the years. It's not a baby language. With True BASIC I personally wrote 10,000- and 20,000-line programs, and it expands quite well, and I could write 30,000- or 40,000-line programs and there wouldn't be any problem, and it wouldn't cause the runtime to become inefficient, either.

The implementation of the language is separate from the design of the language.

The design of the language is what the user has to type to get his work done. Once you allow the possibility of libraries, then you can do anything you want. Then it's a question of the implementation of the language whether it supports programs of infinitely large size, and True BASIC does.

This is different from other versions of BASIC. For example Microsoft BASIC and Visual Basic, that is based on it, have some limitations. Other versions of BASIC that have been floating around had other limitations, but those are in the implementation, not in the design of the language.

### Which features of True BASIC made it possible for you to write large programs?

**Tom:** There's only one, the encapsulation, the module. We call our encapsulating structures *modules*.

That was actually standardized by the BASIC Committee, believe it or not, before they went out of business. That happened in the early days of True BASIC. That feature was added to the language standard, and that was about 1990 or so, 1991.

Modern computers have lots of memory and very fast chips and so there's no problem implementing that kind of stuff.

### Even though you're back to two passes now in the compiler.

**Tom:** The linker is also written in True BASIC. It's actually a crude version of True BASIC, or a simplified version of True BASIC. That's compiled into this B code, like the Pascal P code.

To actually do the linking, you execute those B code instructions and there's a very fast interpreter that executes B code instructions. True BASIC, like the original BASIC, is compiled. The original BASIC was compiled into direct machine instructions, in one stage. In True BASIC we compile into B code, and the B code is very simple, so the execution of B code by a very fast C written loop, as it is now, was originally written for the DOS platforms.

That's very fast. It's not as fast as a language designed for speed, but it's pretty darn fast. As I said, there are two-address instructions in the B code, and so it's very fast.

In the early days, interpretation didn't slow things down because we had to do floating point in software. We insisted that True BASIC and original Dartmouth BASIC always dealt with double-position numbers, so that 99% of the users didn't have to worry about the precision. Now, of course, we use the IEEE standard that's provided automatically by all chips.

### Do you think that the only difference between a language designed to teach and one designed to build professional software is that the first is easier to learn?

**Tom:** No, it's just the way that things developed. C came at an appropriate time and gave access to the hardware. Now the current object-oriented languages that are around, what they are teaching and what the professionals are doing, are derivatives of that environment, and so those languages are very hard to learn.

It means that people who use these derivative languages and are professionally trained and are members of programming teams can put together much more sophisticated applications, such those used to do movies, sounds, and things of this sort. It is just much easier to do that with an object-oriented language like Objective-C, but if that's not your goal, and you just want to write a large application program, you could use True BASIC, which comes from Dartmouth BASIC.

*What is the final goal of making a programming language easier to use? Will we ever be able to build a language so simple that every computer user could write his own programs?*

**Tom:** No, a lot of the stuff we based on BASIC at Dartmouth can now be handled by other applications such as spreadsheets. You can do quite complicated calculations with spreadsheets. Furthermore, some of the mathematical applications we had in mind can now be done using libraries of programs put out by professional societies.

The details of the programming language don't really matter because you can learn new languages in one day. It is easy to learn a new language if there is proper documentation. I just don't see what is the need of any new language alleged to be the perfect language. Without a specific field in mind, you can't have a good language; it's a self-contradicting idea! It's like asking what is the best spoken and written language around the world? Is it Italian? English? Or what is it? Could you define one? No, because all written and spoken languages derive from how life is in that place where the language is used, so there is no such thing as the perfect language. There is no perfect programming language, either.

*Did you always intend that people would write a hundred very small programs and then call themselves programmers?*

**Tom:** That was our purpose, but the odd thing about it is, as the language grew, without getting too complex, it became possible to write 10,000-line programs. That's because we kept things very simple. The whole idea, and you see, the trick in time sharing is that the turnaround time is so quick, you don't worry about optimizing the program. You worry about optimizing person time.

I had an experience when I was writing a program for the MIT computer several years before we invented BASIC. That was using a symbolic assembly program, SAP, for the IBM 704. I tried to write this program and I tried to do everything that made sense, and I used sense lights to optimize it, so I didn't repeat calculations that weren't necessary. I did everything. Well, the damn thing didn't work and it took me a month to find out that it didn't work, because I went down every two weeks. The turnaround time was two weeks.

I used I don't know how many minutes or hours of computer time in the process. Then the next year when FORTRAN came out, I switched and wrote a FORTRAN program and I think I used five minutes of computer time, all told.

The whole business of optimizing and coding is absolutely wrong. You don't do that. You optimize only if you have to and you do it later. Higher-level languages optimize computer time automatically because you make fewer errors.

*That's a point I hear infrequently.*

**Tom:** Computer scientists are kind of stupid in that respect. When we're computer programmers we're concentrating on the intricate little fascinating details of programming and we don't take a broad engineering point of view about trying to optimize the total system. You try to optimize the bits and bytes.

At any rate, that's just an editorial comment. I'm not sure I could back it up.

*Did the evolution of the hardware influence the evolution of the language?*

**Tom:** No, because we thought the language was a protection from knowing about the hardware. When we designed BASIC we made it hardware-independent; there is nothing in the language or in the features that came in later that reflects the hardware.

This is not true with some of the early personal computer versions of BASIC, which were based only in a loose sense on what we did at Dartmouth. For example, in one personal computer version of BASIC they had a way to set or interrogate the content of a certain memory location. In our own BASIC at Dartmouth, we never had that. So of course those personal computer BASICs were terribly dependent on the hardware capabilities, and the design of those personal computer languages reflected the hardware that was available to them.

If you were talking to people who did Microsoft BASIC, they would say yes, the features of the language were influenced by the hardware, but this didn't happen at Dartmouth with the original original BASIC.

*You chose to perform all arithmetic as floating point to make things easier for the user. What is your opinion on the way modern programming languages handle numbers? Should we move to an exact form of representation using arbitrary-precision numbers, where you consider them as a sort of "array of digits"?*

**Tom:** There are lots of ways to represent numbers. It is true that most languages at that time, and modern languages as well, reflect the availability of the type of number representations that are available on today's hardware.

For example, if you program in C today, there are number types that correspond to the numeric representation available on hardware, such as single-precision floating point, double-precision floating point, single-precision integer, double-precision integer, etc. Those are all aspects of the C language because it was designed to get at the hardware, so they have to provide access to whatever the number representations are in the computer.

Now, what numbers can be represented in computers? Well, in a fixed-length number of binary digits, binary bits—with which most computers work—are at least a finite number of decimal digits, you have a limitation on the type and numbers you can represent, and that's well known to lead to certain types of rounding errors.

Some languages provide access to an unlimited precision, like 300 decimal digits, for example, but they do that with software by representing very large numbers as potentially infinite arrays of digits, but that's all done by a software and consequently is very slow.

Our approach in BASIC was simply to say a number is a number, "3" is a number but also "1.5" is a number. We haven't bothered our students with that distinction; whatever they put as a number, we tried our best to represent that number in the floating-point hardware that was available on the machine.

One thing to say about that is when we were first considering which computers to get (of course we ended up with the GE computer in 1964), we insisted that the computer had floating-point hardware because we didn't want to mess around with having to do software arithmetic, and so that's how we represented the numbers. Of course there is a certain imprecision in that, but that's what you have to live with.

*Were the GOTO and the GOSUB statements just a choice given the hardware at the time? Should modern programming languages provide them as well?*

**Tom:** I don't think the hardware was the issue; it's irrelevant.

Some structured languages required it, but that was in the old days, 20 or 30 years ago, so I don't really think that's an issue.

The thing was important at the time because that was how people wrote programs for computers in machine language and assembly language. When we did BASIC the idea of structured programming had not yet surfaced; also, we patterned BASIC after FORTRAN, and FORTRAN had the GOTO statement.

*During the evolution of BASIC, what criteria did you use when considering new features to add to the language?*

**Tom:** Well, whatever was needed at the time—nothing very theoretical.

For example, one of the things we did after BASIC saw the light of day in early 1964 was to add the ability to handle nonnumerical information, strings of character information. We allowed character strings so that when people were writing programs such as to play games, they could type "yes" or "no" instead of "1" or "0". In the original BASIC, "1" meant "yes," and "0" meant "no," but very soon we added the ability to handle strings of characters. And that was just because it was needed.

## Compiler Design

*When you wrote the first version of BASIC, you were able to write a single-pass compiler while everyone else was doing a multipass compiler. How did you do that?*

**Tom:** It's very simple, if the design of the language is relatively simple. A lot of languages are simple in that respect. Everything was known, and the only thing we had to put off to what we call the pass and a half was filling in for forward transfers. That was the only thing that really prevented a complete single-pass compiler.

*In the first hundred lines of a program you have a GOTO to something in the first thousand lines. It's a linking stage then.*

**Tom:** That's what we did. It was the equivalent of the linking list. Now, we didn't actually use a linked list structure in the assembly language of the computer we were working with, but it was basically that. It might have been a little table that was set up with addresses that are filled in later.

*Were you able to parse and generate code at the same point then?*

**Tom:** Yes. The other part about it was that the language was deliberately made simple for the first go-round so that a single-pass parsing was possible. In other words, variable names are very limited. A letter or a letter followed by a digit, and array names, one- and two-dimensional arrays were always single letters followed by a left parenthesis. The parsing was trivial. There was no table lookup and furthermore, what we did was to adopt a simple strategy that a single letter, or a single letter followed by a digit, gives you what, 26 times 11 variable names. We preallocated space, fixed space for the locations for the values of those variables, if and when they had values.

We didn't even use a symbol table.

*Did you require variable declarations?*

**Tom:** No, absolutely not. In fact, arrays always were single letters followed by left parenthesis, so that was in fact the declaration. Let me see if I can remember this correctly. If you used an array, like you used a(3), then it was automatically an array from, oh, let's see, I think it was 0 to 10. Automatic default declarations, in other words, and starting at 0 because, being mathematicians, when you represent the coefficients of a polynomial, the first one has a 0 subscript.

*Did you find that simple to implement?*

**Tom:** Trivial to implement. In fact, there are a lot of things in compiler writing that are not too hard at all. Even later on when a more advanced version of BASIC was floating around that used a symbol table lookup, but that's not so hard, either.

*It's the optimizations that hurt.*

**Tom:** We didn't worry about optimization, because 99% of all the programs that were being written by students and by faculty members at that time were little teeny, little trivial things. It didn't make any sense to optimize.

*You've said that polymorphism implies runtime interpretation.*

**Tom:** I believe that's true, but nobody has challenged me on that statement because I haven't discussed it. Polymorphism means that you write a certain program and it behaves differently depending on the data that it operates on. Now, if you don't pull that in as a source program, then at execution time that piece of program doesn't know what it's doing until it actually starts executing, that's runtime interpretation. Am I wrong on that?

*Consider Smalltalk, where arguably you have the source available. If you make really late binding decisions, does that count as runtime binding?*

**Tom:** That's a tricky question. There's early binding, late binding, and runtime binding. It's really tricky, and I imagine you can figure out ways of getting around this.

For example, suppose you're writing a sorting routine. If you're sorting numbers, the comparison between which number is less and so on is obvious. If you're sorting character strings, then it's less obvious, because you don't know whether you want ASCII sorting or whether you want dictionary ordering or whether you want some other ordering.

If you're writing a sorting routine, you know which one you want, so that's how you make your comparison. If you're writing a general purpose sorting routine, then you have to call a subroutine or do something like that to determine whether item A is less than item B, whatever that is. If you're trying to sort keys to records or something, then you have to know the ordering of whatever it is you're sorting. They may be different kinds of things. Sometimes they may be character strings, but think of what the possibilities are. When you write the sorting algorithm, you don't know any of that stuff, which means it has to be put in later. If it's done at runtime, of course, then it's runtime interpretation.

That can be done efficiently, don't get me wrong, because you can have a little program, a subroutine, and then all the person has to do is, in the subroutine, to write the rules for ordering the elements that he's sorting. But it isn't automatic.

*You don't get polymorphism for free. You have to write the polymorphic variants.*

**Tom:** Somebody has to worry about it.

The other thing that the object-oriented people talk about is inheritance. That's only important if you have data typing in your language. I've read the introductions to a number of object-oriented books, and they talk about a guy writing a circle routine. Somebody else might use it for some other purpose, but that's extremely rare. The problem that I've always felt about stuff like that is that if you want to write a routine that's general-purpose enough that other people might want to use it, then you've got to document the hell out of it, and you have to make it available. I mean there's a whole raft of considerations. You're almost writing a complete application with documentation.

For the kind of programs I do, that's overrated. I don't know what happens in the industry. That's another matter.

*Would you call that idea of cheap and easy code reuse premature generalization?*

**Tom:** It's an idea that may have relevance in the programming profession, but it does not have relevance to the wider group of amateurs who might write programs. As a matter of fact, most people don't write programs these days. Much of what we used to write programs for is now done by an application that you can buy or you can put it into a spreadsheet, or whatever. Having nonprofessional programmers, people in other fields, write programs is not done very much anymore.

One of the things that bothers me about the education of programming primarily in secondary schools, where they have an advanced placement in computer science, is that it's much too complicated. I don't know what languages they teach these days, I haven't looked at it.

I once looked at how I would structure a first college course in computer science using BASIC. It could do practically everything I'd ever want to do in a beginning computer science course except deal with pointers and allocated storage. That's sort of a complexity. If you use Pascal for the language, you may have to get into pointers and allocated storage when people don't even know what a computer program is, but that's neither here nor there. I never pushed my views. I'm one against many.

*People are starting to believe that you don't have to deal with allocated memory and pointers much anymore unless you're writing virtual machines. Those who write compilers do, but that's our job.*

**Tom:** Let the compiler do it; you don't have to do it.

We got portability in True BASIC. A couple of young men who were really brilliant did the design. I just was with the company and did application programming. They designed an intermediate language that was in the fashion of the P code of Pascal. Instead of being two address, it was three address, because it turned out that practically all instructions in BASIC are three address, LET A = 3. That's three things, the opcode and the two addresses. Then they built a compiler using BASIC itself, and built a very crude support to actually compile that compiler. The compiler itself is written in True BASIC, and it runs on any machine for which there is a True BASIC engine, which we call the interpreter.

The language is interpreted at the execution level, not at the scanning level. So there's three stages in the execution of the program. The first is the compiler stage, the second is the linking/loading stage, and the third is the execution. But the user doesn't know that. The user just types run or hits run or something and bang, it happens.

The compiled code is also machine-independent. It can transport that across boundaries.

It's really quite a sophisticated language environment. We were on multiple platforms, four or five different platforms for a while, but most platforms lived a short time and died, of course. Now there's only two major platforms or three major platforms left: Unix, Microsoft, and, for us, Apple—an interesting platform because Dartmouth was always an Apple school.

Doing the porting to those platforms turned out to be a dog. The windowing support and the gadgets and the buttons and all that kind of stuff, they all do it differently, and you have to get down to the detail of how they do it. Sometimes they do it at a very low level, so you have to build all that stuff up yourself.

The old, original Mac, it had a Mac toolbox. For a while, we used a layering software, XVT out of Boulder, Colorado, which claimed to target Windows and also the classic Mac. We were able to get some mileage out of that. Before the company went defunct, the programmer put out a version for Windows; it goes directly to the Windows application environment.

The trouble with those is that when we have a single programmer doing all of that stuff, it takes a while, and new versions of the operating system come out and you run across new bugs and have to track them down. It was almost impossible for a small outfit like we were. At one point we had three programmers, then down to two, and then down to one. That's really just too much for one programmer to handle.

The underlying code, now that it's largely C, contains tons of #ifdefs in it.

## Language and Programming Practice

*What is the link between the design of a language and the design of a software written with that language?*

**Tom:** Very tight. Most languages were designed with specific types of software in mind. A prime example was APT, a language for controlling Automatic Programmed Tools.

*You added the REM statement for comments in the early days. Has your opinion on comments and software documentation changed over the years?*

**Tom:** No, it's a kind of self-defense mechanism. When I write programs in True BASIC, I do add comments to remind me whatever I was thinking when I wrote the code. So I think that comments play a role, and the role is different depending on what kind of programs you are writing, whether you work in a group or no other people read your code. I believe in comments but only insofar as they are necessary.

*Do you have any suggestions for people writing software in teams?*

**Tom:** No, because we have never done it. All the software we have done in our environment has been solo work. In True BASIC we had maybe two or three people writing code, but they were really working on completely separate projects. I just don't have any experience working in teams.

*You had a time-sharing machine, so you suggested that users should plan their session at the teletype before sitting there. The motto was: typing is no substitute for thinking. Is this true today?*

**Tom:** I think probably that thinking does take place. When a major company is going to develop a new software product, they do a lot of thinking before it, so I think that's done.

One of the things I do personally is not thinking too much ahead but just start writing the program. Then I will discover that it is not quite working out, so I will scrap the whole thing and start over. That's the equivalent to thinking. I usually start coding just to see what the problems are going to be, and then throw that version away.

It is important to think about what you are doing—very important. I am not sure, but I think Richard Hamming stated that "typing is no substitute for thinking." Those are the early days of computing and very few people knew how to do it, so there was a lot of advice like that floating around.

*What is the best way to learn a new programming language?*

**Tom:** Once one knows how to program, and knows the concepts (i.e., how storage is allocated), learning a new language is straightforward if one has access to a reference manual, and a decent implementation (i.e., compiler). I've done it many times.

Attending a class is pretty much a waste of time.

Any programmer worth her salt will know many languages in her professional lifetime. (I probably have used more than 20 in mine.) The way to learn new languages is to read the manual. With few exceptions, most programming languages are similar in structure and in the way they operate, so new languages are fairly easy to learn, if there is a reasonable manual available.

Once you get over the jargon hurdle (what does *polymorphism* mean?), things are really fairly simple.

One problem with today's programming style is that there are no manuals—just interface building tools. They are designed so that programmers don't have to type, letter by letter, many of the instructions, but behave like the engineers' CAD and CAM tools. To old-time programmers like me, that is anathema—I want to type all the code, letter by letter.

There have been attempts in the past to simplify the typing (for poor typists or students) by providing macros (such as a single keystroke for the keyword LET), but they never caught on.

I am now attempting to learn a language that is supposedly "object-oriented." No reference manual exists, at least that I have found. The manuals that are available develop what appear to be almost trivial examples, and spend perhaps 90% of the space pointing out how OOP is such a superior "religion." I have friends who took a C++ course, and it was a disaster from a pedagogical point of view. My opinion is that OOP is one of the great frauds perpetrated on the community. All languages were originally designed for a certain class of users—FORTRAN for extended numerical computations, etc. OOP was designed so that its clients could claim superior wisdom for being on the "inside." The truth of the matter is that the single most important aspect of OOP is an approach devised decades ago: encapsulation of subroutines and data. All the rest is frosting.

## Language Design

*Do you think Microsoft's current Visual Basic is a full-fledged object-oriented language, and if so, do you approve of this aspect of it (given your dismissal of the object-oriented paradigm)?*

**Tom:** I don't know. With a few simple experiments, I found Visual Basic relatively easy to use. I doubt that anyone outside of Microsoft would define VB as an OOL. As a matter of fact, True BASIC is just as much object-oriented as VB, perhaps more so. True BASIC included modules, which are collections of subroutines and data; they provide the single most important feature of OOP, namely, data encapsulation. (True BASIC does not have inherited types, since it doesn't have user-defined types, other than array dimensions. Hardly any language has polymorphism, which, in fact, implies runtime interpretation.)

*You mentioned that Visual Basic as compared to True BASIC had some severe limitations. Do you mean that Visual Basic lacked something like your module system?*

**Tom:** I don't know. I only wrote some sample programs in—well, I didn't write anything in Visual Basic. I just convinced myself that I could do it. It had a fairly simple user interface to it. This is in contrast to some of the others I tried to use once. Visual Basic was the old Microsoft BASIC and they claim it was object-oriented but it really wasn't, just by adding the front-end interface builder to it.

*You also made an interesting comment about some of the bigger systems people are building for video and audio. You said it's easier to put together a sophisticated app like that with an object-oriented language like Objective-C.*

**Tom:** Yeah, probably because the language environment is made sufficient for that.

I'm trying to learn Objective-C right now without success, but at any rate, you have that environment. If you know what you're doing you can access all of that stuff that's on the platform, visual and audio, in some sort of a reasonable way. I haven't tried it, so I don't know how hard it is, but it's included in the language development environment.

*It's not necessarily a feature of the language itself; it's a feature of the environment around the language.*

**Tom:** It doesn't really have anything to do with the language per se, but it's the language environment. If the language environment is currently being used by a lot of people, then there's maybe a hundred programmers back in the factory making sure it works right.

*What do the lessons about the invention, further development, and adoption of your language say to people developing computer systems today and in the foreseeable future?*

**Tom:** Nothing.

From the early 60s I recall the Burroughs 5500 computer. Its hardware was designed to allow pushdown stack applications, such as Algol compilers, to be more efficient.

Today, the trend seems to be in the other direction, toward RISC machines.

For most programming languages, nothing special is needed. Part of the reason is that the speed of computers is so great, and getting greater, that the compiling and processing time of a particular language is a nonissue.

The reverse might be true. For example, to process large arrays, you might build an array-processing computer, which would then require you to develop a suitable programming language.

*If today you had to create a completely new programming language for teaching, how similiar would it be to BASIC?*

**Tom:** Very, because the principles that we followed are still valid. For instance, we tried to make a language that was easy to remember, so if a person didn't use it for a long time, they were still able to sit down and remember how to use it.

We tried to make a language that had a minimum of esoteric requirements. For example, in FORTRAN if you wanted to print a number, you had to use a format statement and indicate exactly how was it to be printed. That's an esoteric subject for people to learn, particularly if they don't use the language that often, so what we were doing in BASIC was just print the number in a way that we thought would be the best way to print it. If it was an integer number, in fact, even though we use internal floating point, we would print it out as an integer value without the decimal point. If you wanted to type in a number, you didn't have to worry about the format; you would have just written your favourite formula and it would have gone in—you weren't restricted to some particular format for entering data.

Most of the time this is followed by spreadsheets; they are good at this type of thing. You can specify if you want a fixed-point output for numbers that are displayed in a particular column, or if you don't care you get the general form. I think that's more or less what we did with BASIC. We allow character input, and we do it in a very simple way: you just type it in; there is no rule to follow.

During the 70s and 80s we developed structured programming versions of BASIC at Dartmouth and we added the elements to get the capabilities of object-oriented programming. We would not have done anything differently.

### Is encapsulation what you like about object orientation?

**Tom:** That is absolutely correct. I used to say that encapsulation is 70% of what object programming provides, but I think I'm changing that to 90%. That's the main thing, to merge together routines and their data. That's really important. I don't write much anymore, but everything that I've written when I was working for True BASIC and so on, I encapsulated them.

We had a way of encapsulating groups of subroutines in what we called *modules*, which is the same thing, but grouping the subroutines together and then they're isolated from the rest of the programming except through their calling sequence. In fact, they had their own private data. That turned out to be extremely handy to isolate functionality, that type of thing.

*One of the things that I've asked many of these designers of languages and systems is to what degree they like this notion of a mathematical formalism. Take Scheme, which expresses the lambda calculus very effectively. You have six primitives and everything is just beautifully built on top of that. That seems like the mathematician approach.*

**Tom:** Yeah, that's very interesting. That's an interesting mathematical problem, but if you're designing a computer language, you don't have to do that stuff, because every computer language that I've ever seen is much simpler than that. Even FORTRAN. Algol is simple; it uses recursive definitions, but that's fairly simple and straightforward.

I never studied the theory of programming languages, so I can't make any more comments than that.

*Do you consider the people who will use a language and the biggest problems they're going to have to solve?*

**Tom:** Yeah. The biggest problem for the people that we were designing for was remembering the language from week to week, but they only wrote one program every two weeks. We also wanted a programming language and a system environment that we could teach in a matter of a couple of hours, so you don't have to take a course.

*That's how I and a lot of my peers learned to program. We had Microsoft BASIC on the PCs of the early 80s—the Commodore 64 and the Apple II. They were line BASICs with subroutines, but not much else.*

**Tom:** There are oddities floating around. They actually had some tricky stuff to it. For example, I used Apple Soft BASIC. I don't know if Microsoft did it or whether somebody else did it, but all of those were copied from Dartmouth BASIC startup. They introduced the idea of a multicharacter variable name, but they didn't parse it correctly. If you happened to have a keyword buried inside your multiple-character variable name, it would throw the thing off.

*Was this because of whitespace insensitivity?*

**Tom:** No, because they claimed to have multicharacter variable names, but they didn't. They faked it. If you had a multiple-character variable name which was, let's say, TOT, they would recognize the TO as a keyword. It was a marketing gimmick. Those languages, little features were designed for the market. They thought that multiple-character variable names would be a good gimmick. People that used the language managed to get around that by not using multiple characters very much.

*That's not a process that's discoverable reading the manual.*

**Tom:** The errors in it are not, no.

*How did whitespace insensitivity come about?*

**Tom:** The only thing I know about it was published, and the reason for space insensitivity is partly because John Kemeny was a poor typist. I don't know if that was really the reason. We codesigned the language, but a feature like that is something that he did.

Because variable names are unique and do not look like keywords, spaces are not needed. You can add spaces or remove them ad lib.

Things develop. Now when I write programs, there are still versions of True BASIC floating around that run on various machines. That's the only language I use, and I use spaces to improve clarity.

*Not to work around computer limitations; it's solely a human factors issue for you?*

**Tom:** That's right, because the main thing about a program, you know, if it's a serious program you're writing and you're going to be working on it, is to make sure that if you put it aside for six months and pick it up again that you'll be able to understand it by reading it. It's very important to choose variable names that suggest the quantities they represent or to build a structure; I'm thinking primarily the fact of using single-purpose subroutines and then giving them a name that suggests what they do.

With multicharacter variable names of arbitrary length now a part of all computer languages, even if there are 20 letters in the subroutine name, nonetheless it tells what it does. Someone can come back six months later and understand it.

*Chuck Moore says that in Forth you build up a vocabulary of words so that you can write in the language of the domain if you've chosen the words correctly. It's interesting how that idea has come up so many times.*

**Tom:** A computer language like BASIC is designed for people who are not professional programmers. If you are a person in some field and you decide to write an application program for your field, you would prefer a simpler programming language to work with than somebody who is a professional. I'm thinking in particular of these object-oriented languages that are floating around.

I have a little bit of experience with one of them, and it's grotesquely complicated. It's the only computer language in my life that I have not been able to figure out, and I've written programs in maybe 30 computer languages.

*How would a WYSIWYG eliminate the need for line numbers? You suggested they existed only as targets of GOTO statements. Are line numbers also needed so programmers can refer to lines when editing a file?*

**Tom:** Absolutely not (to the last question). Line-numbered editing has long since gone.

*How would WYSIWYG change programming?*

**Tom:** Not at all. The WYSIWYG editors are now sophisticated and closely associated with the language they serve (in terms of indentation, use of color, etc.).

*Is there anything we miss in computer science education today? Some people have said that there's no engineering focus, for example.*

**Tom:** Well, I don't know because I don't know how they teach computer science today. I retired 15 years ago and I didn't teach anything but statistics and computer science, so I have no idea of how the field has since developed.

*How should debugging be taught?*

**Tom:** Well, the best thing to do is to prevent it in the first place, and you do that by thinking ahead better.

One of our former students become an Apple fellow doing some very significant work for them and then retired. Before that he worked at Dartmouth in the computer center. He wrote a PL/1 compiler, and it's a big thing, and he checked it, and looked at it, and so on, but he never tested it, he never ran it until it was all done. You know, 20,000 or 30,000 lines of code, and the only test he did was to read it. Then he ran it and it worked the first time!

That's an oddity in the whole history of computer science! I mean somebody writes a 20,000- or 30,000-line program and it works correctly the first time, that's bizarre, OK? But he did it, and that's the way to do it. He worked solo; he didn't work in a team. You are always more productive when you work alone. So he was very careful about how the various parts of the programs worked together and he read code very carefully, and this means that when you read the code what you are really doing is emulating what the computer is going to do, so you check every step—this is right, this is right, etc.

So when he pressed the "go" button and it worked, that's crazy, nobody does that, but that's the idea. You reduce bugs by keeping them out in the first place.

A lot of commercial software around these days is tremendously buggy because it is not written by good programmers, it is written by teams, and the design of what it does is determined by the marketing department. It has to come out in a certain period of time with a certain program with certain capabilities, so it's full of bugs. For the software companies, most of the users just use superficial features in their computers, so they don't run into many bugs.

*Would you draw a line between what you think is good to incorporate into the language as opposed to a library?*

**Tom:** Well, we paid a lot of attention to that, too. Anything that was a little bit esoteric that only a fraction of the users would want to know about, we would put into a library. That's the way the language developed over the years. So we had a library for doing a lot of things; in the modern version of BASIC, which is True BASIC, we use a library of subroutines to access the objects of object-oriented programming such as push buttons, dialog boxes, and things of that sort. We use a library routine, and the access of that kind of stuff is not included in the language per se, so you have to call a subroutine to do these things and the subroutines are contained in a number of libraries. That is something we thought quite hard about at the beginning.

*When people write software in teams, they often build common libraries for everyone to use. Do you have any advice to build such libraries in True BASIC?*

**Tom:** Well, I have written libraries myself, but I don't have any particular advice besides try to keep it simple. You know, these are techniques everybody knows about: keep things simple and try to avoid introducing bugs.

Single-purpose subroutines, for example, are important. Don't have subroutines that do something on the side because it seems like a good idea. Side effects can be disastrous. There are lots of ways to write libraries that can reduce or eliminate future bugs or errors. There are well-known techniques for reducing errors, but I don't know how much they follow them in the industry, because in the industry the programs they write are dictated largely by the marketing department.

## Work Goals

*How do you define success in terms of your work?*

**Tom:** For many years because of our work—because it was so open, because we gave unlimited access to students who were part of the project—Dartmouth had one of the best computer reputations around the world. People visited us from Russia, Japan, and other places, just to see what it was like. And this was before the days of common personal computers. Now everyone has a personal computer, so it's not an issue anymore, but in those days it was a very interesting issue that we allowed students, any student, to do any computing, anytime they wanted, without prior permission. That was novel in those days. That gave Dartmouth a reputation that lasted 10 or 15 years and was to its advantage in terms of fundraising, attracting students, and recruiting faculty.

The other success was that many students who went to Dartmouth and learned how to do computing were able to build extraordinary careers out of the fact that they knew how to do it. These were people not in the computing center of the corporations; they were working in other departments. There are quite a few Dartmouth students that became millionaires just because they knew how to use a computer!

That's the main measure of our success.

*What should young people learn from your experience?*

**Tom:** They should be aware of the eventual users of the software, the people that are going to use their software. Many of the applications that we use these days are really very hard to use.

I know that a number of years ago, people at Microsoft tried to introduce the idea of user friendliness through a program called "Bob" or something like that, but they didn't understand it; they thought that "user friendly" meant "patronizing," as if you are talking to a child. That's not what user friendly means.

I am afraid that the industry at large doesn't know what user friendly means. I don't know if people doing computer science these days would even understand what the words mean.

My advice is to be concerned about the people who are going to use your software.

*Should we build an interface that is easy to learn like BASIC was easy to learn?*

**Tom:** Yes, easy to learn, simple to describe in a manual of some sort, and which does more or less what you expect it to do when you use it, so there are no surprises.

*You also said that you're always more productive when you work alone, and I want to understand what you mean by productive there.*

**Tom:** I mean in very simple terms. I think there's a lot of evidence that supports that. I have never worked on a programming team in my life. I've always said, "OK, this needs to be done, I'm going to write a program for it." Everything I've written has been capable of being managed by me, a single programmer.

I've used stuff that other people have written but I've never been part of a development team. I've written, oh, I don't know how many lines of programs, but I've got several things out there that I'm still using that are 10,000 lines long. They're easy to write. They're easy to debug. If you find a feature that you don't like, it's easy to change—and you don't have to write memos if you're working by yourself. I don't mind doing the documentation, either, if it has documentation. Most of my stuff doesn't because it's for my own use, but I'm a believer in everything that Fred Brooks ever wrote about programming in his book *The Mythical Man-Month*.

I like the one he says about estimating how long it takes to write a program. A programmer writes three lines of documented code per day or something like that, and they discovered that their applications were just taking too long. They couldn't figure out what was wrong with them. Then they discovered the reason was programmers only work 20 hours a week. They're in the factory for 40 hours, but 20 hours are spent doing nonproductive things, going to staff meetings.

That's the thing I hate the most: staff meetings. Sometimes they're absolutely necessary. I remember when the original BASIC was being developed for the GE225, GE235 computers. The student programmers would meet for a weekly meeting of about one hour. John Kemeny would chair that meeting, and as he liked to say, he made all of the unimportant decisions, like who is favored in the scheduling algorithm and so forth and so on, but the students made all the important decisions, like which bit is used for what purpose.

We had a two-machine environment in those days, and so there was one student on each machine. They were sophomores, and so they had to work together, they had to communicate. By and large they did their own work. Anytime we were writing a compiler or an editor, that was a single-person job.

*You made this comment in the context of the discussion about the student who wrote a PL/1 compiler, and the first time he ran it, it worked.*

**Tom:** That's Phil Koch, and he's an Apple fellow. He's retired from Apple now, living in Maine. He was an astonishing programmer. It took him a long time and he read code religiously.

*If there is one lesson you'd like people to learn from your vast and varied experiences over the years, what is that?*

**Tom:** Make it easy for your users to use your software.

You can say user friendly if you want, but part of that is that the industry has defined user friendly to be, in my view, condescending. The real issue on user friendliness is to have reasonable defaults in whatever application you're doing, so the person who's just come to it fresh doesn't have to learn about all of the variations and degrees of freedom that are possible. He or she can just sit down and start to do it. Then if they want to do something different, make it relatively easy to get at that.

In order to do that, you have to have some sort of an idea of what your user base is going to be.

I've used Microsoft Word frequently, but by my standards, it's not user friendly at all. Then Microsoft came out with that Bob thing about 10 years ago, and that was the wrong idea. They didn't understand what user friendly really means.

Some applications, I think, are user friendly, but the big thing now is website design. People that design websites, sometimes they do a good job and sometimes they don't do a good job. If you go to a website and you can't figure out what to do to get more information, that's a lousy design.

That stuff's hard to teach.

Ben Shniederman, a specialist in human factors in computer science at the University of Maryland, actually did some studies* that suggested that what we had chosen in BASIC for our structures for DO, LOOP, and IF were easier in the sense of user friendliness than some of the other structures that were using the other languages, like the semicolon in Algol or Pascal to end a sentence.

People normally don't use semicolons to end sentences, so that's something that you have to learn specifically. I remember in FORTRAN, for example, there were places where a comma is needed and places where a comma isn't needed. As a result, there was a bug in a program down at the space station in Florida where they lost a rocket because there was a missing comma. I think Ed Tufte actually documented that. Try to stay away from stuff that's possibly ambiguous.

---

* Shneiderman, B. "When children learn programming: Antecedents, concepts, and outcomes," *The Computing Teacher*, volume 5: 14–17 (1985).

I keep saying to the world at large, Kemeny and I failed because we didn't make other people's computers user friendly, but we did a good job with our own students because for 20 or so years, our students were going out and getting very cushy jobs in the industry because they knew how to do things.

*That is a good type of success to have.*

**Tom:** If you're a teacher, that's really the main thing.

# CHAPTER SIX

# AWK

The Unix philosophy of many small tools, powerful in their combination, is evident in the AWK programming language. Its inventors (Al Aho, Peter Weinberger, and Brian Kernighan) describe it as a language for syntax-driven pattern matching. Its straightforward syntax and clever selection of useful features make it easy to slice and dice text through one-liners without having to understand parsers and grammars and finite automata. Though its inspiration has spread to general-purpose languages such as Perl, any modern Unix box still has AWK installed and quietly, effectively, working away.

# The Life of Algorithms

*How do you define AWK?*

**Al Aho:** I would say AWK is an easy-to-learn and easy-to-use scripting language that excels at routine data-processing applications.

*What was your role in the development of AWK?*

**Al:** I was doing research into efficient parsing and string pattern matching algorithms in the 1970s. Brian Kernighan and I had been talking about generalizations of grep to be able to do more general pattern matching and text processing for many data-processing applications we had in mind. Peter Weinberger came along and expressed great interest in this project, so we quickly implemented the first version of AWK in 1977.

The language then evolved considerably for a few years as a number of our colleagues started to use it for a large variety of data-processing tasks, many of which we had not anticipated.

*In what context is AWK most appropriate?*

**Al:** I think AWK is still unbeatable for simple routine data-processing applications. Our AWK book has dozens of practical examples of where a one- or two-line AWK program can do what would take dozens or hundreds of C or Java lines to implement.

*What should people keep in mind when designing software written in AWK?*

**Al:** AWK is a scripting language that was designed for writing short programs for common data-processing applications. We didn't intend it to be used to program large applications, but we often found people were doing this because the language was so easy to use. For large applications I'd recommend the usual good software engineering practices: good modularization, good variable names, good comments, and so forth. These practices are also good for short programs.

*How does the availability of hardware resources affect the mindset of programmers?*

**Al:** It's certainly true that fast hardware, plenty of memory, and good IDEs have made programming more enjoyable. Also, programs can be applied to much larger datasets than ever before in the past. I now routinely run AWK programs on inputs that are several orders of magnitude larger than in the past, so fast hardware has made me more productive as a user.

However, there is a tradeoff: improvements in hardware have led to explosions in the size and complexity of software systems. Software does become more useful as hardware improves, but it also becomes more complex—I don't know which side is winning.

*When you developed the algorithms behind AWK, how did you estimate the size of data with which your code would work?*

**Al:** Whenever possible, we implemented algorithms that were linear in time, in either the worst case or the average case. This way AWK could gracefully scale to handle larger and larger inputs.

We tested AWK on various sizes of datasets to measure how performance would scale as the size of the input grew. We tried to make our implementation as efficient as we knew how, using real data to test how well we were doing.

### Did you consider how the size of data would grow in the future?

**Al:** When we designed AWK, I thought a megabyte dataset was huge. If we consider the exabytes of data now available on the Internet, we were many orders of magnitude off in what's now considered a large dataset. Of course, even a linear-time scan of a terabyte of data is far too slow, so a whole new approach is necessary to process relevant data on the Internet.

### I've heard AWK described as a "pattern-matching language suitable for simple data-processing tasks." Considering that AWK was created more than 30 years ago, what has changed since then in pattern matching?

**Al:** The scale and diversity of pattern matching has exploded in the past 30 years. The parameters of the problems have broadened significantly; the patterns have become more complex and the size of the datasets has vastly increased. Today we routinely use search engines to look for textual patterns in all of the web pages on the Internet. We are also interested in *data mining*—looking for patterns of all kinds in huge digital libraries such as genomic databases and scientific archives. It is fair to say that string pattern matching is one of the most fundamental applications in computer science.

### Are there better pattern-matching algorithms and implementations of them today?

**Al:** Pattern matching in AWK was done using a fast, compact, lazy state-transition construction algorithm to build from a regular expression the transitions of a deterministic finite automaton needed to do the pattern matching. The algorithm is documented in the Red Dragon book.* The running time of the algorithm is basically linear in the length of the regular expression and in the size of the input text. This is the best known expected running time for regular expressions. We could have implemented a Boyer-Moore algorithm or an Aho-Corasick algorithm for the special cases when a regular expression is a single keyword or a finite set of keywords. We did not do this since we did not know the characteristics of regular expressions that people would use in AWK programs.

I might mention that there is a dark side to using complex algorithms in software systems. The algorithms may not be understandable by others (or even the original author, after a long passage of time). I had incorporated some sophisticated regular expression pattern-matching technology into AWK. Although it is documented in the Red Dragon book, Brian Kernighan once took took a look at the pattern-matching module that I had written and his only addition to that module was putting a comment in ancient Italian: "abandon all hope, ye who enter here."† As a consequence, neither Kernighan or Weinberger would touch that part of the code. I was the one that always had to make the bug fixes to that module!

---

* Aho, Alfred V. et al. *Compilers: Principles, Techniques, and Tools* (Addison-Wesley, 1986).

† *Lasciate ogne speranza, voi ch'intrate* is the inscription on the gate of Hell in Canto III, Inferno, *The Divine Comedy*, by Dante Alighieri.

## Language Design

*Do you have any advice for designers of programming languages?*

**Al:** Always keep your users in mind. Having others say they used your tool to solve a problem is very rewarding. It's also satisfying having others build on your work to create more powerful tools.

*How did Kernighan and Weinberger think about language design?*

**Al:** If I had to choose a word to describe our centering forces in language design, I'd say Kernighan emphasized ease of learning; Weinberger, soundness of implementation; and I, utility. I think AWK has all three of these properties.

*How do you make design decisions with utility in mind? How does that affect the way you think about design?*

**Al:** I don't know whether it's conscious or unconscious, but certainly the things that survive are things that are useful. It reinforces the notion of Darwinism. You create notions and dictions that are useful for solving problems that you're interested in, but if they're not good at solving the problems that others are interested in, they wither away. It's survival of the fittest ideas that create utility. We don't keep languages that aren't useful.

*Unless we're art historians, there's a dichotomy between a program that is beautiful or a program that is functional.*

**Al:** Can't you have both?

*People seem to want to draw the line there. The question is whether programming is a creative endeavor, whether it's art or craft.*

**Al:** Knuth of course was very interested in programming as an art. He thought that programs should be beautiful. Almost all of the programmers that I know feel that there should be elegance in the programs that you write.

*A craftsman woodworker might say, "Here's a chair. You can sit on it or you can stand on it. You can stack phone books on it, but look at the elegant design, look at the wonderful joints, look at the wonderful carvings." There's artistry, even if it's a functional tool.*

**Al:** But there can also be beauty in minimalism, so we don't need all sorts of ornamentation or rococo architecture to make things beautiful.

*How can someone become a better programmer?*

**Al:** My number one suggestion is to think before you program. Then I would advocate writing lots of code, having experts critique your code, reading good code written by others, and participating in code reviews. If you're really brave, you could try to teach students to write good code.

I have found that there's no better way to learn a subject than teaching it to others. In the process of teaching, you have to organize the material and the presentation in such a manner that the subject becomes clear to others. When you're doing this in a classroom setting, students will ask you questions that will expose different ways of thinking about the problems than you had initially thought about. Your insights deepen and become far sharper than they used to be.

This is certainly true about programming. If you are teaching programming, students will ask, "Couldn't we solve it this way, couldn't we solve it that way?" Then you realize, "Yes, there are many ways to solve that problem with a program." You recognize that people think very differently, and because they think differently, they have different approaches to solving problems, and through that, you get a much better appreciation for different approaches to solving the problem.

I have certainly found that in every book that I have written with programs in it, the programs have gotten more efficient and shorter with the writing of the book. During the year we wrote the AWK book, many of the programs in it became 50% shorter. This is because we learned how to use the abstractions in AWK even more effectively than we initially had thought.

*Did you find deficiencies in the design of AWK when you wrote the book?*

**Al:** When people started using AWK for many other tasks than we initially thought, it exposed certain aspects of the language where we hadn't intended it to be a general-purpose programming language. I wouldn't call these "deficiencies," but it showed that AWK was a specialized language that was not intended for some of the applications that people were trying to use it for.

*Were you able to address some of those, or did you strongly resist making AWK more general purpose?*

**Al:** After the initial version of AWK was created, the language evolved for about a decade with the addition of new constructs and new operators, but it stayed a pattern-action language, a language that was intended for solving data-processing problems. We didn't take it out of that domain.

*How do you make the idea of syntax-driven transformations accessible to users who might not know very much or anything at all about finite-state machines and push-down automata?*

**Al:** Certainly as a user of AWK, you don't need to know about these concepts. On the other hand, if you're into language design and implementation, knowledge of finite-state machines and context-free grammars is essential.

*Should a user of lex or yacc understand the context-free grammar even if the programs they produce don't require their users to understand them?*

**Al:** Most users of lex can use lex without understanding what a finite-state machine is. A user of yacc is really writing a context-free grammar, so from that perspective, the user of yacc certainly gets to appreciate grammars, but the user doesn't have to become a formal language theorist to use yacc.

*Otherwise you suffer through pages of pages of shift/reduce conflict errors.*

**Al:** One useful aspect of yacc is that since it automates the construction of a deterministic parser from a grammar, it informs programming language designers about constructs in their language that are ambiguous or difficult to parse. Without the tool, they might not have noticed these infelicitous constructs. With yacc, language designers often said, "Oh, I didn't realize that there were two ways to interpret this grammatical construct!" Then they eliminated or modified the questionable construct. Ambiguities in precedence and associativity were easily resolved by simple mechanisms that specified "I'd like to have this order of precedence for the operators in the language, and this order of associativity."

*How do you build a debugging-friendly language? When designing a language, how do you think about features you need to add or remove to aid the debugging phase?*

**Al:** The trend in programming language design has been to create languages that enhance software reliability and programmer productivity. What we should do is develop languages alongside sound software-engineering practices so that the task of developing reliable programs is distributed throughout the software lifecycle, especially into the early phases of systems design.

Systems cannot be developed assuming that human beings will be able to write millions of lines of code without making mistakes, and debugging alone is not an efficient way to develop reliable systems. Regularity of syntax and semantics is a good way to eliminate accidental errors.

## Unix and Its Culture

*Early Unix culture seemed to promote the idea that when you have a problem, you write a little compiler or a little language to solve it. At what point do you decide it's the right approach to create a language to solve a specific problem instead of a program in another language?*

**Al:** There are thousands and thousands of programming languages in the world today, and one can ask why these languages arose. Virtually every area of human endeavor has its own jargon. Musicians have a special notation for writing music; lawyers use jargon to talk about the law; chemists have special diagrams for describing atoms and molecules and how they get combined. It's not unnatural for people to say, "Let's create a language around these notations for solving problems arising in a given area."

You can use a general-purpose programming language to express any algorithm, but on the other hand, it's often more convenient, more economical, and perhaps even more suggestive of solutions to have a specialized language to solve a specific class of problems. It becomes a judgment call when to create a new language, but if the area is of interest and there are special dictions that are amenable to automation, then it's only natural that a programming language would arise for expressing solutions to problems in a given area.

### Economical in terms of programmer investment or hardware time?

**Al:** Languages, at least in the early days, came about because people recognized certain important classes of problems that they needed to solve, and then they devised hardware-efficient programming languages to create programs for solving problems in those areas. As hardware has become cheaper and faster, languages have tended to become higher-level and hardware efficiency less relevant.

### Did you consider AWK strong enough in its niche on its own?

**Al:** The pattern-action paradigm that's embedded in AWK is very natural for solving large classes of commonly occurring data-processing problems. Changing this paradigm would vitiate the language and not make it as appealing for the class of problems that we had in mind. The language is also very useful for Unix command-line programming.

### That sounds like the Unix philosophy of combining many small tools that are each very good at what they do.

**Al:** I think that's a very apt description.

### Most of the places I've seen AWK are command lines or shell scripts.

**Al:** Applications where you can compose problems on the command line, or create shell scripts that are a combination of Unix commands, are very popular AWK programs. This style of problem solving epitomized early AWK applications on Unix, and even many Unix applications today.

### In Unix, "everything is a file." Do you have a vision of what might be considered the "file" of the Internet?

**Al:** Files are a nice simple abstraction that should be used wherever they are appropriate. The Internet of today, however, has become much richer in data types and programs often have to deal with streams of concurrent interactive multimedia data. Today the best solution seems to be to use standardized, well-defined APIs for dealing with data, and security programs need to be concerned with how to react properly to ill-formed data.

### What limits do you see in command-line tools and in graphical interfaces?

**Al:** AWK is very useful for converting the output format of one program so that it can be used as input to another. If a graphical interface has preprogrammed this kind of data conversion as a mouse-click, then that is clearly more convenient. If it hasn't, then it may be very difficult to get at the internal formats to do the needed data conversions.

*Is there a connection between that idea of composing programs together from the command line through pipes and the idea of writing little languages, each for a specific domain?*

**Al:** I think there's a connection. Certainly in the early days of Unix, pipes facilitated function composition on the command line. You could take an input, perform some transformation on it, and then pipe the output into another program. This provided a very powerful way of quickly creating new functionality with simple compositions of programs. People started thinking how to solve problems along these lines. Larry Wall's language Perl, which I think of as a descendant of AWK and other Unix tools, combined many aspects of this kind of program composition into a single language.

*When you say "function composition," that brings to mind the mathematical approach of function composition.*

**Al:** That's exactly what I mean.

*Was that mathematical formalism in mind at the invention of the pipe, or was that a metaphor added later when someone realized it worked the same way?*

**Al:** I think it was right there from the start. Doug McIlroy, at least in my book, deserves the credit for pipes. He thought like a mathematician and I think he had this connection right from the start. I think of the Unix command line as a prototypical functional language.

*To what degree is formalizing the semantics and ideas of a language useful? Is there an underlying formalism in AWK?*

**Al:** AWK was designed around a syntax-directed translation scheme. I was very interested in compilers and compiler theory, so when we created AWK, the implementation was done as a syntax-directed translation. We had a formal syntax for AWK in the form of a context-free grammar, and the translation from the source language to the target language was done in terms of semantic actions based on that formal grammar. This facilitated the growth and development of AWK. We had at our disposal the newly created compiler construction tools, lex and yacc, which greatly aided experimentation with and development of the language.

*Simon Peyton Jones from Haskell said that they had formalisms for 80/85% of the language, but beyond that it just wasn't worth their time to formalize the rest because of diminishing returns.*

**Al:** Because of security, specificity is becoming a much more important issue in language and systems design. Hackers often exploit the unusual or unspecified parts of a system to compromise security.

*Add into that the problem of library design, and suddenly the problem gets even larger. "I've specified the formalisms of my language, but now I need a library to interact with the Internet; have I quantified the formalisms of that library? Do they fit the formalisms? Do they violate the formalisms and guarantees of the language?"*

**Al:** Having worked in the telecommunications industry, I noticed virtually all of the interface specifications for which Bell Labs constructed equipment conformed to an international standard. Having said this, many of the standards were written in English and so they were often ambiguous, incomplete, and inconsistent. But in spite of these difficulties, the international telecommunications network and Internet interoperate and work well largely due to well-defined interfaces between systems.

Third parties often create device drivers and applications for other vendors' operating systems. If a device driver or application is buggy, the systems vendor gets a bad rap for poor software quality when it isn't their fault. Recently, the research community has made great strides in building software verification tools using model checking and other powerful verification techniques that can check to make sure that programs written by device-driver vendors and other application developers use systems APIs correctly. These new software verification tools are having a pronounced benefit on software quality.

*Would languages benefit from this formalism?*

**Al:** Almost every language today admits of some kind of formal grammatical description. The big problem is how completely we are able to, or willing to, describe the semantics of the language using the current formalisms for describing programming language semantics. The semantic formalisms are not nearly as mechanizable as constructing a parser from a context-free grammar. Even though describing semantics is tedious, I'm a big believer in the benefits of planning and describing and outlining the semantics of a language before implementing it.

*I think of two stories: the canonical story about Make, where Stuart Feldman decided he couldn't remove tabs because he already had 12 users, as well as Dick Gabriel's "Worse Is Better" paper,* where he described the New Jersey approach and the MIT approach. Unix and C and the New Jersey approach won.*

**Al:** I've always expressed that as the success of Darwinism. I believe that successful languages grow and evolve based on usage by real programmers. Languages that need a ponderous committee for their initial design are by-and-large ignored by programmers. Unless their use is mandated, they don't seem to survive.

One perhaps alarming aspect of popular languages is that they are relentlessly becoming bigger. We don't know how to take features out of existing languages. The major languages of today, such C++ and Java, are much much bigger now than when they were initially created, and there seems to be no abatement in sight for the future sizes of these languages. No single individual can really understand all of the language any more and the compilers for these languages are measured in millions of lines of code.

* *http://www.dreamsongs.com/WorseIsBetter.html*

*That seems to be an open question in systems research: how do you make a language that is extensible beyond its initial problem domain without necessarily having to modify the language itself? Do you have an extension mechanism?*

**Al:** Libraries are the time-honored approach to doing that.

*Even C++ and Java have upcoming language changes.*

**Al:** That's true. Even the core languages are growing, but there is a centering force to keep the core language compatible with the past, so you don't break existing programs. That stops unmitigated evolution of these language.

*Is that necessarily a good thing in and of itself?*

**Al:** Certainly being able to run programs from the past is very desirable. At one time I wrote an article for *Science Magazine* entitled "Software and the Future of Programming Languages." In it I tried to estimate how much software the world uses to run its affairs, taking into account all distinct software systems used by organizations and people around the world.

I estimated between a half a trillion and a trillion source lines of software. Assuming it costs $10 to $100 to create a finished line of software, I concluded that we simply cannot afford to reprogram a substantial portion of the legacy base. What this means is that the existing languages and systems will continue to be with us for a long period of time. In many ways hardware is more portable than software, because we always want to create faster hardware that'll run the old programs.

*With Unix, you had an operating system that was suddenly very portable. Was that because they could port it, or because they had a desire to migrate existing software to different hardware platforms as they changed?*

**Al:** As Unix evolved, computers evolved even faster. One of the big developments in Unix occurred when Dennis Ritchie created the C language to build the third version of Unix. This made Unix portable. In a relatively few years when I was at Bell Labs, we had Unix running on everything from minicomputers to the world's biggest supercomputers because it had been written in C, and we had portable compiler technology, which could be used to make C compilers quickly for new machines.

A strong focus of Unix was to create a system that would facilitate software development, one that programmers liked and would be willing to use to develop new programs. I think it was eminently successful at that.

*Most of the best tools and most of the best software written do that.*

**Al:** It's an interesting question: are the best toolmakers the artisans or the toolsmiths? I don't think there's a clear-cut answer to this, but certainly in the early days of Unix, many of the most useful tools were created by programmers who had devised innovative tools to to solve problems that they were interested in. This was one of the reasons why AWK was born. Brian, Peter, and I had certain classes of application programs we wanted to write, but we wanted to write them with really short programs.

*Did the presence of tools and the rapidity of practical feedback push people to research better tools and better algorithms?*

**Al:** If you look at the early history of Unix and my early research career, I was very strongly motivated by Knuth's statement that the best theory is motivated by practice, and the best practice by theory. I wrote dozens of papers looking at how to make parsing more efficient and being able to parse constructs that appear in real programming languages in a convenient and efficient way. Steve Johnson, Jeff Ullman, and I collaborated very closely in the development of this theory and of yacc, so yacc was a great marriage of theory and practice.

## The Role of Documentation

*When I write documentation, or a tutorial or paper, for a piece of software I've written, I often find places where the design is difficult or embarrassing to explain, and that leads me to refine the program. Do you find something similar?*

**Al:** Very much so. My experience with AWK had a profound impact on how I teach the programming languages and compilers course at Columbia. As part of the course there is a semester-long project in which students work in teams of five to create their own little language and build a compiler for it.

In the 20 years or so that I've been teaching the compilers course, never has a team failed to deliver a working compiler by the end of the semester. This success has not come about by accident but by my experiences working on AWK, seeing how software development was done at Bell Labs, recognizing the importance of a lightweight software engineering process for a project of this kind, and listening to my students.

The software engineering process that accompanies the compiler project is vital to the success of creating a new language and building a working compiler for it in 15 weeks. Students get two weeks to decide whether they want to take the course. After two weeks the students form teams, and after another two weeks they have to write a short white paper (patterned after the Java white paper) describing the language they want to create. The white paper really a value-proposition for the language stating why their language is needed and what properties it should have. The most important aspect of the white paper is that it forces the students to quickly decide what kind of language they want to create.

After a month, the students write a language tutorial and a language reference manual. The tutorial is patterned after Chapter 1 of Kernighan and Ritchie's *The C Programming Language* [Prentice-Hall], and the reference manual is patterned after Appendix A of the same book. I critique both the tutorial and the language reference manual very carefully because at this point the students don't realize how hard it is to create a working compiler even for a small language.

I ask the students to state what features they guarantee to implement and what features they will implement if they have extra time. (Never have the students implemented any of the extra features.) The purpose of this exercise is to define the scope the project so that it can be done in the course of a semester and is equivalent in effort to the other projects.

As soon as the teams are formed, the students elect for their team a project manager, a systems architect, a systems integrator, a verification person, and a language guru. Each of these people play a critical role in creating and delivering a working compiler.

The project manager's responsibility is to create and enforce a timeline for the deliverables of the project. The system architect creates the block diagram for the compiler and the systems integrator defines the tools and development environment that will be used to create the compiler. As soon as the language reference manual gets written, the verification person creates a test plan and test suite for the entire language. The language guru makes sure the properties defined in the white paper for the language actually get implemented.

We created a regression test suite for AWK, perhaps a little belatedly. Our test suite was invaluable. As we developed the language, we always ran the regression test suite before submitting our deltas to the master directory. In this way we always had a working version of the compiler at all times. Before we added new features to the language, we created and added the tests for the features to the regression test suite.

I mentioned that no student team has ever failed to deliver a working compiler at the end of the semester. The regression test suite is key to achieving this goal: the students deliver at the end of the semester what they have working at that time. But the working compiler needs to implement the language features promised in the language reference manual.

The systems architect produces a block diagram for the compiler, what the interface specifications are, and who is going to implement which component by when. Every member of the team has to produce at least 500 lines of original source code for the project, and everybody, including the project manager, has to do some implementation. It's very salubrious (and challenging) for students to create programs that have to interface with other people's code.

The system integrator has to specify the platform on which the compiler will be built, and what tools like lex, yacc, ANTLR, or their equivalents are going to be used. He also has to learn how to use the tools and teach the rest of the team about their proper use, so that there is a tools person resource on every team.

The language guru has the most interesting job. He is responsible for the intellectual integrity of the language, so that the properties that were stated in the language white paper actually get implemented. He needs to baseline design and coding changes so that if the team makes a change to the language design, these changes get recorded and disseminated to the entire team and the regression test suite.

Through the project students learn three important skills: project management, teamwork, and communication, both oral and written. At the end of the course, I ask the students what is the most important thing they have learned during the course. Frequently they cite one or another of these skills. Documentation drives the project and students get lots of practice writing and talking about software. The students have to give an in-class presentation on their language, the primary goal of which is to convince their fellow students that everybody in the world should use their language. I rehearse with the first team on how to give a successful presentation. Subsequent teams always try to outdo the first team in their presentations because the students are so enthusiastic about their languages. The languages created have ranged from simulating quantum computers to composing music, to producing comics, to simulating civilizations, to doing fast matrix computations, to generating graphics.

At the end of the course the students have to deliver a final project report, which has as chapters: the language white paper, the language tutorial, the language reference manual, a chapter written by the project manager on how the project was managed, a chapter by the system architect giving the block diagram and interface specifications, a chapter by the systems integrator describing the development platform and tools, a chapter by the verification person with the test plan and test suites, and then a chapter by the language guru talking about language-baselining process. The final chapter is entitled "Lessons Learned" and answers the questions "What did you learn as a team? What did you learn as an individual? If I were to offer the course again next year, what things would you suggest I keep the same; what things would you suggest I change?" An appendix contains the code listing, with the authors signing each module that they wrote.

If you make something better over a long period of time, it usually becomes pretty good. I've heeded the advice students have given me, and a few years ago I received the Great Teacher Award from the Society of Columbia Graduates for this course.

Many recruiters interviewing students who have taken this course have said they wished their software systems were developed with this kind of process.

### Which grade level are the students in this class?

**Al:** They're mostly seniors and first-year graduate students, but there are a lot of prerequisites for this course: advanced programming, computer science theory, and data structures and algorithms. What impresses me about the students is that they end up doing distributed software development, so they're using things like wikis and advanced IDEs. Many of the students have interned in industry.

One thing I strongly emphasize is for the students to keep the regression test suite up to date as the language evolves. The regression test suite makes the students much more productive, because the bugs they find tend to be their own, rather than those of some other person on the team.

### When and how should debugging be taught?

**Al:** I think debugging should be taught along with programming. Brian in his various books has sound pragmatic advice on debugging. However, I don't know of any good general theory for debugging. The techniques one would use to debug a compiler are very different from those used to debug a numerical analysis program, so maybe the best approach is to stress examples of unit tests, systematic testing processes, and use of debugging tools, as part of every programming course. I also think it is salubrious to get students to write specifications for what their programs are supposed to do before they write the program.

One of the mistakes we made with AWK is that we didn't institute rigorous testing right from the start. We did start rigorous testing after the project began, but in hindsight we would have been much more productive had we created and evolved the rigorous test suites right from the beginning.

*What factors should developers measure during the evolution of a codebase and in what way?*

**Al:** The correctness of the implementation is the most important concern, but there is no royal road to correctness. It involves diverse tasks such as thinking of invariants, testing, and code reviews. Optimization should be done, but not prematurely. Keeping the documentation and comments consonant with the code is important, but all too easy to neglect. A modern IDE with good software development tools is a must.

*How do you resume a programming session when you haven't touched it in a few days? After several months?*

**Al:** When one is writing a programming system (or a book, for that matter), one needs to keep the entire system paged in one's mind. Interruptions break one's chain of thought but if the interruption is short, one can usually page in the system after some code review. After an interruption of months or years, I frequently find myself referring to papers, books, or notes in which I have documented my algorithms to refresh my memory of what I previously coded.

I guess what I am saying is that good comments and documentation are a great benefit to the original system designers as well as others who have to maintain the code for long periods of time. Brian maintained a log of major decisions we made as we designed the language. I found his log invaluable.

# Computer Science

*What constitutes research in computer science?*

**Al:** This is a wonderful question, and one that does not have a well-defined answer. I think computer science research has broadened enormously in its scope. We still have the deep, unsolved, quintessential questions of computer science: how do we prove that a problem like factoring or an NP-complete problem is actually hard; how do we model complex systems like a human cell or the human brain; how can we construct scalable, trustworthy systems; how can programmers build arbitrarily reliable software; how can we make software with human-friendly characteristics like emotion or intelligence; how far can we extend Moore's Law?

Today, the scale and scope of computing has exploded. We are trying to organize and access all of the world's information, and computers and computation are affecting all areas of daily life. As a consequence, whole new areas of computer science research have emerged in interdisciplinary applications combining computation with other areas of science and human endeavor. Examples of these new areas include fields like computational biology, robotics, cyberphysical systems. We don't know how best to deploy computers in education or health. Privacy and security have become more important than ever. I believe computer science is as exciting a research field as any.

### What is the role of math in computer science and programming?

**Al:** I think the best engineering is done on top of a solid scientific foundation. With AWK we designed the language around a number of elegant abstractions rooted in computer science theory, such as regular expressions and associative arrays. These constructs were subsequently adopted by the major scripting languages: Perl, JavaScript, Python, and Ruby. We also used efficient algorithms based on finite automata to implement the string-matching primitives. All in all, I think AWK was a nice marriage of good theory and sound engineering practice.

### You worked on automata theory and its applications to programming languages. What surprised you the most when you started implementing the results of your studies?

**Al:** Perhaps the greatest surprise has been its broad applicability. Let me interpret automata theory as formal languages and the automata that recognize them. Automata theory provides useful notations, particularly regular expressions and context-free grammars, for describing the important syntactic features of programming languages. The automata that recognize these formal languages, such as finite-state machines and push-down automata, can serve as models for the algorithms used by compilers to scan and parse programs. Perhaps the greatest benefit of automata theory to compiling comes from being able to build compiler-construction tools such as lex and yacc that automate the construction of efficient scanners and parsers based on these automata.

### What is preventing us from building a compiler (and/or a language) that identify all potential bugs? Where is the line between the bugs linked to a wrong design of the program and the bugs that could have been spotted or prevented if the language were more proactive?

**Al:** Undecidability makes it impossible to design a compiler that will find all the bugs in programs. We have, however, made great strides in creating useful software verification tools employing powerful techniques like model checking to find important classes of bugs in programs. I think the software development environment of the future will have a large variety of verification tools that a programmer can harness to pinpoint many common causes of bugs in programs.

My long-term vision is that through the use of stronger languages, more powerful verification tools, and better software-engineering practices, software will improve in reliability and quality.

### How can we design pattern-matching algorithms that take advantage of concurrency in multicore hardware?

**Al:** This is currently an active research area. Many researchers are exploring parallel hardware and software implementations of pattern-matching algorithms like the Aho-Corasick algorithm or finite-state algorithms. Some of the strong motivators are genomic analyses and intrusion detection systems.

*What motivated you and Corasick to develop the Aho-Corasick algorithm?*

**Al:** The origin has a very interesting story behind it. I was working on the book *The Design and Analysis of Computer Algorithms* [Addison-Wesley] with John Hopcroft and Jeffrey Ullman back in the early 70s. I was giving a lecture at Bell Labs on algorithm design techniques. Margaret Corasick from Bell Labs's technical information libraries was in the audience. At the end of my lecture she came to me saying she had written a bibliographic search program for Boolean functions of keywords and phrases. However, on some complex searches, running the program could exceed the $600 limit for searches.

Her initial implementation of the search program used a straightforward pattern-matching algorithm. I suggested that she might look for the keywords in parallel using a finite automaton, and that there was a way of efficiently constructing the pattern-matching automaton in linear time from any set of keywords.

She reappeared in my office a few weeks later and said, "Remember that $600 program search? I've implemented the algorithm you suggested. That search now costs $25. In fact, every search now costs $25; this is the cost of reading the tape." This was the birth of the Aho-Corasick algorithm.

On learning this, my lab director, Sam Morgan said, "Why don't you keep working on algorithms? I think they'll be useful sometime in the future." That was the magic of Bell Labs at the time: there were people with problems and people with unconventional ways of thinking about those problems. When you brought these people together, amazing inventions would result.

## Breeding Little Languages

*What hooked you on programming?*

**Brian Kernighan:** I don't really recall any specific event. I didn't even see my first computer until I was about a junior in college, and I didn't really learn to program (in FORTRAN) until a year or so after that. I think that the most fun I had programming was a summer job at Project MAC at MIT in the summer of 1966, where I worked on a program that created a job tape for the brand new GE 645 in the earliest days of Multics. I was writing in MAD, which was much easier and more pleasant than the FORTRAN and COBOL that I had written earlier, and I was using CTSS, the first time-sharing system, which was infinitely easier and more pleasant than punch cards. That was the point where the puzzle-solving aspects of programming became really enjoyable, because the mechanical details didn't get in the way nearly so much.

*How do you learn a new language?*

**Brian:** I find it easiest to learn a new language from well-chosen examples that do some task that's close to what I want to do. I copy an example, adapt it to what I need, then expand my knowledge as the specific application drives it. I poke around in enough different languages that after a while they start to blur, and it takes a while to shift gears when I shift from one to another, especially if they are not ones like C that I learned long ago. It's good to have good compilers that complain about suspicious constructions as well as illegal ones; languages with strong type systems like C++ and Java are helpful here, and the options that enforce strict conformance to standards are good, too.

More generally, there's nothing like writing a lot of code, preferably good code that other people use. Next best, though less frequently done, is reading a lot of good code to see how other people write. Finally, breadth of experience helps—each new problem, new language, new tool, and new system helps you get better, and creates links with whatever you know already.

### How should a manual for a new programming language be organized?

**Brian:** A manual should make it easy to find things. That means that the index has to be really good, the tables of things like operators and library functions have to be concise and complete (and easy to find), and the examples should be short and crystal clear.

This is different from a tutorial, which should definitely not be the same as a manual. I think the best approach for a tutorial is a sort of "spiral," in which a small set of useful basic things is presented, but enough to write complete and useful programs. The next rotation of the spiral should cover another level of detail or perhaps alternative ways of saying the same kinds of things and the examples should still be useful but can be bigger. Then put a good reference manual at the end.

### Should examples—even beginner examples—include the error-handling code?

**Brian:** I'm torn on this. Error-handling code tends to be bulky and very uninteresting and uninstructive, so it often gets in the way of learning and understanding the basic language constructs. At the same time, it's important to remind programmers that errors do happen and that their code has to be able to cope with errors.

My personal preference is to pretty much ignore error handling in the earlier parts of a tutorial, other than to mention that errors can happen, and similarly to ignore errors in most examples in reference manuals unless the point of some section is errors. But this can reinforce the unconscious belief that it's safe to ignore errors, which is always a bad idea.

### What did you think of the idea for the Unix manual to cite bugs? Does this practice make sense today, too?

**Brian:** I liked the BUGS sections, but that was when programs were small and rather simple and it was possible to identify single bugs. The BUGS were often features that were not yet provided or things that were not properly implemented, not bugs in the usual sense of walking off the end of an array or the like. I don't think this would be feasible for most of the kinds of errors one would find in really big modern systems, at least not in a manual. Online bug repositories are a fine tool for managing software development, but it's not likely that they will help ordinary users.

*Do current programmers need to be aware of the lessons you collected in your book about programming style,* The Elements of Programming Style *[Computing McGraw-Hill]?*

**Brian:** Yes! The basic ideas of good style, which are fundamentally to write clearly and simply, are just as important now as they were 35 years ago when Bill Plauger and I first wrote about them. The details are different in minor ways, to some extent depending on properties of different languages, but the basics are the same now as then. Simple, straightforward code is just plain easier to work with and less likely to have problems. So as programs get bigger and more complicated, it's even more important to have clean, simple code.

*Does the way you can write text influence the way you write software?*

**Brian:** It might. In both text and programs, I tend to work over the material many times until it feels right. There's a lot more of this in prose, of course, but it's the same desire, to have the words or the code be as clear and clean as possible.

*How does knowing the problems that software will solve for the user help the developer write better software?*

**Brian:** Unless the developer has a really good idea of what the software is going to be used for, there's a very high probability that the software will turn out badly.

In some fortunate cases, the developer understands the user because the developer is also going to be a user. One of the reasons why the early Unix system was so good, so well suited to the needs of programmers, was that its creators, Ken Thompson and Dennis Ritchie, wanted a system for their own software development; as a result, Unix was just great for programmers writing new programs. The same is true of the C programming language.

If the developers don't know and understand the application well, then it's crucial to get as much user input and experience as possible. It is really instructive to watch new users of your software—within a minute, a typical newcomer will try do something or make some assumption that you never thought of and your program will make their life harder. But if you don't monitor your users when they first encounter your software, you won't see their problems; if you see them later, they've probably adapted to your bad design.

*How can programmers improve their programming?*

**Brian:** Write more code! And then think about the code you wrote and try to rework it to make it better. Get other people to read it too if you can, whether as part of your job or as part of an open source project. It's also helpful to write different kinds of code, and to write in different languages, since that broadens your repertoire of techniques and gives you more ways to approach some programming problem. Read other people's code, for example, to try to add features or fix bugs; that will show you how other people approach problems. Finally, there's nothing like teaching others to program to help you improve your own code.

*Everyone knows that debugging is twice as hard as writing the software, so how should debugging be taught?*

**Brian:** I'm not sure that debugging can be taught, but one can certainly try to tell people how to do it systematically. There's a whole chapter on this in *The Practice of Programming* [Addison-Wesley], which Rob Pike and I wrote to try to explain how to be more effective at debugging.

Debugging is an art, but it's definitely possible to improve your skill as a debugger. New programmers make careless mistakes, like walking off the start or end of an array, or mismatching types in function calls, or (in C) using the wrong conversion characters in printf and scanf. Fortunately, these are usually easy to catch because they cause very distinctive failures. Even better, they are easy to eliminate as you write the code in the first place, by boundary condition checking, which amounts to thinking about what can go wrong as you write. Bugs usually appear in the code you wrote most recently or that you started to test, so that's a good place to concentrate your efforts.

As bugs get more complicated or subtle, more effort is called for. One effective approach is to "divide and conquer," attempting to eliminate part of the data or part of the program so that the bug is localized in a smaller and smaller region. There's also often a pattern to a bug; the "numerology" of failing inputs or faulty output is often a very big clue to what's going wrong.

The hardest bugs are those where your mental model of the situation is just wrong, so you can't see the problem at all. For these, I prefer to take a break, read a listing, explain the problem to someone else, use a debugger. All of these help me to see the problem a different way, and that's often enough to pin it down. But, sadly, debugging will always be hard. The best way to avoid tough debugging is to write things very carefully in the first place.

*How do hardware resources affect the mindset of programmers?*

**Brian:** Having more hardware resources is almost always a good thing—it means, for example, that one doesn't have to worry much about memory management, which used to be an infinite pain and source of errors 20 or 30 years ago (and certainly was when we were writing AWK). It means that one can use potentially inefficient code, especially general-purpose libraries, because runtime is not nearly as much of an issue as it was 20 or 30 years ago. For example, I think nothing today of running AWK over 10 or even 100 MB files, which would have been very unlikely long ago. As processors continue to get faster and memory capacities rise, it's easier to do quick experiments and even write production code in interpreted languages (like AWK) that would not have been feasible a few decades ago. All of this is a great win.

At the same time, the ready availability of resources often leads to very bloated designs and implementations, systems that could be faster and easier to use if a bit more restraint had gone into their design. Modern operating systems certainly have this problem; it seems to take longer and longer for my machines to boot, even though, thanks to Moore's Law, they are noticeably faster than the previous ones. All that software is slowing me down.

*What is your opinion on domain-specific languages (DSL)?*

**Brian:** I worked on a lot of what are now most often called domain-specific languages, though I usually called them "little languages," and others refer to "application-specific languages." The idea is that by focusing a language on a specific and usually narrow domain, you can make its syntax match the domain well, so that it's easy to write code to solve problems within that domain. There are lots of examples—SQL would be an instance, and of course AWK itself is a fine example, a language for specifying certain kinds of file processing very easily and compactly.

The big problem with little languages is that they tend to grow. If they are at all useful, people want to apply them more broadly, pushing the envelope of what the original language was meant for. That usually implies adding more features to the language. For instance, a language might originally be purely declarative (no if tests, no loops) and it might have no variables or arithmetic expressions. All of those are useful, however, so they tend to get added. But when they are added, the language grows (it's no longer so little), and gradually the language starts to look like any other general-purpose language, but with different syntax and semantics and sometimes a weaker implementation as well.

Several of the little languages I worked on were for document preparation. The first, with Lorinda Cherry, was called EQN, and was for typesetting mathematical expressions. It was pretty successful, and as our typesetting equipment became more capable, I also did a language for drawing figures and diagrams, which was called PIC. PIC started out only able to draw, but it rapidly became clear that it needed arithmetic expressions to handle computations on coordinates and the like, and it needed variables to store results, and it needed loops to create repetitive structures. All of these were added, but each one was kind of awkward and shaky. In the end, PIC was quite powerful, a Turing-complete language, but one wouldn't want to write a lot of code in it.

*How do you define success in terms of your work?*

**Brian:** One of the most rewarding things is to have someone say that they used your language or tool and found that it helped them get their job done better. That's really satisfying. Of course it's sometimes followed by a report of problems or of missing features, but even those are valuable.

*In which contexts is AWK still powerful and useful?*

**Brian:** AWK still seems to be best for quick and dirty data analysis: find all the lines that have some property, or summarize some aspect of the data, or make some simple transformation on it. I can often get more done with a couple of lines of AWK than others can with 5 or 10 lines of Perl or Python, and empirically, my code will run almost as fast.

I have a collection of small AWK scripts that do things like add up all the fields in all the lines or compute the ranges of all fields (a way to get a quick look at a dataset). I have an AWK program that fills arbitrary text lines into at most 70 character lines that I probably use 100 times a day for cleaning up mail messages and the like. Any of these could be easily written in some other scripting language and would work just as well, but they're easier in AWK.

*What should people keep in mind when writing AWK programs?*

**Brian:** The language was originally meant for writing programs that were only one or two lines long. If you're writing something big, AWK might well not be the right language, since it has no mechanisms that help with big programs, and some design decisions can lead to hard to find bugs—for example, the fact that variables are not declared and are automatically initialized is very convenient for a one-line program, but it means that spelling mistakes and typos are undetectable in a big program.

# Designing a New Language

*How would you go about creating a new programming language?*

**Brian:** Presumably you have some set of tasks, some domain of application, for which you think a new programming language would be better than any existing language. Think about what people want to be able to say. What are the problems, the applications, that this programming language is going to be used for? How would you like to express them in that language? What would be the most natural way to write them down? What are the most important examples, the simplest ones that would get somebody started? Try to make those as straightforward as possible.

Fundamentally, the idea is to try to write things in the language before it exists. How would you say something? I think this applied to AWK pretty well because everything in the design of that language was intended to make it easy to write useful programs without having to say very much. That meant we didn't have declarations, partly because we didn't have types. It meant that we didn't have explicit input statements because the input was completely implicit, it just happened. It meant that we didn't have statements for splitting input lines into fields because that happened automatically. All the properties of the language came from the goal of trying to make it really easy to say really simple things.

The standard examples that we used in the AWK paper that we wrote originally, and in the manual and so on, were all basically one-liners. I want to print all the lines that have length greater than 80 characters, so by writing "length > 80", I'm done. In that particular language, it was clear enough what we were trying to do, and then of course later on you discover all the things that you left out that you really need, like the ability to read from specific input files by name, so we had to add that. Constructs that were needed when programs got longer than a few lines, like functions, were added later.

The EQN language that Lorinda Cherry and I worked on is a completely different example. EQN is a language for describing mathematical expressions so they could be printed.

The goal was to make the language as close as possible to the way that people would speak mathematics out loud. If I were to try to describe the formula to you over the telephone, what would I say? Or if I were writing a formula on the blackboard in a class, what would I be saying as I wrote the expression on the board? Or in my case, I was recording textbooks for blind people. How did I read the mathematical expressions so that somebody who couldn't see them might be able to understand them? EQN was entirely focused on making it easy to write mathematics as it was spoken, and it didn't worry much about the quality of the output. Compare that to TeX, which is not as easy to type, with a lot of syntax, but it is a very powerful language that gives you far more control over the output, at the price of being rather harder to use.

*When you designed the language, how much did you think about the implementation?*

**Brian:** A fair amount, because I've always been involved with both design and implementation; if I can't see how to implement something, I won't pursue the design.

For almost every language I have done, either the language has been simple enough that it could be parsed by a straightforward ad hoc parser, or if it had a richer syntactic structure, I've been able to use yacc to specify the grammar.

I think if I had had to do languages like EQN or AWK without the benefit of yacc, they would never have happened, because it's too hard to write parsers by hand. Not that you can't do it, but it's a real nuisance. Writing them with a tool like yacc made it possible to do interesting, adventurous things easily and change the design quickly if something didn't seem to be right, because all you had to do was rewrite a bit of the grammar; you didn't have to change any significant amount of code to make a substantial change in the language, or to add some new feature. It was really easy with a tool like yacc, and would have been much harder with a conventional recursive descent parser.

*Should language designers enforce a preferred style to avoid some recurrent mistakes? For example, Python's source code formatting, or Java's lack of pointer arithmetic.*

**Brian:** I have mixed feelings about that, though mostly the enforced discipline is helpful once one gets used to it. I found Python's indentation rules irritating at first, but once I got used to them, it was not a problem.

One should try to design the language so that it has the right constructs to make it easy for people to say what they want to say, and there isn't ambiguity or too many different ways to say it. No matter what, people will find the most natural way of expressing things. So if Java omits pointers, that's a major change from C or C++, but it provides references, which are a reasonable alternative for many situations. Java doesn't provide a goto statement.

I've never felt that that was a problem. C provides a goto statement that I don't typically use, but every once in a while, it makes sense. So I'm comfortable either way with those kinds of decisions.

I mentioned the PIC language for drawing pictures. It was good for simple pictures like arrows and boxes and flowcharts. But people wanted to draw pictures with regular structures. For those, I somewhat reluctantly added a while loop and a for loop and even an if statement. Of course, they were an afterthought, with somewhat irregular syntax that didn't quite fit the PIC language, but they were not the same as in any conventional language, either. The result was useful but awkward.

It seems that the language starts out simple, and then it grows, and additions gradually make it take on all of the character of a full-blown programming language with variables and expressions, and the if statements and while loops and functions that any full-blown programming language has. But usually the constructions are sort of awkward, the syntax is irregular or at least different, the mechanisms may not work very well, and the whole thing feels wrong.

*Was this due to their genesis as little languages, without consideration of evolving them into general-purpose languages?*

**Brian:** Yes, I think that's what it is. I'm speaking only for myself on this, but the mental picture that I have started out with is almost always a little language, something very small and simple, not meant to do big things, not meant to be a general-purpose programming language. But if it's useful, people start to push its limits and they want more. And typically the things they want are the features of general-purpose programming languages that make them programmable rather than just declarative. They want ways to repeat things, they want ways to avoid having to say the same thing over and over again, and these lead to loops and macros or functions.

*How can we design a language that works for everybody? You mentioned little languages that are focused on a particular goal, but I also have the impression that you like the idea that a developer writes a language to satisfy his own needs. Once you have something that works, how can you grow it to make it more useful to other people?*

**Brian:** There isn't likely to ever be a language that is satisfactory for everybody for every application or even relatively large groups with large collections of applications.

We have a lot of good general-purpose languages now. C is fine for some jobs; C++, Java, Python—each does a good job in its area and can be pushed into almost all the other areas. But I don't think I would try to write an operating system in Python, and I don't want to write text-processing code in C anymore.

*How do you recognize the area where a language is particularly useful or strong? For example, you said Python is not good to write an operating system. Is that particular to the language or the implementation?*

**Brian:** I think it's probably both. The implementation is likely to mean that things would be too slow. But if I were writing a toy or demonstration operating system, Python might be absolutely fine. It might in some ways be better. But I don't think I would write an operating system that would support, let's say, Google's infrastructure, using Python.

Real programmers don't have the luxury of choice sometimes. They have to do whatever the local environment requires. So if I am a programmer at a big financial operation on Wall Street, they will be programming in a particular language or a very small set of languages, perhaps C++ and Java. I am not going to be able to say, "Oh, I just want to write C," nor am I going to be able to say, "Well, I think Python would be better for that." In one company I know, the set of languages is C++, Java, and Python. Ruby might really be better for some things, but you're not going to write Ruby. A lot of people don't have a free choice in what they write.

On the other hand, if they have to do a particular job, the choice might be free among C++, Java, or Python. Then the technical considerations could be evaluated in deciding which one to use.

*Maybe everybody should have a personal language.*

**Brian:** One that's really their own and nobody else uses?

*Where everyone has a personal syntax that is translated to a general byte code, and then it's universal.*

**Brian:** It's going to make it hard to do collaborative development. :)

*After you built the first prototype, what should people do?*

**Brian**: First try to write code yourself in this proposed language. What does it feel like to write the kinds of things that you personally want to write and that you think people around you would probably want to write? For EQN, it was crystal clear. How do mathematicians speak? I'm not a mathematician, but I had a pretty good idea because I'd taken a lot of math courses. You want to use it yourself and then, as quickly as possible, you want other users to try it, but you want users who are going to be really good critics, that is, people who will try it, push it, and tell you what they found.

One of the wonderful things about Bell Labs in the 70s and 80s was that there were a bunch of people in and around the Unix group who were just incredibly good at this kind of critical evaluation of what other people did. The criticism was often very blunt, but there was good feedback, very quickly, about what was good and what was not.

We all profited from that because the criticism helped smooth off the rough edges, kept systems culturally compatible, and weeded out the really bad ideas.

I think it's harder to get that in some ways now. You can get criticism from a broader collection of people more widely distributed because of the Internet, but you may not get as focused criticism from a group of people who are extremely talented with whom you are very close, where you could meet them in the hall on an hourly basis, where you step out of your office and into their office.

*How did you manage all your ideas and experiments, and at the same time, build a unique and stable system?*

**Brian:** It wasn't that hard because AWK was so small. The first version was only perhaps 3,000 lines of code. I think Peter Weinberger wrote the first version. The grammar was done with yacc, which was very easy. The lexical part was done with lex. And semantics at that point were pretty regular. We had several different versions of the interpreter machine, but it wasn't very big. It was pretty easy to make changes quickly and maintain control of it. And in fact it's still quite small; the version that I distribute is not much over 6,000 lines at this point, 30 years later.

*Is it true that each one of you had to write test modules for every new feature that you wanted to include?*

**Brian:** No. Absolutely not. About the time the book was published in 1988, we started to be more systematic about collecting test cases. It was probably some years after that when I started to be more orderly in collecting tests, and somewhere in that period I decided that if I added a feature, I was going to add a few tests that would make sure that feature actually worked. I have not added new features for quite a while, but the collection of tests has continued to grow because when somebody finds a bug, I add a test or two that would have found the bug earlier and make sure that it doesn't come back again.

I think that's good practice. It's something that I wish we had done more carefully and systematically much earlier in the game. The test suite today includes essentially all of the programs in the first and second chapters of the AWK book. But those obviously came after the book, which was well after the language itself.

*In the past 40 years, there has been a lot of research in computer science and also on programming languages. Have you seen any improvement in the language design part beyond tool improvements?*

**Brian:** I'm not sure I know enough to give a proper answer on that. For some languages, let's say scripting languages, the language design process is still pretty idiosyncratic based on the preferences and interests and beliefs of the language designer. So we have dozens of scripting languages, and I don't think that those have profited directly from research in things like type theory.

*In the 70s, every type of language was available: C, Smalltalk—very different types of languages. Today we have a very different range of languages, but we still have C, C++, and Smalltalk. Did you expect more innovation and improvements in the way we design languages and interact with computers?*

**Brian:** I guess I don't know enough about the whole area. I think probably we will get better at getting the machine to do more of the work for us. That means that languages may become even higher level and more declarative so that we don't have to spell out so many details. One hopes that the languages will become more safe, so that it's harder to write programs that don't work. Perhaps languages that will be easier to translate into a very efficient runnable form. But beyond that, I honestly don't know.

*Can we have a science of language design? Can we approach the language design with a scientific method so that we can learn from the previous discoveries or inventions and keep improving? Will it always include the designer's personal taste?*

**Brian:** I think that there's always going to be a very large amount of personal taste and intuition about what works in language design. Almost all languages are really the product of one or two people, maybe three. There's hardly any language you can name that was a group effort. And so that just says it's likely to be personal.

At the same time, our understanding of almost every aspect of programming languages is better and is likely to continue getting better. That suggests that new languages will be based on sound principles, and their properties will be mostly well understood. And in that sense, it will be more scientifically based than might have happened say 10 or 20, well certainly 30 years ago, where things really didn't have much basis. But I will guess that much language design will still be determined by individual taste.

People are going to come up with things that appeal to them, and some of those will appeal to lots of other people as well. But there will be more and more things that a language has to have because their existence will be taken for granted. So, for example, any significant language today is almost surely going to have some kind of object mechanism, and it will be designed into it from the beginning, not glued on afterward. Concurrency is another important area, because we're getting machines that have lots of processors, and languages will have to deal with concurrency in the language itself, not just some library add-on.

*As we understand the situation better, we try to build systems that are always bigger, so in some ways we are more powerful, but we always try to set the bar higher. We keep building bigger teams.*

**Brian:** I think your basic observation is absolutely correct. We're always trying to do bigger things, so we're always up to our armpits in alligators. As we get more hardware, as we get more understand of how to write programs, as we get better programming languages, we take on bigger things. Tasks that in the 1970s might have taken a team of a couple hundred people a year or two to build can today be knocked off by an undergraduate in a couple of weeks because there's so much support, so much infrastructure, so much horsepower also in the computers, and so much existing software that you can build on. So I think in some sense we're always going to be up against that.

Are we going to have big teams like the thousands that Microsoft had working on Vista? Probably, but we're clearly going to need to find ways to make big projects into a bunch of small projects that cooperate with each other in a safe and well-organized way.

Some of this will require improvements in languages, and some of it will require better mechanisms for gluing together components no matter what languages they were written in, and for packaging information as it passes across interfaces.

*Previously you said that a modern programming language should absolutely support OOP. Is OOP good as it is? Is there anything else that we could try to do or invent or add to simplify the process of building large systems?*

**Brian:** Object orientation is very useful in some settings. If you're writing Java, you have no choice; if you're writing Python or C++, you can use it or not. I think that's probably the right model: you can use it or not use it depending on the specific application. As languages evolve, there will surely be other mechanisms for packaging up computational units and organizing a program.

If you look at COM, Microsoft's component object model, that's based on object-oriented programming, but it's more than that because a component is a bunch of objects, not just one. How do you deal with that in a somewhat more orderly way than perhaps COM provides so that there's more of a notion of how these things are related?

We need mechanisms to deal with huge numbers of objects. We're dealing with quite complicated structures of objects, as we deal with bigger programs or programs whose pieces come from more places.

*Unix takes the C language that didn't have any OO support, and then you build components—objects—as little tools easily combined to build complex features. Instead of putting the concept of objects inside the language, perhaps we should build objects or components that are little tools as separate programs. If you think of a spreadsheet program, generally that's a huge program built with objects, maybe it supports plug-ins or add-ons, but the idea is that the objects are inside, integrated, and managed with the language.*

**Brian:** Excel is a fine example because it packages up a huge number of objects and their associated methods and properties. You can write code that will control Excel, so in effect, Excel becomes a giant subroutine, or just another computational unit. The plumbing isn't quite as neat as it is with, say, a Unix pipeline, but it could be pretty close and would not be very hard to have Excel be part of a pipeline.

Mashups have some of that flavor: there are large building blocks that can be glued together in ad hoc ways. It's not quite as easy as a Unix pipeline, but it's the same idea of combining large, self-contained pieces into larger systems.

Yahoo! Pipes is a nice example. It is a really interesting approach to saying, "How can we take fairly complicated operations and glue them together?" They put a beautiful graphical front end on the whole thing, but you can imagine doing the same with text-based mechanisms, and thus having a system that would let you put together arbitrary collections of computations just by writing text-based programs again. Figuring out how to do this well is definitely something that's worth working on. How do we effectively build systems out of existing components and how do we get programming languages to help us do it?

*During the command-line era, you had to communicate with the computer using written language: enter text as input and read text as output. Today we interact with the keyboard but also the mouse, and we get partially graphical and partially textual output. Is the best way to communicate with a computer still a language? Was the command line in some way a better way to communicate because of the use of language?*

**Brian:** Graphical interfaces are very good for unskilled users, for users who are new to some system, or for applications that you don't use very often or that are intrinsically graphical, like creating a document. But after a while, you find yourself doing the same thing over and over and over again. Computers are great at repetive operations. Wouldn't it be much nicer if we could say to the computer: do this over and over again?

There are mechanisms for that right now, such as macros in Word or Excel. But we're seeing programmable APIs for systems like Google or Yahoo! or Amazon or Facebook. You can take whatever operations you might have been doing with your keyboard and mouse, and you can mechanize them. And you can do it without the screen scraping and HTML parsing that you had to do 10 years ago.

In effect, that's going back to the command line, where pure text-based manipulation is best. You may not know what you want to do until you've done some of the mouse and keyboard-based operations, but once you start to see the repetitive operations, then the command-line interface and these APIs mechanize the process rather than requiring a human being in the loop.

*When designing the language, do you consider the debuggability of features? One critique of AWK is that variables are automatically initialized without declaration. This is convenient, but if you make spelling mistakes or typos, it can be very hard to find problems.*

**Brian:** It's a tradeoff. Every language has tradeoffs, and in AWK we made tradeoffs in the direction of making it really, really easy to use. A one-line program was the goal, because we thought that most programs would only be one or two lines long. Variables that weren't declared and had automatically initialized values were consistent with that, because if you had to declare it and initialize it, you tripled the size of the program. That worked beautifully for small programs, but is bad for big programs. So what might you do?

Perl has a mode that warns you; it says, "Tell me when I've done something stupid." You could be more careful the way that Python does. You do have to initialize variables in Python, but you can usually get away without much declaration. Or you could have some separate tool off to the side, a lint for AWK programs that would say, "You have two variables whose names are extremely similar; did you really mean that?"

A more dubious design decision in AWK is that concatenation was expressed by adjacency, without an explicit operator; a sequence of adjacent values is just concatenated. If you couple that with the fact that variables aren't declared, nearly anything you write is a valid AWK program. It's just too easy to make mistakes.

I think that that's an example of stupid design. It didn't save us anything—we should have used an operator. Automatically initialized variables was a conscious design tradeoff, which works beautifully for little things and doesn't scale.

## Legacy Culture

*Suppose I write a new little language that has to run in two megabytes of memory, for a cell phone or embedded device. To what degree do issues of implementation like that affect the interface level? When a user uses my program, is he or she going to understand some of my design choices, or have we moved away from those types of limitations now?*

**Brian:** I think we're a lot more away from it than we used to be. If you look at the history of early Unix programs, and certainly AWK among them, you can see lots of places where the fact that memory was extremely tight showed up in the language or various pieces of the operating system.

For example, for many years AWK had internal limits: you could only have this many files open, only have this many elements in an associative array, and so on. They were all coping with the fact that memory was really tight and processes weren't all that fast. Those constraints have gradually gone away. In my implementation, there are no fixed limits anymore. Fixed limits are a place where resource limitations bubble up and become visible to the ultimate user.

AWK tries to preserve the state of a variable so that if a variable has been used as a number and then is coerced to a string for printing, AWK knows that both the numeric value and the string value are current so it doesn't have to do the coercion again. In a modern machine running 1,000 times faster, you wouldn't do that at all. You would just coerce the value when it was needed.

Even originally, it was probably a silly thing to do, since there's a lot of intricate code, very delicately balanced and probably not always correct, to manage this state. If I were doing it today, I wouldn't think about it at all. I'm sure if I run Perl or Python, they're not worrying about that.

*Perl 5 still uses that trick, oddly enough.*

**Brian:** The first version of Perl was written less than 10 years after AWK, and there were still plenty of resource constraints. Anyway, those are examples of things where tight resources forced you to do things that, in retrospect, you would probably do differently.

I started out on machines that had, if I remember correctly, 64k bytes total. That was when we were well into the Unix world.

*Peter Weinberger said that in the early Unix days there was always a sense that you could rewrite a program next year. It didn't have to be perfect because it wasn't big or complicated. You could always rewrite it. Was that your experience?*

**Brian:** Programs did get rewritten a fair amount. I don't know whether they got rewritten from scratch. In my own experience, I don't think anything I ever did got rewritten in the sense of just toss it away and start over again. My changes were more incremental, but there was a lot of rethinking, and it definitely was part of the culture to see if there were ways where you could make the program smaller.

*He gave me the impression that this was a cultural thing. The design consideration was never that a program would last for 10, 20, or 40 years. Did you see a shift from short-term to long-term thinking?*

**Brian:** I don't know whether anyone thinks long term in software today, but some people did in the early days. Some people do because they have to. If, for example, I was in a telephone company making switching software, in the good old days that code was going to last for a long while and it had to be compatible with the code that was there before. You had to do things more cautiously. Maybe we were just more realistic about the fact that you can't rewrite it. There isn't enough time.

The other thing, at least in my memory of the Unix of the 70s, was that there were so many interesting new things to do that people just went in and kept changing programs. I don't think anybody thought of themselves as writing for the ages. If you had told Al or Peter or me in 1978 that we would be having conversations about AWK 30 years later, we would not have believed it.

*The Unix kernel has really evolved. Many people may wish otherwise, but the C language is still one of the best options for software like AWK and kernels. Why do things like this survive when other things don't?*

**Brian:** Partly the survival is because they're really good at what they do. C found a sweet spot for system implementation. It's incredibly expressive, but at the same time, it's not complicated or big, and it's efficient, and that's will always matter at some level. It's a nice language to work with because if you want to say something, there aren't too many different ways to say it. I will look at your code and say, "I see what you are doing." I don't think that's true of languages like Perl and C++. I'll look at your Perl code and I'll say "Huh?" because there's no one way to write it.

C++ is big and intricate and there are many different ways that you can say something. If you and I were writing C++, we might come up with rather different ways to express a big computation. C doesn't have that. C survives because it found the right balance of expressiveness and efficiency, and for core applications, it's still the best tool.

*That's why we've never replaced the X Window system on Unix. Everything uses Xlib or something that uses Xlib. Baroque as Xlib may be, it's pervasive.*

**Brian:** Exactly. It does the job. It does it well enough. To do it over from scratch is just too big a job.

*When you look at C++ now, one of the original design goals was backward compatibility with C, for good or ill. The theory goes if you want to replace X, then we need something that can run X program strings transparently. C++ did not displace C in a lot of places, though it had that nominal goal.*

**Brian:** Bjarne killed himself to try and make it compatible with C as much as he possibly could. One of the reasons that C++ succeeded where other languages did not is that compatibility was good, both source and object, and that meant that you didn't have to buy in to a whole new way of doing business to use C++ in a C environment.

I'm sure those decisions that Bjarne made on compatibility have come back in some ways to haunt him just because people say, "Oh, it's awful because…." He made them very consciously and after a lot of thought because the compatibility with the existing world was important, and it was more likely to succeed in the long run.

*Some of its biggest sins are that it hews too closely to C.*

**Brian:** Perhaps, but the further from C, the less likely it would have succeeded. It's a difficult balance, and I think he did a very good job.

*To what degree can you pursue backward compatibility versus trying to introduce something new and revolutionary?*

**Brian:** That's a dilemma in absolutely every field, and I don't see any way out of it.

*You mentioned that a lot of little languages started adding features and becoming Turing-complete and losing their conceptual purity. Are there design principles to apply if you're taking a little language and making it more general purpose without losing its way?*

**Brian:** I guess. I remember saying that on a variety of occasions, and I often wondered how much of it was a parochial view. That is, all of the languages I had touched had this property and maybe nothing else did. Perhaps I was just seeing my own problem. In hindsight, in most cases I would've been better off to be sure that new features were syntactically compatible with existing languages so that people didn't have to learn a brand-new syntax.

*Is there or will there be a resurgence of little languages?*

**Brian:** I'm not sure that "resurgence" is the right word, but little languages will continue to be developed.

What might drive this to some degree is the proliferation of APIs for web services. Everybody has an API that will let you drive their web service from a program rather than from your fingertips. Most of those are, at this point, packaged as JavaScript APIs, but I can imagine ways in which they would be more accessible and run from Unix or Windows command lines rather than writing JavaScript that sits inside a browser, where you still have to click to get it started.

*It almost sounds like you're talking a resurgence of the Unix command line that operates on the Internet as a whole.*

**Brian:** That's a great way of saying it. Wouldn't that be neat?

## Transformative Technologies

*You mentioned that yacc made experimentation with the syntax of a language easier, because you could update your grammar and run that again, rather than tweaking a hand-rolled direct descent parser. Was yacc a transformative technology?*

**Brian:** Certainly for language development, yacc was an enormous influence. Speaking personally, I would never gotten off the ground doing language work without it, because for whatever reason, I wasn't any good at writing recursive descent parsers. I always had trouble with precedence and associativity.

With yacc you didn't have to think about that. You could write down a grammar that made sense, and then you could say "This is the precedence and the associativity, and here's how you handle ugly cases like unary operators that are spelled the same as binary operators." All of those things were so much easier. Just the existence of that tool made it possible to think about doing things from a language point of view that otherwise would have been too hard.

Certainly, yacc worked extremely well for EQN. The grammar was not very complicated, but it had weird constructs. Some of them had not been thought of in a programming language context before, and in fact EQN was declarative, not procedural. There was even discussion of it in CACM at some point—the trickiness of putting subscripts and superscripts on the same entity, which could be handled well in a yacc grammar and was very hard to do other ways.

yacc was an amazing piece of work from the theoretical standpoint—that is, taking this language technology, this understanding of how to parse things and converting it into a program—but it was also extremely well engineered, much better than anything else from that time. For a long time, nothing came close to the engineering that yacc provided.

lex had some of that same property, but somehow didn't take off to the same degree, probably because it's easier to roll your own lexical analyzers. In AWK we originally had a lex lexical analyzer, but as time passed, I found it hard to support in different environments, and so I replaced it by a handcrafted C lexical analyzer. That was the source of all the bugs in the program for years afterward.

*Did other technologies beside lex and yacc make it simpler or easier or more powerful to develop languages or programs?*

**Brian:** After that, having Unix as the operating system underneath meant that all kinds of computing tasks were easy. The ability to create shell scripts, the ability to run a program and capture its output, think about it, perhaps edit and make it into something different, at a time when machines were slow—these made quite a difference. Overall, having these tools around, and especially core ones like sort, grep, and diff, made it possible to see what you were doing and keep track of little pieces.

*I can't imagine compiling programs without Make, but of course I can't imagine a world without patch either, and that was '86 or '87.*

**Brian:** Until I started teaching, I never used patch because I never wrote anything that was so big that patching made more sense than just having the whole source. I decided a few years ago that students in my class ought to know something about patch because that's the way so much code, especially in the Linux world, is shipped around. One of the assignments in my class asks the students to download my version of AWK from the Web, add a specific feature like repeat until, invent some tests and run them with shell scripts, and then send us the patch file. It gives them the whole experience of going to some open source program, fiddling it in a minor way, and sending it back. I had never thought of using patch. I used to get them to send me the source.

*It's easier to review in patch form.*

**Brian:** I guess that's the other thing. Patch files are much more compact and you can see what they did much more quickly.

*You brought up testing. Would you write code differently now to facilitate unit testing?*

**Brian:** For the kind of programs that I have written over the years, unit testing doesn't make much sense because the programs themselves are too small and they're self contained. The idea of a unit test, a bunch of little "call this function and see what it does" inside a fake main for testing, makes no sense for these programs, so I do not do unit testing at that level. I've tried it in my class a few times and it has failed miserably.

For small programs, I prefer to do end-to-end black-box testing. Make up a bunch of test cases, usually a form of a very specialized little language, and then write a program that will run the test cases automatically and report the things that don't work. That's good for bits and pieces of AWK; that's excellent for regular expressions. It's fine for Base64 encoders and decoders, which I sometimes ask students to do. For all of those things, I do outside testing, not inside testing. I don't put things inside the program for testing.

On the other hand, one thing that I would do differently today is to make it easier to do internal consistency checking, with assertions and sanity-checking functions, and maybe more test points or ways to get internal state out to the outside without having to work too hard, rather like the built-in self-test that the hardware people do.

*That sounds almost as much like debugging code as it does testing code. Maybe there's no sharp difference between the two.*

**Brian:** The idea of assertions, for me, is that you're pretty sure that something is right at this particular point, but you're not absolutely sure, so you put on a parachute to make sure that if things fall apart, you can land safely. That's a badly mixed metaphor. Assertions and sanity checks are useful because if something goes wrong, your debugging will be far easier because you know where to start probing to figure out what was wrong. It also tells you what kind of test that you probably should have had that you didn't.

I once tried to get my students to build an associative array class that was basically the same idea as the associative arrays in AWK. They were writing it in C, which meant that the string handling was the place where things would usually go wrong. When I was writing my own version, I wrote a separate sanity-checking function to go through the data structures and make sure that the number of elements that you got by counting on the inside of the data structure was the same as you got from dead reckoning on the outside.

I guess it's like versions of `malloc` that check the arena before and after every transaction. The checking says, "If I'm going to go wrong, this is the place where it's going to happen, so let me just make sure." I would do much more of that.

*Is that partly because of your maturity as a developer that you've seen the kind of bugs that can create, or because it's a lot less expensive to do that?*

**Brian:** I don't think I could claim maturity as a developer. I write less code than I would like almost all the time and when I do, it's often shoddy, in spite of what I say. It's more like "Do as I say, not as I do."

*Our editor heard you praise both Tcl and Visual Basic at a conference once. What do you think of those languages now?*

**Brian:** In the early 90s, I did extensive Tcl/Tk programming. I really understood it inside and out, and I wrote some systems that were at least briefly used inside Bell Labs. I could make interfaces very fast. Tcl/Tk is a wonderful environment for building user interfaces and a vast improvement over all its successors.

Tcl as a standalone language is somewhat idiosyncratic. It was good at what it was meant to do, but it was unusual enough that I think a lot of people had trouble with it, and it might have disappeared if it were not for Tk, which is great for building interfaces.

Visual Basic in its early days was a nice language and environment for writing Windows applications. At one point, VB was one of the most popular programming languages around.

It was so easy to get graphical interfaces up and running, so in the Windows world it was doing the same thing as Tk was doing in the X11 Unix world, a way to build interfaces quickly. Microsoft has slowly killed Visual Basic, and at this point, I wouldn't use it for anything new. C# would be the natural choice.

*What's your feeling on when you can drop a feature or an idea and ask people to upgrade to a new version?*

**Brian:** Unfortunately, that's one of those things where there is no right answer; no matter what, somebody will be unhappy. If it's my program, then I want people to follow me, and if it's somebody else's program, then I want them to maintain whatever purely idiosyncratic construct I've been using. I've been on both sides of this. One of the sore points for me for many years has been the different versions of AWK that came from Bell Labs. Al, Peter, and I had one, and there was a variant called NAWK from another group. They wanted to evolve the language differently, and so we wound up with two somewhat incompatible versions.

*That's a consistent opinion. The question is "What makes your life easier?" If getting rid of a feature that is hard to maintain or hard to explain makes it easier for you to maintain a program long term, that's certainly one aspect. If upgrading to a new version of the program makes you rewrite a bunch of code, that's a different kind of angst.*

**Brian:** In some settings it can be managed. Microsoft for example, had a conversion wizard that would take VB 6 into VB.NET. The early version of that wizard was not really up to the job, but the newer versions got a lot better and so, at that point, it became more of a feasible operation.

*To what degree should a designer consider an elegant interface a prime goal of an implementation? Is that always something to keep in the forefront of your mind, or does it depend on your other goals?*

**Brian:** If it's a programming language, you have to think about how people are going to write programs. What programs are they going to write? You want to have tried many examples yourself before you freeze it. If it's an API, then you really have to think about how people are going to use that API and how it handles difficult questions like who owns what resources.

Michi Henning wrote a very nice article about API design in the May 2007 issue of *ACM Queue*, an article that I reread before I try to talk about APIs in class. One of the points he makes is that APIs are more important now, because there are more of them and they're dealing with more complicated functionality.

Web service APIs are examples. For example, the API for Google Maps is quite big now. I don't remember it being that big when I first played with it three years ago; it seems to have grown. It's well done, as far as I can see. Other interfaces are less easy to use. Getting those right is hard work. Then of course, if you change your mind, what do you do?

*You can have a flag day where you upgrade all your servers.*

**Brian:** Or you change a bunch of names so it's upward compatible?

*Is that something you can evolve? Was it Stuart Feldman who said, "I can't change the tabs in Make—I have 12 users!"?*

**Brian:** Right. That's one of the awkward points about Make, and I'm sure Stu is just as unhappy with it now as he was then. It's very hard to change once you get real users. Joshua Bloch gives a talk about API design where he says, "APIs are forever." Once you've done it, it's hard to change. You can sometimes do converters. We talked about the VB converter. Mike Lesk changed TBL long ago. Tables used to be done by columns and he decided it was better by rows, so he wrote a converter. It didn't do a perfect job, but it was enough that you could take an existing table and map it to the new one. That approach helps for some things. There's an AWK-to-Perl translator that does a pretty limited job, but it's enough to get you off the ground.

*If there's one lesson you've learned over the years of your experience, what is it?*

**Brian:** Think really hard about what you're doing, but then keep playing with it and trying it and keep revising it and fixing it up until you're satisfied. Don't ship the first thing you did.

With some systems you get the feeling that somebody sent out their first version. You know from publishing that that just doesn't fly. Consider a genius like Beethoven. His manuscripts are a mess. Mozart was probably the only composer who could write music down perfectly the first time.

*There's a real line between the staggering work of once-in-a-millennium genius and the rest of us.*

**Brian:** In Isaac Asimov's autobiography, he said that he just wrote the words down and then published it, and most of his writing was actually pretty decent. He said he never rewrote, and that's fine for him, but I don't think that that's the norm.

On the wall of a room here at the university, there is a poem by Paul Muldoon that reminds me of the Beethoven manuscripts. There is endless scratching out and reworking and writing over again, all on one piece of paper; somebody framed it and put it on the wall as a reminder of how hard it is to do things right the first time. Programming is the same. Don't ship the first thing you write.

# Bits That Change the Universe

*Is it true that the beginning of AWK was a discussion that you had with Al Aho about adding a parser for extensible languages to your database project?*

**Peter Weinberger:** That's not how I remember it, although memory is fallible. I worked in a department that dealt with data (on Univac computers), and Al and Brian were interested in adding something database-ish to the Unix commands. It's possible that they had started with even more ambitious plans, but my recollection is that we decided early that scanning data was a productive way to go.

*Why did you choose to focus on a tool to extract information from files? Why did you avoid the feature to insert data, for example?*

**Peter:** One of the unifying features of Unix command-line tools was that they dealt with files made up of lines (and it was ASCII in those days). One would (and did) do insertion with an editor, and otherwise updating a file usually meant making a new file with modified contents. Other things were possible, and were done, but they weren't main line.

*I heard that you focused on reading data because you didn't want to deal with concurrency in writing.*

**Peter:** Well, not exactly; that's not the way it came out. :)

*Would you make the same decision today?*

**Peter:** No, I think if we were writing it today, and remembered to not get overambitious, I don't think there would be any user-visible concurrency stuff in it, but I'm sure it would be built to exploit whatever sort of local multicore or parallelism there was. I'm sure it would have caused us some trouble, but then we would've overcome it. There's an interesting question there, or possibly interesting question, which is: how much would that have changed the language design at all?

I don't know; you'd have to think about that. If you think you have free CPU, lots of free CPU, there's several things you can do. One is you could say, well, we're not going to use it; we'll just leave it for whatever else is running. Which in the case of AWK, or something like AWK, is not a bad choice, because if you believe that mostly it's designed to be used in pipelines then the other things in the pipeline need CPU processing time, too.

On the other hand, if you think it's going to be used for relatively complicated file transforming, you might put in things that could use several processors running on them at once, which of course we didn't do, because that's not the way machines were then.

*In what contexts do you see AWK as a better fit than SQL, for example?*

**Peter:** Well, they are essentially incomparable. AWK has no explicit types, SQL is badly overrun with them. That is, AWK reads and writes strings, but it's prepared to consider some strings as numbers when asked to. SQL does joins, but to do the same thing in AWK, one would run a program in front of it, probably 'join'. SQL does sorting and aggregation, but in the Unix context these are done by sort, and then piping through AWK again, or another Unix command. In short AWK was meant to be used as part of a sequence of commands piped together. SQL was meant to be used with data hidden away in an opaque structure, with some sort of schema known to the user. Finally, there's years of query optimization work done to support SQL while in AWK, what you see is what you get.

*What advantages do you see in storing (Unix) logs in text files and manipulating them with AWK?*

**Peter:** Text files are a big win. It requires no special tools to look at them, and all those Unix commands are there to help. If that's not enough, it's easy to transform them and load them into some other program. They are a universal type of input to all sorts of software. Further, they are independent of CPU byte order. Even so small an optimization as keeping them compressed implies that people remember which compression command was used, and there are usually several choices. As for manipulating them with AWK, that's fine if a pipeline of commands does what's needed. Otherwise a scripting language like Perl or Python reads text files just fine. Finally, so do C and Java.

Text files for logs are great. In the old days, one argument against them was that they had to be parsed, and numbers converted to binary and so forth. But the latter is barely noticeable in CPU time, and lines of text are trivial to parse compared to XML. On the other side, fixed-size binary structs don't need parsing but that's very unusual, and it's a rare case where it makes a difference.

*AWK was one of the early proofs of the power of the Unix concept of many small programs working together. These programs were largely text-oriented. How does the concept apply to nontext forms of data and multimedia?*

**Peter:** It's useful to tease out what the "Unix concept" really was. It was a style in which many programs were useful with one input and one output, together with command-line syntax, and system support that made all input and output uniform (read and write system calls, no matter what the device) and system support (pipes) that avoided having to name and allocate temporary files. Transcoding and compression are examples of things that the idea applies to perfectly well, even when the data is audio or video. But even with text, there are lots of applications that don't work that way, particularly if human beings need to interact with them. For instance, the spell command produced a list of words it thought were misspelled, but it wasn't interactive; the users had to go back and edit their document.

So the essence of your question might be, "If we only have command lines, what commands would be used to process data or multimedia?" But this is a counterfactual. We now have other ways of interacting with computing, and more choices for dividing up tasks. The new ways aren't necessarily better or worse than the old ones, just different. One example is TeX versus programs like Word. Is one better than the other? I doubt that there is a consensus.

*What limits do you see in command-line tools and in graphical interfaces?*

**Peter:** This is an old old topic and the boundaries have become a little blurred. Perhaps it needs a thoughtful essay. Here's a superficial answer. If I need to combine a bunch of programs, then a shell script invoking command-line tools works well. It's also a way of making sure the options and preferences for the various components are consistent. But graphical interfaces are a lot better at letting me see and choose among a modest number of options and potentially better at keeping all the information organized.

*Many interviewees underlined the importance of learning math to be a better programmer. I wonder to what degree we can study what we need right when we need it. For example, with the Internet you can find and learn things pretty quickly, right?*

**Peter:** Yes and no. Unfortunately to learn some things, you not only have to think about them but you have to sort of practice, so there's some stuff—you can go to the Internet and you read it and you say, "Oh, yeah, that works." And then there's some stuff where there's just no substitute for years of hard work. So here you are in the middle of some project and you decide you need to understand linear programming to solve your problem; probably what you'll get from the Internet will not be helpful, and if you have to solve this problem within a week, you're unlikely to choose a method that requires a lot of work to learn unless you already know about that—even if it were much better. And that happens.

*What is the role of math in computer science and programming in particular?*

**Peter:** My degree is in math, so I'd like to believe that math is fundamental. But there are many parts of computer science, and many kinds of programming, where one can be quite successful without any mathematics at all. The use (or usefulness) of mathematics comes in layers. People with no feeling for statistics or randomness will be misled over and over again by real-world data. There's mathematics in graphics, there's lots of mathematics in machine learning (which I think statisticians think of as a form of regression), and there's all sorts of number theory in cryptography. Without some mathematics, people are just cut off from understanding large parts of computer science.

*What differences do you see between working on the theorems and building an implementation?*

**Peter:** At the highest level, when you prove a theorem, you know something about the universe that you only suspected was true before. It's unconditional knowledge. When you write a program, you can do something you might not have been able to do before.

In some sense, you've changed the universe. Mostly the changes are very, very small. Mathematics and programming are quite different. Maybe the easiest way to see that is to compare mathematics papers, and the proofs of theorems or programs that theorem provers produce. The papers are short and frequently convey insight. The machine proofs are neither. Writing a program has some of the character of the machine-generated proofs, in that all the tiny details have to be right, a huge burden on the programmer's understanding, and testing skills, too.

### Does building the implementation teach you something more?

**Peter:** Sure. Typically you learn that you should throw it out and implement it again. Any project has dozens, or more, design decisions, most of which either seem neutral at the time, or the alternative is chosen on the basis of intuition. Almost invariably, when the code runs for real, it is obvious that the decisions could have been made better. And then over time the code is used in unexpected circumstances, and more of the decisions look bad.

### Would functional programming help?

**Peter:** If the question is whether functional programs, being more mathematical, would somehow express results better than ordinary programs, I don't see a big difference. Any single-assignment language is easier to reason about, but that doesn't make the programs easier to write, nor is there persuasive evidence that programs are easier to write. In fact, most comparative questions about languages, coding techniques, development methodologies, and software engineering in general, are appallingly unscientific.

Here's a quote from R. Bausell's *Snake Oil Science* [Oxford University Press]:

> Carefully controlled research (such as randomized, controlled trials) involving numerical data has proved more dependable for showing us what works and what does not than has reliance upon expert opinions, experience, hunches, or the teachings of those we revere.

Software is still a craft, rather like furniture making. There are Chippendales, there are craftsmen, and there are lesser practitioners. I'm a little far off your original question here.

### What are your suggestions to become a better programmer?

**Peter:** How about "learn mathematics"? Oh well, perhaps another answer would be better. How about "understand floating point"? Maybe not that one, either. People vary a lot on this.

I think it is important to learn new techniques and algorithms. Without that, I think people quickly become overspecialized and narrow. In addition, these days one ought to be up on writing secure and robust code. There's a lot of attacks on users and systems, and you'd like to make sure it's not your code that is vulnerable. This is especially tricky for websites.

*When should debugging be taught? And how?*

**Peter:** Talking about debugging should be integral to all programming courses (and integral to all language design as well). It's hard enough to write correct sequential programs running on isolated machines. Writing multithreaded code is even harder, and the debugging tools are not yet very satisfactory. One consideration in design needs to be whether it makes debugging easier. It's not much of an exaggeration to say that as a programmer either I am trying to decide what to do next, or I am debugging. Everything else takes hardly any time.

*Is there something you consider the biggest mistake you've made with regard to design or programming? What did you learn from it?*

**Peter:** I don't know that there's a single biggest mistake. People make mistakes all the time. From mistakes you learn (perhaps without being able to state them clearly) a set of design priniciples that generally work. Then you push them too far, and they break, and perhaps the new lessons can be incorporated in them, or perhaps your code always bears the scars of your obsolescent design rules. I find I do not put enough useful explanation in error messages, and generally end up going back and adding details. There's a typical conflict here: if the error occurs, you want complete useful information. If it doesn't occur that's a lot of typing, and a lot of space taken up on the screen. It's a balance.

*What do you regret most about AWK?*

**Peter:** I think the brainstorm of using whitespace for string concatenation didn't work out as well as we hoped. An explicit operator would have made things clearer. The syntax also generally suffers from the conflict between wanting to encourage short command lines and allowing big programs. We didn't think of the latter at first, so some of our choices are uninspired.

*What has become popular (or useful) to your surprise?*

**Peter:** The whole language became much more popular than we expected, or than I expected. One of the ideas that guided the design was that it should be easy to learn for people who already knew Unix-like things, particularly C and grep. That doesn't drive it to a mass audience of secretaries (as they used to be called) or sheep farmers. But I met a sheep farmer at a wedding in the early 90s who used Unix to keep his records, and was a great fan of AWK. I suspect he's by now moved on.

*How do you stimulate creativity in a software development team?*

**Peter:** The best path to high-quality software is talented experts who share a pretty clear sense of what they want to produce. There are other ways, but they are more work. I have no idea how to produce good software without talented programmers, though presumably it's possible.

*How did you develop a language as a team?*

**Peter:** We all talked about syntax and semantics, and then each of us would write code. Then any of us would change the code. For most of it, it's not any one person's code, although Brian has tended it over the years. We also had limited ambitions. I think we were helped by the target machine, which only had 128k bytes of memory.

For design we sat around and talked and wrote on the board, and then in coding it might turn out that we'd missed something important. That would call for informal discussion.

*When you find a recurring problem in a codebase, how do you recognize if the best solution is a local workaround or a global fix?*

**Peter:** There are two kinds of software projects: those that fail, and those that turn into legacy horrors. The only way to avoid the second would be to rewrite the code as its environment changes. The trouble is that that's a luxury most projects can't afford, so the pressure of reality forces people to put in local fixes. After enough local fixes, the code becomes rigid and really hard to maintain. Without the original developers, or remarkably good specifications, it becomes really hard to rewrite the code, too. Life can be hard.

*If you had one piece of advice, what should readers most learn from your experiences?*

**Peter:** Quoting, or perhaps misquoting, Einstein: "As simple as possible, but no simpler."

The trick is not being self-indulgent, which it's very easy to become. If for sure people are going to start asking for something, then you might as well put it in. It requires judgment to get simple but no simpler than necessary, whatever the quote is.

*The simplest thing that can possibly work? That was Kent Beck, I think. How do you recognize simplicity and resist adding things that you don't need right now?*

**Peter:** It depends on who you've got around you. For many people, "Can you explain it to your parents?" would be a good test. Sometimes that may not be possible, but as a starting point it seems quite reasonable to me. A more general test is if you think about the people you expect to use it, "Can you explain it to the median user?" as opposed to "Will the smartest user figure it out?"

## Theory and Practice

*You taught math before joining Bell Labs. Should we teach computer science in the same way we teach math?*

**Peter:** We teach math for a couple of different reasons. One of them is for future mathematicians, which is sort of what I was doing when I was teaching math. One of them is because mathematics is so useful. But it's a little clearer, I think, what mathematics is than what computer science is.

In computer science there are various kinds of programming and it's hard to know what to think about that. There's all those data structures and there's the sort of algorithms and complexity part. It's somewhat less clear what different users of computer science need than it is, at least what people think about, what potential users of mathematics need. So when you're teaching mathematics you know what the engineers need; nowadays I suppose you know what people who will be doing statistics or economics or something need, but I think the problems are somewhat simpler for the mathematicians.

On the other hand I think computer scientists ought to know more mathematics, so there's some leftovers from when I was a mathematician.

So there's this question versus what we might loosely call reality: computer science departments, at least in this country, have had some trouble attracting majors, at least over the last several years; it's not clear why, but some of the ones who have succeeded in attracting more majors have changed their curricula a lot. So, what computer science should be taught is changing.

*From your previous answers I have the impression that you suggest that the sweet spot of programming is between a pure theoretical approach, where you might be too far from the real-life needs, and a full pragmatic approach, where you might solve the problem assembling pieces of code from various sources. Does this make sense?*

**Peter:** Well, yes, but I think the bigger problem is it's very hard to know where to draw the various lines. It depends on what your ambitions for your code are. If you expect people to use it for a long time, then it has to be written so that it's very easy to fix bugs.

The other thing that's difficult is if you get too many users too soon, it means it's too hard to fix any design problems. If I write it just for myself, then every time I don't like the way it is, I just fix it or change it. If you write it for a fairly small group, then it takes a while before people complain when you make incompatible changes, because they know it's experimental. But if you write for a large group or if it's used by a large group, it becomes much harder to make an incompatible changes, so you're stuck with whatever choices you made.

*This might be one of the problems with legacy software, when people take pieces of code from various sources such that problems in that code propagate and stay alive for decades.*

**Peter:** Yes, I think that a lot of code that's still around that was written a long time ago by people who had no idea it would last this long.

*One factor that keeps AWK alive is that so many users take scripts written by someone else and modify them to do something else.*

**Peter:** Yes, that's right and in fact that was a design goal. That's sort of the way that we thought it would be used, we thought that it would be used a lot. People would take things that did almost what they want and just modify them.

*Is this idea of programming by example applicable to larger projects?*

**Peter:** I think not too much larger, because the example has to be small enough to see to understand. The level at which you can do it, it's easiest if it's a few lines of code. Maybe you could get up to sort of a screenful, and expect people to follow what's going on. Pretty much it needs to be simple enough so that you could just look at the code and see what needs to be changed, or at least see enough of what needs to be changed so that you could run experiments to see if you've got it right.

*The idea to write very short "throwaway" scripts sounds very seductive. Has your experience with big codebases and other programming languages taught you when to rework a codebase, and when to restart it?*

**Peter:** It's hard to restart from scratch, in practice. If your user community is small, you can talk to them. Otherwise, if your code has a well-defined interface, then it's possible. If the interfaces aren't well defined and the user community is large, it seems really hard to avoid breaking things. Unfortunately this is true of less-drastic upgrades, too. So that's actually the good news, namely that since any substantial upgrade will break things, it's not too much worse for the users to do a major reimplementation. After a few years, new code will almost certainly need to be totally rewritten. Users will use it in ways that the developers hadn't thought of, and many of the implementation decisions will turn out to be suboptimal, especially for new hardware.

The AWK experience is a little different. We did rewrite it several times, but then we declared it finished. It would have been possible to upgrade it, but all our ideas seemed incompatible with the basic principles. I think that was nearly the right decision. We all went on to other things, rather than expanding the range of the system. The only thing that I think is missing for its tiny niche in the modern world is using UTF-8 as input.

*Brian said that you were a very fast implementer. What's your secret?*

**Peter:** I don't think there is a secret. People are just different. I'm not sure, for instance, if I had to do it now, that I would be quite as fast. Part of it was optimistic ignorance, I think. That's the belief that you can just write it down and it will be enough. Part of it is how one is with the tools, and language, that are available. Some people find the tools comfortable, and some don't. It's like the ability to match colors with watercolors, which some find easy, and some find difficult.

One of the things that I think that's true is that if you are going to write code professionally, for a living, you should find it fairly easy to write; otherwise, you're just struggling all the time. It's like writing short stories: if you don't find it easy to do them at a certain level, I think you are going to find it very hard to do at all, although I don't know since I can't do that kind of writing. It's a lot of work getting things into their final shape.

*Do you write the prototype and then modify it to get professional-quality code? Or do you experiment with the idea, but then rewrite completely to create the finished work?*

**Peter:** I think you can't tell in advance. When you start writing the prototype, you can tell sometimes what kind of compromises you're making. Sometimes those compromises mean that the prototype will be inconsistent with being easily converted into a production program. Anyway, there's all kind of things that you might do that would make it hard, and in that case you're just going to have to rewrite it, but if you're lucky, then maybe you can transform it sort of step by step. You ought to expect to have to throw it away, and redo it.

For one thing, it's unlikely you'll make enough right decisions. You write it and you start experimenting with it and you change things. After a while, unless you were very lucky, the code starts looking terrible. It really needs to be at least refactored, but probably just rewritten. That's what I would probably expect; you'd really end up rewriting it. Certainly the first AWK implementation was purely a proof-of-concept thing because it generated C code; of course that's completely inconsistent with how you would want to use it.

*Tom Kurtz, creator of BASIC, said that writing code makes you understand aspects of the problem that you didn't think of.*

**Peter:** That's right, stuff you weren't smart enough to think about until you had to face it. I think one of the things you look for when you're hiring people is whether or not writing code is a natural form of expression for them. Is this how they express their sort of algorithmic ideas?

*What differences are there between writing software and creating a language?*

**Peter:** In some ways writing a language is simpler than the general software, but I'm not sure that's really true. It concentrates your choices, I think, because it has to fit together and there's a relatively modest number of ways to do each thing. Once you've decided on the big features of the language, there's a lot of framework that's already in your head: how functions will work, and are you going to do garbage collection, or whatever. What are the primitives of the language? The implementation comes in layers. I think that tends to be somewhat easier. Of course, if, sort of late in the thing, you've discovered you made some really bad choice, you have to throw it all away.

*Does the implementation affect the design of the language?*

**Peter:** Oh, sure. I think you can see that undoubtedly. I think, for instance, for a long time it was a relatively special thing to do garbage collection. The Lisp guys worked at it and some of the functional programming guys worked at it and lots of other people just sort of waited because it wasn't quite clear how it would work in, say, C-like languages. Then, for instance, the Java guys just said that's what we're going to do. It was quite a different tradeoff, by making a relative small change in features of the language; I'm not saying this is what happened to Java, but by giving up on actual memory address as being accessible to programmers, you could decide whether you wanted to try garbage collection or compacting garbage collectors and stuff.

I think now languages without that really suffer a lot comparatively, even though garbage collection is far from perfect. Fighting with memory allocations is a big annoyance, so it's never quite totally trivial, but there's lots more known now about how to implement languages and you have a much wider choice of things to do, especially if you're doing something lightweight.

If you want a feature in your language that's hard to implement, it's not clear that it's worthwhile because it's hard to implement and you're trying to do something lightweight. If you're trying to do a language that makes doing difficult things possible, then there might be a list of things that you have to do and then you have to put up with whatever the troubles are.

*How much does the language influence programmers' productivity? How much does the ability of the programmer makes a difference?*

**Peter:** Boy, I wish I knew the answer to that. I used to think I knew the answers to those questions. It's clear that programmers vary some huge amount in ability. There's really more than a factor of 10, maybe much more than a factor of 10. This is sort of software engineering, so there's no empirical evidence for any of it, and my belief is that the languages shouldn't matter. That is, given a group of people and some project, it really doesn't matter what the language is, but for individual programmers I suspect it does matter. I think people, for personality, or what they learn first, or whatever, find some kinds of languages easier to adapt to than others. This is where you get these funny debates.

It's clear that there are, for instance, Lisp applications that would be really hard to achieve the same functionally in C, and for that matter C applications where it would be really hard to achieve the same thing in Lisp. But for a range of programs you could use lots of languages, but I'm not sure even with practice all programmers would be equally comfortable across a wide range of languages, and I don't know why. But of course it takes time to become expert in a language. On the other hand, for some people it takes less time in some languages than other languages.

People have these big debates about languages and which of the many desirable features they implement and which ones they don't, and how awful that they don't and stuff like that. But it's not clear that it really matters. To put it much more controversially: you can write Mars Lander software in any language; each one of them will have properties and it will depend much more on the people who wrote it and how they organized it than what the language is. Everybody will argue fiercely for their choice, but I just don't believe it.

*C doesn't support objects, but at the same time you built little tools, components of the Unix system, that could be used together to build complex features. To what degree does building objects inside the language as part of a big program work better than building components that are part of the system?*

**Peter:** That raises two questions in my mind. One of them is sort of a binding question or a modularity question. The question is what you put inside one language as opposed to what you try to compose out of tools. You get a much tighter and of course more complex relationship among the components if they are all within a language. Some of that is just computational efficiency, but I think some of it is conceptual consistency also.

The other question has to do with "object-oriented" as a general idea and I think it's possible to be overenthusiastic about the success of object-oriented this and that. Leaving that aside, which is somewhat controversial, if you look across languages a lot of them say, "We're object-oriented," and then when you look closely, you notice they all do quite different things. It's not always clear what the term means. In fact, people get into these very confusing discussions, because there's a natural temptation to believe that whatever your language does about objects, is what object-oriented means. I think it's basically a term that does not have a simple, relatively straightforward, widely accepted definition.

### How does choice of programming language affect code security?

**Peter:** You certainly need something to help you with all the various things that are involved in security. I guess, roughly speaking, two kinds of things go wrong in programs that are connected with security. One of them is logic errors of one sort, so that there's something that you can say to the program and it makes a mistake and it gives you privileges or does things it's just not supposed to do at all. The other is the whole buffer overflow stuff, which is implementation errors of various sorts that are exploitable, actual bugs that people didn't think about. And I think most of those just shouldn't be there. Low-level languages support buffer overflow with careless programming of various sorts, so it's not easy to get right.

I thought there was a time when it was rumored that Microsoft for what became Vista was just going to rewrite all the C and C++ into C#, and at that point you weren't going to get buffer overflows, because you can't get buffer overflows. But of course that didn't work out. Instead they do these enormously elaborate things with machine-language executables, to attempt to make it hard to exploit buffer overflows and other similar things.

Then there is another kind of security problem, which happens at seams between programs, because a lot of the interfaces aren't all that well specified, or not specified at all in some sense, except very informally, such as HTTP and XML cross-site scripting and those things. We need to do something about security, but I really don't know what.

### How much does it help if the language makes it difficult to create certain problems?

**Peter:** Yeah, as much as possible, but like our earlier discussion, it's not clear how much that helps. It was a time when I was writing a fair amount of Python, and I had these amusing bugs, which of course are caused by careless thinking and bad style. But the thing about the indentation in Python was that as soon as the loop became too long—I had a nested loop—to get at the bottom of the loop, I needed to go back two tabs to get out of the loop and do some work, and I didn't give it two tabs; I gave it one tab because I thought that was enough because that is what it looked like on the screen, and that of course meant I was doing this expensive thing every time through the outer loop, which was very silly. Although the program was still correct, it was very slow.

I guess the moral is no matter how well designed the language is, it's always possible for the programmer to make dumb mistakes. And the question of whether or not you can be relatively scientific about ways you can make it less likely or more likely, I don't know. Software engineering is in many ways a very pathetic field, because so much of it is anecdotal and based on people's judgments or even people's aesthetic judgments. It's not clear to me how many of the criteria people use to talk about languages, in programming languages, are directly and irreducibly relevant to writing correct programs or maintainable programs, or programs that can be changed easily.

*Research generally helps the implementation, but the design aspects generally reflect the personal preferences of the designer.*

**Peter:** Yes, in fact, I think the really successful languages have little things in them that weren't directly examples of what had appeared in the literature. People decided that something would be interesting to do. All the stuff that is in programming language is useful for thinking about languages, and talking about languages, but it's not clear what you would do, either in the language or in how you use languages, to make the code, to make a programming process better, the maintenance process better. Everybody has strong views on this, but it is not clear to me why we should believe what. There doesn't seem to be any science.

*It's difficult to use a scientific approach for the design of the language partly because we don't have a scientific way to measure the good and the bad of a language.*

**Peter:** Yeah, I think that's right, or the good and the bad of programming in general, not just languages. There are lots of people who think they know solutions but it's not quite clear to me why they should be believed because it's clear there's lots of different successful ways of developing programs.

*How do you choose the right syntax for a language? Do you focus more on corner cases or on the average user experience?*

**Peter:** The not-so-surprising answer is "both." It should be as sensible as we humans of bounded intelligence can make it, but it should be clear what the semantics are in corner cases, too. A successful language will be used by lots of people, most of whom don't share the designer's point of view or aesthetic judgment, and it's best if they aren't gratuitously misled by strange features or edge cases. And, people will write programs that generate programs in the new language, and that will come as a surprise to the implementation.

*When designing a language, do you consider debugging when evaluating potential features?*

**Peter:** That's a tricky question. What you hope for is a fair amount of help from the development environment for what's easy to do. The stuff we know how to do is giving guesses as to what the completions might be and show you what the parameters are, and it can show you other references if it's good, and find the definitions. It's harder of course to find a function you don't know the name of that does something, I mean you're sure somewhere in this mess is a function that formats numbers in a machine-readable way and puts commas in or something like that, right? But how do you remember the name? How do you find the names of these functions? And so when people write these libraries, they try naming conventions, informal naming conventions and things like that. But a lot of that stuff just doesn't scale very well.

### How about good error messages?

**Peter:** Well, that would be nice. My usual complaint about error messages is that they read like notes from the program to itself, as opposed to suggesting to the user what you might fix, and in some cases they're much worse than that.

### How much detail do error messages need?

**Peter:** Well, they should be as helpful as possible, but that doesn't actually answer the question. Certain kinds of errors in programming languages are much harder to be intelligent about than others, although you can certainly understand heuristics. So in C-like languages mistakes in separators and braces really tend to confuse the compilers a lot and it's hard for them to explain, and so people learn to recognize what your compiler says when you've left out the semicolon between a class definition and the next function. You just recognize that this imbecilic error message has nothing to do with what actually happened. The compiler has gone too far into the next function before it noticed it was a mistake. And if you leave out a closing curly brace, you get the same kind of incomprehensible error messages; you just sort of learn what their shape is. It's possible to do better but it seems to be a lot of work, and it's not clear that it's worth it.

There's another way of asking this question, which is would you like stupid error messages that give you a hint about what the program thought was going wrong, or would you like helpful error messages that remind you of those hints that Microsoft used to put in Word to give you help that were never very useful and always seemed to be wrong?

I think if you're going to do fancy error messages, you have to work hard at getting them so that they're mostly right; but that's partly because we're used to mediocre error messages from which we can sort of figure out what's going on.

## Waiting for a Breakthrough

### How would you change AWK to improve the support for big programs?

**Peter:** Given all that's happened in between, the question is, would we have come up with Perl or would we have come up with something else? Well, I don't think we have the right kind of minds to have come up with all of Perl, but if you look at the spirit of what was going on AWK, if you thought it should be used for big programs, something like that would be possible.

I think the other answer is we stopped when we stopped because it seemed like a good place to stop. I don't know if I've told this story—I think it's only months, but in retrospect, it might have been a couple years after AWK had been released internally—I got a call from somebody in the computer center who was having some trouble with AWK, and I went down to look at his program and we had thought of AWK as I described it, short one-liners, little things, OK? And he had written an assembler for some esoteric piece of hardware in AWK and it was 55 pages of code. We were just stunned. In fact it's not so strange you can do that; people certainly wrote longer programs in languages with less structure, but it was quite surprising to us.

*Brian said that essentially every time you design a little language, people start using it and then they ask for loops and whatever, so every time you have to stop, otherwise the language would become…*

**Peter:** …bigger and bigger, and you have to decide whether you want to go down that road or not.

*If you want to build a general-purpose language, start with that goal in mind, instead of starting from a little language and going big after it becomes successful.*

**Peter:** I think that's right, too. That was another thing, which is another story I may have told. Bigness is that people write programs and, say, languages, parsers, or compilers, and they think of people as typing the input, but for many reasons you may discover people writing programs to produce the input. I think typically the first time that happens is the compiler case because, say, in a C-like language nobody ever saw an 80,000 case switch statement before. They don't think of a human being able to type a 80,000 case switch statement. Maybe the code generator never saw a switch statement with so many cases. These things happen at all levels even for general-purpose languages.

*What about extensible languages where users can modify the language?*

**Peter:** Well, it depends exactly what that means, I think. I mean basically, yeah, sure, but there's a lot of limitations you get unless you mean something like Lisp, where people can add these things to the language using macros. There's lots of reasons people want to add stuff to languages, for either expressibility or because you need to include libraries written in other languages that do complicated things.

This is another question that of course we didn't have to face in AWK at all, thank you, which is how hard is it to incorporate subroutines or packages written in other languages into your language? The answers to that question vary a lot.

*There seems to be a divide between mathematicians and nonmathematicians. Is there a difference between mathematics and software development? C won; Scheme didn't. C won; Lisp didn't. It's the "worse is better" approach again.*

**Peter:** I think there may be a difference between the mathematician-designed languages and the nonmathematician-designed languages, but the differences between Scheme and C are much more the difference between languages that attempt to have a simple foundation and languages that don't. There's nothing absolute in this; we don't know what's going on.

There's certainly no general agreement on what makes languages successful, but there are a lot of factors. Everyone has favorite facets and aspects, and no one knows how to encompass them all. Original Lisp, to be purist, had a very simple model of what was going on, and was for that surprisingly powerful. One might ask, why did they have to make the language more complicated? What was it that they weren't doing that needed extra complication? Certainly all the intermediate Lisps, and then Scheme, and then finally Common Lisp, have extra complications.

There's probably two things. This may not work out because I haven't thought it through but let me just push right on. One thing is programmer convenience. Another thing is program performance. We'll get to other languages eventually but I think that languages like Lisp give a lot of clarity to some of these issues.

One of the big differences between original Lisp, I believe, and Common Lisp is the extra data types, hash tables, and stuff. Those are in there essentially for performance. At the other end of this—my history is really weak on this instance; I do not actually know a lot about Lisp—at some point the Lisp guys started putting macros in. In one way, macros are a very natural thing. There's just a different evaluation environment for them, but—and that's a question of programmer convenience—there's nothing macros do that programmers couldn't have written themselves.

*They're a force multiplier.*

**Peter:** That's the expectation. But you also get a force confusion multiplier and you use it extensively; it means that your code is essentially unreadable by anyone else. It makes it much harder to say what your language does, even informally. There's a lot of funny corner cases. Even in this relatively pure environment, you can see the tensions between what you might call mathematical purity and getting the damn job done.

All the Lisp languages and all those other languages, many of which have very formal semantic definitions, have exactly the same problem. There are people involved in at least at two phases of the life of the program, plus there's a computer involved. To make the program satisfactory to the computer, you need a quite precise definition of what the stuff the people write means. The people need something that's not hard to write. Once the program has been alive for a while and used, it's quite likely the people changing the program, the maintainers, have to be able to read the code and change it.

In my—as we say, "humble, but correct"—opinion, many of the features of some languages that make it convenient to write the code make it very difficult for maintainers. Just for greater shock value we can pick on almost all object-oriented languages. These sorts of pragmatic languages, where the precise semantics are only clear to the compiler and the compiler writer, are quite valuable to the writer of new code. Languages that allow you to express your intent in a way that's clear to people who have no other guidance but the code, that would be nice, too. I'm hard-put to think of any examples. Although, of course I haven't written in every language. But among the languages with which I'm familiar, there may be slightly better and slightly worse languages for this.

*You're talking about two different axes.*

**Peter:** Yes, I am. That's right. However we were writing code in the good old days, when giants walked the earth and all that sort of stuff. Pygmies walked the earth, but they were in big boxes. Nobody thought that their code would last for 30 years. If you had said "Unix will still be here," or "FORTRAN will still be here," the natural answer from all of us would have been "Yes, and we would rewrite it." That's the way we lived. You put it out, and you rewrote it. It was slightly incompatible and somewhat better each time, until you fell victim to the Second System Effect, in which case it was very incompatible and a lot worse. We sort of understood abstractly the idea that there are only two kinds of software projects: failures and future legacy horrors.

We didn't understand the fact that you couldn't keep writing software year after year and rewriting it also. It adds up and either you spend all your time rewriting the old software, or you let it slide. You can't do both. The maintenance problem to some extent looms larger and larger, although I say that because that's what I spend a fair amount of time doing with Google, where it looms pretty large to me.

Leaving aside this unsolved case—the earlier comments on my distinction between languages of the mathematical sort of languages and the nonmathematical sort—there's also languages designed by mathematicians or ex-mathematicians or people who think like mathematicians, and languages that are not. I would expect the former to be nearly completely specified, even if informally. You would really write down what it's supposed to do in all the circumstances you could think of. You'd actually write down the lexical story, as opposed to hint at it. You try to write down the rest of it, and you might not succeed.

*Simon Peyton Jones said they managed to specify about 85% of the first version of Haskell, but beyond that it just wasn't worth their time.*

**Peter:** Sometimes you can be too careful. One of the things that hasn't worked as well as it might have in C short int or long. You had two choices there.

*You also have signedness.*

**Peter:** Please, we will not even start on signedness or const, for that matter. You could have said, "We will have int8, int16, int24, int36, int64, whatever those all are, and the language will either promise to do exactly that or we'll do our best but round up."

This is all in retrospect. I'm not sure that I could have done it even as well starting up ab initio. Or you say "Listen, we've got short int and long, and we'll tell you what they are and bug off. For other things, you just have to cope yourself somehow." That wouldn't have surprised the compiler writers that want to give every last bit of efficiency to their users. You see in GCC where they've graciously gifted you with plenty of types. Then there's the unsigned guys and the pointer-sized guys and all that other stuff, which is just too much to contemplate.

Also strings are an interesting example. After you've come that far, you realize that if you allowed arbitrary characters in them as opposed to making them say UTF-8 strings or ASCII strings, then you can't print them. While it doesn't sound bad to say "Yes, all my structures that my language and program supports are binary except the ones that are explicitly made into printable format," it's a big pain in the neck.

We need some real conceptual breakthroughs. It's been a long time, and I'm pessimistic.

*You've made me pessimistic.*

**Peter:** I'm sorry. What's amazing is that all this stuff actually sort of functions, and you can actually rely on it. It doesn't come with any guarantees but effectively you can rely on it. You know, your car long ago lost any ability to function without the computers, and there's a lot of code in your car. It mostly works almost all of the time. I know there's no guarantee, and I know there are stories where the computers need to reboot themselves while you're on the highway and all that stuff, but fundamentally you rely on it. At one level I'm just complaining about inefficiencies as opposed to fundamental flaws—but they're annoying.

*What type of breakthrough we would need to start solving these problems?*

**Peter:** I think not only "No!" but "Of course not!", but let me try some observations. On the one hand, we have huge amounts of computer power on the machines that we write the software on. Most of the computer power just sits there in some idle loop. Some astonishingly large fraction of it goes in to running the user interface. Then if you're compiling C, for instance, a huge amount of it goes into reading stuff in to memory and then writing out various versions of intermediate files so that they can be read into memory again.

OK? For a language with modest structural integrity, where you can actually tell about aliasing and many other things, you would think the compilers could do a much better job. That means the programmer's got to have some way to express their intent, which we haven't quite figured out yet. In fact it's gotten worse. It would be exceptionally generous-spirited to describe threads and object-oriented as orthogonal. Instead you'd be much closer to describe them as hideously intertangled. We've got all this stuff. You would have to clean up a lot of the stuff that makes it very hard to tell what programs are doing. That's going to become especially difficult in the world of multicore.

Maybe there's lots of very bright people out there doing very interesting work. Maybe something will develop. The only tool we have is to ask computers to help our programs be safer and cleaner, and starting from better languages when we think them up. It's hard to see which; it's a giant ball of yarn, and it's hard to see which of these little loops sticking out you start pulling on. Find an end. I don't know. I'm not eternally optimistic.

On the other hand, it's not all bad. It's just sort of annoying.

*How do you define success in terms of your work?*

**Peter:** When we were doing AWK and things like that, it seemed (it may not have been), it seemed like you could have an idea and do a pretty moderate amount of work and if your idea was good and your implementation was good, you had a big impact on computing. So that set a standard that I think would be extremely hard to match any more. It was easy to have a fairly substantial impact on what turned out to be a significant part of the computing world then, and I think that just isn't true any more.

I think the number of small groups that have a big impact is relatively small. It's hard to have a big impact. It's not impossible to be successful, that is numbers of people who use your stuff, people think it's good, but you can't have the same kind of impact, I think. It's very hard to see—the extreme example of that is Unix, where a relatively small core group produced this thing that really made a big difference. And now maybe one of your readers will explain how there's some examples of that that I missed in 5 or 10 years, but I don't think so. I think now it takes bigger groups and it's much harder.

I think the answer to your question is: we were lucky and had a lot of impact for relatively little work. What a great moment, what a great benchmark for success it was. Now I think for people who are much more talented than we were, that kind of success would be hard to achieve. Of course that is good in many ways. It means there's been a great deal of progress, but it also means that individuals have to settle for less.

## Programming by Example

*You mentioned that AWK is a language that lives because of programming by example.*

**Peter:** That was a deliberate design decision. There's many things; some of them bad, some of them good. AWK has a collection of interesting—which is a very polite way of describing it—syntactic choices, of which I think only a couple are real mistakes. Mostly the idea was it would look a lot like C because then we wouldn't have to explain it to the people we worked with.

Then the question is now what? Our view was that since all AWK programs would be one line or at most a few lines, the way to program AWK was to look and find examples that did something like you wanted. Just change them. If you wanted something more complicated, you'd do it incrementally and that would all work out. At the same time we were doing AWK there was a project at Xerox PARC, whose name I've forgotten unfortunately, which was in vaguely the same space as AWK. It was supposed to process files. The Xerox PARC systems didn't think of their files with any lines and stuff, but it was close. They meant it to be used by secretaries. The page you wrote on was two columns. You wrote the program on the left, and a worked example on the right. The compiler checked that your program did what the example said it should do.

*That's clever.*

**Peter:** It was clever, and furthermore they worked hard to make the syntax approachable by secretaries. Of course it failed. It was not widely successful and AWK was for many reasons. Unix spread and whatever system this was written didn't, and so on and so forth. Our version of that was this idea that you find some program that did something roughly like what you want to do. AWK always was quite deliberately intended for programmers.

That's not the way it worked out, of course, but the fact that it was relatively simple, and there were examples you could look at, and you could get the AWK book and look at examples in, I think helped a lot.

*In copying and pasting and tweaking a program, you learn the semantics of the language by osmosis at best.*

**Peter:** Except the idea of the AWK book is that between the informal introduction and all the examples, there was supposed to be a fairly complete description of what the language was and what it did. I think there is and I think that's the way it worked out.

*Do people read that?*

**Peter:** Some do, some don't. Let me put it slightly differently, OK? Whether or not you read it, you can do it by example in AWK, right? That's an empirical fact. How about Ada?

*I've never tried.*

**Peter:** My guess is that you'd be really hard-put to do Ada programs just by examples. It's quite possible it would be hard to do C++ programs from example. At some level of simplicity, you could get some ways into it.

*People aren't running one-liner C programs, either.*

**Peter:** That's the difference, of course. It's very hard to write a one-liner aside from screen issues. The small examples are intrinsically large.

*As is the scope of the problems you're trying to solve.*

**Peter:** That's right. They're general purpose and AWK is not. One of the early programs written in AWK was an assembler for some attached processor. I was horrified. He didn't clearly explain why he was doing it that way, but it was clear that it was a lot easier to get started with an interpreted language, and the shell wasn't powerful enough.

*I'd like to see programming become more accessible to everyday people, but I also like programs that become more reliable and easier to compose them into larger metaprograms. It's difficult to resolve those ideas.*

**Peter:** Some composability can be helped by language design and idiom. Reliability, well, that's hard. Clean design is hard, too.

*How do you recognize a clean design?*

**Peter:** There's a sort of metaissue here. I used to be a lot more confident in my judgments than I am now. You look at it and you try to write small examples. You think about what the people are saying about it. One of the things that's essentially always true is that the clean examples that people use in text books are completely unrealistic. There may be a class that looks like the ones in introduction to object-oriented programming, but I don't believe it. They all have many, many members, which are capable of responding to many messages. The useful object that you can put into programs and understand what the state of your program is a lot of stuff. I think you put up with a certain amount of complication if the reward seems great enough.

*Or the perceived reward.*

**Peter:** Right. That's all you get. This is software engineering. There's nothing quantitative. Perceived and real are the same because we can't measure real, or at least have shown no inclination to measure real.

*We can't even measure productivity, and that makes it difficult to measure better or worse.*

**Peter:** It does, but I don't think that's the point. If you're in a real engineering field, you measure the results. You do bridges. How much did this bridge cost? How hard was it to build? Does it stand up?

For programs, you can measure how hard it was to build, how much money you spent building it, but the rest of it is just a complete mystery. Does it do what it says well? How would we know? How would you describe what it's supposed to do?

*We don't have a material science for software.*

**Peter:** I have this expectation that when the hardware people finally run out of oomph, it is possible there will be more of an engineering principle to software. Everything's been changing so fast. It's a sort of doubtful analogy, but if the properties of concrete and steel were changing 10% every year, structural engineering would look a lot different.

That's a speculation because there's no reason it would have to look different. It's just the models would say 2007, 2008, 2009. Since we never had any models in software, I guess we can't do that.

*We talk about software. We don't have atoms. We don't have physical properties.*

**Peter:** That's right. It's not quite like mathematics. It doesn't live completely in people's heads. It's almost completely humanly constructed, and the constraints on it are some combination of mathematics that has to do with computability and algorithm complexity, and whatever the hardware guys give us. That part's been changing rapidly.

*Another point you made was that there's a real difference between a computer programmer and a theorem. You can prove a theorem and then you know something, but you write a computer program and all of the sudden you can do something you couldn't do before.*

**Peter:** I still think that's mostly valid. Of course the more modern versions of theorems sometimes come with algorithms, not surprisingly, because computing things turns out to be so useful the boundaries have become a little blurred.

People before the age of computers thought about how hard it was to compute. There was stuff they computed. Scientific literature has a number of places where you look into the notebooks of some of these guys and they did amazing calculations by hand, just elaborate calculations, and then here's the answer. I don't think the distinction is totally categorical. At the time it had struck me since I started out as a mathematician.

*Will there be a computing revolution where we start thinking of components as theorems?*

**Peter:** Not until we learn how to describe them. The kinds of descriptions that have been most widely used are purely functional. This is how the input is transformed into the output. It says nothing or hardly anything about how long it takes. It says almost nothing about how much memory it requires. It's a little vague on what kind of environment it needs to run in. The theorems, to be fair, they're human as opposed to machine theorems, but they do come with hypothesis and conclusions. That's open to only modest interpretation, whereas with the software, you need to interpret a lot.

There are plenty of nasty examples. That list I gave even left out things like a real careful specification of the input. There are programs that are known to have failed when you move them from 16 bits to 32 bits, because someplace in them was intrinsically 16 bit, and you didn't know that. It's hard to describe all that stuff. It's not fair, but the favorite example of that is programs that have been proved correct which have bugs. Unfortunately there was something about it that didn't model reality. People never noticed.

The type guys have this problem. They want to be able to do a type induction guarantee, which keeps the strength of the system fairly weak. At one other extreme in this multidimensional space is a C++ template, which can compute anything at compile time with just the speed you can expect, but since you can compute anything, it's going to be slow anyway.

*That's a more interesting answer to what's bothering us about computer science. Computers aren't getting faster. They're getting wider.*

**Peter:** Exponential growth of goodness is a good environment to live in.

*I realized recently that when the growth in data since the 70s has dwarfed the growth in processor speeds. Take SQL, designed then, and it can still cope with this huge explosion in data sizes. Other languages don't fare as well.*

**Peter:** I would say there's roughly a thousand times gain in CPU speed since then. That's not the number in data. The experience in computing I think is that you get some $10^n$ improvement over time. It's not a bad approximation to say $10^{n/2}$ of that was in hardware, and $10^{n/2}$ of that was in algorithms. I think that's true here.

A lot of work has gone into making query optimizers and better understanding of database design to make it possible for them to have these terabyte databases.

### How do hardware resources affect the mindset of software programmers?

**Peter:** Programmers are too varied a class to generalize about. You have to be aware of the constraints. For instance, the speed of light is what it is, and is not improving. Some things that work well locally are disastrous remotely. All those layers of abstraction and helpful libraries allow us to get programs nearly working quickly, but have pernicious effects on speed and robustness.

### Do you first identify the right algorithms and then make them run faster, or do you focus on speed from the beginning?

**Peter:** If it's a problem you have some understanding of, you build the algorithm in a way that keeps the performance good in the parts you think need it, and then it's possible to tune it if necessary. Generally it's more important that the algorithm work, and it's harder to rearrange the implementation after a lot of tuning. But it's not unusual to discover that something is bigger, or used more often, than expected, so that quadratic algorithms are intolerable, or even that too much time is spent copying and sorting. Many sorts of programs perform adequately without much work. Modern computers are very fast, and a lot of the perceived delay is in networks or I/O.

### How do you search for problems in software?

**Peter:** The trick is finding problems you can solve. There are plenty of problems in software that turn out to be too hard, and for many of the ones that aren't, just scale them up a couple of powers of 10, and the old solutions frequently don't work so well.

### Once you have something that mostly works, what do you do?

**Peter:** If it's for my own use, I just stop there, hoping I'll remember enough context to upgrade it. For professional things, one really ought to document it, try to harden it against various sorts of bad situations, and add enough comments to the code that someone else could easily maintain it (or as easily as I could). This last thing is hard. Well-commented code is rare.

*There is a Unix philosophy that says, "If you don't know how to do something well, you don't do it." Can this artistic approach spread beyond Unix?*

**Peter:** This is a lot bigger question than just software. Most of our lives, we have to do things we don't know how to do well. It was a luxury we got in Unix, plus the original Unix folks figured out how to do many things very well.

It might be interesting to explore the hard-nosed hypothesis that when businesses don't follow this approach they don't do as well, but I doubt the data would be convincing, one way or the other. The natural (and no doubt shallow) comparison is between Microsoft and Apple, but how do you measure, critical acclaim or cumulative profits?

# CHAPTER SEVEN

# Lua

Lua is a very small, self-contained dynamic language created by Roberto Ierusalimschy, Luiz Henrique de Figueiredo, and Waldemar Celes in 1993. Lua's small set of powerful features and easy-to-use C API make the language easy to embed and extend to express domain-specific concepts. Lua is prominent in the world of proprietary software, where games such as Blizzard's *World of Warcraft* and Crytek GmbH's *Crysis*, as well as Adobe's Photoshop Lightroom, use it for scripting and UI work. Its predecessors are Lisp, Scheme, and perhaps AWK; it has design similarities to JavaScript, Icon, and Tcl.

# The Power of Scripting

*How do you define Lua?*

**Luiz Henrique de Figueiredo:** An embeddable, lightweight, fast, powerful scripting language.

**Roberto Ierusalimschy:** Unfortunately, more and more people use "scripting language" as a synonym for "dynamic language." Nowadays even Erlang or Scheme are called scripting languages. That is sad, because we lose the precision to describe a particular class of dynamic languages. Lua is a scripting language in the original meaning of the expression. A language to control other components, usually written in another language.

*What should people keep in mind when designing software with Lua?*

**Luiz:** That there probably is a Lua way of doing things. It's not recommended to try to emulate all practices from other languages. You have to really use the features of your language, although I guess that is true for any language. In the case of Lua, those features are mainly tables for everything and metamethods for elegant solutions. Also coroutines.

*Who should use Lua?*

**Roberto:** I think that most applications without a scripting facility could benefit from Lua.

**Luiz:** The problem is that most designers do not see this need untill much later, when much code has already been written in say C or C++, and they feel that it's too late now. Application designers should consider scripting from the start. This will give them much more flexibility. It will also give them better perspective about performance, by forcing them to think where the application *needs* raw performance and where it does not matter at all, and so can be delegated to the easier, shorter development cycle of scripting.

*From a security point of view, what does Lua offer to the programmer?*

**Roberto:** The core of the Lua interpreter is built as a "freestanding application." This is a term from ISO C that basically means that the program does not use anything from the environment (no `stdio`, `malloc`, etc.). All those facilities are provided by external libraries. With this architecture, it is very easy to create programs with limited access to external resources. For instance, we can create sandboxes within Lua itself, just erasing from its environment whatever we consider dangerous (e.g., `fileopen`).

**Luiz:** Lua also offers user-defined debug hooks that can be used to monitor the execution of a Lua program and so, for instance, abort it if it takes too long or uses too much memory.

*What are the limits of Lua?*

**Roberto:** I think the main limits of Lua are what I consider the limits of any dynamic language. First, even with the most advanced JIT technology (and Lua has one of the best JITs among dynamic languages), you cannot get the performance of a good static language. Second, several complex programs really can benefit from static analysis (mainly static typing).

## Why did you decide to use a garbage collector?

**Roberto:** Lua has always used a garbage collector, since day-one. I would say that, for an interpreted language, a garbage collector can be much more compact and robust than reference counting, not to mention that it does not leave garbage around. Given that an interpreted language usually already has self-described data (values with tags and things like that), a simple mark-and-sweep collector can be really simple, and almost does not affect the rest of the interpreter.

And for an untyped language, reference counting can be very heavy. Without static typing, every single assignment may change counts, and so needs a dynamic check both in the old and in the new value of a variable. Later experiences with reference count in Lua did not improve performance at all.

## Are you satisfied with the way Lua manages numbers?

**Roberto:** In my experience, numbers in computers will always be a source of occasional surprises (as they are outside computers, too!). I consider the use of a double as the single numeric type in Lua a reasonable compromise for Lua. We have considered many other options, but most are too slow, too complex, or too memory-hungry for Lua. Even using double is not a reasonable choice for embedded systems, so we can compile the interpreter with an alternative numerical type, such as long.

## Why did you choose tables as the unifying data constructor in Lua?

**Roberto:** From my side, I was inspired by VDM (a formal method mainly for software specification), something I was involved when we started Lua. VDM offers three forms of collections: sets, sequences, and maps. But both sets and sequences are easily expressed as maps, so I had this idea of maps as a unifying constructor. Luiz brought his own reasons, too.

**Luiz:** Yes, I liked AWK a lot, especially its associative arrays.

## What value do programmers derive from first-class functions in Lua?

**Roberto:** Under different names, from subroutines to methods, "functions" have been a staple of programming languages for more than 50 years, so a good support for functions is an asset in any language. The support that Lua offers allows programmers to use several powerful techniques from the functional-programming world, such as representing data as functions. For instance, a shape may be represented by a function that, given $x$ and $y$, tells whether that point lies within the shape. This representation makes trivial operations like union and intersection.

Lua uses functions also in some unconventional ways, and the fact that they are first class simplifies those uses. For instance, every chunk (any piece of code that we feed to the interpreter) is compiled like a function body, so any conventional function definition in Lua is always nested inside an outer function. That means that even trivial Lua programs need first-class functions.

## Why did you implement closures?

**Roberto:** Closures are the kind of construct we always want in Lua: simple, generic, and powerful. Since version 1, Lua has had functions as first-class values, and they proved to be really useful, even for "regular" programmers without previous experience with functional programming, but without closures, the use of first-class functions is somewhat restricted. By the way, the term *closure* refers to an implementation technique, not the feature itself, which is "first-class functions with lexical scoping," but *closure* is certainly shorter. :)

## How do you plan to deal with concurrency?

**Roberto:** We do not believe in multithreading, that is, shared memory with preemption. In the HOPL paper,* we wrote, "We still think that no one can write correct programs in a language where $a=a+1$ is not deterministic." We can avoid this problem by removing either preemption or shared memory, and Lua offers support for both approaches.

With coroutines, we have shared memory without preemption, but this is of no use for multicore machines. But multiple "processes" can explore quite effectively those machines. By "process" I mean a C thread with its own Lua state, so that, at the Lua level, there is no memory sharing. In the second edition of *Programming in Lua* [Lua.org], I already presented a prototype of such implementation, and recently we have seen libraries to support this approach (e.g., Lua Lanes and luaproc).

## You don't support concurrency, but you did implement an interesting solution for multitasking—namely, asymmetrical coroutines. How do they work?

**Roberto:** I had some experience with Modula 2 (my wife wrote a full interpreter for M-code during her Master's work), and I always liked the idea of using coroutines as a basis for cooperative concurrency and other control structures. However, symmetrical coroutines, as provided by Modula 2, would not work in Lua.

**Luiz:** In our HOPL paper we explained all those design decisions in great detail.

**Roberto:** We ended up with this asymmetrical model. The underlying idea is really simple. We create a coroutine with an explicit call to a `coroutine.create` function, giving a function to be executed as the coroutine body. When we resume the coroutine, it starts running its body and goes until it ends or it yields; a coroutine only yields by explicitly calling the yield function. Then, later, we can resume it again, and it will continue from where it stopped.

The general idea is very similar to Python's generators, but with a key difference: a Lua coroutine can yield inside nested calls, while in Python a generator can only yield from its main function. Thinking about the implementation, this means that a coroutine must

---

\* R. Ierusalimschy, L. H. de Figueiredo, and W. Celes, "The evolution of Lua," Proceedings of ACM HOPL III (2007).

have an independent stack, just like a thread. What is surprising is how much more powerful these "stackful" coroutines are, compared with "flat" generators. For instance, we can implement one-shot continuations on top of them.

## Experience

*How do you define success in terms of your work?*

**Luiz:** The success of a language depends on the number of programmers using it and on the success of the applications that use it. We don't really know how many people program in Lua, but there certainly are many successful applications using Lua, including several very successful games. Also, the range of applications that use Lua, from desktop image processing to embedded control of robots, shows that there is a clear niche for Lua. Finally, Lua is the only language created in a developing country to have achieved such global relevance. It is the only such language to have ever been featured in ACM HOPL.

**Roberto:** This is difficult. I work in several fronts, and at each of them I feel success differently. Overall, I would say that common to most of these definitions is "to be known." It is always a great pleasure to be introduced to someone, or to contact someone, and to be recognized.

*Do you have any regrets about the language?*

**Luiz:** I don't really have any regrets. In hindsight we could have done some things earlier if we knew how to do them as we do now!

**Roberto:** I am not sure I regret something specific, but language design involves several tough decisions. For me, the most difficult decisions are those about ease of use. One of the aims of Lua is to be easy for nonprofessional programmers. I do not fit into this category. So, several decisions about the language are not the ideal ones from my perspective as a user. A typical example is Lua's syntax: many uses of Lua benefit from its verbose syntax, but for my own taste I would rather use a more compact notation.

*Did you make mistakes of design or implementation?*

**Luiz:** I don't think that we have made any big mistakes in designing or implementing Lua. We just learned how to evolve a language, which is much more than merely defining its syntax and semantics and implementing it. There are also important social issues, such as creating and supporting a community, with manuals, books, websites, mailing lists, chat rooms, etc. We certainly learned the value of supporting a community and also about the hard work that has to be put into that as well as into designing and coding.

**Roberto:** Luckily we did not make big mistakes, but I think we made many small ones along the way. But we had the chance to correct them as Lua evolved. Of course this annoyed some users, because of incompatibilities between versions, but now Lua is quite stable.

### What do you suggest to become a better programmer?

**Luiz:** Never be afraid to start over, which of course is much easier said than done. Never underestimate the need for attention to detail. Don't add functionality that you *think* will be useful some time in the future: adding it now may prevent you from adding a much better feature later on, when it's really needed. Finally, always aim for the simpler solution. As simple as possible, but not simpler, as Einstein said.

**Roberto:** Learn new programming languages, but only from good books! Haskell is a language that all programmers should know. Study computer science: new algorithms, new formalisms (lambda calculus, if you do not know it yet, pi calculus, CSP, etc.). Always try to improve your own code.

### What's the biggest problem with computer science and how we teach it?

**Roberto:** I guess there is no such thing as "computer science" as a well-understood corpus of knowledge. Not that computer science is not science, but what is computer science and what is not (and what is important and what is not) is still too ill defined. Many people in computer science do not have a formal background in computer science.

**Luiz:** I consider myself as a mathematician interested in the role of computers in mathematics, but of course I do like computers a lot. :)

**Roberto:** Even among those with a formal background there is no uniformity, we miss a common ground. Many people think Java created monitors, virtual machines, interfaces (as opposed to classes), etc.

### Are a lot of CS programs glorified job-training programs?

**Roberto:** Yes. And many programmers do not even have a CS degree.

**Luiz:** I don't think so, but I'm not employed as a programmer. On the other hand, I think it would be wrong to require programmers to have CS degrees, or certifications, or anything of that sort. A CS degree is no guarantee that one can program well, and many good programmers don't have a CS degree (perhaps this was true when I started; I'm probably too old now). My point is that a CS degree is no guarantee that one can program well.

**Roberto:** It is wrong to require most professionals to have degrees, but what I meant was that the "culture" in the area is too weak. There are very few things you can assume people must know. Of course a hirer may demand whatever he wants, but there should not be laws requiring degrees.

### What is the role of math in computer science and programming in particular?

**Luiz:** Well, I'm a mathematician. I see math everywhere. I was attracted to programming probably because it definitely has mathematical qualities: precision, abstraction, elegance. A program is a proof of a complicated theorem that you can continually refine and improve, and it actually does something!

Of course I don't think in those terms at all when programming, but I think that learning math is very important to programming in general. It helps you get into a certain frame of mind. It's much easier to program if you're used to thinking about abstract things that have their own rules.

**Roberto:** According to Christos H. Papadimitriou, "computer science is the new math." A programmer can only go so far without math. In a broader view, both math and programming share the same key mental discipline: abstraction. They also share a key tool: formal logic. A good programmer uses "math" all the time, establishing code invariants, models for interfaces, etc.

*A lot of programming languages are created by mathematicians—maybe that is why programming is difficult!*

**Roberto:** I will leave this question to our mathematician. :)

**Luiz:** Well, I've said before that programming definitely has mathematical qualities: precision, abstraction, elegance. Designing programming languages feels to me like building a mathematical theory: you provide powerful tools to enable others to do good work. I've always been attracted to programming languages that are small and powerful. There's beauty in having powerful primitives and constructs, just like there is beauty in having powerful definitions and basic theorems.

*How do you recognize a good programmer?*

**Luiz:** You just know it. Nowadays, I tend to recognize bad programmers more easily—not because their programs are bad (although they frequently are a complicated, unstable mess), but because you can sense they are not comfortable at programming, as if their own programs were a burden and a mystery to them.

*How should debugging be taught?*

**Luiz:** I don't think debugging can be taught, at least not formally, but it can be learned by doing it when you are in a debugging session with someone else, perhaps more experienced than you are. You can then learn debugging strategies from them: how to narrow down the problem, how to make predictions and assess outcomes, what is useless and just adds to noise, etc.

**Roberto:** Debugging is essentially problem solving. It is an activity where you may have to use all intellectual tools you ever learned. Of course there are some useful tricks (e.g., avoid a debugger if you can, use a memory checker if programming in a low-level language like C), but these tricks are only a small part of debugging. You should learn debugging as you learn to program.

*How do you test and debug your code?*

**Luiz:** I try mainly to construct and test it piece by piece. I rarely use a debugger. When I do, it's for C code, never for Lua code. For Lua, a few well-placed `print` statements usually work just fine.

**Roberto:** I follow a similar approach. When I use a debugger, frequently it's only to do a *where* to find where the code is crashing. For C code, a tool like Valgrind or Purify is essential.

## What is the role of comments in the source code?

**Roberto:** Very small. I usually consider that if something needs comments, it is not well written. For me, a comment is almost a note like "I should try to rewrite this code later." I think clear code is much more readable than commented code.

**Luiz:** I agree. I stick to comments that say something that the code does not make obvious.

## How should a project be documented?

**Roberto:** Brute force. No amount of tools is a substitute for well-written and well-thought-out documentation.

**Luiz:** But producing good documentation about the evolution of a project is only possible if we have that in mind from the start. That did not happen with Lua; we never planned Lua to grow so much and be as widely used as it is today. When we were writing the HOPL paper (which took almost two years!), we found it hard to recall how some design decisions had been made. On the other hand, if in the early days we had had meetings with formal records, we would probably have lost some of the spontaneity and missed some of the fun.

## What factors do you measure during the evolution of a codebase?

**Luiz:** I would have to say "simplicity of the implementation." With this comes speed and correctness of the implementation. At the same time, flexibility is also an important point, so that you can change an implementation if needed.

## How do available hardware resources affect the mindset of programmers?

**Luiz:** I'm an old guy. :-) I learned programming on an IBM 370. It took hours between punching cards, submitting it to the queue, and getting the printouts. I have seen all kind of slow machines. I think programmers should be exposed to them, because not everyone in the world has the fastest machines. People programming applications for the masses should try them on slow machines to get a feel for the wider user experience. Of course, they can use the best machines for development: it's not fun having to wait a long time for a compilation to finish. In these days of global Internet, web developers should try slow connections, not the hyperfast ones they have at work. Aiming for an average platform will make your product faster, simpler, and better.

In the case of Lua, the "hardware" is the C compiler. One thing that we learned in implementing Lua is that aiming for portability does pay. Almost from the beginning, we have implemented Lua in very strict ANSI/ISO C (C89). This has allowed Lua to run in special hardware, such as robots, printer firmware, network routers, etc., none of which was ever an actual target for us.

**Roberto:** One golden principle is that you should always treat hardware resources as limited. Of course they are *always* limited. "Nature abhors a vacuum"; any program tends to expand until it uses all available resources. Moreover, at the same time that resources become cheaper in established platforms, new platforms emerge with severe restrictions. It happened with the microcomputer; it happened with mobile phones; it is happening all the time. If you want to be the first to market, you'd better be prepared to be very conscious about what resources your programs need.

*What do the lessons about the invention, further development, and adoption of your language say to people developing computer systems today and in the foreseeable future?*

**Luiz:** I think that one has to keep in mind that not all applications are going run in powerful desktop machines or laptops. Many applications are going to run in constrained devices such as cell phones or even smaller devices. People that design and implement software tools should be especially concerned about this issue, because you can never tell where and how your tool is going to be used. So, design for using minimal resources, and you may be pleasantly surprised to see your tool used in many contexts that you did not have as a primary goal and some that you did not even know existed. This has happened with Lua! And for a good reason; we have an internal joke, which is not really a joke: when we discuss the inclusion of a feature in Lua, we ask ourselves, "OK, but will it run in a microwave oven?"

## Language Design

*Lua is easy to embed and requires very few resources. How do you design for limited resources of hardware, memory, and software?*

**Roberto:** When we started, we did not have those goals very clear. We just had to meet them to deliver our project. As we evolved, those goals became more clear to us. Now, I guess the main point is to be economic in all aspects, all the time. Whenever someone suggests some new feature, for instance, the first question is how much it will cost.

*Have you rejected features because they were too expensive?*

**Roberto:** Almost all features are "too expensive" to what they bring to the language. As an example, even a simple `continue` statement did not pass our criteria.

*How much benefit does a feature have to add to be worth its expense?*

**Roberto:** No fixed rules, but a good rule is whether the feature "surprises" us; that is, it is useful for things other than its initial motivation. That remind me of another rule of thumb: how many users would benefit from the feature. Some features are useful for only a small fraction of users, while others are useful to mostly everyone.

*Do you have an example of a feature you added that is useful to more people?*

**Roberto:** The `for` loop. We resisted even this, but when it appeared, it changed *all the examples* in the book! Weak tables are also surprisingly useful. Not many people use them, but they should.

*You waited seven years after version 1.0 before adding the* `for` *loop. What made you keep it out? What made you include it?*

**Roberto:** We kept it out because we could not find a format for the `for` loop that was both generic and simple. We included it when we found a good format, using generator functions. Actually, closures were a key ingredient to make generators easy and generic enough to use, because with closures the generator function itself can keep internal state during a loop.

*Is that another area of expense: updating code to take advantage of new features and newly discovered best practices?*

**Roberto:** People do not have to use new features.

*Do people choose one version of Lua and stick with it throughout the lifetime of the project, never upgrading?*

**Roberto:** I guess most people in games do exactly that, but in other areas I think several projects evolve the Lua version they use. As a counterexample, *World of Warcraft* did change from Lua 5.0 to Lua 5.1! However, keep in mind that Lua now is much more stable than when it was younger.

*How do you share development responsibilities—in particular, writing code?*

**Luiz:** The first versions of Lua were coded by Waldemar in 1993. Since around 1995, Roberto has written and maintained the bulk of the code. I'm responsible for a small part of the code: the bytecode dump/undump modules and the standalone compiler, luac. We have always done code revisions and sent suggestions by email to the others about changes to the code, and we have long meetings about new features and their implementation.

*Do you get much feedback on the language or the implementation from the users? Do you have a formal mechanism for including user feedback in the language and its revisions?*

**Roberto:** We joke that whatever we do not remember was not that important in the first place. The Lua discussion list is quite active, but some people equate open software with a community project. Once I sent the following message to the Lua list, which summarizes our approach:

> Lua is open software, but it has never been open developed. That does not mean we do not listen to other people. We read practically every message in the mailing list. Several important features in Lua started or evolved from outside contributions (e.g., metatables, coroutines, and the implementation of closures, to name just some big ones), but ultimately we decide. We do not do this because we consider our judgment better than others'. It is only because we want Lua to be the language we want it to be, not to be the most popular language in the world.
>
> Because of this development style, we prefer not to have a public repository for Lua. We do not want to have to explain every single change we make to the code. We do not want to keep documentation updated all the time. We want freedom to follow strange ideas and then to give up without having to explain every move.

*Why do you like to get suggestions and ideas, but not code? One thing that comes to my mind is that maybe writing the code on your own allows you to learn something more about the problem/solution.*

**Roberto:** It is something like that. We like to fully understand what is going on in Lua, so a piece of code is not a big contribution. A piece of code does not explain why it is the way it is, but once we understand the underlying ideas, writing the code is fun we do not want to miss.

**Luiz:** I think we also had concerns about including third-party code about which we could not guarantee ownership. We certainly did not want to get drowned in the legal processes of having people license their code to us.

*Will Lua reach a point where you've added all of the features you want to add, and the only changes are refinements to the implementation (LuaJIT, for example)?*

**Roberto:** I feel we are at such a point now. We have added if not all, most of the features we wanted.

*How do you handle smoke testing and regression testing? One of the big benefits I've seen from having an open repository is that you can get people performing automated testing against almost every revision.*

**Luiz:** Lua releases are not that frequent, so when a release does come out, it has been tested a lot. We only release work versions (pre-alpha) when it's already pretty solid, so that people can see what the new features are.

**Roberto:** We do perform strong regression testing. The point is that, because our code is ANSI C, we usually have very few portability problems. We do not need to test changes in several different machines. I perform all regression tests whenever I change anything in the code, but it is all automated; all I have to do is type test all.

*When you find a recurrent problem, how do you recognize if the best solution is a local workaround or a global fix?*

**Luiz:** We always try to provide bug fixes as soon as bugs are found. However, since we don't release new versions of Lua frequently, we tend to wait until there are enough fixes to justify the release of a minor version. We leave all improvements that are not bug fixes to major versions. If the issue is complicated (which is quite infrequent), we provide a local workaround in the minor version and a global fix in the next major version.

**Roberto:** Usually, a local workaround will get you really soon. We should go for a workaround only if it is really impossible to do a global fix—for instance, if a global fix demands a new, incompatible interface.

*Would you still design for limited resources now, some years after you started?*

**Roberto:** Sure, our mind is always focused on that. We consider even the order of fields inside C structures to save a few bytes. :)

**Luiz:** And there are more people putting Lua in small devices today than ever before.

*How does the desire for simplicity affect the language design from a user perspective? I think of the support for Lua classes, which reminds me a lot of OO in C in some ways (but much less annoying).*

**Roberto:** Currently we have a rule of "mechanisms instead of policies." That keeps the language simple, but as you said, the user must provide his own policies. This is the case with classes. There are many ways to implement them. Some users love this; others hate it.

**Luiz:** It does give Lua a do-it-yourself flavor.

*Tcl took a similar approach, but it led to fragmentation, as every library or shop had its own approach. Is fragmentation less of an issue because of Lua's intended purpose?*

**Roberto:** Yes. Sometimes it is a problem, but for many kinds of uses (e.g., games) this is not an issue. Lua is mostly used embedded in some other application, and so the application provides a firmer framework for unifying programming styles. You have Lua/Lightroom, Lua/WoW, Lua/Wireshark—each has its own internal culture.

*Do you consider Lua's "we provide mechanisms" style of malleability a tremendous benefit then?*

**Roberto:** Not exactly. As most other things, it is a compromise. Sometimes it is very useful to have policies ready for use. "We provide mechanisms" is quite flexible, but needs more work and brings fragmentation of styles. It is also quite economic.

**Luiz:** On the other hand, sometimes it's hard to explain this to users. I mean, to make them understand what the mechanisms are and what the rationale for them is.

*Does that work against code sharing between projects?*

**Roberto:** Yes, frequently. It has hindered the growth of independent libraries, too. For instance, WoW has tons of libraries (they even have an implementation for the traveling salesman problem using genetic programming), but nobody uses that outside WoW.

*Do you worry that Lua has splintered somewhat into WoW/Lua, Lightroom/Lua, etc., because of this?*

**Luiz:** We do not worry: the language remains the same. The available functions differ. I guess these applications benefit from this in some ways.

*Are serious Lua users writing their own dialects on top of Lua?*

**Roberto:** Maybe. At least we do not have macros. I guess with macros you could create a real new dialect.

**Luiz:** Not a language dialect per se, but a dialect as domain-specific language implemented with functions, yes. That was the goal of Lua. When Lua is used just for data files, it can look like it's a dialect, but of course they are just Lua tables. There are some projects that do macros, more or less. I recall metalua, for instance. This is a problem with Lisp.

*Why did you choose to provide extensible semantics?*

**Roberto:** It started as a way to provide OO features. We did not want to add OO mechanisms to Lua, but users wanted them, so we came up with this idea of providing enough mechanisms for users to implement their own OO mechanisms. We still think this was a good decision. Although this makes OO programming in Lua more difficult for beginners, it brings a lot of flexibility to the language. In particular, when we use Lua mixed with other languages (a Lua hallmark), this flexibility allows the programmer to fit Lua's object model with the object model of the external language.

*How does the current environment of hardware, software, services, and networks differ from the environment in which your system was originally designed? How do these changes affect your system and call for further adaptations?*

**Roberto:** Because Lua aims to a very high degree of portability, I would say that the current "environments" are not that different from old ones. For instance, when we started the development of Lua, DOS/Windows 3 were 16-bit machines; some old machines were still 8 bit. Currently we do not have 16-bit desktops, but several platforms where Lua is used (embedded systems) are still 16 bits or even 8 bits.  ·

One big change was in C. When we started Lua, back in 1993, ISO (ANSI) C was not yet as established as it is today. Many platforms still used K&R C, and many applications had some complex scheme of macros to be compiled with K&R C and with ANSI C, the main difference being the declaration of function headers. At that time, it was a bold decision to stick with ANSI C.

**Luiz:** And we still haven't felt the need to move to C99. Lua is implemented in C89. Perhaps we'll have to use some parts of C99 (especially the new size-specific types) if glitches surface in the transition to 64-bit machines, but I don't expect any.

*If you could build the Lua VM all over again, would you stick with ANSI C, or do you wish there were a better language for low-level cross-platform development?*

**Roberto:** No. ANSI C is the most portable language I know (currently).

**Luiz:** There are excellent ANSI C compilers out there, but even using their extensions does not give us much improved performance.

**Roberto:** It is not easy to improve ANSI C and keep its portability and performance.

*This is C89/90, by the way?*

**Roberto:** Yes. C99 is not very well established yet.

**Luiz:** Plus I'm not sure C99 would bring us many additional features. I am especially thinking about labeled gotos available in gcc as an alternative to switch (in the main switch of the vm execution).

**Roberto:** This is something that could improve performance in many machines.

**Luiz:** We tested it early on, and someone else tested it recently, and the gains are not spectacular.

**Roberto:** In part because of our register-based architecture. It favors less opcodes with more work in each one. This decreases the impact of the dispatcher.

*Why did you build a register-based VM?*

**Roberto:** To avoid all those getlocal/setlocal instructions. We also wanted to play with the idea. We thought that, if it did not work well, we could at least write some papers about it. In the end, it worked quite well, and we wrote only one paper. :)

*Does running in a VM help with debugging?*

**Roberto:** It does not "help"; it changes the whole concept of debugging. Anyone who has ever debugged programs in both compiled and interpreted languages (e.g., C versus Java) knows they are miles apart. A good VM makes the language safe, in the sense that errors can always be understood in terms of the language itself, not in term of the underlying machine (e.g., segmentation fault).

*When a language is platform-independent, how does this affect the debugging?*

**Roberto:** Usually it eases debugging, because the more platform-independent a language is, the more it needs a solid abstract description and behavior.

*Considering that we are humans and we know for sure we are going to make mistakes when writing software, have you ever thought about which features you needed to add or remove to the language just to aid the debugging phase?*

**Roberto:** Sure. A first step to aid debugging is good error messages.

**Luiz:** Error messages in Lua have improved since the earlier versions. We have moved from the dreaded "call expression not a function" error message, which existed up until Lua 3.2, to much better error messages such as "attempt to call global 'f' (a nil value)". Since Lua 5.0, we use symbolic execution of the bytecode to try and provide useful error messages.

**Roberto:** In the design of the language itself, we always try to avoid constructs with complex explanations. If it is hard to understand, it is harder to debug.

*What is the link between the design of the language and the design of programs written with that language?*

**Roberto:** At least for me, a main component when designing a language is *user cases*, that is, considerations about how users would use each feature and the combination of features of the language. Of course programmers will always find new ways to use a language, and a good language should allow unanticipated usages, but the "normal" use of the language follows what the designers intended when they created the language.

*How much does the implementation of the language affect the design of the language?*

**Roberto:** This is a two-way street. The implementation has a huge impact on the language: we should not design what we cannot implement efficiently. Some people forget it, but efficiency is always a (or the) main constraint in the design of any software. However the design also may have a huge impact on the implementation. At first sight, several distinctive aspects of Lua come from its implementation (small size, good API with C, portability), but the design of Lua plays a key role to enable such implementation.

*I read in one of your papers that "Lua uses a handwritten scanner and a handwritten recursive descent parser." How did you start thinking about the idea of building a parser by hand? Was it clear since the beginning that it could have been much better than the yacc-generated one?*

**Roberto:** The first versions of Lua used both lex and yacc, but one of the main original goals of Lua was to be used as a data-description language, not unlike XML.

**Luiz:** But much earlier.

**Roberto:** Soon people started using Lua in data files with several megabytes, and the lex-generated scanner quickly became a bottleneck. It is quite easy to write a good scanner by hand and that single change improved Lua performance by something like 30%.

The decision to change from yacc to a handwritten parser came much later, and was not that easy. It started with problems with the skeleton code that most yacc/bison implementations use.

They were not quite portable at the time (e.g., several used malloc.h, a non-ANSI C header), and we did not have a good control of their overall quality (e.g., how they handled stack overflows or memory-allocation errors), and they were not reentrant (in the sense of calling the parser during parsing). Also, a bottom-up parser is not as good as a top-down one when you want to generate code on the fly, as Lua does, because it is difficult to handle "inherited attributes." After we made the change, we saw that our handwritten parser was a little faster and smaller than the yacc-generated one, but that was not a main reason for the change.

**Luiz:** A top-down parser also allows better error messages.

**Roberto:** However I would never recommend a handwritten parser of any kind for a language without a mature syntax. And for sure LR(1) (or LALR or even SRL) is much more powerful than LL(1). Even for a simple syntax like Lua's, we had to make some tricks to have a decent parser. For instance, the routines for binary expressions do not follow the original grammar at all, but instead we use a smart recursive priority-based approach. In my compiler classes, I always recommend yacc to my students.

*Do you have any interesting anecdote from your teaching experience?*

**Roberto:** When I started teaching programming, the main computer facility for our students was a mainframe. Once it happened that a program assignment from a very good group failed even to compile. I talked to them, and they swore they tested their program carefully, with several test cases, and it was working OK. Of course they and I were using exactly the same environment, the mainframe. The mystery remained until a few weeks later, when I learned that the Pascal compiler had been upgraded. The upgrade happened between they finished their task and I started correction. Their program had a very small syntactic error (an extra semicolon, if I recall correctly) that the old compiler did not detect!

# CHAPTER EIGHT

# Haskell

Haskell is a purely functional, lazy language, originally designed as an open standard for modern functional languages. This first Haskell Report appeared in 1990, and a "standard" was adopted in 1998. But the language has evolved considerably over the years, in particular with respect to its type system, which has many novel features. Haskell has grown in popularity recently, with numerous and substantive libraries, many real-world applications, significant improvements in implementations (most notably, the preeminent Glasgow Haskell Compiler [GHC]), and a burgeoning, supportive community of users. Haskell is particularly interesting for research into domain-specific languages, concurrency, and the disciplined control of state. The high level of abstractions it provides for solving problems is unparelleled—at least, once you understand the Haskell approach to software design.

*Editors' Note: This interview is based on email exchanges with Paul Hudak, John Hughes, Simon Peyton Jones, and Philip Wadler, and then integrated with a phone interview with Simon Peyton Jones.*

# A Functional Team

*How do you develop a language in a team?*

**Simon Peyton Jones:** We were fortunate in having a shared goal (that of developing a common lazy functional programming language) and having broadly compatible technical agendas. Our paper on the history of Haskell* describes various tactics that we employed (face-to-face meetings, email, having an Editor and Syntax Tzar). We were also unencumbered by having existing users with the accompanying need for backward compatibility. There were no companies involved, thus freeing us from dealing with (incompatible) corporate goals.

**John Hughes:** We shared a vision. We were all passionate about functional programming—there was tremendous excitement in the field at that time, and we all wanted to contribute everything we could to make the functional programming dream a reality. Not only that, but we respected each other very highly. I think both the passion and the respect were essential to get us through the many inevitable awkward decisions that we had to take.

**Paul Hudak:** You start with a common vision. Without that, I doubt that you'd get very far. The original members of the Haskell Committee had a spectacularly common vision.

Add to that a lot of energy. The Haskell Committee had a ridiculous amount of energy. They were like a herd of wild animals.

You also need humility. Like the mythical man-month, having more workers doesn't mean that things get done more quickly, because, despite the common vision, there will be differences. We had plenty of differences, but we had enough humility to make compromises.

Finally, you need leadership. We were lucky in that we were able to share the leadership—I think that's pretty unusual. There was always one person who was driving the action, we always knew who that person was, and we trusted him to get the job done.

*How did you merge your ideas into a cohesive whole?*

**Simon:** We argued a lot, mostly by email. We wrote technical arguments in favour of our point of view and circulated them. We were willing to compromise, because getting a language was the important thing. And because we recognized that there were valid arguments on the other side of the compromise, too.

**John:** Sometimes we included two overlapping approaches, as in the equational versus expression style, both of which Haskell supports. Mostly, though, we would have long technical discussions of competing ideas, hammering out a consensus in the end. I think semantics played an important role here—although we never produced a complete formal

---

\* "Being Lazy with Class: the history of Haskell," Proc Third ACM Conference on the History of Programming Languages (HOPL III), *http://research.microsoft.com/~simonpj/papers/history-of-haskell/index.htm*.

semantics for all of Haskell, we regularly formalised fragments of the design, and semantic ugliness was always a powerful argument against any proposal. Keeping one eye on formal semantics helped guide us to a clean design.

**Paul:** Through debate—mostly at a technical level, where "right" and "wrong" were often obvious, but also at a subjective/aesthetic/sometimes-deeply-personal level, where there was no right or wrong. These debates seemed endless (some are still raging today), but somehow we pushed through them. On seemingly insignificant issues we would often rely on our leadership to make final decisions. For example, we had a "syntax czar" who would make final decisions on syntactic minutiae.

*How do you recognize the best ideas, and how do you "manage" features that you don't like?*

**Paul:** The best ideas were obvious—as were the worst! The harder issues were those with no clear best solution.

**Simon:** For features we didn't like, we just argued against them. If enough people did that, it was hard for the idea to make headway. But in fact I can't recall an idea that was strongly pushed by one person or a small subgroup but was ultimately voted out. Perhaps that's a measure of the shared technical background that we brought to the project.

In sort, disagreement was not the problem, for the most part. Rather, the hard thing was finding willing volunteers to do the minutiae. Languages have lots and lots and lots of details. What happens in this or that obscure case? Libraries have lots of details. This is not romantic stuff, but it's important.

**John:** You spot the best ideas by acclamation! The class system was one of those: when we saw it, we all just drooled. That's not to say there wasn't a lot of hard work after that, though, dealing with details like default instances and the interaction with modules.

As for features we don't like, almost by definition they are the most intensively discussed. Users complain about them all the time, and every time the language is revised someone is bound to say, "Can't we finally get rid of X?", whatever X may be, and the feature gets discussed all over again. That means, at least, that we know very clearly why we have the features we don't like, and why we can't get rid of them.

In some cases, we got these things right from the start—for example, the ever-unpopular "monomorphism restriction" has remained in the same form since the beginning, quite simply because it solves a real problem, and no one has found a better way to do it. In other cases, we revised decisions in the light of experience from the field. We changed the treatment of explicit strictness after the initial design proved to hinder program evolution—at a slight cost in semantic elegance, one of the few occasions we've done that. We removed overloading of list comprehensions after it proved confusing to beginning programmers. The fact that we've been able to go back and fix mistakes in the light of experience, even making incompatible changes to the language, has improved the design in the end.

*Were there advantages in being in a group? Did it oblige you to compromise?*

**Simon:** Being a group was the *most* important thing! We each had our own languages, and we believed that having a *common* language would stop us duplicating effort, and help our users believe in us because we all supported one language. This hope has been amply repaid—Haskell has been a tremendous success by any measure, and dramatically so in terms of our original expectations.

**Paul:** It was a clear advantage. Despite (again) the common vision, we each brought a different skill set to the table. We trusted one another, and learned a lot from each other. It was a fantastic interaction between bright, energetic, and hardworking individuals. Haskell could not possibly have been designed by a single person.

**John:** Compromise can be a good thing!

Working as a group was definitely a big advantage. We had complementary experience and skills, and I think designing a language as a broader group definitely led to a more broadly useful result than any one of us would have achieved alone. One person might have designed a smaller, simpler, perhaps even more elegant language—but I don't think it would have been as useful.

Also, every tricky design decision could be, and was, examined and reexamined from many possible angles. Many heads are better than one. A decision that looks quite sensible to one person may be obviously flawed to another—time and time again we would reject an idea after a serious flaw was exposed in this way, only to find a better idea as a result. I think the care we took is reflected strongly in the quality of the design. It sounds quite dialectical, doesn't it: thesis + antithesis = synthesis.

## Trajectory of Functional Programming

*What makes functional programming languages different from other languages?*

**Simon:** Oh, that's easy: control of side effects.

**John:** Well, careful control of side effects, obviously. First-class functions (although these are finding their way into more and more imperative languages, too). Concise notations for purely functional operations—everything from creating a data structure, to list comprehensions. I think lightweight type systems are also very important—whether they're the purely dynamic type systems of Scheme and Erlang, or the polymorphic inference-based systems of Haskell and ML. Both are lightweight in the sense that the types don't get in your way, even when you make heavy use of higher-order functions—and that's really at the heart of functional programming.

I think lazy evaluation is also important, but of course it's not found in every functional language.

**Paul:** Abstraction, abstraction, and abstraction—which, for me, includes higher-order functions, monads (an abstraction of control), various type abstractions, and so on.

## What are the advantages of writing in a language without side effects?

**Simon:** You only have to reason about *values* and not about *state*. If you give a function the same input, it'll give you the same output, every time. This has implications for reasoning, for compiling, for parallelism.

As David Balaban (from Amgen, Inc.) puts it, "FP shortens the brain-to-code gap, and that is more important than anything else."

**John:** Well, now, there are virtually no such languages. Haskell programs can have side effects, if they have the right type, or use "unsafe" operations. ML and Erlang programs can have side effects. It's just that, rather than being the basis for all programming, side effects in these languages are the exception; they are discouraged, and carefully controlled. So I'm going to reinterpret your question as: what are the advantages of programming largely without side effects?

Many people would start talking about reasoning now, and so will I, but from a very practical perspective. Think of testing a function in an imperative language. When you test code, you need to supply a variety of different inputs, and check that the outputs are consistent with the spec. But in the presence of side effects, those inputs consist not only of the function's parameters, but also of those parts of the global state which the function reads. Likewise the outputs consist not only of the function's result, but of all those parts of the state which it modifies. To test the function effectively, you need to be able to place test inputs in the parts of the state that it reads, and read the parts of the state that it modifies...but you may not even have access to those parts directly, so you end up having to construct the test state you want indirectly, by a sequence of other function calls, and observing the effect of the function by making more calls after the function you tested, to extract the information you expect it to have changed. You may not even *know* exactly which parts of the state are read and written! And in general, to check a function's postcondition, you need access to both the state *before* it ran, and the state *afterward*—at the same time! So you should really copy the state before the test, so you have access to all the relevant information afterward.

Compare this to testing a pure function, which only depends on its arguments, and whose only effect is to deliver its result. Life is much, much simpler. Even for programs that must perform a lot of side effects, it makes sense to factor out as much as possible of the functionality into highly testable side effect-free code, with a thin side-effecting wrapper around it. Don Stewart gives a lovely description of this approach applied to the XMonad window manager in a recent blog post.*

Passing everything a function depends on as arguments tends to clarify dependencies, too. Even in Haskell, you *can* write programs that manipulate one big state, which is passed as an argument to all your functions and returned as a result by all those that modify it. But you tend not to do that: you pass in only the information the function needs, and let it

* *http://cgi.cse.unsw.edu.au/~dons/blog/2007/06/02#xmonad-0.2*

return just the information the function itself generates. That makes dependencies much clearer than in imperative code, where any function could in principle depend on any part of the state. And forgetting about such dependencies is precisely what can cause the most troublesome bugs!

Finally, as soon as you start programming with side effects, evaluation order becomes important. For example, you must open a file handle before doing any file operations on it, you must remember to close it exactly once, and you must not use it after closing it. Every stateful object imposes restrictions on the order in which you may use its API, and those restrictions are then inherited by larger code fragments—for example, such-and-such a function must be called before the logfile is closed, because it sometimes writes a log entry. If you forget one of those restrictions, and invoke functions in the wrong order, then BANG!, your program fails. This is an important source of bugs. Microsoft's Static Driver Verifier, for example, is essentially checking that you respect the restrictions imposed by stateful objects in the Windows kernel. Program without side effects, and you just don't have to worry about this.

The most awkward bugs I've had to deal with recently can be traced to Erlang libraries with a stateful API, which I'm using in code with a very complex and dynamically deter-mined execution order. In the end, the only way I could make my code work was to build a side effect-free API on top of the standard one. I'm afraid I'm just not clever enough to make side-effecting code work! (Wait a minute, perhaps imperative programming would be easier without years of functional programming experience....) :-)

Oh, and did I mention easy parallelization?

**Paul:** Sanity, and the joy of solving a puzzle! :-)

*John mentioned parallelism. Are there other changes in the computer field that make functional programming even more desirable and needed than before?*

**Simon:** I believe that a long-term trend is that it will become more and more important to control side effects, in programming languages of all kinds. This five-minute video explains what I mean:

> *http://channel9.msdn.com/ShowPost.aspx?PostID=326762*

*Is the desire for a lack of side effects a natural evolution of the development of structured programming, as when we moved to higher languages with higher-order control structures and loops instead of just jumps,* goto *statements. Is programming without side effects the next step beyond that?*

**Simon:** That could be one lens through which you might look at it. The reason I'm a little cautious is because people mean very different things when they say "structured program-ming." I always think you have to be rather careful just to get your vocabulary straight before you start making what seems to be compact sound bites.

If you recall Dijkstra's classic letter, "Goto Considered Harmful," he was saying, "Take away goto in order to make your programs easier to comprehend, easier to compile, and so forth." Then you could regard purity as a way to take away assignment in order to make your programs easier to read about. But I think it's a mistake to regard functional programming as solely an exercise in aestheticism ("we'll take away these sinful, bad things and leave you with a boring and difficult life").

Rather than just saying, "We're going to take things away from you," we say, "We'll take some things away from you, but we'll give you in exchange lazy evaluation and higher-order functions and an extremely rich type system and this monad story." This change does force you to think very differently about programming, so it's a not a painless transition, but it is one that is rich in rewards.

### How does error handling change in functional programming?

**Simon:** You can think about errors in a new way, more like "error values" than "exception propagation." An error value is like a NaN in floating point. This gives a more value-oriented and less control-flow-oriented view of error handling, which is on the whole a good thing. In consequence, the type of function is much more likely to express its error behaviour. For example, rather than:

```
item lookup( key ) /* May throw not-found */
```

we have:

```
lookup :: Map -> Key -> Maybe Item
```

where the Maybe data type expresses the possibility of failure, through the medium of values.

### How does debugging change in functional programming?

**Paul:** Well, first of all, I've always felt that the "execution trace" method of debugging in imperative languages was broken, even for imperative programs! Indeed, some well-known imperative programmers eschewed this method in favor of more rigorous methods based on testing or verification.

Now, one nice thing about functional languages, especially lazy functional languages, is that it doesn't have any particularly useful notion of an "execution trace," so that method of debugging isn't a very good option. GHC has a trace facility for the graph reduction engine that underlies its evaluation mechanism, but in my opinion this reveals far too much about the evaluation process. Instead, people have designed debuggers such as Buddha based on "data dependencies," which is much more in line with the declarative principles of functional programming. But, perhaps surprisingly, in all my years of Haskell programming, I have never in fact used Buddha, or GHC's debugger, or any debugger at all for that matter. I find that testing works just fine; test small pieces of code using QuickCheck or a similar tool to make things more rigorous, and then—the key step—simply study the code to see why things don't work the way I expect them to. I suspect that a lot of people program similarly, otherwise there would be a lot more research on Haskell debuggers, which was a popular topic for a while, but not anymore. It would be interesting to do a survey to find out how people actually debug Haskell programs.

That said, there is another kind of debugging that has gotten a lot more attention, namely, *profiling* of both time and space, but in particular space. Space leaks are the hidden scourge of lazy functional programming, and space profiling is an important tool for getting rid of them.

*Would functional programming languages be easier to learn if we came to them without years of imperative language experience?*

**Simon:** I'm not sure. The ability to learn FP seems to be strongly correlated with being a smart programmer generally. There certainly is some brain-rewiring to do, but smart programmers can do that. It think it's a cop-out to blame the niche-status of FP on the fact that most programmers have their initial training in imperative techniques.

A stronger reason is that there's a tremendous lock-in effect. Lots of people use C++, so C++ is fantastically well supported by compilers, tools, the programmer pool, etc. But even that isn't a very strong reason: look at the rapid success of Python or Ruby.

**John:** No, this is a myth. A huge amount of experience transfers straight over—whether it's understanding the importance of abstraction in programming, knowledge of algorithms and data structures, or even just understanding that programming languages are formal languages. The C/C++ hackers that I teach Haskell to do significantly better in general than raw beginners. They understand what a "syntax error" is; they may not understand the type system, but they know what a type error is; they know that giving variables suggestive names will not help the computer "understand" their program and fix their bugs!

I think the myth arises because imperative programmers find functional programming *more difficult than they expect*. Experienced programmers are used to picking up new languages easily, because they can directly transfer basic concepts such as variables, assignments, and loops. That doesn't work with a functional language: even experienced programmers find they need to learn some new concepts before they can do anything at all. So they think functional programming is "difficult"—at the same time as they are picking it up much faster and more easily than complete beginners do!

**Paul:** I used to say that entrenched habits made the move hard, but I'm not so sure anymore. I think that the best, smartest, most experienced programmers (of any kind) find it easy to learn and love Haskell. Their experience helps them to appreciate abstraction, the rigorous control of effects, a strong type system, and so on. Less experienced programmers often do not.

*Why do you think no functional programming language has entered the mainstream?*

**John:** Poor marketing!

I don't mean propaganda; we've had plenty of that. I mean a careful choice of a target market niche to dominate, followed by a determined effort to make functional programming by far the most effective way to address that niche. In the happy days of the 80s, we thought functional programming was good for everything—but calling new technology "good for everything" is the same as calling it "particularly good at nothing." What's the brand supposed to be? This is a problem that John Launchbury described very clearly in his invited talk at ICFP. Galois Connections nearly went under when their brand was "software in functional languages," but they've gone from strength to strength since focusing on "high-assurance software."

Many people have no idea how technological innovation happens, and expect that better technology will simply become dominant all by itself (the "better mousetrap" effect), but the world's just not like that.

Books such as Moore's *Crossing the Chasm* [HarperBusiness] and Christensen's *The Innovator's Dilemma* [Collins Business] have influenced my thinking on this tremendously. If there was a target niche back in the 80s, it was parallel programming—but that turned out not to be at all important until just recently (with the advent of multicores), thanks to the immense ingenuity of computer architects. I think this was more important than technological problems, admittedly also important, such as low performance.

**Paul:** Because it's too radically different from conventional programming. That difference makes it hard to accept, hard to learn, and hard to support (with libraries, implementations, etc.).

## Is that situation changing?

**Simon:** Functional programming is a long-term bet. It's a radically different way to think about the whole enterprise of programming. That makes it hard for people to learn; and even when learnt, it's hard to adopt because it's revolutionary rather than evolutionary.

It's still not clear whether FP will ultimately become mainstream. What *is* clear is that FP has influenced mainstream languages, and furthermore that influence is increasing. Examples include: garbage collection, polymorphic types ("generics"), iterators, LINQ, anonymous functions, and more.

There are two reasons FP is becoming more influential. First, as programs scale up, and people care more and more about correctness, the costs of unrestricted side effects and the benefits of a more functional style become more apparent. Second (although perhaps of more short-term impact), multicores and parallelism have renewed interest in pure computation, or at least computation where side effects are carefully controlled. A recent example is Software Transactional Memory (STM).

All that said, there has been substantial growth in the Haskell community of late, and it's not out of the question that some recognizably functional language might eventually make it into the mainstream. (But my guess is that even if it does it will be called Java3 and will look syntactically like an OO language.)

**John:** Sure. Look at Erlang—a language focused single-mindedly on a very specific niche, the robust distributed systems needed in telecom systems, with a huge collection of libraries for every telecom-related task, and the great good fortune that Internet servers need essentially the same characteristics. Erlang may not be mainstream yet even in telecoms, but it has a heck of a lot of users there, and exponential growth. Choosing Erlang for a telecom application needn't be a controversial choice today—it's proven technology.

Haskell is not quite as far along, but the level of interest is rising fast, and all kinds of unexpected applications are popping up. Likewise OCaml.

Multicores provide a unique opportunity for functional programming—there's a widespread recognition that we don't know how to program them, and many, many people are starting to consider alternative ways of programming parallel systems, including functional programming. The funny thing is that you still hear automatic parallelization of legacy code described as a "short-term" solution, whereas functional programming is described as an attractive "long-term" approach. But the fact is that if you started developing a product today that must exploit eight cores when it is released in a year's time, then writing sequential C and hoping for automatic parallelization to solve your problems would be an *extremely* high-risk strategy. Choosing Concurrent Haskell or SMP Erlang is no-risk, because the technology already works today.

There are already dual-core Erlang products on the market that go twice as fast, thanks to the extra core. In a few short years from now, easy parallelization is going to be a critical advantage, and functional languages have an opportunity to come out of the resulting sea change very well indeed.

**Paul:** Yes, the environment for potential adoption is changing for several reasons:

- Other languages have adopted some of the good ideas, so it's no longer as radical a change.

- Programmers entering the workforce for the past 15 years have had more exposure to modern PL ideas, to mathematics, to formal methods—thus again making the ideas not quite as radical.

- There are many more libraries, implementations, and related tools to make using the language easier and more practical.

- There is now a nontrivial body of successful applications written in Haskell (or other FL), thus giving people confidence that It Will Work.

*Does the fact that we still find functional programming useful after 50 years tell us something about the state of computing?*

**Simon:** I think it tells us something about functional programming. I love FP because it is both principled—staying true to its foundations—*and* practically applicable.

By "principled" I mean that the languages and their implementations (especially pure languages like Haskell) are based very closely on unusually simple mathematical foundations, unlike powerful but much more ad hoc languages like Python or Java. That means that FP isn't going to go out of fashion—FP represents a fundamental way of thinking about computation, so it's not a fashion item at all.

By "practically applicable" I mean that FP is much, much more usable now than it was even 10 years ago, because of vastly improved implementations and libraries. That makes the benefits of a principled approach available to a much wider audience.

As people become more concerned about:

- Security

- Parallelism

- Bugs due to side effects

FP is going to be more and more visible and useful. If you like, computing is moving on to the point where the costs of FP are less important than they were, and the benefits are more valuable.

## The Haskell Language

*Referring back to John's earlier answer, what made you "drool" when you were designing the class system?*

**Simon:** We knew we had a bunch of problems surrounding how to take equality over arbitrary types, how to show and print arbitrary types, and how to do numerics. We knew we wanted integers and floats and double-precision numbers and arbitrary position integers. We did not want the programmer to have to write plus int and plus float and plus arbitrary precision integer.

We knew we wanted some way you could just write A + B and get whatever was correct. The ML solution to that problem was to allow you to write A + B, but the type of addition has to be resolved locally. If you write f(x,y) = x + y + 1, the system says, "Ah, you need to tell me more. You need to give a type signature to f( ) so I can know whether this plus is an integer plus or a float plus or a double plus."

*That makes you carry type information around in lots of places in your program.*

**Simon:** Worse than that. It might be useful to call this particular function on floats or on integers or on doubles. It's a pain to have to fix it to be one type.

You lose the genericity. Instead, you must write three functions: f float, f double, and f integer, all with the same body but different type signatures. Then when you call them, well, which one of these should the compiler call? You've got the plus int problem back again, but one level up.

That hurt us. That didn't feel beautiful. That didn't feel right. That is what the class system solved, because it said you can write f(x,y) = x + y + 1 once for all. It gets the type Num a => a -> a -> a, and it'll work for any numeric type, including ones you haven't yet thought of!

They must be instances of Num, but the beautiful thing is that you can invent a type later—
10 years after the Haskell standard was nailed down and the Num class was defined and this
f function was written. You can make it an instance of Num and your old function will work
with it.

That's where the drooling came from. We had what seemed like an intractable problem
that was just solved. The original work was by Philip Wadler and Stephen Blott.

It solved the equality problem, too. ML has a different solution for equality. If you define a
member with type member :: [a] -> Bool that asks you whether a value is a member of a list,
the operation requires you to compare the values of type a for equality. One possible solution is to say every value supports equality, but we don't like that. You can't reasonably
compare functions for equality.

ML says "Ah, we'll give you a special kind of type variable called 'a. Member has type
member :: a -> ['a] -> Bool. This 'a is called an equality-type variable. It ranges only over
types that admit equality. So now you can apply member to an integer or to a character,
but you cannot apply member to a function, because then 'a will be instantiated by a
function; that's not legal.

Their ML has a different solution from the one for overloaded numerics, but it also pervades the type system, so these 'as go everywhere in the description. It solves a very specific problem of checking equality in a completely different way, but it doesn't help you
with ordering. What happens if you wanted to sort a list? Now you don't have just equality but ordering. Type classes have solved that problem, too. In Haskell you write

```
member :: Eq a => a -> [a] -> Bool
sort :: Ord a => [a] -> [a]
```

thereby saying precisely what properties the type a must have (equality or ordering,
respectively).

That's why we drooled, because it was a single powerful type system-level mechanism
that solved multiple problems to which we had otherwise seen only ad hoc and varying
solutions. One hammer that cracked a whole bunch of nuts, and no nut with good solution, even considered by itself.

**Philip Wadler:** One nice thing about type classes is that they went on to influence the
way that generics work in Java. A Java method like:

```
public static <T extends Comparable<T>> T min (T x, T y) {
    if (x.compare(y) < 0)
        x;
    else
        y;
}
```

is very similar to the Haskell method:

```
min :: Ord a => a -> a -> a
min x y  = if x < y then x else y
```

save that the latter is shorter. In general, saying that a type variable extends an interface (which usually is parameterized over the same type variable) in Java serves the same role as saying that the type variable belongs to a type class in Haskell.

I'm pretty sure there was a direct influence here, because (with Martin Odersky, Gilad Bracha, and many others) I was involved in the team that designed generics for Java. I think that generics in C# were in turn influenced by this design, but I wasn't involved, so I can't say for sure. The new idea of "concepts" in C++ is also very similar, and their papers cite type classes in Haskell for purposes of comparison.

### When do you think Haskell programmers appreciate its strong typing?

**Simon:** Haskell's type system is rich enough to express a lot of the design.

Type checking is not just a way to avoid stupid mistakes like 5+True. It gives you a whole level of abstraction for describing and talking about a program's design and architecture, because where OO folk draw UML diagrams, Haskell folk write type definitions (and ML folk write module signatures). This is much, much better, because it's precise and machine checkable.

**Philip:** Here's an old anecdote.* Software AG marketed a commercial database product called Natural Expert, where data was queried and manipulated by their own home-grown functional language, similar to Haskell. They had a training course that lasted one week. At the beginning of the course, developers would complain that the type checker was giving them an awful lot of type errors. By the end of the course, they discovered that most of the programs they wrote worked perfectly as soon as they got them past the type checker. So the types were giving them all the debugging they needed. In short, at the beginning of the week they were thinking of types as their enemy, but by the end they were thinking of them as their friend.

I'm not trying to say that *any* program you write will work as soon as you get it through the type checker. But types do catch an incredible number of errors and make debugging an awful lot easier.

Types seem to be particularly important as one begins to make use of more sophisticated features. For instance, using higher-order functions is much easier when you have types to keep things straight. Polymorphic functions reveal a huge amount of information in their type. For instance, if you know that something has type

```
l :: (Int -> Int) -> [Int] -> [Int]
```

(take a function from integer to bool and a list of integers, and return a list of integers), it could be doing almost anything, but if it has type

```
m :: forall a b. (a -> b) -> [a] -> [b]
```

* Hutchison, Nigel et al. "Natural Expert: a commercial functional programming environment," *Journal of Functional Programming* 7(2), March 1997.

(for any types a and b, take a function from a to b and a list of a and return a list of b) then you know an awful lot about it. In fact, the type itself furnishes a theorem* that the function satisfies, and from this type you can prove that:

```
m f xs = map f (m id xs) = m id (map f xs)
```

where map applies a function to each element of a list to get a new list, and id is the identity function. Most likely m is itself just map, so (m id) will be the identity. But possibly m also rearranges elements—for instance, it might reverse the input list and then apply the function, or apply the function and then take every other element of the result. But that's all it can do. The types guarantee that it *must* apply the function to an element of the input list to get an element of the output list, and that it *cannot* look at the value of an element to decide what to do with it, only where it is in the list.

The most incredible thing to me about type systems is that they have this very tight connection to logic. There is this deep and beautiful property, called "propositions-as-types" or the Curry-Howard isomorphism, that declares that every program is like a proof of a proposition, and that the type of the program is like the proposition that the program proves, and that evaluating a program is just like simplifying a proof. The most fundamental ways of structuring data—records, variants, and functions—correspond exactly to the three most fundamental constructs in logic—conjunction, disjunction, and implication.[†]

It turns out that this works for all sorts of logical systems and programs, so it is not just a fragile coincidence but a deep and valuable principle for designing typed programming languages. Indeed, it gives you a recipe for design: think of a type, add constructors to the language to build values of that type and add deconstructors to the language to take apart values of that type, while adhering to the law that if you build something and take it apart you get back what you started with (this is called a *beta law*) and if you take something apart and build it up again you also get what you started with (this is called an *eta law*). It is just incredibly powerful and beautiful. Lots of time, when designing something, it feels arbitrary, that there are five different ways you could do it and it is not clear what is best. But this tells us that there is a core to functional languages that is not arbitrary at all.

Now we are just getting to the point where it is beginning to become common for computer scientists to type their proofs into a computer, so the computer can check whether they are true, and the procedure is based on the same principles and type systems that functional languages are based on, because of this deep connection between programs and proofs, and between types and propositions. So we are beginning to see things merge, and types will let you describe more and more of how your program behaves, and the compiler will be able to ensure more and more properties of your programs, and it will slowly become more common to prove properties of your program as you write it. The U.S. government sometimes insists on proofs of security properties for military software.

---

* Wadler, Philip. "Theorems for Free," 4th International Conference on Functional Programming and Computer Architecture, London, 1989.

† Wadler, Philip. "New Languages, Old Logic," *Dr. Dobb's Journal,* December 2000.

We will see this trend continue. Right now, operating systems don't give very strong guarantees about security, but I think we will see that change, and type systems will be a very important part of that.

## Is laziness exportable to other programming languages, or does it fit better in Haskell because of all its other features?

**John:** Laziness results in complex and unpredictable control flow. That's not a problem in Haskell, because evaluation order can't affect the result—you can let the control flow get as complex as you like, and it doesn't affect how easy or difficult it is to get your code working. Laziness can be, and has been, added to other languages, and it's not that hard to simulate, either. But when laziness and side effects mix, all hell breaks loose. Making that kind of code work is virtually impossible, because you just cannot hope to understand why the side effects are occurring in the order they do. I've experienced this in Erlang, in which I was simulating laziness in code that used a library with a side-effecting interface. In the end, the only way I could make the code behave the way I wanted it to was to build a purely functional interface to the library on top of the side-effecting one, so that my lazy code could be side effect-free.

So I think the answer to your question is: yes, laziness can be exported to other languages—but programmers who use it will have to avoid side effects in that part of their code. LINQ is a good example, of course.

## Are there other features of Haskell that other languages might borrow to make them more useful or safer?

**Philip:** Several features from Haskell have been incorporated or are being incorporated into a number of mainstream languages.

Functional closures (lambda expressions) have appeared in a large number of languages, including Perl, JavaScript, Python, C#, Visual Basic, and Scala. Inner classes were introduced to Java as a way to simulate closures, and there is a widely debated proposal for adding proper closures (similar to those in Scala) to Java. The influence toward closures comes not just from Haskell, but from all functional languages, including Scheme and the ML family.

List comprehensions appear in Python, C#, and Visual Basic (both in connection with LINQ), and Scala, and are planned for Perl and JavaScript. Haskell did not introduce list comprehensions, but did a lot to popularize them. The comprehensions in C#, Visual Basic, and Scala also apply to structures other than lists, so they more closely resemble monad comprehensions or "do" notation, both of which were introduced in Haskell.

The generic types in Java were strongly influenced by polymorphic types and type classes in Haskell; I helped design the generics in Java, and also coauthored a book about them published by O'Reilly.* The features in Java in turn inspired those in C# and Visual Basic.

* Naftalin, Maurice and Philip Wadler. *Java Generics and Collections* (O'Reilly, 2000).

Type classes also appear in Scala. Now C++ is looking at incorporating a feature called "concepts" that is also closely related to type classes. Haskell has also influenced a number of less widely used languages, including Cayenne, Clean, Mercury, Curry, Escher, Hal, and Isabelle.

**John:** In addition: anonymous delegates in C# and list comprehensions in Python. Functional programming ideas are popping up all over the place.

**Paul:** I have read many accounts of people who learn Haskell but rarely use it in their real programming jobs, but claim that it changes (for the better) the way they think and program in an imperative language. And Haskell's influence on mainstream languages, and more recent new languages, has been huge. So we must be doing something right, and we seem to have influenced the mainstream, even if we are not in the mainstream.

### What is the link between the design of a language and the design of a software written with that language?

**Simon:** The language in which you write profoundly affects the design of programs written in that language. For example, in the OO world, many people use UML to sketch a design. In Haskell or ML, one writes type signatures instead. Much of the initial design phase of a functional program consists of writing type definitions. Unlike UML, though, all this design is incorporated in the final product, and is machine-checked throughout.

Type definitions also make a great place to write down invariants of the type; e.g., "this list is never empty." Currently, these claims are not machine-checked, but I expect they increasingly will be.

Robust types change the face of program maintenance. You can change a data type and know that the compiler will point to all the places that must change in consequence of it. For me, this is one of the biggest single reasons to have expressive types; I cannot imagine making substantial changes to a large dynamically typed program with nearly the same degree of confidence.

Using a functional language dramatically changes the approach to testing, as John eloquently described earlier.

Using a functional language strongly pushes one in the direction of purely functional data structures, rather than data structures that are mutated in place. That can have a profound effect on the design of the program. You can write imperative programs in Haskell, but they look clumsy, and that guides programmers in the direction of purity where possible.

**Paul:** I like Simon's reply, although he is focusing mostly on how Haskell (or other FL) affects the design of software. The dual question is, how does a software application affect the design of the language? Haskell, and most other FLs, is meant to be general purpose, of course, but one of the cool things about applications written in Haskell in recent years is how many of them are based on a domain-specific language (DSL) "embedded" in Haskell (we often call these "DSELs"). There are tons of examples of this—in graphics, animation, computer music, signal processing, parsing, printing, financial contracts, robotics, and many more—and a ton of libraries whose designs are based on this concept.

Like the real-estate agent who says that "location, location, location" are the three most important things in real estate, I think that "abstraction, abstraction, abstraction" are the three most important things in programming. And to me, a well-designed DSL is the *ultimate* abstraction of a domain—it captures just the right amount of information, no more and no less. What is so great about Haskell is that it provides a framework for creating these DSLs easily and effectively. It's not a perfect methodology, but it's pretty darn good.

**Philip:** Functional languages make it easy to extend the language within the language. Lisp and Scheme are brilliant examples of this; read Paul Graham* on how Lisp was the secret weapon in building one of the earliest web applications (which later became a Yahoo! product), and in particular how Lisp macros were key to building this software. Haskell also provides a number of features that make it easy to extend the power of the language, including lambda expressions, laziness, monad notation, and (in GHC) template Haskell for metaprogramming.

Paul already mentioned how this makes Haskell a favorite language for embedding domain-specific languages. But it also shows up at a less grandiose level, when one builds small libraries for parser combinators or pretty printing. If someone wants to truly understand the power of functional programming, those two examples are a great place to start.

Laziness in Haskell also has a profound effect on how one writes programs, as it allows you to decompose your problem in ways that are hard to achieve otherwise. One way I like to think of it is that laziness allows one to transmute time into space. For instance, instead of thinking of how to deliver values in sequence (time), I can return a list containing all the values (space)—laziness guarantees that in fact the values in the list will be computed one by one, as needed.

Thinking about space is often easier than thinking about time: space can be visualised directly, whereas visualising time requires animation. Contrast browsing a schedule of events for the day with watching a video of the day's occurrences! So exploiting laziness can profoundly change how you approach a problem. One example is the parser combinators mentioned earlier, which return a list of all the possible parses; laziness guarantees that this list is computed as it is needed. In particular, if you are happy with the first parse, none of the others are ever generated.

* Graham, Paul. *Hackers & Painters* (O'Reilly, 2004).

# Spreading (Functional) Education

*What have you learned teaching programming to college students?*

**Paul:** For many years, and perhaps even so today, functional languages were found mainly in introductory classes, because they are easy to learn and abstract away from the many details of imperative computation. I now think that, in the long run, this may have been a mistake! The reason is that students quickly conclude that FLs are toy languages, since, after all, they were used in their intro classes, mostly on toy examples. And once they discover the "power" of side effects, many of them never turn back. What a shame!

It seems to me that the best things about FP aren't often appreciated by beginners. It's only after you've programmed for awhile that the benefits become apparent.

At Yale, we have a course on functional programming, and it is taken mostly by advanced majors. I don't have any problem throwing hard and large problems at them, as well as advanced mathematics, to show them the real power of FP. And more importantly, I can say, "Put that in your imperative pipe and smoke it," and often we do—compare the Haskell code against C code—and it's quite enlightening, and is something that you just can't do with students for whom Haskell is their first language.

*What's wrong with computer science and how we teach it? How would you fix it?*

**Paul:** I wanted to write about a personal educational objective of mine that I hope others will find interesting, perhaps even challenging.

There are literally hundreds of books that teach how to program, or how to write programs in a particular language. These books typically use examples drawn from a variety of sources, but the examples are often pretty lame, ranging from Fibonacci and factorial, to string and text processing, to simple puzzles and games. What I'm wondering is whether it's possible to write a book whose main topic is something other than programming, but which uses a programming language as the primary vehicle to teach the main concepts.

I suppose that you could say that a book on operating systems, networking, graphics, or compilers is such a book, if it uses a language extensively to explain the material, but I'm interested in topics further removed from core computer science. So I'm thinking about things like certain sciences—physics, chemistry, astronomy—or even social sciences, economics in particular. And I wonder whether it's possible to go one step further and teach aspects of various disciplines in the arts—music in particular.

I would think that a functional language, especially a language such as Haskell that offers such great support for domain-specific embedded languages, would be an excellent vehicle to teach concepts other than programming. The great thing about programming is that it forces you to be precise, and the great thing about functional programming is that you can be concisely precise. The pedagogy for many of the disciplines I mentioned could benefit from both.

**Simon:** This touches on something in which I'm quite involved in the U.K., particularly at school. I'm a governor at the school; each school has a board of governors. The way that computing is taught at school at the moment is dismal. There's essentially no computer science. It's all essentially information technology.

When I say information technology, I mean spreadsheet and databases upward. It's like saying, "Here's a car, and here's how to drive it." That's how to use a spreadsheet. "And now that you can drive it, we're going to discuss with you where you might want to go with it. Do you want to go to Birmingham? If you want to go to Birmingham, here's how I think you might plan your route and who you might take with you."

You get into project planning and requirements analysis and systems integration and that kind of stuff. At the moment, at school, you do not learn what's under the bonnet of the car. To a certain extent, that's defensible because that means that in some sense, everybody should learn to drive a car, right? Furthermore, you should have some clue about where you might want to go with it and how to avoid mowing down pedestrians.

Not everybody should be interested in how cars work. It's perfectly fair that most people just drive them, but some people should be interested in how cars work. There is a discipline to computer science or computing that should be taught at school, at least to kids who are interested in it. At the moment what happens is they get told, "This is what computers are about," but they're essentially turned off by it because it's so boring.

I'm involved in a U.K.-based working group that is trying to support teachers to teach computing or computer science at a school level. Certainly at secondary school, which in Britain is ages 11 to 16. At A level, there is a computing A level where there is some real computer science. That's the 16 to 18 range, but by then, they've already been turned off.

Numbers are falling for computer science study in secondary schools, and they're falling even more shortly for university entrants, just as they are in the United States. That's partly because every child has a computer these days, so they already know a lot of this IT stuff. When they're taught it and taught it repeatedly in different contexts at schools, they think, "This is just dull. Why should I be interested in this?"

I think that's primarily what's wrong with the way computing is taught at school. For many people who are not really going to be interested in the technology, it's fair enough to teach them how to drive. That should be modest and it should be integrated with other subjects. It's a useful tool, and there you go. It's no big deal. But for some kids, we teach them about physics, which of course is ultimately going to be interesting only to a minority. Most of them are not going to go around knowing about coefficient of expansions or care about it. In the same way, I think there's a discipline of computing I'd like them to have some notion about, and be fired up by, because it's so exciting.

# Formalism and Evolution

*What value do you see in defining formal semantics for a language?*

**Simon:** Formal semantics underwrite everything that we've done with Haskell. If you look at my publications, for example, you'll see that most papers will contain some formalism that tries to explain what's going on. Even for something as imperative as transactional memory, that paper had a formal semantics for what transactions meant.

Formal semantics is a fantastic way to get a handle on an idea, to try to nail down some of the details and flush some of the tricky corners out into the open. But in a real language, when everything plays together, to actually formalize everything for the whole of your language is quite burdensome. I take my hat off to the Definition of Standard ML because I think it's a tour de force. It's pretty much the only language that has a rather complete formal description.

I suppose the extent to which I'd question it is to ask what the benefit is. There's a high cost to the last 10% of turning the language from a collection of formal fragments describing aspects of the language into a complete formal description as a whole language. That's a lot of work. It might be 70% of the work. How much benefit do you get from that final 70% of the work? Maybe only 20% or something. I don't know quite how it plays out. It seems to me that the cost/benefit ratio increases quite sharply as you go toward formalizing the whole language rather than pieces of it. That's true even the first time.

Then you're trying to say, "But what if the language evolves?" We keep changing Haskell. If I have to formalize every aspect of that change, that is quite a big brake on the changes in the language, and that's actually happened to ML. It's quite hard to change ML, precisely because it has a formal description.

Formalism can be a brake on innovation, perhaps. It's a spur to innovation because it helps you to understand what the innovation is, but it's a brake on innovation if there's somehow a sort of an environment dictating that everything has to be formalized completely across the whole language.

## Is there a middle ground, perhaps a semiformalism where you wear jeans with a sports coat?

**Simon:** I think that's the ground that Haskell occupies. The language definition is pretty much entirely in English, but if you look in the accompanying research papers, you find lots of formalism for fragments of the language. So it's not codified in the report, certainly not as a full description. For a language that does not have a formal description, you'll find much more material that is formalized than for C++, which is exclusively informal, although enormous efforts have been lavished on that informal description.

It's a funny balance. I really, really think that formalism has made a huge difference to keeping Haskell clean. We haven't just lobbed things in without regard. Everything has had to sort of fit in, in a principled way. It gives you a fantastic way to say, "This just looks messy. Are you sure it has to be like that?" If it looks messy, chances are, it's going to be hard to implement and hard for the programmer to figure out what you've implemented.

**Philip:** The initial paper on type classes was by myself and Stephen Blott, and appeared in the proceedings of the Symposium on Principles of Programming Languages in 1989.* It formalized the core of type classes, and we tried to keep it as simple and small as possible. Later, Cordy Hall, Kevin Hammond, Simon, and myself tried to write down a much more complete model.† That appeared in ESOP in 1994, so you can see that it took five years to get around to it! We didn't formalize all of Haskell, but we tried to formalize all the details of type classes. So there are different levels of modeling appropriate for different purposes.

The ESOP paper served as a direct model for implementation in GHC, notably the use of higher-order lambda calculus as an intermediate language, which is now central to GHC. That's one nice thing about formalization. It is a lot of work to do the formalization, but once you've done it, it provides a great guide to implementation. It's often the case that something seems hard to implement, but once you've put in the effort to formalize it, the implementation becomes a lot simpler.

Another example of formalization is Featherweight Java, which I developed with Atsushi Igarashi and Benjamin Pierce, published in OOPSLA in 1999 (and republished in TOPLAS in 2001).‡ At this time, lots of people were publishing formal models of Java and they were trying to make them as complete as possible. Our goal with Featherweight Java was instead to make it as simple as possible—we tried to get everything down to a tiny syntax with just one page of rules. And that turned out to be a good idea, because the model was so simple it was a good basis for people to use when they wanted to add one new feature and model that. So the paper has generated a huge number of citations.

On the other hand, it turned out there was a bug in the initial design of generics having to do with assignment and arrays, and we didn't catch that, because we didn't include either assignment or arrays in Featherweight Java. So there's a tradeoff between a simple model that gives you insight, and a more complete model that can help you catch more errors. Both are important!

I was also involved in formalizing part of the definition of XQuery, which is a query language for XML, a W3C standard.§ Of course, you get a lot of arguments on standardization committees; in our case lots of folk said, "What is all this formalization stuff? How am I supposed to read that?" They didn't want to make the formalization the canonical standard; they wanted to make English prose canonical because they thought it was easier for their developers to read. But parts of the type system were easy to write in the formalization and very hard to write out in English, so they decided that for those parts the formal spec would be canonical.

\* Wadler, Philip and Stephen Blott. "How to make ad-hoc polymorphism less ad hoc," 16th Symposium on Principles of Programming Languages, Austin, Texas: ACM Press (January 1989).

† Hall, Cordelia et al. "Type classes in Haskell," European Symposium On Programming, LNCS 788, *Springer Verlag*: 241–256 (April 1994).

‡ Igarashi, Atsushi et al. "Featherweight Java: A minimal core calculus for Java and GJ," TOPLAS, 23(3):396–450 (May 2001).

§ Simeon, Jerome and Philip Wadler. "The Essence of XML," Preliminary version: POPL 2003, New Orleans (January 2003).

At one point, someone suggested a change to the design. And an interesting thing was that despite these complaints, the committee asked the group of us who were working on formalization to formalize this change. So we did this, and discovered that even though the proposal for the change written in English was supposed to be precise, there were 10 places where we didn't know how to formalize it because the prose could be interpreted in more than one way. So we resolved these questions and then presented a formal spec. After we presented the formalism at the next meeting, the change was accepted unanimously—there was no argument at all—which is something that *never* happens at standardization meetings. So in this case, the use of formalism was really a big success.

As Simon said about Haskell, it's usually more effort than it's worth to formalize absolutely everything. So with XQuery, we formalized about 80% of it, but there was another 20% that was important but would be a huge amount of work to formalize, so we didn't do it.

That said, I think we got a lot of value out of what we did formalize.

Apart from this story, that formalization became the core of Galax, implemented by my colleagues Mary Fernandez and Jerome Simeon, which is now one of key implementations of XQuery. So, again, this is an example of how formalization can make implementation easier.

*All the mathematicians I know say if math's not beautiful, it's probably wrong.*

**Simon:** Right. To take an example, we're busy adding type-level functions to Haskell at the moment, and we're really trying to figure out the formalism for that. We've got an ICFP paper this year about it, but still I'm not completely satisfied with it. So we're beating away on this. This has direct consequences for the implementation. We could just throw together an implementation. Say, "It is what it is; try it out." Then we'd have a good chance that people would come back the next day and say, "Well, here's a program that I thought would type check but doesn't, so should it?" Then we have to say, "Well, you know, the implementation doesn't type check it, so maybe not. But you have a right to ask."

I'm not unhappy with the fact that we never formalized the entire language as a whole. But that's is not to say that there's no benefit from doing it, right? The last 70% of the effort does produce some benefit. Maybe the cost/benefit ratio isn't as good, but there are benefits. Maybe there are interactions between language features that you hadn't understood. You formalized aspects, but you didn't know that if you had a cunning plan A and tricky feature B that they'd mutually destroy each other. We're all a bit vulnerable to that.

*If you have a large language community in some aspect, people will run into that eventually and file bugs.*

**Simon:** Right, and then you may embarrassingly say, "Well, ah, yes," and "If only we'd gone further with formalizing a larger sort of subset to the language, we'd have been in better shape." It's terribly important. But after a bit, we consciously didn't do what ML did.

*When this happens, do you have a technique for handling backward compatibility concerns?*

**Simon:** I guess we're still evolving one, but in the past, we've more or less ignored it. That's less true today. About 10 years ago we established this language we called Haskell 98 as a kind of stable subset language. It was a language we were certain we weren't going to change. Haskell compilers by default accept Haskell 98. If you want anything other than Haskell 98, you have to give them some flags that say: accept this after the other extension.

One flag used to say: switch everything on, and nowadays it has been broken down into about 30 separate extensions. The old single flag just expands into some 15 of those. If you look at a source module, you can usually see which language extensions it's actually using. In effect, we've become more careful about inviting programmers to identify which language they're using.

The constraint tends to be that you should not break old programs, although this not exclusively the case. Some of these extensions switch on the extra keywords like forall. In Haskell 98, you could have forall as a type variable in a type—but when you switch on the high-ranked types, forall becomes a keyword, and you can't have a type variable named forall.

People very seldom do that anyway. For the most part, the extensions are upward compatible. But, as I say, there will definitely be Haskell 98 programs that break when you switch on enough extensions.

*Is there a point in the future where a Haskell 2009 or 2010 codifies all of these into a new standard?*

**Simon:** Yes. There's a well-advanced process of this called Haskell Prime, where the "Prime" is the tick to a variable name, mainly meaning we haven't yet decided what to call it. What we originally envisioned was a group of people debating in public and emerging with a new language, sort of standard that we could plant in the ground and say, "That's Haskell 2010," rather as we did with Haskell 98. In fact, it's difficult to get enough people to devote enough effort to make that happen.

I suppose that's because it's a bit of a kind of success disaster. GHC, by virtue of being the most widely used Haskell compiler, has become a bit of a de facto standard. That means that in practice, people don't come across too much difficulty because of language incompatibilities between different compilers. I don't think that's ultimately healthy for the language, but it reduces the impetus for people to devote their most precious commodity—their time—to codify the language standard.

*Will there ever be competing implementations that follow GHC's language standard closely?*

**Simon:** There already are competing implementations that tend to be a bit more specialized toward particular areas. In fact, just recently at ICFP, the functional programming conference a couple of weeks ago, we shifted gears. Rather than trying to produce a single monolith, which is Haskell Prime, we're instead going to try to codify language extensions. Rather than have them defined by GHC, we're going to invite people to suggest what language extensions they think should be codified, debate them a bit, and then get a person or a small group of people to write up essentially a kind of addendum to the report that says: "Here is a standalone description of what this language extension is supposed to do."

Then we'll be able to say that Haskell 2010 is this set of mutually coherent extensions. We can proceed, as it were, first of all by codifying and naming extensions, and then by grouping them into a named group, rather like Glasgow extensions, but a bit more coherently.

We're hoping, as far as the language design is concerned, that it's a bit more like what the open source community does when they're releasing a new version of GNOME or Linux or something. There's lots of stuff going on in the background, but eventually somebody wraps a bit of sticky tape around it and says, "All the pieces work together and this particular collection of pieces is called GNOME 2.9."

*A loose collection of progress joined at a common philosophy with a nice bow on it.*

**Simon:** Right, and a promise that they're mutually compatible. That's what we're doing on the language side. The language is almost defined by an implementation, so there's quite a lot of order to that process already. If anything, the reason the impetus is lacking is because it's too ordered.

On the library side, it's the complete reverse. There are lots of people developing libraries. Do you know about Hackage? There's about a new library in there every day. We're up to 700-something at the moment. What that means is that it's quite difficult to say, "Does this library actually work at all? Is it compatible with that one?" That's quite a serious question if you're just Joe User trying to use Haskell.

At the moment, the goal for me, as a compiler writer, is to get out of the business of library design and maintenance. Instead, a different bunch of people are going to do the same process that we just described but for libraries. They're going to call it the Haskell Platform. It'll essentially be a bunch of libraries that are codified. Again, this is quite conventional, I think. The Haskell Platform will essentially be a meta library that depends on particular versions of dozens of other libraries. It will say, "If you get the Haskell Platform, you get a bunch of libraries, all of which have a kind of kite mark of quality control, and all of which are somehow mutually compatible."

One way in which they can be incompatible is that two libraries might depend on different versions of the same common base library. If you glom them together, you'd have two copies of the base library, and you probably don't want that. If the base library defines a type, the two different copies of the library might create different versions of the type that are mutually incompatible. Things that you might expect to work wouldn't. They wouldn't just fail one type, but give a perplexing type error; it would say that T from Module M in Package P1 version 8 doesn't match T from Module M in Package P1 version 9.

I guess this is a long way of answering your question about backward compatibility. We're beginning to take it much more seriously. We still have the problem, when releasing a new version of GHC, that the compiler is rather tightly coupled to a base package of libraries.

*Everybody depends on the Prelude as well.*

**Simon:** Yes, but that's because the Prelude is very useful. It defines a lot of useful functions. When I say "tightly coupled," I mean the compiler knows the exact implementation of map and knows its name and where it's defined. There are some libraries that GHC is deeply in bed with.

*Is that in order to cheat in the compiling stages?*

**Simon:** Yeah. Somehow, if the compiler's going to emit code that calls library functions, it has to know that those functions exist and what their types are. That knowledge ends up being baked into the compiler. That's one way of thinking about it.

What that means is that if we change the interface to the base package, as is likely to be the case from version to version, in future releases we're going to include a kind of shim around the new base package that provides the same API as the old base package so that you can be insulated from the changes if you want. All of this is sweaty backward compatibility stuff that we didn't have to do before. But it's the problem of not obeying the motto, "Avoid success at all costs."

*Popularity has its own set of problems.*

**Simon:** That's right, but they're nice problems to have in a way.

*What do the lessons about the invention, further development, and adoption of your language say to people developing computer systems today and in the foreseeable future?*

**Simon:** Functional programming is a laboratory where lots and lots of interesting ideas are explored. Because the basic setting is simpler, we can go a lot further in exploring promising ideas (examples: type systems, generic programming, reactive programming, continuations). So if you walk into the FP laboratory, you'll find lots of interesting stuff lying around. It may or may not be *directly* useful to you, but the future is happening right now in this lab.

**Paul:** The most interesting lesson I learned is that sticking to an ideal—purity, in the case of designing Haskell—can have big payoffs. It might take a while to find the right solution, and it might take even longer to see the payoff, but it will come. Shortsightedness may yield a quicker payoff, but if you compromise your principles in the process, you will lose out in the end.

# CHAPTER NINE

# ML

ML is a general-purpose functional language developed by Robin Milner and the team he led at the University of Edinburgh in the 1970s. It grew from a metalanguage project designed to describe mathematical proofs. ML's most valuable contribution to language design may be the Hindley-Milner type inference algorithm used in many static, latent type systems. The language inspired Standard ML, Caml, Haskell, and F#, among others.

# The Soundness of Theorems

*You created LCF, one of the first tools for automated theorem proving, and the programming language ML to run the proving. How did it work?*

**Robin Milner:** There were other efforts at machine-assisted proof around in 1970. They were at two extremes: either fully inventive (e.g., using Robinson's famous resolution principle) in searching for a proof, or fully noninventive in the sense that they would only check that each small step performed by a human was logically valid (as in de Bruijn's Automath system). Both these approaches, by the way, contribute a lot to today's proof technology.

I looked for something in between, where a human would design a tactic (or a strategy built from little tactics) and submit it to the machine together with the thing to be proved. There would be interaction; if one tactic failed or partly failed then the machine would say so, and the human could suggest another. The key thing was that, although the tactics could be adventurous, the machine would only claim success if a real proof was found. In fact, in a successful case the machine could proudly export the proof that was found so that another independently written program (of the fully noninventive kind) could check it.

The key to why it works was that ML, the metalanguage in which clever users would write the tactics they thought of, had a type system (somewhat but not completely novel) which made the language resolutely refuse to claim success unless it (thanks to the clever user's tactics) could fill in every detail of the proof which the tactic merely sketched. So ML was the vehicle for a cooperation between hopeful human and meticulous machine.

*What are the limits of LCF?*

**Robin:** I don't see obvious limits. Nowadays systems people express quite adventurous tactics to systems like HOL and COQ and Isabelle, and the problems solved are slowly getting harder. HOL actually achieved a proof that the type system of ML was sound, which is like confirming that your parents' reproductive system was OK. But we're a long way from being able to capture the mathematicians inspired thoughts as a tactic. I suspect that bigger advances will come mainly from building a tower of simpler theorems from which more complex ones can be deduced, which is how most mathematical theories are built anyway.

As for proving that programs work, this is already quite possible when the user is able to annotate his program-to-be-proved with assertions (as pioneered by Floyd and Hoare right back in the early 70s), which say things like "every time *this* point is reached in execution *these* relationships will hold between the program variables."

*Can this approach analyze the source code of a program to prove that it contains no bugs?*

**Robin:** Yes! It's done a lot, especially for small critical programs that are embodied in real products like the brakes of a car. The biggest problems come when people can't (or refuse to) formulate the desired property in a rigorous form!

*How much effort is needed to define these properties in a rigorous form?*

**Robin:** This is really a question for those who deal with logics in which the properties can be expressed. The role of ML is not to be such a logic, but to be a medium in which proofs in these logics can be expressed, as well as heuristic algorithms for finding those proofs. So ML is a host to such logics. The original logic for which ML was a host was LCF, a logic of computable functions due to Dana Scott. In this logic we used ML (and its predecessor) to find and/or check some theorems; I'm glad to say that one of these theorems was the (almost completed) proof of correctness of a compiler from a very simple source language to a very simple target language.

*Is this portable to other programming languages?*

**Robin:** Having explained ML's role (as a host to logics) I suppose the closest question to this one that I can answer is this: can other languages be equally good hosts to logics for proof? I'm sure they can, if they have a rich and flexible type system and handle both higher-order functions and imperative features. ML was fortunate to be the host chosen by some successful logic developers, and this means that people continue to choose it.

*Why are higher-order functions necessary for a language to be a good host for what you call logics of proof?*

**Robin:** You implement inference rules as functions from theorems to theorems. So that's the first-order type. Your theorems are essentially sentences, so an inference rule is essentially a function from strings to strings. We invented these things called *tactics*—you express a goal, your sentence, that you'd like to prove, and what you get back is a set of subgoals together with a function that will, given the proof of those subgoals, produce a proof of the goal. So a tactic is a second-order function.

We had some of these tactics. We programmed them, and then we wanted things that would stick them together to get bigger tactics. We then had third-order functions, which we called *tacticals*, which would take tactics and produce bigger tactics. Such a tactic might say, "Well, first of all, get rid of all the implications and put them into the assumption list and then apply the induction rule, then apply simplification rules." That was quite a complex tactic, which we called a *strategy*, and that would demolish several theorems.

When I was working for John McCarthy in Stanford, I said, "Look, I've done something nice, I've got this strategy, this tactic, and here's a property of strings that it proves. I just express this goal, which is a fact about strings, and then I apply my tactic and it produces that assertion as a theorem." He then said to me, "How general is your tactic? What else will it apply to? I've got an idea." He said, "What about this particular thing that I'd like to prove?" He came up with another example. Secretly I had already proved that second example with the same tactic, but I didn't tell him, so we applied the tactic to it and, sure enough, it worked, to which he simply didn't say anything because that was the way he agreed with things. I was able to show that we had a polymorphic tactic; they could do more than one thing.

*You also developed a theoretical framework for analyzing concurrent systems, the Calculus of Communicating Systems (CCS), and its successor, the pi calculus. Can this help to study and improve the way we handle concurrency in modern hardware and software?*

**Robin:** I began to think about communicating systems when I was in McCarthy's AI lab at Stanford, 1971–1972. It struck me that there was hardly anything in existing languages that dealt with them nicely. Mainly I was looking for a mathematical theory, that languages could use as their semantics—this implies the need for something modular; you should be able to assemble a (concurrent) communicating system from smaller ones.

At that time there was already a beautiful model by Carl Adam Petri—Petri nets—that treated causality very well; there was also the Actor model of Carl Hewitt. Petri nets were not modular, and I wanted to get closer to a kind of concurrent theory of automata than in Hewitt's model; also to take the notion of synchronized communication (handshake) as primitive. Also automata theory, with its semantics as formal languages (sets of strings of symbols), did not treat nondeterminism and interaction well. So CCS was my attempt.

My main excitement was to get an algebraic treatment—first for the statics, and then for the dynamics. Many years were spent doing this better, including a major step prompted by David Park, to introduce the notion of bisimilarity based upon maximal fixed points. At the very beginning, I wanted to model systems that reconfigure their state; for example, A and B may not be able to communicate until C, who is in touch with both, sends A the address of B. At first, in discussion with Mogens Nielsen, we failed (mathematically); then Mogens put right something that we had not thought out properly; this led to the pi calculus, developed with Joachim Parrow and David Walker.

The excitement here was that pi not only dealt with reconfiguration but also was capable—without any addition—of representing data types. So it looks like a basic calculus for mobile concurrent systems, much as the lambda calculus is for sequential systems.

Pi seems to be used a lot, and is even useful for biological systems. But more importantly a whole new range of calculi are coming forward that model distributed systems more directly, handling such things as mobility and stochastic behaviour. Instead of polishing off the theory of concurrent processes, we seem to have opened a very useful can of worms.

*Is it possible to understand a system scientifically before you design and build it?*

**Robin:** I've been thinking a lot about this in relation to ubiquitous computing lately, but I think it's general. You have to have some kind of model of how the system is going to work. At the very simplest level you have the von Neumann machine, which is a scientific or formal or rigorous model that actually gave rise to FORTRAN and a whole sequence of sequential languages. That's a scientific model. It's a very simple one; that was its beauty.

You need a model from which the programming language is, as it were, extracted or defined. For ubiquitous systems, this model may be very far from the von Neumann machine; it has to be something that deals in general populations of agents all interacting and moving about, and sensors and so on.

*It sounds like you're talking about a series of metalanguages that express semantics.*

**Robin:** I'm not keen to use the word "language" until we have a model. Of course, that completely goes contrary to what happens all the time; languages get defined and they do get defined in metalanguages, and very often that's before there's a good model, unless of course the metalanguage actually provides that model. Maybe metalanguage is a synonym for model in this case. We used it when we defined Standard ML. We used the metalanguage, which was a kind of inductive inference of what would be admissible instructions and what they would do. I suppose that's what a generic model is. I agree with you; I'm talking about a series or a kind of unknown family of metalanguages. Each of those gets specialized to a particular system, which we could call a program.

*In this sense, is computing the definition and formalization of models at several different layers that allow you to build models at higher layers?*

**Robin:** Yes. This is very much my concern with ubiquitous computing because there are so many concepts you want to be reflected by the behavior of a particular system, but you may not be able to include all those concepts directly in one model. I've been talking about a tower of models where at the bottom you might have a rather elementary machine. As you go up, you get into more interesting or more humanoid or more subtle concepts, like failure management and self-awareness and trust and security and so on. Somehow one wants to build models in a layered way so that in each model you talk about a fairly manageable set of concepts, and then you implement them in a lower-level model.

*Lisp and Forth often talk about extracting and building systems out of reusable concepts of meaning. In a sense, you develop a rich language to solve your problem.*

**Robin:** As I think of a stack of models, at the lower levels you have things that would be called programs. At the higher levels, you have specifications or descriptions of what can and can't, or should and shouldn't happen. They might be in all sorts of forms, in a logical form, even in natural language. When you get to the lower levels, you get familiar things called programs, and they can be just regarded as particular models.

*Are they a sop to the idea that our computing models are inherently procedural?*

**Robin:** Yes. When you get to the more dynamically explicit models, then they're procedural, I suppose. You can have a model of specifications. It may consist of logical predicates; that's a model, it's not a very dynamic model, but then you can use pairs of predicate formulae to represent pre- and postconditions and you can assess the soundness of an implementation by whether you can verify it logically. You move from a specification or model that isn't obviously dynamic to one which is dynamic further down. That's interesting, I don't think I quite understand the shift from dynamic lower down to descriptive higher up, but it does seem to happen.

Alternatively, as in the method known as abstract interpretation, you still have a dynamic model at a higher level but working with some abstraction of the data. It isn't really the program but it is dynamic. That's what the French people have used in verifying the European Airbus embedded software. It is an interesting and involved question as to when a model is dynamic and when it's just descriptive.

*Perhaps that shift occurs when we have to acknowledge the laws of physics—the behavior of NAND gates, for example. We understand these physical processes, but there's a point at which the models we build subsume that level.*

**Robin:** Yes. There's the circuit diagrams for a computer and they're talking about electronics, and then up above them you have the assembly code and you're no longer talking about electronics. But as you're moving upward you're still retaining a dynamic element in the program as if it were translated into the dynamic element in the circuit diagrams. You seem to be able to move through, as it were, different dynamic notions while still retaining the dynamicity, but it becomes of a very different nature as you go further up.

Often logical models have a dynamic element as well. For example, the so-called modal logics are defined in terms of possible worlds, and moving from one world to another. There you have a dynamic element but it's slightly cloaked.

*I can imagine people objecting that errors or elements of undecidability in lower levels may affect the computability possibilities at upper levels.*

**Robin:** That seems to be just a fact of life. You may not be able to damp down the undecidability at a lower level, but at a higher level this is done in type checking. Types are an abstract model, and there you may have decidability because it's a weak abstraction and you don't have the ingredients that lead to undecidability. Of course they only talk about some one aspect of a program, so you only gain decidability as you go up at the expense of detail.

*I hadn't thought of it that way.*

**Robin:** Nor had I terribly much. In terms of type checking, you do have type systems for which it's decidable whether the program is well typed and what type it has, and then you do something quite minor to it and then it turns out to be undecidable. You just add a little bit more detail to your type system. This happened to the type system which we used in ML; the type system was basically decidable but if you add so-called conjunctive types it gets to be undecidable.

There's this sort of tension between what's useful to have and what is totally manageable. A lot of the time even if you can't always check something against an conjunctive type system, you can have an awful lot of success with a sufficiently intelligent theorem prover.

One can express all this with the notion of what I call a tower of models. As you go upward you lose more information. You may gain some analytic capability, and it may be valuable because you're analyzing a property of the programs that is going to be useful to know about even if you're not getting the whole story.

*I've heard that you can go the other way. An expression in the model at an upper level means you can remove a whole lot of undecidability from lower levels when you can prove that certain conditions never happen.*

**Robin:** Oh, I see, yes. The lower level consists of a basically undecidable model, but under certain constraints on the elements you're considering, it could attain decidability.

*Is undecidability not as universally bad as it sounds?*

**Robin:** No, but it's an interesting topic to bring up in order to see what models do for you and how they affect the undecidability. I think it's a good topic.

*How should we as informaticians, computer scientists, or working programmers teach concepts of theorems and provability and typefulness to people who just want to get stuff done?*

**Robin:** It's probably fatal to do it too early in the degree programme. That's something we're up against, and it happens in maths as well. You do things that you're later going to do in a more abstract way, but you do them in a more concrete way early on and then people can vaguely understand them. You do Euclidean geometry and you shut up about all the other geometries there are. Later on, maybe in the second year at university, you can begin to understand what another geometry might be like, whereas that level of abstraction just isn't available to a 17-year-old, mostly. It would be unwise to work under any assumptions that enough of them would have it to justify teaching it.

I know I'm making mistakes also in the degree programme by trying to teach things to the final year of an undergraduate programme that are still too abstract. A lot of the computation theory is too abstract even at that level. That's something we just have to live with. The trouble is that to get proper understanding of the subject without these abstractions, you have to have a kind of hierarchy of understanding. Some people will never want to talk about the abstractions. Other people will love them, and all you've got to do is make sure they can talk together about something.

*Does this limit the applicability to practical programmers? Can we expect that up to 20% of them will be interested in theory?*

**Robin:** It's reasonable that they shouldn't have to understand the theory. Language is a tool, and there are all kinds of tools. Model checking is a tool that people used to avoid having to understand too many details. That's fine, provided there are some people who do understand and who know that the model-checking tool is sound. Essentially we seem to have a lot of tools in our discipline that are there just to relieve people of certain kinds of understanding because they've got better things to do. They've got bigger and more urgent things to do, and that's exactly where a high-level programming language comes in. What I really like about some theories is that you can extract a programming language from them.

I'm working with a graphical model for ubiquitous computing. It's a descriptive mechanism, which is possibly difficult for many people to understand, but you can extract a language from it, which will be, I think, quite easy to understand. When you extract the language, you're using kinds of metaphors—sometimes they're special metaphors, sometimes they're structural limitations, and so on—so that the step from the abstract model into the programming language is a comfort-providing step which gives people some protection from things they don't want to have to bother with. Type systems, for example, give you protection from some things you would rather not know for most cases. Isn't that the nature of our subject: that we go up this tower of models, we get more and more abstract, and each person is prepared to go up—or down—a certain distance and no further?

As you go up the tower of models, you don't necessarily get more abstract, but you may get more restrictive. One beautiful example is the model of message sequence charts, which described finite fragments of concurrent behavior of message-passing and what can happen and what can't happen. That seems to me like a restrictive model, which is readily translatable into a more complex model, which deals with recursion cycles and all sorts of horrible things that you don't want to think about like race conditions. The beauty of the message sequence charts model is that your executives can understand it, so as you go up the model tower, not only do you abstract to make it easier to understand theoretically, but you may also restrict somehow to make the model more accessible to less-specialized people.

*In some ways it's more general, but in some ways it's more specific.*

**Robin:** Yes, exactly. That's a puzzle, I think. You might want to put the more specific thing lower rather than higher, but I've been putting it higher. The main thing is it's different and it serves the purpose of making things more accessible to some people at the price of generality. It seems to be a worthwhile thing to do.

*If a model is a collection of theorems built up from more fundamental principles, how does it affect the ideas you can express using that particular model?*

**Robin:** I've got an example. I hope it's not too far-fetched, but it happens in the model I'm working with. You have a model of mobile systems, systems where messages move about and sensors and actuators move about, the sort of thing that happens in ubiquitous computing. You can set up the model so that you can say a lot about it. You can express the invariants so that there never comes a state when you've got more than 15 people in the same room or something of that kind. But in one version of the model you can't track a particular individual and say, "This person was never in this room."

It seems like a screwy example, but it's quite simple, really: there's nothing in that model that tracks the identity of an individual through various events and reconfigurations. You cannot even formulate the question, "Was this person ever in this room?" because you don't know how to say "this" person—"this" implies identity persisting through time, especially if it's connected with verbs in certain tenses.

That's a case of a model in which there are some things that you can't even express, and I'm very much intrigued with this because that seems to be an advantage for some purposes. It's a great advantage in applying this model to biological systems, where you're talking about populations of millions of molecules, and you're not concerned about which molecule is which; you're just concerned that you can say something about how many molecules there will be in 15 minutes or something like that. The model can be very useful for biology without having to express the identity of particular molecules.

### Identity is not as important as the stochastic description?

**Robin:** That's right, in this particular case, where it might not be for many purposes. Of course, I've been making an analogy between biological and ubiquitous systems in which people or agents of some kind moving around in a city or in some controlled environment. In this latter case, you're very much more likely to want to talk about the identity of a particular individual. He was never in this pub where the crime was committed. You might want to say that, and so you've got to know about what "he" means through time.

In models, again for ubiquitous computing, you might be talking about space in an entirely discrete manner, so you don't say anything about distance. You only talk about some entities being adjacent to each other or being nested inside each other. You may not wish to model the continuity of space, so you forget all about that. It does seem that there are lots of features that models may cheerfully do without for certain purposes and then need to refine themselves for other purposes.

### Suppose I write an API. The better my design choices, the more expressive and easier to understand the model. As well, I may be able to make the system much easier to use correctly than to misuse.

**Robin:** This probably happens with whatever family of systems you're considering. You might be talking about security systems, and in a particular model you might be unable to express some aspects of security, but able to argue about other aspects. Or the model may express security properties but not be able to say anything about privacy. Properties like authenticity, privacy, security, and safety are all subtly different. Most models can only express some of them.

*To borrow the biological metaphor again, I don't have to understand the process of ATP conversion in my cells to understand how to pick up and pet my cat, but those cells don't know anything about the cat. As far as they're concerned, it's a bunch of other cells.*

**Robin:** We're not too different from natural science in this way. You can do Newtonian mechanics about moving bodies, but you can ignore friction.

*Are we in for a renaissance of provability?*

**Robin:** I think it'll continue, as long as people go on designing languages with an explicit semantics. That semantics won't be of any use at all unless there are some theorems that you can prove about it, like "No program will ever do anything stupid of this kind," or possibly more positive things like "Programs will always take a polynomial amount of memory."

*That might be an impetus for people that design new languages to make those kinds of proofs.*

**Robin:** I wish they would. Generally languages get designed without that in mind particularly. That's something I would like to change, but that's the way the languages get designed and usually by a mixed committee of people. Some of the designs are excellent, but they don't generally have proof in mind. You get faults like the fault in Pascal about variant records where the type discipline is violated. Nontheorems like that about languages are quite common.

I think we're probably making progress, because we do see these proofs about languages happening, and happening without a huge amount of effort because of the efficiency of proof systems, so this will allow feedback from provers to designers. That would be nice.

## The Theory of Meaning

*What is the link between the design of a language and the design of software written with that language?*

**Robin:** This is an enormous question. Long ago, I think in the 60s and 70s, there was hope for a single UNiversal Computer Oriented Language (UNCOL), which never came into existence. The idea was that you would use UNCOL for everything. If it existed, there couldn't be a meaningful link between the design of a language and of programs!

Now (and before then) we have seen a progression of languages, almost all favouring certain applications. Prolog favoured applications where actions can be conveniently described by logical formulae, so the design of a Prolog program would be structured on logical terms. ML and Haskell have rich type structure, so the design of ML and Haskell programs will often be closely linked to type structure. And so on. Every task can be written in many different languages, and it may be that the structure in the programmer's mind is the same, but that each language will do better in rendering explicit some parts of the structure, leaving other parts implicit; the parts that can be made explicit will differ from language to language.

Faced with a particular task, I think a programmer often picks the language that makes explicit the aspects of the task that he considers most important. However, some languages achieve more: they actually influence the way that the programmer thinks about the task. Object-oriented languages have done very well from this viewpoint, because the notion of object helps to clarify thought in a remarkable variety of applications.

*Do paradigms besides OOP influence the way a programmer designs and thinks?*

**Robin:** Yes, I think that logic programming and functional programming have had that influence. I hope that the paradigms of process calculi also have an influence. They certainly did in Lotos—a specification language—and I think they did in Ada, via the notion of ALT commands, among other things.

*Instead of having to choose a language for each task, will each programmer use his own programming language? Will we converge on a few language families?*

**Robin:** It would be anarchy for each programmer to use his own language, if this language were not constrained in its meaning by an accepted theory. After all, how would the meaning of his language be defined, other than in terms of an accepted theory? Once the theory exists, a programmer can invent syntactic phrases that are explained by the theory. So he would be using "his own" syntax, but with meaning drawn from a theory, and when he describes his language, he refers explicitly to that theory. Nothing wrong with that. But, because the theory will be behind these languages, one expects them to have a lot in common.

*How do you define the idea of designing a programming language? Is it a tool to express ideas or a tool to express goals?*

**Robin:** If you consider the nice example of functional programming and also logic programming, there was already a theory, for functional programming the theory of functions, the theory of types, of values, and for logic programming the well-developed theory of first-order logic. This theory was there before the language arose and the language was more or less based on that theory, so there are examples of theories that came before the languages, and I think we probably need more of those; I don't know how many different ones we need.

*We might say that the goal that someone wants to achieve is fundamental to designing a language.*

**Robin:** It might be that you need to express the goal or you express the properties of the behaviour of programs in a different language or using a different theoretical tool. For example, you might want to write your specifications in some kinds of logic, and the programming language would be more algebraic kind of language, but the two—the algebra and the logic—would be already pleasingly linked before you even design parts of them as a programming language.

I think the tool that you use for expressing goals and expressing desiderable properties doesn't have to be the same as the one that you used to express the program, but they ought to be linked in a theory of some kind which exists perhaps not just in order to produce programs, but exists even to understand natural phenomena like in the case of biology I mentioned. It seems that if we can understand informatics we can understand natural systems from an informatic point of view, and that is what a natural scientist does. But perhaps we can also use the same formalisms, the same mathematical constructions and properties to define languages and therefore bring in artifacts that are not natural phenomena. So I don't see why the informatic description of natural systems should be separated from the informatic description of programming systems or software systems.

*Suppose today you found a bug in the system you'd done five years ago. You have a specification synchronized with the implementation. What if there's a bug in the language design? What if a fault leads to a particular type of error?*

**Robin:** I'm very glad to say that hasn't happened, and I don't know what we would do. I think probably we would say you've got to live with it. We would publish something that said, "OK, this goes wrong but if you do this, this, and this then you'll never have to worry." These definitions are pretty sensitive. I mean some people are working on the idea of making definitional mechanisms less sensitive and more modular, and I think that's really quite difficult. I don't know how that's done. I would be inclined now not to change it but simply to tell people that it's there, the problem. It's just a practical move, so as not to tear your hair out.

*Given a language with a rich type system, such as ML or Haskell, what ideas does the type system make explicit within the design of programs written in those languages?*

**Robin:** If their system gets through the compiler—that is, the type checker—then certain things cannot happen. They do know that there won't be any of certain types of runtime error. They won't know that you won't get array overflow and they won't know all kinds of other nasty things that can happen like silly endless loops and so on, but they will know quite a bit.

For the application we had, the proving of mathematical theorems, it was marvelous to be able to say, "If you think you've proved a theorem in ML, and you think your representation of the inference rules of your logic in ML has been well done and the ML program comes up with a proof of a theorem, then the theorem is certainly proved." That's because of the abstract types mechanism, which allows you to express the type of theorems as being something that is only manipulable by the inference rules. Whatever clever tricks you might want to do to search for possible inferences, if one of your searches for a possible inference sequence succeeds, then you have actually to perform that inference and you have to perform that inference at the type of theorem. You know that the only things you can do there are valid inferences. You may never succeed within certain searches for possible inference sequences, but if you do succeed then you perform those inferences, or the system does it for you. Within the verification of the soundness of the implementation and soundness of the language design, then you do know it's a theorem. If you had a typeless language, you wouldn't.

*You just have a collection of operations.*

**Robin:** The system would say, "I've got a theorem" and you'd say, "how am I to be sure of that?" That's really serious. I remember early days at Stanford when we designed the first version of—not even ML, actually. We were working with automated inference system and we believed that we automated it correctly and the only things that could be inferred were inferable by the inference rules. I remember thinking at midnight once that something came out and the theorem came through and says, "I am a theorem," and I didn't have to worry because I trusted the types, I trusted the implementation. I trusted it to the extent that even though I'd been doing crazy things at the terminal, none of that could affect the robustness of the system.

It's really quite a really strong feature and has been all along, I think, with systems like Isabel and HOL, and all those other systems that now exist. That side of it is amazingly liberating because there's a point at which you don't have to worry.

*The question then is: how do we convince the computer to tell us what our program means?*

**Robin:** A particular program presumably means something like: if you do this to me, then this will happen; if you do that to me, then this will happen. Types allow you to make firm statements of that kind. That's where the computer does help you, the compiler helps you via its type checker. Of course, this doesn't have to be a decidable type checker; this could be a type checker which, if it does conclude the program is well typed, then it certainly is, but it may not conclude anything for some programs. You can have very rich type systems that have undecidability, but still have what you call positive safety: if the theorem comes through, then it is the theorem.

*What do you suggest to someone who wants to be a better software designer?*

**Robin:** Decide if they want to make money or whether they want to do science. You can't advise somebody which of those to do, but there are plenty of ways of making money and avoiding doing science. And vice versa.

If I am advising somebody who wants to do the science, then I would say talk to people who are doing the designs, and don't sit in a vacuous room designing a theory that looks beautiful, but make sure it's going to have some relevance to practice.

*You've described the millennium bug as a good example of a situation in which we didn't know what type of problems we were about to face. How can we prevent similar structural problems during the design phase?*

**Robin:** I don't know. The market is so hungry for software products that if you spend time analyzing what you are going to sell, then somebody else will get the contract. That sounds very cynical, but I think it's actually true. If you are going into the real world, you really don't succeed if you try to bring in analytical tools, even when they do exist. Of course, very often they don't yet exist.

In the face of the millennium bug, we actually had all the theory we needed to completely avoid the problem if we had written the programs in appropriate ways; all it needed was the care to use a type theory that had been around for 20 years. Of course there are a lot of conjectures about why that theory had been ignored, but I think it's largely because of market forces.

### Maybe documentation might have helped. How should developers write documentation?

**Robin:** Well, they should certainly write comments in the code, but there should also be some kind of rigorous basis. The difficulty of making an adequate commentary increases nonlinearly with the size of programs, I believe, so when you get to a million lines, then it's really far beyond what may be adequate for a program that is only a few thousand lines long. Things become much more difficult; the increase in complexity of the interactions between the different parts is greater than linear, therefore the need for rigorous specification is much greater for what you might call real programs.

By the way, we wrote down the complete formal specification of ML in the form of inference rules. We laid down the formal definition of the language. What we didn't do was write down how implementations should relate to that formal specification, but because we had the formal specification we knew very much what we were trying to implement. First of all we had a very clear specification, and secondly we did not intend to change it, at least only very, very slowly.

Now what happens with real-life programs is that they have to provide the possibility of changing or removing parts, adapting parts, introducing other parts, because the specification is going to change. So for real programs in real life there is an additional reason for being very careful about the relation between the specification and the implementation, because you are going to change the specification and you want to know exactly what that is going to imply for the change in the implementation.

### Do you have any interesting anecdote regarding the development of ML?

**Robin:** Well, one thing is that we spent much more time arguing about syntax than we did about semantics. We agreed on the functional understanding of the language to a very large extent, but very often when it came to matters of taste like which word would be used in the syntax, then we would argue indefinitely because we had no scientific basis on which to base the decision.

Another story: we gave ML a very carefully thought-out type system which was modest compared to some of the type theories that were already around. We were using ML for purpose of doing formal proofs using mathematical logic and one of the things we had to do was to make it efficient to implement what we called the "simplification rules." When you transform a complicated expression into an expression in some particular form, sometimes called *normal form* or *canonical form*, you have a lot of rules that dictate the transformations. To do those transformations quickly you have to implement them rather cleverly, so that you can be looking through all the rules which might apply and matching them somehow simultaneously.

We were implementing this simultaneous matching in ML, and we discovered that something wasn't quite efficient, and it turned out to be because our type system was a little bit limiting. For this particular bit of the implementation—which was actually the implementation of an analytical tool, a theorem prover—we decided to suspend the rule in ML and we made it much more efficient. As a matter of fact, it wasn't too bad because the more generous type system we used was fairly well understood anyway, but it was more complicated; we wanted ML to have a simple type system, and we needed a slightly more generous but slightly more complicated one to do some of the work that we wanted to do efficiently.

*If you were to start over and design ML today, would the advances in computing or your understanding change the design in dramatic ways or would it turn out mostly the same?*

**Robin:** We designed it for theorem proving. It turned out that theorem proving was such a demanding sort of task that it became a general-purpose language. That makes me ask, "What would I be designing it for now?" If I were designing it for theorem proving again, the same problems would be there. You want something where state can be changed. You don't want a pure functional language because you want to change the state of it often; you want to manage the inference tree or whatever it is that you're growing or the tree of goals and subgoals. You want to change that.

Having moved from that world into dealing with much more explicitly dynamic systems like ubiquitous computing, I'd feel lost if I were using a functional language. If I were designing the language for theorem proving, then maybe the facilities in Haskell, the monads by which they deal with sequence, might be a better idea—but I'm not sure. I'd have to know very much what I was designing it for.

What puzzles me is how people can design languages without having some preferred domain of application, some kind of specific things that they want to make easy to do. Java probably had a good idea about that and so it turned out to be a good language. But the space of possible application domains is pretty large now. That's why you seem to get a lot of different languages for different purposes. Purpose is the missing parameter. If I were designing it for the same purpose, then I might well come up with the same language.

*I've looked at your work, and it seems like you take the approach "Within this problem I want to create a set of reusable primitives—my theorems—and then I will build other theorems on top of those."*

**Robin:** I think you can use ML without having many theorems in mind, but maybe you're talking about a designer rather than a user. Certainly when we were designing the thing and using the operational structures and semantics that we did, it was in mind that we would want to prove certain theorems about the whole language—for example, that there would be no dangling references. There were quite a few things that we wished to be true, and in fact later have been proved by automatic proof systems or semiautomatic proof systems. To my relief!

We knew informally that there wouldn't be any dangling references, but it's nice to have a formal proof of the fact, to be sure you didn't make a bad mistake. On the other hand we did get into trouble with reference types, types of assignable variables. A couple of people showed that we had trouble with these in the type system. If we had inposed a certain constraint on the language then we wouldn't have had that trouble. On investigation they found that only 3% of programs would be affected by the constraint! If we were happy with the other 97%, then we could avoid the trouble. We revised the language to impose the constraint, and that triggered the revision that we did in '97, as opposed to '90 when the first semantics came out.

*When you revise a language, is a formal revision the only way to keep implementation and specification synchronized?*

**Robin:** I suppose we kept them synchronized. We were able to show that we were upward compatible. In other words, old implementations were OK as long as they were only implementing the slightly restricted form of programs. Upward compatibility was a real question in revision.

As a matter of fact I almost wish we hadn't done the revision, but it was such a tempting thing to get right and also to do something more simply that these people had suggested. What happened was because we were doing a revision, we revised various other things as well. The revision took us more effort than we really had wanted. On the whole we could so nearly not have bothered to do the revision. But on balance I'm glad that we did it, because something had been exposed about the type system that was clearly a valuable thing to know, and we were able to do that side of things more simply.

# Beyond Informatics

*What are the major problems in computer science today?*

**Robin:** What I have been working on lately is the notion of a structure of models. If you work in a high-level programming language, then that's expressed in terms of entities of lower-level languages, then that's expressed in lower-level assembly code, and the way assembly code behaves is expressed in terms of logic diagrams underneath, and so you have then a model that is no longer a software model, but a model of electronic objects. And that in turn is an explanation of the artifact that is the computer, which eventually is going to run your program, which is about four levels up in the hierarchy of models. That isn't the end of the story, because you could go higher than that from a programming language to a specification language, which is in some sense a higher model, so you already have five levels.

Think about ubiquitous computing, the kind of systems that are going to manage your household shopping and fill your refrigerator for you, or that will monitor the health of individuals by attaching to their body or even traveling inside them. To understand those systems you are going to need many levels of modeling, because people talk about software agents as negotiating with each other, requesting resources from each other, trusting each other, and reflecting on their own behaviour, in other words exhibiting all kinds of semihuman properties. Some of the behaviour of these systems is going to be expressed in a very high kind of logic that has to do with trust, knowledge, belief, and so on. So you are going to need a theory of those logics, explaining how to specify programs in terms of more basic behaviour. These specifications will be of the normal kind, which has to do with the operational behaviour of the program. but then at high levels you would ask such questions as, "is it true that this program trusts that one?", or "how do you implement the notion of trust between computing agents?" or "how do you understand the way in which an agent can be said to believe what another agent wishes to do, or to believe that the other agent is a threat to its own aspirations?"

I can see those questions living perhaps three levels higher than the normal level of specification that we have for ordinary programs. Whatever the models are, they model software, or they model other models that explain software some level lower. Besides this, if you build something like the European Airbus, then you are combining the model of the software with the electromechanical model of how the plane would work, and possibly even the model of atmospheric conditions or the weather, which is going to be met by the plane when it flies. So we have this challenge to combine models, sometimes models from natural science like meteorological models, or electromechanical engineering models, and then the software models, and these all interact. At the level of such combined models, you should be able to predict how this Airbus is going to perform.

I like the idea that we have a combination of the natural and the artificial, but we have the same notion of modeling applied to both; it's just in the case of the artificial that the model precedes the artifact, whereas in the natural case the natural phenomenon comes first and the modeling is done later. It's a sort of integrity between informatics and natural science.

*When you design hardware, you can actually test it physically. In software, sometimes we fail during the implementation step, before we have any users. How can we combine these different steps of design, implementation, and real-world use?*

**Robin:** If you look at the models that natural science has built, ultimately they only validate them by observation, by observing that the real world behaves in the ways their models predict. This means that they can never fully validate their models; they can only falsify them by discovering that what is observed on some occasions is not what they predicted. They could never observe that every possible phenomenon is as they predicted, because that is an infinite amount of work.

We have a better situation if, for example, we are implementing a high-level programming language in terms of a lower-level one. We have a formal description of how each of these behaves, and so we can validate the implementation that is the translation of the higher-level programs into the lower-level ones by seeing that the scientific or theoretical explanation of the behaviour at the higher level is actually consistent with the explanation at the lower level. So we have a chance of validating the way in which one model is realized by another one at a lower level. It's only when we get down to implementing the lower-level programs as physical artifacts that we cannot do this kind of mathematical proofs, but at every higher level, we have a chance, provided the models are well expressed, and provided the meaning of the entities at each level are a part of the model at that level. At each level, you have entities and then you have the explanation of how they behave, and that's the medium by which you expect to validate the implementation of a high-level model by some kind of lower-level implementation.

That's the way I have been trying to persuade people to think. For example, one of my recent talks was called "Ubiquitous computing: shall we understand it?", and what I meant with "understand" was precisely that we would like to specify the behaviour of one of these systems, like something that is monitoring the behaviour of your body, and we would like to understand how the specification of the behaviour of that system is actually implemented by the agents.

I don't think it's very easy to persuade people of this; they tend to say it's going to be impossible because the systems are going to be so large that you can't do it. In fact I read a European report that said no one would be able to analyze the behaviour of ubiquitous computing systems. It seems to me that that was an entirely wrong thing to be said. It's up to us whether we design systems that can be analyzed or not, so we should create them in such a form that the analysis is possible.

### What links do you see between engineering and informatics?

**Robin:** Well, engineering is very often already supported by a natural science that came first. A lot of chemical engineering has arrived since the chemical theories were designed and tested against reality, so chemical engineering arises as a result of the science chemistry, which was observing natural phenomena, so you then begin to be able to engineer using the understanding that comes from the natural science.

I think the same thing is true in physics, but in software it seems to be different, there is no such thing as naturally occurring software, as far as I can see it's too much of a stretch to try to pretend that software exists inside our minds or whatever, so we don't have a developed science that can be the basis for software engineering. So I think the link between engineering and software is precisely not a link as much as a contrast; we don't have software engineering based on a well-accepted science, whereas in most other forms of engineering they are based on well-accepted science.

### What's the role of math in computer science?

**Robin:** There are various parts of math that get used. We use logic, we use algebra, we use probability theory; in hybrid systems, which mix up continuous phenomena with discrete behaviour, we use the differential calculus. So there seems to be a role for more and more varied parts of mathematics. What's not so clear is how you pick a part. Are you picking it because you like to do probability theory or you like stochastics? Or are you picking it because you envision some kind of computer system or informatic system that is going to explain?

As a mathematician, you can choose what you like to study; for us I think you have to look at practically occurring systems, whether they are natural or artificial, and then ask what do I need to explain that?

Lately I had to understand stochastic analysis, which is the probability of duration, time elapse, and so on. That seems absolutely necessary if we are going to use some of our models to explain biological phenomena. I have been moved to do learning I never did before in order to understand how that theory works. Also I have been understanding some more abstract parts of math like algebra, category theory, and so on. You usually find that you are only going to use a part of that, so you are not going to develop the very sophisticated pure theories that the mathematicians develop, you are going to pick a bit here and there, and these parts may be already well understood, or they may be less known because they are not beautiful enough, so you may be eventually a contributor to the pure theories, even though your aim is to explain something real.

## Do you define yourself as a computer scientist or a researcher?

**Robin:** I don't like the term "computer scientist" because it puts too much emphasis on the computer, and I think the computer is just an instance of informatic behaviour, so I would say "informatic scientist." Of course it depends on what you mean by informatics. I tend to think it means acts of calculation and communication, communication being very important.

## What is your role as informatic scientist?

**Robin:** My role, I think, is to try to create a conceptual framework within which analysis can happen. To do this you have to take account of what is actually happening in software, like for example this notion of ubiquitous system, but you try to abstract from that in some ways. This is truly difficult; you will make mistakes, you will invent the wrong concepts, they won't fly in a sense, they won't scale up. You are looking for elementary notions that can be scaled up, so that they can actually be used to explain existing or proposed large software systems.

I think this notion of communication among agents is very important because it is one of the first concepts to be isolated in computation theory that the logicians hadn't already studied. The idea of a structured population of interactive agents: what should be the structure? How are they going to be linked to each other? Which ones can communicate with which other ones? Can they create new ones? Can they adapt their behaviour according to their neighbours' requests or behaviour? You come across a huge range of questions that can only be asked when you have populations of agents rather than, as in the early days of programming, just a single program that was supposed to do just a single task.

*Can the Internet help us find solutions?*

**Robin:** I think the Internet might create problems. To understand it is a problem in itself. It might help if we create conceptual tools that can be used to analyze the Internet behaviour, then they may be the ones that we need to understand other kinds of populations of agents, like agents monitoring your body, or controlling traffic on a motorway.

A lot of what has happened on the Internet has been excellently designed. It's a good example to study because it has worked in practice extraordinary well, so I think it's part of the solution as well as part of the problem.

*How do you see the computer science research field today?*

**Robin:** I see it very widely spread. People who build large systems are not using rigorous ways of specifying them. Also the people who work at the lower levels or at the more formal levels, if you like, they sometime get absorbed into pure mathematics and they don't perhaps like to make concessions to the world's realities, so you get a bifurcation of the communities. Well, in fact there is a spectrum as you move from the front line of application back to theories, and you can find people all the way along that rather long path, who find it difficult to understand the people to the left or to the right of them.

I see it not very well connected. We designed a Grand Challenge for computing in the U.K. called "Ubiquitous computing: Experience, Design and Science." By experience, we mean the kind of experiments that people do with instruments in environments of some kind. They might instrument a building by putting a computer in every room that might recognize people when they arrive, or report their movements. So you can have the people who are experimenting with alternative designs; then you have people in the background who are implementing those things in a way according to good engineering principles; then below them, you have the scientists who are relating more abstract models to the engineering work, while the engineers use what they build as the tools for experiment in the real world. These three levels—experiment, design, and science—try to bridge the gap that I was talking about.

I began to talk to people I wouldn't have normally talked to, the people who think of the social impact of ubiquitous systems, and they really think of the systems as not systems for use by humans, but systems in which humans are some of the components. You have these very concrete levels of understanding the systems, and you have to fight your way back through engineering principles right down to some concepts that might be used as the basis for analyzing the whole thing.

*Do you see any difference in the way research is done today and the way it was done in the 60s and 70s?*

**Robin:** Well, there is much more interest in these ubiquitous systems, which will be much more embedded in our environments, and that's a big difference. Think in particular of the real-time critical software that is inside vehicles or some other critical machinery. The kind of analysis that you have to do to validate real-time software is very different; the relationship between computing and real time used to be less of a concern.

Of course today, engineers building the Airbus or any pervasive system are very much concerned with what is happening in real time, just like in physics when you know how long things take.

## Will pervasive computing provide improvements or breakthroughs to AI?

**Robin:** Yes, but I think that we should approach AI indirectly. I have never been very happy with the emphasis that was placed on AI in the 60s or 70s. It seems to me that some of the hopes were being overstated.

As we begin to use words like "belief," and "knowledge," and so on, in understanding populations of agents, we begin to regard artificial intelligence not as something that either exists or doesn't exist, but as something that you gradually approach. Your systems become more and more intelligent, and become what's called "reflective," which means that they can report on their own activity and they can analyze their own behaviour, and so gradually concepts that are regarded as part of AI will be found in small quantities and perhaps in even larger quantities as we develop more of these systems.

So I am not sure that all the work that has been done on AI is going to be helpful. I think it's going to be more that, as we design our big systems, we use more human-centric words like "belief" in order to describe the events. Then the problem of the difference between an intelligent and a unintelligent being gets softened because you have degrees.

## Is there any lesson from the research field that you don't see applied?

**Robin:** Most programming languages have been designed without first thinking about the theory on which the meaning would be based. So, very often a language get designed and implemented, and then what it means, what it is supposed to happen when every program is run, is not necessarily predicted. Of course it was in some cases wonderfully predicted, for example, in ALGOL60; the ALGOL60 report of 1960 was so accurate that one could follow it and find out what was going to happen. This isn't always the case. Even in the good languages, the formal basis is not there before the language arrives, so what people do is later to retrofit a theory of meaning to the language, and maybe that means that the design could not take advantage of theoretical understanding.

Other examples of retrofitted analysis are large software systems. There are plenty of examples in the U.K.; they cause an enormous amount of delay and sometimes a disaster. Large systems will gain greatly from rigorous specification and some kind of scientific analysis.

## What do you mean when you say a language has a "theory of meaning"?

**Robin:** It's a theory of what an implementation will do. ML has a theory of meaning because I can prove from its operational semantics that there will be no dangling references. People have been showing lately all kinds of things about semantics of C, creating a theory of meaning for C. You have the semantics of C and then you prove certain theorems about all possible C programs using that semantics. There's been really quite a lot of success lately. Things are getting off the ground, I think.

*For a programming language, you mean the specification and design of the language itself. Could this prevent some mistakes by users of the language?*

**Robin:** Yes, it will mean that the user mistakes can be checked against the specifications and then a mismatch can be found before the program is ever run or ever used in practice.

What I am working on now is a behavioural theory of populations of interacting agents. It can describe how a population of people and machines might live in a built environment communicating among themselves. The same theory can be used, I hope, for understanding biological systems—for example, how a cell can produce a new cell as a kind of bubble on its surface.

There is the possibility of a general science of informatics that doesn't depend on particular applications. Before you ever get to a programming language, you hope to have a theory which then guides your design of a programming language. I want to create the theory before the language becomes fixed.

# CHAPTER TEN

# SQL

Given a large collection of structured data, how can you provide an efficient way to
gather, retrieve, and update information when you don't know what kind of operations people will need? That's the fundamental idea behind the relational model,
invented by E. F. (Ted) Codd. SQL is the most visible implementation of the relational model—a declarative language where you describe what you want, not how
to do it. Donald Chamberlin and Raymond Boyce developed SQL based on Codd's
ideas.

# A Seminal Paper

*How was SQL designed?*

**Don Chamberlin:** In the early 1970s, integrated database systems were just beginning to be widely deployed. Trends in technology and economics were making it possible for the first time for businesses to view their data as a corporate resource to be shared among many applications. This new perspective on data created an opportunity for development of a new generation of data management technology.

In the 1970s, IBM's mainstream database product was IMS, but in addition to the IMS development group, small research groups in several IBM locations were studying the database problem. Dr. E. F. (Ted) Codd was a leader of one of these groups, located at the IBM Research Laboratory in San Jose, California. Ray Boyce and I were members of another of small research group, located at IBM's Watson Research Center in Yorktown Heights, New York. Ray and I were studying database query languages, trying to find ways to improve the languages that were in common usage at the time.

In June of 1970, Ted Codd published a seminal paper* introducing the relational model of data and describing its advantages for data independence and application development. Codd's paper attracted a great deal of attention, both inside and outside IBM.

Ray Boyce and I attended a symposium on the relational data model organized by Codd at Watson Research Center in 1972. This symposium served as a "conversion experience" for Ray and myself. We were impressed with the elegance and simplicity of storing data in relational form, and we could see that many kinds of queries were easy to express in relational form. After the symposium, Ray and I engaged in a "query game" in which we challenged each other to design languages that were flexible enough to express many kinds of queries.

In 1973, Codd's ideas had gained such prominence that IBM decided to consolidate its database research efforts at Codd's location, San Jose, and to develop an industrial-strength prototype, called System R, as a proof of the relational concept. Ray Boyce and I, along with several other IBM researchers from Yorktown and Cambridge, moved to California to join the System R team. Since Ray and I were interested in languages, our first task was to design a query language to serve as the user interface for System R. We studied the relational languages that had been proposed by Codd and others, and set the following objectives for ourselves:

- We wanted to design a language that was based on common English keywords and was easy to type on a keyboard. We wanted the language to be based on familiar concepts such as tables with rows and columns. Like Codd's original language proposals, we wanted our language to be declarative rather than procedural. We wanted to capture

---

* Codd, E. F. "A Relational Model of Data for Large Shared Data Banks," Communications of the ACM, June 1970.

the power of the relational approach while avoiding some of the mathematical concepts and terminology, such as universal quantifiers and relational division operators, that had appeared in Codd's early papers. We also wanted to include some high-level query concepts, such as grouping, that we felt were not easily expressed in other relational languages.

- In addition to query, we wanted the language to provide other functionality. The most obvious extension was to include operations for inserting, deleting, and updating data. We also wanted to address tasks that had traditionally been handled by database administrators, such as creating new tables and views, controlling access to data, and defining constraints and triggers to maintain database integrity. We wanted all these tasks to be accomplished in a uniform syntactic framework. We wanted authorized users to be able to perform administrative tasks such as defining new views of data without stopping the system and invoking special tools. In other words, we saw query, update, and database administration as different aspects of a single language. In this respect, we had a unique opportunity because our users were creating their relational databases from scratch and were not constrained by backward compatibility.

- We wanted our language to be used both as a standalone query language for decision support, and as a development language for more complex applications. The latter goal required us to find ways to interface our new language to various popular application programming languages.

Based in part on our earlier experience with the "query game," Ray and I developed an initial proposal for a relational query language named SEQUEL (an acronym for "Structured English Query Language"), and published the proposal in a 16-page paper* at the annual ACM SIGFIDET (precursor to SIGMOD) conference in May 1974 (the same conference that featured the famous debate between Ted Codd and Charles Bachman). Shortly after publication of that initial paper, Ray Boyce died suddenly and tragically from the effects of a brain aneurysm.

After publication of the initial SEQUEL proposal, the language went through a phase of validation and refinement that spanned approximately 1974 through 1979. During this period, SEQUEL was implemented as part of the experimental System R database project at IBM San Jose Research Laboratory. System R was investigating several aspects of database management, including B-tree indexes, join methods, cost-based optimization, and transaction consistency. This implementation experience fed back into the evolving design of the language. SEQUEL was also influenced by feedback from three IBM customers who installed the System R prototype and used it on an experimental basis. The System R team met quarterly with the customer teams to discuss ways to improve the language and its implementation.

---

* Chamberlin, Don and Ray Boyce. "SEQUEL: A Structured English Query Language," Proceedings of ACM SIGFIDET (precursor to SIGMOD) Conference, Ann Arbor, MI, May 1974.

The SEQUEL language evolved significantly during the span of the System R project. The name of the language was shortened from SEQUEL to SQL to avoid a trademark infringement. A general-purpose join facility, missing in the original proposal, was added. The grouping facility was improved and a HAVING clause was added to filter groups. In order to deal with missing information, null values and three-valued logic were added to the language. Some new kinds of predicates were added, including a "Like" predicate for partial matching and an "Exists" predicate to test for a nonempty subquery. Additional papers were published to document the evolution of the language.[*†] During this phase of the language design, decisions tended to be made on a pragmatic basis, according to our implementation experience and the needs of our experimental users.

The research phase of SQL at IBM ended in 1979 with the completion of the System R project. At this point, responsibility for the language passed to development teams, who converted the System R prototype into commercial products on various IBM platforms. However, the first commercial product based on SQL was released in 1979, not by IBM but by a small company called Relational Software, Inc. The product was called Oracle, a name that was later adopted by the company, which is no longer small. The Oracle product was soon followed by SQL implementations from IBM and eventually from all major database vendors. SQL is now the world's most widely used database query language.

In order to promote portability of applications among various SQL implementations, the American National Standards Institute (ANSI) undertook a project to develop a standard specification for SQL. The result, called Database Language SQL, was published as an ANSI Standard in 1986[‡] and as an ISO Standard in 1987.[§] The SQL standard has served as a focus for continuing evolution of SQL, as new features have been added to the language to meet changing requirements. New versions of the SQL standard were published by ISO in 1989, 1992, 1999, 2003, and 2006.

*Adin Falkoff worked on APL with Ken Iverson. His work was similar to your work on SQL; both grew from the expression of a rigorously defined model. Does a formalism like Iverson's notation or Ted Codd's relational model help create a successful programming language?*

**Don:** I think the relational data model was fundamental to the design of SQL. I think that any programming language that computes deterministic results needs a well-defined set of objects and operators, which you might call a formal data model. I think that is the foundation of deterministic programming.

---

* Chamberlin, Don et al. "SEQUEL 2: A Unified Approach to Data Definition, Manipulation, and Control." *IBM Journal of Research and Development*, November 1976.

† Chamberlin, Don. "A Summary of User Experience with the SQL Data Sublanguage." Proceedings of the International Conference on Databases, Aberdeen, Scotland, July 1989.

‡ American National Standards Institute. "Database Language SQL," Standard No. X3.135 (1986 and subsequent updates).

§ International Organization for Standardization "Information Technology—Database Language SQL," Standard No. ISO/IEC 9075 (1987 and subsequent updates).

Even if you look at loosely typed languages like Python, you will find that they have a well-defined data model underlying them. It's more flexible than the relational model, but it must be well defined to be used as the base for the language semantics.

*If I were to create a new language myself, would you recommend I start from a rigorous data model, or is it something you can retrofit into a language as it grows?*

**Don:** In principle, I think you could do it either way, but you don't always have the flexibility to design a new data model concurrently with defining a new language. For example, the designers of XQuery didn't get to invent XML—they had to work with the data model that had already been defined by XML Schema and other W3C standards.

# The Language

*Why did you become interested in the query languages?*

**Don:** I have always been interested in languages.

*Do you speak other languages (beyond English)?*

**Don:** No, I don't speak any other human language, but I like to read and write, and I find languages a fascinating subject. I was very lucky in my career to be at the right place at the right time, when Ted Codd had his groundbreaking ideas about the relational data model. It was a once-in-a-lifetime opportunity to be a participant in a project that had the impact of our early relational database research. My existing interest in languages helped me to find a niche in this project, and I'm very grateful to have had that opportunity.

*One of the early design decisions was that you wanted SQL to be declarative, not procedural. What were the important criteria for this choice?*

**Don:** There were several reasons for this. The first is that we wanted the language to be optimizable. If the user tells the system in detailed steps what algorithm to use to process a query, then the optimizer has no flexibility to make changes, like choosing an alternative access path or choosing a better join order. A declarative language is much more optimizer-friendly than a lower-level procedural language.

The second reason is that we were very interested in data independence, meaning that system administrators should be free to add or delete indexes, change the organization of the data, and create new views of data. You should be able to write applications in such a way that they don't have dependencies on the physical organization of the data and the access paths that are available at the physical storage level. So, data independence is a second important reason why we wanted a declarative language.

The third reason has to do with user productivity. We thought that it would be easier for users to express their intent at a high level using familiar terminology rather than having to express their queries based on low-level machine concepts that were less familiar.

So we thought that declarative languages had important advantages for optimization, data independence, and user productivity.

*Were these widely held beliefs within your group at that time?*

**Don:** I think that the general advantages of declarative languages were pretty well understood, but I think there was significant uncertainty about whether a declarative language as complex as SQL could be implemented with the degree of performance required for commercial applications.

*Views abstract away the physical structure of data stored on disks. Was it a goal at the time that users might interact with data through views rather than directly through tables?*

**Don:** We thought that views would be widely used for querying data, because different applications would need to access data in different ways. For example, different applications may view data at different levels of aggregation, and may be authorized to view different parts of the data. Views provide a very natural mechanism for implementing these differences in access to data.

For updates, on the other hand, the situation is much more difficult, because when you update through a view, the system needs to map your updates onto the underlying stored data. In some cases that can be done, but in some cases there isn't a unique mapping that can be derived. For example, it's fine to query a view that aggregates average salaries by department, but if you try to update that view, I don't know what it means to change the average salary of a department. So we found that the use of views is much more widespread in querying applications than in updating applications.

*SQL was one of the first languages that had to deal with concurrent access to shared data. What impact did this issue have on the design of SQL?*

**Don:** Maintaining database consistency in a concurrent-update environment was one of the most important research issues addressed in the System R project at IBM Research. The ultimate result of this work was a rigorous definition of the "ACID" properties of electronic transactions, for which Jim Gray received the ACM Turing Award in 1999. These transaction properties were supported in System R (and other relational systems) by a system of locks and logs that is largely transparent to SQL users.

Concurrent access to shared data is reflected in SQL mainly by the concepts of transactions and degrees of isolation (isolation is the "I" in the ACID properties). Degrees of isolation allow application developers to control the tradeoff between protecting users from each other and maximizing the number of users who can be supported concurrently. An application that is performing a statistical survey, for example, might specify a low degree of isolation in order to avoid locking up large portions of the database. A banking transaction, on the other hand, might specify a high degree of isolation to make sure that all the transactions that affect a given account are serializable.

Concurrent updates are also visible to SQL programmers in the form of potential deadlocks. Under certain circumstances, two concurrent SQL transactions can encounter a deadlock; in this case, one of the transactions will receive a return code indicating that its effects have been rolled back.

*I read that there's an interesting Halloween story from the System R days involving Pat Selinger and Morton Astrahan.*

**Don:** On the occasion of the Halloween holiday in, I believe, 1975, Pat Sèlinger and Morton Astrahan were working on the optimizer for the first SQL implementation, which had to choose an access path to use when doing a bulk update such as giving a pay increase to all underpaid employees. Initially Pat and Morton thought that if you are looking for employees who earn less than a certain salary, it would be efficient to find them by using an index on their salary attribute. So the optimizer used an index to scan through employees in order of increasing salaries, updating the salaries as it went along. But we observed that when an employee's salary changes, he moves to a new place in the index, and as the scan continues it may encounter the same employee again and give him another pay increase. This problem was leading to incorrect and unpredictable results in this early experiment.

This problem was discovered by Pat and Morton on a Friday afternoon on Halloween, an American holiday. Pat came into my office and asked, "What are we going to do about this?" and I said "Pat, it's Friday afternoon, we can't solve this problem today; let's just remember it as the Halloween problem, and work on it next week."

Somehow that name became attached to the problem that you can't access data using an index on an attribute that's being changed or modified. Since this is a problem that has to be solved by all relational database optimizers, somehow this name has become fairly well known in the industry.

*What do the lessons about the invention, further development, and adoption of your language say to people developing computer languages today and in the forseeable future?*

**Don:** I think the history of SQL illustrates the importance of having a specific set of principles that guide the process of language design. I've made a list of some principles that I think (in hindsight) are important in designing a computer language. I'm not claiming here that all of these principles were well observed in the design of SQL; in fact, as various people have observed, some of them represent areas of deficiency in the original SQL design. To a considerable extent, these early deficiencies have been mitigated as the language has evolved.

Here's my list of design principles. Many of them seem like common sense, but applying them in practice is more difficult than it looks.

*Closure*

The language should be defined in terms of a data model consisting of a set of objects with well-defined properties. Each operator in the language should be defined in terms of its operands and its result as data model objects. The semantics of each operator should specify the effects of the operator on all the properties of the participating objects.

*Completeness*

Each kind of object in the data model should have operators to construct it, to decompose it into its more primitive parts (if any), and to compare it with other objects of a similar kind.

*Orthogonality*

The concepts of the language should be defined independently and should not be subject to special rules constraining their use. For example, if a scalar value is a concept in the language, any expression that returns a scalar value should be usable in any context where a scalar value is expected.

*Consistency*

Common tasks, such as extracting a component from a structured object, should be handled in a consistent way wherever they appear in various parts of the language.

*Simplicity*

The language should be defined in terms of a small number of relatively simple concepts. Designers should avoid the temptation to add special-purpose features. If the language is successful, keeping it simple will require discipline and determination to push back against many requests for "improvements." This ongoing struggle will be made easier if the language has a good extensibility mechanism (see the next item).

*Extensibility*

The language should have a well-defined, general-purpose mechanism whereby new functionality can be added, ideally with little or no impact on the syntax of the language. For example, a database query language might provide a facility for adding user-defined functions written in a separate Turing-complete programming language.

*Abstraction*

The language should not expose or depend on aspects of a specific implementation. For example, eliminating duplicates from a set of values should be specified in terms of an abstract concept such as a "primary key" rather than a physical strategy such as a "unique index." (This was a flaw in some of the earliest versions of SQL.) In the database world, this concept is sometimes called *data independence*.

*Optimizability*

The language should not place unnecessary constraints on algorithms for executing its expressions. For example, the definition of the language should allow some flexibility in the order of predicate evaluation. Where possible, the semantic specification of the language should be declarative rather than procedural, in order to provide opportunities for automatic optimization. In some cases, it is helpful to tolerate some indeterminacy (for example, in processing a given query, an error may or may not be raised depending on order of predicate evaluation).

*Resilience*

Not all programs are correct. The language should be designed in such a way that many programming errors can be detected and clearly identified at "compile" time (i.e., in the absence of actual input data). Also, the language should provide a mechanism that enables programmers to handle exceptional conditions at runtime.

# Feedback and Evolution

*Ted Codd's original paper on the relational data model was published in the open literature and influenced people outside IBM such as Larry Ellison, and Mike Stonebraker's group at UC Berkeley. Was this process similar to the "open source" model? How did external visibility affect the development of SQL?*

**Don:** In the 1970s, the relational data model was a new idea. It was a subject for advanced research and prototyping and it was not generally available commercially. SQL was developed as part of an experimental research project called System R that was independent of IBM's normal product development process. The research division at IBM traditionally publishes the results of its exploratory research in the open literature and that's what we did with the SQL language and other parts of System R.

We did not release the source code for our SQL implementation, so this is quite different from today's model of open source software. We didn't give away any software, but we described some of the interfaces and techniques that were used in our experimental implementation of SQL. For example, some of our optimization techniques were described in the open literature, and as you know some of these papers have been influential for other people in the industry who were developing similar kinds of software.

This process of sharing ideas was not a one-way street. In the early days of research in relational databases, ideas were shared freely among several organizations including IBM, UC Berkeley, and others, to their mutual benefit.

## Why did SQL become popular?

**Don:** I think that the main reason for the popularity of SQL derives from the power and simplicity of Ted Codd's relational data model. Codd was responsible for the conceptual breakthrough that revolutionized database management—SQL was simply an attempt to encapsulate Codd's concepts in an accessible format. Compared to other existing technology, relational databases provided a quantum improvement in user productivity for creating and maintaining database applications.

Of course, SQL was not the only language based on Codd's ideas that was proposed during the 1970s. I think that some of the specific reasons why SQL became successful include the following:

- The fact that SQL supported a complete set of database administration tasks was important to the acceptance of the language. Using SQL, any authorized user could create or drop tables, views, and indexes at any time by using simple commands. These tasks had traditionally required the services of a database administrator, shutting down the database and incurring significant costs and delays. SQL liberated end users from database administrators and allowed them to freely experiment with alternative database designs.

- SQL was reasonably easy to learn. A subset of SQL sufficient to accomplish simple tasks could be learned in a few hours. Users could then pick up the more complex and powerful aspects of the language as needed.

- SQL was available in robust, multiuser implementations from at least two vendors (IBM and Oracle), and on multiple platforms including OS/370 and Unix. As the language gained popularity, additional implementations became available, creating a snowball effect.

- SQL supported interfaces to popular programming languages. Together with these host languages, SQL was able to scale up to support complex applications.

- The early work at ANSI and ISO on standardization of SQL gave users confidence that their SQL applications would be portable from one implementation to another. This confidence was reinforced by the creation of an SQL conformance test suite by the National Institute of Standards and Technology (NIST). Some agencies of the U.S. government required their database procurements to conform to an SQL-based Federal Information Processing Standard (FIPS-127).

- The development of SQL took place at a propitious time, just as many enterprises were developing or converting their critical applications to use integrated corporate databases. Application developers and database administrators were in short supply. The productivity improvements provided by SQL-enabled organizations to deal effectively with their application development backlog.

### Why has SQL remained popular?

**Don:** Many of the languages that were popular 25 years ago have effectively disappeared, including some languages that had the support of large corporations. I think the reasons why SQL remains in widespread use include the following:

- The ISO SQL standard has provided a way in which the language can evolve in a controlled fashion to meet changing user requirements. The standard is maintained by a committee that includes both users and vendors, and the vendors have committed resources to keep their implementations in conformance with the evolving standard. Over the years, the SQL standard has corrected flaws in the original language design and added important new functionality such as outer join, recursive queries, stored procedures, object-relational functionality, and OLAP (online analytical processing). The SQL standard has also served to focus the industry's attention and resources, providing a common framework in which individuals and companies could develop tools, write books, teach courses, and provide consulting services.

- SQL manages persistent data, which has a long lifetime. Enterprises that have an investment in SQL databases are inclined to build on that investment rather than starting over with a different approach.

- SQL is robust enough to solve real problems. It spans a broad spectrum of usage from business intelligence to transaction processing. It is supported on many platforms and in many processing environments. Despite some criticism about its lack of elegance,

SQL has been used successfully by many organizations to develop critical, real-world applications. I believe that this success reflects the origin of the language in an experimental prototype that was responsive to the needs of real users from the earliest days. It also reflects the pragmatic decisions that have been made throughout the history of the language as it has evolved to meet changing requirements.

*Systems written in C today are perhaps a few orders of magnitude larger than systems written in C in the 70s, but the datasets of today are much, much larger. A handful of lines of SQL can still operate on a dataset as it grows huge; it seems that SQL can scale with data much better. Is that true? If so, why?*

**Don:** Maybe this gets back to an additional advantage of declarative languages, in that they are more susceptible to parallel processing than procedural languages. If you are performing an operation over a large dataset and it is described in a nonprocedural way, the system has more opportunities to split up the work across multiple processors. The relational data model and the high level of abstraction that it supports have been very helpful in that kind of scaling. SQL, as a declarative language, provides opportunities for compilers to take advantage of implicit parallelization opportunities.

*Did you get feedback during these years from users of products based on your research?*

**Don:** Since IBM's mainline database products began to support SQL in the 1980s, IBM has conducted periodic reviews called "customer advisory councils," where we collect feedback from our users about SQL and other aspects of our database products. There is also an independent user group called IDUG, the International DB2 User Group, that has a meeting once a year in America, Europe, and Asia, and at those IDUG conferences there is a lot of exchange of information between DB2 users and IBM. Much of that feedback comes back to the research and development teams in IBM and it is used to help us plan future enhancements to the products. This is the origin of many new features like the object relational extensions and the OLAP extensions.

Another source of ideas is the ANSI and ISO committees that maintain the SQL language standards, which include representatives from both users and implementors of the language. These sources of feedback have helped the language to evolve over the years to meet the changing needs of the user community.

*You also conducted some usability tests with a psychologist named Phyllis Reisner for two languages, SQUARE and SEQUEL. What did you learn during those tests?*

**Don:** Yes, Phyllis Reisner was an experimental psychologist who worked with the System R group to test our language ideas on college students. SQUARE was an early attempt at a relational database language based on a mathematical notation, whereas SEQUEL was a similar language that used an English keyword notation.

Phyllis did an experiment in which she taught both of these languages to college students to find out which approach was easier to learn and could be used with the fewest errors. I think that overall the English keyword notation proved to be easier to learn and use than the mathematical notation.

It was interesting though that the majority of the mistakes that were made by the college students didn't have much to do with the structure of the language. They had to do with things like whether strings of data were enclosed in quotes or not, or whether the data was capitalized or not—things that you might consider to be trivial or inconsequential errors, not really related to the structure of the language or the data. Nevertheless those kinds of details were hard for users to get right.

*Today there are a lot of SQL injection attacks against web services that don't correctly filter the input before it's included in the queries to their databases. Any thoughts?*

**Don:** SQL injection attacks are a good example of something that we never dreamed of in the early days. We didn't anticipate that queries would be constructed from user input from web browsers. I guess the lesson here is that software should always take a careful look at user input before processing it.

*Did SQL evolve in ways that were unexpected during its initial design?*

**Don:** SQL was intended to be a declarative, nonprocedural language, and it still retains that character. But over the years, the language has evolved to become much more complex than we originally imagined. It's been used for many things that we never thought of in the early days. Features such as Data Cubes and OLAP analysis have been added to the language. It's been turned into an object-relational language, with user-defined types and methods. We didn't anticipate all these new applications. SQL users today have to deal with more complexity and need more technical sophistication than we expected in the early days.

Ray Boyce and I hoped that SQL would have an impact on the database industry, but its impact did not come in the way we expected. Ray and I thought that we were developing a language that would be used mainly by "casual users" to pose ad hoc queries for decision support applications. We were trying to make databases accessible to a new class of users who were not trained computer scientists. We expected to see SQL used directly by financial analysts, urban planners, and other professionals who needed access to data but did not want to write computer programs. These expectations proved to be too optimistic.

Since the beginning, SQL has been used primarily by trained computer programmers. In fact, over the years a great deal of SQL code has been generated by automatic tools, a development that was not foreseen in the early days. The nonprogramming professionals who Ray and I thought would use SQL directly are more likely to use forms-based interfaces supported by application programs with back-end access to an SQL database. Direct access to data by casual users had to wait for the development of spreadsheets and search engines.

*You have worked on relational systems, and also on a document-processing tool called Quill that isolates users from the physical representation of documents. Spreadsheets like Excel also present data in a very intuitive, user-oriented way. Do these systems have something in common? Can this kind of data independence be extended to encompass the Web?*

**Don:** Quill and Excel both support what we might call direct manipulation user interfaces that allow users to operate on a visual representation of data that has an underlying logical structure. This has proved to be a very powerful metaphor. There's an analogy here with relational databases: the user operates on data at a high level of abstraction that is independent of the underlying data structures. Direct manipulation interfaces are easy to learn and use, but at some level they still need to be supported by specialized underlying data structures. Some kind of optimizing compiler or interpreter is needed to map the user's intent into the underlying data.

As far as the Web as a whole is concerned, it is what it is, and we don't have an opportunity to redesign the Web at this point, but all the popular search engines isolate their users from the details of processing requests for information. I'm sure that search engines will continue to evolve to support higher levels of abstraction, and to discover and exploit the semantics of information on the Web.

*You tried to develop a tool that would be useful to regular users, but for the most part only programmers use it.*

**Don:** I think we proved to be a little bit naïvely optimistic in our goals in the original design of the language. I worked with Ted Codd in the early days of the relational data model, and in those days Ted was working on a project called Rendezvous, which was a natural-language question-answering system based on the relational model. I didn't think that it was feasible at that time to go all the way in a natural language, but what I did hope was that we could design a human interface that was understandable enough that people could use it with very little training.

I think for the most part that didn't happen. SQL quickly grew to a level of complexity that made it a programming language and required a level of training that was consistent with other programming languages, so it has been used primarily by professionals.

I have the greatest respect for more recent web-based applications like Google that can be used to retrieve useful information without any training at all. We just didn't have the technology to support that back in the 70s.

*Is the difficulty in explaining how SQL works, or in exposing the ideas of the relational model that people may not have been prepared for?*

**Don:** I think both of those were factors that led to the requirement of a certain level of technical expertise among SQL users. Another factor relates to the difference between precise and imprecise queries.

When you throw a handful of search terms into Google, you are willing to accept an imprecise result. In other words, Google makes its best effort to find the documents that are most relevant to your list of search terms. That's a nondeterministic process, and the result in most cases is very useful.

With SQL we were working on a different kind of a problem in which the answers are deterministic, and for deterministic answers you need a query language with a higher degree of precision. You need to understand very explicitly the difference between "and" and "or," for example. In Google the semantics of queries can afford to be a little fuzzier than they are in the structured query domain where SQL is used.

*The cost of making a mistake or the cost of getting imprecise answers back from a web search is much smaller than the cost of getting the wrong salary figure for your employees.*

**Don:** That's right, and if you misspell something, or don't remember exactly what the join column is in a table, your query might not work at all in SQL, whereas less deterministic interfaces like Google are much more forgiving on small mistakes like that.

*You believe in the importance of determinism. When I write a line of code, I need to rely on understanding what it's going to do.*

**Don:** Well, there are applications where determinism is important and applications where it is not. Traditionally there has been a dividing line between what you might call databases and what you might call information retrieval. Certainly both of those are flourishing fields and they have their respective uses.

## XQuery and XML

*Will XML affect the way we use search engines in the future?*

**Don:** I think it's possible. Search engines already exploit the kinds of metadata that are included in HTML tags such as hyperlinks. As you know, XML is a more extensible markup language than HTML. As we begin to see more XML-based standards for marking up specialized documents such as medical and business documents, I think that search engines will learn to take advantage of the semantic information in that markup.

*You are now working on a new language called XQuery for accessing XML data. XML is different from relational data because it includes metadata. What challenges have you encountered when designing a query language for XML?*

**Don:** One of the greatest strengths of XML is that XML documents are self-describing. This makes it possible for XML documents to differ in their structures, and for these differences to be observable by reading the metadata in the form of XML tags that are included in the documents themselves. This makes XML a very rich and flexible format for representing information. In today's business applications where we exchange documents that are not all similar in structure, the internal metadata that is included in the XML format is very important. One of the main purposes of the XQuery language is to exploit this flexibility so that queries can operate on data and on metadata at the same time.

One of the challenges that we faced in designing XQuery is that there are many different environments in which the language needs to be used. There are some applications in which types are very important. In these applications, you want a strongly typed language that does a lot of type checking and raises errors if an object turns out not to conform to the expected type. But there are also other environments, sometimes referred to as Schema Chaos environments, in which data types are less important. In these environments you may be willing to accept data of unknown type or heterogeneous type, and you may want the language to be very flexible and to work on data of many different kinds.

It was difficult to design a language that could span this spectrum of usage from strongly typed to loosely typed. Also, the type system of XML Schema is much more complex than the type system of the relational data model, and designing a language to be used with this complex type system was very challenging.

The result is a language that's more complex than SQL. I think XQuery is harder to learn than SQL, but the payoff for dealing with this complexity is the ability to deal with the richer and more flexible data format that's offered by XML.

*You have participated in the standardization of two query languages, SQL and XQuery. What have you learned from these experiences about the standardization process?*

**Don:** First, I learned that standards have great value in providing a formal language definition, a focus for user feedback, and a mechanism for controlled evolution of a language to meet changing requirements. The standards process brings together people with varying points of view and expertise. The resulting collaboration is notoriously slow, but I believe it tends to produce a relatively robust language definition.

In my experience, the following practices are important to the effectiveness of a language standardization committee:

- The committee should maintain a reference parser at all times during language development, and should use this parser to validate all the examples and use cases used in the language specification and related documents. A surprising number of errors are exposed by this simple process. Maintenance of a reference parser exposes usability and implementation issues, and ensures that no ambiguities or other anomalies are introduced into the language grammar.

- The committee should maintain a formal set of use cases that illustrate the intended usage of the language. These use cases are helpful in exploring alternative approaches during the design process, and can ultimately serve as examples of "best practices" in language usage.

- The language definition should be backed up by a conformance test suite, and at least one reference implementation should be required to demonstrate conformance before adoption of the standard. This practice tends to expose "edge" cases and to ensure that the semantic description of the language is complete and unambiguous. A standard without an objective measure of conformance is of little value.

## How did XQuery feel different from inventing SQL?

**Don:** I did notice some differences. We had many more constraints in designing XQuery than in designing SQL, and there were a couple of reasons for that.

One was that a lot of people were interested in XQuery right from the beginning. We were designing the language in the context of an international standards organization that had representatives from about 25 different companies, and they all had preconceived notions of how the language should turn out. We were doing this work in the full glare of publicity with all our working drafts published on the Web. As a result, we got a lot of feedback, much of which proved to be helpful.

SQL was a very different experience. We were designing the language in a very small group, and nobody was interested outside IBM and not very many people inside, so we had a lot more flexibility to make autonomous decisions without having to explain them and justify them to lots of people that had strong opinions.

## Having a low profile can be kind of liberating, I found.

**Don:** Yes, it has many advantages!

## Does the size of the team affect the results?

**Don:** Yes, I find that, for me, the ideal size of a team is 8 to 10 people. A team of that size can accomplish a lot, but it's small enough that everyone can understand what everyone else is doing and information can propagate easily without a lot of friction and overhead. That's about the size of the System R team that built the first experimental SQL implementation.

## What is the best way to stimulate an R & D team?

**Don:** I think the best way to stimulate a research and development team is to give them an opportunity for their work to have an impact. If people can see that their work is going to make a difference in the world, they will be very motivated and work very hard. This is an advantage that I think small start-up companies tend to have: they are often doing something revolutionary and don't have a legacy that places limitations on their work.

In larger companies, opportunities of that kind are more unusual, but they do exist. I personally found it very motivating to be a part of the early development of relational database technology. It was something that we could see had the potential for a revolutionary impact. Working on a project that has that potential motivates people to do their best work.

## How do you define success in your field?

**Don:** That's a wonderful question. I would define success in research as having a lasting impact on technology. If we can develop theories or interfaces or methods that are widely used and survive the test of time, I think we can claim that our research has some value.

One of the best examples of this is the work of Ted Codd. Ted came up with ideas that were simple enough for everyone to understand and powerful enough that nearly 40 years later, they still dominate the information management industry. Not many of us can aspire to that level of success, but that's how I would define an ideal outcome of a research project.

CHAPTER ELEVEN

# Objective-C

Objective-C is a combination of the C and Smalltalk programming languages with Smalltalk's object support added. Tom Love and Brad Cox developed this system in the 80s. Its popularity grew with the rise of Steve Jobs's NeXT systems in 1988, and it is currently most prevalent in Apple's Mac OS X. Unlike other OO systems at the time, Objective-C used a very small runtime library instead of a virtual machine. Objective-C's influence is present in the Java programming language, and Apple's Objective-C 2.0 is popular for Mac OS X and iPhone applications.

# Engineering Objective-C

*Why did you extend an existing language instead of creating a new one?*

**Tom Love:** That was very important because of the requirements for compatibility in large organizations. It was a very important decision early on that you could take a C program and run through the Objective-C compiler and nothing would be changed. Nothing that you could do in C would be prohibited, and nothing that you did in Objective-C would be incompatible with C. That was a big constraint, but it was a very important constraint. It allowed for mixing and matching easily, too.

*Why did you choose C?*

**Tom:** Probably because we were using Unix systems in a research environment originally and programming in C and we were trying to do things that were difficult to do in C. The August 1981 issue of *Byte* magazine showed up and started describing to most of the world for the first time what one could do with Smalltalk. Brad basically said, "I think most of the capabilities that they're talking about in Smalltalk I could figure out how to add to C."

We were a research group in ITT building distributed programming environments to help software engineers build telecommunications systems. So we were looking for the right tools to build a set of what today might be referred to as CAD tools—but it was more than just CAD tools.

*From today's perspective, is Objective-C better than Smalltalk in some ways?*

**Tom:** The Objective-C that exists today and the libraries that exist today are very different than what existed in the fall of 1984 or 1983 when the first version actually came out. We talked earlier about a set of given applications for which a language is appropriate and a set for which it's not. Smalltalk absolutely is a wonderful language for learning about object-oriented programming, and I'm actually surprised that it's not being used a lot more often in academic environments because it's a beautiful way to learn the basic concepts. By contrast, if I were responsible for writing a new operating system, I wouldn't choose Smalltalk as the language for writing an operating system. If I'm doing certain kinds of research models or prototypes or something like that, Smalltalk is a beautiful solution. I think there's a range of appropriate solutions for which any given language works well and there's an overlap between the two.

*Objective-C and C++ both started from C, but they went in two very different directions. Which approach do you prefer now?*

**Tom:** There's the successful direction, and then there's the approach that Bjarne took with C++. In one case, it was a small, simple—dare I say, elegant—programming language that was very crisp and well defined. In the other case it was a pretty ugly, complicated, difficult language that had some really troublesome features. I think those are the distinctions between the two.

*Is C++ too complex in some ways?*

**Tom:** Oh, absolutely.

*It's still evolving. They are still adding things today.*

**Tom:** Well, and go to it. I happen to like my languages really simple. APL is a nice programming language because it's incredibly simple but outrageously powerful for doing certain kinds of applications. If I'm writing a statistical package, then APL is a dandy language to be using because it really does matrix algebra better than anything I know of. But, you know, it's just an example.

*Why do you think that C++ was used more frequently than Objective-C?*

**Tom:** It had the AT&T moniker behind it.

*Just that?*

**Tom:** I think so.

*What do you think about Objective-C today?*

**Tom:** It still exists. How about that?

*Objective-C 2.0 adds a lot of interesting features—Apple is certainly keeping it alive.*

**Tom:** I was just talking to someone last night who is programming for the iPhone. He was describing that he had downloaded the Developers Kit for the iPhone, and it's Objective-C through and through. It stays alive.

*Did you have any idea during its early development that people would use the language on mobile phones and small devices?*

**Tom:** We first met when I hired Brad into an advanced technology research group for the telephone industry—ITT. Our job was to look 10 years ahead at that time. One of the things that we learned about looking 10 years ahead was that we weren't very good at it; particularly, we weren't very good at the software aspects of it. It turned out we were spectacularly good at predicting where hardware technology was going to be 10 years out, and we were 10 years optimistic about software. By that, I mean we thought things would happen by 1990 that didn't happen until 10 years later.

*Even in the late 90s, people were still dubious about some of the ideas that Lisp and other languages had invented and had used successfully for 30 or 40 years by that point.*

**Tom:** Right. Of course programmers are legendary for being optimists. Another thing is that that the population keeps turning over. We develop PCs and we develop PDAs, and we develop programmable telephones, and the set of people that are programming those different devices is often different. It's not like the same people keep using the same technology. A long time ago the tradition was that the mainframers were different than the minicomputer guys who were different from the PC guys who were different from the workstation guys. Each of them independently had to go learn some of the same lessons. We keep doing that.

Listen to a group of people that are at a conference doing iPhone development applications. They won't look at all like the crowd that will show up at a mainframe conference these days, or even a Windows development conference. The .NET programmers are not only a different crowd but a different generation as well.

*Do you see that in hardware as well?*

**Tom:** I don't think that the learning is as distinct.

*Why can we speculate about 10 years in the future of hardware, but not software?*

**Tom:** We have good quantifiable data for hardware. For software, we don't have such quantification. As you might know about me, I'm big on counting stuff. I like numbers. It has been a bit of an avocation of mine for 30 years of trying to figure out how long does it take a programmer to write a class, and how long is it being tested, and how many testers do you need per programmer, and how many tests need to be written for every class, and how many lines of code fit in a box of paper: 100,000.

## Growing a Language

*Do you believe in growing and evolving a language?*

**Tom:** Slowly. The interesting and complicated question has to do with proprietary languages versus languages in the public domain versus open source languages, and those are reasonably difficult things to resolve. If you have a single authority responsible for making changes to the language and those changes happen slowly and methodically, that's probably a good thing—but some people don't like the fact that they have to pay for their compilers or pay annual maintenance charges on a compiler that's not changing very often. We struggled with these questions for years. It is one of the issues when trying to design and deploy a programming language—same problem with operating systems, of course.

*How do you decide whether to add a feature to a language?*

**Tom:** You want as few features as possible to give you a maximum amount of functionality and flexibility.

*You've said that object-oriented languages are somewhat limited in their applicability. Are there ways to reduce this limit?*

**Tom:** Any language that you choose has a range of systems for which it's appropriate and systems that are outside that range. There are still people writing very tight assembly language code for certain special-purpose applications because they need absolute maximum runtime efficiency. I don't think this happens as much anymore, but there are simply physical space constraints that one has to be aware of. My view is that no matter how wide the range, you can find examples that are outside it. So I don't mean to imply that object-oriented languages have especially small range. For example, if you're building some kind of onboard avionics system for some remotely piloted vehicle and you have a tiny little processor and tiny little system on board that is essentially a model airplane, it's going to be a different problem than if you're designing software to run on a Boeing Dreamliner.

*I can see why you chose Smalltalk; it was clearly the best choice. Even now it's a good choice.*

**Tom:** It's an elegant language. I know some of the earlier languages like APL. APL has, like Smalltalk, one really gigantic simplifying principle around which it was designed and built. That was hugely important. Objective-C started off life with the idea of being a hybrid language, and we rigorously upheld the notion that we wouldn't take away anything from C, we would only add to it. Therefore we weren't creating a C-derivative language, but rather a hybrid based upon C.

Some of those early decisions were actually really important, for the fact that it's still around. I often refer to myself as the guy responsible for the square brackets in Objective-C, because Brad and I had a long conversation about. Do we have a C syntax that is consistently C, or do we create a hybrid language where I describe it as "the square bracket is a gear shift into the object land"? Our view was that if you had a hybrid language, you could build a set of foundation classes so that at some point most of the work is actually done inside the square brackets. This allows a lot of details to be hidden from a typical application programmer.

The square brackets are an indication of a message sent in Objective-C. The original idea was that once you built up a set of libraries of classes, then you're going to spend most of your time actually operating inside the square brackets, so you're really doing object-oriented programming using an underlying framework of objects that were developed in the hybrid language, which was a combination of procedural and object-oriented language. Then as you began to build up libraries of functionality, there's less and less requirement to drop into the procedural world and you could stay within the square brackets. It was a deliberate decision to design a language that essentially had two levels— once you had built up enough capability, you could operate at the higher level. I actually think that's one of the reasons. Had we chosen a very C-like syntax, I'm not sure anybody would know the name of the language anymore and it wouldn't likely still be in use anywhere.

The other two goals at the time were sort of simplicity and elegance. Back in those days, people in the business had probably written a program in 20 different program languages. I found for myself that when you try to do something serious in APL you begin to learn its real power, and see, it turns out to be a grand program for these applications.

My first home computer was an IBM 5100, which was actually an APL machine. I thought it would be interesting to see if you could do something like a full-screen text editor using APL, and that turned out to be a really hard problem.

*You'd have to treat your screen as a matrix of characters...that would be tricky.*

**Tom:** Right. It was a poor match. A lot of us in this generation came along and spent some time at least with a string-processing language, a Lisp processing language, a matrix-manipulation language, and an object-oriented language. For me, I felt like I learned important fundamental concepts each time I added a language to my repertoire.

*I can see how that builds the desire for a good, general-purpose language. Was your motivation to start from C and add Smalltalk trappings?*

**Tom:** We were trying to figure out what is the right programming language to use to build programming environments for large international teams building telephone switching systems. We weren't completely happy with any of the choices available in those days.

When the August 1981 issue of *Byte* magazine came out on Smalltalk, we all went out and read it from cover to cover a few times. Brad walked in my office one day and said, "Can I take this computer home for about a week? I think in about a week I can come back and show you that I can build something real close to Smalltalk as an extension to C language."

I allowed him to do something hugely unusual at the time, which was to take a computer home. That computer was about the size of a box that a pair of cowboy boots might come in those days. It was an Onyx computer, a computer company lost in computer history for most people.

*I have the Smalltalk 80 book from '83 right here. It looks like more than a week's work, but the compiler itself is not that complicated.*

**Tom:** No, it isn't. Languages that have clean underpinnings aren't themselves that complicated. By contrast you can well imagine that a C++ compiler is just a really ugly thing, because it's not a tidy language. It's got all sorts of special and unusual constructs that are not completely consistent, and that's a problem.

*Several other interviewees have said you really want to start with a very small core set of ideas and then build everything on top of those. Is that your experience or your impression as well?*

**Tom:** I think this is a reasonable thing to do. I would start with a few examples of really simple, really pure languages, and Smalltalk and APL would be two obvious candidates. You could probably think of some others. Lisp is also another candidate.

For contrast, you might want to consider a really ugly language. I'll give you a candidate, which is more important than you might think. It's the MUMPS programming language. It's actually a simple language. It's rather ugly and untidy and very unconventional, but it turns out to be a good language for building things like electronic medical record systems.

It is really a programming environment, not just a programming language. The environment is really helpful when building high-performance electronic medical record systems. The largest existing system in production is wall-to-wall MUMPS, built by the Department of Veteran Affairs.

Of 108 applications, about 100 of them are written MUMPS. It's about 11 million lines of code, and it's intractable, and it doesn't look like anything you've ever seen before. Since electronic medical records are really, really important right now to this country and to the world, and the largest known production system happens to be written in this language, it actually is more important than most people realize.

*One of my colleagues has always said the spreadsheet is the world's most popular programming language anyway. Why should we be surprised by things like that?*

**Tom:** I'll tell you an example of programming language pathology you probably haven't heard of. It turned out that I worked at a little low-key and relaxed firm called Morgan Stanley once upon a time, and they were involved in doing trading systems, which probably does not come as a surprise to you.

One guy there decided that, that among the world's programming languages there were, there was not one that was ideal for doing really high-performance trading systems. He decided to design his own programming language. It was actually designed very much in the spirit of APL, but he had this very firm belief that any language compiler worth its salt could be written in 10 pages of code or less.

As more and more features got added to the language and to the environment, he kept trying to figure out how to squeeze it into his 10-page constraint. At a certain point he started shortening the variable names in order to put more on each line. After about 15 years, you looked at those 10 pages of code and it looked like a core dump. It was the mid-90s. Every bond trading system in Morgan Stanley was programmed in this language called A+.

When I arrived at Morgan Stanley, I had 250 people working for me in three different geographies: Tokyo, London, and New York. I started a process where I spent at least 30 minutes at the desk of every one of the 250 people.

I began to notice the variety of programming languages that they were actually using. I started tabulating a list and it turned out that when all was said and done, I had a list of 32 procedural programming languages. These were not query languages. These were not command languages. These were all programming languages. I said to the group, "Don't you think we could get by with 16?"

I started a variety reduction campaign, and I took all 32 languages and put them on a big chart on my wall, and I had each one printed on a card. The idea was the name was on one side and you flip it over and there was a name with a slash through it, which means we had decommissioned the programming language. At one point a guy working for me called up from London. "OK, Tom. Go put your telephone on speakerphone and walk over to your wall. We're going to have a little ceremony. We have as of today officially decommissioned the following programming language." I don't actually remember which one it was. I looked on the wall and my response was, "Oh, no." He said, "Why do you say that?" I said, "It wasn't on the wall. We're back to 32. The good news, we just decommissioned an unnecessary programming language. The bad news is we still have 32."

That's a humorous story, but imagine the problem of having 250 people writing in 32 different programming languages, and think about the human capital problems and the resource allocation problems. You've got 15 people that are available to do work, but not in the four programming languages that are going to be used on the next project. That's just an incredibly expensive way to run an organization.

More is not better in this business.

### If you were to design a new language today, what would it look like?

**Tom:** Remember, I'm not fond of adding to the technical variety unless it's absolutely necessary. I would start with the question of "Do I really, really, really need it?" A language that we haven't mentioned is Ruby. It's a clean language that can be reasonably efficient—sufficiently efficient to do lots of things. It's got a nice clean structure to it.

I don't feel a need for a new language. I'm spending most of my days, worrying about what happens before you get the first line of code.

I just handed out to some of my friends this week a big pile of buttons with the word REQUIREMENTS and a red slash through it like a European road sign. On the back of the button are 14 acceptable alternatives to that word. Lots of discussions go on between individuals or between groups of the form of "I couldn't do this work because you didn't give me the requirements yet," or "We need to have a group of people that goes out and gathers the requirements for this new system."

The term is simply too imprecise. You need to have more precise terms as an alternative. On a big project that I've been involved in we have imposed a requirements tax. If anybody uses the word "requirements" standalone, they have to add $2.00 to the entertainment fund. If they want to talk about use cases, or if they want to talk about story cards, or they want to talk about performance metrics, or they want to talk about business cases or business process models, those are all acceptable terms. They don't incur a tax, because now if you say, "I need to have the use cases or the functional specification, or a mockup of the application that needs to be developed," that's a precise request.

I see projects getting into trouble when they don't get that part right. Writing the code doesn't seem like the hard part anymore. The hard part is figuring out what the code should be doing.

### Do you believe we've reached a productivity level where languages and tools and platforms and libraries don't matter as much to success as we thought 20 years ago?

**Tom:** I think that's a true statement. It took me a long time to realize that when you write a class in an object-oriented programming language, what you're actually doing is extending the programming language.

In some languages that's a little more obvious than in others. It's pretty obvious in Smalltalk, for example—a little less obvious in a language like C++.

Since we have the ability to essentially create specialized languages by virtue of developing frameworks or class libraries that are available, the problem moves to other parts of the development cycle. I would highlight both in the "what is it that we need to do?" front end of the process, and the back end of the process, which is the testing.

I was talking to somebody the other week who's building an application where they expect to have on a daily basis 40,000 users of the application. I said, "Tell me about the stress testing that you're going to do to convince yourself that the system will be able to accommodate those 40,000 people when they all hit the return key at the same time."

It's probably because of my brief stay in the telephone industry that I think of it as a system-engineering problem. In the medical world, I was sitting with a group of people who were talking about shipping electronic medical records from a central database around the country with subsecond response times. I said, "Do you know how large a current-day MRI file is? It's five gigabytes."

When you start talking about what does the pipe need to look like to be able to ship 5 gigabytes in subsecond time across the country, that's expensive. You actually can do it, but it's not cheap. It's almost never the case that it's really necessary.

## Education and Training

### What do you recommend to manage complex technical concepts?

**Tom:** I think we look to European trades in the olden days as an example. A person should have a career progression in this business that starts off understanding some of the simple aspects of what needs to be done, how to write test cases, how to develop functional specifications for projects up through the more technical how to actually design the solutions, how to implement those solutions, and how to do more complicated things like stress testing of systems or actually deploying large-scale systems. I think we have a tendency to bring people into jobs for which they're not actually qualified and then are surprised that they're not successful with the job.

I happen to know a little more about Germany than I do about Italy, but my understanding is that, in Germany, in order to be a certified architect you have to spend a period of time—I think six months—in a variety of building trades. You have to understand something about how plumbing actually works and how electricity actually works and something about how you actually frame a house before you're allowed to be certified as an architect to legally do such things, I think. In the software business, we're missing that process of getting people the proper academic training and practical experience—but even after academic training, the proper on-the-job training.

### How important is real-life experience?

**Tom:** I draw an analogy also to the aviation business where you have to go through a very methodical well-defined legal process of flying little airplanes, little larger airplanes, then little larger airplanes and little faster airplanes before you finally get up to where you're sitting in the front seat of a 757 flying 300 people across the Atlantic Ocean. Of course, the aviation business got to that set of regulations off the back of a lot of people who got killed doing it the other way. So those regulations didn't come about before the requirement to regulate happened.

## Which topics should students study more?

**Tom:** I was just in a meeting last week with several old-timers in the software engineering business and we were asking the question about what are the best schools in the United States to learn about software engineering and how well regarded they are and how well funded they are by national research grants. The news is not very good, actually. I make a clear distinction between software engineering education and computer science education. I'm not talking about here how to design a compiler or how to write an operating system, but rather how to plan a project and run a project and succeed at projects in a variety of roles.

I'm not as well versed as I once was about the educational systems in Europe for software engineering, but I think in the United States it's pretty weak right now. I had the experience recently that a Swedish friend of mine said, "I'm going to take over responsibility for a software organization. What books should I read about software engineering to help me do my job?" I gave him a list of five books and then he said, "Where can I get these?" I said, "You could go to Amazon or something, but I'm actually going to a major university's bookstore tomorrow if you'd like me to pick them up and send them to you."

I went to Yale University and I had my list of five books and it turned out that not one of the five was in the bookstore, which was really quite revealing. Yale is not the most prestigious computer science school in the Ivy League, let alone the United States, but it's a well-respected program and has been around a long, long time. Yet they didn't even have the books available for the students, let alone classes in which they might learn something a little more than is just in the books. I saw something funny yesterday. I saw a new product that was advertised and as part of the advertising line it said it's written 100% in Objective-C.

## How would you train a software developer?

**Tom:** I would start off by putting them in a testing group and teach them how to test code and how to read code. The software business is one of the few places we teach people to write before we teach them to read. That's really a mistake. It's nothing like picking up a really awful piece of code and trying to figure it out. It turns out to be very instructive. I would also encourage them to become familiar with existing software products that are well designed and well architected so that they are gaining that experience from the inside as contrasted from the outside.

Here's an example of a very well-written product in our company. Take a look at the well-written product and well-designed product and compare that with the one you're currently working on. I'd begin to give them more and more responsibility but in very short cycles so there's the opportunity to judge their progress and success and also to give them help when they need it.

*How do you hire a good programmer?*

**Tom:** There's a big topic. You might or might not know that my dissertation was a study on the psychological characteristics of successful programmers in the 1970s.

*Some of them are still active.*

**Tom:** Yes, there are actually some that are still alive. It's quite amazing. There are certain cognitive psychological traits that you look for: memory ability, attention to detail. I also look for things like communication skills, both written and oral. Working in a team; it's important that you be able to communicate effectively with the rest of the team and then it's also important if you obtain leadership roles that you be able to communicate with customers or subject matter experts or other operations and maintenance teams that you need to interact with as you start to deploy products. I don't make it a requirement, but I look for correlations like really excellent programmers, if I'm trying to hire somebody to be a chief designer and architect for a project, I'll pay attention to their hobbies. If they're very proficient in music, that's a very good thing—proficient means has studied classical music and can perform a piano sonata from memory. That's a pretty good test of their memory ability and attention to detail, and it should sound pretty good, too!

## Project Management and Legacy Software

*You've said that a programmer can maintain about half a box of paper.*

**Tom:** That's right. I'm involved in a lot of projects with the federal government these days. It's amazing how helpful that one little fact turns out to be. 100,000 lines of code is a box of printout. It cost $3 million to develop. It takes two people to maintain it. The number of test cases to fully test that box of code is another two or three boxes of code.

*Is that independent of language?*

**Tom:** Almost. It seems to hold true across the object-oriented languages at least. In a moderate object-oriented language, it actually takes more people testing than writing code, because the languages are powerful enough. I'm dealing with a project right now with three-quarters of a million lines of code, and more than half of the code was acquired externally. This is not even anything close to leading-edge technology, actually. Looked at from that perspective, if you said, "I'm going to have one tester for every programmer," you would wildly underestimate the real effort that's required, because the programmer is actually bringing in a lot of untested code from the outside that, in the case of a medical application, you've got to thoroughly test.

You may end up with four or five or six testers for every programmer in those kinds of circumstances. In the early 1980s in a C language environment, for example, you might have had six programmers for every tester in that environment.

*Is that due to the C language and its level of abstraction or reusability of code?*

**Tom:** It's the extent of the library that you're bringing on board. I did a lot of analysis back in the early days of Objective-C of if you take a big C program and redo it in Objective-C, how many lines of code do you end up with? The number oscillated around five; you had one-fifth the number of lines of code.

*That's a good compression ratio.*

**Tom:** It's a big number. We did a project about four years ago where it was actually a combination of COBOL and C++ code, but 11 million lines of code ended up being compressed to half a million lines of Java. That's a 20 to 1 savings in annual maintenance. It doesn't take long before that ends up being an interesting number.

*Part of that is due to lessons learned in reimplementing a system.*

**Tom:** It's always true. I tell that story the following way. It is in fact always easier to build a second version of a system than the first version of the system. One of the reasons is because you don't have to spend any time asking the question of whether it is possible. You know that which exists is not impossible.

You probably know this story about the Russians getting a B-29 bomber—the plane that dropped the atomic bomb. They made an exact clone, down to the level of making sure a patch on the wing was actually beautifully and exactly replicated in the model, and they did it in two years and for a lot less than the $3 billion spent in the U.S. over five years to build the first B-29—it was more expensive than the Manhattan Project!*

It really is true that the second time around, things get a lot faster.

*Of course, you're talking about more than an order of magnitude of difference in the lines of source code. Can a programmer maintain about the same number of lines of code, regardless of language?*

**Tom:** I have had a lot of conversations with good programmers about that topic. There's a lot of variants around that number. I think the average is well established. On the other hand, I think there's a pretty good spread. It is possible for there to be code written so that it is really clean and tidy and well organized, and a person can maintain 200,000 lines of code. That's rare, but it's for sure possible.

Equally you can have a rat's nest where a person works their buns off to try to keep 10,000 lines of code working. There's a greater tendency to observe that than there is the former. We often find it interesting that if you do a really good job of architecture and design of some new system, and then you turn it over to the organization that paid you to do the work, it's astonishing how fast that orderliness gets lost in the application. People that don't know what they're doing go in and start whacking, and they can do a lot of damage in a short period of time.

* *http://www.rb-29.net/HTML/03RelatedStories/03.03shortstories/03.03.10contss.htm*

*Were you thinking about these organizational principles when you developed Objective-C?*

**Tom:** We actually were. The research group originally at ITT was chartered to help a large international telephone company build a distributed, object-oriented digital telephone switching system, and to do that with what had to be distributed development teams.

We were steeped in those issues. I had come to ITT from General Electric, where I was involved in the same kind of activities. At GE I called the thing the Software Psychology Research Group. We were looking not only at the order of the characteristics of programming languages that make them easier for people to read, understand, and maintain, but also the organizational structures for development teams and the organizational issues associated with doing large-scale development.

*The software industry would change dramatically if governments made the software developers responsible for security problems.*

**Tom:** Yes, absolutely, and one of my rules when I'm looking at people to take on projects is that they don't take on a project that's more than 20% different from a project that they've been successful on before.

*This means that you need lots of experience before becoming an architect over a large project.*

**Tom:** Well, it does have that characteristic, doesn't it? The alternative actually is to do very short projects. But there is that constraint that some of these projects take three years to do and, exaggerating for a moment, if you work for 40 years, there's only a relatively small number of projects that you can do. There's the same problem in aviation. The solution to the problem is realistic simulators and that's something that I've argued for in the case of project managers. In fact there is a problem of being able to live long enough to do 100 projects, but if you could simulate some of the decisions and experiences so that you could build your resume based on simulated projects as contrasted to real projects, that would also be another way to solve the problem.

*Does productivity depend more on the quality of the programmer or the characteristics of the programming language?*

**Tom:** The effect of individual differences will far outweigh any effect of the programming language. Studies from the 1970s show for programmers with the same educational background and same number of years' experience, the number was 26:1 individual differences. I don't think anybody claims that their programming language is 26 times better than somebody else's.

*You've said that you are now an expert in reengineering legacy software, and that requires understanding three words: agile, legacy, and reengineering. What did you mean?*

**Tom:** Let's analyze the words backward. Let's talk about reengineering first. When I use the word "reengineering," by that I mean to replace very close to exactly that functionality using modern design techniques and modern technologies. I make the clear distinction between a reengineering project and a modernization project. Modernization projects suffer from the long ago described Second System Effect that Fred Brooks described in *The Mythical Man-Month* [Addison-Wesley Professional]: let's try to do everything in this iteration that we couldn't figure out how to do in the first iteration and do it in half the time. Guess what? Those projects routinely get into trouble. I'm still searching for a modernization project in the U.S. government that was actually successful. It's exceedingly easy to find ones that are unsuccessful, but I have yet to find one that was actually successful.

I'm using the word "reengineering" as a major scoping constraint on the project. I'm not saying we're going to look at the old system and think about the new system and go with a clean sheet of paper and start all over. If we can reuse the workflow or reuse the screen definitions or reuse the data models or the data elements at least or if we can reuse test cases or reuse documentation or reuse training courses, there's a huge amount of time and effort to be saved and a lot of risk to be removed from the project.

A gigantic advantage of a reengineering project is you have a working system there that you can query from time to time to find answers to questions that you couldn't otherwise find out answers to. That gets one of the three words.

"Legacy" of course is just simply referring to an existing system, often an enterprise-scale system. They're not necessarily 20-year-old systems built in antique procedural programming languages or worse. I've heard of examples of legacy Smalltalk applications that need to be redone and reengineered in Java for example. The distinction of legacy systems is it's an existing system that is deployed, that is working, that is important to the organization and it does need to be replaced for some set of reasons. The reasons could be that it's running on an antique operating system that's about to be decommissioned and no longer supported. It could be in a programming language that you can't find any programmers who are still alive that understand, or all sorts of reasons. It could be that the business has changed that you need all of that functionality but you need it packaged in a different way or it could be that you need completely different functionality and that would not be a reengineering project. That's a new application development project.

The third word is "agile," and that simply is a process that has been demonstrated to work repeatedly and at scale and therefore a risk-adverse project manager should be looking very seriously at that as a way of doing business.

### How can we prevent legacy problems in software under development today?

**Tom:** I'm not sure that you prevent it. Any product that you build has a useful life. Often in the software business, a useful life is many decades longer than the original developers imagined and what would have been helpful is if that code had been well structured, well documented, and well tested. I'm currently working with a government client that has 11 million lines of code, some of which is 25 years old, for which there are no test cases. There's no system-level documentation. They even stripped out the comments in the code as an efficiency measure a few years ago, and it's not under configuration control, and they issue about 50 patches per month for the system and have been doing so since 1996. That's a problem.

You can take all those things and reverse them and say, don't do this, and don't do that, and don't do that, and that'd be the right thing to be doing.

### How about modularity of design?

**Tom:** The better designed the system, the more modular the system, the better the object model that has been developed for the system, the longer the useful life is in all probability. Of course, you can have a beautifully designed system, and if the business changes, then you may or may not have anticipated the extent of the change.

### Do you have a rule of thumb as to how many programming languages an organization should have?

**Tom:** I have a rule for project managers, but it's not exactly that. A project manager has to have reading knowledge of every programming language being used on the project that he or she is managing, which is by the way almost never the case. I believe it's one of the fundamental reasons that so many projects get in trouble.

I had a project manager come to me and say, "We're supposed to be using six languages on this project. You don't really expect me to gain a reading knowledge of those six programming languages, do you?" I said, "No, no, that's not the only way you can solve the problem. The other way you can solve the problem is to get rid of some of the languages."

He finally realized I was serious. I have sat in so many meetings in which a programmer is having a discussion about the effort that it takes to write a class and the project manager has no idea what a class is in a modern programming language.

### Do you still use Styrofoam balls to model your systems, where each ball represents a class?

**Tom:** We do, actually. We've also done a 3D animation version of it, which we found to be nowhere near as useful as the Styrofoam balls. There's something about a physical, conspicuous structure hanging from the ceiling right in the middle of a development project that's regularly updated to provide not only the structure of the system that you're building, but also the current status of each one of the classes.

We've done it on 19 projects the last time I've counted. One of them was 1,856 classes, which is big—actually, probably bigger than it should be. It was a big commercial project, so it needed to be somewhat big.

### Does a class still represent a fundamental unit of progress in a system?

**Tom:** It's the most stable thing I've found to count. You have to define what the nature of the class is that you're writing. If you're just writing an initial prototype of a class, a person can do that in a week. A real class as a part of a production application is more like a person month of effort. A highly reusable class is a two- to four-person month of effort.

*Does that include testing and documenting?*

**Tom:** The whole nine yards.

It takes about a day to read and understand a class. That's where a lot of projects nowadays get in trouble, because you're going to use this class library, the Swing classes, or take your current favorite, and nobody actually sits down and says if all the programmers actually need to understand 365 classes, then it's going to be 365 business days before we can get ready to write the first line of code.

By contrast, if you forget that time to understand the code in the beginning, you can have pretty big slips in a schedule.

*You spend that time during debugging, for example.*

**Tom:** Well, somewhere. You're going to have to incur that overhead somewhere along the way. That's a big number. If you're doing a six-month project, then you're going to have a two-year delay to get started.

*Is it worth it?*

**Tom:** It might be, but there's several things you can do. One, you can hire people that already know the classes. Another is you can partition it up so that not everybody has to know everything, which is almost always a good idea. You need to be having those kinds of thoughts. You don't want to be surprised by that.

Look at some of these modern projects in the Java world. They could easily be starting off with 2,000 classes that they're relying on. You can get about 200 business days in a year, so that's only a 10-year hit on the schedule.

*You've said that the time to write code has remained consistent over the years, but you've also mentioned that other factors make us more productive now. Some productivity gains require an investment of time and effort to learn.*

**Tom:** Isn't it better to spend a person-day to understand a class than a person-month to rewrite it? It's expensive, but you're starting off with huge amounts of functionality that in the olden days we had to start from scratch and write.

*You might be 20 times more productive if there are 20 business days in a month. That's a good tradeoff.*

**Tom:** It's huge. Let's just pick some number that I think might be a normal number these days. Imagine that you need to understand 500 classes in order to some serious application in the modern world. It's not 500 completely new classes every time you start a project. You probably didn't go from 0 to 500 in one step. You probably did it in five steps at least, or more.

*How do you recognize simplicity in a design?*

**Tom:** In the olden days the measure was how many pages of BNF description were there in order to describe the language, which is not a bad measure, because it ends up allowing you to be able to distinguish the complicated languages from the simple languages.

You know when you stand and squint your eyes in just the right way at an APL program or a Smalltalk program, there isn't much of the language there. It's almost like the language goes away, and that's a good thing.

How large is the reference manual for the language? How much is included? The Objective-C programming language is not very complicated, but the class libraries that had been built with it over the years are complicated. Describing all of that detail is hard and bulky, and error prone. Hard to test, hard to document.

*Even a language as simple as C can have complex semantics—whose responsibility is it to manage memory for this particular library?*

**Tom:** Exactly. What do you think the chances are that Microsoft applications get slower and slower because they haven't managed memory properly? Have you ever met a three-year-old Microsoft operating system that you wanted to use? I actually operate with a laptop that has a Microsoft-free zone. It's amazing how much more productive I am than other people sitting in the same room with Microsoft computers. My machine is on, and I've done my work, and I've closed it down before they've gotten to their first Excel spreadsheet.

*What's the most important piece of advice you can offer from your experience?*

**Tom:** I could boil that down to four words. Make interesting new mistakes.

We don't need to regurgitate history, but appreciate where we've come from. How many 25-year-olds coming out of a computer science program do you know that have written an APL program?

I don't know, but I think it's almost none. Yet that's an important experience, because admittedly this may be a specialized language for doing certain kinds of applications, but an accomplished APL programmer writing a statistics application is going to beat the pants off anybody else using anything else, I think.

I was having a conversation with some people at the Software Engineering Institute about the issue of how software engineers are being trained, if they are at all, and how few graduate programs there are that really make a conscientious effort to train people about system-building experiences as contrasted to algorithm design. I don't think we're very good at that.

Wouldn't it be great—I do this nowadays—if you were hiring a project manager, if the project manager showed up with a certified log book that said here are all the projects that I've managed, and here's who to contact to find out details of each project, and here's what quantitative measures about each one of those projects that I can look at. How many lines of code, how many classes, how many test cases, compliance in schedule, you know, all that kind of stuff.

I happen to be a general aviation pilot and I spend a little time doing this stuff. There are rules that grew up around failed experiences almost always resulting in a loss of life that has resulted in the rules and regulations that exist around aviation in this country as well as the world.

In any given point in a typical day, there are something like 56,000 flights in the air in the United States, and there have been years recently in which there was not a single accident of a commercial airliner in a year's time. That's a pretty amazing record actually.

They have actually figured out some stuff, like pilots should be sober when they're taking off in their airplane. They ought to have flown with a pilot that knows this particular airplane, once or twice before. When this industry matures, we will end up with something in that same spirit. One of the reasons that organizations spend so little time thinking about either building new applications or even reengineering existing applications is because they're scared to death. They assume that any project they're going to start is going to be a failure, and they don't want it to happen on their watch.

If they could become convinced instead that they've got a 90% chance or a 95% chance, or—God forbid—a 99% chance of being successful, and they could know what it's going to cost before they got started, it would be a much more robust industry.

*What do you mean by "success"?*

**Tom:** You hear various numbers. Let's imagine a project that's going to end up with a million lines of code or more. The probability of those projects being successful in the United States these days is very low—well under 50%. That's debatable. I don't know where people get reliable data for that kind of stuff, because people don't like to advertise that information. Various competent people have gone around trying to find out that information. But I just point out that it's actually hard to get, but not impossible. Just hard.

## Objective-C and Other Languages

*Why did you extend an existing language instead of creating a new one?*

**Brad Cox:** I was quite satisfied with C, apart from well-known but livable limitations. Reinventing the base language to do OOP would have been a waste of time.

*Why did you choose C?*

**Brad:** That's what we had. Ada was unthinkable, Pascal was (regarded as) a toy for researchers. Which leaves COBOL and FORTRAN. Enough said. Oh, yes, there was Chill (a telephony language). The only plausible alternative to C was Smalltalk, and Xerox wouldn't sell that.

Our goal was to move OOP from the research lab to the factory floor. C was the only credible option.

## Why emulate Smalltalk?

**Brad:** It hit me as an epiphany over all of 15 minutes. Like a load of bricks. What had annoyed me so much about trying to build large projects in C was no encapsulation anywhere and wrapping data and procedures into what looked to me like methods—a ha. That's it.

## When did you see C++ for the first time, and what did you think of it?

**Brad:** Bjarne heard of my work and invited me to Bell Labs before either of our languages was quite on the air. He was focused entirely on using static binding and upgrading C. I was focused on adding dynamic binding to plain old C in the simplest, least-disrupted manner I could manage. Bjarne was targeting an ambitious language: a complex software fabrication line with an emphasis on gate-level fabrication. I was targeting something much simpler: a software soldering iron capable of assembling software ICs fabricated in plain C.

## How do you explain the different diffusion rates of the two languages?

**Brad:** Objective-C was the initial product of a small company with no other revenue sources than the compiler and its support libraries. AT&T built C++ for other reasons than revenue and could well afford to give it away. Free trumps paid most every time.

## Have you been involved in the project announced by Apple as Objective-C 2.0?

**Brad:** I have no relationship with Apple other than that I like their products.

## What is your opinion on garbage collectors?

**Brad:** I think they're great. Always have. I did have to struggle with marketeers who thought of it as a language "feature" that could be painted onto C with little effort and no impact on those who chose C for performance.

## Why does Objective-C forbid multiple inheritance?

**Brad:** The historical reason is that Objective-C was a direct descendant of Smalltalk, which doesn't support inheritance, either. If I revisited that decision today, I might even go so far as to remove single inheritance as well. Inheritance just isn't all that important. Encapsulation is OOP's lasting contribution.

## Why did Objective-C not support namespaces?

**Brad:** When I was directly involved, my goal was to copy Smalltalk and it had no notion of namespaces.

What you know as Objective-C today is just as much a product of Apple as it is of me. Most of my work is in XML and Java today.

*Was the notion of protocols unique to Objective-C?*

**Brad:** I wish I could take credit for that. That idea was one of the things added on top of the plain Objective-C backbone—by which I mean the smallest set of stuff I could imagine taking from Smalltalk. Smalltalk didn't have anything like protocol in those days and that was added by Steve Naroff, who's now in charge of the Objective-C at Apple. I think he got it from SAIL if I remember right.

*It seems that Java was influenced by your design, as single inheritance was carried over into Java. Could single inheritance be removed from Java, too?*

**Brad:** Probably could. But it won't be and shouldn't. It's there, it works, it does what it claims. It's just abusable, like any language feature, and not as important as encapsulation.

At first I used inheritance heavily, experimenting to find its bounds. Then I realized that encapsulation was the real contribution of OOP and that it could be used manually to do almost everything I'd been using inheritance for, but more cleanly.

My focus has since gravitated to objects with higher levels of granularity (OOP and JBI/SCA), which, tellingly, don't support inheritance at all.

*How do you decide whether a feature belongs in a project? For example, a garbage collector may slow some C applications, but it offers many advantages.*

**Brad:** Absolutely. In fact, we developed one at Stepstone similar to the one Apple has now. Even had an Objective-C interpereter. But the marketeers wanted something automatic to compete head to head with Smalltalk, not something that looked so much like C.

*Do you believe in default settings and limited configurability?*

**Brad:** We could, and did. What I objected to was trying to bend C to marketing's wish list.

*Several language designers start by describing a very small, formalized core, then build on top of that. Did you do that for Objective C, or did you decide to borrow what Smalltalk and C provided?*

**Brad:** Yeah, I definitely was not starting from a formal foundation. I was thinking about silicon. We were doing a lot of consulting with a large silicon foundry and visited their factories. I was reflecting on how they did it versus how we did it, and I saw that everything they did revolved around reuse of silicon components. They all thought long and hard about the components and not at all about their soldering irons. For us, of course, the language is the soldering iron.

I saw everybody concentrating on languages or soldering irons and nobody concentrating on components. It just seemed backward to me. It turns out why the chip manufacturers held their perspective is very important, because silicon components are made of atoms and there's a business model for buying and selling them. That business model for software components is very ephemeral, indeed.

*Software itself is ephemeral.*

**Brad:** Indeed, but that's why we focus on languages and not on components. We essentially don't have components in any kind of robust sense. If you think about a housing analogy, it's like we're back in cave days where the way we built houses was to find some monolithic pile of stuff—volcanic ash, for example—and I'm afraid that leads us to the Java class loader. The way you build a cave house is: you start with a pile of stuff and remove what you don't need and that's essentially a class loader model. My energy right now is going into small granularity components where you start with nothing and add what you need, the way we build houses today.

*We describe biology and chemistry with English. Maybe the problem is that the programming languages we use are not as powerful as the English language.*

**Brad:** If computers were as smart as human beings, I would have confidence in that approach. We are talking about something that is as dumb as a brick—computers—and they haven't really changed in any fundamental way since I started using them in the 1970s.

On the other hand, there are some fascinating new languages out there, such as functional languages, that might help with things like multicore computers. I keep hearing people claiming that it will help, and I have no reason to doubt them.

*How does a focus on concurrency affect the OO paradigm? Are there changes necessary to OO approaches?*

**Brad:** Despite OOP's Simula heritage, I've always thought that programming languages should offer just enough thread support to build higher-level components that exhibit concurrency in a limited but controllable manner. For example, Unix filters support concurrency, implemented in plain C, in a controllable manner. I spent considerable time on a similar approach for Objective-C: a multitasking library called TaskMaster based on nothing more than the setjmp( ) mechanism.

Another example is the Defense Modeling and Simulation Office's HLA, widely used for military simulations. It's implemented in several languages—C++ and Java, to name two. It supports an event-driven concurrency model that doesn't rely on thread support from either language, as far as I know.

A final example is the one I'm most involved in now. SOA supports large-grained, network-resident objects that are intrinsically concurrent because they typically reside on different machines. Sun's JBI and OASIS's SCA enhance this model with finer-grained objects/components that are assembled to build SOA objects. This is the first sign in software construction of the multigranular approach that's the norm in hardware engineering: fine-grained objects (gates) assembled into intermediate-grained objects (chips; like the famous Software-ICs) which are ultimately assembled into even higher-granularity objects (cards) which are…so it goes. The main difference is that in tangible domains the system is truly fractal, with many more levels than this, while we have only those three. Today.

Granted, there are applications that need tighter integration. This just wasn't a problem I was addressing at the time. That omission was at least partially driven by my own inability to manage highly concurrent systems, and my doubts that anyone truly can.

*The complexity and size of applications seems to continue to grow. Does OOP help or hurt? In my experience, the idea of making reusable objects adds complexity and doubles the amount of work. First, you write a reusable object. Then you have to modify it and fit something different in the same hole it leaves.*

**Brad:** You're right—if by OOP you mean Objective-C/Java-style encapsulation; what I called *chip-level integration* in my second book, *Superdistribution* [Addison-Wesley Professional]. Not if you see chip-level integration as just one level of the kind of multilevel integration tool suite that is the norm in hardware engineering, with gate-level objects coexisting in perfect harmony in a fractal world of gate-, chip-, card-, and higher-level encapsulation options.

Which is exactly why I'm focused on SOA (chassis-level) and JBI (bus-level) today. These support encapsulation as much as traditional OOP. Even better; they encapsulate not just data + procedures, but even the entire thread of control that powers them.

Best of all, multilevel integration costs nothing and is known to work at arbitrary scales in other industries. The only gotcha is that it's hard to get across to unilevel OOP advocates. Been there, done that—back then with OOP versus traditional procedural programming and today with SOA versus JBI versus Java.

Everybody's stuck on the myth that new technologies "obsolete" older ones like OOP. Never happens, never will. New builds on top of old, every time.

*We seem to be entering a new era of experimentation in languages and willingness by programmers to try paradigms they're unused to, such as Rails and functional programming. As language designers upgrade languages or create new ones, what lessons can you offer from Objective-C?*

**Brad:** I've tried, but not yet managed, to get my head around the syntax of languages like Haskell—at least not well enough to have a strong opinion on it. I do use XQuery fairly heavily and that's a functional language. And I find XQuery far more congenial to read than XSLT.

I guess I am capable of new approaches—but Haskell in particular, I just can't get my head around its syntax. I had much the same problem with Lisp. That said, I've been impressed by a Navy project that expresses complex authorization and authentication policy in Haskell rules that can be proved by inspection.

The future, to me, is not continually proliferating ever more notations for doing exactly the same thing we've been doing for decades—writing procedural code. That's not saying that working at this level is not important; it's where the higher-level components come from in the end and that's not likely to change. I'm only saying that new ways of writing procedural code are not on the cusp of innovation.

What I do find exciting is the introduction of new kinds of notations for doing entirely new things, namely composing ever higher-level systems from libraries of preexisting components. BPEL is one specific example, which can be applied at two levels of integration: SOA for largest-granularity objects, and JBI (Sun) or SCA (OASYS). For example, see the BPEL editor in NetBeans. OMG has done excellent work in this area with the model-driven architecture.

## Components, Sand, and Bricks

*What do the lessons about the invention, further development, and adoption of your language say to people developing computer systems today and in the foreseeable future?*

**Brad:** I've been interested in multilevel integration (aka encapsulation) for as long as I can recall: the ability to subdivide work so that it can be allocated to specialists, then use their work products with little or no need to break the encapsulation, to know "what's inside" to use it successfully.

I've used the common wooden pencil in some of my writing as an example. When I ask audiences which is "simpler," a digital pencil like Microsoft Word or a wooden pencil, people agree the wooden variety is simpler. Until I point out that Microsoft Word was written by eight programmers, while the wooden variety involved thousands, none of whom could appreciate the full complexity of harvesting lumber, mining graphite, smelting metals, making lacquer, growing rapeseed for oil, etc. The complexity was there in the pencil, but hidden from the user.

My complaint with C (and similar languages) is that programmers were fully exposed to each program's complexity, except the modest amount that could be encapsulated in functions. The only real encapsulation boundary was the entire process space, which amounts to a tremendously effective higher-level capsule, heavily exploited by Unix as two-level encapsulation via shell scripting and the "pipes and filters" notion.

In trying to explain the advantages of object-oriented programming, I often used the term "Software-IC" to refer to a new level of integration, larger than C functions (gate-level) and smaller than a Unix program (chassis-level). My main motivation for developing Objective-C was to get a simple software "soldering iron" for assembling large (chassis-scale) units of functionality from reusable Software-ICs. By contrast, C++ emerged from a rather different vision; a vast and automated factory capable of making tightly coupled assemblies of gate-level units. Interpreting the hardware metaphor for programming, chip-level integration occurs mainly at link time; gate-level integration at compile time.

At that time (mid-1980s), lightweight threads were not widely known and there was nothing smaller than a Unix-style process ("heavyweight thread"). I spent some time building out an Objective-C library, called Taskmaster, to support lightweight threads as a basis for card-level integration. The advent of RISC computing put a stop to this; such low-level tinkering with stack frames made it too hard to support this portably.

The big change since then was ubiquitous networking, which opened up new levels of integration larger than the Unix process space. In a service-oriented architecture (SOA), for example, the Internet is like the cabling between the components of a HiFi system, with services (programs) on disparate servers functioning like the components themselves. I found this tremendously exciting because it is the first level of integration that approximates the separation of concerns we take for granted in everyday life. There is little temptation or need to view the source code of each service we use, when that service runs on a remote server that belongs to somebody else.

Significantly, this is also the first level of integration that makes it possible to solve a fatal flaw with the Software-IC idea: the ability to provide an incentive for others to provide components. Pencils (and the many subcomponents used to make them) get produced because conservation of mass works for tangible goods. Nothing comparable existed for digital goods until SOA made it feasible to deploy a useful service and charge for it while it is used.

Within the last two years, I've become aware of a fundamental problem with "plain ol' SOA" and am currently focusing largely on that. In large SOA deployments (for example, DISA's NCES and Army's FCS), there is strong resistance to reaching the kinds of consensus needed to build fully homogeneous SOA systems that use compatible transport mechanisms for land, sea, submarine, and air vehicles, not to mention compatible definitions for confidentiality, integrity, nonrepudiation, etc. And even if the "enterprise" were expanded to include all of the Department of Defense's (DOD) vast system of systems, what about Allied forces? What about compatibility with other government agencies? What about states? What about first responders? No matter how you define the enterprise, you're leaving out something that you might need to communicate with someday. Making each service developer responsible for all this just doesn't scale.

So I'm currently looking at Sun's JBI (Java Business Integration) and its multilanguage successor, SCA (Software Component Architecture), as a way to support a smaller level of integration that can be composed to build plain ol' SOA services.

### Do we need hardware assistance to create such a system?

**Brad:** Hardware certainly provides a robust example we could aspire to. Computer hardware is one of many examples of engineering excellence, 200 years since the industrial revolution. People have gotten extremely good at building hardware, so as a model to which to aspire I think hardware has a lot to teach us. But there are no easy lessons, no easy button to push to improve quality.

Lately, I've been using a different example to illustrate what I mean when I say software is primitive. Consider home construction. People have been doing that for millennia. In fact, in some places they're still doing in the original primitive way, with each construction team packing mud into frames to make their own mud bricks to assemble to make a home.

Although there are signs of recent advancement, by and large, we make software systems in exactly the same way. For example, to build a SOA service, every development team starts with raw materials from the java.net quarry to meet fundamental requirements of any SOA service.

Consider security, for example, which is fundamentally what the walls of a house provides. The DOD has extremely stringent security requirements that are mandated by policy. It has also invested heavily in security standards like the WS-Security suite. And it has recently rolled out Certification and Accreditation (C&A) processes that each and every web service must pass. C&A is fundamentally a laborious and expensive process that each and every web service must now undergo independently to ensure that it is in fact secure enough to install on sensitive networks.

These web services are like mud brick homes. The policies and standards amount to instructions that each developer should follow in making his or her own bricks. But those bricks still cannot be trusted by others because their quality still depends on whoever made them. Did they really abide by the standards? Did they implement them correctly? Sure, mud bricks are free, but no one can trust them because their quality is known only by the team that made them.

The construction industry long ago advanced to the relatively sophisticated form of production that we take for granted today. Construction crews no longer make their own bricks, since no one would trust them. The standards and policies remain, and as do the C&A processes (industrial brick-testing labs). However, few of us ever see them. We can rely on these invisible processes to ensure that any bricks on the market won't weather and will continue to hold up the roof.

That evolutionary process from mud bricks to real bricks wasn't even mainly technical. It was mainly about creating trust. We have grown to understand that there are independent standards for what a brick should do, how long it should be, how it should resist weather. And there are independent testing labs that we count on implicitly. Most of us don't know that there are brick-testing labs out there—we don't have to know; we can just trust the bricks to do all that we need!

Which takes us full circle to why economic systems are important. Trusted bricks exist because there is an incentive structure for providing them: pay by the brick. Everybody except the few brick-making specialists can forget the complexity of making them and get on with the creative parts of building houses.

See *http://bradjcox.blogspot.com/* for more on the distinction between mud brick versus real brick architecture.

To end on a more optimistic note, this situation is beginning to improve. Several companies have started building SOA security components and are beginning the long struggle to have them regarded as trusted components by DOD. The most mature example I know of is OpenSSL, but Sun, Boeing, and several others recently started similar initiatives specifically for SOA security.

*Are encapsulation and separation of concerns the drivers for designing software?*

**Brad:** I think so. That's largely based on how other industries handle complexity. That seems to be a human pattern of using encapsulation to wrestle complexity to the ground.

*Are SOA and your initiatives attempts to bring componentization to software?*

**Brad:** Absolutely. That's exactly what I've been chasing my whole career.

*Was it something you'd always considered, or did you see how the popular approaches to software development don't match the real world?*

**Brad:** I started from the latter and started looking for how other people deal with it. I started from the realization that software was broken.

*Is the practical, large-component approach at odds with the heavily mathematical, computer science view of software?*

**Brad:** Probably. I just don't want to get into criticizing computer science. I just have never seen it as being lined up with how human beings solve problems, and that springs from a characteristic difference in viewpoint. Computer scientists start from the view that there is a science of software and that their purpose is to document it and teach it. I've always started from the point of view that there is no such thing. There's a science of house building and there's a science of silicon engineering, and our job is to learn what they've learned over thousands of years and start creating a science of software. To me, the glass is totally empty and to them the glass is worth noticing.

*You've mentioned a couple of times that you think the economic model of software breaks down.*

**Brad:** It's not that it broke down. That statement implies that there was a model and now it's decomposing. There never was one. You can't get it off the ground because software spreads like vapor. The human race has just not invented a way of building economics on that. It's becoming barely imaginable, so with SOA services, it's easy to imagine an economic model for services, because the software is nailed down on some server over yonder and they can charge for access.

These objects with small granularity: I used to be hopeful that there was a way to deal with fine-grained stuff, the sand and gravel objects of computing, java.net objects, but the human complexity of setting up a solution there just got overwhelming. In the middle ground, those mid-level prospects with intermediate scaled objects made a nucleus for us. So at the SOA level, there's some hope. And at the next level down, maybe. The word's still out on that. I think there's no hope for objects of really small granularity.

*Is that middle level the level of frameworks?*

**Brad:** Those are the cave-dwelling objects, monolithic components where you start with something very large and switch on functionality. I suppose there's a model there. JBoss supports that, for example. You fundamentally give the bits away and sell the trust. That is a very complicated thing to do.

### What does it mean to be able to trust a piece of software?

**Brad:** Well, the DOD is right in the middle of that and they have answers for that. It's very laborious and impossibly expensive, unsatisfactory in every way you can imagine, but they do have an answer for that.

However, the DOD is so focused on SOA that they don't realized that SOA alone is insufficient. There's also a need for smaller-granularity components that can be reused to solve recurring problems that SOA alone cannot solve. Like security and interoperability, to use DOD's terminology. So my current work is providing sub-SOA components that can be assembled to address the boring, repetitive parts of building SOA services. I'm hoping someday to advance these mud bricks through DOD's C&A processes so they become real bricks that can be implicitly trusted, much as we trust bricks for our homes.

Security is an example of something every DOD SOA application needs. It's a requirement, by policy. The only thing that the SOA application builder they has to go on is standards and policies. DOD has no brick supplier. There are no trusted components—real bricks, if you will—that you can take or ultimately buy and that you can put together without having to be fully informed about SOA standards, security policies, the minutiae of using java.net components to meet DOD security requirements.

### How do these multiple levels of abstraction look from a security standpoint?

**Brad:** I'm not sure I understand your question. It's like asking, "How does specialization of labor in the auto industry affect driving safety?" I suppose that with specialization, each product depends on more people who are working at arms length from each other, and some fraction of those might be bad guys. But their product at each level has to withstand acceptance tests at all higher levels, so there's less chance of bad effects getting through than in monolithic construction.

Note that multilevel integration is not multiple levels of "abstraction." It's really multilevel "concretion": higher-level components assembled from reusable, off-the-shelf, pretested components. For example, consider secure SOA services assembled from a library of JBI subcomponents by wrapping the SOA services' core functionality in JBI components that each provide SOA security attributes: authentication, authorization, confidentiality, nonrepudiation, integrity, etc. The result is more secure simply because now you can afford to do it well.

### Are there answers the rest of us might find satisfactory?

**Brad:** I think so. If you look at the difference between a mud brick and a real brick, why don't we build houses from mud bricks? It turns out we can't trust them. It's just like software. The quality of that mud brick depends totally on whoever built it, the skill of the builder. Let's ignore the technical differences between real bricks and mud bricks. The fundamental difference, beyond the fact that you bake one at a high temperature, is that real bricks have testing and certification labs. To be a real brick provider, you have to get through the maze. That's basically DOD's trust model.

The certification and authorization are basically very laborious testing procedures. One of the names for that is "common criteria." It's in place now, and I think that's probably where we're going to end up after a few thousand years of complaining about mud bricks. "We," you know, means the industry at large, because there's a lot of complaining about software security right now and not many solutions out there. Ultimately, people don't trust software. They never will. Ultimately, it will come down to a trust model that applies to the people that provide software.

Look at Sun. Sun is basically trying to create a totally new business model. You're aware they recently went to an open source approach. They're very taken with that analogy I mentioned earlier, where old business model involved selling bits and their new business model involves selling trust. They really resonated to that idea. That's fundamentally what they're doing: the bits are now free. You can download almost anything Sun makes right now today and use it if you want. They're betting that, given that choice, that people are going to choose to buy the bits that come with indemnity and support and some other things I haven't dug into in this interview. Time will tell whether that works, but I think there's a plausible chance.

*You've probably heard about the problems that the state of California recently had with their systems written in COBOL. Could having a system built with little "bricks" help us avoid the problem of legacy software in the future?*

**Brad:** I believe very strongly in components, but I don't want to oversell the idea—components don't solve everything. Components are how people solve problems above a modest scale; it's one thing that separates us from chimpanzees. We invented a way of solving problems by simply making it the other guy's problem. It's called specialization of labor, and it's as simple as that. That's how the humans differ from chimpanzees: they never invented that. They know how to make tools, they have a language, so for most of the obvious things there are no differences between chimps and humans. We discovered how to solve problems by making it the other guy's problem—through an economic system.

*If we discover an answer, will it be something built on the past or something completely new?*

**Brad:** Evolution is slow-motion revolution. There is no binary distinction between them. But the article you mentioned about COBOL also mentioned that the most recent COBOL standard supported object-oriented extensions. I don't track COBOL these days, but in the 80s I advocated that very thing: take COBOL and add OO to it, much as I did for C.

That's an example of how I see thing always happening. They didn't throw out COBOL and replace it with something new. They simply added whatever was missing, and kept on keeping on.

*Do you still think superdistribution is the way to go? What about web applications?*

**Brad:** Superdistribution (as I use the term) applies to fine-grained objects. Simpler ways work for more coarse-grained ones, such as SOA services. I definitely think robust incentives are needed. But there are now easier places to begin than with OOP-scale objects—SOA services in particular. These didn't exist back then (apart from a lot of hype about "thin clients").

Problem is, that's like saying that learning to get along is the solution to the Palestinian conflict. It's obviously true, since that solution was used and found effective in the U.S. and South Africa. But its also completely irrelevant in the middle of a shooting war on between owners and users of digital goods. Neither side is going to compromise and just learn to get along. Wheeling out superdistribution as "the solution" to such a conflict will only get you shot at—by both sides.

*Is the ubiquitous availability of a network a prerequisite for building the cities of your analogy?*

**Brad:** If houses are SOAs, the network is certainly a prerequisite to doing that. You can't have an SOA without a network. But as a practical matter, you can't do squat without a network these days.

*Robin Milner from ML wants to have lots of very tiny, very stupid machines working in parallel. Is that similar to your goal?*

**Brad:** It's an interesting idea. I've spent a lot of time in military simulations and it's very attractive for that kind of problem. There may be other applicable problems that I haven't thought about.

## Quality As an Economic Phenomenon

*How can we improve the quality of software?*

**Brad:** One way is to keep software on servers, as we see in Software as a Service (SaaS). There may be hope for an economic answer there, although that approach also has obvious tradeoffs (privacy, security, performance, etc.).

I spent a number of years working on the opposite approach, creating an economic system around components that run locally on the end user's machine, but I have grown pessimistic about this approach because the discussion ends up in digital rights management fight and that could go on forever. I don't see any way to reconcile those who want to produce and own property with those who want to take it. Without physical conservation laws backing up what ownership means, we're left with only laws, courts, and lawyers, which ultimately escalates to police-state tactics. Imagine banks deciding to dispense with safes and locks, leaving money in the streets at night, and prosecuting those who steal it. Not a pretty picture.

Another economic solution is the one in widespread use today—advertising. Here, users are neither fisherman nor the fish, but the bait. Google's successes notwithstanding, I don't see how this can lead to anything good. We've all seen what that model did to radio and television, and exactly the same thing is happening to the Internet.

The final way is the open source model in its many different versions and refinements, from freeware to shareware to beerware, etc. This is largely the model I work within today. This is not because it's the best model imaginable, but because it's the only one left standing, and it does address one of the DOD's many self-inflicted wounds: proprietary lock-in.

*What are we missing to create software objects with the same "quality" as real objects?*

**Brad:** An economic system for rewarding improvements.

*Just that?*

**Brad:** That's the engine that drives the ship, but other innovations will be needed once a caloric (economic) system is in hand. Robust examples can also be found in biology. For example, Java has primitive notions of encapsulation, which are comparable to biological mitochondria, cells, tissues, organs, etc. In Java, the largest granularity capsule is a full JVM and the smallest is a Java class. The only level between them is the Java package (*.jar*). Various tricks can be played with class loaders to support a few others (servlets, to name one, used for SOA services).

I've recently become attracted to OSGI as the first serious attempt to create a mature level of encapsulation between Java classes and the JVM. For example, my sub-SOA security and interoperability components are packaged as OSGI bundles.

*Do you think that we need better incentives to make better software?*

**Brad:** If you look at forces that improved products like socks, sweaters, and Twinkies, the engine that drives that system is economics.

It's economics that breaks down for software so that it remains indefinitely in its present primitive stage of evolution.

*A drug company will spend billions of dollars for research because it gets tens or hundreds of billions of dollars from selling the drugs that result. There's a monetization factor in that science, even though so much research is public.*

**Brad:** Yeah, that is a way to nail down the bits so you can own them. With bricks and silicon chips, you relied on laws of nature for protecting the economics. That approach relies on the law of mankind. In other words, go get some lawyers and lawsuits and patents and trade secrets and all that and that model might work someday. It's just so unpleasant.

All the knowledge you have, you can imagine banks leaving gold in the street at nights and prosecuting those who steal it instead of locking things up in safes. It's a very inhumane picture that comes out of that, and there's a pretty good chance we're going to end up there with the DMCA stuff. DMCA, RIAA, all that's going on in that area; I just hate to be associated with it.

*Could the open access of the open source model improve the situation?*

**Brad:** Well, open source is the best economic model going right now. Most of what I do is involved in open source; that's because it's the best model going until this SOA thing matures and becomes a reality to count on.

But basically when I talk about a mud brick business, I am really talking about open source. Materials are free to make mud bricks, but the result is that everybody who does anything with those mud bricks has to suffer through the appalling documentation problem of open source.

The whole point of the mud brick analogy is that it's OK in the absence of other options: mud bricks are better than nothing at all. But that's our only option and it's primitive.

*What role do the Internet and networking play in the way we design software?*

**Brad:** These days you can't do software without the Internet; it is just not even thinkable.

But to flip to the controversial side of that, without an economic model behind either the Internet or software, the quality of what we have there is going to be way less than what we get from tangible marketplaces.

*Does looking at software in terms of services and components at a higher level than the language change the economics of writing software? By selling trust, do you destroy the market for selling bits?*

**Brad:** My crystal ball is not that good. I don't know. In thousands of years…it took the building industry that long; why do we think we can do it any faster? I think that's where it will end up in thousands of years, but I'll be dead and buried by then. It's hard to predict that far out.

*Some people might object that we don't have the laws of physics standing in our way.*

**Brad:** Yeah, that should be an advantage. It seems to hurt us more than it helps us. It cut down that economic model just for starters, and that's pretty big damage.

*If you built Objective-C today, would it be an open source project?*

**Brad:** There are too many ifs in that to respond to. Open source wasn't an option then and we had to pay the mortgage somehow. If I had a secure job today that wasn't too demanding, I'd probably spend the slack time on open source. But ultimately, revenue is just like gravity; the weakest force and thus easily overpowered by stronger forces (like self-actualization). But revenue is also the longest-range criterion, and thus utterly inescapable in the long term.

*Do you mean that an open source project isn't a serious alternative to commercial software without financial support?*

**Brad:** No, I meant just what I said. Revenue comes in many forms; reputation chits satisfy that need, too, for many of us.

*Is the web applications phenomenon a good thing?*

**Brad:** SOA puts software on servers where it is not under control of end users. That might someday lead to an economic system for SaaS.

That approach has barely given us any results to look at because SaaS is still in its infancy, but I can see how that approach could lead to an economic system that might improve software in the way tangible things are improving, through economic forces.

## Education

*You have a Bachelor's degree in organic chemistry and mathematics, and a Ph.D. in mathematical biology. How did you go from there to creating a programming language?*

**Brad:** After my postdoc, I took a look around and realized that I was more interested in computers than in the kind of openings that were available then.

*Does your university background influence your vision of software design?*

**Brad:** Absolutely. Constantly.

If you examine ecological systems, you see software as an ecological system in all respects except that the system lacks anything like physical conservation laws—no conservation of mass or energy. The product of our labor is made of bits that can be copied so easily that it's hard to buy, sell, and own them. The economic system, the ecology, breaks down.

If a leopard could replicate its food as we replicate software, there would be no improvement by either the leopard or its prey.

It's a constant problem in software, how to own and be compensated for the products and for your efforts.

*Did the agenda for computer science research shift from academia to industry?*

**Brad:** I've never considered myself a "computer science researcher" or an academic (although I did spend some time in that environment). All my other work was in industrial settings, so my biases naturally lie there.

That said, I've never been impressed by academia's research prowess until recently, when I've noticed increasing academic involvement in standards-setting bodies like W3C, Oasis, etc. That's tremendously exciting in my view.

*I like this quote from virtualschool.edu:*

> Thus computer science isn't dead. Computer science has never existed.

> The core concept of this new paradigm I'm trying to bring about in my new book is that the virus that's causing the disease that's causing the symptoms we call the software crisis is that we're dealing with a substance that is made of bits instead of atoms, that originates entirely from people, not nature.

> But since this substance doesn't abide by conservation of mass laws, the commercial mechanisms that incentivize people to work together for building pencils or baggage handling conveyor belts, entirely break down. Without commerce, advanced social orders can't evolve, so we're stuck in the primitive state where every nerd fabricates everything from first principles.

> Thus everything is unique, so there is nothing above the level of the bit that is consistent to warrant experimental study. This is why there's no such thing as computer science.

## Ten years later, is computer science still dead?

**Brad:** Apart from the line of observation you quoted, I don't have much to add. And after all, that question depends on how one defines "computer science" and "dead"…and how much desire one has to antagonize one group or the other, fairly or not; a desire I lack completely.

The only thing substantive I can add is that so long as software is unique and not governed by physical law (but note that the growing use of standards tempers this claim, which was written years ago), that makes it a kind of social science, which is very different from physical sciences.

## How did your thinking change with regard to OOP and superdistributions and SOA?

**Brad:** The thread you seem to be looking for is that my interests aren't in programming languages at all, but in why software is so hard compared to other things people manage effortlessly. Like feeding lunch to millions of New Yorkers, keeping up with Moore's Law, obliterating planets (this one for now) to keep up with car production, etc. It's really a remarkable phenomenon, one that no other species has mastered. I keep trying to understand how it works to make it work for software.

In fact, the ability to manage those types of complexity is so widespread that I'd call it innate were it not for vestiges of hunter-gatherer societies that haven't discovered it and everyone is homogeneous…everyone grows their own gardens, hunts their own meat, builds their own houses. But even then encapsulation and specialization of labor can be found: wives cook, men hunt, children help, old people advise.

But in modern life, specialization is rampant: that peculiar human ability to carve off some piece of my problem and make it somebody else's. I'll cook lunch if you run the store, somebody else hauls supplies, somebody else grows the wheat, somebody else makes fertilizer, and so forth ad infinitum, down to digging ore from the mines. It's so obvious that we take it for granted, as evidenced by the lack of vocabulary for even talking about the many levels of production involved in something as common as putting lunch on the table. Notice the two parts: 1) ability to carve off, i.e., *define*, a carvable piece of my problem, and 2) the ability to make it somebody else's. I'll come back to those later.

Before OOP, the ability to delimit a problem was very deficient. The more people who worked on a problem, the more the problem grew out of control. File after file with confusing names (Hungarian notation), external variable conflicts, almost no encapsulation at all. Exactly like the problem gate-level designers face when designing big chips. Their solution? Encapsulate a bunch of gates inside a chip. I'll handle chip design. You solder them together. Objective-C was precisely that notion.

Of course, that was just the beginning, not the end (which is why I sometimes lose patience with language-centric thinking). Languages are tools, things to be picked up or laid aside according to the problem at hand. And the same problem repeats at every level. For example, 20 years later, the same problem recurs with Java libraries, which have grown way beyond the ability of anyone to comprehend and use them effectively (J2EE, I'm talking about you).

Back to superdistribution, which comes from the ability to make my problems somebody else's, when we're talking about goods made of bits which don't abide by the conservation laws upon which compensation has been based since antiquity. Why should you undertake to solve my problems? What's in it for you, when I can just take what you produce and use it to suit my own needs? My superdistribution book explained one answer in the context of small-granularity OOP objects, basing compensation on metering usage of the bits, not acquisition of the bits as we do today.

But usage metering is a tedious and difficult problem for goods so exposed to interference by unscrupulous users. SOA services, in contrast, are not. They run on a server that the owner controls, not the user, where usage can be monitored without having to address so many opportunities for scamming. You still have the problem of supporting fair exchange of revenue for all levels of the structure of production, but that's just an accounting problem, not a matter of armor-plating an object against tampering.

Interestingly, all the old computer science problems are still present as you proceed up the hierarchy from OOP to JBI/SCA to SOA. The only difference is that standard data representations (XML schemas) eliminate the need for custom parsers for each representation. That leaves code generation working off DOM trees built by standard XML parsers driven by increasingly graphical "languages" like UML, DODAF, etc. The stuff going on there is exciting, at least compared to endless debates as to which OOP language is "best."

Been there, done that (with C, Objective-C, Perl, Pascal, Java, Ruby, etc.). IT got boring, so I moved on to interesting problems.

*Do we miss anything in the way we teach software development?*

**Brad:** My own teaching tried to bring the lack of robust economic forces on software quality into awareness. As a rule, the economic problem is lost and ignored in the computer science and software-engineering curricula, and given no attention at all.

*Why is computer science not a real science?*

**Brad:** Each time you encounter a new piece of software, you encounter something completely new and unique. How can you have a science where everything is unique?

If you study gold or lead from day to day, you can measure the properties and employ scientific methods to study them. With software, there is none of that.

# CHAPTER TWELVE

# Java

The Java language grew out of a project to run on small devices. It gained popularity with the rise of web browsers and applets, but with automatic memory management, a virtual machine, a large set of bundled libraries, and some degree of "Write Once, Run Anywhere," it's grown into a general-purpose programming language. Though Sun Microsystems has released the source code as free software, the company still retains some degree of control over the evolution of the language and libraries though the Java Community Process.

# Power or Simplicity

*You've said that simplicity and power are evil twin brothers. Can you elaborate?*

**James Gosling:** Often systems that are really powerful tend to get complicated. Take something like the Java EE spec. It's got all this stuff about transactions and persistence and those are really, really powerful. But in the early days of Java, we didn't have any of that.

The system was really pretty simple, and people could sit down and they could understand it pretty easily. If you restrict yourself to Java the language and the basic APIs, it still is very simple. But as soon as you start using some of these more powerful subsystems like Swing and Java EE and the rest of them, you get the sort of feeling that you're drowning in stuff. Look at the OpenGL libraries, it's really powerful the kind of stuff you can do with OpenGL. But oh my God, it sure isn't simple.

*Especially in OpenGL, you need a strong sense of how idealized graphics hardware works.*

**James:** Right. I think it was Einstein who had this quote that was essentially systems should be as simple as possible but no simpler.

*Is simplicity or complexity a constant throughout the system? Larry Wall talks about a waterbed theory of complexity; if you push down complexity in one part of the language, it pops up elsewhere. In making the Java core language itself very simple, does complexity show up in places like the libraries?*

**James:** The phrase I like to use for it is "whack-a-mole." Often when people say, "Oh, I solved the problem," if you poke around a bit, you discover they haven't actually solved the problem; they've just moved it.

One of the issues with addressing some of these things in the language is that the language is used by everybody. If you put specialized transaction support into the language, you might make transactions a little bit simpler for people doing transactions, but you would probably make life much harder for everybody else who is not using transactions.

*They pay the conceptual overhead there.*

**James:** Well, they certainly pay the conceptual overhead, and depending on how it's done, they may pay other overheads.

*Java's a mature platform now, widely used for over a decade. Is there a way to redesign simplicity back into a system like that?*

**James:** I don't know; I guess it's kind of a yes and a no answer.

It's sort of no in the sense that there's piles of code that uses all of this stuff. We would just love to get rid of various bits of complexity that have been around. The problem is, if you survey the apps out there, they tend to use them a lot.

*You had one shot at replacing AWT with Swing, but AWT is still around.*

**James:** Yeah, and it is amazing how many people still use AWT. A part of that is because AWT lived on in cell phones.

But part of it is that, despite press reports to the contrary, Java is used in desktop applications unbelievably heavily, mostly building enterprise applications. There are tens of thousands of them out there that were built using beta libraries, and they work perfectly well, so people have very little incentive to get rid of them.

The answer is sort of yes in the sense that one of the nice things about having an object-oriented system with decent abstraction is that when the world changes and you figure out a better way to do things, you can do it that way, and it doesn't collide with the old stuff.

*You have namespaces, abstractions, and encapsulation.*

**James:** Right. In Java EE with EE5, we went through a fairly major revolution in simplicity. If you look at Java EE today, if you just pick up an EE5 manual, it's actually not bad in terms of complexity. But if you pick up the old EE manuals, and you try to make sense of both of them, then it's just hideous. We did a reasonably good job of moving EE forward, unless you have to live with one foot in both camps. Then life is unpleasant.

*Backward compatibility is always difficult. Is it a deliberate Sun engineering discussion to allow people to run very old Java 1.1 programs on the most modern JVM?*

**James:** One of the things that is sort of funny is that the JVM itself is actually kind of outside of all of this discussion, because the JVM has been remarkably stable. Where all the pain and anguish has been is in the libraries. The libraries are much more manageable in the core VM. They're designed to be modular. They come in; they come out. You can actually build class loaders that partition the namespace so that you can have actually two versions of Java AWT. There's lots of tools to manage that. Once you get down to the actual virtual machine itself, life becomes much more difficult. But there just haven't been many issues down there.

The bytecodes have actually been pretty stable. Where all the VM work has been is in building these rocket science optimizers.

*Well, I've heard it said that effectively you have two compilers in the Java world. You have the compiler to Java bytecode, and then you have your JIT, which basically recompiles everything specifically again. All of your scary optimizations are in the JIT.*

**James:** Exactly. These days we're beating the really good C and C++ compilers pretty much always. When you go to the dynamic compiler, you get two advantages when the compiler's running right at the last moment. One is you know exactly what chipset you're running on. So many times when people are compiling a piece of C code, they have to compile it to run on kind of the generic x86 architecture. Almost none of the binaries you get are particularly well tuned for any of them. You download the latest copy of Mozilla, and it'll run on pretty much any Intel architecture CPU. There's pretty much one Linux binary. It's pretty generic, and it's compiled with GCC, which is not a very good C compiler.

When HotSpot runs, it knows exactly what chipset you're running on. It knows exactly how the cache works. It knows exactly how the memory hierarchy works. It knows exactly how all the pipeline interlocks work in the CPU. It knows what instruction set extensions this chip has got. It optimizes for precisely what machine you're on. Then the other half of it is that it actually sees the application as it's running. It's able to have statistics that know which things are important. It's able to inline things that a C compiler could never do. The kind of stuff that gets inlined in the Java world is pretty amazing. Then you tack onto that the way the storage management works with the modern garbage collectors. With a modern garbage collector, storage allocation is extremely fast.

### You're just bumping a pointer.

**James:** It literally is just bumping a pointer. New in the Java world costs about as much as malloc( ) in the C world. There are benchmarks where it's a factor of 10 better than malloc( ). For things that involve large numbers of small objects, malloc( ) tends to do a pretty bad job for anybody's malloc( ).

### Speaking of C, how do you design a system programming language? What does a designer need to consider when he builds something that may become a system programming language?

**James:** I tend to not think about languages and features much. In the times when I've done language design, which is tragically too often, it's always motivated by a problem. What is the context in which it is going to be run? What are people going to do with it? Kind of what is different about the universe? With Java, the things that were different were the network. The whole pervasive network makes you think about things a little bit differently because it has a lot of spinoff things. One of the components of that was computing in your grandmother's living room.

### Or a handheld device that doesn't look like a computer.

**James:** On the long list of things that that changes, you don't ever want to see a blue screen of death. You don't want to have complex installation features. So Java ended up with really strong fault-isolation mechanisms. Most people don't think of them that way, but they're there; things like the way that memory pointers work and garbage collections work and exceptions work are really about fault isolation. That ends up being about making sure that things keep running, even if there's a little hiccup. If you're driving down the road in your car and your doorknob gets loose, the car keeps going down the road. One of the problems with most C programs is you do something completely innocuous, it turns into a rogue pointer dereference, and bam! It's shrapnel all over the place.

*You have absolutely no way to predict what gets corrupted and where and if or when you're going to crash.*

**James:** Right. That's always struck me as completely unacceptable. In the days when C was built and the early days at Sun, performance mattered above everything. Anything that was like a check for array out of bounds or whatever it was was completely unacceptable. When the Java spec came out, it had this thing about "array subscript checking cannot be turned off." There is no "no subscript checking thing." For one thing, it was somewhat a radical departure from C in that C doesn't have subscript checking at all, and it's kind of an intrinsic part of the language spec.

*It barely has arrays, if you want to think about it that way.*

**James:** Yeah. It has addition and then kind of a weird syntax for addition. One of the magics of modern compilers is that they're able to theorem prove a way potentially all subscript checks. Though you might think that something like, you know, pointer checking can never be turned off is a bad thing, in fact, it's not a bad thing. It's actually a very good thing. It doesn't have a negative performance impact. You might do a little bit of checking on the outside of the loop, but inside the loop, it just screams.

*If C had only fixed its string problem where you don't know the length of the string because it's null-terminated, we probably could've had faster C for 40 years. That's my worst problem with C these days.*

**James:** Yeah. I love C. I was a professional C developer for years and years and years. I switched to C long before anybody else was using C. The first C compilers ran on machines that had 32K of RAM, and for something that would run in 32K of RAM, the original C compilers were astonishing, but it's really hard to find a watch with only 32K of RAM. Your average credit card has more than 32K.

## A Matter of Taste

*How does ubiquitous Internet connectivity change the concept of a programming language?*

**James:** The issue of how does the network impact the design of a programming language is huge. As soon as you've got a network, you have to deal with diversity; you have to deal with communication; you really have to think about how failures affect things; you have to worry a lot more about reliability.

In particular, you have to worry about how to build systems that can be robust and continue operating in the face of partial failures, because most of the systems that people are building that are of any interest are ones where there's always something that's broken.

And the traditional view of software has been that it's sort of an all-or-nothing thing; it's working, or it's not. And a lot of those sort of concerns feed into things like the Java exception mechanism, the strong type system, the garbage collector, the virtual machine, and on and on. I mean, the network had really profound effects on the design of Java, the language and the virtual machine.

*What's the biggest influence that you credit for your views on design and programming? Is there a way that you can point to something and say this is the Gosling trademark when I look at a system that you've designed or worked on?*

**James:** Yeah. I wish life were that simple.

I've met several architects who say "I have a trademark design," sort of a way that they tend to approach things. I tend to be much more sort of trademark-free. If I have anything of a trademark, if you talk to people who had looked at the code that I write, I tend to drive people nuts who have to maintain code that I write because I tend to over-obsess on performance.

I won't do aggressive inlining, but I'll use complicated algorithms when something really simple would've been just fine. I will move heaven and earth to—I'll tend to do more caching than most people do. I'll throw a cache in somewhere just out of reflex, just because if there isn't a cache, I get all nervous.

*That reminds me of a quote about one where someone asked, "Why use a linear search through an array? Quicksort is faster!" The response was, "There will only ever be at most seven elements in here; writing quicksort has too much overhead."*

**James:** I certainly wouldn't do a complex data structure for seven.

*A lot of programmers never consider the practical implications of these things.*

**James:** The sort of thing that drives me nuts is that, you know, people will be building a system for all of their development work; it's fine to do a simple linear search. They know that when it gets deployed, it's going to be 100,000 elements. I'm testing it on only 10 things, so I might as well just do a linear search, and they always say, "someday I'll put in the performance tweaks." It's one of those Robert Frost moments: "Knowing how way leads on to way, I know I never shall come back." Lots of code is that way. I tend to have this feeling like coming back to fix things up too often doesn't happen, and the world is filled with systems that are just incredibly slow.

*Is that time constraints or laziness or the fact that programming keeps geting simpler for nonprogrammers?*

**James:** It's a little bit of all of them. It also helps that these machines have three gigahertz clocks, and you can do an infinite loop in finite time now. :)

*Why did you choose to use a virtual machine for Java in the beginning?*

**James:** It helps tremendously with the portability story. It helps surprisingly with reliability, and oddly enough, it helps hugely with performance. It's much easier to get high performance when you're doing the just-in-time compilation. So it helps all over the place. It helps with debugging hugely.

*Is there anything you'd do differently about the JVM design, or are you satisfied with how it works?*

**James:** I'm actually pretty darn satisfied with it. The JVM design has been probably the most stable part of the whole system architecture. If I were going to go off and find a problem to solve, I wouldn't charge in there because it's in good enough shape; there's nothing in there that's an issue that's high enough to be worth bothering with. It's also had a crew of really bright people working on it for like a decade, basically a lot of Ph.D. compiler jockeys.

*Would you have designed the JVM any differently based on its current popularity among other languages?*

**James:** Well, there may be some things I would have tweaked somewhat. We are going through a round of language-design questions around that issue right now, and it's actually surprisingly hard to find the things that you could do differently in the VM that would really help other languages.

The places where we tend to have the big issues are ones that are sort of philosophical problems or philosophical issues with the virtual machine. So, for instance, it's really hard to implement languages like C and C++ on the Java virtual machine because we don't allow naked pointers.

Allowing naked pointers would be a huge reliability problem, and we decided that we would never allow naked pointers. I mean, the kind of issues that you get both with reliability and security from that is just too awful. So C and C++ on the JVM? Nope.

*You used the example that if you are driving a car, it doesn't stop if something like the radio stops working. Do we need new building blocks for software to avoid this fundamental problem that when something goes wrong, everything stops working?*

**James:** A lot of that is the way that kind of low-level plumbing in some of these language systems is built. "Everything comes to a screeching halt" is one of the big issues in C, because of the way that they do pointers.

As soon as you get any kind of memory error through your pointers, the system core dumps and bam, you're gone. Whereas in Java, on the one hand it's somewhat less likely that you'll get a pointer bug, and on the other hand, when a fault happens, you can actually contain it.

The exception system is really good at limiting the extent of damage so that when the car radio goes off, you can maybe just disconnect the car radio.

And people who build these big enterprise systems in Java actually spend a fair amount of time making it so that the various components are reasonably firewalled against each other so that the pieces can fail gracefully.

If you look at things like the Java Enterprise spec, there are all kinds of things in the way that that framework works that works really well with fault containment.

*Is the object-oriented paradigm still complete and correct in this way?*

**James:** Object-oriented programming is working very well for people these days. There are all kinds of debates about things on the edge—people are getting into all kinds of language-theory debates about basically tweaks on the side—but the basic notion of object-oriented programming has just been fabulously successful, and is not really showing any big cracks.

*Sometimes it seems that developers have to work twice as hard with objects. First they have to design a reusable component. If they make a change later, they have to write something that fits precisely in the hole left by the old component. Essentially, I see a very thin line between using objects to achieve good design and having objects that make everything more complicated.*

**James:** Well, it's certainly the case that object-oriented design requires a certain amount of good taste. The world is filled with examples of people who got way out of control, and things got a little crazy, but that's actually remarkably limited. The use of interfaces and objects has been just dramatically successful, and the fact that it forces you to think about how subsystems relate to each other, that alone as an intellectual exercise is very important.

The whole issue of making it so that things can be decomposed so that the parts of your system can be pulled apart helps hugely with evolution, and debugging, and fault containment, and a host of other issues.

And yeah, it requires a certain amount of good taste to use it properly, but it's not that hard. And it's proven to be very, very valuable—much more valuable than the kind of stuff that people do with spaghetti code, where everything is directly integrated with everything else, and if you try to change any one thing, then everything else has to change. It just gets horrible.

That's a really, really awful world to live in, when you're not doing things in an object-oriented way. Where object-oriented programming really starts to shine is when systems start to get large, when they have large teams, and when they evolve over time.

The more modular you can keep things and the more sort of isolated the various programmers tasks are, the boundaries of things that have to change when something else changes, it's just tremendously useful.

# Concurrency

*People talk a lot about the end of Moore's Law, in that systems are getting wider but not necessarily faster. Do you agree?*

**James:** Yeah. Moore's Law was all about gate count, and it's pretty easy to see how gate count has got a pretty good chance of growth in following Moore's Law for a lot of years. But how that translates to clock rate, it's almost been an accident that it's been able to be interpreted as clock rate for so long.

*Does the need for better concurrency change the implementation or also the design?*

**James:** Oh, it changes the design of things tremendously, although there is a certain amount of variability as you go from problem domain to problem domain.

So like in most mathematical software, to make some piece of mathematical software work in a multithreaded world, you really do have to change the algorithm tremendously. In a lot of enterprise software, though, the software's often running inside frameworks.

Like in the Java world, there's the applications server frameworks, Java EE, and in the EE framework, the apps hardly have to be aware that they're running in a multithreaded world; it's actually the container, the app server, that knows everything about multithreading and how to deal with clusters and multiprocesses and all that.

Those problems are just abstracted away from you and you don't have to worry about it, but that works really well for enterprise software, which tends to be characterized by lots of little transactions that have nothing to do with each other, and they just happen, bang, bang, bang.

Mathematical software where things are tightly interrelated, they share common data, yada yada, things get much more difficult. So there's not a clean answer there.

*Do we need new languages, or can we get by with new tools or libraries to address this? Is it just retraining all of the existing programmers to think in a different way?*

**James:** Well, it depends. I think it's extremely domain-specific. In most enterprise applications, which are heavily transaction-based, you can do frameworks like Java EE, which take care of multithreading completely straightforwardly. If you're running on a 128-core Sun machine, which oddly enough you can actually get, developers are not even aware of it and it uses all of them just perfectly and it's not even hard.

*It doesn't necessarily depend on the skill of the programmer; you can have a decent programmer who may not be an expert on multithreading, but in that case Java will take care of it for you.*

**James:** Right. The frameworks pretty much abstract away all the threading issues. It gets harder when you get into some of the more numerical things, you know—if you're doing various kinds of simulations and such. Any of these graph algorithms and numerical things, breaking them up into multithreaded situations is just intrinsically hard.

Some of it is because you have to do data structure access and locking and all of that. Often it's just intrinsically hard in terms of the data structures, and getting the algorithm right. Travelling salesman is a particularly tough one. Some of them are easier, like ray-traced image rendering, but there it's one where you've got a domain-specific observation namely that you can take individual pixels and they're completely independent.

*It's parallelizable down to a pixel level if you have that much hardware.*

**James:** Right. That actually works pretty well. Most of the good ray-trace renders, they do that. Some things like computational fluid dynamics, which is the underlying algorithm set in things like weather prediction and figuring out whether or not an airplane is going to fall out of the sky, those are harder because there's a lot of communication between different parts of the fluid. There it's pretty easy to break up into a shared address space system, but really hard to break up into a cluster where you've got address spaces that aren't shared. For CFD algorithms, you know, they pretty quickly die just on communication costs between nodes in the cluster. They work much better in multicore, but it tends to get excruciatingly algorithm-specific.

One of the things I like about functional languages like Scala is that if you write a numerical algorithm in Scala, then the compiler has a lot more ability to reason about what your program is doing. It can do more automatic mapping of the algorithm to a multithreaded, multicore distributed system.

*Is this because Scala is a pure functional language?*

**James:** It's not pure functional. One of the reasons that it works as well as it does for most people is that it's kind of both. You can program it kind of as if it were Java or you can program it functionally.

*Are there problem domains in which shared-memory multithreading works better than functional?*

**James:** For enterprise applications, the framework-based approach to multicore distributed systems actually works really, really well. I don't think that there's a huge advantage to a system like Scala. Things get really interesting when you're doing something like a travelling salesman algorithm.

*A deliberate decision that seemed to come from the Green Project or the Oak Project is that designing a language that works with the network in a pervasively network world with multithreading means that you need primitives for synchronization, and the core libraries need to be thread-safe.*

**James:** We have an immense amount of mechanism for thread safety. Actually, this one is sort of a weird case because normally what it means is that when you're running on systems that only have one CPU, you pay a certain price. But in this particular case, I mean this is one of these things where abstraction kind of comes to the rescue because the more abstract APIs and interfaces can be, things like the Java Virtual Machine are quite abstract compared to the real machine. The underlying mechanisms can do a lot of adaptation.

In the multithreaded logging case, it turns out that the HotSpot VM magically understands that single-core machines are different.

*When you're JITing, you can say, "I don't really need to worry about synchronizing this part because I know for a fact that we're never going to have a deadlock; we're never going to have thread contention for this particular piece of memory."*

**James:** Yeah, and that just happens magically and transparently. Nobody is aware of it. There's a similar issue with 64-bit pointers.

People in the C world get all wrapped around when they have to make their apps work in 64-bit. With Java apps, there's absolutely nothing you have to do.

## Designing a Language

*If it weren't for Java, would Scala be your language of choice?*

**James:** Yeah, probably.

*What do you think of all of these new languages that are not just research projects, that appear to be very serious attempts to build a real powerful language on top of the JVM?*

**James:** I think they're pretty cool.

*You don't feel threatened, as if they take all of your good ideas and bypass you?*

**James:** No, all the important bits of Java are in the VM. It's what makes the interoperability work. In some sense, Java and the ASCII syntax was designed as something that would make C and C++ programmers comfortable. It does that pretty well. Most C and C++ programmers can look at a piece of Java code and go, "Oh, I understand that."

*Tactically I see what it's doing, even if I don't know the details of the APIs.*

**James:** One of the big design goals was exactly that. In some abstract world of "what is the world's best possible programming language," that wasn't actually a goal. I personally think that Scala is pretty darn interesting. The problem with Scala is that it's a functional programming language and most people have a hard time thinking that way.

If I were to go off and design a programming language that was just for me, it would probably drive most other people completely nuts.

*Lisp then?*

**James:** It probably wouldn't be Lisp, but there are bits and pieces that would kind of be like Lisp.

*Bill Joy once said your goal was to drag C++ programmers kicking and screaming halfway to Common Lisp.*

**James:** In some sense that was true, if you look at what's on the sheets from the JVM.

*The idea that a VM doesn't have to be slow, or the idea that pervasive garbage collection is very productive for programmers.*

**James:** One of the things that people really didn't appreciate was that garbage collection is very good for reliability and security. Look at where bugs come from in typical large systems: memory-management bugs all the time. I went through a period of collecting statistics on all the bugs I found, and in particular, the number of hours spent. One of the things about memory-corruption bugs is that they tended to take an inordinate amount of time to track down. I swore to myself that I never wanted to waste another hour doing that again.

I wrote the first two garbage collectors in the JVM. Garbage collectors are a pain in the ass to debug, but once they're done, they're done, and they just work. Now we've got several serious rocket-science garbage collectors.

*What kind of GC did you write initially?*

**James:** I needed to do one that would work in very small address spaces. It was conceptually a basic mark and sweep with compaction and a certain ability to run asynchronously. There wasn't enough space to do any of the sort of more modern design. If someone had handles, which is what helped the compaction.

*An extra pointer indirection, but it lets you copy stuff around.*

**James:** Because I was trying to work with C libraries, the initial versions of it were semi-exact. It was exact for all pointers in the heap, but then it was inexact on the stack because it actually would scan the C stack to see if there was anything that looked like it might be a pointer.

*That's the only way I've seen handling the C stack well, unless you want to not use a C stack at all, which has advantages and disadvantages.*

**James:** Right. Which is actually what the JVM does now. It doesn't use the C stack. I mean it has its own stack mechanism. When you dive in to C code, you're on a separate stack. One of the things that's sort of painful about JNI is making the transition between the worlds.

*Considering that C# was inspired by Java, do you think that there are other features of Java that could be taken by other programming languages?*

**James:** Well, I mean, C# basically took everything, although they oddly decided to take away the security and reliability stuff by adding all these sort of unsafe pointers, which strikes me as grotesquely stupid, but people have used most of the features of Java somewhere.

*You wrote a garbage collector to stop wasting time debugging memory-management bugs. What's your opinion on pointers as implemented in C++ compared to references in Java?*

**James:** Pointers in C++ are a disaster. They are just an invitation to errors. It's not so much the implementation of pointers directly, but it's the fact that you have to manually take care of garbage, and most importantly that you can cast between pointers and integers—and the way many APIs are set up, you have to!

*Did you design references in Java to solve all these problems and still provide the same advantages of C++ pointers?*

**James:** Yes, you can do all your important stuff in Java that you can do in C++ using pointers.

*Do you see any other recurrent problem that might be avoided by implementing a general solution into the language?*

**James:** Things like that are all over the language in Java. One example is the exception mechanism. One of the things that people do in C++ is completely ignoring error codes that they get from all kind of things. Java makes it easy for you to deal with errors when they happen.

Java programs tend to be a lot more reliable partly because people are strongly encouraged to actually take errors into account as much as possible, in part because when errors do happen, you are pretty sure they are contained.

*Can well-chosen defaults help programmers write better code without looking for external libraries or add-ons?*

**James:** Over the years, most languages have cleaned up most of these stuff. One of the most problematic over the years in C++ has been multithreading. Multithreading is very tightly designed into the code of Java and the consequence is that Java can deal with multicore machines very, very well.

*What is the link between the design of the language and the design of the software written with that language?*

**James:** Oh, there are subtle linkages everywhere. I mean, an object-oriented language really encourages you to build very modular systems. You know, when you've got a strong exception-handling system, it encourages you to build systems that are robust. Basically every feature of a language you can think of has within it a subtle push toward a certain software design.

*Is there any other feature that you would like to include in the standard language? What about automatic code checking?*

**James:** Well, we do a lot of that kind of stuff in the tool. If you look at what makeme(?) does, it basically does like a real-time LINT, you know, all kinds of high-level things. These days you can't just consider a language alone, you have to pick the language and the tool together.

*When designing a language, do you consider how people will debug the language?*

**James:** There are a bunch of things that are important for building reliable software, but they are not particularly about debugging itself. For debugging we have a bunch of standards, things like how the system communicates with the debugging system.

You actually do a lot of stuff in the language to avoid ever getting in a situation where you need to debug; that's why things like the memory manager, strong type system, the threading model, it's all over the place in Java and these are things that help you even before you get to the debugger.

*When a language is platform-independent, how does this affect the debugging?*

**James:** Well, from a developer point of view, debugging is completely seamless, you know, running on a Mac debugging something on a Linux server—it works perfectly.

*How do you debug your Java code?*

**James:** I just use NetBeans.

*Do you have any advice for Java programmers?*

**James:** Use NetBeans, sprinkle assert statements all over the place, be really careful building tasks—there is JUnit, which is pretty popular—and pull them together and they work pretty well.

*What do college students in computer science miss?*

**James:** Most universities focus on the technical side of things. A lot of software engineering is about, "OK, here you've got a piece of software, find a bug in it," and your average college assignment is, "Write a piece of software to do this," where what you start with is a blank sheet of paper so you can do anything you want.

And also a lot of software engineering is just the social dynamics of working in a team, and a lot of that is not taught at all.

*What's your view on software documentation?*

**James:** The more, the better.

One of the sort of unique facilities that Java pioneered was documentation that's integrated into the code.

And for Java APIs, there's this tool called Javadoc, which extracts documentation from your source code. One of the big issues that people often have with software documentation is that the documentation is not up to date with the actual APIs. And so by having a lot of the boilerplate automatically extracted, things stay in sync a lot better, and even if you write no comments at all, Javadoc actually does a plausible job of generating usable API documentation.

So the single most important thing that people can do as far as documenting their code is just use the Javadoc tool, and then the more that you can do in putting the right comments into your code, it just helps everybody.

*Do you believe in specifying a project formally or fully before you build it?*

**James:** I guess I sort of have mixed feelings about formal specifications. It's one of those things that in theory, I think they're great; in practice, they don't seem to work out very well. They can often be OK for fairly small things, but the larger you get, the less useful formal specifications get, if only because they don't scale very well.

And more importantly, often doing formal specifications doesn't actually solve a problem; it moves the problem; it moves the issue of bugs in your software to finding bugs in your specification. And bugs in a specification can be really hard to find.

Even if you're not doing formal specifications, you're just doing sort of requirements analysis—a lot of organizations do these kind of waterfall things, where there's a group that comes up with a requirements document, and then they hand it off to the people who actually have to build the thing.

The requirements document is often just filled with problems, and unless there's a really tight feedback loop, you don't find bugs in the requirements; you don't find bugs in the specifications. So while I'm generally a big fan of doing specifications and requirements and that kind of thing, I tend to not take them all that seriously, and I certainly don't expect them to solve huge problems.

*I've also been interviewing the people from UML, and other languages, and one of the thing that sounded very interesting to me is the idea of using one of these very high-level design languages to build the logic behind the software. They mention the possibility of discovering logic mistakes in the model even before writing code.*

**James:** Yeah, there are a lot of high-level tools that are model-based in the Java world. The kind of high-level modeling that you find in lots of web application frameworks in UI frameworks, in UML frameworks can be very powerful.

If you get a copy of NetBeans, you'll see it's got a fairly sophisticated UML modeling system. You can use that both to initially specify a piece of software in terms of UML model, and then have it automatically generate the software, or you can use the UML modeler as kind of an archaeology tool to let you peer into a piece of software, so they help, but there are still issues.

## Feedback Loop

*How much feedback do you get on the language itself, not the implementation?*

**James:** Boy, we get lots of feedback with the language.

*How do you approach that?*

**James:** If we get one or two people asking for some feature, we tend to ignore it.

Because one of the things about a language is you've gotta be fairly judicious about what you change. The barrier's a little bit easier in APIs, but in general, we don't do anything unless there's a really strong demand for something.

So if many people ask for the same thing, that's like, "Oh, OK, then, that maybe makes sense to do." But if just one out of millions of developers asks for something, then it's like, "Probably would do more harm than help."

*What's your experience after freeing the source code to Java?*

**James:** Oh, we've had lots of good interactions. I mean, we made the source available for Java since 1995, and people have been downloading the source and using it in everything from thesis projects to security audits, and it's been a very powerful thing.

*Is that polishing the implementation or cooperative evolution of the language?*

**James:** Having multiple contributors is a good thing. It ends up being a conversation.

*Can you design a language in a democratic fashion?*

**James:** It's a very, very fine line because if you're sort of too democratic, what you end up with is just rubbish. But if you're sort of too much of a central dictator, you end up with something that doesn't make sense to anybody because it's just that one person's views.

And so it is really important to have a conversation with lots of people, and to have a reasonably tight decision-making process.

*Do you believe in the idea of growing a language, or do you think that since you have a goal, once you build something that can achieve that goal, you should just write a new language?*

**James:** I guess bits of both. I have no problem with growing a language, but I think that there needs to be a fairly high barrier to just jerking things around. For things that have real demonstrated value, it's fine to grow the language. On things where the value isn't really huge, things like random syntactic changes are just kind of pointless. If you woke up one morning and decided that braces were evil, that would be dumb, but for things that really affected people's ability to build software, we went through a few years ago the whole exercise of adding generics to Java, and that's been profoundly good.

*How did you choose what to put inside the language and what to keep as an external library?*

**James:** That's pretty much always decided based on sort of how generally applicable the feature is. So things that are useful only to small communities really are best off in a library. And in general anything that you can do in a library ought to be done in a library, and language changes should be reserved for things that really don't fit in any kind of a library.

*What criteria do you use when designing an API?*

**James:** I mean, my number one principle is keep it as small as possible. And I guess my number two principle is to design based on use cases. One of the failure modes that people often get in designing an API is that they design an API just kind of in a vacuum, and they sit around saying, "Well, somebody might want to do this," or, "Somebody might want to do that," and that just causes APIs to mushroom and get way more complicated than they need to be.

Whereas when you actually go through, "So what would people want to do with this?" Look at other systems where people have tried to draw menus or make network connections. You know, what has worked in other places? What have people actually used as opposed to what's written in the API?

You can do a lot of interesting things about API design and language design just by doing statistical analysis on software written in other languages.

### Is there any lesson that you would like other people to learn from your experience designing Java?

**James:** Designing languages isn't terribly hard. The most important thing in designing a language is not designing a language, but figuring out what the language is for. What is the context? What are the tasks that people are trying to do?

The thing that really made Java different was starting out with the network. What are the implications of networking on programming language design? It turns out to be pretty profound, and in some sense, the language design choices were pretty simple once one sort of went through the implications of networking.

### Did Java influence how the public thinks about platform independence?

**James:** I don't think the public thinks about platform independence. I mean, it's one of these funny things that, from my kind of weird point of view as an engineer building these large-scale systems, the public should not even be aware of.

When you go and you use your Visa card in an ATM or a cash register, the fact that there arc almost certainly big bags of Java code behind that, running on Sun machines and IBM machines and Dell machines and HP machines, and things with x86 architectures and PowerPC architectures and whatever, all of that kind of stuff, you don't notice that when you swipe your card on the reader.

And yet, a lot of those mechanisms are going on behind the scenes. You get onto the subway; if you're using one of these proximity cards, like the Oyster cards on the London Underground, that's a Java-based system.

You really used all the platform-independence stuff in it, and if consumers were forced to be aware of the programming language used to build the system, that would be a real failure to the system. One of our goals is to be completely transparent and to get out of people's way. Of course, this drives the marketing people nuts. They would like to have a Java logo in front of you every time you get on the London Underground, but that would be crazy.

# CHAPTER THIRTEEN

# C#

When Microsoft settled a lawsuit from Sun Microsystems over changes to the Java programming language, they turned to veteran language designer Anders Hejlsberg to design a new object-oriented language backed by a powerful virtual machine. The result was C#—and a replacement for both Visual C++ and Visual Basic within the Microsoft ecosystem. Although comparisons to Java are still inevitable in syntax, implementation, and semantics, the language itself has evolved past its roots, absorbing features from functional languages such as Haskell and ML.

# Language and Design

*You've created and maintained several languages. You started as an implementer of Turbo Pascal; is there a natural progression from implementor to designer?*

**Anders Hejlsberg:** I think it's a very natural progression. The first compiler I wrote was for a subset of Pascal, and then Turbo Pascal was the first almost full implementation of Pascal. But Pascal was always meant as a teaching language and lacked a bunch of pretty common features that are necessary to write real word apps. In order to be commercially viable, we immediately had to dabble in extending in a variety of ways.

*It's surprising that a teaching language would be so successful in bridging the gap between teaching and commercial success.*

**Anders:** There are many different teaching languages. If you look at Niklaus Wirth's history—Niklaus Wirth designed Pascal, later Modula and Oberon—he always valued simplicity. Teaching languages can be teaching languages because they're good at teaching a particular concept, but they're not really real other than that; or they can be full-fledged languages that truly teach you the basics of programming. That was always Pascal's intent.

*There seem to be two schools of thought. Some schools—MIT, for example—start with Scheme. Other schools seem to take a "practical" focus. For a while, they taught C++. Now it's Java, and some use C#. What would you do?*

**Anders:** I've certainly always been in the more practical camp. I'm an engineer more than I'm a scientist, if you will. It's my belief that if you teach people something, teach them something they can use later for something practical.

Like always, the answer is not at the extreme. It's somewhere in between. Continually in the programming language practice, in the implementation of programming languages for the industry, we borrow from academia. Right now, we're seeing a great harvesting of ideas from functional programming which has been going on in academia for God knows how long. I think the magic here is you've got to do both.

*Is your language-design philosophy to take ideas from where you can and make them practical?*

**Anders:** Well, in a sense. I think you probably have to start with some guiding principles. Simplicity is always a good guiding principle. Also, I'm a great fan of evolving as opposed to just starting out new.

You might fall in love with one particular idea, and then in order to implement it, you go create a brand-new language that's great at this new thing. Then, by the way, the 90% that every language must have, it kind of sucks at. There's just so much of that, whereas if you can evolve an existing language—for example, with C# most recently we've really evolved it a lot toward functional programming—it's all gravy at that point, I feel. You have a huge user base that gets to just pick up on this stuff. There's a bit of a complexity tax, but it is certainly much less than having to learn a whole new language and a whole new execution environment in order to pick up a particular style of programming.

*It's hard to draw the line between a language per se and its ecosystem.*

**Anders:** Well, yeah, and certainly these days more and more. The language used to dominate your learning curve, if you go back say 20, 30 years. Learning a programming environment was all about learning the language. Then the language had a little runtime library. The OS had maybe a few things, if you could even get to the OS. Now you look at these gigantic frameworks that we have like .NET or Java, and these programming environments are so dominated by the sheer size of the framework APIs that the language itself is almost an afterthought. It's not entirely true, but it's certainly much more about the environment than it is about the language and its syntax.

*Does that make the job of the library designer more important?*

**Anders:** The platform designer's job becomes very important because where you really get maximum leverage here is if you can ensure longevity of the platform and the ability to implement multiple different languages on top of the platform, which is something that we've always put a lot of value in. .NET is engineered from the beginning as a multilanguage platform, and you see it now hosting all sorts of different languages on it—static languages, dynamic languages, functional languages, declarative languages like XAML, and what have you. Yet, underneath it all is the same framework, the same APIs, and the leverage there is just tremendous. If these were all autonomous silos, you'd just die a slow death in interop and resource consumption.

*Do you favor a polyglot virtual machine in general?*

**Anders:** I think it has to be that way. The way I look at it is, you go back to the good old 8-bit days, where you had 64K of memory. It was all about filling those 64K, and that happened pretty quickly. It's not like you were going to build systems for years there.

You could implement for a month or two and then that was that; 640K, maybe six months and you'd filled it up. Now it's basically a bottomless pit. Users demand more and more, and there's no way we can rewrite it all. It's about leveraging and making things that exist interoperate. Otherwise, you're just forever in this treadmill, just trying to do the basics.

If you can put a common substrate below it all and get much higher degree of interoperability and efficiencies out of shared system services, then it's the way to go. Take interoperability between managed code and unmanaged code, for example. There are all sorts of challenges there. But better we solve it than every distinct programming environment trying to solve it. The most challenging kinds of apps to build are these hybrid apps where half of the app is managed and the other half is unmanaged, and you have garbage collection on one side of the fence and none on the other.

*There seems to be a design goal in the JVM never to break backward compatibility with earlier versions of the bytecode. That limits certain design decisions they can make. They can make a design decision at the language level, but in the actual implementation of generics, for example, they have to do type erasure.*

**Anders:** You know what? I think their design goal wasn't just to be backward compatible. You could add new bytecodes and still be backward compatible. Their design goal was to not do anything to the bytecode, to the VM at all. That is very different. Effectively, the design goal was no evolution. That totally limits you. In .NET, we had the backward compatibility design goal, so we added new capabilities, new metadata information. A few new instructions, new libraries, and so forth, but every .NET 1.0 API continued to run on .NET 2.0.

It's always puzzled me that they chose that path. I can understand how that gets you there right now on what's there, but if you look at the history of this industry, it's all about evolving. The minute you stop evolving, you've signed your own death sentence. It's just a matter of time.

Our choice to do reified generics versus erasure is one that I am supremely comfortable with, and it is paying off in spades. All of the work we did with LINQ would simply not be possible, I would argue, without reified generics. All of the dynamic stuff that we do in ASP.NET, all of the dynamic code generation we do in practically every product that we ship so deeply benefits from the fact that generics are truly represented at runtime and that there is symmetry between the compile time and runtime environment. That is just so important.

*One of the criticisms of Delphi was that there was a strong reluctance to break code, which informed some language decisions.*

**Anders:** Let's step back then. When you say break code, that must first of all mean that you're talking about an evolution of something. You're talking about a version $N + 1$ of something. You could argue that sometimes it's good to break code, but by and large, when you sum it up, I've never been able to justify breakage. The only argument I hear for breakage, because they're not really good arguments, is "It's cleaner that way" or "It's architecturally more sound" or "It'll prepare us better for the future" or whatever. I go, "Well, you know, platforms live maybe 10, 15 years and then they cave in under their own weight, one way or the other."

They become more or less legacy, maybe 20 years. At that point, there's enough new around them and enough new without any overhead. If you're going to break it, then break it good. Break everything. Get to the very front of the line. Don't like move up a couple of slots. That's pointless.

*That sounds like a game of leapfrog where the turns take 5 or 10 years.*

**Anders:** You either play leapfrog or you be super cognizant of backward compatibility, and you bring your entire community with you every time.

*Managed code does that to some degree. You can use your existing components in process.*

**Anders:** Certainly from the inception of .NET we have remained backward compatible at every release. We fix some bugs that caused some code to break, but I mean there has to be some definition by which it is okay to break people's code.

In the name of security or in the name of correct program behavior or whatever, yes, we will sometimes break, but it is rare, and generally it reveals a design error in the user's program or something that they're actually glad to have fixed because they weren't aware that that was a problem. It's good at that point, but gratuitous breakage in the name of more beautiful code or whatever, I think it is a mistake. I've done that enough in my early years to know that that just gets you nowhere with your customers.

*It's hard to make the argument from just good taste.*

**Anders:** Yeah. Well, sorry. My good taste is not your good taste.

*If you look back on the languages you were involved in, from Turbo Pascal through Delphi, J++, Cool, and C#, are there themes in your work? I can listen to early Mozart and then to his Requiem, and say, "Those are both distinctly Mozart."*

**Anders:** Everything is a picture of the time that you're in. I've grown up with object orientation and whatever. Certainly ever since the middle of Turbo Pascal up until now everything I've worked on has at the core been an object-oriented language. A lot of evolution happened there that has carried forward. In Delphi, we did a bunch of work on a more component-oriented programming model, with properties and events and so forth.

That carried forward into the work that I've done with C#, and certainly that's recognizable. I try to always keep a finger on the pulse of the community and try to be there with the relevant new. Well, Turbo Pascal was the innovative development environment, and Delphi was the visual programming—RAD. C# and .NET has all been about managed execution environments, type safety, and so forth. You learn from all of the stuff that's around you, be it in your ecosystem or competitive ecosystems. You really try to distill what is good about those, and what didn't work for them. In this business, we all stand on the shoulders of giants. It's fascinating actually how slowly programming languages evolve when you compare to the evolution that we've seen in hardware. It is astounding.

*Since Smalltalk-80, we've had between 15 or 20 generations of hardware!*

**Anders:** One every 18 months practically, and yet, there's not really a massive difference between the programming language we use today and those that were conceived, say, 30 years ago.

*They're still arguing over old concepts such as higher-order functions in Java. That's probably going to be a 10-year debate.*

**Anders:** Which is unfortunate, because I think they could move a bit faster on that one. I don't think there's really a question of whether it's valuable. It's more a question of whether there's too much process and overhead in the Java community to get it done.

*If going to a continuation passing style and exposing "call with current continuation" at the language level gives you a huge advantage, would you do that, even if only 10% of programmers might ever understand it?*

**Anders:** If, yes—but that's a big if. I don't think that that's the case, but look at what we did with LINQ. I truly believe that that will benefit the vast majority of our C# programmers. The ability to write more declarative styles of queries and have a uniformly applicable query language across different domains of data, it's super valuable. It's like the Holy Grail language and database integration in some ways. We may have not solved the entire problem there, but I think we made sufficient progress that it justifies the extra learning, and there are ways you can expose that to people without having them figure out the lambda calculus from first principles.

I think it's a great example of a practical application of functional programming. You can happily use it and never even know that you're doing functional programming, or that there are functional programming principles powering it underneath. I'm very happy with where we ended up on that one.

*You used the word "practical." How do you decide which features to add and which features to exclude? What are your criteria for deciding what to add and what to keep out?*

**Anders:** I don't know. Over time, you get a knack for telling whether this is going to benefit enough of your users to merit the conceptual baggage that it creates, right? Trust me, we see lots of interesting proposals from our user base of, "Oh, if we could only do this," or "I'd love to do that," but often it's too narrowly focused on solving one particular problem and adds little value as an abstract concept.

Certainly the best languages are designed by small groups of people, or single individuals.

*Is there a difference between language design and library design?*

**Anders:** Very much so. The APIs are obviously much more domain-specific than languages, and languages really are a level of abstraction above APIs if you will. Languages put in place the framework, the quarks and the atoms and the molecules, if you will, of API design. They dictate how you put together the APIs but not what the APIs do.

In that sense, I think there's a big difference. This actually gets me back to what I wanted to talk about before. Whenever we look at adding a new feature to the language, I always try to make it applicable in more than one domain. The hallmark of a good language feature is that you can use it in more than just one way.

Again, I'll use LINQ as an example here. If you break down the work we did with LINQ, it's actually about six or seven language features like extension methods and lambdas and type inference and so forth. You can then put them together and create a new kind of API. In particular, you can create these query engines implemented as APIs if you will, but the language features themselves are quite useful for all sorts of other things. People are using extension methods for all sorts of other interesting stuff. Local variable type inference is a very nice feature to have, and so forth.

We could've probably shipped something like LINQ much quicker if we said, "Let's just jam SQL in there or something that is totally SQL Server-specific, and we'll just talk to a database and then we'll have it," but it's not general enough to merit existence in a general-purpose programming language. You very quickly then become a domain-specific programming language, and you live and die by that domain.

*You turn your nice 3GL into a 4GL, which is a general-purpose death.*

**Anders:** Yeah. I'm very cognizant of that. Now one of the big things we're looking at is concurrency. Everybody's looking at concurrency because they have to. It's not a question of want to; it's a question of have to. Again, in the concurrency domain we could have the language dictate a particular model for concurrency—but it would be the wrong thing to do. We have to step above it and find what are the capabilities that are lacking in the language that would enable people to implement great libraries for concurrency and great programming models for concurrency. We somehow need treatment in the language to give us better state isolation. We need function purity. We need immutability as core concepts. If you can add those as core concepts, then we can leave it to the OS and framework designers to experiment with different models of concurrency because lo and behold, they all need these things. Then we don't have to guess at who will be the winner. Rather we can coast by when one blows up and it turns out that the other one was more successful.

We're still relevant.

*It sounds like you want to give people tools to build great things, rather than dictating the kinds of things they're going to build.*

**Anders:** I want to. You get much better leverage of community innovation that way.

*Where do you see that in the C# community? Do people bring code to you? Do you go visit customers? Do you have your MVPs trolling newsgroups and user groups?*

**Anders:** It's a mixture of all of the above plus some more. We have code-sharing things like Codeplex. There are all sorts of communities. There's commercial communities. There's open source. There's lots of open source .NET code. It's from all over. I don't think there is a single point of influx, so to speak. It's a varied and complex ecosystem out there.

You always run across stuff where you go, "Wow, how did they come up with this?" or "That's amazing." You can appreciate how much work this was for someone to do. It might not be commercially viable, but boy, it's a beautiful piece of work.

I certainly try to follow lots of blogs that are relevant to C# and LINQ.

Those are some of my favorite keywords when I go blog trolling, just to see what's happening out there. It gives you good insight in whether people are picking up on the work that you've done in the right way or not. It teaches you something for the future.

## Growing a Language

*How do you recognize simplicity?*

**Anders:** There's true simplicity and then there's this thing that I call *simplexity*, which I see a lot of. It is when you first build something super complex and then you go, "Wow, people will never get this. This is way too complicated but we have to have all this power in here. Let's try to build a simple system on top of it. Let's just try to like wrap it all up in a simple interface."

Then, the minute you have to do something that isn't quite what the system was designed to do, boom! You fall into this big morass of complexity underneath because all you were looking at was just a thin veneer on top of something that's very complicated as opposed to something that is truly simple all the way down. I don't know if this makes a lot of sense to you, but I tend to think of it like that. Simplicity often just means that you're doing more with less. There's just less there, but it does the same as something else or it even does more than something else. It's all about do more with less. It's not about doing more with more with a simple layer on top.

*Would you follow this principle if you were to create a new programming language today?*

**Anders:** Oh, certainly. I've created lots of programming languages by now or certainly lots of implementations. I think it's very important before you embark on creating a new language you have to be very, very clear about why you're doing it and what is the problem that you want to solve.

Often the mistake people make with new programming languages is that they get enamored with a particular problem they want to solve. Maybe the programming language is the right place to solve it, and so they set about solving that part of the problem and maybe they do a wonderful job of that. Then every programming language—and I mean every programming language—consists of 10% new and 90% stuff that is just bread and butter for programming and that just has to be there. A lot of these new innovative solutions that we see in new programming languages are great at the 10% new, but then they are terrible at the 90% that every language must do in order for you to really be able to write programs, and therefore they fail.

It's very, very important to understand that there's a bunch of boring standard stuff that has to be in every programming language. If you don't get that right, you will fail. Conversely it means that if instead of creating a new programming language, you can evolve an existing programming language, then the equation looks very different because then you already have the 90% covered. In fact you have 100% covered. You're just trying to add the new thing.

*Like C++.*

**Anders:** Like C++, which was a great example of an evolution of C or of the different versions of C# that we've done and so forth. I'm very much a believer in evolving. Then, of course, there comes a time when you just can't stuff more in there—there's so much tension between the new things you add and the old way of doing it in the language that you just can't move it anymore. Creating a new language is really more of an exception to the rule than it is the rule.

*Would you create a general-purpose language or a domain-specific language?*

**Anders:** I think the real answer there is "neither." How I would address that problem is I would create a general-purpose programming language that is great at creating domain-specific languages. Again, the devil that we face with all of these domain-specific languages is that they may get the domain right but then they get the general-purposeness wrong. There are certain general-purpose features that literally every domain-specific language ends up needing. Unless the domain-specific language is purely just a data definition language where you're just stating data, and at that point in my opinion you might as well use XML then.

If you're really a programming language where there's logic or predicates or rules or whatever, then you have to have expressions and expressions have operators and maybe you have to have standard functions and your customers are going to want to do things that you never even thought of. There's just a bunch of standard stuff that you need. If you can instead create your domain-specific language out of a base that is a general-purpose programming language, then I think you're much better off than starting out fresh every time.

One of the things that is problematic with general-purpose programming languages today is they're getting better at creating internal DSLs, and you could view LINQ as an example of that. But what they're not good at currently is capturing the correct usage patterns of those internal DSLs. In some ways, when you create internal DSLs you actually want to limit the things that you can do with the general-purpose programming language. You want to be able to shut off the general-purposeness of the language, and you want to only reveal it in certain spots in your DSL. That's one thing that general-purpose programming languages are not very good at right now. That might be something that would be useful to look at.

*Brian Kernighan said that if you want to create a general-purpose language, you should start from the beginning with that goal in mind. Otherwise, if you create a little language, as soon as people start using it, they are going to ask to add features to it. Growing a DSL generally doesn't work very well.*

**Anders:** Oh yeah. I think Gosling said that every configuration file ends up being its own programming language. It's very true, and you want to be real careful about that.

*You said that in some ways the platform is more important than the language. Are we going to produce reusable components?*

**Anders:** Well, the reason I said that is if you look at the evolution over the last 25, 30 years of languages, tools, and frameworks, it's quite remarkable how little programming languages have changed. It's equally remarkable how much larger our frameworks and run times have gotten. They're probably three orders of magnitude larger today than they were, say, 25, 30 years ago. When I started with Turbo Pascal, there were like maybe 100, 150 standard functions in the runtime library and that was that. Now we have the .NET Framework with 10,000 types with a combined 100,000 members. Obviously leveraging all of that work is increasingly important. It's important because it shapes the way we think about problems, but the framework is getting increasingly important because it is the stuff that we leverage in our programs.

Leverage is everything today. Your computer is, from a programming perspective, basically a bottomless pit. You could write code from now until the day you die and you would never fill it up. There's so much capacity, and end user expectations keep going up and up and up. The only way you really succeed is by finding smart ways to leverage work that has already been done. That wasn't the case if you go back 25, 30 years ago. You had 64k of memory, well, gee, that would fill up in a month or two.

*How much does the language influence the programmer's productivity, and how much is it the ability of the programmer that makes the difference?*

**Anders:** I think the two go hand in hand. I think the language tends to influence the way we think. The programmer's job is to do the thinking, if you will. That's the raw material, the raw power that goes into the process. The language is the thing that shapes your thinking—its function is really to help you think in productive ways. That's how, for example, languages with object-oriented support cause you to think about a problem in a certain way. Functional languages cause you to think about the problem in another way. Dynamic languages might cause you to think about it in a third way. They're different hats you put on that cause you to think differently. Sometimes it's useful to try and put both hats on and approach it from various viewpoints.

*Would you prefer adding a language feature that make everyone a bit more productive or one that makes just a few developers much more productive?*

**Anders:** For a general-purpose programming language, it's not a good idea to add features that only help a few because you end up being a grab bag of strange things. The hallmark of any good language feature is that it has many good uses, not just one good use. If you look at all of the stuff we added to the language in C# 3.0, all of the stuff that collectively forms this concept called language-integrated query or LINQ, that actually breaks down to about six or seven discrete language features that in and of themselves have many good uses. They don't benefit just one particular programmer. They're at a more abstract level than that. For every good language feature, you have to be able to show how it's going to benefit you in several scenarios or else it may not be right for the language. It might be better to just have that be an API feature.

*Do you consider which features to add or remove to make debugging easier? Do you consider the debugging experience during the design process of the language?*

**Anders:** Oh, absolutely. If you look at the whole underpinning of C#, the language is a type-safe language, which means there is no such thing as an array overrun or a stray pointer. Everything has well-defined behavior. There is no such thing as undefined behavior in C#. Error handling is done with exceptions as opposed to return codes that you could ignore and so forth. So each of those underpinnings like type safety, memory safety, and exception handling all help tremendously in eliminating whole classes of bugs or making whole classes of bugs much easier to find. That's something we think about all the time.

*How do you try to prevent these recurrent problems without limiting the developers? How do you choose between safety and freedom for the developer?*

**Anders:** I think each language puts itself somewhere on the spectrum of power versus productivity, if you will. C# is definitely a much safer and more protected environment than C++, which in turn is safer and more protective than if you're writing assembly code. The general trend for programming languages throughout their entire history really has been for us to keep moving the level of abstraction up and to make the program environment safer, if you will, or put more and more of the housekeeping that programmers have to do in the hands of the machines and allow programmers to focus on the creative part of the process, which really is where they add value. Programmers are terrible at doing memory management as a rule. They're terrible at doing type-safety analysis; therefore, we have bugs.

To the extent that we can put that in the hands of the machine instead and have the programmers do the creative thinking, that, I think, is a good tradeoff. It costs just a little bit of performance but boy, it's not all that much. Today in a typical .NET application, if you profile a program execution and look at where the program spent its time, garbage collection rarely even shows up. Yet your program is safe and will have no memory leaks. That's a wonderful tradeoff. That's just fantastic compared to the kinds of stuff we had to deal with in manually memory-managed systems like C++ or C.

*Could we use a scientific approach in the way we design and grow a language? I can see improvements given by research results in the implementation, but language design sounds like a matter of the designer's personal preferences.*

**Anders:** I think programming language design is an interesting combination of art and science. There's clearly a lot of science in it, mathematical formalism in notation for parsing and semantics and type systems, and what have you, code generation, blah, blah, blah. There's lots of science. There's lots of engineering.

Then there's the art of it. What does the language feel like? What is this process that happens in your head when you program in this language versus the other language and how is it different? What's going to be easier for people to understand and what's going to be hard for people to understand? I don't think we'll ever be able to measure those.

It'll never be scientific. It will always be an angle of language design that is purely an art. Just like there are good paintings and bad paintings and you can sort of scientifically talk about, "Well, the composition wasn't done right. Maybe he didn't use the right kind of paint." But ultimately it's in the eye of the beholder. There's just something about it that you cannot formalize.

*Do you think that the fact that you speak at least two languages in some ways might help? Sometimes in Italian I can describe with one word a concept that in English requires a sentence, and obviously sometimes the reverse happens.*

**Anders:** I don't know. That's a good question. I never thought of that. Possibly. I certainly think that to be a good language designer you have to understand multiple programming languages, no doubt about it. Whether it helps to understand multiple spoken languages, I I don't know. Could very well be the two are connected. On the design team we definitely have people that speak many languages or there are people that are good at music. They do seem to be connected somehow, but I'm not quite sure how.

## C#

*How long is the future of C#? You've been on it for almost 10 years.*

**Anders:** C# the project started in late December of '98, so we're coming up on our 10-year anniversary. That's not 10 years of existing in the industry, but it's 10 years since inception internally. I'd say we've got another 10 years at least, but it all depends. I've said I've long given up predicting the far-off future of this industry because no one ever gets it right anyway. But I certainly see a strong healthy future for C#. We're not done innovating, and there's plenty of work still to do.

*When I look at the evolution of C# from an application domain standpoint, I see the desire to replace C++ as a systems programming language.*

**Anders:** It can be used for that, but there are a lot of uses for which a managed execution environment like .NET or Java is more appropriate.

*When I compare C# to Java, C# seems to have a stronger push toward evolution. The Java people seem to want a baseline where everyone's code looks more or less the same. Whether you've programmed Java for a decade, never programmed before, or just graduated from a six-month course on Java, all of your code will look the same. C# seems to pull in new ideas from Haskell or from F#. Is there a desire to add new features that people who've just finished the six-month C# course haven't seen and won't immediately understand?*

**Anders:** I am not in this to engineer the next COBOL; let's just put it that way.

What is it that powers the Internet revolution and the electronic revolution that we've seen? It's the fact that we're constantly evolving. I bring it back to that. The minute you stop evolving, I don't know that you're adding any value. This is, again, taking it to the extreme. Of course, there is value in stability of the platform, but I think you provide that value by ensuring backward compatibility. You are free to get off the bus at C# 1.0 and just not move any further. For those people that really want to be more productive and want to build newer kinds of apps like SOA or whatever and get into more dynamic styles of programming—adaptable programs and more declarative styles of programming like we're doing with LINQ—then you've got to evolve or get out of the way, or something else will replace you.

### Do you get feedback regarding the C# language, not just the implementation?

**Anders:** We get feedback every day on the language in many different ways. It could be people mail me. I read people's blogs, I read forums where people ask technical questions, go to conferences—all sorts of ways that we get feedback daily on what works and what doesn't in the language. We take that feedback back to the design team and we maintain a long laundry list of all of the crazy ideas. Some of them will never make it into the language, but we keep them on the list because there's something there that maybe someday we'll get a good idea around this area. We know that we don't have it right yet, but there's a desire to do something.

Then gradually we find solutions to problems. Some of them are just simple things that people ask and that we just go do. Others are things that are bigger problems that people never really said anything about like LINQ. It's not like someone ever asked us, "We'd love to have queries built into the language," because you don't really think about the notion that you could.

I wouldn't say that there's one particular way we get the feedback. It's a very organic process and we get it from many different places. Certainly there's no way we could design the language without all this feedback, so it's all based on listening to what people do with the product.

### How do you manage the design team? How do you make decisions?

**Anders:** First of all, when you get feedback from customers, very often customers will tell you, "We would really like for you if you could add this particular feature." As you dig, it turns out that, oh, they're trying to do such and such, and typically people will tell you what they think is the solution to the problem. Now it is your job to discover what their real problem is, and then try to fit that into the bigger framework of the language. In a sense the first part of getting feedback is to do a little bit of detective work and understand what's really behind this solution that the customer is asking for. What is their true problem?

Then I think in terms of deciding what to do about it. As you evolve a language, you always have to be careful about just willy-nilly adding a bunch of features to a language, because the more features you add the more you age the language. Eventually the language just caves in under its own weight. There's too much stuff—too many conflicting things.

You have to be very, very judicious about what you add because you really don't want to end up with three different ways of doing the same thing that all there only for historical reasons.

So there are many times where we go, "Yeah, if we could start over we would definitely include this feature that people are asking for right now." Since we can't start over, we're not going to do it because it's fundamental or foundational enough that we can't fundamentally change the nature of the beast by peppering on. We can only make it a dual-headed beast and we don't want that.

In terms of the design process itself, we have a very strong C# design team consisting typically of between six and eight people who meet regularly. We have met regularly for the past 10 years from 1:00 to 3:00 every Monday, Wednesday, Friday afternoon. Some of the meetings get cancelled, but that is a slot that we have all had on our calendars for 10 years and it continues to be there. The people who are in the process have changed. I've been there throughout. Scott Wiltamuth has as well pretty much. Other people have come and gone, but the process has existed for that long.

We use this as our design function. That is where we do our ongoing design work. In order to have continuity in a product it's very important to have design as a continuously going process. Very often people will do stuff in spurts, "Oh, it's time to do the next version. Let's have some meetings and decide what it's going to be." Then you have a bunch of meetings and then people go away and you don't do any design work for a year. By the time a year's gone by and it's time for the next version, you can't even get the same people together anymore. You end up with this sort of schizophrenic product where every release feels different. If you keep the design ongoing, there's almost like a personality of the product that you keep alive.

Also good ideas don't happen on a schedule. They just happen. If you don't have a process to capture the good idea, if you're not designing right now, well then maybe that idea is lost. We're always doing continuous discussion of the next version that we're about to ship and the one after that, in an ongoing fashion. I think that works really well.

### C# has an ECMA standardization process, which is rare for languages. What was the motivation for that?

**Anders:** Standardization for many people is a requirement for adoption. There are certainly places—not so much businesses—but if you look at government, standardization is actually a requirement. Academic as well. It actually has interesting benefits, for Microsoft to standardize. Whenever we build a technology like .NET, there will invariably be implementations of that technology built by third parties for other platforms, and you can then choose to have them randomly try to replicate what you've created and get it wrong, and then have a poor experience there. That means also a poor experience for those customers that, by and large, rely on yours but need this other implementation for legacy hardware they have or whatever.

When you sum it all up, it actually makes sense to do it, even from a business standpoint. It also works as a great forcing function in being very precise about what it is you're building which has lots of advantages internally. The fact that we standardized C# meant that we had to write a very concise specification of the language. That very precise specification of the language—that investment—has come back to us manyfold already just from an internal standpoint.

In terms of having better test frameworks from our QA department, having better vehicles in research for implementing new language features, because prototype compilers, it's entirely clear what they're supposed to do. For teachability of the language, the fact that there is a very concise specification means that people can always consult that as a reference as opposed to just guessing.

It helps us in ensuring that code remains backward compatible. So anyway, lots of benefits there that you might think immediately are not there, but in reality they are. By going through a standardization process, you get the eyes of a very savvy community on your product. We've gotten lots of feedback from the other companies and individuals involved in the standardization process and that made C# a better language. That's valuable, too. I'm not sure that these organizations and individuals would've taken an interest if it wasn't because we standardized.

*Standardization lags behind language evolution, though.*

**Anders:** Right. Standardization does to some extent slow you down. It sort of depends on how you word it. Some standards are worded as, "You must implement this and nothing else, and it is a violation of the standard to have extensions to what we specify here." I have never much believed in that. Standards are supposed to establish a common baseline, and arguably, also a way to ensure that you are adhering to the baseline and not overstepping it. But standards should definitely leave freedom for innovation in them because that is how you're going to produce v2 of the standard—by picking up some of those innovations. You can't outlaw it.

For C#, there's a standard, but that standard has not kept us from evolving. Rather a process of evolution happens outside the standards process, because you're not going to get innovation out of a standards community. That's not its purpose. Whatever framework you're operating in must allow for that innovation to occur elsewhere.

*What is your opinion on the formal aspect of the design of the language? Some people suggest that you should start with a formal specification on a piece of paper and then write the code. Some people just ignore the formal specification totally.*

**Anders:** The answer is rarely at the extreme. I think languages with no formal specification at all generally tend to be a mess. Languages where you first formally specify everything and then implement the compiler as an afterthought also tend to be not very pleasant to use. The way we developed C# is we would in parallel write the compiler and the language specification, and the two deeply influenced each other. We would run into issues in writing the compiler that we would have to go back and address in the specification. Or in writing the specification and trying to rigorously analyze all the possibilities we would find stuff that, "Whoa. Maybe we should just try to do this differently in the compiler because there's these other cases that we didn't think of."

I think both are important. I'm happy that we did the standardization work because it forced us to be very explicit about what the language is and how it works. Then it forced us to have a formal specification, which, like you said, some languages don't; that is just not a good thing. When the source code is the specification that means that in order for you to understand what's going to happen in this particular program, you have to go look at a source code for the compiler. Not a lot of people are capable of doing that. Your only other alternative is to guess or to write tests and see what happens and hopefully you caught all the corner cases. I don't think that's the right way to do it.

### By the way, how do you debug your C# code?

**Anders:** My primary debugging tool is `Console.Writeline`. To be honest I think that's true of a lot of programmers. For the more complicated cases, I'll use a debugger because I need to look at a stack trace or what happened to my locals here or whatever. But quite often you can quickly get to the bottom of it just with some simple little probes.

### Do you follow any principles to design an API?

**Anders:** Well, first of all I would say keep them simple, but what does that mean? I mean that sounds stupid, right? I am a great believer in APIs that have as few methods as possible and as few classes as possible. Some people believe more is better. I'm not one of those. I think it's important to look at what is it that you think people will typically be doing with your API. Find the typical five scenarios that they're going to be doing and then make sure that the API makes that as easy as possible. Ideally that it's just one call to the API. It shouldn't be that in order to do the typical scenario you have to write many lines of code against the API. At that point it is not at the right level of abstraction.

However, I also think it's important in APIs to always leave an out. You want to flow from the very simple use of the API and seamlessly move into the more advanced uses if you need to. A lot of APIs have sort of this step function. Yes, there's some simple methods you can call, but then the minute you want to do something that's a little more advanced then, boom, then you fall off a cliff. Now you have to learn about all these other things that you didn't care about in order to do the little more advanced stuff. I'm very much a believer in sort of more of a gradual easing into it.

### What about documentation?

**Anders:** The state of documentation in software in general is terrible. I always urge programmers and try to advocate internally as well, and I'm not always successful, but I tell programmers half the value you deliver to customers is good documentation for your APIs. A great API is worthless without documentation that explains what it does and how it's supposed to be used. It's a tough one. Lots of companies like to have the programmers write the code and the documentation people write the documentation, and the two never talk. You end up with documentation that just says "MoveWidget moves the widget," or states the obvious in as many words as possible. That's a shame. I think programmers should write more documentation than they do.

*Do you like the idea of comments inside the code or you were thinking of some external document?*

**Anders:** I've always been an advocate of having XML documentation comments in the code. If you put it in code, then chances are the programmer who's working on it will notice that whatever it says up there in that documentation comment isn't right. Maybe he'll go fix it. If you put it in a different file somewhere, then the programmer will never look at it, and so it'll never be correct.

It's all about trying to bring the two as close together as possible. It's not perfect by any means, but we try.

*What do you suggest to become a better C# programmer?*

**Anders:** It's hard. There are many good books out there on C# programming and I would encourage people to pick up one of the better books. I'm not going to start naming names here, but there are many good books out there that will help you become a better C# programmer and help you better understand the .NET Framework. There are many things available online that also help. There are things like Codeplex. There's a bunch of open source projects that you can grab and look at and learn from and so forth.

To become a better programmer in general, one of the things that have helped me is to look at different styles of programming and different kinds of programming languages. I have learned in the last 5, 10 years a lot from looking at functional programming, which is a very different way of programming, but it teaches you a bunch of things. It's obviously about programming, but it comes at it from a different angle, and that gives you a different viewpoint on problems that I find to be very, very useful.

## The Future of Computer Science

*What do you consider the outstanding problems in computer science?*

**Anders:** If you look even at a metalevel above that, the ongoing trend in language evolution has always been this constant increase of abstraction level. If you go all the way back to plugboards and machine code and then symbolic assemblers and then C and then C++ and now managed execution environments and so forth, each step we moved a level of abstraction up. The key challenge always is to look for the next level of abstraction.

There are several contenders right now that appear to be big challenges. One we already talked about is concurrency: producing meaningful programming models for concurrency that are understandable by the broad masses of programmers as opposed to a few high priests of parallelism. That's kind of the world we're in right now. Even the high priests at times get surprised by their own code today. We have a big challenge there.

Also there's a lot of talk about domain-specific languages and metaprogramming in the community these days. In my opinion, there's more talk than reality there. I don't think we know what the answers are. You see things like aspect-oriented programming and intentional programming, but we have yet to really nail it.

Depending on who you ask, people go either, "Oh, there are no domain-specific languages," or "Oh, domain-specific languages are everywhere." We can't even agree on what a domain-specific language is, in a sense—but there's clearly a there there when it comes to devising more declarative ways of expressing yourself. In some ways, we've run out the line all the way on imperative styles of programming. We're not going to get much further with our imperative programming languages. It's not like there are new statements that we could add that would make you 10 times more productive all of the sudden.

I think one of the things that are true of most programming languages today is that they force you to overspecify the solution to your problem. You're down there writing nested for loops and if statements and whatever, and really all you wanted to do was a join between two pieces of data. But there's nothing that allows you to say that. You have to get down and dirty and do hash tables and dictionaries, blah, blah, blah.

The question is how do we move to that more declarative level of programming. Of course, the more you move it up, the more concepts you end up having because you get more domain-specific. There's a lot of truism to this dream of domain-specific languages, yet we somehow have not found the right vehicle to implement them, I feel like. Yet. So that does remain a challenge.

Right now, we're seeing this interesting resurgence of dynamic programming languages. I actually feel it is really in spite of the languages being dynamic and more because they have great metaprogramming capabilities. Like if you look at Ruby on Rails, it's all powered by Ruby's metaprogramming capabilities, not so much the fact that it's dynamic. It just so happens that eval and metaprogramming are a lot easier in a dynamic language than in a static language.

On the other hand, it's a high price to pay to give up your statement completion and your compile-time error checking and so forth.

*The argument I've seen from lots of people who've been around dynamic languages for a while is Smalltalk's browser.*

**Anders:** I'm not sure I buy that. That works when your problem is small enough, and it used to be that problems were small enough back when Smalltalk first appeared. Now with the size of the frameworks, it is unfathomable to think that people actually know all of the APIs that exist on a particular object or even care to know. Tools like statement completion and Intellisense and refactoring driven by compile-time metadata or static typing are just invaluable. They're going to continue to be more valuable because the world is going to keep getting more complex. Right now we're seeing a surge of dynamic programming languages, but I think in large part it is powered 1) by the metaprogramming angle, and 2) it's in many ways just a reaction to the complexity of the J2EE environment.

I've certainly seen lots of Java programmers defect to Ruby just because they're dying in frameworks and Struts and Spring and Hibernate and what have you. Unless you are a grand wizard of technology, you're not going to be able to put all of these things together yourself.

*Should programming be more accessible to people who aren't and have no aspiration ever to be grand wizards?*

**Anders:** I think so. It all depends on what you mean by programming also. Because in a sense, is using a spreadsheet programming? If you can make people program without them even realizing they're programming, then, oh my God, that's wonderful. I harbor no aspirations that we've got to teach the world users how to write programs in the kinds of programming environments that we use as developers today. Certainly, programming, yes, but at a much higher level.

## What's facing us now and in five years?

**Anders:** Concurrency is the big one right now. That thing is right in our face, and we've got to find solutions to that problem. One of my biggest challenges in the foreseeable future is having our team work that issue.

Again, we'd like to do it in an evolutionary fashion, but how do you deal with the shared state problem and side effects without breaking all the existing code? We don't know yet, but it very well may be that that concurrency is a big enough paradigm change that whole new languages are needed or whole new frameworks are needed. Although I don't think we're at that point yet.

I think there's a lot of ground that we can gain from making it possible for people to write APIs that internally are massively parallel and written by people that really understand a particular domain, be it transformations or numeric processing or signal processing or bitmaps or image manipulation. And yet, put APIs on it that look largely synchronous from the outside and in a sense, wall off the concurrency to inside the APIs.

There are things that are required in our programming languages today in order for us to be able to do that properly. One of them we already have, which is the ability to pass code as parameters. As APIs get more and more complex in their capabilities, you can't just pass in flat values or data structures to the API. You've got to pass in pieces of code that the API then orchestrates and executes.

## You need higher-order functions and abstractions such as map, fold, and reduce.

**Anders:** Higher-order functions. Exactly. In order to be able to do that, you need stuff like lambdas and closures and so on. In order for you to be able to do that in a concurrent environment, you also need guarantees on whether these lambdas are pure, or do they have side effects. Could I just automatically run this in parallel, or are there side effects that would cause that not to be possible. How can I know that? Those are things that we don't have in our languages today, but we can certainly speculate about adding these. Of course, the trick is adding them in a way that doesn't constrain you too much and that doesn't break too much of your existing code. That's a big challenge.

That is something our team thinks about daily.

*Does the need for concurrency change the implementation or also the design of the language?*

**Anders:** Oh, it certainly changes the design. A lot of people have harbored hope that one could just have a slash parallel switch on the compiler and you would just say, "Compile it for parallel" and then it would run faster and automatically be parallel. That's just never going to happen. People have tried and it really doesn't work with the kind of imperative programming styles that we do in mainstream languages like C++ and C# and Java. Those languages are very hard to parallelize automatically because people rely heavily on side effects in their programs.

You need to do several things. You need to first of all construct modern APIs for concurrency that are at a higher level than threads and locks and monitors and where we're at now.

Then there are certain things you need from the language to make that style of programming easier and safer, like guaranteed immutability of objects, pure functions where you know there are no side effects, analysis around isolation of object graphs so you know whether a particular reference to an object graph has ever been shared with anybody else, and if it hasn't, then you can safely mutate it, but if it has then there might be side effects. Things like that; things of that nature where the compiler can do some analysis and help provide safeties, like we have type safety today and memory safety and so forth.

Those are some of the things that I think need to happen in the next 5 or 10 years in order for us to better be able to program in these concurrent systems.

*Essentially you are telling the computer what to do.*

**Anders:** That's one of the big problems with the very imperative style of programming that we do now is that it is indeed very overspecified. And that's why it's hard to automatically parallelize.

*In the future, might we let the framework do the work to deal with concurrency?*

**Anders:** Oh, I think so. There are many different kinds of concurrency, but if you're talking about data-parallel kinds of concurrency where you're going to do operations on large datasets like image manipulation or voice recognition or numerical processing, then I think it's very likely or very appropriate for us to have a model where you just view it as an API. You have a higher-level API where you can say to the API, "Here's the data and here are the operations I want to have applied. You go away and do it and do it as quick as you can given the number of CPUs that are available."

It's interesting there because today it's pretty easy for you to just say, "Here's the data." You can just give it a reference to some big array or some object or whatever. Specifying what the operations are would typically involve you giving references to pieces of code, if you will delegates or lambdas, and it sure would be nice if the compiler could analyze and guarantee that these lambdas have no side effects and warn you if they do. That's part of what I'm talking about, but that's just one kind of concurrency. There are other kinds of concurrency for more asynchronous distributed systems, which is a different kind of concurrency where we could also benefit from support in the programming languages. If you look at a language like Erlang, which is used in very highly scalable distributed systems. They have a very, very different model of programming that's much more functional and that's based on asynchronous agents and message passing and so forth. There are some interesting things that I think we could all learn from also in our languages.

### Does the object-oriented paradigm create problems?

**Anders:** You know, it depends on what you group under the object-oriented paradigm. Polymorphism and encapsulation and inheritance are as such not a problem, although functional languages typically have a different view of how you do polymorphism with their algebraic data types. Aside from that, I think the biggest problem typically with object-oriented programming is that people do their object-oriented programming in a very imperative manner where objects encapsulate mutable state and you call methods or send messages to objects that cause them to modify themselves unbeknownst to other people that are referencing these objects. Now you end up with side effects that surprise you that you can't analyze.

In that sense object-oriented programming is a problem, but you could do object-oriented programming with immutable objects. Then you wouldn't have these same problems. That's kind of what functional programming languages are doing, for example.

### Regarding your interest in functional programming, should computer science students study more math and experiment more with functional programming?

**Anders:** Well, I certainly think that it is important to include functional programming in any computer science curricula. Whether you start with it that depends. I'm not sure that your very first introduction to programming should be functional programming, but I definitely think that it ought to be part of a curriculum.

### What lessons should people learn from your experience?

**Anders:** Well, if you look at the first product I worked on, Turbo Pascal, it was very much about not believing the traditional way of doing things. Don't be afraid. Just because people tell you it can't be done, that doesn't necessarily mean that it can't be done. It just means that they can't do it. I think it's always fun to think outside of the box and try to find new solutions to existing problems.

I think simplicity is always a winner. If you can find a simpler solution to something—that has certainly for me been a guiding principle. Always try to make it simpler.

I think to be really good at something, you have to be passionate about it too. That's something you can't learn. That's just something that you have, I think. I got into programming not because I wanted to make lots of money or because someone told me to. I got into it because I just got totally absorbed by it. You just could not stop me. I had to write programs. It was the only thing I wanted to do. I was very, very passionate about it.

You have to have that passion to get really good at something, because that makes you put in the hours, and the hours are the real key. You need to put in a lot of work.

# CHAPTER FOURTEEN

# UML

How do you communicate ideas about the design of software to other people? The world of construction uses blueprints. UML—the Unified Modeling Language—is a graphical language intended to represent the artifacts of a software project. The resulting combination of the object-oriented analysis of James Rumbaugh, the object-oriented design of Grady Booch, and object-oriented software engineering of Ivar Jacobson allows developers and analysts to model their software through specific types of diagrams. Though the language has multiple successive standards, you've likely used some of its concepts in quick whiteboard drawings.

## Learning and Teaching

*I read that you started working at Ericsson knowing nearly nothing about programming. How did you learn?*

**Ivar Jacobson:** I started working at Ericsson without knowing anything about telecommunications. It was a valuable experience. Even though I worked in a division that developed hardware switches, I could abstract from that the whole idea of building large systems. I worked there for almost four years, and I learned how to think about systems in general. That knowledge was very unique, because people who developed software had no experience in building large systems.

I was an electrical engineer—probably the only one who had an academic degree in engineering. Most people there had no academic degree. I had learned at university how to attack problems, and I also obtained a lot of self-confidence that you could solve basically every practical problem.

*You used to take home assembly code, study it in the evening, and prepare some questions about it for the developers.*

**Ivar:** We had almost no documentation; it was done by people who didn't know much about software. They wrote about requirements and documented these requirements in some kind of flowcharts, but these were inconsistent and incomplete.

We had flowcharts, too, developed and used by our people, but they were not componentized, so they became huge diagrams. We added descriptions to every line of assembly code, but people learned primarily by working together, by talking, and by reading code. I would ask people about the code I read at night, basically, "what did you really intend to do here?" and so on.

I probably had to read the same piece of code three to five times before understanding it, but I was very stubborn, so I went over a lot of code that way at night. During the day I was very busy managing the project. My role was a project manager, someone who doesn't really get involved in the technology, but understands the project, and can at least go around and ask people where they are. I was more like a project administrator. I hated that role, and as soon as I learned more I became more involved. It took me only three months to come to the conclusion that what we were doing would never, ever become a product.

Our project had 75 people at that time and what we were doing was absolutely mission-critical to Ericsson. You can imagine the project manager who goes to his boss and says, "this will never, ever become a product."

## How did you come up with the concept of the use case?

**Ivar:** It was quite natural. In the telecom industry, people have something called traffic cases. Traffic cases were like use cases, but applied only to telephone calls. We didn't have any use cases or traffic cases for other features in a switch, even if those features actually represented more than 80% of the code, such as operation and maintenance. For this software we just talked about "features." There was a long list of features, and it was very hard to see how they related to one another.

We had these two different concepts in traffic cases and features. They had been in use in the telecom industry for at least 50 years, but they were not easy to combine. I thought very hard to find one unifying concept that we could use to describe all kinds of interactions with a system. I started to look at the system from the outside, as if it were a black box. I tried to identify all the scenarios that seemed useful to the users. The concept in Swedish is called *usage case*, but my translation was not good so it became just use case—and I am happy for that.

By April 1986, my use cases needed to stand on their own, so I made them classlike. Use cases can be thought of as objects that live as long as the transaction goes on between the user and the system. They may interact with other users as well, as in telephone calls. One of my important goals was to be able to reuse use cases, so I needed a more abstract use case system comparable to abstract classes in object orientation. Making the analogy with objects and classes helped me to find a unifying concept (use case) that could be applied to describe both traffic cases and features.

It took a while before the concept settled, but by 1992 I had identified everything important about use cases. After I wrote the book *Object-Oriented Software Engineering* [Addison-Wesley], I don't know anyone who has contributed something really substantially new since then. Other people have explained them in better ways, such as in the book written by Kurt Bittner and Ian Spence [*Use Case Modeling*; Addison-Wesley Professional]. Both of these individuals now work in my company. Their book is a better book to introduce and detail the idea.

The discovery of aspect orientation was new, of course, as was the discovery that use cases are really good aspects. That resulted in the book *Aspect-Oriented Software Development with Use Cases* (together with Pan Wei Ng, also in my new company), published in 2005 [Addison-Wesley Professional].

## What happened when you presented the idea to the developers at Ericsson?

**Ivar:** The first reaction from my friends and the top guys at Ericsson when it comes to methodology was "this is really nothing new." I could tell they just didn't see it: I saw immediately that use cases are also test cases, so if you specify your use cases up front, you have many of the test cases. That was really a new thing in 1986. We could use use-case-driven development, meaning every use case describes some set of scenarios where you describe how they are implemented by collaborations among classes or components.

*How can we share experiences like yours in the software field?*

**Ivar:** That is a very special problem that I have spent the last five years solving. You need to understand the knowledge you have, so you can describe it. It's difficult for other people to learn ad hoc ideas. Even if you have the best process in the world, you still have to transfer that knowledge to other people. You need systematic ideas, and then transfer your knowledge by transferring a knowledge system. There are better and worse ways of doing so.

Fifteen years ago, we had Objectory. That evolved into the Rational Unified Process, and of course a lot of new knowledge was added, but the whole technology of capturing knowledge was not yet very approachable. It was the best we could do at that time. It was unique because it had never been done before to such an extent.

Now we promote "practice-based" knowledge transfer. Instead of transferring knowledge about everything you need to know about software development, you transfer one practice at a time, and only when other people most need it. The practices are small and approachable, and everything inside a practice fits logically together so it's easy to learn, whereas in a process you have all kinds of stuff you need to keep in mind all the time. You may say that a process in the past was just a soup of ideas. We make the process a bag of practices instead.

## How should we approach computer science in education?

**Ivar:** The problem we have is that most university professors really know very little about engineering. When it comes to software, few of them have developed any useful software themselves. Maybe they have developed some compiler, but most of these compilers were very academic. Maybe they have developed some software for training purposes. We cannot really expect them to teach software engineering.

You can learn to do Java programming at a university level, or any other language they might have taught if you go back in time, but if you really want to understand software, you need to have competencies in many other different areas, such as requirements, architecture, testing, unit testing, integration testing, system testing, performance testing, not to mention configuration management, version control, differences between building frameworks and building applications, building reusable software, services-oriented architecture, product line architecture, and so on.

You can't learn the really hard things in universities.

## Do students need more practical experience, such as participating in an open source project or doing an internship in a big corporation?

**Ivar:** Training at universities takes place primarily through education and building simple things.

I don't have a fair picture of the whole world here, of course, but compare that situation with other engineering disciplines—for example, the construction industry. There they have architectural education, which is very separate from building things. Several different disciplines go together. If you educate people to be architects, they still have to build things, too; otherwise they are not useful architects. You can always dream, but if you cannot realize your dreams, they are not very useful.

We really don't educate people in engineering. Building software is much more engineering than art. Many people would like to see it differently, but very few professional programmers can spend time on art. Most of them are engineers. That doesn't mean they are not creative. Would anyone believe that people who have an education in machinery, like building various types of machines, are not creative? If I build ships, am I not creative? Or houses? Of course I am. Architects are very creative, too.

Thus, we need to realize that software development is engineering and not an art. You need to educate engineers in engineering. However, many universities in the U.S. and Europe have a long tradition of letting their professors be truly just academics. The fundamental problem, as I see it, is that we really don't have a theory for software engineering. To most people, software engineering is just a soup of ad hoc ideas. This is one of the most important problems to fix.

*Please explore why you think this is such an important problem.*

**Ivar:** Our view on how software should be developed seems to change dramatically every second or third year, more frequently than the whims of fashion. Big companies around the world carelessly discard expensive process and tool investments, almost before they have even tried them. Instead of learning from experience, they heedlessly start with something they believe is fundamentally new. In reality, very little has changed. As in the fashion world, there is much ado about next to nothing. In something as trivial as clothing this may be acceptable, but with the size of our investment in software this is wasteful, expensive, and absurd.

The latest trend is "being agile" (as exemplified by Scrum). The "agile" movement has reminded us that people matter first and foremost when developing software. This is not really new—this theme resurfaces every decade or so as naïve managers try to mechanize and commoditize what is basically an exercise in creative problem solving. It is important that we not lose track of how to work as a team, how to collaborate, how to document what we do, and how to plan our work on daily, weekly, and monthly timescales, etc. But in bringing these things back to focus, much is lost or obscured by new terms for old things, creating the illusion of something completely new.

The result of this is a lot of wasted effort as old truths are rediscovered but cloaked in apparent new clothing. Younger and less experienced coworkers promote new trends, following new gurus, supported by the hype of a media always hungry for "news." Managers who have lost touch with actual development find themselves in a hopeless situation: resist the newest fashion, and they brand themselves as out of touch. Pilot projects are run to force proof of merit for the new approach, but motivated developers can make anything work on a small scale. As a result, the new approach overtakes the old, and all that was working with the old approach is thrown out along with the parts that were not. Only too late do they discover that the new approach itself has parts that don't work along with the parts that do.

At the root of this problem is a deep misunderstanding of the nature of software development. Researchers have tried to attack this problem with new theories like formalism to prove correctness of programs, or through formal languages that never have been adopted outside the academic world. Industry efforts have spent years standardizing swollen meta-models that defy easy understanding.

Universities and technical institutes teach us a particular way of working. Every project adopts a special method that we must first learn and master before we can begin to work. Every time we change jobs, we have to learn a new approach before we can get on with the real task at hand. This is not effective; we cannot learn from experience as we are forever starting over.

We need to stop forever chasing after fads and easy answers that forever disappoint us. But how? This is a problem I have thought about for at the least 10 years, and now I have a concrete idea on how we can get there.

### What is your solution?

**Ivar:** We need a basic theory concerning what software development actually is. In my opinion, this theory is right in front of our noses. We just need to grab it. Start with all these methods, processes, and practices and find the "truth" of software development. For instance, we could do what we have done in my company and what now has been used by hundreds of companies around the world.

First we need to find that core of things which we always have or which we always do when we build software. For instance, we always write code, we always test it (although sometimes we fail to document how we're testing it), we always think about requirements (documented or undocumented), we always have a backlog (explicit or implicit), and we always have a plan on a paper or in our heads. You might borrow an overused metaphor and say that we must find the DNA for software development.

With my colleagues, I have identified some 20+ such elements by studying about 50 methods, including XP and Scrum. On the surface, there may appear to be large differences in these methods and the ways we work with them. As an example, you can capture requirements with features or with use cases. But there is a common basis for the two methods, which I capture in my kernel elements.

Then we draw on this kernel element to describe widely used and proven methods and practices: architecture, Scrum, components, iterations, etc. Today around 15 such practices have been developed. Since the kernel is agnostic in relation to any specific practice, we can simply find out what is the actual difference between different practices, not just on the surface but in depth. This decreases the element of religion in which every method is embedded. The education will become more logical since it focuses on individual ideas instead of the particular soup of ideas that forms every method, process, or methodology. I believe students will love it.

It would be excellent if our technical institutes or universities would educate students in the basics of software engineering, followed up by training the students in a set of good practices using that base. There is also space for a lot of relevant research here.

Remember Kurt Lewin's words: "there is nothing as practical as a good theory." A good theory makes it easy to learn and develop your knowledge without going overly religious.

*You travel a lot. Have you noticed different approaches to programming or design in various parts of the world?*

**Ivar:** Of course, but what's happening right now in the U.S. is about to happen in the rest of the world, too. Perhaps the U.S. is a little ahead trying new things faster than others, but they also throw out things they have. Many companies in the U.S. are more prepared to give up what they have to run after new things, whereas in Europe people think twice before doing so.

In East Asia they are lagging behind a couple of years in terms of new technologies, but on the other hand, they might not necessarily make the same mistakes.

I have seen one trend very clearly in China. They want to follow India, and so adoption of CMMI became very popular, peaking around five years ago. They have now seen that CMMI handles only the process improvement part of the problem. However, before you improve a process, you need to have one worth a name, so they are now finding that they need good practices to help them develop good software quickly at a low cost.

*How much is the culture involved in the way we design software?*

**Ivar:** I don't know. I typically see that Finnish people have in some ways more a cowboy mentality than the rest of Scandinavia. They are more down to earth and they get results. A special word in Finnish, *sisu*, means "never give up," and they take this concept seriously, so they don't do unnecessary things. Many people would probably say that the Finnish nature is very close to Agile, and that's a positive thing.

The rest of Scandinavia has also been very good at developing software. You can take Ericsson as an example, but I don't think we should exaggerate this topic because I don't have enough evidence to elaborate.

# The Role of the People

*How can we know if someone is the right person to be the architect of a software project?*

**Ivar:** Let me be very clear. I think architecture is very important, but I am cautious about labeling individuals as architects, for many reasons. Many times I have seen companies with a team of architects that they send to other organizations to work on projects. That may be fine if they work inside a particular project, but companies such as big banks usually have a group of enterprise architects that sit and draw representations of the architecture.

Then they throw this over the wall to the developers. The developers just ask themselves: "What is this? It's useless." In many companies, enterprise architects sit in an ivory tower without doing anything useful.

I never believed that we should have architects as a special class of people, because software is developed by teams, not by stove-piped organizations.

Many companies try to organize software development as a number of departments, divisions, or groups. They have one group for requirements, one group for architecture and design, one for coding, one for testing, and maybe others. Then they throw all kinds of projects into this organization, so you have a project manager who works with these different groups. The responsibility for requirements is in the hands of the leader of the requirements group. Testing is in the hands of the leader of the testing group. These are not teams, just groups, so you really don't know where the project is. The project manager is just an administrator, not a manager who can give directions. The result is very slow and expensive development of poor software, because the requirements written by the requirements group are difficult for other people to understand.

Instead we work with teams that include people who are competent to manage requirements, or competent to design software, and so on. The team is lead by a manager or a coach, and the team is self-organized. It's like a soccer team: you have people that are forwards, defenders, and goalkeepers, but they switch around as needed. Sometimes a forward defends or a defender scores a goal. This is the model we need in software.

We need to have a team that fights together, and where people help each other, and where the people who write requirements understand the difficulties of the people who do development. The requirements people can then make sure that the requirements are testable, not written for the sake of filling a document.

We have a new model: the team model, instead of the organization model.

### How do you define the term "social engineering"?

**Ivar:** Social engineering is about making people work together. It's about organizing a team. It's about organizing your time daily, weekly, monthly, etc. It's not about technology; it's about how you make your people motivated and excited about what they are doing, and about how to get results.

We have always had a lot of management books in this space, but it's a new area in the software space. The Agile movement, which is primarily about just that, came about when methodologies like CMMI and RUP stiffed the organizations.

I never believed that people would work according to RUP as people have tried to do, because you have to use RUP more as a knowledge base, a thinking base, and then work according to what makes sense for people. I have always said that. Unfortunately, RUP became understood as a prescriptive methodology like cooking food. None of us who have developed software would even dream that you really do it step by step, following a checklist.

*Why are we so slowly improving programming methods and processes?*

**Ivar:** That is the real question. From my perspective, the industry is very immature. It's little more mature than it was 20 years ago, but we build much more complex systems today. Twenty years ago we started from a programming language and an operating system. Now we have all kinds of frameworks.

The software industry is the most fashion-conscious industry I know of. People want to have a new buzz every two to three years; otherwise they don't see any progress. The way we take in new ideas is not only to throw out bad or old ideas we need to replace, but basically to throw out everything and start all over. We don't move forward by systematically changing what we have and adding new stuff, so we stand still in a way. We don't really feel progress.

The new, popular methodologies today are not very different from what we had 20 or 30 years ago, but they have a new emphasis and new ways of talking about them. We've also seen counterreactions to the big processes that have been quite successful, like CMMI and RUP. The counterreaction means that everything that belongs to these or other similar camps are bad, and now we need something new and fresh—but it's not really new and fresh. These new methodologies are not really new, but just variations of what we already had.

Actually, Agile does embody something new: the heightened emphasis on people and social engineering. Even this is familiar to most people who developed successful software in the past. People are the most important asset when it comes to software development. Having competent and motivated people is the most important prerequisite to get good software quickly and at a low cost. Sometimes we forget about that.

Another problem I think we have is that the people who come from universities are educated in the latest silver bullets, but really don't know how to deal with commercial software they've inherited from past practices. When they come out young and fresh and energetic, we cannot make them start with something that they consider old-fashioned. They would just not take the job, particularly in good times. These young and inexperienced but well-studied people become quite dominant in organizations and the result is that we don't move forward.

*How can we approach the problem of legacy software?*

**Ivar:** Software traditionally has been developed by people who never had any explicit methodology. They couldn't describe what they were doing. They didn't document what they did. It is still very hard to understand the system structure if you come in later, so you don't understand the architecture or the ideas behind the system. Having new people to take over that kind of system is very, very difficult.

If in a business all the people leave at the same time, the business will die. Even if you have money to recruit other people, they would not know what to do. There is nothing special about software. This is the nature of doing business. It helps if you have a system that is understandable—if you have a way to train people in the system—but there's no magic here.

We need software that is understandable, good architecture, and good models. We know that code without a visible architecture is almost impossible to manage.

A major challenge for most big companies is to change legacy systems and the way they are developed and/or extended. There are inherent practices linked to these systems that have evolved over time, and many of those practices are not Agile, or compatible with Agile. Changing development methods for new systems or products is much less of a challenge. The approach to be used should be optimized for legacy systems. My view is expressed in this statement: product development is a change management process, changing from something to something more. New development is just a special case, changing from nothing to something. This view should penetrate everything you do and the practices that you deploy when developing software.

There are basically two approaches to managing legacy systems and improve them.

The first is to just deploy practices that don't really change the product but improve the way you work, such as iterative development, continuous integration, test-driven development, use-case-driven development, user stories, pair programming, and cross-cutting teams. The cost and risks of introducing such practices are marginal, but for big companies still substantial.

The second approach is more fundamental: change the actual product via practices such as architecture (at a simple level), enterprise architecture, product-line architecture, components, etc. You do major reengineering. The costs and the risks are greater, but the return on investment dramatically higher.

### Would using the right method avoid the problem of managing a system without a visible architecture?

**Ivar:** No, not avoid, but reduce it. Documenting your software might not have much effect, because people don't read documentation anyway. Even so, sound documentation focusing on the essentials is useful because it makes the system more approachable. For example, being able to describe your architecture means that you actually have an architecture!

Still, you can't expect that people can just leave and other people come in and take over. You need to have a transition that lets new people learn the structure they will have to work with. No matter how much you teach people, if there is no visible architecture, there is no easy way to transfer knowledge about the system.

## What is the best format to transfer knowledge?

**Ivar:** In general, people that work with software don't read books or manuals. It's only at universities that people really read, if anywhere. Saying that people use books and manuals while they work is just a myth.

I have written a couple of books, and I am very happy that people buy my books, but as for all other books, they don't read them. It is a law of nature that people read neither process books nor language books.

Instead of learning big methodologies or big languages like UML or Java, focus on practices. Practices are more manageable. You can become an expert in a practice without being an expert in a complete methodology. Most of my colleagues that wrote books about methodologies were not really experts on more than minor pieces of the methodology—practices.

Instead of working on a big methodology or a language, focus on working with one practice at a time. No single human individual can know all good, useful practices, but possibly you can compose practices into some way of working. I have been working for the last five years to make practices much simpler, and keep them separate, but in such a way that others can compose larger processes (or ways of working) from them.

## I also read about the use of cards.

**Ivar:** Every methodology starts from some new interesting ideas, borrows some other interesting idea from others, makes a soup of all of it, and calls that soup a methodology, process, approach, or whatever.

It is great to be able to do that and be consistent, complete, and correct. Some people have done so successfully. Some have become recognized gurus.

However, doing this is the simple part of the problem. The real difficulty is to get other people to adopt it. Another problem is to be able to change what you have when new ideas appear on the frontier.

Thus, we have not been successful in rolling out methods by and large.

People in my company (in particular, Brian Kerr and Ian Spence) have come up with some important innovations to do this. One of these innovations is to use cards to describe the essentials about something you do or something you produce when developing software.

Using cards is an agile way to describe practices. They hold the essentials; you can figure out the rest by yourself.

# UML

*How do you define UML?*

**Ivar:** UML is a blueprint language for software applied to specifying, architecting, designing, testing, and using it.

*How does it interact with different software engineering methods?*

**Ivar:** All the different software engineering methodologies that OMG identified in the early 1990s (26 methodologies, as I recall it) had their own notation, but most of them have now adopted UML.

*Did your group of three designers provide design advantages, or did it just oblige you all to compromise?*

**Ivar:** We had our passionate discussions, but these discussions helped us to design a better language than anyone of us would have done individually. We wouldn't have been able to do what we did without the contributions from people such as David Harel, Jim Odell, Cris Kobryn, Martin Griss, Gunnar Overgaard, Steve Cook, Bran Selic, and Guus Ramacker.

*What would you change in the future? What might change in UML?*

**Ivar:** The most important are:

- The language is too complex. We need to change that. Eighty percent of all applications can be designed with less than 20% of UML. In my company we have defined a pure subset of UML to become the Essential Unified Modeling Language. We also use a very different way of describing UML that is much more attractive to ordinary users. Traditional UML is designed for methodologists or tool vendors.

- I would love to restructure UML as a set of domain-specific languages (DSLs). I would like to do that similar to the way we redesigned the Unified Process in my company. A DSL is an aspect of a modeling language (of which UML is an example). You create your modeling language as a composition of many such DSLs (aspects) in a way similar to how you compose a software system from many cross-cutting concerns. While I claim that the language was not designed for users but for methodologists and for tool vendors, I claim it was not even good for the latter groups. The semantics of UML are poorly defined. UML—in particular, UML 2.0—has included so many constructs from so many different methodological camps that it became impossible to define its semantics clearly. Like many other languages, UML became, as John Backus said about Ada, "fat and flabby."

  The focus was on concrete syntax (icons) and to some extent on static semantics, but we left the operational semantics undefined. I expected that we would get this critique since standard language design practice at that time was to use techniques like denotational semantics. We didn't. We just wrote page after page that we knew were very hard to understand. We could have used the same practices used to define SDL (the telecom modeling standard was defined using VDM already back in 1984).

SDL became a modeling language with a well-defined semantics. Even if major portions of SDL were adopted in UML, we didn't adopt the language design practices that were used more than 15 years earlier. Sad!

Having said that, even if UML is not formally defined, it was far better designed than most other popular OO modeling languages. Basically all competing languages were abandoned when UML became available. If used right, UML can really help developers to become successful. Friends of UML shouldn't fear; there is a great future, but UML should be given a better structure and it needs a formal definition.

### How do you figure out which elements can be removed from UML? What process would you use to simplify the language?

**Ivar:** I would start with the basics of the language. I wouldn't start from the whole language and remove individual pieces. I know which language constructs are really useful and which are not. There are language constructs I wouldn't even bother to look at. I don't want to go into particulars, but we have already identified this 20%, at least to some rough level.

When we teach UML, we teach Essential UML, which is based on our experience. We use the same ideas for describing language elements as we use to describe process or practice elements; we use cards, and every card represents a language construct such as a component, an interface, and so on. We are talking about pedagogy. We are not talking about anything new, or any new language construct. We have just learned that people really don't read and don't like thick language specifications, so we need to find a more approachable way of learning. You learn object by object, interfaces, classes, components, etc.

### How would you "restructure UML as a set of domain-specific languages"?

**Ivar:** We have a basic universally applicable core in UML. I would identify aspects of that core, and describe UML by adding aspect after aspect. These aspects of UML are what we call practices when it comes to processes, and these practice-like things of UML would be domain-specific languages.

A domain-specific language would, as the name suggests, support a particular domain, such as a vertical industry sector (enterprise systems, telecom systems, healthcare systems, etc.) or a discipline (requirements, design, real-time, test, etc.). A rather small aspect of UML would constitute one domain-specific language. In that way you would compose UML from different domain-specific languages. These domain-specific languages need to have a common core and a common semantic, otherwise we'll have a very difficult problem in translating between things in different domains.

### Are there practices used to design SDL that you could use to improve UML?

**Ivar:** Fifteen to twenty years earlier when we designed SDL, we used the Vienna Development Method (VDM), developed by people at IBM in the late 60s or 70s. It is a language that can mathematically describe notions such as a language, an operating system, or any other system. It relies on discrete mathematics: set theory, maps, and so on. In that way you can actually define mathematically the meaning of every language construct.

We first identified an abstract syntax, and we described the abstract syntax using discrete mathematics. Then we used that to define domains of elements. We defined static semantics by describing what kind of conditions would be true and false for elements in these domains. Next, we described the operational semantics by describing the meaning of a particular statement. That was a mathematical way to describe a language. Then finally we mapped the graphical notation to the abstract syntax.

I was involved quite heavily in SDL, but I couldn't convince my UML colleagues to do anything in that direction for UML. They felt it was just academic. With my experience from working on SDL, I disagreed because as soon as you want to build tools, you need to know the exact semantics. Otherwise people have to guess.

When Steve Cook from IBM and Bran Selic from Objectime (later acquired by Rational) joined the team, they said, "This is unprofessional. We are not going to join without defining the language in a more formal way," so I suggested a variant in order to compromise. I said, "Let's define the abstract syntax and the static semantics mathematically, but let's describe the operational semantics using just English." UML 2.0 is better than UML 1.0, but it's not enough if you really want to understand every detail.

### What do you think of using UML to generate implementation code?

**Ivar:** There is no fundamental need for two kinds of languages. Why have a language just to express your design, given that your design is an abstraction of the implementation? And then why have another language to describe the implementation? This is the situation today, and it creates overlap.

There are several reasons why we have these two languages. Maybe the most important is because we have not been able to get computer scientists in general to see the value of a modeling language; they feel that a programming language is enough. The reality is that code is a language designed for machines (compilers, etc.), and doesn't use all the abilities of the human brain.

At some point I think we will be able to clearly demonstrate the value of visual modeling and persuade computer scientists to perform research in this area. A lot of research is done on UML, so there is no fundamental reason why we should have two kinds of languages—but we are not there yet.

### Is it just a matter of persuading people to focus there?

**Ivar:** It's a matter of getting university people to understand that not everything is well expressed by code. Many of them already understand that, but not enough. We need to show more successes.

UML is fundamentally better than anything we had before. SDL has been very useful in the telecom industry, but UML is a more universal language (includes important language constructs not available in SDL). UML was created in the late 90s, so because there is nothing fundamentally better, you can expect that it will take another 20–30 years before UML will be replaced. However, until then, we can improve the way we teach UML.

I believe the value of UML will be proved as time goes by. We need something like UML to help people scale software development. Maybe more people with real experience in software development will go into research. Maybe they will demonstrate that how we teach new students now is not scalable.

*Is there a size for a software project under which using UML might add more complexity and work without adding benefits?*

**Ivar:** If, to the cost of the project, you add training and education in UML, and training and education in tools to use and support UML, it might be too expensive to motivate the adoption of UML. But if people starting a new project are forced to understand UML and how to use at least one tool that supports UML, you have a different situation.

If you want to teach people basic software engineering during normal working hours, it might be hard to motivate them, especially in an existing small project. For large projects the motivation is very different, because the risks involved in not doing proper modeling are so high.

*Suppose that I am wary of using of UML. What could you say to persuade me that it would help my team?*

**Ivar:** The answer to this question depends on who you are.

If you know nothing about software, it is rather easy to say that you need a drawing language because writing code is not a good way for humans to work. Code is good for machines to interpret but not for humans to work with.

If you are an experienced programmer, I would ask how you describe your system, the components, and how they interact. How do you describe a particular scenario from a user perspective? Will it be implemented through interactions between your components or your objects? No programming language can do that in a reasonable way, and so that's an example of where you can use UML. There are plenty of similar examples.

Some people I would never be able to convince because they have worked with code for many, many years. But if you ask them how they would feel if they had to work with a completely unfamiliar language like Prolog, or a new class of languages such as declarative languages, or functional programming languages like Scheme or Lisp, they would probably feel that they would get a lot of help by using graphical language as well.

I never had a real problem convincing people to use UML once they have understood the demands of systems they are building.

# Knowledge

*How much knowledge of software engineering is linked to a particular programming language?*

**Ivar:** Very little. Universities teach programming languages, so people believe that the language is the central point. The real problem is understanding software in general.

How do you capture requirements? How do you know if you are building the right system? How do you test whether you have built the system right? How do you do configuration management and version control? How do you do the 30 or 40 practices that you don't learn at school?

People learn the easy things at school. That's why they're taught at school. Programming languages are relatively easy to teach and learn. When I was at MIT, I took the class 6001, where we used Scheme, a variant of Lisp, to describe several phenomena in the computer science world. People took that class directly from high school—they wrote code during the class—and it was one of the most fantastic classes I have taken. You used a language to describe phenomena such as compilation, execution, interpretation, and many of the interesting phenomena in the computer science world. You also learned the basic ideas of programming, so programming actually became simple.

Now we have frameworks, but learning a framework is much harder. Still these things are relatively easy; they are just one of the several things you need to know to be a good software developer. We have to raise our competence level in software engineering.

### We should find a way to deliver the knowledge when we need it instead of before.

**Ivar:** Yes, and you should not throw away what you have. Start from where you are. Everyone that develops software today has some practices that are not that good, but are still useful. We should not try to change everything at once, but improve what needs the most improvement.

It might be that they know how to do programming or configuration management, but maybe they really don't know how to do good requirements and testing. There are practices for that. They can keep the things they are doing today and change what they need to change without throwing out everything they have just to incorporate something new. This is a natural evolution of process.

### I read that you see a future where intelligent agents will partner with us for pair programming. How?

**Ivar:** Developing software is not rocket science. Look at the 5–10 million people who call themselves software developers. Very few of them really do anything creative or fundamentally new. Unfortunately the outside world thinks that programmers are creative and brilliant people, and that's far from reality.

There is scientific evidence that 80% of what a software developer does in a day—different steps and small microsteps—it's not brain work. They do what they have done 50, 100, 1,000 times before. They just apply a pattern to new situations.

Of course there is creative work, but most people don't do that. Twenty percent is brain work. It is still not rocket science; they might have to think in a way they might not necessarily have thought in before.

Eighty percent of work is rule-based. Given a particular context, you can apply pattern after pattern to develop software. These patterns are not necessarily defined, so you may actually apply the wrong patterns and thus develop bad software. People don't always apply the same patterns, so some of their software is good and some software is bad.

There is a way to describe and apply these rules through tools. This is the idea behind intelligent agents. Intelligent agents understand the context and the activity you need to apply, and they apply that activity. They might do a lot of things by themselves because they know these are trivial rules, or they might ask advice from the developer working with the agent.

The company I founded, Ivar Jacobson International, developed intelligent agents to support software development and achieved dramatic results. Tata Consulting Services cut their costs by 20% with a rather small set of rules. They increased quality and shortened training time for programmers and developers. They could quickly get their new employees up to speed to do something useful.

In my mind there is no doubt that this technology works. The problem is that we still have so many diverse platforms and many different kinds of tools people want to use. If you really want to develop this kind of software, you have to adapt it to a lot of tools and many different kinds of platforms, so developing these agents is hard to do for a small company. It becomes feasible when you reach the scale of a big company such as TCS.

Potentially, an 80% cut in the costs is achievable using a technique like intelligent agents. For example, we have intelligent agents to specify use cases, to design use cases, to test use cases, and so on. That is just the beginning. I have no doubt: the technology is there, the problem is there, the money is there.

*Is the final goal that everyone will be able to interact with the computer and ask it what to do, or we will always have a strong difference between programmers and users?*

**Ivar:** I think that more and more work will be done by the user community instead of the programmers. One method to do that is by using rule-based programming. With rule-based programming, you don't really have to understand execution; you just have to write your rules. A rule engine will interpret them. This is something the AI community has taught for 40 years, so it is not fundamentally new. Object technology has helped us understand more how to build modelers. Twenty to thirty years ago, the rule-based systems were monolithic and very hard to change. Now using agents you have a kind of object-oriented expert system, and it's much easier to change.

*How do you recognize simplicity?*

**Ivar:** Simplicity is the core idea behind being smart, doing something smart, or general smartness. Einstein said something like "things should be as simple as possible, but no simpler." I agree fully. That is what I call smart.

If you are smart, you make something as simple as possible, but no simpler. Everything you do should be done in a smart way. When you do your architecture, you should model as little as possible, but as much as you need. If you don't model, you will spend a lot of energy trying to describe what you are doing, and you won't have a necessary overview.

Doing requirements up front, for instance, and trying to identify all the requirements before you start building anything is not smart. To identify the key use cases, or the key features and to start implementing them so you get some feedback, is smart. I have identified about 10–15 such smart cases.

We need to become smart when we work and develop software. Smart is an extension of agile. Agile is primarily social engineering, although people now have added more things into it. You don't need to be smart to be agile, but to be smart you need to be agile. My new talk is about how to become smart.

## Be Ready for Change

*You have a B.S. in physics from MIT, an M.S. in astronomy from Caltech, and a Ph.D. in computer science from MIT. How does your university background affect the way you think about software design?*

**James Rumbaugh:** I think my varied background adds insights and synergy beyond a straight computer science curriculum. In physics the concept of symmetry is fundamental, really at the heart of modern physics. I tried to apply this concept to modeling. For example, associations provide a more symmetric viewpoint on a situation than the more traditional approach of pointers incorporated by most programming languages. In my computer science studies at MIT, I worked in the Computing Structures Group of Professor Jack Dennis, one of the first groups to investigate fundamental models of computing. That ferment of ideas with intellectual rigor was a stimulating environment that informs my thinking even now.

*Which topics should students study more?*

**James:** I'm not intimately familiar with current academic programs, but it is my impression that many colleges have adopted a narrow focus for computing science, with an emphasis on specific programming languages and systems rather than understanding the important principles underlying computation. For example, I rarely have met a programmer who understands the principles of computational complexity and puts them into practice. Instead they fuss with all kinds of pointless suboptimizations that are "penny wise and pound foolish."

I think the most important skill in computing (as in physics and other creative fields) is the ability for abstraction. Unfortunately my experience has shown me that less than 50% of programmers can abstract properly. A colleague suggested it was really less than 10%. He may be right. Unfortunately, many people in the software field may not have the basic skills needed to do the job right.

*What is the best format to share knowledge in the software field? I am not sure people really read thousand-page manuals.*

**James:** If you need to have a thousand pages at your fingertips, there is something wrong with the system you are working with. It isn't partitioned well. Unfortunately many people in this field worship complexity. IBM made a religion out of complexity. Of course, that helps in selling consultants.

Engineers learn a variety of skills during their training, first in university classes and then in on-the-job training working on real-world projects. Most important is to learn general principles. In engineering that includes the laws of physics and engineering principles of a particular discipline. In computing that would mean computer science principles such as algorithms, data structures, and complexity theory, as well as the principles of software engineering. In any field, it is important to develop a feel for how things are done. If software applications follow expected norms and are consistently designed, the skillful developer can often intuit the structure and behavior of a new system without searching piles of manuals.

It's also important to provide guidance on how a system works. It's not enough to list the constituent parts and assume someone can figure out how it is all supposed to work when put together. If you are trying to learn a complicated application such as Photoshop, a tutorial that shows how to put together basic commands to accomplish common useful tasks is the best way to get started. You can always use the comprehensive command list to check details, but it's a bad way to learn a system. But how many system developers think they have done their jobs when they simply provide a comprehensive list of commands or procedures that constitute the system? That doesn't help people understand how a system works. So the biggest lack in conveying system knowledge is a focus on overly static decomposition information rather than usage patterns. The Pattern Movement had the right idea in focusing on usage, although they sometimes took too narrow a view of patterns.

*How do you identify the right person to be the architect of a software project?*

**James:** It's a tricky balance. Good architects have to be able to balance theory and practice; they need to balance elegance and efficiency; they need to balance experience and vision. The job of the architect is to get the overall structure of the system correct, to make the decisions that have global impact. That includes the decomposition into modules, the major data structures, the communications mechanisms, and the goals to be optimized. An architect who is obsessed with detailed coding is likely to get the big picture wrong.

An architect must be able to communicate effectively so that the developers and programmers are all working together. The last thing you need is an architect who is a genius but can't explain things clearly to ordinary people. Political skills are a definite plus; part of the job of the architect is to get rival factions working together smoothly.

An architect needs experience having worked on large systems. You can't learn it all from university classes and books; you need hands-on experience before getting the big job for the first time.

*How can we transmit experience in the software field?*

**James:** I used to say that the problem with software compared to other creative fields is that there is no program museum. If you are a painter, you study paintings by famous artists through the ages, in books and by viewing the original pictures in museums. If you are an architect, you can visit many different kinds of buildings. In programming, programmers were on their own.

The Pattern Movement provided catalogs of useful techniques that can be adapted to many different situations. That's a good way to capture best practices from the top programmers so that everybody else can benefit.

However, people also need large examples of how everything goes together in a complete application. More recently, the open source movement has provided examples of large programs that anybody can examine. But not everything in a system is equally good, and novice developers need someone to walk them through. What we need are annotated case studies so that software developers can understand what is good and what is bad in those systems, like a commentary on chess games or a business school case study of a company. These should illustrate examples of good practice and also point out things that may not be done so well. As in learning any skill, it is important to see examples of bad practices to avoid.

*How much is the knowledge of software engineering linked to a particular programming language?*

**James:** Unfortunately far too much effort goes into thinking about specific programming languages. Most of the effort to design a program can be done in a way that is independent of the programming language. Of course, you can't ignore the programming language, and at the strategic level you have to be aware of the fundamental properties of the language, such as how it treats storage, concurrency, etc. But most of the design involves issues such as data structures, computational complexity, and decomposition into separate threads of control that transcend a particular programming language.

It's like natural languages. You can outline a news article without much effect from the language. If you're writing poetry, then the language matters a great deal from the beginning. If you are writing programs like poetry, then you are far too self-indulgent. But when you sit down to write the actual words or the code, you don't translate them from your outline, you use your knowledge of the language to choose a good expression.

*Will we always see a difference between programmers and so-called users, or will everyone be able to tell a computer what to do?*

**James:** I have noticed that some people can express themselves clearly in natural language and some can't, so even if you could speak to the computer in your native language, some people would have a hard time being understood because they just don't think clearly. So there will always be a difference between people who can think and express themselves clearly and those who can't.

Also some ways of expressing ideas are a lot more concise when the topic is restricted. Music notation is a wonderfully compact way to capture music, and chess notation is excellent for chess games. Drawing blueprints is a lot better way to ensure that you get the building you want than trying to talk to carpenters entirely in natural language. So you need people who can think clearly and precisely and express themselves using specialized languages.

I'm not holding my breath that we are going to be able to speak to computers in natural language any time in the foreseeable future. Remember that COBOL was supposed to be a way to communicate to computers using English! So there has been a lot of over-optimism about natural-language communication for a long time.

*What do the lessons about the invention, further development, and adoption of your language say to people developing computer systems today and in the foreseeable future?*

**James:** First, you need some luck to be successful. I was in the right place at the right time. We developed OMT as one of the first OO methods and had the good fortune to write a book that explained things in a simple enough way. Later methods may have been equally good, but they missed the window. I also had the luck to be working at GE Research during a period when GE had no serious business in software. I don't know why they let us keep working on it so long, but we were able to work on it without having to tout a bunch of company products, which gave us credibility compared to most other methods.

My experience at Rational Software was more mixed. Bringing together the inventors of three leading OO methods gave us the ability to forge UML and get it widely accepted. It's not that UML was that much better than many of the existing methods (although it did manage to round off some of the rough edges that individual methods had), but it got most people working on the same page, rather than arguing about the merits of different symbol shapes and various other arcane differences. Unfortunately Rational wasn't able to follow up the methodology success by building effective, easy-to-use tools quickly enough. I don't believe the upper management or most of the developers really believed in modeling—they still believed in Heroic Programming—and it showed in the tools. Why should you buy a tool from people who won't use it themselves? When that attitude changed, it was too late. Another lesson is, you have to believe in what you are doing or it won't work.

The OMG (Object Management Group) is a case study in how political meddling can damage any good idea. The first version of UML was simple enough, because people didn't have time to add a lot of clutter. Its main fault was an inconsistent viewpoint—some things were pretty high-level and others were closely aligned to particular programming languages. That's what the second version should have cleared up. Unfortunately, a lot of people who were jealous of our initial success got involved in the second version.

They felt they could have done just as well as we did. (As things turned out, they couldn't.) The OMG process allowed all kinds of special interests to stuff things into UML 2.0, and since the process is mainly based on consensus, it is almost impossible to kill bad ideas. So UML 2.0 became a bloated monstrosity, with far too much dubious content, and still no consistent viewpoint and no way to define one. It's kind of like a bad appropriations bill with all kinds of goodies stuffed in. It shows the limitations of trying to do creative activity by committee.

The whole process illustrates Brooks's Second System Effect. If you've never read Fred Brooks's *Mythical Man-Month* [Addison-Wesley Professional], then get it today and read it. It's absolutely the best book ever written on software engineering. The sad thing is that most of the problems he cites in this 30-year-old book are still happening today. Managers keep trying to add manpower to late projects which makes them even later, just like Brooks said.

Maybe this is a good way to state the main problem facing the computing field: most of its practitioners have no understanding of computing history and so, as Toynbee said about world history, they are condemned to repeat the same mistakes. Unlike scientists and engineers who build upon past discoveries, too many computing practitioners treat each system or language as a new thing, unaware that similar things have been done before. At the first OOPSLA conference in 1986, the highlight was a presentation of Ivan Sutherland's Sketchpad system invented in 1963. It incorporated some of the first OO ideas long before OO was invented, and did them better than most OO systems do now. It looked fresh in 1986 and still does over 20 years later. So why do we still have many graphical tools that are inferior to Sketchpad today?

Why do we still have buffer overflow errors—a prolific source of loopholes for malware—in operating systems today? Why do we still use languages like C and C++ that don't understand the concept of bounded arrays and so facilitate buffer overflow errors? Sure, C++ can define bounded arrays, but programmers still use naked pointers far too much. It's all ignorance, laziness, or arrogance on the part of developers. Computing is difficult, and it is impossible to avoid logical mistakes in complicated systems, but there is no excuse for still making this kind of rookie mistake after all these years.

So what are the big questions to ask about development of a new system? First of all, understand what it is for and who it will serve. Don't get too ambitious at first—better to get something useful out the door quickly and then add onto it, rather than trying to think out everything you might ever need. That's a good principle from Agile Development. You can't be all things to all people, so be prepared to make some hard choices, but also understand that if a system is successful, it will evolve in ways that you can't predict, so expect and plan for unexpected change.

# Using UML

*What do you think of using UML to generate implementation code?*

**James:** I think it's a terrible idea. I know that I disagree with many other UML experts, but there is no magic about UML. If you can generate code from a model, then it is a programming language. And UML is not a well-designed programming language.

The most important reason is that it lacks a well-defined point of view, partly by intent and partly because of the tyranny of the OMG standardization process that tries to provide everything to everybody. It doesn't have a well-defined underlying set of assumptions about memory, storage, concurrency, or almost anything else. How can you program in such a language?

The fact is that UML and other modeling languages are not meant to be executable. The point of models is that they are imprecise and ambiguous. This drove many theoreticians crazy so they tried to make UML "precise," but models are imprecise for a reason: we leave out things that have a small effect so we can concentrate on the things that have big or global effects. That's how it works in physics models: you model the big effects (such as the gravitation from the sun) and then you treat the smaller effects as perturbations to the basic model (such as the effects of the planets on each other). If you tried to solve the entire set of equations directly in full detail, you couldn't do anything.

I think a lot of the recent work on UML has been misguided. It never was meant to be a programming language. Use it to get the strategy right and write the final program in a suitable programming language.

Unfortunately I don't know any really good programming languages. They all have a lot of flaws that encourage mistakes. The whole C family (C, C++, Java, etc.) is sorely lacking (the syntax is almost unparseable), but we are stuck with them whether we like it or not. A lot of new faddish languages demonstrate the ignorance of any serious language theory on the part of their developers. On the other hand, many of the more academic languages are too elegant for their own good and disdain important features, such as the need for multiple teams to work separately on the same system.

*What does a language need to be usable by multiple teams of developers?*

**James:** Let me go back to Algol-60, an early programming language that was one of the first that I used (probably before many of the readers of this interview were born). It introduced many important concepts, such as BNF syntax notation, recursive subroutines, and structured control constructs. In many ways, it was a much cleaner language than FORTRAN. But it had four major flaws that made it unusable in practice: it had no built-in input/output constructs; it did not support double precision and matrix arithmetic; it did not support separate compilation of subroutines; and there was no standard way to interface with machine language and FORTRAN subroutines. These are all fairly minor issues theoretically, but major software engineering barriers.

Lots of academic languages make the same mistake: they solve the interesting mathematical issues, but overlook the pragmatic issues of how a language will be used in context because the pragmatic issues aren't theoretically interesting. It's these small things that determine the usability of a language.

First of all, developers need to be able to work on parts of a system in isolation without either the declarations or the code for the rest of the system. Then they need a way to put the parts together and make sure that they work as a system; I think this requires some notion of declared typing. You need to accommodate various kinds of communications mechanisms, as systems are now highly concurrent. Most languages have no good way to describe or declare dynamic behavior. I think you need debugging tools that are better integrated with the language but can be turned on or off at runtime. There is too much of a separation between coding and testing right now.

### Is UML just a tool to coordinate work in a large team of developers?

**James:** It is first and foremost a tool for guiding and organizing the thinking of individual developers. You need to work at different levels of abstraction; code is a particular level, but not the most useful level for understanding how systems work. You need to work at a higher level, which means getting away from all the details of the code to the things that are important at the higher level. That's why it's a mistake to make UML executable; that would destroy the whole point of abstraction.

### Speaking of architects, you stress the importance of good communications. Does UML help to solve that problem?

**James:** It provides a common set of concepts and notation. That helps communication. You can't communicate if you don't share the same vocabulary, or rather, you think you are communicating and instead different people mean different things, which is even worse than no communication.

### Can an architect communicate better using UML?

**James:** Well, that's the whole point, isn't it?

When I first started pushing object orientation within GE, I paid a visit to GE Aircraft Engines. We had a great deal of trouble convincing the programmers that OO was a good idea—they were stuck on existing concepts (such as FORTRAN programming) and didn't understand what we were talking about. Several of the aircraft engineers, however, understood exactly what we were talking about and got excited about the idea of OO. In their work, they were used to making models and abstracting high-level concepts, such as "engine performance curve" or "stall speed versus angle of attack." They were used to creating mental objects to represent physical concepts. The programmers could not see the forest for the trees—they were stuck in the code and did not realize that the purpose of code is to represent higher-level concepts. Many of them still don't realize that.

*Robin Milner, the creator of ML, illustrated the idea of a hierarchy of models linking together everything from high-level design languages such as UML to low-level assembly code, to the physics model behind the hardware, to additional models as part of the environment where the hardware was used. He gave the example of an airplane, where you have the high-level code that goes down to the hardware, the hardware with its own models, and then the whole airplane "hardware" is designed according to the aerodynamics and physics and weather models! When a pilot pushes a button, all these models are involved.*

*Should we reduce the number of levels (toward one universal model/language), or increase the abstraction (and the number of levels)?*

**James:** Excellent point. One of the major concepts from physics (or rather, science in general) is the idea of multiple levels of emergent views. Each view is built on top of the one below it but, once built, is self-consistent and self-meaningful. So we have levels such as quantum physics, chemistry, microbiology, biological organisms, populations, ecosystems, environments. Another hierarchical tower is computation: physics of materials, semiconductors, circuits, digital systems, computers, firmware, operating systems, application frameworks, applications, networks. No one level is the "right" or "true" or "fundamental" level. Each is meaningful in its own terms and can be defined in terms of the next lower level. But that doesn't mean it can be understood at the lower level. The meaning of each level is unique and can only be understood at that level. That's an emergent system: the meaning of each level emerges from a simple lower level but must be understood in its own terms. So to understand any complex system (the universe being the ultimate example, of course), we need to work on multiple levels simultaneously, no one of which can claim to be primary.

The tower of emergent levels is something that modeling languages have not captured well. We need a way to model a system on multiple levels simultaneously. I'm not talking about the OMG 4-level metamodel. It came about because some people made the same mistake as Bertrand Russell in assuming that you can't model something in terms of itself. You can, of course; see Douglas Hofstadter's writings, such as *I Am a Strange Loop* [Basic Books]. There is also the failure of code hackers who disdain modeling. They think that the code is the only thing that matters. That's like saying circuits are the only thing that matters, or semiconductor physics is the only thing that matters. All the levels matter, and you need to work at the right level for a particular purpose. I would submit that the code level is a poor level to understand how a large, complex system performs useful activities for humans.

A single universal language won't work. What we need is a framework that allows us to work at multiple levels of abstraction. That's what UML 2.0 should have done, and it didn't. It's not that the added details are wrong, but they make things more complicated; the cost/benefit analysis is bad. The major thing that is lacking is a clean way to build layers of emergent models, keeping the various levels separate.

For example, UML contains fairly low-level concepts more suitable for programming languages, such as permissions or pointers, as well as high-level concepts, but there is no good way to separate the low-level concepts from the high-level concepts. Profiles were an attempt, but they don't really do the trick. A lot of the fights during the construction of UML as well as its schizophrenia were caused by this tension between programming-language concepts and high-level logical concepts.

The other major issue is a difference in tone between different parts developed by different people. For example, the message sequence chart contribution to UML was very helpful, but it has a very different style from the activity diagram stuff.

### What process would you use to simplify the language?

**James:** I doubt it can be simplified through a standards process, such as the OMG process that produced UML 2.0. There are too many competing interests all trying to stuff their own ideas into the pie. The problem is that standardization processes place too little emphasis on consistency, simplicity, and uniform style; instead they overemphasize excessive content. In fact, I'm not a big believer in standardization bodies; they tend to produce overstuffed products lacking in elegance and usability. I was reluctant to get involved in them in the first place; my fears about their negative effects have been realized.

The best approach would be for one or more people to make up their own cut-down versions of UML and let the public decide through usage. The result would not necessarily be called "UML," because that term may have particular legal and emotional baggage. It is important that any language developers clearly state the purpose of their versions, rather than trying to be all things to all people.

### How do you recognize simplicity?

**James:** It requires a willingness to do too little rather than doing too much. Remember, a modeling language is not a programming language; if some capability is missing from the language, the modeler can always make up something to bridge the gap. If you have to carry around a large scorecard to remember all the features in the language, it isn't simple. If you constantly are faced with four or five alternate ways to model a straightforward situation, it isn't simple.

### Suppose that I am skeptical about UML. How would you persuade me that it can help me?

**James:** I'm skeptical about a lot of it myself. I think it has gotten terribly bloated by too many cooks in the OMG kitchen. Also people have tried to promote it as the answer to all things for all people. The whole computing field has a tendency to hype any new development beyond reason. There is also a tendency to look for a single solution for all problems. Life and computing are too complicated for simple solutions.

UML is a very useful tool for data structure design, moderately useful for decomposition of systems into layered modules, not so useful for dynamic things that it doesn't handle so well. It's helpful, but it doesn't solve all of your problems. You need many other skills and tools as well.

*Is there a size for a software project under which using UML might add more complexity and work without adding benefits?*

**James:** No, but that doesn't mean that you would use it the same way on very small and very large projects. On a small project, you would have a lot less "ceremony" in the use of tools, models, software processes, etc. On a small project, class diagrams of the classes and data structures would still be useful, but maybe not so much round-trip design. So UML provides a way to sketch out the initial design, but eventually you end up in a programming language and stay there.

On a large project, half or more of the development process is communication rather than just capturing the design. In that case, it is essential to have tools and processes for decomposing the system, controlling access to models and code, and keeping track of progress; otherwise, people will step on each others' toes all the time. I know that a lot of programmers whine about having to subject themselves to this kind of discipline. In sports, building construction, newspaper writing, rocketship design, or almost any other kind of large cooperative venture, these whiners would be kicked off the team with little regret. It's time we adopt that kind of attitude in software if we want to have it taken seriously.

## Layers and Languages

*In one of your first answers, you said that you think the pattern movement did some great things, but they had too narrow a view of patterns. Can you expand on that?*

**James:** At a workshop I once attended that included some of the Hillside Group, it came out that they had this very narrow, almost quasi-religious view of what patterns were, and they really didn't want to expand it. They were very protective of their official view of patterns and this sort of worship of the architect Alexander. They viewed patterns as this very specific thing, and I think patterns can be applied at many different levels.

Not everyone follows this specific view of small- to medium-range patterns that appear in things like the Gang of Four's* *Design Patterns* book and Hillside Group stuff. Actually, even within the pattern movement there were some divisions, but I think the idea caught on, and that was the main thing.

What the pattern people are saying is the same thing that people have said in many other disciplines, that we should gather up experience from highly skilled people and write it up in catalogs for more ordinary people to follow. This has happened in things like engineering and painting and building architecture, in almost any creative field. The computing field was a bit slow to adopt this concept of learning from the past and it still is. That was one of my complaints. The computing field has a lot of people that think very well of themselves and seem to forget that there is any past to build upon. A lot of people keep reinventing things that have already been discovered.

---

* This term refers to Erich Gamma, Richard Helm, Ralph Johnson, and John Vlissides, authors of the book *Design Patterns: Elements of Reusable Object-Oriented Software* (Addison-Wesley Professional).

I think the pattern view goes to counter that problem by saying, "Look, there are things that we can capture and understand and make available to the broader mass of people in the field who may not be able to create these things, but if they're described properly they can use them."

That's true with any field. The number of people that make great breakthroughs is very small in any field. After the initial breakthrough, other people take the idea and expand it. It's been said once the idea is out there, the inventor loses control over it. You can't let an inner group control what an idea means. New people will find additional meanings that the originators did not intend.

*I want to draw a parallel to some of the things you've already said about your background in physics, where there are lots of layers. What's applicable and appropriate in one layer is not necessarily appropriate at the other layer, but you also can't deny the reality of the other layers.*

**James:** That's the whole concept of emergent systems. That's what science is all about and language is all about. That's one of the concepts from the concept of complexity theory. You get the sense of emergence, and there's no one fundamental layer. Certainly people have understood that in computing for a long time. You have multiple layers, and no one of them is the true layer.

*When you say the pattern movement has left itself very narrow on purpose, do you think it's stuck at one layer when it should address the whole stack?*

**James:** Let me be fair to the pattern movement; there are people that worked at different layers. For example, there are several books on architectural patterns. Maybe the original Hillside Group had a particular view of what constituted a pattern and tied it into this whole concept of Alexander's pattern language. I think you need to apply the word in a broader way.

*One pervasive criticism about the* Design Patterns *book is that a lot of these patterns aren't really effective in languages other than C++ or Java.*

**James:** One of the points of patterns is that they have to be specific to what you're working with. You can't take everything and soften it out to a very general approach. If you're writing programming-language patterns, many of them are specific to a particular programming language, and some may be general and work across a wide range of programming languages. That works in engineering, too: some things work for steel and not for wood and vice versa, and some things go across.

Maybe that was my complaint about modeling. The thing that UML didn't do well was differentiate among various uses. There are uses of modeling that apply to specific programming languages, and there are uses of modeling that apply to more logical things. UML contained both, and it jumbled them all together in one bag. I'll take part of the responsibility for that. In the first version we mixed a lot of different things together. That happens in first versions—you don't have the experience to know how to divide things up.

I had hoped in the second version we'd clean it up, so it would allow you to say, "These features here apply to C or C++," because there are features in there that smack of C and C++ and similar languages. It's OK to have them in there, but they're not as general as certain other features that apply across a wide range of languages, and it would be good to know which is which

There are modeling features that apply at high levels and at low levels. The profiling mechanism was intended to allow features to be defined for a particular viewpoint, but unfortunately the profiling mechanism is kind of clunky. It doesn't allow you to do layering properly. It says "Here's a domain," but that's in a sense a one-level thing. There's no way to do organize them cleanly into modeling levels.

*Suppose that you were able to create UML 3.0 and break backward compatibility. How do you do that without annoying absolutely everybody?*

**James:** By your premises you just guaranteed you're going to annoy everybody. Of course, this is the trouble that Microsoft and Apple are always faced with. Do you maintain compatibility like Microsoft did over a number of generations or do you break it occasionally as Apple did? There are advantages and disadvantages to both.

You can't maintain compatibility forever. It just isn't possible. In any field, you eventually have to say "I'm sorry, we don't do it that way anymore," and "Sorry, you've got to buy something new." Look at analog television sets. After June 2009 in the U.S., they're not going to work off antennas anymore. A lot of people aren't going to find that out until the change occurs. Most of the people reading these kind of articles are aware of that kind of thing, but there's no easy or painless way to break compatibility. It's just like the issue of heritage systems.

People keep wanting some magic solution to the heritage problem and the fact is there is no easy solution. It's a big, messy problem. You have to roll up your sleeves and dig in. It's not like it's a specific problem. You're trying to do two incompatible things and it's always going to take pain and work and making some decisions about when you make people unhappy.

*Do you prefer doing that in big steps, once in a very infrequent while, or a very little bit of unhappiness frequently?*

**James:** On any new system, you find that you made mistakes. You can make local changes for a while, but eventually you find that some of your basic assumptions and architecture decisions don't hold up any more, and you've got to make some major changes and completely rearrange the thing, because otherwise it can't keep growing. I call that "taking an earthquake." You can do that once per system. Twice is kind of pushing it, because you have too many built-in commitments. Eventually you end up ossifying in a way that you can't make major changes anymore. I think that happens in many systems—in computer systems, in other various systems we see in the world around us, where things just get locked up. Eventually somebody comes through with an Alexandrian sword and finds a new solution that replaces the old approach. It's not that the old thing gets fixed. Somebody comes around with something new and makes the old issues moot.

I think that's certainly true of computing. The world's a hard place, but you've got to deal with it as it is. I don't know why that should be depressing. The fact is that we're not stuck with the same things forever, because people do come along with new things. If you looked at our transportation problems in the 19th century, you would have said, "We project that there's going to be so many horses everywhere, we'll have horse manure all over the streets and we can't lodge all the horses!" In the 20th century, there was talk about how everybody would be a telephone operator eventually. That comes because people can't think beyond the way they're doing it right now.

What happens is somebody comes up with a new way of doing things that people hadn't thought before that makes the old problems moot. I think that's encouraging. It may be discouraging for people who have committed their whole lives to a particular way of doing things and can't change. If anything, the last 50 years have shown us that you can't pick a career and stick with it without making changes; the days of working at one company all your life or expecting to retire in the same field that you graduated are over. You have to be prepared to change.

### Heinlein said "Specialization is for insects."

**James:** Insects reproduce rapidly and die in large numbers. That's not a very good human life. It discourages me that a lot of companies seem to be hiring that way. They want to hire insects. They hire people specialized to know some very narrow system. They want them to come running out of the box. They want to cast them aside when they're done. I think that's a discouraging trend. I don't think it serves us well for the long run. We need people who can think and change and learn what they need to learn. I don't see much value in going to school to learn a particular programming language. You go to school to learn the concept of a programming language. Learning a new language is easy. We need people who are able to change. People need to watch what's happening. It's been said everybody needs to continue to educate themselves these days, and that's true.

### Is it possible to fix some of your criticisms of UML?

**James:** Sure it is. I think this whole concept of standardization was more of a marketing thing than anything else. Why do you need a standardized model language? You need to standardize things that you actually execute. I think this whole concept of standardization is greatly oversold. You don't need standards to do modeling. If UML is too bloated, people will carve out the parts that they need to use. Everybody uses class models and a lot of people use things such as sequence charts and use cases. There are parts of UML that few people use. That shows the danger of getting too many smart people together with little ways to enforce decision. They'll come up with a lot of ideas that seem useful, and there's no way to say, "That's a nice idea, but it's not useful enough to put in this large pot that is going to serve a large number of people."

People will use what they want. It's really no different than using something like Photoshop. I can use Photoshop, but I'm not an expert. I don't remember how to use most of it—I can look it up if I have to, but I know how to adjust levels and make selections and other things that I need to do all the time. If I have to do something else I can look it up. A professional graphics designer would know a lot more. That's the way people use most large applications or devices such as cell phones. They don't know how to use every feature, because most of the features are put in there just to be sales bullets on the box in the store.

*It's hard to evaluate modeling languages for usability. I can ask someone to use a programming language to solve a real problem and give me feedback on how well it works.*

**James:** If you look at the program languages out there, I would argue that a lot of them did not follow that paradigm. In many cases, the developers thought of clever ideas and put them in the language without making good usability tests, causing all kinds of problems down the road.

Language designers come up with these thought experiments that they feel they have to solve. Sometimes you should just say, "Well, we don't need to solve that problem; people can just work around it another way. It's not important enough to be part of the language."

In something like a modeling language, programming language, or application system, you want to include features if they're useful enough to justify the need for people to remember how they work, and then you need to test them to make sure they work in practice. If you cram too much in there, nobody can remember how to use it, so it actually becomes a burden. It's more likely to cause problems for the system because there's more for the developers to test and more things to go wrong. You can't just ask whether something is useful; you have to ask if it is useful enough, compared to everything else, to be worth the cost of remembering how to use it.

One way UML could evolve is for people to use subsets of it, which certainly is what's happened all along. I doubt the OMG process is going to resolve anything, because it just doesn't lead to decisiveness. I don't think UML 3.0 done with the OMG would accomplish anything because you'd just have too many competing interests. Too many people want to stuff things in that you can't keep it simple.

*I'll give you your stupid feature if you give me my stupid feature.*

**James:** Exactly. It's too much of a tradeoff. The other way it could go is that somebody comes up with something new that's sort of based on UML but has a new name and some different basic design decisions. Of course, that's what eventually happens to almost everything. Or else people could decide this is not where the action is anymore and move on to something else.

# A Bit of Reusability

*It seems that the average complexity and size of software grows year after year. Does OOP scale well in this situation or does it make things more complicated?*

**James:** First of all, it is unclear how fast the size of systems is growing. You can't just measure the number of bytes in a program. If you generate code, then it is the number of source lines that matter, not the number of generated lines or bytes or whatever. If you use higher-level procedures, then complexity depends on the number of calls, not the amount of code executed. As we work at higher levels, we get larger systems, but their inherent complexity may not be all that much greater.

Even if you don't buy that (and I don't buy it entirely—systems do seem to be getting more complex), OO systems are a good way to proceed. But you need to separate OO from a primary focus on reusability. I know that building reusable parts was put at the center of OO by the original Smalltalk developers, but I think that is a mistake. You can have OO structure without focusing obsessively on trying to build a library of reusable parts containing every class you use in an application. Reusability is good, but it's not really the main goal in most systems. It's really hard to build good reusable libraries—most programmers can't do it very well and shouldn't be encouraged to try. It's a separate task from system building. In designing a system, use OO structure to build a clean application made of classes that are easy to modify if needed, without insisting that they be immediately reusable by somebody else. If you find that you end up using variations on a class a lot, then you can go to the trouble of making it truly reusable.

You also have to know when to stop. I've seen plenty of beginners fuss over making reusable objects out of every line of code. When you can express a straightforward algorithm in natural language and just write the code, then don't bother with chopping it into smaller pieces—just write the code. OO is all about providing higher-level structure when things are not so straightforward, not about sweating the small stuff.

## How can we be sure that the advantages of OO are more valuable that the disadvantages?

**James:** As I said before, you can always use OO structure. The problem is in knowing how low to go with it. The true believers always want to push it all the way down. There are a lot of other issues in computing besides OO structure, such as good algorithms, good data structures, acceptable computational complexity, understandability, etc. It's not all about OO; in fact, OO is just a small part of the whole picture. OO provides a useful framework for organizing designs and programs. That's important, because otherwise you can get overwhelmed and confused by the problem. But the essential content of any design is not OO at all—it's all the other things I mentioned.

*You mentioned that reusability isn't the focus of object orientation.*

**James:** I don't think it should be. Reusability is greatly oversold and has been from the beginning. It was the marketing point that convinced a lot of managers to buy into it. Reusability is damned hard. To make things that are truly reusable is a far higher skill level than most people possess. Someone said, I think it was Brooks or Parnas, that it's three times harder to make something work in production than in a laboratory prototype, and another three times harder to make it work on a reusable basis. To insist when you do something on a one-shot basis that it be reusable is actually a waste of time and effort most of the time

You can take some precautions to make changes easier in the future, however. First, don't do something in a very specific way if you could do it in a bit more general way. Don't paint yourself into corners if you don't need to. If you can see a way to generalize it without too much additional trouble, go ahead and do it. Design things with an eye to the fact that you will have to change them. It doesn't mean that when you write the first version you have to do all that generalization. You leave the door open. You put in the hooks for making changes. You write things as methods that can be substituted but you don't go and write all those overgeneralized methods right off until you know you need them. The problem is that it's very hard to guess what your needs are going to be in the future and often the guesses are wrong. If you spend a lot of time generalizing one area, you may find out that's not the area where the changes need to be.

It's just like optimization. I really think too many programmers have worried about making things run fast in the wrong places. It's been an obsession in this field for years and years. Even though computers have gotten so much faster, that doesn't matter. They're still obsessed with what I'll call the micro-optimizations. They don't know complexity theory, they don't understand the "order-of" stuff, but they're worried about little, itty-bitty speed improvements.

I wrote a subroutine package and then I went and profiled it. You can't always guess where you need to optimize, you've got to go measure, and then you fix those problems. One subroutine took 30% of the time. I fixed that subroutine.

People overoptimize. It makes the program more likely to fail, and it may not be a place where it matters. I think here's an area where people just don't get it. People say, "Efficiency's important. Embedded things, you know." Nonsense. Everything's gotten faster. Excessive optimization is not worth it at the cost of all the bugs it causes. I just don't understand why people fail to do the simple things they could do. Something's badly wrong with the mindset of a lot of developers that these things are still happening. I think some of them like to do it the hard way, like rock climbers without ropes. But if they climbed the way they program, they'd be dead.

*If reuse isn't the goal of object orientation, is there a goal?*

**James:** Reuse is facilitated by object orientation, but I think the main goal of object orientation is use, not reuse. If you structure things in this way it'll be easier to get it right the first time and it also will give you modifiability. You may get some reuse, but that's just a bonus.

You know you're going to have to change any application, but you don't know where, so building things in an object-oriented fashion helps to facilitate future change because it produces a structure that's easier to modify. The point is to make it changeable, but not usually to build a reusable library. You don't start building an application with the expectation that everybody else in your company is going to use every class in your application. Somebody else in your company, it may be you or it may be somebody else, is eventually going to have to modify that program you wrote. You know for certain that's going to happen. Object orientation facilitates future change. I think that's its main value. Writing something the first time, it's just as easy to use any approach. It's the second version where OO pays off.

*Because you've encapsulated things?*

**James:** Right, you've actually got a cleaner design that's less intertwined. This way of structuring things tends to keep the functionality from tying itself in knots as much. That's the real problem that people have a hard time dealing with: very complex functionality. In a sense you're reusing it on the next edition of the same application. Call that reusability if you want. Only a little bit will be reused across many different projects.

Before you start reusing something on a wide basis, you really need to use it three times. Once is always a special case, twice could be a coincidence, three times, OK, now you begin to see some patterns in things. Now maybe it's worth going to the trouble of pulling out parts of it and making them really robust. You don't need to reuse everything. You find the things that are most useful and reuse them.

*This reminds me of SOA, where the assumption seems to be that you can define services that are reusable across a whole enterprise.*

**James:** To my mind, SOA was more of a marketing tool than anything else. I never quite saw much deeper substance in it. It's pretty superficial.

A lot of these things are marketing tools. Of course you have to get things adopted. I learned on an early project that a good name is worth a year of inactivity on a project. I came up with one great name in my career, but it helped a lot. People are affected by these things. OMT and UML—trouble is, we couldn't come up with great names there. I don't tend to like acronyms if you can avoid them, but sometimes it's the best you can do.

*What links do you see between the OO paradigm and the new focus on concurrency?*

**James:** The concept of an object as a self-contained package of data structure and behavior is ideal for concurrency. In the real world, everything is self-contained and everything is concurrent, so the idea of objects in modeling is perfect for concurrency.

That doesn't automatically follow in programming languages, however. Almost all of the programming languages that people learn are essentially sequential. There may be a few academic languages that are inherently concurrent, but that's not what most people learn to program. You can add in concurrency features to languages like Smalltalk or C++ or Java, but the underlying computational models and mindset are inherently sequential.

So the problem is not with the OO paradigm, it is with the programming languages and systems. Sure, you can design concurrent languages. I did one for my Ph.D. thesis in 1975, and so did several of my fellow grad students in Jack Dennis's Computation Structures Group at MIT in the early 1970s. It's not hard to make up new languages (although it's hard to make up ones that are easy to use over a wide range of practical problems). What is hard is getting them adopted.

There is no money in inventing languages—the essence of a popular language is wide use, and people don't want to use a language that is proprietary. It's hard for a company to devote the resources needed if they have to give it away (or else you may suspect their motives if they do give it away). Don't believe the nonsense about inventing a better mousetrap—it takes serious marketing to get something adopted. So I'm not very hopeful that a good concurrent programming language will get widely adopted—I don't see the path to motivate it happening.

*How can we design an inherently concurrent programming language?*

**James:** I worked with Professor Jack Dennis and his other students at MIT on data flow languages and computers on my Ph.D. thesis. These were inherently extremely concurrent languages. They were very innovative and spawned a lot of follow-on work over the years. Unfortunately, there were a few problems that I didn't solve, and neither did anybody else. So here was a promising idea, but it just didn't quite work in the long run. I pulled some of those ideas into UML, but data flow architecture doesn't seem to replace von Neumann architecture in most cases. So I had my shot and didn't quite make it.

There are also cellular automata. I think over half of my fellow grad students tried to build on them a highly parallel computer. That has to be the right approach, because that's how the universe is constructed. (Or maybe not. Modern physics is stranger than fiction. The latest speculations suggest that space and time arise out of something more primitive.) But cellular automata seem suited to only certain geometric problems, very important problems to be sure, but not general-case problems. People haven't figured out how to program them for the general case. Maybe there is no general case.

The critical issue seems to be the interface between control flow and data structure. Highly concurrent control flow doesn't mesh with large chunks of data, and it is unclear how to make the data concurrent and still perform the kind of computations we are accustomed to. Probably we need to perform new kinds of computations. The brain is a highly concurrent computer that does not run von Neumann algorithms, but we have no idea how to program something organized like the brain. Probably you can't program it: the concept of effective programmability and extreme concurrency may be mutually exclusive. Maybe it's a kind of Heisenberg uncertainty at a higher level (there's the physics background again).

*When you talk about programming languages that are adapted for concurrency, it seems an obvious connection to functional languages. What are the weaknesses of functional languages and why won't they provide the clue to easy concurrency?*

**James:** Functional languages are very good for expressing a world that is so concurrent that you don't need to talk about concurrency. The problem is that in the real world, often you need a middle ground in which you need to talk about some kinds of concurrency explicitly. I guess this is another one of those broken symmetries. However, functional languages have a lot of advantages; it would be good to be able to use them selectively within more imperative languages.

## Symmetric Relationships

*You said that associations provide a more symmetric viewpoint on a situation than pointers in most programming languages. Can you elaborate?*

**James:** In the real world, relationships are relationships. They're not usually encapsulated to only work in one direction. Occasionally they are, but mostly if A is related to B, then B is related to A.

### Is it a bidirectional relationship?

**James:** Well, it's a relationship. Relationships are inherently bidirectional. Mathematical relations are bidirectional. Even saying bidirectional implies that one is thinking of pointers. Relationship is relationship. The things are related and neither side takes precedence, maybe that's how to say it. Bidirectional doesn't mean symmetric, of course—man bites dog is different from dog bites man.

Thinking of your data structure and your system structure in terms of relations is a good way to start, rather than starting to think of how you're going to encapsulate them in terms of pointers.

At the line of code level, sure, you're in a specific programming language. At that point you should be thinking of whatever your programming language provides.

I once made a programming language in which relations were built in, and it worked great. You didn't have to make a commitment to directionality—you could go either direction quite easily. The cost wasn't that great. I'm surprised more languages don't provide that.

*Was this a dataflow language?*

**James:** It was actually a data structure package. I called it DSM, Data Structure Manager. It was basically a set of data structure procedures, but I set it up so that you could easily think in relational terms and go either way. If you want to delete tuple from a relation, you just delete a tuple. I optimized it so you can work from either end and used hashing to make it of linear complexity, so you didn't take a major performance hit.

All these techniques are well known, but the average person can't program them on the spot. You need to get them out of libraries or built into the language. I doubt that most of programmers now would know how to use hashing. This wasn't a big language, but we included one approach to do hashing for sets and relations and extendable arrays. If you filled up the array, it doubled in size. It kept the cost linear at the expense of some memory. Again, we didn't rewrite a whole language, we sort of did an overlay on something else. It made a lot of things much easier. We never had the buffer overflow problem. This kind of approach can be very powerful.

I'm surprised people don't do more of it. I know that in C++ some former colleagues of mine built generic template classes. I'm not sure they got used so much. Maybe the whole mechanism was too hard to use in C++, or maybe programmers were just too lazy to bother learning them.

One complaint I have is we have this great divide in computing between programming languages and databases. You have the programming language people who are pointer-based and obsessive about efficiency and everything, and they have all kind of problems with programs that have nasty errors in them.

You have the database people who are relational-based. They understand the concept of relations. That's where I got the concept of relationships from originally. They are not so obsessed about efficiency. In a sense a database is highly inefficient from a programming point of view, but it's worth it because they want it to be robust. They want the data to be secure, they don't want it to crash. There doesn't seem to be anybody in the middle. It's maybe like our political system now, you have people on the ends and we've frozen out the people in the middle. I tried to approach the database people and they didn't seem to appreciate the value of anything that's going on in programming languages and vice versa.

I really think it would help if these two sides would come together and we wouldn't have such a strong division. If we have languages where you could do these relational database types of things easily. You could do the procedural types of things easily and go back and forth between the two approaches easily, and do things in a safe way most of the time, using built-in things. That would give you computational complexity efficiency that the average person couldn't write out of the box, and with less obsession on this program-it-yourself micro bit pushing. I think people think they're getting more efficient. They aren't, because they blow the high-level efficiency; don't see the forest for the trees. They end up micro-optimizing, but it's much less efficient at the high levels.

*I think it's* The Practice of Programming *[Addison-Wesley Professional] where Kernighan said that in one of these old Unix utilities, they used a simple linear scan.*

**James:** Exactly. Why is it we're still using Unix? What year is this, 2009? Now when was Unix invented? Forty years of Unix and it's still got some of the same assumptions in it, like bytes for characters. You can't encode a character in a byte. We've gone beyond that and we're still thinking of strings as arrays of bytes. That doesn't work these days.

Sure, they've updated some of them, but Unix was built originally on the concept of a PDP-7, with a 64K memory of 18-bit words (not the puny 16-bit stuff) where you would swap out the entire memory every now and then. I don't know how many of those concepts are still buried in there waiting to cause problems.

Again, it's the same problem: some people tried to make new operating systems, but it's hard to get them adopted. Here we are using these old things. Windows has code that goes back to the 1980s. I guess that's only 20 years. Wow, I'm getting old. When you say it's only 20 years, I guess that shows I've been around a while.

If you remember history, a lot of the stuff coming out now doesn't seem so novel anymore, because you've seen it happen three or four times already. People keep making the same great discovery and thinking it's new. I've seen that happen many times before. To quote Elrond, "My memory reaches back to the Elder days, and I've seen many defeats and many fruitless victories."

Let me throw out a different idea here. I know a lot of people have sold the idea that there's a software crisis. A lot of the modeling stuff was sold on that basis. I've been guilty of that myself. On the other hand, I can go to Fry's Electronics and buy devices and software that keep getting more and more complicated every year. It costs less each year. Somehow people keep cranking out new applications. Maybe there is no software crisis. Maybe it's overplayed for shock value.

You could also argue about things like security. We'll get security when people decide it's important enough. They say it's important, but the evidence is people don't think it's important enough to pay for. If it's important enough, vendors will pay attention to it. It doesn't matter what people say if they're not willing to spend extra for it, cash and cycles and memory and things like that.

*If security is an important consideration, will it be worth it not to write in C or C++ with their dangerous pointers?*

**James:** Sure. People get what they pay for. Take databases—the database that loses or corrupts your data doesn't stay in business very long. When developers are writing a database manager, they spend a lot of effort to make sure it doesn't lose data. Crashing is one thing, but if it loses or corrupts your data, that's much worse.

In projects, people often talk about prioritizing bugs before a release. A fatal bug, one that crashes the application, is usually considered the most important to fix. I think that's a misguided approach. Something that corrupts your data and doesn't crash the system is a far more serious problem than something that just crashes the system, because you don't realize you have a problem and you lose data. In fact, something that's inconvenient can be much more serious than a fatal bug.

I built an early modeling tool. I made a list of priorities. It turns out that something low on the list was hard to do, and you had to do it all the time. This supposedly minor thing was so annoying in practice that I moved it to number one on the list. Something you do all the time that annoys you may be much more serious than a bug that crashes the system, because if it crashes the system, you restart it and go on. If it annoys you every single time you click on the screen, you won't use the tool at all.

### Most of the credit I've received for bugs I've fixed has been those kinds of bugs.

**James:** Right. You mean the ones that really annoy you. I don't know if you've ever read Edward Tufte's books. He talked about "chartjunk," which is the kind of graphs that Excel puts out—you have ink all over the page showing very little information. His concept is you want the least ink per amount of information on the screen.

You can apply that same concept to user interfaces. I've always felt that the best applications are ones that make you click the least. If you have to click all over the place, if you have to do two clicks when one would suffice, it's a bad design. It's one of these annoyance things that stops you from using something.

### If there is one lesson that designers and developers should take from your experience, what is it?

**James:** The one lesson is that everything is going to change. That's the number one lesson in life in general. Everything changes.

You need to build for change. When you're writing applications, you need to write with a certainty that it will change in the next version. When you're educating yourself, you need to educate yourself with a certainty that what you learn in college won't be the only thing you're using by the time you retire, and you may go through several different careers in your lifetime.

The needs of the business world will change. The problems of today won't necessarily go away but they may become insignificant in relation to new problems. Change is everywhere. You need to expect it, embrace it, and learn to live with it, and you'll succeed. Those people that can deal with change are the ones that both have a good success and have a good life. If you can't, you're going to be in trouble. It doesn't matter if you're in computing or something else, that's true of everything these days.

# UML

*How do you define UML?*

**Grady Booch:** The Unified Modeling Language is a graphical language used to visualize, specify, reason about, document, and construct the artifacts of a software-intensive system. In my use of the UML, the UML is not a programming language but rather a language with deep semantics that transcends traditional programming languages, and permits one to work at a level of abstraction equal to and/or above code.

*During which phases of development is UML most effective?*

**Grady:** The UML is suitable for the entire lifecycle of a software-intensive system, from birth to death to rebirth. My particular bias is that the UML is especially useful in reasoning about the architecture of a system. I'm also biased to Kruchten's 4+1 model view, and in my work in the Handbook of Software Architecture, I've not found a single system for which the UML has not been sufficient for me to capture valuable design decisions.

*How does it interact with different software engineering methods?*

**Grady:** While Jim, Ivar, and I had particular methodological perspectives, there's really nothing that we put in the UML that binds it to any reasonable software engineering process.

*Suppose that I am skeptical about UML. How would you convince me that it's useful?*

**Grady:** Two things: use it to document a system you've written, and see if it helps you communicate things that transcend the code; also, scour the Web for examples of its use, and study how others are using it (from MediaWiki to embedded systems and many things in between).

*What is your opinion on using UML to generate the implementation code?*

**Grady:** The UML was designed—and is still appropriate for—the visualization, specification, construction, and documentation of software-intensive systems. To that end, model-driven development has proven useful in treating the UML as a programming language from which one can generate executables. At the same time, I'm a greater fan of using the UML to visualize the design of an as-built or evolving system (the inverse of model-driven).

*I've read that hospitals only have rooms with two or four beds because discussions among groups of three often turn into two against one, where the one person is always the same. Did working on the UML as a group of three present similar difficulties?*

**Grady:** Remember, though, that for about a year it was just two (Jim and I), then for another year it was three (Jim, Ivar, and I) but after that, it was dozens and then hundreds (as the UML migrated to become a public standard). As such, the dynamics of the parties involved varied widely. At any rate, what was interesting was not so much the nature of compromise, but rather that we did achieve convergence in the presence of many passionate people who approached the problem from a variety of perspectives. This diversity and the subsequent public exposure are what have made the UML so broadly accepted.

*If you were to revise UML into UML 3.0, how would you approach the process?*

**Grady:** I can tell you exactly because I've given some thought to that. First I'd begin with the set of use cases for which I want to apply to UML 3.0. One of the things that I lament in the 1.x and 2.0 process is that a lot of what's in the UML now came from the bottom up and it was not driven by exemplars as saying, "Here are problems. Here are points of pain. How do we solve this? Here's how we do it in the current UML. Here's how we can improve it."

I'd begin by canvassing a set of use cases from the industry as to what are the kinds of things we'd like to model. Having done that, I would make an intentional effort to engineer a 3.0 to support those use cases as well as intentionally work on refactoring the metamodel to simplify it.

*What would you change?*

**Grady:** The UML still needs to be made simpler, but this is always one of the hardest things to do, for there is no end to the elements that one may wish to add in support for a specific problem. Additionally, I see the UML growing to become more suitable as a system language.

*Is there 20% of UML that everyone uses all the time?*

**Grady:** That's exactly what I'd say. In the handbook work I've done thus far it's the classic 80/20 rule. There's probably about 20% of the UML that I need for the work I do. There's 80% that covers lots of corner cases and details, but it's really that core that's the sufficient part for my purposes.

Remember that there are lots of ways different people use the UML. If I'm using the UML drive to create code, then boy, I need a lot of those details. On the other hand, if I'm just using it to reason about a system, to visualize, to make informed decisions, then I don't need those details. It is kind of the tyranny of the minority. I'll put it that way. Because there are some uses of the UML, particularly from DD, that drive a lot of the complexity in 2.0 and that does complicate it for some other things.

*Most of what I've seen is a lot of ad hoc whiteboard discussions. Here are my class models. Here are my entity models. Here are the relationships between them.*

**Grady:** When I began the Booch method, I certainly never intended it to become a programming language. If you go down that path and make a visual programming language, there are lots of things you need to do that haven't been done. For example, really nailing the semantics of the notation and the meta model. That doesn't exist, and it surprises me that it hasn't really been an effort for some time.

If I have a box, what does it mean? There honestly is no formal specification of what a box means. While there's been focus upon the formal semantics of the UML meta model, not as much work done between the notation to UML meta model coupling.

*Are there possible changes to take advantage of distributed development and teamwork?*

**Grady:** I can't think of a thing. I've been cataloging a variety of design patterns for distributed systems, and there's no concept that I can't fit in the UML as it exists today. As for teamwork, I'm spending a great deal of time on the problems of collaborative development environments, including some exotic stuff in virtual worlds such as Second Life; the UML helps, and there's nothing I'd really change in the language itself, for in temporally and geographically distributed development is the social dynamics that trump the technical issues.

*What should developers learn from the invention, evolution, and adoption of the UML?*

**Grady:** A phrase I often use is that the entire history of software engineering can be characterized by rising levels of abstraction. We see this in our tools, our methods, our languages, our frameworks. The UML, in this context, is simply a natural point on this evolution. In the earliest generations of computing, the hardware platform dominated; in the next generation, the choice of language dominated; in the current generation, issues of software platform have persisted (primarily manifest in the operating system wars, especially if one takes a broad view and sees the Web as a peer platform). This is not to say that vestiges of these earlier concerns do not exist. Nay, they all still play a role in contemporary systems, to one degree or another. Returning to the UML, it came at a time where the complexity of software systems was on such a trajectory that the failure or success of a project relied less on problems of language and programming and more on problems of architecture and collaboration.

Another phrase I've used is that software development has been, is, and will remain fundamentally hard. There is, as Dr. Brooks so eloquently states, an essential complexity to software that will not go away. Thus, we know that, however far our vision might reach, all future advances will rely on software yet to be written (yet building on software that currently is). The software-intensive systems of the past appear trivial to us today but in their time they stressed the state of the practice—just as contemporary systems that although challenging to us, will likely pale in comparison to the systems of systems of the future. It is these forces that impel us to keep improving the practice and the profession of software engineering.

## Language Design

*What is the link between the design of a language and the design of software written with that language?*

**Grady:** The question you raise is an old one, albeit cast in a new form: linguists and cognitive scientists have pondered that very question for decades, with much of the controversy swirling around what is called the Sapir-Whorf hypothesis. Edward Tufte similarly points out that the right representation can collapse complexity, making it possible to meaningfully reason about complex information in an abstract way.

To explain further, the Sapir-Whorf hypothesis (from the linquists Edward Sapir and Benjamin Whorf) posits a connection between language and thought: the syntactic and semantic elements of a spoken language impacts how a person can perceive the world and reason about it (and vice versa). Contemporary linquists such as George Lakoff (author of *Women, Fire, and Dangerous Things* [University of Chicago Press]) agree. Tufte's work (*The Visual Display of Quantitative Information* [Graphics Press]) focuses on the visualization of complex data, and through numerous examples makes the point that effective graphics can make the difference between understandability and obscurity.

How, do you ask, do I know about these issues? Well, building crisp abstractions is a fundamental principle of object-oriented development, abstraction is primarily a problem of classification, and linguists such as Chomsky and Lakoff have influenced my thinking about classification.

Anyway, to reframe your question to "is there a link between language and software design?"—assuming that by language we mean both classical textual programming languages such as Java as well as graphical ones such as the UML—I would answer "probably."

It is the case that languages that encourage algorithmic decomposition (such as FORTRAN and C) will lead to particular program organizational styles that are quite distinct from those that encourage object-oriented decomposition (e.g., Java) or perhaps even functionally oriented. In my experience, however, there are many other factors that influence design to a greater degree: the culture of the development team, the historical context, the particular forces that weigh upon a system at any given moment. One could argue that language is some one of a First Cause, but I'd argue otherwise, suggesting that these other forces dominate.

### What differences are there between developing a programming language and developing a "normal" software project?

**Grady:** The same difference, perhaps, between drafting some law on public policy and making that law manifest: they are related, but very different things indeed. A language—be it a human one or a programming one—does not have unlimited degrees of freedom, but rather, technical, business, social, historical, and pragmatic forces shape it. For programming languages in particular, one must be precise of its syntax and semantics, as ultimately we use these languages to create artifacts that execute. I don't know if there's any such thing as a "common" software project, but therein so many more ambiguities exist. A language, once defined, is relatively stable; a software project, if its economically interesting at all, lives in an environment of constant motion. Thus, while both the language and the project are essentially engineering problems to be solved the resolution of the forces around them, the forces on a project tend to be far more diverse and far more dynamic.

*Do you believe that it's important to start with some degree of formal specification of a core of a language and evolve from there?*

**Grady:** Absolutely. In fact, that's how Jim and I began when we began trying to really nail the semantics of what would become UML and unifying the OMT and the Booch methods. We began by writing a meta model using UML itself. And so the challenge is one person's formal is another person's informal. For us the issue was "Is it sufficient formality to do what we needed to do?" And the answer was yes.

*How do you recognize that sufficiency?*

**Grady:** There was a chief justice—this is an oft-quoted story—that was once asked a question about how you judge what pornography is. His answer was—you've probably heard this story—"I know it when I see it." So there you go. You run into these incredibly metaphysical discussions when you start talking about the meaning of meaning because what really is formality? Because you can get yourself into a very deep hole of saying, "What does meaning mean?" There's a point even in formalisms where one has to stop.

*A lot of people might say, "We can rely on Turing completeness or the Lambda calculus, and beyond this point I know how to apply a function to an argument."*

**Grady:** I'm very happy that there are such people that care about those things in the world, but imagine if we applied that same kind of rigor to Java or Vista and how much stuff is actually written in those languages and those platforms for which there exists no formalisms. There are operational semantics. We run these things and know how they work. That's really good enough for the large part of what we develop software with these days. That's not to say that there's not a place for formalisms. There is. There are certain— and I'm going to use these words carefully—certain very narrow corners of the industry for which deep formalisms are very important.

*Is it worthwhile to distinguish between language with which people can build systems and that for which you might want some degree of formalism?*

**Grady:** Sure. But is there a formal semantics for Linux? Is there a formal semantics for C++? Sure. I would imagine people have worked on some elements of those but it hasn't stopped people from building real things.

*There's a very practical concern there, too, then.*

**Grady:** Absolutely. I'm a pragmatist. If it works and it's good, then I use it, which is what leads me to using about 20% of the UML. It's good enough for my purposes.

*Your 20% might not be my 20%.*

**Grady:** I would imagine there's probably going to be a fair degree of overlap. Maybe your 19% and my 19% match.

*That's a pretty good match, honestly.*

**Grady:** Yeah. It is indeed.

*Where would you start looking for the use cases for that 19%?*

**Grady:** I would look at the way that people have been using the UML. I'd go to real projects that have been trying to apply the UML and ask them the questions, "Give me some common cases. Give me the central cases in which you use it, and let's make sure it's easy to do easy things in the UML. Then let's start looking at some of those corner cases." I would go from real use as opposed to expected use.

This is a time for consolidation and simplification. A language that's in version 3 and is used in so many places—while there is value in innovation, there's also value in refactoring. UML 2.0 to some degree, and I'll say this a little bit harshly, suffered a bit of a second system effect in that there were great opportunities and special interest groups, if you will, clamoring for certain specific features which added to the bloat of UML 2.0. Now is a time to step back and refactor and simplify. In any meaningful system, you do see this growth and collapse. Now is the time for simplification.

*Is there a pattern of even, odd, even, odd?*

**Grady:** I'm just thinking out loud right now in terms of the Microsoft operating system releases. As I look at Windows 7, yeah, there might be something to that effect, yes.

*Or the* Star Trek *movie effect.*

**Grady:** Now that one certainly is worth lots of formal studies.

*To what degree is backward compatibility with UML 2.0 a factor?*

**Grady:** Remember that there are a lot of things in UML 2.0 which if we were to be constantly moving forward and having complete, as you said, being able to have complete compatibility with the past, it's going to keep growing in size. There are probably some small cases where I would be willing to break it to say, "Wow, this thing adds a lot of complexity. It's simply not worth it. Sorry, I'm going to offend a few folks. Here's some workarounds for it."

If you look at the core in which people are using UML for that 20%, we're not going to break those. Having backward compatibility of that—sure, that's very important.

*Just about every programming language designer tries to walk that line, and there are lots of different approaches. Lisp almost says, "We're not going to give you an object system; you can build one. We're not going to give you certain control structures; you can build them." Then everybody went off and did, and they started sharing code. Then Common Lisp tried to nail down what everyone should use.*

**Grady:** That's a good model to describe that.

*To some degree that's also an evolutionary or a simulated annealing algorithm, where the community figures out what looks good and the designers bring that back into the core.*

**Grady:** Absolutely. Which is why I pointed out going to the use cases from industry itself. How have people actually used this? Look at it from the enterprise side where people have looked at some really large systems. Let's look at some small ones as well, too.

*What's your view of the standardization process, having gone through this?*

**Grady:** I've been involved in a variety of standardizations processes and it is a wonderful, interesting process that I'd imagine legions of sociologists would have a fun time following. It's hard to generalize in terms of the standards process. There are some standards, and I'm not going to name any, that get pushed by specific industries and they become specific companies, they become de facto standards. There are others that are true group efforts. There are some that are obviously politically motivated and get rammed down the throats of others. So there's a whole spectrum of how standards come to be.

The really delightful thing is that despite all of the complaints people have about the standard systems, it does have its value and it does work. So I'm grateful for organizations such as the OMG who are willing to spend the resources to shepherd such things and create a forum for their evolution. Without such standards, the Web wouldn't exist.

It's a painful process and many people involved in these processes, they're passionate, they have their own particular view of the world, they know that view of the world is right; such is the nature of the human experience.

*Is it your experience that everyone comes away slightly disappointed, but feeling that everybody else is slightly disappointed, too, so it works out?*

**Grady:** I'm not sure it's necessarily that bad, but standards are a degree of compromise all the way around. Every standard you can imagine is such a case. There will always be somebody who will walk away disappointed. In fact, there are still people that are disappointed in Obama's election and they're happy that Bush is around. But go figure. There are people that like Britney Spears's music—no accounting for taste. Again, part of the human experience and let's hear it for diversity.

*On the Linux kernel, there's no real standard there beyond POSIX. There's this taste of Linus Torvalds and his lieutenants.*

**Grady:** Well, I think that's a good comparison. In the case of Linux, Linus has been on the forefront of being its leader for some time. In the case of the UML, Jim Rumbaugh and I moved away from the standards process and let go of it. There hasn't been as much of a driving force, and I think that makes a bit of a difference. Look at C++; Bjarne is still very much in the midst of C++'s evolution. That steady hand does continue to offer a degree of intellectual integrity and consistency.

*They're working through the standardization process on the new version, too.*

**Grady:** Correct. But like Linux's case, you have a voice that has great experience and there's great expectations from said person and that person has proven themselves. While they're not the only voice, they're a strong clear voice.

*Maybe this is two questions. What value is there in pursuing standardization for an idea? To what degree do you need a strong leader with a strong vision to help you achieve success?*

**Grady:** On the latter, you can ask that question to any human endeavor. Look at the way changes happen in the world. I'm not comparing our effort to any of these people, but look at what a Gandhi has done, or a Martin Luther King. The power of an individual to bring about change is extraordinary in this world.

From a technical perspective you can think of a variety of technical leaders that have made things happen. Look at Larry and Serge of Google who brought their notions from Stanford to bear, and now it's a whole empire. The presence of a strong visionary has proven itself in so many domains to make a difference.

*I don't want to put those forward as competing ideas.*

**Grady:** It's just an example that the power of an individual or a small set of people to bring about fundamental change is proven in many places.

*Suppose I were to create a programming language. What value should I expect from pursuing standardization?*

**Grady:** In producing anything new like that, ultimately the marketplace decides independent of whether or not you make it a standard. Many of the scripting languages did not start through the standards bodies but they simply grew out from the grassroots and as there was sufficient critical mass people realized, "Oh, we need to more precisely standardize these things because we need interoperability." The point here is that you have to consider in any of these kinds of things what is the value that you're providing and how is the marketplace going to react to it. The standards process can then help you get some critical mass behind making it real, but ultimately the market is going to decide.

The challenge of any new language is that I may come up with the most perfect technical design but there is a myriad of other things, mostly social, that impact whether or not that language is going to be successful. Can I build a community of practice? Does it address the points of pain that are alive and real at that moment for that particular community? Is there sufficient interest by individuals in organizations to contribute to it in a case where as it's in a fledgling state, there's no obvious business model for it, but it just seems right.

Many of these kinds of early developments start on faith, if you will, and they're in the right place at the right time. That's certainly true of the Booch method and probably if you ask the same thing of Jim Rumbaugh, the same thing's true of Objectory and OMT, to which UML came to bear. We were at the right place in the right time addressing a point of pain in the marketplace.

Now today, does the world need another language? You may come to mind of what about M, which Microsoft has brought to the marketplace? Will M be successful? It's technically very interesting, but whether or not it succeeds will be based upon does it have some traction in the marketplace. Even though it may be standardized, even though it may be a de facto standard because of what Microsoft has done, the marketplace will decide.

*It sounds like there's a lot of pragmatism beyond that visionary status.*

**Grady:** Oh, absolutely. I believe that's true that again, even the best idea, the most technically well formed, fully formal, well thought-out, completely documented thing will fall flat if it does not solve real problems for real projects.

*People might not like to hear that; there seems to be a real tech-utopianism that still believes that the best technical project has to win.*

**Grady:** I'm delighted that such people exist because of their optimism. Their optimism tends to drive us. But I'm more of a solver engineer, where I deal with pragmatics. I am not a computer scientist. I'm more of an engineer. It's delightful that we have both worldviews because this dance, this tension, makes both parties more and more honest. I am driven by my pragmatism, but on the other hand, the pure computer scientist pushes me to be pure and more formal and that's not a bad thing. Similarly, I push him to be pragmatic.

*Is there a creative tension between those two poles?*

**Grady:** Absolutely. I believe there should be. Part of the issue of creativity is in my mind the presence of tension, because creativity that tension focuses our creativity to solve real problems. There's a delightful site called Gaping Void. He's basically a PR-type person and his claim to fame is he does art on the back of business cards. But he has this riff which has been very popular about how to be creative. You might point your readers to that one.* It's quite interesting because it really talks about the importance of that kind of pragmatic tension.

## Training Developers

*Why are we moving so slowly in the improvements of programming methods and processes?*

**Grady:** Well, I object to the premise of your question. Perhaps it seems slow because from the inside of the industry, we know there is much more we can do, and do better. But consider that our industry has literally transformed the world in, essentially, one generation. To me, that's fast, not slow.

* *www.gapingvoid.com*

*How can we transmit experience in the software field?*

**Grady:** In the Middle Ages, guilds served as a primary mechanism for the transmission of tribal memory; today, we lack such apprenticeships in software. Still, a considerable amount of experience is transmitted via the Web (consider Slashdot, for example), books, blogs, and technical meetings. It is also that case that raw, running, naked source code is a source of knowledge from the past—and this is one of the reasons I've worked with the Computer History Museum to preserve the code of classic software for future generations.

*What should today's students study more?*

**Grady:** I'll answer that question in two ways. From the lens of software, any good course of study will teach you the basic skills of programming and design. However, I'd recommend three things: learn how to abstract, learn how to work as part of a team, and study the code of others. From a wider lens, I urge students to pursue their passion with abandon, but never forget the value in growing as a whole person.

Study outside your domain (there's more to the world than software), develop the ability to continuously learn (for this field will continuously change), and fan your spark of curiosity and risk taking (for from such things comes innovation).

*What single best piece of advice could you give a novice programmer, drawing on your experience?*

**Grady:** This is a question that was just asked of me by a student at USC. I gave some lectures at Cal Poly and USC a few weeks ago. I've had some followups from some of those students, so I'll offer the same answer that I offered for them back then.

The first is follow your passion and be sure you have fun. There is certainly value in pursuing a career and pursing a livelihood but in the end development and all the things we do, it's a human experience and you want to be a whole person in this process. So enjoy, live fully, gain life experiences; please do that. Follow your passion because it's easy to find really crappy jobs out there where you can find yourself in a place you just hate. Please don't do that. That's what I encourage.

The second thing I encourage is gain some experience. Get yourself involved in some open source projects. Find something of interest to you and just do it. Don't be afraid to try new things and expose yourself to diversity, insofar as you get exposed to new ideas in different domains. Frankly that's going to help you out no matter what domain you enter.

*The idea of music comes up time and time again. The idea of creative arts—especially writing—does, too.*

**Grady:** Speaking of writing, a question I often ask academics is, "How many of you have reading courses in software?" I've had two people that have said yes. If you're an English Lit major, you read the works of the masters. If you want to be an architect in the civil space, then you look at Vitruvius and Frank Lloyd Wright and Christopher Rennin and Frank Gehry and others. We don't do this in software. We don't look at the works of the masters. I encourage people to look at the work others have done and learn from them.

*It would be nice if we had a pattern of body of literature to say, "Here is what a great-looking Pascal program looks like."*

**Grady:** That's what Andy Oram and Greg Wilson's *Beautiful Code* from O'Reilly is attempting to be. There's a book out by a guy in New Zealand who's developed a reading list as well, too. He's one of the two people that I've encountered that have actually done this.

We don't have a body of knowledge for software literary criticism. The work that Knuth did on literate programming, I think, was one of the early attempts to try to do that. Most code is really poorly written. It's like at the third grade reading level of sentence structure and the like, if you want to put it. But beautiful code is full of drama and beauty and elegance and it's well written. I've had the opportunity to look at the source code for Mac Paint, about 10,000 lines of Object Pascal, and it reads beautifully. We don't have such examples like that that we give out to the world very much.

Then the challenge is, if I've got a system that's like the Linux kernel, 10 million lines of code, I'm not going to read that. It's like reading *War and Peace* over and over again. What do I do to expose its beauty and elegance? There's a conference coming up this January, Rebooting Computing, led by Peter Denning and Alan Kay—and others are in it—and I'll be there. We're talking about that's one of the problems. How does one take these incredibly invisible intellectually complex things and expose their beauty to the world?

We have a similar problem with the Computer History Museum. I'm on the Board of Trustees. We've started a Software Collections Committee and we have all these wonderful artifacts. How do you expose the beauty that's in Vista? There is beauty. How do you expose, how do you let people read what's inside there? In civil architecture you can show them a building. You can show them a painting. They can listen to a piece of music. How do we expose the music that's in software?

*Maybe we need to document algorithms and data structures.*

**Grady:** I think that's too low a level. My thesis is you need to document the patterns that sweep through the system itself.

## Creativity, Refinement, and Patterns

*How can we address the problem of legacy software?*

**Grady:** The phrase I often use is that while the code is the truth, it's not the whole truth: there is a loss of information from vision to execution. My experience is that there are nine things you can do with old software: abandon it, give it away, ignore it, put it on life support, rewrite it, harvest from it, wrap it up, transform it, or preserve it. Each of these things has both technical as well as social elements. From a technical perspective, there's interesting research underway to harvest patterns from code; from a social perspective, the techniques of oral histories can contribute to a solution.

*Where do you find inspiration for design?*

**Grady:** I find inspiration in the elegance of complex things. These things may be software (one of the goals of the Handbook is to be able to codify a set of architectural patterns and to explain their beauty); others may be organic systems (really, any organic system: a system that has evolved from millions of years of forces upon it clearly has some things we can learn); art (there is great beauty in many artists in many mediums); music, product engineering, quantum physics…the list goes on and on for me.

*To what degree do you see creativity as necessary in programming?*

**Grady:** A lot of programming doesn't require a lot of creativity because you're solving known problems and you're trying to do them in interesting ways. It's not unlike somebody building an extension to my house. There are certain constraints in which they live and there are certain best practices they need to follow. I'm going to hire somebody who's not totally out of the box but I want to hire somebody who can follow those best practices. He or she will need to innovate along the way. It's like, "Oh, wow, this doesn't quite line up, and so I need to think of some innovative ways to do X." That's where innovation comes in for the small, individual developer.

A lot of what we do in software development does not require that much innovation. We have known technology upon which we're building it. We need to apply it in novel ways. We need to shape it, sand off the edges, add a new slot here and there. That's part of the fun in the puzzle of so doing. No doubt.

There are certainly places for which unbridled innovation is necessary. We didn't know the right way to build software for huge globally scalable searching systems and Serge and Larry went off and they prototyped it and thus Google was born. We don't know the right ways to look at all the data feeds from the tens of thousands, if not millions, of video cameras that are placed in corners around the world in London and New York and Beijing. What's the right architecture to do that? We have no good models to do so, and so wild innovation, unbridled innovation is necessary.

But once you start converging upon the right kind of architecture, then you've constrained a problem and you start innovating in the small.

*You used the words "innovation" and "constraining" again. It seems like a direct parallel to the evolution of a language.*

**Grady:** Absolutely. The thing that a painter or I as a writer or anyone in the creative field hates the most is a completely blank page because there are no constraints. There's nothing to guide me. The moment you start putting constraints on it, in a way it's a curious thing. You're freed because now you can begin working within those constraints and applying all of your innovative skills to resolve those constraints.

If I am a musician and I say, "Wow, I can do anything." Well, being unconstrained it's like, "Gosh, should I do the piano or should I play something else? Should I do whatever?"

It's actually an embarrassment of riches and it doesn't focus you. I may say, "Gosh, I could build my own piano." Or like Don Knuth did, "I'm writing this book and I don't like the way it lays out, so I'm going to stop for a few years and write a language text to actually lay out books." Not to condemn what Don did because he did some wonderful things there, but in the face of no constraints it's really hard to focus one's skills.

*Do you suggest that we first identify the constraints when we seek to build a new system and then embrace them?*

**Grady:** I don't think you can always first do that. You sort of live under them and you may choose some constraints; every decision I make then makes a decision to not do other things and that's not a bad thing. So many of the earliest decisions one makes in any of these projects is to establish some constraints via a leap of faith. You can't a priori decide what all those constraints are and you have to make an attempt to try something, throw it out in the world, and then follow it. For example, very simple case, I might say, "Gee, I want to devise a new graphical programming language." And so I begin. Well, all of a sudden I've just made some decisions like, "Wow, it's maybe like a 2D language as opposed to a 3D language." Maybe I make the decision that color is important for me and all of a sudden I realize, "Wow, I've just alienated the whole community of color-blind programmers." Every one of those things becomes a constraint that I have to work out, and I have to deal with the consequences of those constraints.

*That argues for an iterative process.*

**Grady:** Absolutely. All of life is iterative. It goes back to the point I made earlier, which is you can't a priori know enough to even ask the right questions. One has to take a leap of faith and move forward in the presence of imperfect information.

*Is it likely we'll see a break-out visual programming language or system in the next 10 years?*

**Grady:** Oh, it already exists. It's National Instruments' Lab View. The absolutely wickedly coolest visual programming language I've seen. I don't know if you're familiar with it. It's absolutely amazing. You draw your boxes and lines that represent virtual instruments and virtual electronic devices. You can if you need to dive into using, I think, C and C++. Basically you can build virtual instruments and connect them with real-world devices and it's just wickedly cool. Such a thing already exists.

*What type of instruments?*

**Grady:** Oscilloscopes, monitoring instruments. Imagine taking your PC and having on its USB port some D2A converters and parallel serial converters and things like that so I can talk to real world equipment. Now I can build virtual instruments on my PC simply by drawing things together. Maybe I want to have a strip chart or an oscilloscope or do some munging of data and present it in some interesting ways in various meters, trivial to do in Lab View. It is wickedly cool.

If you look at the direction further out where Charles Simonyi is trying to head with Intentional. Charles's notion—and he's gathered some prototypes in his case—if I am an electrical engineer, then I'll use schematics and I can feed that into my system. I have not seen a variety of others of his, but that's one of the classic examples. I choose a visualization that is germane to that particular domain.

*How about for your standard business application? You have a database backend. You have business objects. You have a presentation layer.*

**Grady:** Most enterprise systems are architecturally very dull because they are relatively simple in that regard. They're a state. There's a set of design decisions you have to make, and we know what those decisions are. Why it's been so difficult is because there's a tremendous technology churn that's going on and it's the embarrassment of riches. There are so many ways I could go build something.

I mean, if I were to say today, "Gee, I'm going to start building from scratch a banking system." Well, there's probably a set of standards I need to worry about at first, but gosh I could choose from a countably finite but very large countably finite set of ways to solve that problem. That's where I think much of the challenge and chaos comes into being. Consider the most volatile piece of business applications these days. It's been the presentation layer. How do I deliver this information to people? For a decade or so people were content to do this just printing things, but now we have these wonderfully open ways via the Web and mobile devices, and you see a lot of innovation churn in that area because we haven't converged upon the right models in which people want to collaborate with these systems. That's why you see churn.

The other most volatile piece is the area of business rules. The challenge of the times in the past because we've been so limited by our machines is that we had to throw business rules in some creepy places, stored procedures and you put it in the browser, but they're all over the place. We're realizing that that's a bit of a problem because it makes it difficult for us to react to change when the volatile business rules change very quickly.

You're seeing the refactoring of many enterprise systems where business rules are being pulled out. We find ways that the enterprise system sort of looks at this repository of business rules and reacts to it. But again, we couldn't have known that…we built these first systems; we couldn't have known that's where the most volatile pieces would be, and that's some of the changes that are going on right now in that space.

Is that open for visualization? You bet. We see the opportunity for being able to find new languages to express business rules. My personal opinion is the UML was quite sufficient and we saw some interesting political things happening that led to BPEL (Business Process Execution Language) coming out as a very separate thing from the UML.

*Microsoft might argue that M is an attempt to do that.*

**Grady:** Absolutely, which goes back to the point I raised earlier: will M be successful? The marketplace will decide.

*People might not even realize they want a separate layer for business rules.*

**Grady:** Absolutely. There's a delightful paper written by researchers at IBM called "The Diary of a Datum."* We keep adding these layers that perhaps to some degree help us as humans reason about and visualize these systems, but ultimately in the executability of our systems we're adding incredible layers. In "The Diary of a Datum," they point out we're looking at this simple piece of data, and it was astounding the numbers of ways that that data was transformed, streamed in, streamed out, cached, until something actually real was done to it. There's a cost to the layers of abstraction we add to our system.

*It seems to me that the average complexity and size of software keep growing year after year. Does OO help?*

**Grady:** If by OO you mean particular classes of languages, one could make the case that said languages are indeed more expressive than others and as such represent a higher level of abstraction (and so require fewer lines of code to represent something). If you mean OO as simply a philosophy of decomposition—as contrasted with algorithmic or functional abstractions—then you'd be back to one of Aristotle's issues in his text *Categories*: multiple forms of decomposition are really necessary to express complex things.

I'd observe the complexity is not proven to be isomorphic with size/lines of code. There is another kind of complexity, perhaps best measured by what I call *semantic density* (the ratio of meaning to expression and the measure of the semantic connections among things). Is semantic density increasing? Yes, I think so, but I think that's orthogonal with the means of expression—object-oriented or not—that we use to express such semantics.

*Concurrency in software is a big topic these days.*

**Grady:** It's been an issue for a long time. Simulated concurrency (multitasking) on single processors is an old concept, and the moment more then one computer existed in the world, people began to think about how to make those things work together. Today we have islands of computing, but more often than not, one has loosely coupled distributed concurrency (e.g., the Web) or intimate concurrency (multicore ships to massively parallel computers). In short, this has always been a "big topic" and, frankly, it's a really hard problem. The average developer does not know how to build distributed, concurrent, and secure systems, because these properties require systemic solutions.

*What about concurrency in development? Will we ever be able to reduce development time by adding more people?*

**Grady:** Again, I have to question the premise of your question.

"Reducing development time" is one possible benefit, but other viable ones are "improve quality," "increase functionality," "reduce complexity," and others are desirable results of

---

\* Mitchell, Nick et al. "The Diary of a Datum: Modeling Runtime Complexity in Framework-Based Applications," IBM Research (2007).

adding more people. It is pretty much undeniable that adding people increases available labor cycles but also increases noise, communication overhead, and project memory costs. The reality is that most economically interesting software—intensive systems simply require a goodly handful of people—and really interesting ones require hundreds if not more stakeholders. So, in some ways, you've asked an uninteresting question. :-)

## What limits the effectiveness of collaboration during software development?

**Grady:** My experience suggests that there are a number of points of friction in the daily life of the developer that individually and collectively impact the team's efficiency:

- The cost of startup and ongoing working space organization
- Inefficient work product collaboration
- Maintaining effective group communication, including knowledge and experience, project status, and project memory
- Time starvation across multiple tasks
- Stakeholder negotiation
- Stuff that doesn't work

I wrote about all this in the CDE papers found here: *http://www.booch.com/architecture/blog. jsp?part=Papers*.

## How do you recognize simplicity in a system?

**Grady:** Dave Parness asked me this very question. I wrote an article for our IEEE software recently in my column on architecture dealing with complexity and I started out saying, "Look at a huge multiton boulder of granite. It's huge but it's very simple. Look at a strand of DNA. It's small but it's very complex." Dave wrote me to challenge me on that saying, "Defend why you believe that's so." I quoted back to him some of the work that Herbert Simon has done in *The Sciences of the Artificial* [MIT Press]. Simon notes that if you look at complex systems, complex systems that we can understand tend to have a variety of characteristics in common. They tend to be hierarchical. They're layered in some way or another. There tends to be a tremendous amount of repetition within them.

Simon in his time saw that in terms of structural repetition. I'm going to update his notions to say it's not just repetition of the structures. It's also repetition of the design patterns we see within the system. Having had the opportunity to work with lots and lots of projects in just about every domain you might imagine, I've seen some really gorpy systems. I've seen some beautiful systems. The ones that tend to be beautiful and simple tend to have that commonality through a set of design patterns that transcend the system, that cut across many of the individual component, and offer tremendous simplicity to them.

In fact, if you look at where the folks in DNA research are headed, they're trying to find those common things. We, the royal we, thought there was all this junk encodens we'd find in DNA and we thought, "Oh, this is crap from evolutionary times and it's meaningless." As we dive into it deeper we realize, "Wow, this junk is not necessarily junk."

We called it junk because we didn't understand it. This is the God of the Gaps problem, but I won't get metaphysical on you on that one. As people in that space began to unpack the beautiful, fierce elegance within these systems, there's some amazing patterns that are emerging. That's where I find that simplicity and elegance.

### What do you mean by a "design pattern that transcends the system"?

**Grady:** I'll mention a Wall Street system. I won't mention its name. I went through an archeological dig with these guys recently and we were trying to mine some of the decisions they'd made. This is a huge system. Millions of lines of code written in every conceivable language you might imagine, from assembly language to contemporary languages of today. If you look at the overall architecture of the system, there are some guiding principles that are very common. There's a security aspect of this system. You really don't want people coming in and not knowing that they're doing it, shaving off a thousandth of a percent of a transaction. If you're doing a trillion dollars' worth of transactions every day, nobody's going to notice it.

How do you prevent that kind of thing? Very simple business rule. All state changing things must be in stored procedures in the database so that there can be no way, because this is checked through walkthroughs and a variety of formal mechanisms, there's no way you can inject code that has state-changing ways without doing that. That's a very simple, elegant principle that transcends all that code out there. It's things like that.

Design patterns are ultimately names of societies of classes that work together in a harmonious way. Just by looking at an individual line of code you can't see those kinds of things. That's the challenge of architectural mining, by the way, because the code's not the whole truth and being able to find those things and discover those patterns. It's often locked up in the heads of individuals.

### That almost implies that you can't always look at a system and understand and see its simplicity or see its underlying organization until you understand those constraints or rules or design decisions.

**Grady:** Absolutely. We have to learn by inference, too. You look at a whole bunch of these things and the patterns begin to emerge. You can't look at just one instance and say, "Wow, there's a pattern," because that's not the nature of the patterns themselves. This is one of the areas where I tend to use the UML a lot in visualizing the architecture of as-built systems. There's "green field" development out there, no doubt, but by and large most of the software in the world, to quote a term from Chris Winter, is "brown field." It sounds icky and malodorous. It is to some degree—but most of the interesting systems we build are systems that are adaptations or accretions upon existing systems.

### Maybe we should embrace the term "brown field development."

**Grady:** I think it's a great thing. It's not a bad thing at all. That's where UML comes into play for me because it allows me to visualize things that I can't see in just the individual code itself.

*It's a level of abstraction beyond that where these patterns can become obvious. I can imagine that if you're drawing diagrams or producing UML artifacts for an existing system, there's a very satisfying feeling when you can unify concepts.*

**Grady:** Absolutely.

*You (and many other interviewees) cited OO development as a major element of correct design. How much is it fundamental?*

**Grady:** This may sound very curious coming from me, but OO is, IMHO, an effect and not a first cause. Having had an opportunity to examine many complex systems in many domains, I observe that the best ones—most useful, most elegant, most cunning, most... whatever measure you may choose—have a number of common characteristics in their development, namely a focus on crisp abstractions, a good separation of concerns, and a balanced distributions of responsibilities. Abstraction is largely a problem of classification, and object-oriented mechanisms are particularly well suited to classifying the world.

*At OOPSLA about 20 years ago, Ward Cunningham and Kent Beck first proposed software design patterns, based on the work of the architect Christopher Alexander. Has that been a success, a moderate success?*

**Grady:** My personal opinion, not that of anybody living or dead or my company or anybody yet to be born, is that Alexander's work, I think, is interesting and it has been an inspiration for many in terms of its flow over into the software space. There's a small community that has, I think, benefited from it, but the large community has not. It's also the case that the language of patterns, while I find this in many places, it's probably not as dominant as it could be or should be.

*When you say language of patterns, do you mean something closer to what Alexander said, which was, "Let's create a vocabulary by which we can talk about recurring ideas of design"?*

**Grady:** Absolutely correct. In many of the industries in which I go into, many of the projects into which I go into, the notion of the Gang of Four patterns there might be a reading knowledge of it, but not an actual application to building their systems or their architectures. There are places where it has made a big difference, but it's not gotten as deeply into the roots of mainstream as I would have liked to see. It's not the specifics. It's the way of thinking about the problem.

*What might solve that?*

**Grady:** What I tend to do when I go into projects is help them develop a language of patterns. They need to understand. They need to get the working knowledge of what patterns are all about. Then I try to encourage them to find the patterns and name the patterns that they have developed themselves in their systems and start documenting them, making the patterns their own.

*Some of those patterns might reflect business rules and constraints.*

**Grady:** Some of them might not. It depends upon the nature of that domain. What are the unique value-added ways, the innovative ways they have solved their problems? Those are the design patterns.

I'm working with a satellite project right now. It's only about 50,000 lines of Ada. There are some amazing patterns that are potential, that exist in the minds of these developers. And the challenge has been getting to name those things so they can communicate them well. These are brilliant architects but insofar as you can't name a thing, then it's hard to talk about it and name it and manipulate it and communicate it to others.

*Let's take APL. Certain flows of data in there might not necessarily translate directly to other languages.*

**Grady:** Right. Ada is a wonderful language in so many ways. Look at the features that we see coming into Java and C++ and others. The issues of concurrency built into the language, exception mechanisms, generic mechanisms, abstract data types—Ada was ahead of its time.

# CHAPTER FIFTEEN

# Perl

Perl fans call it the "Pathologically Eclectic Rubbish Lister" and the "Swiss-Army Chainsaw", flaunting the motto, "There's More Than One Way to Do It!" Creator Larry Wall sometimes describes it as a kind of glue language, originally intended as a sweet spot between the Unix shell and C to help people get things done. It incorporates linguistic principles and design decisions from Unix (and sports perhaps the largest repository of libraries of any language in the CPAN). Many programmers anxiously await the long-developed revision of Perl 6, a language designed to last at least 20 years.

# The Language of Revolutions

*How do you define Perl?*

**Larry Wall:** Perl is an ongoing experiment in how best to incorporate some of the principles of natural language into computer language, not at a shallow syntactic level like COBOL, but at a much deeper pragmatic level. Some of the fundamental principles of human language are—well, here, let me paste you a list:

- Expressiveness is more important than learnability.

- It's quite OK to speak in "baby talk" if you happen to be a baby.

- A language can be useful even before you have learned the whole language.

- There are often several good ways to say roughly the same thing.

- Every linguistic utterance gets meaning from many contexts at once.

- Your language is agnostic about which context you should optimize for today.

- Your language does not enforce any particular paradigm in exclusion to others.

- Efficient communication requires a certain amount of linguistic complexity.

- Semantic networks do not generally map well into orthogonal spaces.

- Shortcuts abound; common expressions should be shorter than uncommon expressions.

- Not everything can be easy to express; it's OK if some things are hard but possible.

- Languages naturally have slots for verbs, nouns, adjectives, adverbs, etc.

- Humans are good at syntactic disambiguation when the slots are obvious.

- Languages are naturally punctuated by pauses, intonation, stress, pacing, etc.

- Languages make use of pronouns when the topic of conversation is apparent.

- Languages should ideally express solutions, not talk about their own constructs.

- Healthy culture is more important than specific technology to a language's success.

- The primary purpose of language is to communicate with people who are different from you.

- It's OK to speak with an accent as long as you can make yourself understood.

- Subcultures have special problems and often generate useful dialects or sublanguages.

- People learn to do "frame shifting" when confronting dialectic or accentual differences.

- Frame shifting is more efficient when you can easily tell which sublanguage you're dealing with.

- For any living language, evolution is not preventable over the long term.

- For most communication, worse-is-better is fine, but sometimes better-is-better is better.

- It's particularly important for written documents to be evaluated in historical context.

Each of these principles has had profound influence on the design of Perl over the years. Doubtless each of them could be expanded to a paragraph, or a chapter, or a dissertation. Even ignoring computer languages, linguistics is a huge field with many specialties.

On the other hand, most of these principles have largely been ignored in other computer languages. For various historical reasons, many language designers tend to assume that computer programming is an activity more akin to an axiomatic mathematical proof than to a best-effort attempt at cross-cultural communication.

To be sure, it also goes the other way—concentrating on these linguistic principles has upon occasion led me to ignore some important ideas from computer science. We're working on fixing some of those warts now.

### Which ideas are those?

**Larry:** One of the major places where we kind of fell down in the early design of Perl—or maybe I should be honest and say "I fell down"—is this notion of the proper scoping of things. True, Perl 5 does have lexical scopes for variables, but there are many places where it doesn't really quite have the right scoping. And it still has lots of global variables.

Perl 5 also has a lot of action-at-a-distance. Perl made much the same mistake that languages like Ruby are currently making with monkey typing, that is, reaching in and monkeying with the innards of things, which results in spooky action-at-a-distance.

We've learned that there are a number of different proper scopes for things. Classically we can attach information to an object or a lexical scope or a dynamic scope, of course, but we also have file scopes, process scopes, threads, types, metaclasses, roles, prototypes, events, grammars, and transactions, to name a few. You can even think of things like precedence levels as a strange kind of scope. Each location in space or time has things that are naturally associated or attached to it, and those things are misplaced if attached somewhere else. That's something that I've been learning slowly over time. Some would say too slowly.

Another principle is the importance of knowing which of your data structures are mutable and immutable. That's something that will become even more important in the coming years because of parallelism; you really cannot do a good job with concurrency unless you keep track of what might change when. That's something that Perl has historically swept under the carpet. We treated everything as mutable.

### Mutable even by observing it sometimes.

**Larry:** Yeah. It's a mindset that works well for small programs and naïve users—it doesn't violate the expectations of newcomers if they are not very sophisticated.

On the other hand, it does make it more difficult to scale up to programming in the large, where you have to pay more attention to mutable versus immutable, public versus private, the kinds of distinctions that let you know when you are allowed to change things and when you aren't. These sorts of things have become increasingly important in the design of Perl, especially with Perl 6.

At the same time, we want to try to keep the same feeling and, where possible, hide some of the high-falutin' concepts so that a new user can still pretty much ignore them. But just because they're hidden doesn't mean they aren't there; if Perl's really doing the right thing underneath, then we can at least have some hope of detecting when something is going wrong, and some hope of knowing when it is reasonable to spread the work out over multiple cores without worrying too much about things happening in a bad order. To do that, you have to track the data dependencies. That really implies knowing when a pointer can be treated as a value and when it must be treated as an object.

*Perl was born as a collection of tools to manipulate text and simplify the job of system administration. What is it now?*

**Larry:** Perl is actually two things right now. First, in its Perl 5 form, it's a very stable example of what it started out to be: an API glue language that is really good at text processing (augmented by vast quantifies of extensions lovingly crafted by a pathologically helpful culture). That's why the Web was largely prototyped in Perl—because HTML is text, and people wanted to write HTML that glued in data from various sources including databases. The extensions to do that were already there, or were easy to write.

But Perl is also Perl 6, where we're trying to fix everything that's wrong with Perl 5 without breaking anything that's right with Perl 5. We recognize that this is impossible, but we're going to do it anyway. We're completely redesigning the language while keeping the same underlying design principles.

Even in its current, partially implemented form, Perl 6 is already a spectacularly cool language in many people's opinion, and when it's done it will, hopefully, be both self-describing and self-parsing using highly derivable grammars, and thus optimized to evolve smoothly into any kind of a language we might want 20 years from now. It will come with knobs to adjust its many different dimensions, including the ability to hide all those dimensions that you aren't currently interested in thinking about, depending on which paradigm appeals to you to solve the problem at hand.

Well, that's our dream, anyway....

*How did you go from writing a tool to manipulate text and simplify the life of sysadmins to a complete programming language? Was this a deliberate step or a gradual transition?*

**Larry:** Hmm, those are not mutually exclusive, which is a good thing because I would characterize the process as a deliberate gradual transition. A language is a wonderful playground, and it was obvious to me from the start that I would continue to develop it into whatever I needed for "today". But of necessity such a process must be gradual, regardless of how deliberate it might be, if for no other reason than that you have to wait for "today" to change until you know what you'll really want next.

That being said, there was a point when I realized that Perl was not just about making easy things easy but also about making hard things possible. Perl 2 could only handle textual data, so I said to myself, "Perl is just a text-processing language; if I teach Perl how to handle binary data, who knows where it will stop?" Then I realized that there are a great many problems in the world that are mostly textual, but that require handling a little bit of binary data; adding solutions for that problem space would greatly increase the applicability of Perl, even if the handling of binary data was only rudimentary. So Perl 3 handled binary data, and who knows where it'll stop?

Also, I came to see all this as a continuation of my earlier notion that Perl wasn't going to have any arbitrary limits such as those that plagued early Unix tools. Truncating a string merely because it contains a accidental null character is just about as bad as truncating it because your buffer is too short. You might even say that the process of generalizing a language is simply the removal of various kinds of arbitrary limits, on one level or another.

*Do you prefer freedom or order? Do you prefer one way to do one thing, or a thousand ways to reach the same goal?*

**Larry:** That's not a terribly meaningful question unless you define what you mean by "way" and "reach", which optimizations you allow, and how the various permutations and combinations of options are allowed to multiply. Natural languages are like old-world cities where precious few of the streets meet at right angles, and there are typically several more or less decent ways to get where you're going. Obviously, if you count up all the possible ways to get somewhere, not just the best ones, you have might have a googolplex of them or more.

Even in a completely orthogonal city built on a strict rectangular grid, you can reach your destination in countless different ways, unless you constrain the solution to treat the dimensions as ordered, as in a mathematical vector giving a spatial location, and specify that you want a minimal path. But as a person, your motion in a city is not simply defined as a vector. You optimize for many different kinds of externalities as you navigate through a city or through a language. There may or may not be a single best solution, or a solution at one time of day may not be the right solution for a different time of day. You could optimize for visiting all the parks along the way, or you might just want to stay out of the river. Or in the river.

So, to actually answer your question, either of those extremes is suboptimal. I suspect the fractal dimensionality of natural language is rather larger than 1 but much, much smaller than 1,000. If you really only have one way to say something, then you could be replaced by a robot programmer. If you really have a thousand seemingly equivalent ways to do something, you'll very quickly come up with some kind of razor to trim the choices down to a manageable number at every choice point.

# Language

*Many people credit Perl for being very, very good at text processing. Is there a connection between that and the linguistic concerns you had in mind when you created the language?*

**Larry:** Ooh, that is a good question. One is tempted to say yes, and one would probably be wrong.

The telltale evidence is that, though it was designed to work on certain levels the same way a natural language works, Perl was really no good at parsing Perl code. (It used yacc for that.) I rather suspect that if the answer had been yes to your question then Perl 1 would've been much more aimed toward the sort of language parsing that Perl 6 is now aimed at. But it wasn't. Call it compartmentalization if you will, but the task that Perl 1 was trying to address was a much more limited form of text processing than what we do in our brains when we're thinking about natural language.

*I reviewed the test suite for Perl 1 a few years ago, and even then the code was recognizably Perlish, even considering that many Perlish notions such as context have evolved over time. How much of the intrinsic Perlishness did you have in mind from the start?*

**Larry:** Certainly the notion of context was important from the start, and Perl 4 even had a fairly well-developed notion of context. I think, however, that it only dawned on me gradually how important context is. As a linguist, I've always known about context; under tagmemics, one of my favorite linguistic theories, multiple levels of context are exceedingly important. How a word is classified lexically is very different from how you use it. You know "verb" is a noun even while you're verbing it. So I always had this notion floating around in my brain that you can put a particular construct to use in various ways driven not only by the construct's own structure and type, but also by its semantic and cultural context. I think where the contextual design actually shows up the most in early Perl is not so much in the low-level syntax of things like scalar versus list, but more in the notion that when you are trying to do a job, you are programming in the context of the thing you're trying to accomplish outside the program. Therefore, it is useful to have a language in which there are multiple ways to express things so that you can optimize for externalities.

*In other words, your program should represent the context of your problem more than trying to express the problem in the context of your language.*

**Larry:** Yes, the question is who's to be master, that's all. There will usually be a number of different ways of representing a particular problem, especially if you consider the various programming paradigms. Some of those will more naturally map to some problem spaces, and others will more naturally map to other problem spaces. If you're thinking of your problem as some sort of a mathematical proof, then something more like functional programming is better, something more declarative, where things have universal meaning that never changes—you know, when there's a lot of immutable state built into the concepts you're directly working with. But if you are doing something more like a simulation, then you will be thinking of the problem more in terms of objects that change over time. For a given problem that you're trying to solve, these may be provably isomorphic views, but the different programming paradigms force you into placing your mutable state in one place or another. It's obvious where the state is in objects; that's what objects are for. It's not so obvious where the state is in functional programming—the state is implicitly hidden in the stack and in the way the various monads and function calls have been arranged.

So, one form of context is how you prefer to view such things as a programmer.

It's sort of a weak Sapir-Whorf hypothesis. I don't believe in the strong version of that....

*You were predestined not to believe in strong.*

**Larry:** Yeah. I chose to be predestined. Or maybe it's just that my brain is not wired linguistically in the first place, so I do a lot of nonlinguistic thinking. And therefore I don't think language has control of my brain. Be that as it may, the weaker form of the hypothesis is fine by me: the language in which you choose to express something certainly has some influence on how you choose to express it. Therefore, if you actually want to have a single language that has a better impedance match with many different kinds of problems, then you need a language that does not, in fact, force you to think in any one particular way.

*There are several subtle contexts: the Unix one-liner, where you can express a useful, working Perl program. There's the shell-script context, where you have what looks like a shell script with all of the power of Perl 5 behind it. There's the standalone single-page CGI program context. To some degree, it is a different context for getting things done. You can recognize it both as distinctly Perl and distinctly that style. It's a Perl one-liner or it's a shell script written in Perl.*

**Larry:** In linguistic theory, we call that "pragmatics," a step or two away from semantics toward sociology. Some linguists tend to focus down on the low-level phonology or syntax. You see the same tunnel vision in many computer language designs; the designers haven't really thought much about how utterances are used to do practical things. If you're talking in terms of one-liners and shell scripts, essentially you see the same sorts of things happening in natural language. There are utterances that you can say to somebody at the bus stop that are one-liners that communicate. English is full of pithy utterances. At the other extreme, there are all sorts of literary genres that you might think of as comparable to programming paradigms. There are various levels of discipline that you can exercise in composing literary efforts. These genres have various rules that you are allowed to break from time to time. And sometimes you'd be stupid to break them, but the language itself is not trying to enforce any one particular style.

Natural language is neutral on that score. Language is the servant of the poet—it's the artistic medium in which the artist is trying to do Something Else. That Something Else is what is driving the whole process and should rightfully drive the whole process.

There's a sense in which natural languages are extremely humble. They don't tell you how you have to talk. Your grammar school teacher told you how you have to talk, but by and large, people ignore that, and it's a good thing.

Nevertheless, there are the equivalent of grammar school teachers for computer languages, and for certain kinds of utterances, you should follow the rules unless you know why you're breaking them. All that being said, computer languages also have to be understandable to computers. That imposes additional constraints. In particular, we can't just use a natural language for that, because in most cases when we're communicating with natural language, we are assuming an extreme intelligence on the hearing end who will in turn assume extreme intelligence on the speaking end. If you expect such intelligence from a computer, then you'll be sorely disappointed because we don't know how to program computers to do that yet.

*Even though Perl is the first postmodern computer language, computers are really bad at understanding irony.*

**Larry:** Indeed. They really don't understand when they should ask for feedback. That's because they don't understand when they should be unsure. Mind you, there's a lot of people who do not understand when they should be unsure either, but it's a matter of degree there. Computers are very quickly promoted to the level of their incompetence.

*You've often said something to the effect that computer language designers should pay a lot more attention to linguists than mathematicians because linguists actually know how to communicate with people.*

**Larry:** Let's just say they know how real people communicate.

Mathematicians know how to communicate with each other, but that doesn't say whether you want to consider mathematicians to be real people or not; I'm sure the mathematicians could find some way in terms of set theory to decide that they are real. Nonetheless, I think that linguists pay a little bit more attention to psychology and pragmatics than mathematicians usually do. So maybe linguists can help computers get a little bit smarter about those things.

*Do you believe that the idea of a small, rigorous, and provable model of a programming language may not work in the real world where people have to work with it?*

**Larry:** There will always be some subset of people who are willing to pour their minds through very small funnels. To the extent that you can find people who are willing to do that, a given language will be successful for the problem space that it is intended, barring other catastrophes.

It is not necessarily the case that the opposite holds. A language that is large enough may not achieve success for a number of reasons. It may be too difficult to implement. It may be too difficult to get people over the hump of learning a useful subset. I suppose those are the two main difficulties in getting a larger language accepted.

Nonetheless, none of the computer languages that have been invented so far come anywhere close to the complexity of natural language, I think. And people are demonstrably willing—well, perhaps not Americans—let's say that most people who do not speak English are demonstrably willing to learn multiple languages.

I've tried learning several natural languages, and they're really hard. The lexical complexity, the strange grammatical rules that vary from language to language, the ways in which languages make you think about things in different orders, the way some languages make you say things that other languages don't make you say and vice versa, and so on. It's difficult to learn a natural language. The question is, can one actually make a computer language that is rich enough that people are willing to cross that learning barrier? Can the language be made such that people can usefully learn a pidgin subset of it? We see how pidgins and creoles arise in natural language when people are sufficiently motivated to find a common language somehow.

Can we tap into that dynamic? Can we design the language such that it is no more complicated than it really needs to be? Those are all really good questions that every language designer answers differently. Perl has hierarchical namespaces, but some computer languages just have a flat namespace and put everything into one lexicon. Arguably, English does that. Especially if your name is Webster or Johnson.

### English does support the notion of jargons and implicit communication forms.

**Larry:** Certainly it does. That points out the notion of lexical scoping that is so important to the control of language diversity in Perl 6. It's very important to us at every point in the lexical scope to know exactly which language we are speaking. Not so much because it's important to the human; it is, but the human is smart enough to puzzle it out eventually. The compiler probably isn't that smart, so it's crucially important to the compiler to keep track of which language it's parsing.

If we can keep the compiler from getting confused, I suspect we can keep the people from getting confused, too. Different lexical scopes, different passages in literature—different frames, as they call them in psycholinguistics—use different languages. People do frame shifting all the time. They know when to talk casual, and they know when to speak properly. People make adjustments all the time without being aware of it. It's part of the toolbox of natural language.

*How do you know if the problem you are trying to solve requires a tool or a language to be solved?*

**Larry:** That's really a fuzzy boundary; the notion of single tool blends into the notion of sets of tools, and I suppose you can view a language as a set of tools, so it's not a hard and fast distinction. Is a Swiss Army knife one tool or many?

Perhaps a more important distinction is how well the set of tools plays together. The Swiss Army knife may be a handy set of tools, but it's rather difficult to use multiple bits of it at the same time.

I'd say that languages tend to differ from tools or even sets of tools in how general they *can* be (though of course there are special-purpose languages as well as general-purpose). While a language can be viewed as a mere tool, languages really excel at putting ideas together in unforeseen ways. If your problem requires such composability, and is not overly penalized by the linear nature of language, then defining a language can be a good choice for solving your specific problem—or at least some reasonable subset of your problem.

Beyond that first problem, your language may subsequently provide you with a machine shop that you can make other tools with more easily, and to the extent that it does so, you've improved your life in a permanent way. Sometimes, knowing that in advance, you go out of your way to invent a language even though it might no be the fastest route to solving the first problem you apply it to. But if you're Truly Lazy, you'll figure out how to amortize the extra effort over all the eventual uses of the language.

*How does a language change as it starts to move away from a specialized domain? It may be fair to characterize earlier versions of Perl as a cleaned-up dialect of Unix designed as an API for gluing things together. How does a language change when it moves from a specific purpose like that to something more general?*

**Larry:** In my experience, when you have a domain-specific language like that, you have various constructs which feel very natural but are all, in some sense, defined in an ad hoc fashion. They feel more rational than they perhaps are.

*Is that the human brain trying to make connections with things?*

**Larry:** Yes, and when that happens people will leap to conclusions that don't necessarily follow. You end up with a large set of Frequently Asked Questions. If you look at the Perl set of Frequently Asked Questions, there's quite a few of them, which could be construed as evidence for this process of what you might call false generalization. When you are evolving a language into a more general-purpose language, you go back and look at all of those places and you say "Why did people generalize that way? Should the language have supported that? What are the minimal changes that we can make to how it actually works underneath that will actually do what they expect rather than what they don't expect?"

That process to the *n*th degree is, as you know, the Perl 6 design process. We've been in that mindset for the past few years.

## Can you give an example?

**Larry:** In Perl 5, $var is a scalar, @var is an array, and %var is an associative array. New users often generalize that to think that @var[$index] and %foo{$key} are how you write the indexed forms, but for historical reasons that's not how Perl 5 does it. The documents go through contortions to explain why things aren't the way people expect. In Perl 6, we decided it would be better to fix the language than fix the user.

In Perl 5, various functions default to an argument of $_ (the current topic) if no argument is supplied, and you basically have to memorize the list of functions that do so. If you don't, you're likely to falsely generalize that capability to all functions. In Perl 6, we chose to not have any functions default that way, so there is no longer any danger of false generalization. Instead there is some lightweight but explicit syntax for calling a method on the current topic.

Any time your language compels you to memorize an arbitrary list, the very arbitrariness of the list indicates that someone will think certain things should be in the list that aren't, or vice versa. These things tend to creep into your design gradually. When Unix culture first invented their regular-expression syntax, there were just a very few metacharacters, so they were easy to remember. As people added more features to their pattern matches, they either used up more ASCII symbols as metacharacters, or they used longer sequences that had previously been illegal, in order to preserve backward compatibility. Not surprisingly, the result was a mess. You could see the false generalization right there in many programs; panicking users would backslash anything symbolic in a regex because they couldn't remember which characters were actual metacharacters. In Perl 6, as we were refactoring the syntax of pattern matching we realized that the majority of the ASCII symbols were already metacharacters anyway, so we reserved all of the nonalphanumerics as metacharacters to simplify the cognitive load on the programmer. There's no longer a list of metacharacters, and the syntax is much, much cleaner.

## One word that I use to describe Perl's design is "syncretic." You pick and choose good bits from other places and try to combine them in a coherent whole. How do you balance syncretism with the idea of generality of ideas and coherence between ideas and features?

**Larry:** Badly, some would say.

It is the sad plight of language designers that they can only go by their gut feelings on how to balance those.

## History doesn't support experiments very well.

**Larry:** Agreed, at least in general. It has been a rare privilege in the Perl space to actually have a successful experiment called Perl 5 that would allow us to try a different experiment that is called Perl 6.

We're actively looking to strike a different balance this time based on what we've learned. Certainly, many bad guesses were made, if not in terms of feature set, at least in terms of what the default behavior should be for a given feature. We want to make different mistakes this time.

It will be interesting to see if it works. When we taught people earlier versions of Perl, we had to do a lot of explaining why things had to be the way they were. Now we have to come back and say, "Well, what we were thinking back then was wrong. Which means what you're thinking now is wrong." It becomes an interesting cultural problem whether and to what extent you can lead people out of where you led them into. To use a Biblical metaphor, you led them into Egypt, now you're trying to lead them back out to the Promised Land.

Some people will follow you, and some people will hanker for the leeks and onions.

## Community

*You've always encouraged the community to participate in design and implementation. Was this a necessity for getting things done? Is it a reflection of your style of work or your sense of aesthetics?*

**Larry:** I'm sure it must be a combination of factors.

Certainly the early motivation for building a community is simply to have people both giving you positive and negative feedback. Preferably positive, but the negative also helps.

From a linguistics perspective, a language that has a very small community of speakers is not going to do very well. It was pretty obvious on that level that a community certainly helps the vitality of a project.

More than that, I just wanted my stuff to be used by lots of people because I like to help people. As things progressed, the project got large enough that I needed help, too. About the end of Perl 4, I realized that things were diverging in all directions, and people were compiling up different versions of the Perl executable. It was obvious at that point that Perl was going to need a modular extension mechanism, and that various people would be in charge of various modules.

Pretty soon after Perl 5 itself came out, it became quite clear that even Perl itself was getting too large for any one person to perform as integration manager (let alone designer) for any extended period of time, without completely burning out. That job needed to be handed off. Basically, I figured out in the early stages of Perl 5 that I needed to learn to delegate. The big problem with that, alas, is that I haven't a management bone in my body.

I don't know how to delegate, so I even delegated the delegating, which seems to have worked out quite well. I don't make people do things, but other people step up and exert management force in appropriate directions and come up with to-do lists and coordinate other people. It's been interesting to see that despite my inability to micromanage, or maybe because of my inability to do so, the community is in some ways healthier for it.

It's possible I do have one management skill: I've never hesitated to tell people what they should do, though usually in such abstract terms that they haven't the foggiest idea what I'm talking about.

*You said that you aren't interested in being a manager and you don't think you have capabilities to do so. Yet still you guide the Perl community. Is that your most important job, or do you just want people to get along and you're willing to do what it takes and necessary?*

**Larry:** I probably want people to get along on a slightly deeper level than Rodney King. Mostly I think it's my job to notice when things are kind of going a little wrong and just put a little pressure to keep them from going wronger where I can. I don't often get to the point of having to take drastic actions; only once have I ever called up someone in the Perl community on the phone and yelled at them.

It worked, by the way.

Certainly I think if my management skills were stronger, I would be able to minimize some of the corrosive currents that do, in fact, flow through portions of Perl culture. There are places in Perl Town you shouldn't go after dark, but not even the most benevolent and omniscient and omnipotent ruler can tell everyone what they ought or ought not to do all the time.

Arguably, not even God tries to do that with us. As He says in *Time Bandits*, "I think it has something to do with free will."

*One of the greatest successes of Perl 5 is the CPAN, and that seems to me to be the primary form of extensibility. Did you make specific design decisions to encourage such a thing to form or was it a serendipitous accident of history?*

**Larry:** Well, as usual with this sort of historical question, the answer is yes, I did, and no, I didn't.

It was fairly implicit in the design of the modular system that various people would come up with modules and publish them, and even that there would be repositories of these modules. Other languages have had repositories of reusable software of various sorts. What, of course, I did not anticipate was the scale of the thing and the sheer wackiness of the things that people hooked Perl up to.

From the very beginning, it's always been my concern to try to make Perl talk to as many different APIs as possible, whether that's shell or the environment variables or the operating system directly or the terminal. I was the first person to hack in an XML parser. It's always been important to me at various stages that Perl be a language that is not trying to pull everything into itself, but to connect to the outside world in as many ways as possible. That's the essence of a glue language. Contrast that with a language like Icon, which has tried to define everything internally in an insular fashion.

Now, I don't want to oversimplify; to a greater or lesser extent, all languages reinvent at least part of the wheel.

There's always this pressure to have solutions in 100% Perl or 100% Java or 100% whatever. That simplifies things like configuration and testing. That makes distribution nicer. It may make it easier to hire programmers. On the other hand, if your language is entirely that way and your culture is entirely that way, it's really a damaging form of hubris.

There needs to be a balance. Perl has always tried to err on the side of too many external APIs rather than too few. But it's best to support both approaches.

I built in these philosophies of connectivity and pragmatics. I did not anticipate the scale of the thing when the World Wide Web came about. Perl really took off in a way that I had never anticipated, but in a sense it was implicit there, too.

*You deliberately put mechanisms in place to enable that serendipity to happen or to exploit that when it happened.*

**Larry:** For some definition of deliberate, which may or may not be left-brained or right-brained, hind-brained or fore-brained or mid-brained. Usually pretty scatter-brained. Certainly a lot of this is "out-brained" in the sense of a great deal of the contribution of Perl from the beginning has been from brains outside of my own brain.

*Many languages have library repositories, but CPAN has an advantage in that the implementors (Jarkko, Andreas, et al.) built just enough infrastructure to encourage development without constraining it. Were there features of the language or community you encouraged which made that possible?*

**Larry:** I can't take responsibility for the good choices of the CPAN implementors (or the bad ones either), but I will say that I think CPAN hit some kind of a sweet spot in the application of Sturgeon's Law ("90% of everything is crud."). Especially when you're prototyping something new, it's easy to overdesign it to try to keep out most of the 90% code, with the result that you keep out most of the 10% code as well. Certainly we've seen some of that cruddy code later evolve to be not-so-cruddy, so it often pays to be patient and take the worse-is-better approach. And some people are just late bloomers. We're all learning as we go.

As for what made it possible in the language, that was probably the most important design goal of Perl 5: to allow anyone to extend the language via modules. From the viewpoint of Perl 6 hindsight, I botched the design of Perl 5 modules in various ways, but it was Good Enough, and CPAN was the result. I suppose I also said a few things now and then to encourage the community in that endeavor, though only in the most general of terms. By and large, however, it really just comes down to the fact that most Perl developers are pathologically helpful people. I waved the flag a bit at the start to help nucleate the process, but people mostly just brought themselves to the party and stayed because they found some kindred spirits. And it delights me to see that cooperative spirit spreading to other communities as well.

*Were there surprising community contributions?*

**Larry:** I don't know if there really were or not. I suppose maybe the whole culture of mandatory strictness and warnings was a bit of a surprise to me—people asking for more discipline than was given by default. It became culturally acceptable to the point where we decided to just build it into Perl 6. That was kind of a small surprise.

The biggest surprise to me came when we went to start redesigning Perl for Perl 6. We asked for suggestions in the form of RFCs (Request For Change), and I expected to get maybe 20. We got 361. Part of the surprise was in how much pain there actually was, approximately 15 times more than I expected. The double whammy was how many different things that people thought could be fixed in isolation, which really couldn't be. So the need for a systematic redesign was the biggest surprise from the community for me over the last 20 years. I have also been surprised (positively) at the success of some of the cultural hacks. The original dual-licensing hack in Perl 3 has stood Perl in very good stead, both among the hacker communities who were afraid of corporate culture and the corporate culture that was afraid of the hacker communities.

Both communities found reassurances in that approach without me ever actually having to force anybody to decide whether they were actually following the GPL or the Artistic License.

*I've almost never seen anyone ever actually choose which one they were following.*

**Larry:** Yeah. It was a quantum superposition of licenses that people just didn't observe. I suppose I've been negatively surprised by the fact that we coined the term *dual licensing* for that, and it has since come to mean forcing the user to pick one license or another. You never can coin a term and make it mean what you want it to mean. There's always this dance between what you think you can get and what you can actually get.

## Evolution and Revolution

*In software design and development, what is your approach: evolution or revolution?*

**Larry:** I'm a bear-of-very-little-brain in some ways, so I personally take an evolutionary approach when I'm programming. When developing a Perl program I typically make a change, run it, make another change, with a cycle time of maybe 30 seconds. I don't spend much time debugging because it's usually pretty obvious whether the last thing I did was right or wrong. Every now and then I refactor, but that also tends to be evolutionary, alternating between making a change and making sure that nothing really changed.

As far as language design is concerned, my basic approach has always been similar: to take an evolutionary approach, but "rev up" the mutation rate so that if you took two snapshots far enough apart, it would look like a revolutionary change.

To Unix lovers, Perl 1 looked like a radical change from awk and sed and shell, but actually a great deal of Unix culture was distilled down into Perl at that point in order to keep it acceptable to people. Any new language has to worry about migration, so new languages tend to borrow heavily from existing languages. (We have since regretted some of that borrowed culture; in particular, regex syntax has only gotten cruftier over the years, and Perl 6 will remedy that, we hope.)

To many people, Perl 5 looked like a revolutionary change from Perl 4, but in fact the implementation evolved through various intermediate forms that the outside world never saw. At one point, some of the opcodes were interpreted by the old "stackful" interpreter while others were interpreted by the new "stackless" one. Perl 5 was also still very conservative in its backward compatibility; in fact, Perl 5 still runs most Perl 1 scripts correctly.

With Perl 6 we're finally making a major compatibility break, "throwing out the prototype," as it were, and rapidly evolving the syntactic and semantic design while attempting to preserve the underlying "feel" that makes Perl what it has always been. This time, though, I've done a better job of involving the community in the incremental redesign process.

When we first announced the Perl 6 effort, we got those 361 RFCs, and most of them assumed an incremental change from Perl 5 without any other changes. In a sense, the Perl 6 design is simply the result of summing up, simplifying, unifying, and rationalizing those incremental suggestions, but the actual leap from Perl 5 to Perl 6 will certainly feel revolutionary to anyone who did not participate in the design process. Yet most Perl 6 programs will look quite similar to what you'd write in Perl 5, because the underlying thought process will be similar. At the same time, Perl 6 will also make it much easier to branch out into the functional or OO modes of thought, if that's how you think. Some people will think that's revolutionary.

To me, revolutions are mostly just people pretending they didn't go through all the intermediate steps. Perl is designed to help people go through the intermediate steps as expeditiously as possible so they can pretend to be revolutionaries, which is fun.

### What revolution is this?

**Larry:** I'm talking about private revolutions here. The revolution that happens when somebody who doesn't know Perl comes up to a Perl programmer and says, "I'm trying to do this and I don't know how." And the Perl programmer says, "Oh, that's easy. Here," and writes a little program that is both obvious and fast enough and gets the job done, and the person says, "Oh, cool." Whenever someone says, "Oh, cool," it's a little revolution.

In a sense, it's a continuum from evolution to revolution in it's just how loudly you say, "Oh, cool"—or if you happen to be the aristocracy, "Oh, crap." A good revolution has more people saying "Oh, cool," than "Oh, crap."

I guess I really believe that there can be good revolutions. Maybe that goes back to theology, too, at least on a personal level. I believe that, given the proper nudge, people can reorient themselves drastically in a short period of time.

*Whether they intend to or not.*

**Larry:** Yes. It's like the difference between modern scientists and the Greek philosophers who were trying to puzzle everything out from first principles. They eked out a certain amount of knowledge, but without empirical testing you don't get the unintentional discoveries of science where the serendipitous results come in and knock you upside the head and completely subvert the way you were thinking before in a very nice way.

*Perl 5 on the Web, for example.*

**Larry:** Perl 5 on the Web. Also arguably many of the intermediate forms that crawled onto land or crawled into holes when asteroids hit or any number of other contingencies that existence has thrust upon our ancestry. There's just these general principles that you should be open to, both the small steady improvements and the large epiphanies.

*Are these large epiphanies inductive? That reminds me of the lambda calculus where you start with four or five separate principles, then reason and deduct your way to the world of usable Turing completeness.*

**Larry:** Yeah, but reality usually whacks us by hitting us at a different scale than we were expecting. I might be optimizing for maintaining my current body temperature in a very benign climate, but sometimes asteroids come in size XXXL. Induction will help you with the gradual revelations. It just does not necessarily help you anticipate the changes that will occur when large numbers of your premises are cut out from under you. That's when you want to have a large gene pool. Genes are the tools in your toolbox, and you want lots of them, especially in asteroid context.

*You want to give people tools to use to adapt to new circumstances if they find themselves in those situations.*

**Larry:** It's the whole mutable versus immutable thing again. Induction is built on the notion that your premises are immutable.

*Induction or deduction?*

**Larry:** Both. I think they are kind of two sides of the same coin, and sometimes the coin lands on the edge. Probability theory assumes the probability of that is zero. But it isn't; I've done it myself. It was a most amazing thing. I was a kid playing football with my neighbor, and we were flipping a coin. He said, "Call it." I said, "Edge." And it came down on edge, because it wedged in between the stiff blades of grass. Sometimes context trumps probability theory.

I guess the story of my life has been calling "edge" and being right a good part of the time.

*What's your rationale behind the notion of potentially multiple competing or cooperating implementations of Perl 6?*

**Larry:** There are several parts to the rationale for that. We already mentioned that you want a large gene pool. A healthy gene pool requires the exchange of lots of genes, which can be fun. Another reason is that the different implementations will tend to keep each other honest. Different people will naturally view the specification in different ways and if there's any ambiguity in a specification, they will likely discover it. Then it becomes a process of negotiation among the various implementations as to what the spec really ought to mean.

*That sounds like a parenting strategy: "First, you cut the cake in half, and then your brother picks which slice he wants."*

**Larry:** Yeah. It's a way of foisting off some of the design work onto the implementers, which is a necessity for somebody who is as lousy a designer as I am.

Another facet of the multiple implementation strategy is that people's interests vary. They will want to prototype different parts of the implementation first. Rather than writing half of a project and then discovering that you've made assumptions that make it very difficult to implement the other half because nobody's ever really tried to do it, it's better if different people are playing around with prototypes of the different aspects of the design and can then share with each other the danger points.

We've just seen this in the last week or two with the SMOP folks who really don't have a lot by way of implementation yet, but they're thinking very detailed ways about exactly how lists and captures and signatures and all of these crucial concepts really play together at a low level, and how laziness and iterators and arrays actually ought to work semantically.

It's one of those scientific simplifications: we'll ignore the whole rest of the problem and just examine this particular aspect of it. I think that's very valuable in forcing us to think through the design in places that we haven't thought through yet.

*Is this because they're intended to be full implementations or because someone's prototyping specific parts?*

**Larry:** I almost don't care. If somebody is prototyping a portion of the implementation, it's really up to them how far they want to run with that—how much energy they have, how many other people they can recruit to the effort. That's another example of my delegating the delegation to other people. A new continent has opened up, and people need to explore in every direction.

*By not blessing one potential implementation, you are actually encouraging experimentation.*

**Larry:** Yeah, we're encouraging a flooding algorithm, which is not really what you necessarily want to do if you're someone like a corporation. Instead, you design a project with one major goal in mind, and you have a particular burn rate and it has to be done on such-and-such a date. But the fact is, we've got this great parallel processor called the open source community, and flooding algorithms seem to scale rather nicer to parallel hardware than to serial hardware. But it's not a stupid flooding algorithm; it's more like an ant colony seeking food. So really we're just optimizing the process to the engine that we'll be running on. It's not a symmetric multiprocessor—more like a Beowulf cluster of hackers. And hackers are not all the same architecture.

*Shared memory is also a problem, especially when the state is so immutable.*

**Larry:** It's not just memory—the open source community is a Non-Uniform Everything Architecture, but I think that our approach is playing to the strengths of that rather than the weaknesses of it. And certainly shared memory doesn't seem to be a big problem for the ants.

*Does any particular implementation of Perl 6 constrain what happens at higher semantic levels?*

**Larry:** Well, even if you try to create a Newspeak, no language can exert absolute control over everything, and implementations are just one of the things that a language can't have absolute control over. To the extent that we try to exercise control, the definition of the language really comes down to what we choose to include in the test suite, or exclude from it, and I think those sorts of decisions should primarily be the result of negotiation among the various implementors, with occasional input from the language designer. This is one of the reasons we think it's important to have multiple implementations, because they tend to wear off each other's rough edges.

*Do you have particular concerns about the availability of resources?*

**Larry:** I think that different locuses of effort tend to be self-limiting anyway in terms of how big they can scale usefully. When programming teams they get bigger than six or twelve people, they end up dividing themselves into different subprojects anyway. It's really only a resource drain to the extent that people are reinventing wheels identically without looking at the other work that's going on.

To the extent that they are reinventing wheels differently; well, that's an interesting experiment in widening the gene pool. Certainly, there is some inefficiency in any approach you take. Whether that is amortized across the world of programmers simultaneously or whether it's something that comes back and bites you later because you couldn't do everything first, there's going to be inefficiencies any way you work the project.

There's some argument that spreading the inefficiencies across the world of hackers is actually likelier to get it done sooner than if you try to serialize it. Always assuming you have enough hackers to throw at the problem, and that the problem is parallelizable, and that you can get the volunteers talking to each other.

*You can't tell volunteers what to do. You can, but it doesn't work.*

**Larry:** That's the other major thing. They're going to do whatever they want anyway. So as the saying goes, if you can't fix it, feature it.

*I really like the quote from you: "They say worse is better, but we're just hoping for one better-is-better cycle here with Perl 6."*

**Larry:** Right. That's my current "edge" call. I hope you're feeling edgy.

# CHAPTER SIXTEEN

# PostScript

PostScript is a concatenative programming language most commonly used to describe documents for desktop and electronic publishing. John Warnock and Charles Geschke invented the language after founding Adobe Systems in 1982. Apple's LaserWriter shipped with PostScript in 1985, making desktop publishing possible. PostScript quickly became the de facto standard for document interchange. Since then, its successor PDF has supplanted PostScript in that realm.

# Designed to Last

*How do you define PostScript?*

**Charles Geschke:** PostScript is a programming language whose primary purpose is to provide a high-level description of the content of (printed) pages in a device-independent representation.

**John Warnock:** PostScript is an interpretive programming language that emulates a simple, stack-oriented virtual machine. In addition to the normal operators found in most programming languages, PostScript has a very rich set of image, graphic, and font rendering operators. With PostScript, an application can emit PostScript commands in a resolution-independent manner that will define the appearance of a printed page (or display).

I think PostScript was successful because it is so flexible and has a well-defined underlying imaging model. Other printer protocols of the time attempted to statically define pages with data structures. These protocols invariably would fail at describing some intuitively simple pages.

*What made you create the language PostScript and not a data format? A printer's going to interpret this; what's the effective difference between a language and a data format anyway?*

**John:** When we started doing this at Xerox PARC there was a language called JaM. We were doing research in graphics and wanted an interpretive language where you could run very quick experiments to try things out, and interface into the hardware of the Alto at that time and into the programming interfaces in the Alto, and do experiments without having to go through a huge compile cycle and a lot of program try, program compile, assemble, load, try. We used an interpretive language, and it turned out to be very effective in trying out lots of new ideas.

**Charles:** What this allows you to do over time is if you decide that there are certain key things that you've evolved in your language that are not nearly efficient enough to run interpretatively, you can codify them into a set of extensions to the language by introducing new operators and implement them at a much lower level so that they run more efficiently.

Really the whole idea of language was because we didn't know what kind of devices, what kind of environments, and to a certain extent what new opportunities there would be in the future with the way we would want to control and describe the appearance of a printed page. This gave us an ultimate flexibility that you could never get from data structures.

It has the same operations and controls that other Turing-complete languages contain but, of course, the Church-Turing thesis observes that it cannot be mathematically proven.

**John:** There are many instances of command protocols in our industry that are not full programming languages. It was our judgment at the time, that because how a protocol is used is always open-ended and unknown, a full programming language would allow use to program our way out of things we forgot or did not anticipate. This "completeness" allowed PostScript to have a longevity that even we did not anticipate.

*One of the benefits of a concatenative language is that if you do need to codify a new feature, you can do that in hardware on certain platforms and you can emulate it in software for older platforms. If you define a new word, you can define that word in terms of other word primitives in the language so it runs on older machines, but if you need to have support for that word in the interpreter, you can add it in newer versions. Is that right?*

**Charles:** Yes.

**John:** We actually made it so that even the primitive operators could be redefined. The add instruction can be redefined in PostScript to do anything you want it to do. That piece of flexibility actually made PDF possible because we defined the primitive graphic operators to grab their operand stack and put that out as a static data structure as opposed to retaining the programmatic nature of PostScript.

*Was this partly to work around the possibility of bugs in ROM?*

**John:** Absolutely.

**Charles:** At the time it was produced, the LaserWriter had the largest amount of software ever codified in a ROM.

*Half a megabyte?*

**John:** Yes.

*Was this standard practice at the time?*

**John:** This was a huge piece of software to put in a piece of masked ROM. If you had bugs, you better get yourself some escape hatches. Having to be a programming language where you could really program around errors was extremely useful.

**Charles:** Any project of this sophistication you have to go in with the knowledge that there will be and are bugs. You can't somehow cross your fingers and hope that won't be true.

Basically we put in the mechanism to allow us to patch around bugs, because if you had tens of thousands or hundreds of thousands of printers out there, you couldn't afford to set out a new set of ROMs every month.

**John:** At the cost of masked ROMs in those days, you couldn't afford to send them out at all.

*Was hardware a consideration at the time, beyond the necessity to have a piece of hardware?*

**John:** No, the original language happened at a company called Evans & Sutherland. We were building these huge graphic projection simulators and when the spec for the project came around the hardware wasn't built yet and yet we had to build the databases for this. We had to leave ourselves lots of room to do late binding. The late binding property is just so important because you didn't have an idea of how this thing would evolve and what your target machine would be.

**Charles:** John, you might tell him a little bit about the database. It was the entire port of New York.

**John:** It was all the buildings in Manhattan—not all the buildings in Manhattan, but the skyline of Manhattan, the Statue of Liberty, and it was to train people to bring tankers into the port of New York. It was a miracle project because it got executed in about a year.

*That's a lot of data.*

**John:** It was a lot of data, especially when we were dealing with essentially PDP 15s. They were teeny, teeny, teeny, teeny machines in comparison. You had 32K bytes of memory.

*The leap to a laser printer must have seemed like a luxury.*

**John:** Even the laser printer at the time was the biggest processor that Apple had ever built. For them this was a huge piece of processing equipment. Then they already had the Mac interfaces to the graphics.

We actually used the PostScript programming language to build a sympathetic interface in some sense to their graphics interface so that we could take their data structures and do the equivalent thing in PostScript and those were PostScript programs.

The Mac was just a 256K Mac or a 512K Mac at that point and it had really very little flexibility in what it could do with Mac Draw and what it could do with Write at that time. The LaserWriter actually downloaded a whole set of programs to interpret their commands.

*Did the Mac produce PostScript at that point?*

**John:** It was producing PostScript, but it was sort of the quick-draw version of PostScript.

**Charles:** Right; it was producing PostScript, but through a set of PostScript subroutines that took in Quick Draw and spit out PostScript. Those macros or subroutines were actually running in the printer.

*Did you make changes to PostScript as you supported more devices?*

**John:** We had a hard thing that we had to have laser printers. We did finally port Post-Script to a dot-matrix printer.

**Charles:** It wasn't the most satisfying project.

**John:** No, it wasn't.

*What is like to think in two dimensions (graphically) at the very foundation of a language?*

**Charles:** One must have designed in the mechanisms to support two-dimensional transformations that allow the programmer to program in his/her own coordination system but ultimately transform that space to the coordinate system of the actual device.

**John:** I think it is easy to think in two dimensions when you imagine each two-dimensional construct as being drawn (or imaged) by a subroutine. One of the successes of PostScript is that each object or set of objects can be wrapped in its own coordinate system. By doing this, objects can be instanced around the page in different sizes and orientations without regard to the details within. This simple idea makes it easy to think about how to make up a page or portion of a page.

*You are mathematicians by training. How did your background help during the design of PostScript?*

**Charles:** In terms of understanding the transformational logic of the imaging model, it was obvious to both John and me that that's the way you'd want to have it operate because you wanted to have linear transformation mechanism just built in inherently at the base of the imaging model. That isn't a language-specific thing.

I don't know how much impact it had, but just by happenstance, at least in my background, was not only the mathematics but also a very close familiarity with the entire printing process. My grandfather and my father were letterpress photo engravers. I understood a lot about how printing actually worked, particularly in terms of half-tone generation and things. With a little bit of all of that background, it helped with PostScript, but I would hesitate to say that the mathematics was a major contributor. Having that in your toolkit is always extremely helpful when you're working with abstraction definitions.

*How did you manage your ideas? Did you ever disagree? How did you find common solutions?*

**Charles:** I hired John in 1978, so we have worked together now for 30 years. During that entire time, he and I never parted company angry at one another. We always had sufficient respect for one another's ideas that if our ideas were different, we immediately tried to figure out why they were different and either which idea was better or how to come up with some way of integrating those two things together.

It almost never arose to the level of disagreement, that I can remember. It's a fairly unique partnership in that regard. Very few people have had that experience in their work life. A lot of people have had that experience in friendships or marriage or other places, but in a work environment it's pretty rare that you get that level of mutual respect, as well as the ability to unify around your ideas so quickly.

*A lot of people compare PostScript to Forth because they're both stack-based languages. Was there an influence?*

**John:** No; actually when we'd finished the language at E&S we came across all these discussions of Forth and Forth is quite similar, but in a lot of respects very, very different. So there really wasn't much influence. It was totally coincidence.

**Charles:** I fully agree.

*I'd always assumed a connection, but now it sounds like similar requirements led to similar designs.*

**John:** The cool thing about PostScript is that you can implement it with a very, very small amount of programming because it's emulating a hardware environment. It's very easy to build the basic machinery and then add operators as you need them.

**Charles:** The core interpreter of PostScript was only a few kilobytes.

**John:** Pretty small.

**Charles:** Quite small.

*What problems did the stack-based design solve? Would PostScript have suffered if it were more directly a descriptive language?*

**John:** The stack-based design of PostScript is straightforward to implement, and also can be interpreted and executed quickly. On the machines of the day when PostScript was introduced (Motorola 68000s), this simplicity and efficiency was very important.

I think the following were the most important design decisions in defining PostScript:

- PostScript was a complete programming language with variables, conditionals, iteration, etc.

- PostScript operators can be redefined in the language itself. This capability allowed us to reinterpret existing PostScript files to produce Acrobat (PDF) files. This also allowed us to fix bugs in an implementation that was burned into read-only memory.

- The imaging model allowed one to isolate and graphically manipulate substructures that then could be incorporated into larger elements. For instance, PostScript allows one to take a description of a page, scale it down, and make it a component of another page. This flexibility and ease of use was not present in any other printer protocols.

- PostScript allowed the user to deal with type like any graphical element: it could be scaled, rotated, or transformed like any other graphical element. This capability was introduced with PostScript.

- Although the first PostScript printers were black and white, the design of PostScript anticipated the use of color.

### Was the runtime stack usage bounded?

**John:** I think the execution stack was limited to 256 levels and I think all those stacks were limited by byte length.

**Charles:** The machine it was running on inside the LaserWriter only had—I should say only for its time it was a lot, but it had a megabyte and a half of RAM, one megabyte of which was just the frame buffer. You're running in half a megabyte of RAM for all of the executions.

*Did you have half a megabyte of ROM as well?*

**Charles:** Yes.

**John:** Yes.

*Would you map that ROM into RAM and then runtime patch if necessary?*

**John:** No, what you would do is you would just add an operator with downloaded code into the RAM and that would either supersede the built-in operator, as I said you could redefine operators or it would either supersede it or add new functionality.

*What about formal semantics? Some designers nail down the semantics of the language, then prove a small set of core features.*

**John:** We had a dictionary facility for looking up names and symbols. We had arrays. We had all the number things. We had this very simple stack machine that could take up to 256 operators if you wanted to go that far, but it's a very simple machine, and once you get the basic interpreter working, it's really easy to debug.

I think we were convinced that this was robust. I don't think we went through any formal exercises.

*Did you intend for people to write PostScript by hand?*

**John:** No; a lot of people wrote it by hand. You get used to it after a while. I prefer Java-Script now.

**Charles:** All of the early brochures that we wanted to show off the capability of PostScript on were done by designers who had to learn to program.

I think one of the other reasons that a language can have a long, healthy life is going back to the comment I made earlier about the size of the interpreter. It's small enough. It's hard to imagine that people couldn't take a long coffee weekend and port it anywhere you want to do it.

**John:** It might take more than a weekend.

**Charles:** It's when you do things that are sophisticated in the graphics realm that things get a little more complicated.

**John:** The other thing about PostScript and what made it successful is there was a language part of it, but then there were the problems we actually solved. The scaling of fonts from outlines was by far the biggest thing. It made good-looking type out of outlines and no one had been able to do that.

*Some people thought that was impossible.*

**John:** We weren't sure it was possible.

**Charles:** Yeah; that was a bet-your-future kind of thing. We decided we had to do it that way because the alternative was to hire armies of people to hand-tune bitmaps. That wouldn't fit the whole philosophy of the arbitrary linear transformation mechanisms of PostScript because as soon as you rotated a character a few degrees, you had to do a whole new bitmap.

**John:** There were a couple of key ideas that made all of that work. We were the first to do it.

**Charles:** I think the other area that was very successful with PostScript is the eventual ability to do absolute state-of-the-art quality half-toning for color. There had been a lot of work done in that area, but I think the implementation that evolved with Adobe by the end of the 1980s was clearly understood to be as good or better than the sort of electro-mechanical kind of systems that people used to use.

*Do you credit that to your background researching graphics?*

**Charles:** Well, it wasn't just the two of us.

**John:** No; it wasn't just the two of us. We actually did the first set of half-toning by just emulating what real half-tones do, the mechanical ones, but then we hired some mathematicians—a guy named Steve Schiller who really did a lot of work in half-toning and really understood it at a much more fundamental level.

**Charles:** John and I had both been around printing a lot. My father and grandfather were photo engravers. When I brought some of the early stuff home to my dad he'd look at it and say, "Hm, not so good."

Then Schiller and some of the other guys got involved. Eventually we got to the point where we got even my dad's blessing on it. That was cool.

*Did you have in mind just rotations for bitmap fonts?*

**Charles:** Arbitrary scaling and resolution. It becomes less critical as you get up to very high resolutions and relatively normal point sizes, but for a laser printer, or God forbid, a screen, it wasn't going to work.

**John:** The fundamental idea that made all of this work was people had tried to take the prototypical outline of a character and try to figure out what bits to turn on. We didn't do it that way.

We noted the frequency of the raster image and we morphed the outlines to align with the bitmap and then turned on the obvious bitmaps. That's what made all of the stem weights the same. It made all of the serifs the same. It made all of the bolds work right and it was a very, very simple idea, but no one had ever done it.

**Charles:** You can tolerate something be a little thicker or thinner than something else, except if the element is repetitive within the character your eye will pick out differences.

**John:** Very small differences.

## How do you handle kerning and ligatures?

**John:** You position the start on a raster boundary and then pick the closest thing. If it's pair kerning and sophisticated kerning you still do the same thing. You align the character on a raster boundary and then pick the spacing between that and the next character to the nearest pixel. It works as well as it's ever going to work. Ligatures are just different character designs.

**Charles:** Then you get to do all of this for Chinese and Japanese for the kanji characters.

**John:** We had a guy who worked for us named Bill Paxton. When we started doing the Chinese characters, not only the spaces between the strokes were important, but the holes and little rectangles were important—that they didn't disappear or get overscanned. He built a very complex set of rules of how to distort a character to the raster frequency so that it would preserve all the critical parts of the character.

## Did you have to identify those critical parts for each character?

**John:** Pretty much so, yes.

**Charles:** But you're only going to do it once. Actually designing the PostScript description of a Chinese typeface obviously takes much longer than Roman, simply because there are so many more characters, but once you've paid that price, then it doesn't matter.

## Can you share that information across fonts?

**John:** You build a strategy and you can automate a lot of that stuff and say, "Here is this kind of situation. Deal with it this way."

When TrueType was built, it used the same strategy, but it would do it specifically for every character. Whereas the strategy we used in PostScript was pretty much across an entire alphabet. In other words, on a lowercase *h* you want to identify the left stem and the right stem. Now the left stem and the right stem identification works on a small *n*, it works across the whole thing. The x-height on the character is a constant across the whole font.

We would identify those properties and then the algorithms would deal with that. If you change the design of the *n*, you really didn't have to do much. It was much easier to build a PostScript font than a TrueType font.

## Modern printers can interpret PostScript (as well as PDF) without an intermediate translation. Is this a benefit of the flexibility and elegance of the design of PostScript?

**John:** It is very important to remember, when PostScript was first implemented, the available memory on machines was very small. The original LaserWriter had 1.5 megabytes of memory and 0.5 megabytes of masked read-only memory. One megabyte of RAM was reserved for the page buffer, and therefore we only had 0.5 megabytes for all working storage. The masked ROM was used for the PostScript implementation.

PostScript was designed so that it held very little state. There was not enough memory to hold the entire PostScript program in most cases. That meant that the program processed and printed pages as they were encountered in the PostScript program as it was read by the printer. This strategy allowed us to print very complex jobs without the luxury of much memory.

Acrobat is not like that. The location of each page is found at the end of the file, which means that printers with Acrobat capability must read the file before starting. In today's world of gigabytes, this is not a problem.

Having said that, PostScript and PDF have identical print imaging models, and therefore are closely related.

*Are there features of PostScript's problem domain that make it difficult to write a clear PostScript program?*

**John:** It was really nice in the graphics domain because the stack, the way you nest transformations and the way that there are recursive calls on things is really nice when you're dealing with graphics. You can draw an image and then bottle it up and put transformations around it and it takes care of all of the internal stuff and does all the right stuff.

**Charles:** I can't help but interject a little bit of an anecdote here from the Xerox PARC days. There were always a lot of debate there between a very structured language, Mesa, between the people who loved Lisp and the folks who were just as happy going back to fairly primitive BCPL.

One of our programming languages guys proposed a competition in which people would program the same problem in all three of those and we'd see who could do it the shortest, the fastest and the most elegant kind of thing according to his judgment.

It turned out the only thing we figured out is it all depended where the brightest programmer went, who happened to be Bob Sproull, who did it all in BCPL and he didn't need any of this other fancy stuff. At the end of the day, that's probably so many more order of magnitude more of an impact that the particular language probably doesn't mean much.

*PostScript Level II adds features such as garbage collection. Are there further evolutions in the language you can foresee?*

**John:** Still in JavaScript there are no graphics interfaces that allow me to print a page. Whereas if I want to lay out type I always actually write that stuff in PostScript and run it through the distiller to produce PDF files. Well, I certainly couldn't maintain half of my life without it.

**Charles:** If you're specifically talking about PostScript, my suspicion is there's certainly not going to be any accelerated evolution at this point in its life. What it's doing is morphing the graphics imaging model of PostScript into other environments, like Flash.

**John:** Yeah, for Flash to be able to do all of the text things it's got to have the traditional Adobe text engines. All of that stuff's going to end up on phones.

*Apple uses PDF to describe graphical aspects of the Mac OS X desktop. I read that, essentially, there was a project that used PostScript to do such a thing.*

**Charles:** When we did the original deal with Apple back in 1983, we gave them license rights to Display PostScript as part of the deal. That's something that Steve Jobs really wanted to have as part of that contract. When Steve left Apple, Apple decided to go their own way and drop that, but Steve understood that he wanted to have the same imaging model both on the display as well as on the printed page so there would never be a discontinuity between the two. When he went to NeXT, we did a deal with him and Display PostScript was the graphics imaging model for the NeXT computer environment.

*I can see how that would work from a desktop publishing standpoint, where you want as much accuracy as possible between display devices.*

**John:** Actually from a general system point of view, once we were able to scale the font to screen-display resolutions and that was also Bill Paxton's work; it was really a very consistent graphics model that had a lot of power.

**Charles:** Imagine how much more interesting the Web would have been had HTML started out with a PostScript imaging model instead of all the silliness you have to do now to simulate.

**John:** It's really funny. Adobe today—Flash is getting enhanced so that it can deal with the fonts. It's really interesting. They were never strong on fonts. They were never strong on the graphics engines. Flash is evolving to be much, much stronger in those areas.

**Charles:** In effect it will become we think a Display PostScript for the Web.

*Do you think it might migrate into printers?*

**John:** No.

**Charles:** No.

*Will printers matter?*

**John:** Less and less so.

**Charles:** What we have seen is a lot of the printers now, many of the printers, are actually PDF printers, not PostScript printers, which just means the interpretation is done back in your computer.

**John:** But computers are a little bit different size now than they were then.

**Charles:** The fact that you can drive an ink printer from your computer at 20 pages a minute tells you a lot.

# Research and Education

*Is there anything that really surprised you in the way that software and hardware evolved since the 70s? Many of the ideas in use today were present in the 70s at PARC.*

**Charles:** I think it's important to understand how PARC came to be, what it was. The story begins at the time of the transfer of control of government here in the United States from Eisenhower to Kennedy.

Eisenhower took Kennedy aside and said he had been advised by some of the brighter people in the U.S. defense industry that in order for the U.S. to continue to expand its military presence around the world, it had to convert from analog communications to digital. I don't think either President Eisenhower or President-elect Kennedy probably understood what that statement meant, but Kennedy took him very seriously.

He took the most technical-oriented person in his Cabinet, McNamara, aside and said Eisenhower has told me this. I want you to look into it. You have the biggest budget. I want you to take enough money to have an impact in terms of getting this started, but small enough that Congress isn't going to spend a lot of time asking us questions about it because I want to get it started quickly and effectively.

McNamara, in turn, selected a guy out of MIT. His name was J. C. R. Licklider and he had been hanging around the research labs at MIT where they had started to do research on using computing technology, not to calculate but to communicate. What he saw was that the researchers at MIT had built up a set of relationships with other academic and a few industrial research labs around the country and he went to visit all of them, found them to be exceptionally bright people. They were at places like Caltech, UCLA, Stanford, Berkley, Utah, Michigan, and, of course, a bunch of East Coast places like MIT, Carnegie Tech, and a few others.

He decided to take a few tens of millions of dollars and distribute it in small packages to about a dozen of these universities and a couple of research labs like Bolt Beranek and Newman, and the RAND Corporation. He said "I'm not going to micromanage you. I'm going to give you this money and you can depend on it for a few years to get you up and started and what I want you to do is to do research so that if Congress ever does come and ask us questions, we can point to how the money was being used. But more importantly, especially for the academic institutions, I want you to train a whole new cadre of people who are experts in this field."

If you go through my background, John's background, we were all ARPA students. In fact, if you go through the genealogy of Silicon Valley, almost all of the corporate founders and senior researchers in this field were all educated by the Advanced Research Project Agency of the Defense Department during an era in which, as I said, you were not micromanaging this research.

That's where the principal people came to PARC because what Xerox did is hire the guy who took over from J. C. R. Licklider, a guy named Robert W. Taylor, and he knew where all of us had gone to school. He recruited all these people to come to PARC. PARC was the first industrial manifestation of the quality of the people who had been developed by ARPA during the preceding decade or so. By getting all those people together in one organization at PARC, they had a tremendous impact on the field.

*Charles, you formed the Imaging Sciences Laboratory at Xerox PARC, where you directed research activities. What is your advice on how to direct a research group?*

**Charles:** The most absolute, most important thing is to hire the brightest people you can find. I probably made the best hiring decision in my life by hiring John to come work in that laboratory, plus there were already a couple of researchers in the lab that were also extremely talented. Having those people as a core base for a research activity means that they tend to attract other high-quality people, particularly younger people coming out of, in the case of research, typically graduate degrees. We were able to build a very strong team of people.

From the beginning a lot of our research was not limited to being done just by a group formed within the lab but we reached out to other parts of Xerox and, to a certain extent, the academic research community. That kind of integration is also a very valuable way to do research because it brings a diversity of points of view.

*How do you recognize a good researcher?*

**Charles:** There's no test to give. It's mostly for people who have been in the field for a while by just looking what their impact has been. I had known John by reputation since he got out of graduate school, but he and I had never worked together or actually formally met until I interviewed him. I knew from what he had accomplished at Evans and Sutherland that he had a combination of creative insight and he was a finisher.

He's someone who didn't just propose ideas and let them go off to someone else, but he actually worked through the implementation of his ideas. I always found that to be a very valuable aspect of anyone doing research, that they would take their idea and follow it through to actually developing a really high-quality representation of what the idea was.

*Maybe it's the difference between pure research and applied research.*

**Charles:** I don't think it's the difference between them. I think the same criterion holds in either one. I have found over my career, whether it be researchers or engineers, that in addition to the sort of intellectual skills that they manifest, if they are people who finish what they set out to do, they tend to be much more productive and have a much larger impact.

*How do you recognize which projects look promising?*

**Charles:** Some of it is peer review—whether it attracts the interest of people who are colleagues who want to come and join the activity. I remember when we began working on a project called InterPress for Xerox, where we were developing the precursor of PostScript, we got people from a variety of different places, in addition to Xerox, who wanted to engage in the plan.

We had a professor from Stanford, we had a professor from Carnegie Mellon, a Xerox researcher who was working on his own on the East Coast. Actually, it's interesting. Except for John and myself, the six of us who worked on that project were never in the same physical location until after we completed the project. We did it all by email and using the ARPAnet to transfer information around during the entire design project.

My strategy always was to set general direction. People had an understanding of what the particular focus of the laboratory was to be and then within that it was up to their creativity to decide what to do. My job as their manager to help them shape and represent what they wanted to do and then get them the resources to be able to do it.

In a business where you're running primarily development, there you typically have a much greater focus on getting something done that will eventually go to market, and we try to put a schedule around a set of criteria that make it possible for that particular project to be successful in the marketplace.

*I asked about managing the research lab because I know that you had problems in building a product from InterPress.*

**Charles**: The research management was fine. The problem was there was no attempt to really figure out how you take the ideas out of research and get them effectively implemented in the development part of the corporation and that's really where the slip was, between those two spots. It was a failure at a more senior level of management than just research.

Although in fairness, I think we in research thought if we came up with great ideas that the development people would just flock to them and do them. That gets back to my comment earlier. A really good researcher—this didn't occur to me when I was young—has to take that idea and follow it almost all the way to its final implementation if they really want it to be successful.

*What's the difference between a leader and a manager?*

**Charles:** A leader is a person who has an idea of where he or she wants to go and a pretty good idea of how to get there and has to have the skills to recruit and motivate other people to work with them to achieve that objective. That's what a leader does.

A manager primarily focuses on making sure that sort of the underpinnings of things like budgets and modes of communication and other things occur between the individual working on a project, but that person may have little or no visionary idea of where they want to go.

Any complex organization needs to have both, but it often ends up with disastrous results if you confuse the difference, because some leaders can also be managers. If you think you're hiring someone to be a leader and they really have primarily the skills of a manager, you're probably be disappointed in what they do. Conversely if what you need is to manage a large organization and you pick a leader who spends most of his or her time thinking about great ideas off in the future, they probably won't be a very good manager.

There are different skills and they are both critical, and you can't confuse them when you ask someone to do something. They either have the skills of a leader or a manager and in a few rare cases, both.

## How do you recognize a good programmer?

**Charles:** Mostly by the experience of working either with them, beside them, for them—by having an active working relationship. I don't know of any way to tell it in the abstract.

I've had the good fortune of working with a variety of people. One person—in addition to John—that really sticks in my mind is a guy you may never have heard of. His name is Ed Taft. I first hired Ed in 1973 to work for me at Xerox PARC. The thing about Ed is he is the best programmer that I have ever had the opportunity to work with. He is very careful in his description of what problem we were trying to implement, and he's very determined to do it at a level that allows him the most flexibility for you to change your mind about how you really want it to work.

In some sense, he delays binding just like we talked about PostScript doing, but he is a finisher. When he has a piece of code and he says it's done, it is rock-solid and he is a great finisher. From concept level to completion, he's the full package. If I could clone Ed, I would. It would be a wonderful opportunity to build a great organization.

## Is there any particular topic that college students should focus on regarding computer science?

**Charles:** I've been a fairly conservative person with regards to undergraduate education in computer science. I think you should take as much physics and mathematics as you can while you're an undergraduate and leave more of computer science to a Master's and Ph.D. level, but that's just my attitude. Obviously, universities go wherever their students demand that they go and so I understand why they give undergraduate degrees in computer science.

Unless you have a strong background in math and science, obviously, if you want to go into hardware, you need to have that background and some combination of chemistry and physics. That's just my particular prejudice.

For your general education, I believe very strongly in the liberal arts. What good is it to be a scientist with great ideas in your brain, if you can't communicate them effectively and convince other people to follow your direction? Your ability to write and to speak are absolutely critical to your success. If you don't have all of that, you're really not a fully educated person and I'll think you'll be less effective.

I strongly encourage as much liberal arts education as possible as part of an undergraduate degree program, along with science and math.

## What lesson should other people learn from your experience with PostScript?

**Charles:** One of the beautiful ideas behind PostScript is that you delay binding yourself to something explicit as long as possible. In other words, you compute, calculate, and do most of your work at a reasonably abstract level. It's only at the final moment of deciding which bits you're going to turn on in this raster image or not that you bind yourself to the specific algorithms that do that.

By living at that higher level of abstraction, you're able to build a reasonable high-level description of the image that you want to produce, which is inherently importable to a whole array of devices. It's that same philosophy in imaging model that gives us the opportunity to do something we were talking about much earlier, which is to produce the same kind of imaging model that runs, not only on your personal computer, but on the Web and on all of the digital imaging devices you might have from televisions to telephones to various web appliances, and so on.

That's the beauty of PostScript. You can run at that higher level in terms of how you describe what you want to produce and only bind it at the last moment to a specific device.

## Interfaces to Longevity

*How can a designer think about longevity for a general programming language? Are there specific steps to take?*

**John:** A lot of languages go after a specific problem. Remember the one Atkinson did, HyperCard. He made what I would believe is the most common mistake that people make and that's not to make it a full programming language. You have to have control, you have to have branching, you have to have looping, you have to have all the mathematics and everything that makes up a full programming language or else you'll hit a brick wall at some point in the future.

People would look at us and say, "Why are you putting in all the trig functions? What are you going to use those for?"—and they all got used. An important thing in language design is at the outset recognize that it's got to be complete. You've got to have access to the filesystem. You've got to have all kinds of stuff to make it complete. I think that's really important.

There are PostScript machines 25 years later today that are still running, still the same and still running PostScript. It's enhanced a lot, but the basic program still runs.

**Charles:** I have a second-generation LaserWriter that I keep using because it has the best manual feed of any product I've seen. It still works. But Canon thought there would only be 100,000 prints and then the printer would be thrown away. They clearly way overdesigned it.

*What's the difference in designing a language intended for human consumption versus machine consumption, or human production versus machine production? Are there factors that come to mind when you're designing it when you think it's OK to do this a little bit because no human's going to sit down and unroll this loop this whole way?*

**John:** The one big downside to PostScript is it's very tough to debug. That's because you write the code once and your mind gets around it. After you've done that and try to come back to it six months later, it's a little rough. Whereas the standard infix notation languages where there isn't a lot of state hanging around are much easier to read and much easier to debug.

*You don't have to have the whole state of the stack in your mind.*

**John:** Right.

*Did you address that dichotomy when you designed PostScript?*

**John:** Because it was easy to add new operators, you had a tendency to write very, very short subroutines and try to separate the functionality as cleanly as you could as a programming practice, but no, the syntax just doesn't lend itself to human programming.

*You mentioned that you had designers writing PostScript programs to make brochures. In the 80s, you had administrative assistants writing LaTeX by hand. How was it teaching designers to write a program to write a brochure?*

**John:** That's an interesting question. The little-known fact that Adobe has never communicated to anybody is that every one of our applications has fundamental interfaces into JavaScript. You can script InDesign. You can script Photoshop. You can script Illustrator with JavaScript.

I write JavaScript programs to drive Photoshop all the time. As I say, it's a very little-known fact, but the scripting interfaces are very complete. They give you real access, in the case of InDesign, into the object model if anybody ever wants to go there.

**Charles:** This is not for the faint of heart.

*Even using JavaScript to script the HTML document model is not for the faint of heart sometimes.*

**John:** No, it's not. I do that all the time and it's not for the faint of heart, especially since the character sets are different and almost everything is different about the two environments.

But anyway, people do. If you want to automate document production, the best way to do it is to get into JavaScript and script the incredible typesetting engines inside of InDesign or the incredible imaging engines inside of Photoshop. You can build massive numbers of things in an automated way in a fairly straightforward fashion.

*This sounds like the longevity argument again. Make it general purpose and allow people all these operations and possibilities, but give them control to write loops and control flow.*

**John:** It's really true. There are projects and I've got a couple. I have this one website that is 90,000 pages. If I didn't automate the production of that website, you couldn't do it. It's just too many HTML pages.

*Did designers ask for this, or did someone show them how to do it?*

**John:** In maintaining and extending Photoshop and extending InDesign and extending a lot of these things—for instance, most people don't know that Bridge, which is a program that deals with the file structure and the viewing of images between Illustrator and Photoshop and InDesign, that's all written in JavaScript.

*You're just translating back and forth between object models.*

**John:** That's right. It is a lot of JavaScript, but the fact that it hangs together is amazing. It's completely portable.

*From your point of view, how should developers think of hardware? Does software lead innovation?*

**Charles:** I think it's a yin and a yang. Back in the days when all of this "innovation" was occurring at PARC, it was done on very small machines with relatively little disk storage, only modest-level network performance and so on, and within those constrained environments, a lot of creativity was used to make the software do things that in some sense surprised the people who used those computers because they'd never seen anything quite like that.

Today, we're in a situation in which the environment has changed dramatically and hardware has continued to evolve so quickly that we have gigabytes of storage at very modest costs and we have processor speeds that are lightning-fast.

I think one of the things that's interesting is that when you remove those restrictions of relatively slow performance and relatively modest memory size, it's easy for people to get a little bit lazy in terms of just assuming that they're using all of this. Then they come across an extremely complex problem where all of a sudden, once again, the hardware is the limitation and that's where the creativity and the software has to be really developed in order to be able to solve the particular problem.

There is sort of a balance always going on between the hardware and the software environment. In terms of what applications are, I think Vista is a good example of where development got a little lazy and assumed that these machines would be able to cope with the inherent inefficiencies and the way certain things were done. And it didn't work.

Now they're going back and in some sense restricting their expectations of what the hardware will do for them and they'll probably bring out a better version of Windows, certainly, than the Vista experience has been.

*Is making a language popular easier today?*

**Charles:** No, not really. I think when people are first learning how to develop and program, they tend to come up within some kind of environment which shapes a lot of the way they think about doing software development. It's very hard for them to break that bond between that experience and new tools that come out. In order for a new programming language to become really popular, you have to find an environment in which a lot of people begin using it early on and get them engaged in it. To a certain extent, it comes more out of the educational environment than it does out of a sort of independent organization trying to bring a new language to the market.

We see such an evolution now in the notion of cloud computing, for example, where the distribution of where computing and access to information occurs is broadly spread between someone's desktop and the Internet and servers and a whole variety of things.

It's very conceivable to me, and this is not an area in which I've done any work, but that opens up an opportunity for a language that will allow you to more directly address that diversity of environment than any of the current languages do, maybe. I say maybe because I don't know if it's a language issue or not. Certainly if you look at organizations like Google and Microsoft and to a certain extent, Adobe, which are really focusing a lot on being able to provide our customers a seamless experience in that environment, we may find, over time, that the tools become a limitation to doing that. Whether that's a programming language per se or, more importantly, a language plus—and this always goes along with a programming language—a programming environment in which that language resides, need to be enhanced above the tools that are available today.

Now, the issue is, there aren't a lot of natural environments. There is no longer a Bell Labs like there used to be, or an IBM Research or for that matter, a Xerox PARC. We aren't in any sort of an "industrial labs" where this kind of research and development would be taking place. There certainly are a variety of very high-quality academic environments, but most of them are now being funded by very targeted research projects that are supported by primarily the U.S. government either through NSF or DARPA.

The environment in which a Berkeley Unix was developed or the environment in which, when I was working on my thesis I was working with William Wulf and we developed a higher-level language for doing systems programming called BLISS. We could get the funding because of the way that ARPA managed funds in those days. Today that's not so easily available in a research environment. It's hard for me to know where this kind of development is going to happen.

It's very difficult for a corporation, with its need to generate revenue and profits to put this kind of investment in it unless it has an entity off to the side that it can independently fund as a research organization. Most corporations today, particularly in software and Internet environments, do not have such an entity within the company.

*Maybe an open source project?*

**Charles:** Maybe, but the problem with open source from my point of view, is if a concept is already pretty well developed and a sort of structural integrity has been established and is well understood, then open source contribution can work well. Taking a blank sheet of paper and calling it open source and getting something started, I think would be very difficult to pull off.

*Would you suggest to make it an open standard in any case?*

**Charles:** You've got to do that in this day and age. People need it to be open and, frankly, you need to have a way to have people add their own tools to it. Something you may not be aware of is that, and I can only speak of Adobe because it's what I know best, but all of Adobe's products have an open JavaScript-style interface to every one of them so that third parties can build very sophisticated add-on to any of our products from InDesign to Photoshop to Acrobat and so on, and do it all in a sort of platform-neutral, independent, scripted way. A lot of companies and individual groups do things like that all the time.

It's not open source in the sense of handing out the C code for the guts of Photoshop, but it is a way to maintain the integrity of the core component and then give a lot of freedom to third parties to experiment and add value.

## Standard Wishes

*What is the next outstanding problem to solve in the realm of computer programming or computer science?*

**John:** Well, in the world I live in today I have probably 30 or 40 manuals on my bookshelf that all have to do with the Web. They're all thick and they're all mutually contradictory. I would love to see cleaning up the imaging models, cleaning up the programming environments, cleaning up all the things that make up the Web today, because there really is no reason to have any of that stuff.

The terribleness of the different browsers and dealing with that because of the different implementations with HTML has to go away.

With Flash what we're trying to do is both beef it up and make it robust enough so that at least you can get one language that's platform-independent and will move from platform to platform without hitting you every time you turn around with different semantics.

**Charles:** I totally agree. It is so frustrating that this many years later we're still in an environment where someone says if you really want this to work you have to use Firefox. We should be way past that point by now! The whole point of the universality of the Web would be to not have those kind of distinctions, but we're still living with them.

It's always fascinating to see how long it takes for certain pieces of historical antiquity to die away. The more you put them in the browsers you've codified them as eternal, and that's stupid.

*Do you see this as a failure of the standards process we have today?*

**John:** Well, the standards process is less about solving problems than in codifying history.

**Charles:** My personal attitude is a lot of the standards activity, the sprinkling holy water on what's already a fete complete. It's not there to actually create anything, as John said. It's just to codify it and its historical generation.

Unless there's an active, vibrant organization who takes ownership of the standard and either polices or makes so easily and readily available the implementation of that standard that no one tries to do it on their own, you don't have a standard. That's always the dilemma we dealt with in the early days with PostScript. If the clones had managed to wrest control of PostScript away from us, we would never have gotten to PostScript 3. It would have by that point devolved into a set of incompatibilities that would have made its whole premise pointless.

**John:** The same thing is true of PDF. We finally got the U.S. Archives to adopt it and it's a subset of the current stuff, but at least it's a spec.

When we did Acrobat we said we really have to have it so that these files really live and we sign up for making them completely backward compatible so that really, really old Acrobat files will still be read by the readers. That's a big job. Acrobat is a huge piece of code, but it serves such a purpose on the Web that I can't even imagine the Web not having it.

*Should these standards be driven by one main implementation or can they arise from rough consensus?*

**John:** With PostScript it was our implementation that really defined what the standard was and that's pretty much true of Acrobat, too.

The dilemma is if you had Netscape and then you had Microsoft, Microsoft wasn't in anyway motivated to keep them compatible. I think that's tragic.

**Charles:** They did the same thing with Java.

*Could we have a better Web if we used PostScript instead of HTML and JavaScript?*

**Charles:** Well, we have been working on our new platform for the Web, the current name for it is Adobe AIR. The Adobe Internet Runtime is a way to bring the level of sophistication of the graphics of the Web up to the same level that you see in our applications and you see in the kernel of the PostScript imaging model, bringing that to the Web in such a way that you can build applications that seamlessly sort of blur the distinction between what goes on on the desktop and what goes on on a web application. We believe that that is a way to get PostScript-like imaging and graphics out to the Web in a way that HTML really does not support effectively.

HTML has two problems. It's basically a bitmap-oriented representation of information, number one. Number two, it's not a standard. The way I say it's not a standard is if you take any of the most popular web browsers and point them at a specific HTML page, they'll all produce different results. To me that's just not acceptable because what it means is that if you really want to build a sophisticated website, you have to do browser-specific programming in order to get the website to give the appearance of being the same no matter which browser you use. It's going back in time. It's like the bad old days.

That's happened because HTML was left as sort of an "open standard." I believe that there's an inherent contradiction in that. You can have the implementation of a standard be open, but the standard itself needs to be very well designed and thought out in such a way that you don't see that kind of disparity.

I remember when Java was first introduced by Sun. They eventually did a deal with Microsoft, and one of the first things Microsoft did is change Java. There was no uniformity between various implementations. That sort of flies in the teeth of the whole concept of a standard. If you're going to have a standard, it has to be a standard and everybody has to adhere to it. Typically that means having one fairly autocratic organization maintain the standard, not the implementation.

We think there's some real opportunities to bring the quality of what you can do up on the Web to a whole new level. We've been working in this area. We've got a lot of interesting applications that third parties have already done using the AIR platform, and we're going to continue to focus on that. It makes the operating system and the platform that you're running your local laptop or PC on pretty much irrelevant. It just doesn't matter.

You can see why, to a certain extent, Apple and Microsoft view that as a challenge because they would like you to buy into their implementation of how the seamless integration with the Web goes. What we're saying is it really shouldn't matter. That cloud ought to be accessible by anybody's computer and through any sort of information sitting out on the Web.

# CHAPTER SEVENTEEN

# Eiffel

Eiffel is an object-oriented programming language designed primarily by Bertrand Meyer in 1985, now managed by a standards committee at Ecma International, which produced an ISO standard released in 2006. It provides a wide range of features now considered modern and widespread: garbage collection, generic programming, and type safety. Its most important contribution may be the idea of Design by Contract, where the language enforces interface preconditions, postconditions, and invariants; this improves the reliability and reusability of components. Eiffel's influence is apparent in languages such as Java, Ruby, and C#.

# An Inspired Afternoon

*Why did you choose to create a programming language?*

**Bertrand Meyer:** Very few people create a programming language just for the sake of it. Eiffel was born out of a necessity. I designed a programming language because I needed to write software and everything I had was unsatisfactory.

*Did you need a tool to, for example, implement Design by Contract?*

**Bertrand:** That part was obvious, but in general I needed an object-oriented language. Let me give you the context. We started a company in 1985, Interactive Software Engineering. It is now called Eiffel Software. We were actually going to build software-engineering tools. We were funded by a Japanese company to build a program editor, or a syntax-directed editor, which we did build and which enjoyed moderate success.

This was a very small company. I was still teaching at the University of California, Santa Barbara, so this was kind of a business on the side. We had Unix workstations that had been given to us by the Japanese customers, as they were one of their products. This was '85 and I had already been programming in an object-oriented way for almost 10 years. I had been very fortunate in the 70s to run into Simula 67, which hooked me right away. I knew this was the way to program.

On the kinds of machines we were looking at, there was no Simula compiler, and I liked Simula very much. As Tony Hoare said of Algol, it was an improvement over many of its successors. Still, Simula had neither multiple inheritance nor genericity; by then I understood that you needed both, inheritance and genericity. I explained the reasons in an article presented at the first OOPSLA, "Genericity versus Inheritance." So we looked at what was available. C++ was there, so I opened the book but closed it very quickly—really this was not the kind of thing I had in mind; the idea of making a bit of object-orientation palatable to C programmers was interesting, but surely it could only be a temporary stepping stone to something more consistent. Objective-C was there, too, but it was very Smalltalk-oriented and had little to do with the kind of software engineering principles we were interested in. The same holds for Smalltalk itself. Smalltalk was a fascinating development, but it had little to do with the kind of concerns that we had. Eiffel was born as a combination of object-oriented techniques and software engineering principles and practices that had been developed over the previous decade. Smalltalk had this very nice experimental programming flavor, which we felt was inappropriate for the kind of things that we were going to do; for example, the absence of static typing was already a killer. So there were lots of exciting ideas but nothing around that we really wanted to use.

What I did was to write a report. It was a UC–Santa Barbara report that actually described not the language, but the library of data structures and algorithms, because I was very much into reuse and wanted to have a standard library to cover the fundamental data structures of computer science, what I sometimes call "Knuthware." What later was called

EiffelBase was at that time just called the Data Structures Library. So I wrote this paper describing arrays, linked lists, stacks, queues, and so on; it used that particular notation, and I said we were going to implement it. I thought it would take three weeks to implement it. We are still at it. But this was already Eiffel.

The language was not a focus in itself. The focus was on reusable components, and I had realized that to have good reusable components you needed classes; you needed genericity, which was there right from the beginning; you needed multiple inheritance; and you needed a careful combination of genericity and multiple inheritance, as my OOPSLA paper demonstrated. You needed deferred classes. You needed contracts, of course, which to me were the most trivial thing. Everyone else makes a big fuss about them, but I still today don't understand how people can program without contracts. Also something I knew was needed was a good streaming or serializing mechanism, so this was one of the first things that we built. I actually had learned this from a language called SAIL, Stanford Artificial Intelligence Language, which was very well designed—not object-oriented but very interesting—that I had used at Stanford 10 years earlier. So that was there and absolutely fundamental from the very beginning. Garbage collection, of course, was obviously needed.

*How did you come up with this philosophy? Was your experience as a practical programmer sufficient to identify how to improve how we build software?*

**Bertrand:** Partly that and partly of course reading the literature. When I was a student at Stanford in '73 I read the book *Structured Programming* by Dahl, Dijkstra, and Hoare [Academic Press]. It is really three monographs under a single cover. The first, by Dijkstra, is the famous one about structured programming. The second, by Hoare, is about data structuring, which is also great, and there's the third one. One of the great lessons I have learned about life is that people read the beginning of books, so—actually this is a tip to people who write books—you have to be very careful about what you put in the first 50 pages of your book because 90% of the people will read 50 pages and then stop, even if the book is very good. Most people read the first part of *Structured Programming*, the part by Dijkstra. Some people read the second part by Hoare. I think few people actually went to the end and read the third part, which was by Ole-Johan Dahl with the help of Tony Hoare, called "Hierarchical Programming Structuring." What it really was is an introduction to Simula and object-oriented programming. I was an earnest student: I had been told to read this book, and I read it from beginning to end. I loved the first and second part, and found the last one just as illuminating.

This also explains why a few years later when object-oriented programming came onto the scene and most people said it is what comes after structured methods, to me that made no sense. It was part of structured methods right from the beginning. Structured programming was for programming-in-the-small aspects, and object-oriented programming was for programming-in-the-large, but there was no gap between the two. Having read Dahl's and Hoare's text, I knew this was the right way to program. When I went to industry in the mid-70s, I was fortunate that my boss let me buy a Simula compiler, which was quite expensive, but the compiler was very good. I used it a lot in the company I was working for, to develop quite interesting software. To me it was absolutely obvious that there was no other reasonable way to program, but most other people thought I was completely crazy. Object-oriented programming was still very amorphous at the time.

In the mid-70s, just out of school, I had written a book with my friend Claude Baudoin, in French; it was titled *Méthodes de Programmation* [Eyrolles], "Programming Methods", and was a kind of a compendium of everything we knew, everything we had learned at Stanford and other places. The book was very successful. Actually it is still in print today, which is kind of crazy for a 1978 book. It served to train, I think I can say without exaggeration, a couple of generations of French software engineers—also Russian software engineers because it was translated into Russian in the Soviet Union at that time. It was also quite successful in Russia; I still meet people when I go to Russia who tell me they learned programming through that book. It used a pseudocode to explain programming techniques, to explain algorithms and data structures.

I showed the book to Tony Hoare, who said that he was interested in having it translated into English for his famous international series in computer science at Prentice Hall and so I said, "Yes, sure," and then he said, "You speak some English, so why don't you do the translation yourself?" and I was stupid enough to say yes, instead of insisting that he find someone to translate it. It was really the stupidest thing I did in my life: of course, as I was translating the book, I was rewriting it because it was three or four years after the original publication. I had already matured and I had more ideas. I called the book *Applied Programming Methodology*, and it was never published because I never finished it. I was rewriting every sentence. It was very unproductive, but in writing it I improved the pseudocode that I had used for the first book. In particular I felt I could not really express programs or algorithms properly without contracts. The Eiffel notation for contracts comes from there.

Another event was quite important. I was in industry, but I took a sabbatical in academia at the University of California at Santa Barbara, and so as a visitor I was given some courses that no one wanted to teach. There was a sequence of courses, 130A and 130B, Data Structures and Algorithms, which had a very interesting role because it had really three purposes. The official purpose was to teach data structures and algorithms. But there were two undocumented purposes, the really important ones. One was to make it sufficiently hard that it would fail a good number of students, so the ones who survived would be worthy of being computer science students. The second secret goal was that it should teach students C because they had to know C for other courses.

This was completely absurd because whatever C is good at, it is not a good language for expressing algorithms, let alone teaching them. It was a horrible experience because instead of talking about what I wanted to talk about in the course, I was essentially helping students debug their programs with C pointers gone wild and such. This taught me two things: first, that I never wanted to touch C again as a language for humans. C is a reasonably good language for compilers to generate, but the idea that human beings should program in it is completely absurd. Second, I learned that the only way to present fundamental data structures and algorithms was to equip them throughout with loop invariants, loop variants, and pre- and postconditions all over the place. So to a certain extent, when at the end of that year I had to design a notation for our own work in the company that we had by then just started, I used the language that I would have liked to use for my course at UCSB. More generally, this was all the result of reading a lot, immersing myself for years in modern work on software engineering from Dahl, Dijkstra, Hoare, Wirth, Harlan Mills, David Gries, Barbara Liskov, John Guttag, Jim Horning, people like that, and basically following the evolution of programming languages. To me it was the obvious thing to do. Really I think I can say Eiffel was designed—I was going to say in an afternoon, but not even that. Eiffel was designed in 15 minutes. It was the absolutely obvious thing to do.

*Did the Eiffel language lead you to the idea of Design by Contract?*

**Bertrand:** No, it is more the other way around. That is to say, the concepts were there before. The language is just there to reflect that. To me, this is not a meaningful question to ask, or rather, the question should be directed to people who do not use Design by Contract; they should be asked why. I just cannot understand why people would write software elements without taking the trouble to express what the elements are there for. It's a question to ask Gosling, Stroustrup, Alan Kay, or Hejlsberg. How can they write software, or design a language for people to write software in, without providing this kind of mechanism? I just do not see how anyone can write two lines of code without this. Asking why one uses Design by Contract is like asking people to justify Arabic numerals. It's those using Roman numerals for multiplication who should justify themselves.

*I've heard that design by contract in an OO language enforces a Liskov Substitution Principle. Do you think that's true?*

**Bertrand:** I have never understood what the Liskov Substitution Principle was. The way I see it, it's just polymorphism.

*I think that's true with the catch that you have to have complete substitutability. You can't constrain your inherited type to do less than what the parent tack does, for example. Basically you have to enforce the same contract as the parent class.*

**Bertrand:** Well, I think this was what Eiffel introduced in '85, this idea of weakening the precondition and strengthening the postcondition when you redefine a routine. So if the Liskov Substitution Principle says this, the answer I guess is yes. But Eiffel didn't wait for Barbara Liskov.

*I like those notions of converging discoveries.*

**Bertrand:** The part of Barbara Liskov's work on which we directly rely is the notion of abstract data type, work from '74; that had been seminal. Of course, there was all the work in the CLU language at MIT, which was also influential. But the Liskov Substitution Principle never struck me as anything new.

### How does Design by Contract help a team of developers?

**Bertrand:** It makes it possible for the various parts of the team to know *what* their partners are doing without having to know *how* they are doing it. This enables you to get snapshots of the products of all the teams, based solely on the specification and not tied to particular choices of representation. It is also very good for managers.

### Isn't there a risk of overspecifying the solution?

**Bertrand:** No, actually not. The risk is always to underspecify. People rarely overspecify with contracts. The risk of overspecification arises when people commit early to an implementation instead of staying at the specification level, but that cannot happen with contracts since they describe intent, not realization. The problem with contract-based specification is the reverse: people don't say enough because it's difficult to specify everything.

### I read that when using contracts the code must never try to verify the contract conditions. The whole idea is that the code should fail hard. Could you explain this decision?

**Bertrand:** There may be many people who claim to apply Design by Contract principles and who are not bold enough to apply this rule. The idea is very simple. It applies to preconditions. If you have a precondition to a routine that says, "These are the conditions I want to meet," then the routine's code itself should never check the contracts; that is, any responsibility for checking the contracts at run time, assuming you suspect some clients may be buggy and not ensure the precondition, lies with someone else. It lies with some automatic mechanism that will be used during testing and debugging. But if you are both having a precondition and testing for the same condition in the code and something is wrong, you are doing the same thing twice; it means you are not able to make up your mind as to whether the condition, the constraint, is the responsibility of the client or the supplier. This is the real test of whether people are applying Design by Contract, rather than some kind of defensive programming: are they willing to remove the checks? Few people actually have the guts to do this.

In Design by Contract there is a very clear rule, which is that the precondition is a constraint imposed on the client, on the caller, so if there's a precondition violation, it's the client's fault. It is not the responsibility of the routine. For the postcondition, it's the responsibility of the supplier, of the routine. If you have a precondition, meaning the caller's responsibility, but then the routine itself checks it, then you haven't made up your mind and you are actually going to have lots of useless code. This of course is very dangerous, especially since often this code will not have been exercised during testing and debugging, during development. It's really just a matter of being serious about specification.

### How important is the distinction between specification and implementation?

**Bertrand:** That's a really good question. The distinction is very important, but it's a relative distinction. That is to say, it is absolutely impossible to say that something is specification in the absolute or that something is implementation in the absolute. One of the characteristics of software is that any software element you look at is the specification of something that is more concrete and the implementation of something that is more abstract.

You take even a construct that sounds absolutely like implementation—say, an assignment := A+1 or A := B. Most people would say this is pure implementation. But in fact if you are a compiler writer, for you this is a specification of something to be expanded into maybe a dozen machine-language or C instructions. The distinction is important, but what really creates the difficulty of software is that with a big enough size, at a certain scale, the techniques used to write implementations are very similar to the techniques used to write specifications.

For example, there is a striking phenomenon for anyone who writes formal specifications: when you write big enough formal specifications, you end up doing things and asking yourself questions that are remarkably close to the kind of things you do and the kind of questions you ask if you are writing actual programs. So the distinction is always relative. The reason is that in software we do not deal with physical stuff. We never deal with concrete, tangible, material elements. All that we deal with are abstractions, and so the difference between implementation and specification is fundamentally one of abstraction level. So it is usually meaningless to say that something is an implementation or a specification. What you can say is that X is a specification of Y; in other words, Y is an implementation of X. That is a statement that makes sense; it is falsifiable. But the statements "X is a specification" or "X is an implementation" are not falsifiable. They do not have a precise yes/no answer.

### What is the link between a programming language and the design of software written with that language?

**Bertrand:** One of the really unique aspects of Eiffel—one of the obvious properties of software that no one else seems to consider obvious or even true—is that the chain between concept and realization is completely continuous. That's what we call seamless development, and it probably is the most important aspect of Eiffel. Everything else is there to support it. It is this idea that, for example, there is no real distinction between design and implementation. Implementation, to paraphrase a famous saying, is just design carried out by other means. The difference is only the level of granularity and the level of abstraction. In particular, Eiffel is designed as much to be an analysis and design language as an implementation language. Overall, it is fundamentally a method rather than a language, but the part that is a language is as much for analysis and design as for implementation.

People who use Eiffel typically do not use UML or such tools, which to an Eiffel designer are largely noise with little connection to what's useful for software. Eiffel is a tool that is meant to help you—you're talking about design, but I would say one starts at the level of specification and analysis, continues with design, and then with implementation—to support you in this process. But there is no fundamental gap between the tasks, in my view or in the view of Eiffel developers in general.

The other point to mention is that the language should be as unobtrusive as possible. Many of the languages that are around today are what I would call "high-priest languages," with lots of strange symbols and conventions that you need to understand to be admitted into the inner circle. For example, many of the dominant languages of today essentially go back to C. They are a result of successive additions to and removals from C, and you need to understand a lot of baggage to master them.

The idea with Eiffel—I cannot claim that Eiffel is completely devoid of any baggage, but there's very little—is that when you are doing a design you think about the design and not about the language. The best compliment that I have heard from people using Eiffel is that when they use the language, they are focusing on their problem only. That is the best influence that a language can have on a design.

*Have you ever considered other solutions beyond handling objects at the language level? Maybe components like little tools that built the Unix system and that were put together via pipes to build complex features. After all, when you write a message or a letter to someone and you want to describe something you don't use the idea of objects in French, in Italian, in English, etc.*

**Bertrand:** Certainly the Unix mechanisms are very elegant, but they are too fine-grained for what we need to do in building big software. In my experience objects are the only mechanism that has proved that it can scale up for big systems. The only other approach that I would probably have considered would have been functional programming, but I don't think it works. It is an attractive idea, very elegant, and there is much to be learned from it, but at the highest level it loses to objects. Objects—I should say classes—are much more effective at capturing the large-scale structure of systems.

The analogy is not so much human language; rather, mathematics. Again it is classes more than objects. Classes are nothing more than the transposition to programming of the notion of structure that works so well in mathematics: groups, fields, rings, and so on. That is, mathematics takes objects that can be very different in nature—say, numbers and functions—and shows that in both cases you have the same structure, defined by operations that have the same properties. Then you abstract this into a single notion of, for example, groups or monoid or field. This notion has worked very well for mathematics in the past 200 years. In this respect, classes or objects are not such a new concept. They are just a direct transposition of this standard notion of mathematical structure.

*Many modern systems are componentized and spread out over a network. Should a language reflect those aspects of the network?*

**Bertrand:** It's a desirable property and you can do this in Eiffel, but I would not claim this is the part where Eiffel shines most. There are lots of developments at the moment in dynamic updating and concurrency that will be visible in the next few months, but which are not there yet. Yes, I think it is important. One can argue whether it should be in the language or in the implementation, but some language support will be needed.

*What link do you see between the object-oriented paradigm and concurrency?*

**Bertrand:** I think concurrency is extremely important. I have written extensively about this. There is in particular a whole literature about the so-called SCOOP model of concurrent object-oriented programming that we have developed. A basic operation is that the naïve approaches do not work. There is a certain tendency to say, "Oh yes, concurrency, objects, that's kind of the same idea, that must work very nicely, objects are naturally concurrent," and assume everything into place; this simply just doesn't work. It does not work if you try to combine object-oriented ideas with concurrent ideas on an elementary level.

Let me just say a couple words about SCOOP. The basic realization is that the standard notion of contract cannot have the same interpretation in a concurrent context as in a sequential one. What SCOOP is about is a way to take a sequential object-oriented programming model and extend it in the simplest possible way that will support concurrency. This idea is very different from what many others are doing. For example, if you take all the process calculi, they take exactly the reverse approach: ask what is the best scheme for concurrency, then add the rest of programming on top of it. This gives something that is very different from the usual ways of programming. The idea of SCOOP is that people have trouble reasoning in a concurrent fashion, but can reason much more effectively in a sequential fashion; so SCOOP hides much of the complexity of concurrency in the implementation, in the model. Then it lets programmers program in a concurrent way, but one that is very close to sequential programming and allows them to retain their usual modes of thinking.

*At what level should we deal with concurrency? For example, the JVM manages some things almost transparently.*

**Bertrand:** Obviously Java threading has been very useful for many applications, but the concepts are not closely connected with the object-oriented fabric of things. It's basically semaphores in the Dijkstra sense. Actually there is a library in Eiffel called EiffelThreads, which does more or less the same; I think it's clear to everyone that such solutions are good in the short term but do not scale up. There are still too many possibilities of data races and deadlocks. The goal should be to protect programmers automatically from these problems; this requires working at a higher level of expression. As you indicate, this means that more and more work is going to be done by the implementation.

## Reusability and Genericity

*How does Eiffel deal with change and the evolution of the programs?*

**Bertrand:** Together with reusability, extensibility was a major goal from the start. To a certain extent, this is the reason why Eiffel continued because, as I said, we had initially devised Eiffel as a tool for internal use, not as something that we would sell to the rest of the world. The event that really made us reconsider and think about making Eiffel more widely available was when developers started saying that the big difference with languages that we were using before was that they could change their minds much more easily and not be punished for their hesitations.

I think that several aspects are critical. First, information hiding is done quite carefully in Eiffel to isolate the various modules showing changes in one another. There is no information hiding for descendants because it does not make sense, but there is information hiding for clients. For example, it is really striking and a bit shocking to see that in recent object-oriented languages, you can still assign directly to an attribute, to a field of an object. This you cannot do in Eiffel because it violates information hiding. It's a catastrophe for software.

Then the inheritance mechanism is very flexible and enables you to write software by variation over existing patterns. Genericity gives an extra level of flexibility.

The absence of a language mechanism above the class makes it possible to combine classes in a very flexible fashion. Contracts also help there because what is really important when you change software is to know what you are changing—in particular, whether you are changing aspects of the specification or only aspects of the implementation. When you change software, you have to decide whether this is a purely internal change that will not affect the contracts, in which case you know that the clients are completely unaffected, or whether this also changes the contracts; if so, of course, you have to see exactly how. This gives you a level of granularity in controlling the extent of changes. I think these are some of the mechanisms that are most fundamental in supporting extensibility.

*How should developers think of reusability? I'm asking this because some of the people that I have interviewed essentially have said that even if you are building classes, you should forget the reusability part because it requires a lot of work, and you should focus on reusability only if you discover that you are using a particular class in different types of context a lot of times. At that point, is it worth spending additional time to make it reusable?*

**Bertrand:** I think that is only the case if you are not good at reusability or if you are a novice. It is true that if you do not have any experience in reusability, then when you try to make your software more general than needed by the requirements of the moment, you are going to spend a lot of time, and you might not succeed. But I would contend that once you become good at reusability, once you have had a long experience working with reusable components produced by others and have had experience in making your own software reusable as well, then you just do it right.

I think the mistake that many people make is not to understand that there are two aspects of reusability and that one must precede the other. They are the consumer aspect and the producer aspect. In the consumer form of reuse, you are just reusing existing software for your own applications; many people do this basically to save time. In the producer form of reuse, you make your own software more reusable. If you try to be a reuse producer right from the start, you will fail because producing reusable software indeed requires specific techniques. What you are going to do is spend a lot of time making your stuff more general, but you will have to guess in what directions it might be generalized later on, and usually you will guess wrong because that is difficult.

However, if you take a slightly more humble attitude and start out as a consumer—study high-quality reusable libraries, how they are produced, how they are designed, what their APIs are—then you can apply the style you learned from this experience to your own software. This is very much the way it works in the Eiffel world. People learn to program in Eiffel by looking at the standard libraries like EiffelBase or EiffelVision for graphics; these are quite high-quality libraries that serve as a model for good software. If you study them, then you are able to apply the same principles to your own software and make it much, much better and more reusable in particular. This is the way to go: start as a consumer and learn from your experience to become a producer. In my experience, if you work like this, then it actually works. This was the idea behind my book *Reusable Software* [Prentice-Hall].

With this approach you can make your software reusable. The agile or extreme programming view is that you should not worry about reuse, it's a waste of time. I think it only applies to people who are not very good at reusable programming because they have not taken the trouble to learn how to produce good reusable software by looking at good models.

*Maybe it's also a matter of the programming language that they are using.*

**Bertrand:** It certainly is; you do not need to push me much on this. Eiffel was designed fundamentally to achieve three things. One was of course correctness, and more generally reliability. The second one was extensibility, the ease of changing software, and the third one was reusability. So reuse is built throughout. For example, it is really striking to see that we had generic classes right from the start. This was absolutely fundamental to reusability, but over the years people laughed at this again and again. At the first OOPSLA in 1986, the company had a booth where there was a sign that talked about it, and people were coming to our booth to laugh at this word *genericity*, which they said was not even an English word. No one had a clue what it was about.

Then a few years later C++ introduced templates. When Java came out in 1995, there were no generics, and people were saying it is not necessary, it's one of the complications of object-oriented programming that makes languages messy. Sure enough, 10 years later, genericity was introduced in a complicated and, in my opinion, not fully satisfactory way, not so much because of a bad design but because of the constraints of compatibility. Then I could not believe my eyes when I saw that C# came out without genericity again, even though there had been this experience with Java and sure enough, seven years later or so, genericity was added.

This is the kind of thing that Eiffel had seen right from the start, motivated by reusability. The particular details of the inheritance mechanism, the particular mix of renaming, redefinition, undefinition, that are present in Eiffel, the mechanism for repeated inheritance—all this is justified and motivated by reusability. Contracts, of course, are essential for reusability. I said earlier that I do not understand why people can program without contracts, but something that is even harder to understand is how people can have supposedly reusable components without a clear specification of what the supposed reusable elements do.

Little by little, people are understanding this. You may not have seen it yet, but .NET 4.0 has been announced with a contract library, Code Contracts, and all of the base libraries; Mscorelib is going to be redocumented and rearchitected with contracts. It's only like 23 years after Eiffel. People are finally understanding that you cannot have reuse without contracts. It has taken time. Of course, during that time Eiffel has continued to introduce new ideas to remain ahead of the game.

*When and how did you realize that genericity was as important as classes?*

**Bertrand:** This particular point or this particular realization, I think, came more of the academic context than an immediate industrial need. In my career I have mostly been in industry, but I have had my stints in academia. A couple of times, in 1984 and 1985, I taught a course at USCSB in Santa Barbara entitled "Advanced Concepts in Programming Languages." It was pretty free-ranging.

I wanted to look at what was at that time at the forefront of programming languages. I included both Ada, which was generating a lot of heat, and Simula, which was not generating any heat, but which I knew was the wave of the future thanks to its object-oriented concepts.

The question became even inevitable as I was teaching that course, because one week I would talk about genericity and the next week I would talk about inheritance, or the other way around. The question arose naturally of how these two things compared. I do not recall this being a particular student's question, although it might have been. I just recall asking myself, "Am I going to be Dr. Genericity one week and Mr. Inheritance the next week?"

This led me to ask myself the question, "What can I do with one that I cannot do with the other?" and the converse. Of course, this was the result of many discussions and reflections before, but the programming language community was split between those who thought that Ada was the be-all and end-all of programming language flexibility and the little club of those who had discovered object-oriented programming and inheritance.

These discussions were common in working groups—"I can do better with my language." "No, no I can do better with mine." As far as I can tell, no one had really gone further and tried to understand exactly what the relationship was and how exactly did the expressive power of each mechanism compare.

For my course, I presented a kind of comparative analysis of the two. Then the call for papers for the first OOPSLA came, and this was the obvious thing to submit to OOPSLA.

I sat and wrote down what I thought I had understood, and that was "Genericity versus Inheritance" in the first OOPSLA proceedings.

*You published that paper before most common OO languages even realized that was a problem. Even Smalltalk doesn't take an approach on that.*

**Bertrand:** Smalltalk does not care, because Smalltalk being dynamically typed does not need any of this. Actually it was very strange. I mean this Schopenhauer quote, which is something like first they laugh at you and then they...

*...first they ignore you, then they laugh at you. Yeah.*

**Bertrand:** Actually, it was true, literally. The first OOPSLA, I had my paper under the USCSB umbrella, so it was a truly academic paper, and the company also had a booth, which was quite makeshift, because we didn't have any money at all. The booth signs were handmade, partly hand-written.

People would come to our booth and essentially laugh at us, and then they would bring their friends to share the laugh. As I mentioned earlier, one of the things they laughed at was the word *genericity*. There were these big guys from HP, and when I say "big," I really mean big. Some suits from HP came to our booth several times, bringing a different friend each time, and pointing them to the word. "How do you pronounce this? That must be French or something." They were loudly pretending to try various pronunciations: "It must be generi*sissy*ty!" and so on.

That really was the spirit of the time. Then, of course, 20 years later I get to referee papers that say that genericity was invented by Java. That's part of the fun of life.

## Proofreading Languages

*You speak at least three natural languages I've heard: English, obviously, French, and German. Has being multilingual or a polyglot influenced you as a language designer?*

**Bertrand:** The short answer is yes. My German is actually not great. French is my native tongue. English, I do my best. I speak fairly fluent Russian. Actually I have a Master's degree in Russian, although I don't speak anywhere close to the level of one who has a Master's degree. I speak reasonable Italian. Actually I can lecture in Russian without too much trouble. I can lecture in Italian for 15 minutes, and then my mind kind of overheats. Anyway, that was to be more accurate, but the answer to your question is definitely yes.

I was drawn to computer science partly because of my interest in languages. Knowing that there are several ways to say something, that they are not in one-to-one correspondence with one another, that you can take a different tack at things, that sometimes a noun will be the right solution, sometimes a verb would express the nuance that you are trying to convey—this has definitely influenced and helped me a lot. I also think that you speak your own native tongue better if you know at least one foreign language.

In addition, much of what one does in technical endeavors and in programming in particular is not just writing programs, but writing English or another natural language. Having spent a little time on writing skills and on learning one or more languages helps tremendously.

*Do you approach programming from a mathematical perspective or a linguistic perspective, or some combination of the two?*

**Bertrand:** I wish I would approach programming more mathematically than I do. I'm convinced that 50 years from now, programming will just be a branch of mathematics.

Some people have been promoting the mathematical approach to programming for a long time. It has not really caught on, except in a few select areas when people really do not have a choice when they are building fairly small, life-critical systems. In the end, programming is operational mathematics; mathematics that can be interpreted by a machine. I think programming will be even more mathematical in the future.

As to my own approach, I think it's a mix of what you call a linguistic approach, the more spontaneous and creative and discursive approach, and an attempt to be rigorous and mathematical. Certainly Eiffel is more influenced by mathematics than most other existing languages, except perhaps for functional languages, like Haskell.

*I've asked a lot of designers about starting with a small, rigorous core language and building on that—take the lambda calculus. You can build anything computable once you have function application. What do you think of that approach?*

**Bertrand:** I don't think it helps that much. The problem of programming is the combination of science and engineering. One aspect of programming is essentially scientific, and as I said fundamentally programming is mathematics. But the other side is the engineering side. If you take some of the programs that exist today, they are more complex than just about any artifact that humankind has built before. The big operating systems—like a Linux distribution, Vista, Solaris—are in the tens of millions of lines of codes, often over 50 million; these are incredibly complex engineering constructions. Many of the issues that they have to address are essentially engineering issues.

The difference between science and engineering, to simplify things a bit, is that in science you need a few very smart ideas; in engineering you need to take care of very large amounts of details, most of which are not very complicated, but they are very numerous. The contrast is between a few smart things and a very large number of not particularly difficult things. What is interesting about programming is that you need both. I seem to be contradicting what I said a moment ago, that in a few decades programming would be essentially mathematical, but I think there is no contradiction. Let me try to explain.

Fundamentally programming is nothing more than mathematics, but the emphasis is on the word *fundamentally*. In practice, programming also involves all these engineering issues that you have to take care of. If you are writing an operating system, you must deal with the problem of thousands of device drivers written by naïve programmers and make sure they don't crash your operating system. You have to take care of all the human languages and dialogs that people use. You need to have a very complex set of mechanisms for user interfaces; even though the basic ideas might be simple, the details are numerous.

The difficulty of programming is twofold: the scientific difficulty and the engineering difficulty. Having a very strong mathematical basis, for example, lambda calculus, will help you with the first half, but not with the second one, and it helps you with the part that is the best understood today. Lambda calculus is very good to model the core part of a programming language at a level of something like Pascal or Lisp, but more modern programming languages are far more ambitious than that.

In the end, we must reduce everything to very simple mathematical principles, but the mathematical principles themselves are not enough to tackle the challenges of large-scale programming today.

*Is that the difference between an academic programming language and an industry programming language?*

**Bertrand:** Absolutely. At the time of the design of Ada, people were criticizing it as being too big and too complex, and Jean Ichbiah, its designer, said in an interview that "Small languages solve small problems." There is a certain amount of truth in that. I think he was essentially answering criticism by people like Wirth, who is very much into "small is beautiful," but he was largely right.

*What's in between structured programming and OO? You mentioned that you thought structured programming was a good way to structure small programs and object orientation was a good way to structure large programs. Is there a scope of programs in between, size-wise?*

**Bertrand:** No, I would not use anything other than object-oriented programming. I basically learned the two at the same time, and I see no reason ever to use any non-OO technique for any development except possibly small throw-away scripts. "Object-oriented" simply means applying the mathematical notion of structure to programs, and there is no good argument against that.

*You have either small programs or big programs.*

**Bertrand:** There is no clear reason not to use classes. I am not sure what Dijkstra thought of this. He was never a great proponent of object-oriented programming, but I also did not hear him criticize it; he could be extremely outspoken and loud if he didn't like something.

*You mentioned that one of the things you really needed for Eiffel was a streaming serialization mechanism. Can I ask why you needed that?*

**Bertrand:** The first application we built was the Smart Editor that I mentioned, which was commercialized as ArchiText. All the time what you need to do with an editor is to work on a small data structure, which is in memory, and then to store it. One way is to parse or unparse the text each time, which is an absurd way to go. Assume that you are editing a text and you have reconstructed a small structure for the text, and you have an abstract syntax tree or other effective internal representation; you do not want to unparse it to text and then reparse it the next time around. You want to use the abstract structure all the time. When you need to store it, you just press a button, which is what the streaming mechanism does for you.

That was the first application, but every subsequent application has been like this, too. If you are writing a compiler, it's the same thing. Assume that you have several passes in your compiler; each pass takes the data structure from the previous pass, decorates it, massages it a little more, and then stores the result to disk. You do not want to have to write this in a specific way each time. You just want to press a button. Dozens of applications need this kind of thing.

*You can add more stages in between.*

**Bertrand:** Right. You are not restricted to one particular processing structure.

*You mentioned something called "seamless development," and said this was a real fundamental idea in Eiffel. What is seamless development?*

**Bertrand:** It is the idea that you have unity through the process of constructing software: a single set of issues, a single set of solutions to these issues, and then a single notation to express the results, which is what the Eiffel language tries to be.

This is completely going against the grain of the evolution of the industry for the past 20 years, which I disapprove in this respect. The tendency has been for separation, because it is good for business, because people then have to buy analysis tools and design tools and IDEs, and use consultants at each level.

Also I think it's because people do not realize that, for example, specifications are software in essentially the same way that implementation is software. Historically, programming languages were very low-level, so the idea that you could think in a programming language was absurd, but with what we can do today there is no reason to retain these gaps.

*People have trouble escaping the mindset that we had in the punch card era where you submitted your program as a batch job and came back the next day, and if you had a compilation error you were in trouble. You had to sit and think really, really hard beforehand.*

**Bertrand:** Right. There is nothing wrong in thinking hard beforehand, but it does not mean that you should be using completely different schemes of thinking and then, as a consequence, tools and languages at the different stages.

People see this almost in moral terms. There is this implicit idea that analysis is noble and great, and that implementation is dirty and despicable. This was true to a certain extent when you had to program in assembly language, or even in things like FORTRAN. FORTRAN is a remarkable achievement for its time, but not something that most people would want to think in. Hence this idea that the noble part of the work is this early thinking, and then at some point someone—not necessarily the same person—implements the whole, rolls up his sleeves, and does the lowly work, like opening the hood of the car and starting to dirty his hands.

This was true up to a point, but with modern programming languages, and certainly with Eiffel, it does not have to be that way. Instead of trying to make our analysis and design methods more implementation-oriented, we start from the other end. We start from the programming end and make the programming language so expressive, so elegant, so close to productive modes of thinking, that we can do all of our work in it. The first versions of the program will be abstract and descriptive, then later versions will be more operational and will actually execute. There need not be any gaps between those various stages of the process.

It is the reverse, for example, of model-driven development, which says you have the model and then you have something completely different, the program.

*Your model in that case, whether it's visual or not, is akin to the source code, because it's what you generate, and the source code is sort of an afterthought.*

**Bertrand:** This is good as long as you have the absolute guarantee that no one will ever touch the source code, either to debug it or to change it, for example. This is always what people say initially—"Sure, we only work on the model and no one will ever touch the source code"—but the practice is often quite different.

*The source code is the artifact of the design.*

**Bertrand:** The question is what do you debug? If you really debug the model, then there is nothing to criticize. Then of course it means that what you call the model is just a program. Maybe it is a very high-level program, but it is a program. You have developed a very high-level programming language, and then you need to build a complete development environment around it.

On the other hand, if the program that you debug is the generated program, then you will run into all the difficulties of a split development. This is the key question to ask people who say they do model-driven development: which version do you debug? Which version do you change when the customer wants a new feature for yesterday?

*Can one prove programs or are contracts just for testing?*

With this contract mechanism present right from the start in Eiffel, the idea has always been that contracts would be used to proof programs in the long term, but in the short term they would be used to test programs. One consequence is that you can enable runtime monitoring of contracts, and then when a contract is violated, you get an exception.

The next step, which actually took a long time to carry out, was to say, let's use this as the basis for completely automated testing. This is the research we have done in the past few years in my group at ETH, which is now integrated in the tools.

The basic question was: what is difficult in testing?

One, we have to automate the testing process. This has been solved by JUnit and all these great tools that people use now to automate that part of the process.

There are two more things to automate, which essentially no one else has automated, but they're the most difficult. One is test-case generation, because you need to create all test cases—potentially thousands, or tens of thousands, or hundreds of thousands of them. Third and last, even if you did the first two, you still have a problem, because you are going to run these thousands of tests and someone has to decide whether the test is successful or not, each one of them, so that also has to be automated with test oracles. What we can do with contracts is to have test oracles taken care of simply by saying: if the postcondition or invariant is satisfied, then the test succeeds; if the postcondition or the invariant is violated, then the test has failed. This is automatic.

What remains is generating the test cases, and for this we use the approach that seems the most silly at first, and in fact, works remarkably well: random or quasi-random generation.

The tool creates objects almost randomly, and then it calls all the routines, all the methods of the corresponding classes, with mostly random arguments. Then we just wait. We call this "Test While You Lunch." We start the push-button test, and come back from lunch an hour later, and see the postcondition violations.

This works remarkably well, because basically you have nothing to do. You just wait for the automatic-generation mechanism to exercise your software. But you can only do this with a language that has contracts built in, because otherwise people would have to add on the contracts and the contract-checking mechanism. If you do have support for contracts, it's actually a remarkable way to test your software.

*What do you think about program provability? Is that useful? Is that always going to be a pipe dream?*

**Bertrand:** It is becoming more and more realistic. For the academic part of my work, it occupies a good deal of our efforts. It has been very frustrating, because the basic ideas have been there for almost 40 years, essentially since the publication of Tony Hoare's axiomatic semantics paper in '69. The practical realization has been very slow to come, but no, it is not a pipe dream.

Certainly in the past 5 to 10 years there's been considerable progress. The work at Microsoft Research with Spec# is very interesting. There's the work that we are doing with Eiffel at ETH, which has not registered that much yet because we are very ambitious, so we have to solve lots of problems before we can really impress the world. But I think it is promising.

There's the work on SPARK. It is a very interesting development. They are actually able to produce programs that are proved. Now the catch is that it is a language that no one would want to program in. They call it a subset of Ada. It's really a subset of Pascal, with modules. The price to pay is that you have to renounce all the pleasures of life. No classes, no dynamic object creation, no genericity, no inheritance, no pointers. By taking such a reduced language they have been able to build effective proof tools. That is a real achievement because it makes it possible to build significant systems, typically military or aerospace, and prove their correctness. Now you would not want to program in that language. I would not, and 99% of the programmers in the world would not. Still, it's a major achievement.

What we are trying to do with our proof effort, at ETH, is something similar, but for a language that people will want to program in. The difficulty is to include all the programming language mechanisms that we have come to know and love. Of course, as soon as you have pointers, for example, you have aliasing, and this immediately complicates the problem considerably. The challenge is no longer to prove programs. It is to prove programs written in a modern realistic programming language. It will happen.

One has to realize that we are essentially dealing with undecidable problems. In the end there will always be parts of programs that we cannot prove, and that is also why the other side of what we are doing is tests. The development is going much faster. This is certainly the most exciting thing that we have done for the past two or three years, and it is now completely integrated with the environment. So basically one of the benefits of having contracts is that you can test completely automatically. We have this Eiffel Testing Framework, now completely integrated in Eiffel Studio, which is essentially push-button testing. You don't have to write test cases. You don't have to write test oracles. You just call the Testing Framework, which creates instances of classes and calls the methods on these classes, and then waits for a contract to fail. The other cool side of the Testing Framework is the test synthesis part: when an execution fails, the tool automatically creates a test out of it, which you can rerun to help fix the bug, and keep as part of your regression test suite.

To relate this to your question, there are proofs and there are tests, and the two aspects will always remain necessary. But proofs definitely are becoming possible.

*Proofs and contracts seem like different stops along a sliding scale.*

**Bertrand:** As I mentioned we started with dynamic evaluation of contracts, but the idea has always been that the eventual aim was to prove that classes satisfy their contracts. There was not the industrial possibility until recently. People were just not ready for proofs.

*Should we expect to see this in Eiffel in the next few years?*

**Bertrand:** Absolutely. This is still partly research, so it is difficult to give an exact deadline. The research work on testing started about four years ago and now the first results are part of the environment. For proofs, I think we are going to see the first outcomes in about that same time; I would say three years from now.

*OK, so it's definitely a production goal for you?*

**Bertrand:** Absolutely.

*You mentioned areas of unprovability in code. Haskell uses the concept of monads to separate functionally pure code from impure code—code that has side effects. Could there be a similar mechanism to isolate unprovable code?*

**Bertrand:** We have to separate the parts we can prove from the parts we cannot prove, but I don't think we will use monads for that. Monads are a very interesting concept. They can be used in the context of proving for something else: they make an incremental approach possible by defining a base language that supports provability and then adding more advanced language constructs like exceptions or others in a more incremental way.

## Managing Growth and Evolution

*You said that you designed Eiffel in about an afternoon, but it took about 20 years to implement that vision.*

**Bertrand:** The key ideas really are very simple and all the rest is commentary, as they say. To a certain extent, that's what we did. We have expanded on the basic concept for the past 20 years.

You take classes, you take inheritance, especially multiple inheritance. You take genericity, you take contracts, and then a number of language principles, like for example, something that is very important in Eiffel, which is that you need to provide one good way to do anything. Also the idea of high signal-to-noise ratio: that the language should not pursue small size as such, but should select features on the basis of how much power each feature adds and how little complication it brings. You take a couple dozen ideas like this, some of them language ideas, other meta-ideas about language design, and basically that's it. But to turn this into something that is useful to write applications that simulate the U.S. ballistic missile defense system, or manage billions of dollars, you need the engineering part, which takes a lot of time.

Anyone has limited resources, and it is not a matter of being a small versus a large company, because every innovative design comes from a small group. The only exceptions are projects that are essentially engineering projects. You send a man to the moon; well, this takes thousands of people for a few years. Or maybe the human genome, you know how to do it initially—you just need what I would call engineering. But those are the exceptions.

If you take really innovative ideas, I have never seen a breakthrough product in software that was built by more than 10 people, and usually it is somewhere between 2 and 5. Anyone has limited resources, so the key decisions that you make are what to do and what not to do.

Certainly along the way we have made a few mistakes. For example, we invested in an OS/2 version, which was a complete waste of effort; we should have put the work into making the basic version better. These are the decisions that you have to make on a day-to-day basis, and some of them have been mistakes.

*Did it take 20 years to reach the point where you were satisfied with the language, where the implementation, the polish, and the applicability met your original design goals?*

**Bertrand:** I would not say that, because if you do not have a certain amount of chutzpah, you don't go into something like this. In a way the first implementation was already something that the whole world should have used already. One can also be much more modest and say we are not there yet.

We're working on it every day, improving the implementation and doing things that we think are absolutely indispensable. It's never going to be perfect, certainly not during my lifetime, but the question is what you work on at any particular point in time, what you decide is important, and what you decide is an accessory. One can always revisit past choices and wonder whether the emphasis was the right one or not.

Certainly there have always been aspects of the implementation that people would criticize, often rightly. On the other hand, we have people who have been using Eiffel for 10, 15 years, some almost since the first implementation appeared, and they seem to have been very happy with it all along.

So on the one hand, I'm never satisfied with the implementation; on the other hand, I think that Eiffel throughout its existence has provided an excellent solution, far ahead of the pack, to people who wanted to use it.

*You have to have the chutzpah to believe you can spend 20 years on a project, but you also have to work on a project you think you can love for 20 years.*

**Bertrand:** Right. The decision of what to do and what not to do is very hard, because for example, we were one of the first commercial companies to introduce a version for Linux. At the time this sounded like a completely crazy decision. Take Linux versus OS/2. The effort on OS/2 was for absolutely nothing. On the other hand, someone told me at some point, in '93 I think, really early, "We're using this thing called Linux. Could you have a version for Linux?" No one wanted to do it within the company. I told them it claims to be a variant of Unix—we covered dozens of Unix variants because at the time commercial Unix had many variants, we had worked very hard to develop a highly portable technology—so just try to recompile the stuff under Linux and see if it works, and if it's going to be one month of work, it's not worth it. If it's going to be one day of work, it may be worth it. Actually it was no work at all. The whole thing compiled on Linux at the push of a button. The guy who had asked me for a Linux version was very happy, and then suddenly requests started coming in.

From a conventional wisdom standpoint, Linux was a stupid thing to do and OS/2 was the smart thing to do, and it turned out that it was exactly the reverse. Having an early Linux version helped us tremendously. It's very difficult to make these decisions, and you of course are working with limited information, with people giving you advice who often really do not know what they are talking about.

The lesson is that you have to rely on everyone's input, but in the end you must know what you are doing and can only rely on yourself, on your own judgment.

*What criteria do you use to analyze those decisions?*

**Bertrand:** Consistency. Is it consistent with the idea of the organization? Is this consistent? Is this starting us in a direction that is going to pull us away from our core ideas and competence and pleasure, because you have to take pleasure in what you're doing, or is this going to be a new experience that teaches us something new and adds to what we already know?

*Today, how do you choose which features to add to Eiffel? How do you grow a language?*

**Bertrand:** Until '98, almost 2000–2001, basically I was in charge of the evolution, and then things changed with the creation of the Eiffel standards committee at Ecma, which led to an Ecma standard in 2005 and an ISO standard in 2006. To answer the question administratively, the changes that go into the language are those approved by the committee. Now to answer it more technically, we have been extremely careful about the growth of Eiffel; some of what we have done as a committee and community are fairly original.

First we have this principle that in the language, there should be one good way to do anything. This is the best way we have to resist creeping featurism. It is not that we do not want new features, but we do not want to include new features in the language that are going to be redundant with existing mechanisms. The criterion is that if a programmer wants to do something, he needs to have one good way to do it. As a counterexample, some languages have both dynamic binding and arrays of function pointers. As a programmer, especially as a novice OO programmer, you do not know which of these techniques to use if you have the problem of calling a different function depending on a certain object type. Eiffel causes almost no such dilemmas. The principle cannot be achieved 100%, but we are close.

Another guiding principle is to maximize what one may call the signal-to-noise ratio. It's interesting to compare this with the Niklaus Wirth approach to languages. Wirth really likes to have small languages, and he has this phobia of bloat. I think that many of the mechanisms of Eiffel would seem to him to make the language too big. I greatly admire this view, but Eiffel rests on a slightly different one. A language should not necessarily be small for the sake of size; it's more that the signal-to-noise ratio should be very high, meaning very little noise. What I call "noise" are language features that are not very useful but just complicate the language without bringing a lot of expressive power, and "signal" means expressive power. As an example of this, we added about 12 years ago a notion of "agent" that has proved tremendously successful. It's a form of closures, full-fledged lambda expressions, and there was some concern that it would be redundant with existing mechanisms, but this has not happened. That is an example of a major addition to the language that has proved extremely popular with the users and made possible things we could not do elegantly before. All signal, very little noise.

The third principle is to make sure that everything we do is compatible with the goals of Eiffel and the spirit of Eiffel, and in particular, to improve the reliability of the language and decrease the possibility of errors for programmers. Some really major developments have occurred in this respect in the past two to three years. I think Eiffel is the first commercial language that is void-safe. What that means is no null pointer referencing anymore. This is fully implemented with the latest release, 6.4, with the libraries completely converted. Void safety is the standard problem of object-oriented languages or actually even of C or Pascal that x.f could crash because x is null, or void in Eiffel terminology. For Eiffel programmers the risk is completely gone. I think it is a major achievement because it removes the major potential runtime problem that still exists with object-oriented development. This is the kind of thing that we want to do to increase the reliability of software developers.

There are more principles, but let me mention just one more, which is that the standards committee has been pretty bold. We are not shy about changing the language. In particular, we will not hesitate to remove language mechanisms if we feel that there is a better way to do things. Of course, we do this extremely carefully because there is an installed base and if a customer has millions of lines of code we cannot afford to break the code, so typically the old mechanisms are still supported for several years. We offer migration tools and various aids, but if at some point we come to the conclusion that there was a certain way A of doing things and we have found a way B of achieving the same result that is better (in the sense of being simpler, safer, more extensible, and so on), then we just remove something that was there and replace it by the mechanism that we think is better.

## How do you handle concerns of backward and forward compatibility?

**Bertrand:** This is at the center of our concerns. I would say if you have been in business and have had a product for some time, this quickly becomes one of the dominant considerations, and it takes up an incredible amount of our time.

It is an extremely hard question if you are not the dominant player. If you are the dominant player in the market, you can do whatever you like. All the big names in the industry do this once in a while. They basically change overnight, and customers have no choice but to follow.

The Eiffel community is a little special in this respect in that it is more open to innovation than most other communities—in particular, language communities. People accept that things have to change, but because the people who use Eiffel tend to be forward-looking, interested in really good solutions that are elegant and creative, they accept that things change, even if they have millions of lines of code to manage. What they don't like, and what no one anywhere likes, is for someone to point a pistol at their head and say, "change now or die." If this is your approach to change, you are not going to be very popular with your users.

The strategy that we have in the Ecma committee is to try to see all the ins and outs of the situation and take every issue into consideration. If we decide something has to change, then we change it. We are not going to reject change with the excuse that things have been done one particular way for years. If we have to change, we will change, but change has to be planned very carefully. I'm simplifying, because there are language changes, there are library changes, there are tool changes, and the strategy is not necessarily the same for each case, but these are the basic rules:

- Do your homework and be absolutely convinced that this is the right change.
- Make a plan.
- You have to explain why you are making the change. This is very important. You have to assume that you are talking to intelligent people. If you have indeed done your homework and thought very carefully about the reasons for the change and are able to explain it to and convince your closer colleagues, then you will be able to convince other intelligent people as well.

- Give people time. Almost always a significant language change implies a two-step process, sometimes three steps. There is one release in which the new mechanism is optional and the old one is still the default, but you can try the new mechanism as an option, typically on a class-by-class basis, so that you can try it on parts of your system. Then there is a version that reverses the defaults.

  We very seldom remove something completely. Even if something is deprecated, it still remains available as an option. It is unfortunately not always possible to do this, because sometimes an incompatibility exists between the old mechanism and the new mechanism.

- Provide migrations aids if you can: tools, libraries, whatever can help people move from the old mechanism to the new one.

We have gone through this many times, especially in the past five or six years. If you take the history of the Eiffel language, there have been two major upheavals. The first version was in 1985–1986. The second version was in 1988, but this was essentially additions, so it did not cause any incompatibility problem. Then we moved to Eiffel 3 between 1990 and 1993; this was definitely a major upheaval, but the benefits were so big that it didn't cause too much trouble.

The language did not change very much until the start of the standards process in 2001. The standard was published in 2005 and became an ISO standard in 2006. It introduced some substantial language changes, which took several years to implement; the implementation is almost complete now. We are currently in the midst of probably one of the most difficult instances of the problem, and it is really worth it. It's the attached type mechanism, solving the void safety problem that I brought up earlier, the guarantee that no x.f call will ever be executed if x is null. The compiler catches such cases and rejects the program if it could cause a void call (a null pointer dereferencing). But the mechanism does cause incompatibilities with existing code, if only for the good reason that in existing codes, there are cases in which there could indeed be void calls. The mechanism was essentially implemented for 6.2, and the finishing touches were put in 6.3; the full library conversion to void safety, which turns out to be a large endeavor, is for 6.4. (We work with a "clock cycle" scheme, producing two releases a year, one in the spring, one in the fall.)

Conversion of existing code has turned out to be a delicate issue. We cannot afford to make existing code obsolete, ever. What we can do is to tell users: if you want to take advantage of this new mechanism that is going to be available now, here is what you have to do, and we have done it ourselves, so we know that it's worthwhile, and we also know how much effort it is. We provide you with all the benefits of our experience, and tools to help you do it.

*What should people learn from your experience?*

**Bertrand:** Disregard fashion and choose the solution that is right intellectually.

# Afterword

**A SINGLE WORD DESCRIBES MY CHIEF PLEASURE FROM WORKING ON THIS PROJECT—ENTHUSIASM.**
Every interviewee offered the rewards you might expect—deep knowledge, historical lore, and practical insights—but it was their enthusiasm for the subject of language design, implementation, and growth that proved infectious.

For example, Anders Hejlsberg and James Gosling made me excited about C# and Java again. Chuck Moore and Adin Falkoff convinced me to explore Forth and APL, two languages invented before I was born. Al Aho enticed me by describing his compiler class. Everyone we interviewed gave me multiple ideas I wish I had the time to explore!

My debt of gratitude is great, not just for the time they gave Federico and me, but because they blazed trails to a rich and fertile field of invention. The best lessons I've taken away from this experience are:

- Never underestimate the value of simplicity of design or implementation. You can always add complexity. A master removes it.

- Pursue your curiosity with passion. Many of the best inventions and discoveries occurred when someone was in the right place at the right time, ready to chase the right answer.

- Know the field, past and present. Every one of the interviewees worked with other smart, hardworking people. Our field depends on this sharing of information.

The languages du jour may change continually, but the problems each of these masterminds faced still haunt us—and their answers still apply. How do you maintain software? How do you find the best solution to a problem? How do you surprise and delight users? How do you handle the inevitable desire for change without disrupting solutions that must continue to work?

I have better answers to those questions now. I hope this book has helped you in your own search for wisdom.

—*Shane Warden*

# Contributors

**Alfred V. Aho** is the Lawrence Gussman professor in the computer science department at Columbia University. He served as chair of the department from 1995 to 1997, and in the spring of 2003.

Professor Aho has a B.A.Sc. in engineering physics from the University of Toronto and a Ph.D. in electrical engineering/computer science from Princeton University.

Professor Aho won the Great Teacher Award for 2003 from the Society of Columbia Graduates.

Professor Aho has won the IEEE John von Neumann Medal and is a Member of the U.S. National Academy of Engineering and the American Academy of Arts and Sciences. He received honorary doctorates from the Universities of Helsinki and Waterloo, and is a Fellow of the American Association for the Advancement of Science, the ACM, Bell Labs, and the IEEE.

Professor Aho is well known for his many papers and books on algorithms and data structures, programming languages, compilers, and the foundations of computer science. His book coauthors include John Hopcroft, Brian Kernighan, Monica Lam, Ravi Sethi, Jeff Ullman, and Peter Weinberger.

Professor Aho is the "A" in AWK, a widely used pattern-matching language; "W" is Peter Weinberger; and "K" is Brian Kernighan. The Aho-Corasick string-matching algorithm is used in many bibliographic search and genomic analysis programs. He also wrote the initial versions of the string pattern-matching programs egrep and fgrep that first appeared on Unix.

Professor Aho's current research interests include programming languages, compilers, algorithms, software engineering, and quantum computers. Professor Aho has served as chair of ACM's Special Interest Group on Algorithms and Computability Theory, and chair of the Advisory Committee for the National Science Foundation's Computer and Information Science and Engineering Directorate. He is currently the coeditor-in-chief of the contributed articles section of the *Communications of the ACM*.

Prior to his current position at Columbia, Professor Aho was vice president of the Computing Sciences Research Center at Bell Labs, the lab that invented UNIX, C, and C++. He was also a member of technical staff, department head, and director of this center. Professor Aho was also the general manager of the Information Sciences and Technologies Research Laboratory at Bellcore (now Telcordia).

**Grady Booch** is recognized internationally for his innovative work in software architecture, software engineering, and collaborative development environments. He has devoted his life's work to improving the art and the science of software development. Grady served as chief scientist of Rational Software Corporation since its founding in 1981 and through its acquisition by IBM in 2003. He now is part of the IBM Thomas J. Watson Research Center serving as chief scientist for software engineering, where he continues his work on the Handbook of Software Architecture and also leads several projects in software engineering that are beyond the constraints of immediate product horizons. Grady continues to engage with customers working on real problems and is working to build deep relationships with academia and other research organizations around the world. Grady is one of the original authors of the Unified Modeling Language (UML) and was also one of the original developers of several of Rational's products. Grady has served as architect and architectural mentor for numerous complex software-intensive systems around the world in just about every domain imaginable.

Grady is the author of six bestselling books, including the *UML Users Guide* and the seminal *Object-Oriented Analysis and Design with Applications* (both Addison-Wesley Professional). He writes a regular column on architecture for IEEE Software. Grady has published several hundred articles on software engineering, including papers published in the early 80s that originated the term and practice of object-oriented design (OOD), plus papers published in the early 2000s that originated the term and practice of collaborative development environments (CDE).

Grady is a member of the Association for Computing Machinery (ACM), the American Association for the Advancement of Science (AAAS), and Computer Professionals for

Social Responsibility (CPSR), as well as a senior member of the Institute of Electrical and Electronics Engineers (IEEE). He is an IBM Fellow, an ACM Fellow, a World Technology Network Fellow, a Software Development Forum Visionary, and a recipient of Dr. Dobb's Excellence in Programming award, as well as three Jolt Awards. Grady was a founding board member of the Agile Alliance, the Hillside Group, and the Worldwide Institute of Software Architects, and now also serves on the advisory board of the International Association of Software Architecture. Additionally, Grady serves on the boards of the Iliff School of Theology and the Computer History Museum. He is also a member of the IEEE Software editorial board. Grady helped establish work at the Computer History Museum for the preservation of classic software and therein has conducted several oral histories for luminaries such as John Backus, Fred Brooks, and Linus Torvalds.

Grady received his B.S. from the United States Air Force Academy in 1977 and his M.S. in electrical engineering from the University of California at Santa Barbara in 1979.

**Don Chamberlin** is co-inventor, with Ray Boyce, of SQL, the world's most widely used database query language. He was also one of the managers of System R, the research project that produced the first implementation of SQL and developed much of the basic technology underlying IBM's family of database products.

Don is also a coauthor of the "Quilt" proposal, which became the basis for the XQuery language. He served as IBM's representative to the W3C XML Query Working Group during the development of XQuery and as editor of the XQuery language specification.

Don is currently an adjunct professor of computer science at University of California, Santa Cruz. He is also an IBM Fellow (Emeritus), affiliated with IBM Almaden Research Center, where he worked for many years. For the past 11 years, he has also served as a judge and problem contributor to the annual ACM International Collegiate Programming Contest.

Don holds a B.S. degree in engineering from Harvey Mudd College, and a Ph.D. in electrical engineering from Stanford University. He is an ACM Fellow and a member of the National Academy of Engineering. He is also a recipient of the ACM Software Systems Award for his contributions to the design and implementation of relational database systems.

**Dr. Brad Cox** is currently chief architect for Accenture, where he specializes in SOA security, interoperability, standards, and component-based engineering for clients within government and industry.

He was part of the faculty of the George Mason Program on Social and Organizational Learning (PSOL), an interdisciplinary department that concentrates on overcoming obstacles to change, development, and learning as firms transition to a global information-intensive economy. His interests were in applying Internet, television, and groupware technology to expediting experiential and collaborative learning. Courses included Taming the Electronic Frontier, Internet Literacy, and Advanced Object Technology.

He coauthored the book *Object-Oriented Programming: An Evolutionary Approach* (Addison-Wesley), often credited with today's enthusiasm for object technology and component-based engineering. His second book, *Superdistribution: Objects As Property on the Electronic Frontier* (Addison-Wesley), proposes a technosocial solution to buying, selling and owning property made of bits as distinct from the atoms from which goods have been composed since antiquity.

He was a cofounder of the Stepstone Corporation, where he originated the Objective-C programming language and Software-IC libraries.

At Schlumberger-Doll Research, he applied artificial intelligence, object-oriented, Unix, and workstation technologies to oil field wireline services.

At the Programming Technology Center at ITT, he applied Unix and object-oriented technologies in support of the development of a large, highly distributed telephone switching system, System 1240.

His Ph.D. from the University of Chicago is for theoretical and experimental work in neurophysiology in an area since known as neural networks. His post-graduate experimental studies were at the National Institutes of Health and at the Woods Hole Marine Biological Laboratories.

**Adin D. Falkoff** (B.Ch.E., CCNY 1941; M.A., mathematics, Yale 1963), prior to a stint in U.S. Navy during WWII, worked in the development of materials and methods for the mass manufacture of precision optical instruments. He subsequently worked in the design of airborne antennas for military aircraft, before joining IBM in 1955 where he was the manager of research publications during the formative years of the IBM Research Division. He started work on various aspects of computer science in the late 1950s, and after attending Yale University under the IBM Resident Scholarship Program in 1960, he concentrated on computer science, including APL. He was a member of the visiting faculty at the IBM Systems Research Institute for several years, and a visiting lecturer in computer science at Yale University. From 1970 to 1974, Mr. Falkoff established and managed the IBM Philadelphia Scientific Center, and from 1977 to 1987 was the manager of the APL Design Group at the Thomas J. Watson Research Center. He has received IBM Outstanding Contribution Awards for the development of APL and the development of APL\360, and was the first recipient of the ACM Iverson Award for contributions to APL. He authored or coauthored publications including "Algorithms for Parallel Search Memories," "A Formal Description of System 360," "The Design of APL," "A Note on Pattern Matching: Where do you find the Empty Vector," "A Pictorial Format Function," "Semicolon-bracket notation: A hidden resource in APL," "The IBM Family of APL Systems," and many others. Mr. Falkoff holds patents in materials and methods for manufacture of precision optical instruments and the design of computer systems.

**Luiz Henrique de Figueiredo** holds a D.Sc. in mathematics from IMPA, the National Institute for Pure and Applied Mathematics in Rio de Janeiro, where he is an Associate Researcher and a member of the Vision and Graphics laboratory. He is also a consultant for geometric modeling and software tools at Tecgraf, the Computer Graphics Technology Group of PUC-Rio, where he helped to create Lua.

Besides his work on Lua, his current research interests include computational geometry, geometric modeling, and interval methods in computer graphics, especially applications of affine arithmetic.

He has held post-doctoral positions at the University of Waterloo in Canada and at the National Laboratory for Scientific Computation in Brazil. He is a member of the editorial board of the *Journal of Universal Computer Science*.

**James Gosling** received a B.Sc. in computer science from the University of Calgary, Canada in 1977. He received a Ph.D. in computer science from Carnegie-Mellon University in 1983. The title of his thesis was "The Algebraic Manipulation of Constraints." He is currently a VP & Fellow at Sun Microsystems. He has built satellite data acquisition systems, a multiprocessor version of Unix, several compilers, mail systems, and window managers. He has also built a WYSIWYG text editor, a constraint-based drawing editor and a text editor called Emacs for Unix systems. At Sun, his early activity was as lead engineer of the NeWS window system. He did the original design of the Java programming language and implemented its original compiler and virtual machine. He has been a contributor to the Real-Time Specification for Java, and a researcher at Sun Labs, where his primary interest was software development tools. He was the chief technology officer of Sun's Developer Products Group and is now the CTO of Sun's Client Software Group.

**Charles (Chuck) Geschke** cofounded Adobe Systems Incorporated in 1982. A leader in the software industry for more than 35 years, Geschke retired from his position as president of Adobe in 2000 and continues to share the chairmanship of the board with Adobe's cofounder John Warnock.

Geschke actively participates on several boards of educational institutions, nonprofits, technology companies, and arts organizations. In 1995, he was elected to the National Academy of Engineering. In 2008, he was elected to the American Academy of Arts and Sciences. He recently completed his term as chairman of the Board of Trustees of the University of San Francisco. He is a member of the Board of Governors of the San Francisco Symphony and the board of the Commonwealth Club of California. He also serves on the computer science advisory board of Carnegie-Mellon University, the board of the Egan Maritime Foundation, the board of the National Leadership Roundtable On Church Management, the board of directors of Tableau Software, and the board of the Nantucket Boys and Girls Club.

Prior to cofounding Adobe Systems, Geschke formed the Imaging Sciences Laboratory at the Xerox Palo Alto Research Center (PARC) in 1980, where he directed research activities in the fields of computer science, graphics, image processing, and optics. From 1972 to 1980, he was a principal scientist and researcher at Xerox PARC's Computer Sciences Laboratory. Before beginning full-time graduate studies in 1968, he was on the faculty of the mathematics department of John Carroll University in Cleveland, Ohio.

Industry and business leaders, including the Association for Computing Machinery (ACM), the Institute of Electrical and Electronics Engineers (IEEE), Carnegie-Mellon University, the National Computer Graphics Association, and the Rochester Institute of Technology, have honored Geschke's technical and managerial achievements. He received the regional Entrepreneur of the Year Award in 1991 and the national Entrepreneur of the Year Award in 2003. In 2002, he was elected a Fellow of the Computer History Museum and in 2005 he was given the Exemplary Community Leadership Award by the NCCJ of Silicon Valley. Geschke received the Medal of Achievement from the American Electronics Association (AeA) in 2006. He and John Warnock are the first software leaders to receive this award. In 2007, he received the John W. Gardner Leadership Award. In 2000, Geschke was ranked the seventh most influential graphics person of the last millennium by Graphic Exchange magazine.

Geschke holds a Ph.D. in computer science from Carnegie-Mellon University and an M.S. in mathematics and an A.B. in Latin, both from Xavier University.

**Anders Hejlsberg** is a technical fellow in the Server and Tools Business Unit at Microsoft. Anders is recognized as an influential creator of development tools and programming languages. He is the chief designer of the C# programming language and a key participant in the development of the Microsoft .NET Framework. Since its initial release in 2000, the C# programming language has gained widespread adoption and is now standardized by ECMA and ISO.

Before joining Microsoft in 1996, Anders was one of the first employees of Borland International Inc. As principal engineer, he was the original author of Turbo Pascal, a revolutionary integrated development environment, and chief architect of its successor, Delphi.

Anders coauthored *The C# Programming Language*, published by Addison-Wesley, and has received numerous software patents. In 2001, Anders was the recipient of the prestigious Dr. Dobbs Excellence in Programming Award, and in 2007 he and his team were awarded Microsoft's Technical Recognition Award for Outstanding Technical Achievement. Anders studied engineering at the Technical University of Denmark.

**Paul Hudak** is a professor in the department of computer science at Yale University. He has been on the Yale faculty since 1982, and was chairman from 1999-2005. He received his B.S. in electrical engineering from Vanderbilt University in 1973, his M.S. in electrical engineering and computer science from MIT in 1974, and his Ph.D. in computer science from the University of Utah in 1982.

Professor Hudak's research interests center on programming-language design, theory, and implementation. He helped to organize and chair the Haskell Committee, which in 1988 released the first version of Haskell, a purely functional nonstrict programming language. Hudak was co-editor of the first Haskell Report, and has written a popular tutorial and a textbook on the language. His early work also involved parallel functional programming, abstract interpretation, and declarative approaches to state.

More recently, Professor Hudak has been involved in the design of domain-specific languages for a diverse set of application domains, including mobile and humanoid robotics, graphics and animation, music and sound synthesis, graphical user interfaces, and real-time systems. He has also developed techniques for embedding such languages in Haskell, including the use of abstract models of computation such as monads and arrows. His most recent focus has been on the use of Haskell in computer music and sound synthesis for both education and research.

Professor Hudak has published more than 100 papers and one book. He is editor-in-chief of the *Journal of Functional Programming*, and a founding member of IFIP Working Group 2.8 on Functional Programming. Among his honors, Professor Hudak is an ACM Fellow, and is a recipient of an IBM Faculty Development Award and an NSF Presidential Young Investigator Award.

Born in North Wales in 1958, **John Hughes** spent an influential year (1974–1975) between school and university as a programmer in the late Christopher Strachey's research group at Oxford University. As well as helping Strachey install a modem during the interview, it was here that John was introduced to functional programming, and developed a passion for it that has yet to fade. While studying mathematics at Cambridge, he co-developed perhaps the first compiler for GEDANKEN, John Reynolds's thought-experiment in programming language design. He returned to Oxford for his doctoral studies in 1980, completing a thesis on implementation techniques for functional languages in 1983. There he met his wife, Mary Sheeran, another research student in the same group.

In 1984–1985, John spent a postdoctoral year at Chalmers University in Gothenburg, Sweden, where seminal work on compiling lazy languages like Haskell was under way. He loved both the research environment, and the beauty of western Sweden. When the year ended, John returned briefly to Oxford as a lecturer, then in 1986 took up a Chair at Glasgow University in Scotland.

The Glasgow department was expanding strongly at the time, and John was able to found the Glasgow Functional Programming Group, which grew to be one of the best in the world—including both Phil Wadler and Simon Peyton Jones. The annual research group workshops became well known, and eventually developed into the Trends in Functional Programming symposium, which continues to this day.

But in 1992, John was offered a Chair at Chalmers, and took the opportunity to return to Sweden. There he continues to work in functional programming, and since 1999, on software testing using an automated tool called QuickCheck. In 2006 he founded Quviq, a startup that markets and develops QuickCheck, and he now spends half his time at the company.

John is now a Swedish citizen, and has made a fair attempt at learning both the Swedish language and how to ski—the latter from a very unpromising start! He has two sons, one of whom is both blind and autistic.

**Roberto Ierusalimschy** is an associate professor of computer science at PUC-Rio (Pontifical Chatolic University in Rio de Janeiro), where he works with programming-language design and implementation. He is the leading architect of the Lua programming language and the author of the book *Programming in Lua* (Lua.org; now in its second edition and translated to Chinese, Korean, and German).

Roberto has a M.Sc. Degree (1986) and a D.Sc. Degree (1990) in Computer Science, both from PUC-Rio. He was a visiting researcher at the University of Waterloo, (Canada, 1991), ICSI (CA, USA, 1994), GMD (Germany, 1997), and at UIUC (IL, USA, 2001/2002). As a professor at PUC-Rio, Roberto was the advisor of several students that later became influential members of the Lua community. Lately he has been developing LPEG, a novel pattern-maching package for Lua.

**Dr. Ivar Jacobson** was born in Ystad, Sweden, on September 2, 1939. (His full name is Ivar Hjalmar Jacobson, but he never uses the middle name.) Dr. Jacobson got his Master's of electrical engineering at Chalmers Institute of Technology in Gothenburg in 1962. He received his Ph.D. at the Royal Institute of Technology in Stockholm in 1985 with a thesis on Language Constructs for Large Real-Time Systems. He was a visiting scientist at the Functional Programming and Dataflow Architecture Group at MIT in 1983–1984. On May 3, 2003, he was awarded the Gustaf Dalén Medal by the Chalmers Alumni Association.

Ivar founded the Swedish company Objectory AB, which merged with Rational in 1995. He was with Rational during its outstanding growth until it was acquired by IBM in 2003. Then he departed from Rational as an employee, but he stayed as an executive technical consultant of the company for more than a year, until May 2004.

Concurrently with working for Rational, he has pursued other interesting ideas. One of them involves working at Jaczone AB, a company he founded April 2000 with his daughter Agneta Jacobson. Jaczone is implementing an old vision—make software process active instead of passive. An active process executes and assists the developers in carrying out their project.

Ivar also recognizes that the software development community desperately needs to improve in applying software development capability. In 2004, he founded Ivar Jacobson International, which aims to promote and help project teams across the world apply good software development practices. Ivar Jacobson International is now operating through separate companies in six countries: the U.K., the U.S., Sweden, China, Australia, and Singapore. In 2007, his new company acquired Jaczone, so the two companies are now consolidated.

**Simon Peyton Jones**, M.A., MBCS, CEng, graduated from Trinity College Cambridge in 1980. After two years in industry, he spent seven years as a lecturer at University College London, and nine years as a professor at Glasgow University, before moving to Microsoft Research (Cambridge) in 1998.

His main research interest is in functional programming languages, their implementation, and their application. He has led a succession of research projects focused around the design and implementation of production-quality functional-language systems for both uniprocessors and parallel machines. He was a key contributor to the design of the now-standard functional language Haskell, and is the lead designer of the widely used Glasgow Haskell Compiler (GHC). He has written two textbooks about the implementation of functional languages.

More generally, he is interested in language design, rich type systems, software component architectures, compiler technology, code generation, runtime systems, virtual machines, and garbage collection. He is particularly motivated by direct use of principled theory to practical language design and implementation—that's one reason he loves functional programming so much.

**Brian Kernighan** received his B.A.Sc. from the University of Toronto in 1964 and a Ph.D. in electrical engineering from Princeton in 1969. He was in the Computing Science Research center at Bell Labs until 2000, and is now in the computer science department at Princeton.

He is the author of eight books and some technical papers, and holds four patents. He was elected to the National Academy of Engineering in 2002. His research areas include programming languages, tools, and interfaces that make computers easier to use, often for non-specialist users. He is also interested in technology education for non-technical audiences.

**Thomas E. Kurtz** was born near Chicago, Illinois, on February 22, 1928. He attended Knox College in Illinois, graduating in 1950. He then attended Princeton University, earning a Ph.D. in mathematics in 1956. Kurtz was on the faculty of Dartmouth College from 1956 until retirement in 1993, teaching statistics, numerical analysis, and, eventually, computer science. In 1963–1964, he and John Kemeny (who later became president of Dartmouth College) devised the BASIC programming language. Aided by the Time Sharing and Personal Computer Revolutions, BASIC was for several decades the most widely used programming language around the world. He was the director of the Kiewit Computation Center at Dartmouth from 1966 to 1975.

He has served on numerous boards and committees, and written several books on programming with Dr. Kemeny. Upon his retirement from Dartmouth, he was active in True BASIC, Incorporated, which developed and marketed the BASIC computer language and other educational software products for personal computers.

**Tom Love** earned a Ph.D. in cognitive science from the University of Washington where he studied the cognitive characteristics of successful computer programmers. Tom's first post-graduate job was with General Electric Company doing user interface design for a proprietary text search machine—Google in a box! A few months later he was contacted by the Office of Naval Research to find out whether he was interested in continuing his Ph.D. research. That led to the formation of the Software Psychology group at GE.

Tom was attracted from GE to create a group of leading software researchers at ITT. It was in this group that the first object-oriented extension to C language was conceived and developed by Brad Cox. The ITT group was also exploring groupware, distributed computing, and interactive development environments in 1982! Based upon this experience, Tom subsequently became the first commercial user of Smalltalk in 1982.

In 1983, Tom and Brad Cox founded the first object-oriented products company, Stepstone. At Stepstone, they promoted object technology, originated the Software-IC concept, and marketed the first standalone set of reusable classes, IC-pak 201. Among other accomplishments, they convinced Steve Jobs to use Objective-C as the system programming language for the NeXT Computer (later the basis for Apple's OS X operating system). Tom also had the idea and organized the initial group of volunteers who created ACM's OOPSLA Conference.

After spending five years as a one-person consultant, Tom joined IBM Consulting and founded the Object Technology Practice—an application development organization that did major application development projects for major IBM customers. Based upon this success, he was attracted to Morgan Stanley, where he delivered a redesigned corporate, credit risk-management system two days before the Barings disaster.

In 1997, Tom teamed up with Dr. John Wooten to found ShouldersCorp. At ShouldersCrop, he has led more than a dozen successful 100-day projects, including the largest known Agile Development project, completed in 2001. Many experiences with object technology are recorded in his 1993 book, *Object Lessons*, published by Cambridge University Press.

**Bertrand Meyer** is professor of software engineering at ETH Zurich (the Swiss Federal Institute of Technology), and Chief Architect at Eiffel Software, based in Santa Barbara, California. He pursues a diverse career as software project manager (having overseen the development of tools and libraries totaling several million lines of code), software architect, educator, researcher, book author and consultant.

He has published 10 books including several bestsellers such as *Object-Oriented Software Construction* (Prentice Hall, Jolt Award 1998), and *Eiffel: The Language*, *Object Success*, and *Introduction to the Theory of Programming Languages* (Prentice-Hall PTR). His latest book, an introductory programming textbook using the full extent of object technology and contracts, entitled *Touch of Class: An Introduction to Programming Well* and due for publication by Springer-Verlag in March 2009, is the result of six years of teaching the introductory programming class at ETH.

As a researcher, he has published over 200 papers on software topics; his main contributions have been in the area of software architecture and design (Design by Contract), programming languages (Eiffel, now an ISO standard), testing and formal methods. His main current research areas, in cooperation with members of his group at ETH, are safe and simple programming for concurrent and multicore architecture (SCOOP), automated testing (AutoTest), program proofs, pedagogical tools (Trucstudio), computer science pedagogy, development environments (EiffelStudio, Origo), reuse and component-based development, the software process, and object persistence.

He is the recipient of the ACM Software System Award (2006) and the first Dahl-Nygaard prize for object technology (2005), a fellow of the ACM, and a member of the French Academy of Technologies.

**Robin Milner** graduated from the University of Cambridge in 1958. After short posts, he joined the University of Edinburgh in 1973, where he cofounded the Laboratory for Foundation of Computer Science in 1986. He was elected Fellow of the Royal Society in 1988, and in 1991 won the ACM's AM Turing Award. He rejoined Cambridge University in 1995, headed the Computer Laboratory there for four years, and retired in 2001. His research achievements (often joint) include: the system LCF, a model that underlies many later systems for interactive reasoning; Standard ML, an industry-scale but rigorously based programming language; the Calculus of Communicating Systems (CCS); and the pi calculus.

Currently, he works on Bigraphs, a topographical model for mobile interactive systems. This model combines the power of the Pi Calculus, which emphasizes how mobile agents can modify their linkage, with the power of Mobile Ambients (Cardelli and Gordon), which emphasize how they move in a nested space. The combination of these two features treats them as independent of one another: "Where you are does not affect whom you can talk to." This yields a generic model that not only subsumes many process calculi, but also aims to provide a rigorous platform for the design of ubiquitous computing systems that will dominate computation in the 21st century.

**Charles H. Moore** was born in 1938; grew up in Michigan; received a B.S. in physics from MIT; married Winifred Bellis; has a son, Eric. He presently lives in Incline Village, on beautiful Lake Tahoe; drives a WRX; hikes the Tahoe Rim Trail and the Pacific Crest Trail; reads a lot. He delights in finding simple solutions, changing the problem if necessary.

During the 60s, he worked as a freelance programmer until inventing Forth in 1968. (Forth is a simple, efficient, and versatile computer language of which he's very proud.) He used it to program telescopes at NRAO. And in 1971, cofounded Forth, Inc. to program other real-time applications.

In 1983, fed up with clumsy hardware, he cofounded Novix, Inc. and designed its NC4000 microprocessor chip. This morphed into the Harris RTX2000, which was space-qualified and is orbiting Saturn on Cassini.

As Computer Cowboys, he used custom software to design ShBoom, Mup20, F21 and i21; all Forth-architecture microprocessors. He's equally proud of these small, fast, low-power chips.

In this century, he cofounded IntellaSys and invented colorForth to program design tools for a multicore chip. As of 2008, a 40-core version is being produced and marketed by Intellasys. He is presently porting his design tools to this amazing chip.

**James Rumbaugh** received a B.S. in physics from MIT, an M.S. in astronomy from Caltech, and a Ph.D. in computer science from MIT. His doctorate work at MIT was in Professor Jack Dennis's Computation Structures Group, which pioneered research into fundamental models of computing. His thesis presented a language and hardware architecture for a data flow computer, a maximally concurrent computer architecture.

For 25 years, he worked at the General Electric Research and Development Center in Schenectady, New York, on a wide variety of research projects, including one of the first multiprocessor operating systems, algorithms for the reconstruction of X-ray tomography images, a VLSI design system, an early framework for graphical interfaces, and an object-oriented language. Working with GE colleagues, he developed the Object Modeling Technique (OMT) and wrote the book *Object-Oriented Modeling and Design* (Prentice Hall), which popularized OMT. He wrote a popular monthly column in the *Journal of Object-Oriented Programming* (JOOP) for six years.

In 1994, he joined Rational Software Corporation in Cupertino, California, where he and Grady Booch combined their modeling methods to produce the Unified Modeling Language (UML), with subsequent inputs from Ivar Jacobson and collaborators from the Object Modeling Group (OMG). Standardization of UML by the OMG led to its widespread adoption as the leading software modeling language. Books by Rumbaugh, Booch, and Jacobson presented the UML to the public. He helped guide the further development of UML and evangelized for the use of good engineering principles in the development of software. After Rational was acquired by IBM, he eventually retired in 2006.

James is an expert skier, a poor golfer, and a weekly hiker. He attends opera, theater, ballet, and art museums. He enjoys fine food, traveling, photography, gardening, and foreign languages. He reads about cosmology, evolution, cognitive science, epic poetry, mythology, fantasy, history, and public affairs. He and his wife live in Saratoga, California. They have two sons in college.

**Bjarne Stroustrup** designed and implemented C++. Over the last decade, C++ has become the most widely used language supporting object-oriented programming by making abstraction techniques affordable and manageable for mainstream projects. Using C++ as his tool, Stroustrup has pioneered the use of object-oriented and generic programming techniques in application areas where efficiency is a premium; examples include general systems programming, switching, simulation, graphics, user-interfaces, embedded systems, and scientific computation. The influence of C++ and the ideas it popularized are clearly visible far beyond the C++ community. Languages including C, C#, Java, and Fortran99 provide features pioneered for mainstream use by C++, as do systems such as COM and CORBA.

His book *The C++ Programming Language* (Addison-Wesley, first edition 1985, second edition 1991, third edition 1997, "special" edition 2000) is the most widely read book of its kind and has been translated into at least 19 languages. A later book, *The Design and Evolution of C++* (Addison-Wesley, 1994) broke new ground in the description of the way a programming language was shaped by ideas, ideals, problems, and practical constraints. A new book *Programming Principles and Practice Using C++* is finding a role as a first introduction to programming and C++. In addition to his six books, Stroustrup has published more than a hundred academic and popular papers. He took an active role in the creation of the ANSI/ISO standard for C++ and continues to work on the maintenance and revision of that standard.

Born in Aarhus, Denmark, Bjarne received his Master's degree in mathematics and computer science from the University of Aarhus. His Ph.D. for work on distributed computing is from Cambridge University, England. From 1979 to 2002, he worked as a researcher and later as a manager in Bell Labs and AT&T Labs in New Jersey. He is currently the College of Engineering chair in Computer Science Professor at Texas A&M University. He is a member of the U.S. National Academy of Engineering, an ACM fellow, and an IEEE fellow. He has received numerous professional awards.

**Guido van Rossum** is the creator of Python, one of the major programming languages on and off the Web. The Python community refers to him as the BDFL (Benevolent Dictator For Life), a title that could have been taken from a Monty Python skit (but wasn't).

Guido grew up in the Netherlands and worked for a long time at CWI in Amsterdam, where Python was born. He moved to the U.S. in 1995, where he lived in northern Virginia, got married, and had a son. In 2003, the family moved to California, where Guido now works for Google, spending 50% of his time on the Python open source project and the rest of his time using Python for internal Google projects.

**Philip Wadler** likes to introduce theory into practice, and practice into theory. Two examples of theory into practice: GJ, the basis for Sun's new version of Java with generics, derives from quantifiers in second-order logic. His work on XQuery marks one of the first efforts to apply mathematics to formulate an industrial standard. An example of practice into theory: Featherweight Java specifies the core of Java in less than one page of rules. He is a principal designer of the Haskell programming language, contributing to its two main innovations: type classes and monads.

Wadler is professor of theoretical computer science at the University of Edinburgh. He holds a Royal Society-Wolfson Research Merit Fellowship, is a Fellow of the Royal Society of Edinburgh, and is an ACM Fellow. Previously, he worked or studied at Avaya Labs, Bell Labs, Glasgow, Chalmers, Oxford, CMU, Xerox Parc, and Stanford, and lectured as a guest professor in Paris, Sydney, and Copenhagen. He appears at position 70 on Citeseers list of most-cited authors in computer science, is a winner of the POPL Most Influential Paper Award, served as editor-in-chief of the *Journal of Functional Programming*, and served on the Executive Committee of the ACM Special Interest Group on Programming Languages. His papers include "Listlessness is better than laziness," "How to replace failure by a list of successes," and "Theorems for free," and he is a coauthor of *XQuery from the Experts* (Addison-Wesley, 2004) and *Java Generics and Collections* (O'Reilly, 2006). He has delivered invited talks in locations ranging from Aizu to Zurich.

**Larry Wall** was educated at various places, including the Cornish School of Music, the Seattle Youth Symphony, Seattle Pacific University, Multnomah School of the Bible, SIL International, UC Berkeley, and UCLA. Though trained primarily in music, chemistry, and linguistics, Larry has been working with computers for the last 35 years or so.

He is most famous for writing _rn_, _patch_, and the Perl programming language, but prefers to think of himself as a cultural hacker whose vocation in life is to bring a bit of joy into the dreary existence of programmers. For various definitions of "work for," Larry has worked for Seattle Pacific, MusiComedy Northwest, System Development Corporation, Burroughs, Unisys, the NSA, Telos, ConTel, GTE, JPL, NetLabs, Seagate, Tim O'Reilly, the Perl Foundation, and himself. Larry is currently employed by NetLogic Microsystems in Mountain View, California. To get to work, he walks past both the Computer History Museum and the Googleplex, which must mean something. Preferably something absurd.

**John E. Warnock** is cochairman of the board of directors of Adobe Systems, Inc., a company he cofounded in 1982 with Charles Geschke. Dr. Warnock was president of Adobe for his first two years and chairman and CEO for his remaining 16 years at Adobe. Warnock has pioneered the development of world-renowned graphics, publishing, web, and electronic document technologies that have revolutionized the field of publishing and visual communication. Dr. Warnock holds six patents.

Warnock's entrepreneurial success has been chronicled by some of the country's most influential business and computer industry publications, and he has received numerous awards for technical and managerial achievement. A partial list of awards includes: Entrepreneur of the Year from Ernst & Young, Merrill Lynch, and *Inc. Magazine*; University of Utah Distinguished Alumnus Award; Association for Computing Machinery (ACM) Software Systems Award; Award for Technical Excellence from the National Graphics Association; and the first Rhode Island School of Design Distinguished Service to Art and Design International Award. Dr. Warnock has also received the Edwin H. Land Award from the Optical Society of America, the Bodleian Medal from Oxford University, and the Lovelace Medal from the British Computer Society. Warnock is a distinguished member of the National Academy of Engineering, and a member of the American Academy of Arts and Sciences. He has received honorary degrees from the University of Utah and the American Film Institute.

Warnock has been a member of the board of directors of Adobe Systems Inc., Knight-Ridder, Octavo Corporation, Ebrary Inc., Mongonet Inc., Netscape Communications, and Salon Media Group. He is a past chairman of the Tech Museum of Innovation in San Jose. He also has serves on the Board of Trustees of the American Film Institute, and is on the Board of the Sundance Institute.

Before cofounding Adobe Systems, Warnock was the principal scientist at Xerox Palo Alto Research Center (PARC). Prior to joining Xerox, Warnock held key positions at Evans & Sutherland Computer Corporation, Computer Sciences Corporation, IBM, and the University of Utah.

Warnock holds B.S. and M.S. degrees in mathematics and a PhD in electrical engineering all from the University of Utah.

**Peter Weinberger** has been at Google New York since the middle of 2003, working on various projects that handle or store large amounts of data.

Before that (from the time that AT&T and Lucent split apart), Peter was at Renaissance Technologies, a fabulously successful hedge fund (for which he takes no credit at all), where he started as Head of Technology, responsible for computing, software, and information security. The last year or so, he escaped all that and worked on a trading system (for mortgage-backed securities).

Until AT&T and Lucent split, he was in Computer Science Research at Bell Labs in Murray Hill. Before ending up in management, Peter worked on databases, AWK, network file-systems, compiling, performance and profiling, and no doubt some other Unix stuff. He then slipped into management, for which his penultimate title was Information Sciences Research Vice-President (a title only a large corporation could love). Peter managed about one-third of Research, including mathematics and statistics, computer science, and speech. His last year at AT&T was spent in Consumer Long Distance, trying to look ahead.

Before working at Bell Labs, Peter taught mathematics at the University of Michigan in Ann Arbor, publishing a bunch of papers the last of which was superseded in 2002, making them not even of academic interest.

Peter received his B.S. from Swarthmore College in Swarthmore, Pennsylvania, and his Ph.D. in mathematics (number theory) from the University of California, Berkeley.

# INDEX

APL\360, 44
applications (see programs)
arbitrary precision integers, in Python, 24
architects, identifying, 335
aspect orientation, 319
Aspect-Oriented Software Development with
        Use Cases (Jacobson; Ng), 319
asymmetrical coroutines, in Lua, 164
asynchronous operation, in Forth, 70
audio applications, language environment
        for, 92
automata theory, 115
automatic code checking, 289
AWK, 101, 102
    compared to SQL, 138
    data size handled by, 102
    initial design ideas for, 137
    knowledge required to use, 105
    large programs
        good practices for, 102
        improvements for, 149
    longevity of, rewriting scripts for, 143
    programming advice for, 121
    programming by example, 154–159
    purposes appropriate for use of, 102, 105,
        107, 120
    regrets about, by Peter Weinberger, 141
AWT, 279

# B

backward compatibility, 199
    for potentially redesigned UML, 345
    with Java, 279
    with JVM, 298
    with UML, 361
BASIC, 79
    comments, 90
    compiler
        one pass for, 81, 86
        two passes for, 83
    design of
        considerations for, 80, 86
        holding up over time, 93
    encapsulation, 83
    GOTO statements, 80, 86
    hardware evolution influencing, 85
    large programs, suitability for, 82
    lessons learned from design of, 92
    libraries, building, 97
    line numbers in, 80, 95
    number handling, 80, 85
    performance of, 83
    teaching programming using, 81, 82
    True BASIC, 82, 83
    variable declarations not required in, 87
    whitespace insensitivity, 82, 94
bitmap fonts, handling in PostScript, 402

Booch, Grady, 317, 444
    Ada, 374
    backward compatibility with UML, 361
    benefits of UML, persuading people of, 356
    body of literature for programming, 365
    brown field development, 372
    business rules, 369
    complexity and OOP, 370
    complexity of UML, 357
    concurrency, 370
    constraints contributing to innovation, 367
    creativity and pragmatism, tension
        between, 364
    design of UML, teamwork for, 356
    design patterns, 372, 373
    implementation code, generating with
        UML, 356
    language design compared to
        programming, 359
    language design influencing programs, 358
    language design, inspiration for, 367
    legacy software, approaches for, 366
    lessons learned by design of UML, 358
    OOP influencing correct design, 373
    percentage of UML used all the time, 357,
        360
    purposes of UML, 356
    redesigning UML, possibilities for, 357
    simplicity, recognizing, 371
    standardization of UML, 362–364
    teams, effectiveness of, 371
    training programmers, 364–366
    visual programming languages, 368
books and publications
    Aspect-Oriented Software Development
        with Use Cases (Jacobson; Ng), 319
    The Design and Evolution of
        C++(Stroustrup), 14
    "The Design of APL" (Falkoff; Iverson), 44
    Design Patterns: Elements of Reusable
        Object-Oriented Software (Gamma;
        Helm; Johnson; Vlissides), 344
    The Elements of Programming Style, 118
    "The Formal Description of System 360"
        (Falkoff; Iverson; Sussenguth), 44
    "HOPL-III: The development of the
        Emerald programming language", 11
    "Learning Standard C++ as a New
        Language" (Stroustrup), 7
    literature for programming, 365
    Méthodes de Programmation (Meyer), 420
    "A Note on Pattern Matching: Where do
        you find the match to an empty array"
        (Falkoff), 48
    The Practice of Programming (Kernighan;
        Pike), 119
    A Programming Language (Iverson), 44

Forth, 59, 60
   application design with, 71–77
   asynchronous operation, 70
   colorForth, 62
   comparing to PostScript, 399
   conditionals in, 74
   cooperative multithreading, 70
   customer vocabulary used in, 61
   design of
      influencing program design, 73
      longevity of, 62
   error causes and detection, 65, 74
   for embedded applications, 65
   I/O capabilities of, 69
   indirect-threaded code, 63
   lessons learned from design of, 63
   loops in, 74
   maintainability of, 72
   minimalism in design of, 62
   porting, 69
   postfix operators, 65, 66
   programmers receptive to, 61
   programming in, advice for, 74
   readability of, 62, 65
   "reusable concepts of meaning" with, 207
   simplicity of, 60, 62, 74
   stack management in, 74
   stack-based subroutine calls, 60, 70
   syntax of small words, 60, 62
   word choice in, 72
fourth-generation computer language, Forth
      as, 60
frameworks, learning, 332
functional closures, in Haskell, 191
functional programming, 180–187
   abstraction in, 180
   concurrency and, 352
   debugging in, 183
   error handling in, 183
   in computer science curriculum, 315
   lazy evaluation in, 180, 191
   learning, 184
   longevity of, 186
   parallelism and, 182
   popularity of, 184
   Scala for, 286
   side effects, lack of, 180, 181, 182
   usefulness of, 140
functions
   first class, in Lua, 163
   higher-order, in ML, 205

# G

Gamma, Erich (Design Patterns: Elements of
      Reusable Object-Oriented
      Software), 344
garbage collection, 259
   in JVM, 288
   in Lua, 163
   in Objective-C, 260
   in Python, 35
general arrays, in APL, 52
general resource management, 5
general-purpose languages, 303
generic programming
   as alternative to OOP, 3, 10
   in C++0x, 13
   as paradigm of C++, 8, 9
   reducing complexity, 3
generic types, in Haskell, 191
genericity, 428
generics in Java, 188
Geschke, Charles, 395, 447
   bitmap fonts, handling in PostScript, 402
   bugs in ROM, working around, 397
   computer science, topics that should be
      taught, 409
   concatenative language, benefits of, 397
   design team for PostScript, managing, 399
   font scaling in PostScript, 401
   half-toning for color in PostScript, 402
   hardware considerations, 397, 405, 412
   history of software and hardware
      evolution, 406
   Imaging Sciences Laboratory, formed
      by, 407
   kanji characters in PostScript, 403
   kerning and ligatures in PostScript, 403
   lessons learned from PostScript, 409
   longevity of programming languages, 410
   mathematical background, impact on
      design, 399
   open source projects, success of, 414
   open standards, 414
   popularity of languages, difficulty in
      making, 413
   PostScript as language instead of data
      format, 396
   programmer skill, importance compared to
      language design, 404
   programmers, good, recognizing, 409
   research groups, directing, 407–409
   stack-based design of PostScript, 399
   standardization, problems with, 415
   two-dimensional constructs,
      supporting, 398
   web use of PostScript, 415

loops
  alternatives to, 53
  in Forth, 74
Love, Tom, 241, 451
  appropriate uses of Smalltalk, 242
  classes, modeling and developing, 255
  complexity of C++, 243
  distributed teams, organizing, 253
  hardware, predicting future of, 243, 244
  languages
    evolution of, 244–249
    extensibility of, diminishing need for
      new languages, 248
    new, necessity of, 248
    number of in use, 247
  legacy software, reengineering, 253
  maintaining software, number of
    programmers required for, 251, 252
  managers understanding of languages, 255
  Objective-C as extension of C and
    Smalltalk, 245
  Objective-C as extension of C, reasons
    for, 242
  Objective-C compared to C++, 242
  OOP, limited applications of, 244
  popularity of C++, 243
  productivity
    improving, 256
    programmer quality affecting, 253
  programmers
    advice for, 257
    recognizing good, 251, 253
  programming, predicting future of, 243
  real-life experience, necessity of, for
    programming, 249
  simplicity in design, recognizing, 257
  size of code for Objective-C compared to
    C, 252
  success of a project, measuring, 258
  teaching complex technical concepts, 249
  teaching programming, 250
  training programmers, 250
  uses of Objective-C, 243
Lua, 161, 162
  asymmetrical coroutines in, 164
  closures in, 164
  code sharing with, 172
  concurrency with, 164
  design of, influencing future systems
    design, 169
  dialects of, written by users, 172
  environments used in, changing design
    of, 173
  error messages in, 174
  extensibility of, 173

  feature set completed for, 171
  feedback from users regarding, 170
  for loop, 169
  fragmentation issues with, 172
  garbage collection in, 163
  limitations of, 162
  mistakes in, by designers, 165
  number handling by, 163
  parser for, 175
  platform independence of, affecting
    debugging, 174
  programming in, advice regarding, 162
  purposes appropriate for use of, 162
  regrets about, by designers, 165
  resources used by, 169, 171
  security capabilities of, 162
  simplicity of, effects on users, 172
  tables in, 163
  testing features of, 171
  upgrading during course of
    development, 170
  VM
    choice of ANSI C for, 173
    debugging affected by, 174
    register-based, 174

# M

M language, 364, 369
Make utility, 133
mathematical formalism
  in language design, 94
  pipes used for, 108
mathematicians, languages designed by, 150,
  167
mathematics
  importance of learning, 143
  role in computer science, 48, 115, 139, 166,
    220
  (see also theorems)
metalanguages for models, 207
Méthodes de Programmation (Meyer), 420
Meyer, Bertrand, 417, 452
  adding features to Eiffel, decisions for, 437
  analysis required before
    implementation, 432
  backward and forward compatibility of
    Eiffel, 439
  componentization, language reflecting, 424
  concurrency and OOP, 424
  Design by Contract, 421–422
  evolution of, 436–440
  extensibility of Eiffel, 425
  genericity, 428
  history of Eiffel, 418–421

## P

papers (see books and publications)
paradigms
    influencing programmers, 213
    multiple
        in C++, 2, 8, 9
        in Python, 26
parallel processing, 64
parallelism
    in APL, 53–56
    functional programming and, 182
    uses of, 269
parser for Lua, 175
patch utility, 133
patents for software, 77
pattern matching
    algorithms for, using concurrency, 115
    evolution of, 103
pattern movement, 336, 343
patterns, design, 372, 373
PEP (Python Enhancement Proposal), 22
performance
    influencing design of C++, 6
    of BASIC, 83
    practical implications of, 282
Perl, 375
    APL influencing, 56
    community participation in, 386–389
    context in, 380–382
    CPAN for, 387, 388
    dual licensing, 389
    evolution of, 380, 384, 389–393
    human language principles
        influencing, 376, 380
    multiple implementations of, 393
    multiple ways of doing something, 379
    nicknames for, 375
    purposes of, 378
    scoping in, limitations of, 377
    syncretic design of, 385
    transition from text tool to complete
        language, 378
    version 6, 378, 390, 391, 393
Peters, Tim ("Zen of Python"), 21, 25, 31
physical processes, models affected by, 208
pi calculus, 206
Pike, Rob (The Practice of Programming), 119
pipes
    composing programs using, 108
    used for mathematical formalism, 108
platform independence, Java influencing, 293
pointers
    compiler handling, 89
    in C++, compared to Java, 3
    not used in APL, 55

polyglot virtual machines, 297
polymorphism, requiring runtime
        interpretation, 87
postfix operators, in Forth, 65, 66
PostScript, 395
    for Apple graphics imaging model, 405
    bitmap fonts, handling, 402
    bugs in ROM, working around, 397
    comparing to Forth, 399
    as concatenative language, benefits of, 397
    debugging, difficulty of, 411
    design decisions for, 400
    font scaling in, 401
    fonts, building, 403
    formal semantics not used for, 401
    future evolution of, 404
    half-toning for color in, 402
    hardware considerations, 397, 405
    JavaScript interface, 411
    kanji characters, handling, 403
    kerning in, 403
    as language instead of data format, 396
    lessons learned from, 409
    ligatures in, 403
    for NeXT graphics imaging model, 405
    print imaging models, compared to
        PDF, 403
    purposes of, 396
    stack-based design of, 399
    two-dimensional constructs in, 398
    web use of, 415
    writing by hand, 401
The Practice of Programming (Kernighan;
        Pike), 119
pragmatism and creativity, tension
        between, 364
productivity of programmers
    improving, 256
    language affecting, 304
    measuring, 156
    programmer quality affecting, 253
    programming language affecting, 146
    when working alone, 98
productivity of users, SQL improving, 229,
        233, 234
programmers
    all levels of, features for, 27
    creativity of (see creativity)
    general population as, 313
    good, recognizing, 27, 75, 409
    hiring, 27
    improving skills of, 104, 118, 140, 166,
        215, 311
    knowledge of, tied to language, 331, 336
    paradigms influencing, 213
    productivity of, 98, 146, 156

programmers (*continued*)

    productivity of (see also productivity of programmers), 304

    real-life experience, necessity of, 249

    recognizing good, 167, 251, 253

    skill of, importance compared to language design, 404

    teams of

        Design by Contract helping, 422

        distributed, organizing, 253

        education for, 290

        effectiveness of, 371

        importance of, 75

        in classroom, 111–113

        increasingly larger, 126

        organizing, 323

        productivity of, 98

        size of, 240, 393

        skills required for, 251

        stimulating creativity of, 141, 240

    training, 250, 364–366

    type of

        design considerations for, 26, 45

        receptive to Forth, 61

    users as, 333, 336

programming

    analysis in preparation for, 90, 432

    approaches to, in different parts of the world, 323

    compared to language design, 145

    compared to mathematical theorems work, 139, 157

    compared to writing text, 118

    components in, 260, 263–269

    constraints contributing to innovation in, 367

    creativity involved in, 104

    debugging (see debugging code)

    economic model of, 265, 266, 269–272

    as engineering, 321

    by example, 144, 154–159

    as form of communication, xi

    future of, 243, 414

    hardware availability affecting, 102, 158, 168

    intelligent agents partnering with people for, 332

    linguistic perspective of, 429

    mathematical perspective of, 429

    methods and processes for, improving, 325

    nature of, changed over time, 68

    not doing, if you can't do it well, 159

    resuming after a hiatus, 67, 114

    seamless development, 432

    specialization of labor for, 267, 268, 273

teaching (see computer science education)

testing (see testing code)

users, considering, 97, 99, 118

A Programming Language (Iverson), 44

programming language design, 121–129, 169–176

    backward compatibility versus innovation in, 131

    breakthroughs needed in, 149–154

    bugs in, 214

    by mathematicians, 150, 167

    clean design, 156

    compared to library design, 300

    compared to programming, 145, 359

    data models for, 229

    debugging considerations for, 148

    defining, 213

    designer's preferences influencing, 148

    domain-driven (see domain-driven design)

    environment influencing, 297

    errors reduced by, 122, 147

    by extending existing languages, 2

    for handheld devices, 280

    for system programming, 280

    formalisms for

        benefits of, 228

        mathematical, 94

        usefulness of, 108

    goals for, 293

    implementation affecting, 175

    implementation considerations for, 122, 129, 145

    implementation related to, 296

    improvements to process of, 125, 126

    influencing program design, 51, 73, 90, 174, 192, 212, 289, 358

    inspiration for, 367

    multilingual background influencing, 429

    network issues affecting, 281

    personal approach for, 50

    programmers, considerations for, 94

    prototypes for, 124

    scientific approach for, possibility of, 126, 148, 305

    simplicity in, recognizing, 257, 302

    SQL's influence on, 231

    starting with small core set of functionality, 246, 430

    syntax choices for, 148

    teams for, 142, 178–180, 356

        democratic nature of, 292

        managing, 307, 399

    user considerations, 104

    utility considerations, 104

programming languages

adding features to, 278, 300

adoption of, obstacles to, 41

compared to human languages, xi

compatibility requirements of, 20

debugging, 20

domain-specific (see domain-specific languages)

dropping features in, considerations for, 135

errors reduced by, 224

evolution of, managing, 15, 20, 96, 244–249

experiments of, success of, 385

extensibility of, 40, 110, 150, 248

families of, 213

formal specifications for, 360

general-purpose, ideals for, 123, 150

growth of, 292

implementation of, factors measured during, 168

influencing programs, 423

interface for, elegance of, 135

linguistics as influence on, 382

little

making more general, 131, 150, 303

resurgence of, 132

longevity of, 109, 410

managers required to understand, 255

moving from specialized to general-purpose, 384

new, necessity of, 248

number of in use, 247

popularity of, difficulty in making, 413

productivity affected by, 146, 304

reducing complexity of, 382

revising, 218

safety of, versus creative freedom, 305

simplicity of, goals for, 84

size of, increasing, 109

specific to each programmer, 213

strengths of, recognizing, 124

teaching languages, 296

testing new features of, 125

theory of meaning for, 223

upgrading, considerations for, 135

usability of, 339

validating, 219

(see also specific languages)

Programming: Principles and Practice Using C++ (Stroustrup), 17

programs

beauty or elegance of, 104

complexity of, OOP and, 262, 348, 370

computer's ability to state meaning of, 215

documentation of (see documentation of programs)

as domain-specific languages, 50

large systems, building, 127

legacy, reengineering, 253

little, handling nontext data, 138

local workarounds versus global fixes, 142, 171

maintainability of, 142, 151, 251, 252

performance of, 158

problems in, finding, 158

provability of, possibility of, 434

quality of, improving, 269–272

revising heavily before shipping, 136

reworking versus restarting, 144

rewriting, frequency of, 130, 152

size of, continuing to increase, 126

structural problems in, avoiding, 215

success of, measuring, 258

theory and practice motivating, 111

trusting, 267

written in 1970s, rewriting, 68

protocols, in Objective-C, 260

provability, 209, 212

proving theorems, 204, 214, 217

publications (see books and publications)

Python, 19

adding features to, 20–24

bottom-up versus top-down design, 29

concurrency with, 37

design process using, 29

dynamic features of, 30

elegance philosophy for, 25, 31

experts using, features for, 27

future versions of, 41

garbage collection, 35

learning, 30

lessons learned from design of, 40

macros in, 33

maintainability of, 28

multiple implementations of, 34–36

multiple paradigms in, 26

new versions of, requirements for, 23

novices using, features for, 27

number handling in, 24

prototyping uses of, 29

searching large code bases, 37

security of, 30

simple parser used by, reasons for, 32

strict formatting in, 33

type of programmers using, influencing design of, 26

Python 3.0, 41

Python 3000, 32

Python Enhancement Proposal (PEP), 22

"Pythonic", meaning of, 21

## Q

specifications
    distinct from implementation, 422
    formal (see formal specifications)
SQL, 225, 226–228
    compared to AWK, 138
    complexity of, 236
    concurrent data access issues of, 230
    declarative nature of, 229
    design principles of, 231
    external visibility of, 233
    Halloween problem in, 231
    influencing future language design, 231
    injection attacks on, 236
    knowledge required to use, 237
    popularity of, 233
    scalability of, 235
    standardization of, 239
    updates on indexes, 231
    usability tests on, 235
    user feedback for, 235
    users of, primarily programmers, 237
    views in, uses of, 230
stack management, in Forth, 74
stack-based design, of PostScript, 399
stack-based subroutine calls, in Forth, 60, 70
standardization
    of APL, 47
    of C#, 308
    of UML, 346, 362–364
    problems with, 415
static typing, 25
statically checked interfaces, problems caused
        by, 10
Stroustrup, Bjarne, 1, 454
    academic pursuits of, 16–17
    C++0x FAQ, online, 13
    "close to the hardware" design for C++, 5
    code examples in textbooks, 17
    complexity of C++, compared to Java, 3
    complexity of OOP, 9
    concurrency and network distribution, 12
    concurrency support, in C++, 11
    concurrency, linked to OOP, 10
    creating a new language, considerations
        for, 14
    debugging C++ code, 6
    The Design and Evolution of C++
        (Stroustrup), 14
    embedded applications, C++ for, 7
    extending existing languages, reasons for, 2
    future versions of C++, 13
    general resource management, 5
    industry connections of, 16
    kernels not written in C++, reasons for, 8
    "Learning Standard C++ as a New
        Language", 7
    lessons from design of C++, 14

    moving code from C to C++, reasons for, 8
    multiple paradigms, reasons for supporting
        in C++, 2
    pointers in C++, compared to Java, 3
    Programming: Principles and Practice Using
        C++, 17
    security of software, 6
    system software, C++ for, 7
    testing C++ code, 6
    value semantics, 5
    "Why C++ isn't just an Object-Oriented
        Programming Language", 8
Structured Programming (Dahl; Dijkstra;
        Hoare), 419
structured programming, compared to
        OOP, 431
superdistribution, 268, 274
Sussenguth, E. H. ("The Formal Description of
        System 360"), 44
symmetric relationships, 352–355
System R project, 228
systems
    models for, 207–212
    wider not faster, 285

# T

tables, in Lua, 163
Tcl/Tk, usefulness of, 134
teams of programmers (see programmers,
        teams of)
teams of programming language
        designers, 142, 178–180, 292, 307,
        356, 399
templates, in C++, 10
test cases, as use cases, 319
testing code, 167
    C++, 6
    for Lua, 171
    Python, 37
    writing code to facilitate, 133
theorems
    proving
        as purpose of ML, 217
        with LCF and ML, 204
        with type system, 214
    teaching in computer science, 209
    working on, compared to
        programming, 139, 157
threading
    concurrency and, 261
    indirect-threaded code, in Forth, 63
    lightweight threads, 263
    (see also multithreading)
top-down design
    with C++, 5
    with Python, 29

# ABOUT THE INTERVIEWERS

**Federico Biancuzzi** is a freelance interviewer. His interviews have appeared on online publications such as ONLamp.com, LinuxDevCenter.com, SecurityFocus.com, NewsForge.com, Linux.com, TheRegister.co.uk, and ArsTechnica.com, as well as in the Polish print magazine *BSD Magazine*, and the Italian print magazine *Linux&C*.

**Shane Warden** has a decade of experience developing free software, including contributions to the Perl 5 core, the design of Perl 6, and the Parrot virtual machine. In his spare time, he runs the fiction division of independent publisher Onyx Neon Press. He is coauthor of *The Art of Agile Development* (O'Reilly).

# COLOPHON

The cover fonts are Akzidenz Grotesk, Orator, and Helvetica Neue Ultra Light. The text font is Adobe's Meridien; the heading font is ITC Bailey.

# The O'Reilly Advantage

## Stay Current and Save Money

Order books online:
www.oreilly.com/store/order

Questions about our
products or your order:
order@oreilly.com

Join our email lists: Sign up
to get topic specific email
announcements or new
books, conferences, special
offers and technology news
elists.oreilly.com

For book content
technical questions:
booktech@oreilly.com

To submit new book
proposals to our editors:
proposals@oreilly.com

Contact us:
O'Reilly Media, Inc.
1005 Gravenstein Highway N.
Sebastopol, CA U.S.A. 95472
707-827-7000 or
800-998-9938
www.oreilly.com

Did you know that if you register
your O'Reilly books, you'll get
automatic notification and upgrade
discounts on new editions?

**And that's not all! Once you've registered
your books you can:**

» Win free books, T-shirts and O'Reilly Gear

» Get special offers available only to registered
O'Reilly customers

» Get free catalogs announcing all our new
titles (US and UK Only)

**Registering is easy! Just go to
www.oreilly.com/go/register**

# Try the online edition free for 45 days

Get the information you need when you need it, with Safari Books Online. Safari Books Online contains the complete version of the print book in your hands plus thousands of titles from the best technical publishers, with sample code ready to cut and paste into your applications.

Safari is designed for people in a hurry to get the answers they need so they can get the job done. You can find what you need in the morning, and put it to work in the afternoon. As simple as cut, paste, and program.

**To try out Safari and the online edition of the above title FREE for 45 days, go to www.oreilly.com/go/safarienabled and enter the coupon code TTMOJFH.**

To see the complete Safari Library visit:
safari.oreilly.com

70502